About this book:

The first two editions of this book were acclaimed internationally as the leading texts in their field. This third edition presents the latest applications of management audits. While much of the text of the second edition has been retained, it has been revised and updated to reflect the new trading realities and technology facing management. It also contains much new material as well, dealing, *inter alia,* with cyberspace, environmental, project and value-added auditing, continuous improvement programmes. Accordingly the text is substantially larger than before. Its central focus is on using management audits to reduce or eliminate avoidable costs and improve business results, to make the company ever more competitive and meet the challenges of competition. It is intended as a no nonsense practical guide for both auditor and auditee. It will be a valuable information source to managers and management auditors and a handbook for students of management.

Based on modern business management needs, the author's techniques have helped businesses from many different economic sectors identify opportunities to reduce costs and improve their results. Businesses pursuing continuous improvement programmes will find the book almost indispensible.

About the author:

Allan J. Sayle has nearly thirty years experience of management and auditing and is known internationally as a leading authority in his field, devoted to business improvement. A major contributor to the modern body of knowledge of management audit practices, he has been acknowledged as a pioneer of value-added auditing. He has provided management services for a wide variety of industries, for large and small companies around the world.

Allan Sayle lives in the United States of America.

Other books by the same author:

Meeting ISO 9000 in a TQM World.   ISBN 0-9511739-3-X.

Available through bookstores or from Allan Sayle Associates.
(Internet address, www.sayle.com)

Management Audits

Best wishes

Allan Sayle (signature)

Allan J. Sayle

Third edition

Published by Allan Sayle Associates

Brighton, Michigan, U.S.A.

Management Audits

Library of Congress Catalog Card Number: 97-91977

Author: Allan J. Sayle

First published 1981
Published by Allan J. Sayle 1985
Reprint 1985
Reprint 1986
Reprint 1987 (twice)
Second Edition published by Allan J. Sayle 1988
Reprint 1988 (twice)
Reprint 1989 (twice)
Reprint 1990
Reprint 1991 (twice)
Reprint 1992
Reprint 1994
Third edition published by: Allan Sayle Associates, 1997.
                                Brighton, Michigan, USA.
                                (Internet address: www.sayle.com)

ISBN 0-9511739-0-1

Printed in the United States of America

Contents

And in such indexes, although small pricks
To their subsequent volumes, there is seen
The baby figure of the giant mass
Of things to come at large.

William Shakespeare (Troilus and Cressida)

Preface to the third edition.

Part 1: The assessment of business operations

Why audit? Analogies. What is a *"management audit"*? What type of organization should perform management audits? In-house or hired auditors? Cost of audits. Development of audits. The problem of multiple assessment.

Categories of management audit. Management audit applications. Audit depth. Audit scope. Informal audit. Unannounced audit. Supplier evaluations, third party assessments and pre-award surveys. Just-in-time justifies time.

What has to be done and who will do it? Organization charts. The span of managerial control. Implications of the quality manager's reporting level. Job descriptions. Job specifications. Work flow. The unit concept. Problems of location and size. Virtual organizations, *"doughnuts"* and outsourcing.

Introduction. The task elements, The Person. The item. The equipment. The information. Service.

11. Audit methods.   **247-262**

Seven steps. Following the system. Obtaining objective evidence. Spot checks. Look and see. Two-level auditing and pattern recognition. Cyber auditing. The well equipped modern auditor.

12. Information collection.   **263-278**

Use of the audit guidance tools. The quantity of objective evidence to collect. What to record. Mental notes. Collect the information as you go.

13. Question technique.   **279-300**

Six friends. The seventh friend. The unit concept (analyzing the process). The hypothetical question. "I don't understand". Systematic questioning. The silent question. Non-questions. The obvious question. The unasked question. Inverse questions. Comparison questions. A useful sequence for questioning. An example of question technique. Presentation of questions. Active listening. Sensitive situations. Always give praise where it is due. Personal demeanour. Unavailable information. Gathering opinions at grass roots level. The constructive approach. Two edged swords. The auditor's stature.

14. Auditor conduct.   **301-314**

Projecting the right image. Conducting the proceedings properly.

15. The auditee's conduct.   **315-326**

Time wasters. The "Cook's tour". Provocation. The fixed ballot or loaded dice. The special case. The trial of strength. Insincerity. Pleas for pity. The absentee or indispensable man. Amnesia. Language barrier. The bribe. The right tactics. Desperation.

16. Cyber audits.   **327-334**

The arrival of cyber audits. What is a cyber audit? What are the limitations of performing cyber audits? What kind of competence does the auditor need? Where is the auditor? Audit preparation. What effect does the paperless office have on audit method? Interacting with the auditee. Accessing the auditee's computer system. Security and auditor authority. Hidden files. The exit interview and the audit report.

Attitude towards the audit. Answering the questions. Bluff. Taking action on the spot. Challenging the auditor. Note taking. Preparation. Auditee's personnel. Corrective action requests. Marketing statements. Obvious deficiencies. Escorts.

Part 2. Management Audit applications

Refocussing on the original mission. Quality standards, is registration necessary? The role of the quality movement. The role of the management audit.

Revisiting the elements of price. The nature of costs. Continuous improvement and value-added auditing. Future focus. Audit preparation. Checklists and tools. Audit method. Appraising the nature of the costs. Cutting fat, not muscle. Staff utilization and turnover. Auditing the business performance of systems. The role of auditors. Interface systems capability. What is the avoidable cost? The impact on audit time budgets. The system's use of time. Some indicators of system problems. System time elements. Mathematical techniques. Assessing resource utilization. Assessing energy management. Can a CAR be issued? Exit interviews. Audit reports. Follow-up action. Internal, external, extrinsic and self audits as part of the CI effort. Sharing the gains. Value-added audits and the registrars.

The nature of projects. The role of the auditor. Conduct of the audit. Project controls. Project phases. Virtual organizations.

The importance of software. Problems of procurement. The role of the auditor. Conduct of the audit. The need for controls. Controls implemented during the supply of new or revised software. Controls implemented during the operational life of the computer installation and the software. Loss controls. Virtual organizations. Control of resources.

Preface to the third edition.

There are risks and costs to a program of action.
But they are far less than the long-range risks and costs
of comfortable inaction.

John F. Kennedy

Change surrounds us affecting our personal and business lives. The driving forces of global competition, emerging nations, new trading blocks and applied new technology that are causing the pace of change to accelerate, are well documented. They hit hard at businesses large and small regardless of economic sector. Companies in the industrialized nations have responded with downsizing, restructuring and increased investment in powerful small computers all of which have, to some extent, helped them to regain competitiveness, or at least stave off the consequences of change. Those responses are major contributory factors to the extended Wall Street bull runs of the 1990's since they have affected the fundamentals that influence investors - and they never change. Business progress requires the lubricant of investment which always follows the best prospects of a satisfactory return for its investors. Investors can disappear as quickly as they appear, putting firms into trouble.

If regaining competitiveness is one thing, retaining it is quite another. Retention of competitive edge demands knowledge and a steady stream of pertinent information feeding it. Management audits offer an important source of information.

The changes that impact firms impact auditors too whose duty is to provide a value-added service. It is insufficient to offer the service so typical of audits performed in the name of ISO 9000 and similar standards. Business needs more than superficial walk-abouts culminating in banal reports of isolated minor issues: audits must focus more sharply onto business operations. To do this the auditors must become more savvy and better qualified in management and business operations. Their training schemes need to respond.

Audits need to be net earners, not net spenders. A polarization is developing between auditors offering a value-added service and those who do not. The future is bright only for the former. Another polarization is developing between compliance audits and systems audits. The future is brighter for the latter, the former becoming regarded as low level activities when conducted in a purely inspectorial manner for they add little if any value to the firm. Systems audits performed at the appropriate time are real preventive activities: they can prevent the expenditure of avoidable costs. In this lies the key to the future of management auditing. Not only must audits provide pertinent management information, they must attend to avoidable costs. This is a major thrust within this third edition.

The status of discussion

The preface to the first edition of this book asked for more discussion about management auditing. Twenty years later, as this edition is completed, the need for discussion is more urgent than ever. But one gets the impression that professional discussion and debate about the direction of management auditing, its tools techniques *et al* is stultified. Perhaps the fashion for ISO 9000 style audits and management systems has much to do with that. Recent publications and conferences in the world of the so-called quality profession are disappointing, regurgitating well worn themes, displaying a propensity towards plagiarism. Overall, it seems as if the quality industry, its auditors, its auditor qualifications and its training schemes have either lost focus on the real goal or have lost their way. They cannot expect business and management to await their attempts at catching up for they have the onerous task of securing their own firms' future and meeting the ever changing pressures in their trading world - the real world. Whilst not doubting the good intentions of many in the quality profession, I do doubt the wisdom of its direction.

Who will be the management auditors?

Do I believe the cadre of management auditors needed by hard pressed business will come from the ranks of the quality profession's present day auditors? A few will, most will not, for they are ill-equipped, ill-trained and ill-qualified for understanding the complexities of modern management and business operations. Who will be the management auditors? People trained to at least a bachelor's degree and MBA standard, who understand well the processes they audit and have several years personal hands-on experience of real accountability for managing business results. They will be people for whom continuous professional development is a way of life and a joy.

Issues facing auditors

Traditional industries and sectors will not vanish but, as new technology emerges and develops, new concerns face the management auditor: cyberspace, nanotechnology and biotechnology immediately spring to mind. In their fields they will require their own methods of auditing. How will an auditor regard their associated processes? When challenged my task elements always provided me with a framework for dialogue and communication with auditees in areas I was not originally trained for. They provided me with a sound proven basis for managing the audits assigned to me. My firm belief is that their usefulness will continue for they can and do relate to processes regardless of the technology involved.

But while assessing the technology within an auditee's process will continue to be an essential element of the audit, assessing the operational goals of the auditee's systems and organization is a challenge of growing importance. More than ever before, time is a major competitive battleground for business. The way the organization is structured and the way the systems are engineered, to ensure effective management of time, are key issues demanding the auditor's closest attention. Almost inextricably intertwined with time management is resource management. It too has to be scrutinized during the audit. Lack of time and resources are two of my six real causes of business problems, mentioned in each of the first two editions of this book. The other four are no less relevant. Indeed, avoiding all six are even more essential than ever. This, too, is a recurring theme throughout the text.

Auditors need to be analytical and use a broader range of tools in assessing the business efficacy of the auditee's management systems. This is pointed out in several places within the book. The biggest issue facing auditors is to prove their worth, to provide a value-added service and be not only a catalyst for corporate change but a mentor who can steer auditee's towards information that can improve their operation. To do this effectively, the management auditor will need to spend a considerable amount of time in keeping abreast of a wide variety of topics that affect business. These topics include, inter alia, concepts and applications of new and emerging technologies, business management thinking and innovations, developments and trends affecting the marketplace and trading conditions both locally and globally, product liability matters including pertinent case law affecting the company's activities. To be a management auditor, one has to understand and be current on issues affecting the management of a business: continuous professional development is not only essential, it is unavoidable.

A decade of change

In the almost ten years that have elapsed since the second edition was written many changes occurred and, inevitably, the jargon of everyday business life has altered. Expressions such as *"outsourcing"*, *"re-engineering"*, *"downsizing"*, *"virtual organizations"*, *Internet"*, *"intranet"*, *"world wide web"*, *"Just-in-time"* and *"real time"* programmes and many others caused my readers and seminar delegates to enquire of their impact on the audit and the auditor. These are dealt with in the book. In 1987, when writing the second edition, ISO 9000 registration audits were in birth: they have caused an entire industry to be created. ISO 9000/QS 9000 audits, whilst currently still being in vogue, are not dealt with in any special manner as compliance and system auditing, which are dealt with throughout, predate those audits by decades and will continue to be in use long after those standards lose their attraction. This will happen (indeed, I believe it has already begun to happen) as business grapples with the more substantive issues that will forever face it: continuous improvement of products, processes, performance, people and price, the 5 "P's" that affect value for money, influence customers and protect one's market. When successfully pursued, the sixth and dependant "P" is created - profit. But not before.

Since the second edition was written, the international political, ideological and economic maps have changed almost beyond recognition. The collapse of the soviet empire and of apartheid in South Africa, the accelerating pace of reforms in China brought about by the late Deng Xiaoping, the rise of ASEAN, the powerful Single Market of Europe and its slow move towards monetary unity, the birth of NAFTA and similar trading blocks in other parts of the world, rampant and rapid privatization of nationalized industries (the Margaret Thatcher legacy) as a mantra of governments regardless of their political colour, amongst others, are combining to promote capitalism and marketplace disciplines. Share ownership is expanding apace and adding to the pressure for competitive performance. Stock markets outside the established ones of America, western Europe and Australasia are getting bigger, fueled not only by the improving wealth of their own citizens, benefitting from increases in global trade, but also from richer nations. Aging baby boomers and generation X'ers started to pour money into the world's stock markets in the 1990's demanding stellar performance and returns from the firms they are investing in. These investors, nervous of any potential inadequacy in their personal pension plans needed to take care of them in their old age, and aware of politicians' duplicitous promises in these matters, are building a substantial proportion of their investment portfolios in emerging markets which are thereby enabled to compete even more fiercely with developed, industrialized nations.

Capital drives competition. As it spreads, bringing new sources of supply to the growing global free market, the customer is king as never before. Customers are getting tougher, setting stringent targets for prices, knowing well that someone, somewhere in the exploding free market can and will satisfy their demands. If any one feature of the business world will affect management auditors, it is that one. The management auditors' main effort will be and must be directed at seeking out and eliminating avoidable costs wherever they occur: it is at the heart of continuous improvement.

This third edition

Although a substantial amount of the text within the second edition is retained, for the same reasons explained in its own *"Preface"*, it has been brought up to date throughout and much new material has been added as relevant to present and future management audits, which I hope new and existing readers alike will enjoy. As ever I still refuse to pad out the book with lengthy audit checklists etc., still believing the auditor must be able to consider the audit objectives, the auditee's circumstances and prepare his own. (For those who note the extensive use of the male gender in the text, rest assured there is no intentional discriminatory bias - it is just easier to write that way than to constantly include *"his/her"*, *"he/she"* etc.)

Once again, the book should help those companies wanting to improve their business operations, develop programmes apart from demanding audits. The management auditor has to address management issues and, knowing what those auditors will look for, the auditee then knows much of what has to be done for effective business operations. The book does not attempt to discuss conventional cost budgeting and financial controls, since these matters are well addressed in their own standard texts, but it should help highlight issues that need effective budget planning, cost accounting and control. A continuous theme in both parts of the book is for the management auditor to look to the future, not the past as is typical of the traditional financial audit, for when this is done, the probability of preparing and meeting sensible budgets is increased, as is the likelihood of management meeting its fiduciary responsibilities.

The book has been split into two separate parts. The emerging split was apparent in the second edition as its last chapters dealt with audit applications. Feedback provided by readers, conference and seminar delegates, asking questions about audit applications, convinced me that the split should be more apparent. Part 1 looks at the audit process running from audit preparation through to close out after follow-up action is taken. It describes many commonly used audit tools as well as ways of analyzing different aspects of an auditee's business operations. Part 2 deals with some audit applications: it can not deal with all types of applications for there are so many economic sectors and applied technologies that a full analysis of each and every one would create a voluminous encyclopaedia. The applications selected are those that affect most firms. Part 2 mentions more tools that can be usefully employed by the auditor, especially when performing a value-added audit and trying to secure improvement in the auditee's business operations. A full discussion of the various tools that can be used is not possible within the constraints of this type of book, so, the reader is advised to seek out the many texts available dealing with them. This second part unashamedly focuses on reducing avoidable costs and making the auditee more competitive. That is the original mission of management auditing and it must remain so.

Bouquets

Once again, my sincere thanks to the many people who took the trouble to express their appreciation of the book, to those who requested extra points of clarification for particular topics. There are too many to name, but each and every one has my highest regard.

Above all, throughout the writing of this third edition, the constant encouragement and support of my wife was paramount: mere thanks to her are insufficient.

Thank you for purchasing this book, I earnestly hope you will enjoy it and find it of use.

Allan J. Sayle   Brighton, Michigan, USA, March 1997.

Management Audits

Part 1

The assessment of business operations

1. Audit benefits, audit development and audit costs

Facts do not cease to exist because they are ignored.

Aldous Huxley.

Why audit?

It is proper to deal with this question at the outset. Audits are performed by people and people cost a lot of money to employ. Before deciding to embark on any course, a manager needs to know the justification for committing manpower, time and effort to pursuing it. So what is the justification for performing audits, either within one's own company or that of a supplier? Figure 1.1 presents a list of key reasons why management audits should be performed and the company can benefit from their execution.

---

1. To obtain factual input for management decisions.
2. To obtain unbiased management information.
3. To know factually if the company is at risk.
4. To find opportunities for continuous improvement efforts.
5. To improve communications and motivation.
6. To assess individuals' performance based on facts.
7. To assess the status and capability of fixed assets.
8. To assist with training of company staff.
9. To prevent management and business problems.

Figure 1.1 Reasons to perform management audits

1. To obtain factual input for management decisions.

All managerial decisions and plans, especially those of a long term strategic nature, require factual input. Many companies practise a policy of formulating annual, middle-term and long-term plans. Some

3

managements call their plans "objectives" and operate what are commonly known as *"Management By Objectives"* exercises (MBO). Others prefer to dub them as "strategic". By whatever name they are known, these plans are only of value in so far as the data on which they are based is reliable. An audit is one method of gathering factual information based on an unbiased assessment of objective evidence rather than on subjective opinion. Managerial decisions and plans based on this quality of data will be more meaningful for the enterprise than those with a less firm foundation of fact.

People at all levels in an organization either make, or are involved in the making of, decisions. The real product of anyone's labours is *"the decision"*. The output of any decision making process is, obviously, only as good as the input. Audits are fact finding activities which examine objective evidence in an unbiased manner so as to provide reliable input for decisions. A central purpose of a management audit is to obtain correct information that will provide essential input to assist the decision making process so that business problems can be prevented or rectified, avoidable costs thereby being saved.

Decisions are made at all levels in a company. At the highest level, the strategic decision is of vital importance. The greatest failure cost occurs in any company when these decisions go wrong. For example, if an ill-informed executive decides to enter a market for which the company possesses neither the product nor the capacity to meet jurisdictional requirements, it does not matter how well the existing product is made or whether it is made right first time, the entire production cost and effort is waste: such a result would reduce profit, could cripple the company and damage the share price.

> A major company decided to enter the burgeoning personal computer market with its own product. The general consensus reached by the industry's observers and commentators was extremely favourable with regard to the product's technological features and quality of build. However the market reacted unfavourably to the sticker price, determined at the highest level within the firm, and few were sold. The product was perceived as pricy compared to competitive products and offering less value for money. The associated loss cost many millions of dollars and caused hardship for employees and suppliers alike.

Audits are unbiased fact finding exercises which substantially improve the quality of decisions by helping to reduce the risks associated with them. Audits provide management information.

The value of audits has been recognized by such management notables as A.P. Sloan,[1], Henri Fayol [2] and Harold Geneen[3]. A.P. Sloan was a master at strategic decision making: he built the General Motors empire and from the quotation reproduced in Chapter 8, it can reasonably be stated that audits were of importance in assisting Mr. Sloan in that task.

2. To obtain unbiased management information.

Since an audit systematically analyses objective evidence and presents facts rather than value judgements, it corrects preconceived ideas about the status of a company's management systems, procedures, methods and training requirements. This also involves the correction of peculiar notions about whether or not the various parts of the company are working in a manner which is consistent with the policies and objectives delegated from the board of directors. It is common for senior and middle management to see their own operation through rose-coloured spectacles, sometimes to such an extent that any similarity between the official procedure and actual practice is purely coincidental. Senior managements obtain their information through the channels that run upwards through the organization's hierarchy. As the information is passed from level to level, it is inevitably liable to be distorted and filtered before it ever reaches senior management. This can be disastrous in extreme cases and costly at other times. An audit report bypasses a number of management levels and reaches senior management in its original form, giving an undistorted picture of company operations and the effectiveness of the various departments and managers within the organization.

As companies reorganize and re-engineer, flattening the organization charts, reducing the layers of management in the hierarchy, the problems of distortion and filtering are reduced. Small and medium size firms have an advantage in that their management is naturally closer to the lower levels. Even so, inadequate communications still persist in too many cases.

3. To know factually if the company is at risk.

An audit provides vital feedback to management as to whether the organization is meeting its legal and contractual obligations - an increasingly significant benefit in view of trends in product liability. This reduces the possibility of customer complaints and expensive litigation. Moreover, it provides even more vital feedback concerning the organization's ability to compete in the future and hence the wisdom or otherwise of becoming involved in contracts and product markets which the organization does not currently have the capacity to satisfy. Many companies contract in their problems from pure ignorance of their real capacity in relation to market and other external factors. The audit also determines whether the company is meeting its contractual and legal obligations within the company to its staff. This includes, *inter alia*, assessment of safety practices and compliance with employment legislation.

Environmental responsibility is an area of growing importance to the firm. The business practices, products and materials used, by-products and waste created attract increasing attention from public and media: locally, nationally and internationally. The penalties for irresponsible behaviour, whether wittingly or unwittingly performed, are becoming ever more stringent. The management audit can determine whether the company is meeting its legal and social obligations and includes an assessment of environmental policies and practices relating to the product, materials, by-product creation, waste disposal and end-of-life recycling of the product in the marketplace.

4. To find opportunities for continuous improvement efforts.

The audit analyses objective evidence concerning the effectiveness of the organization and its structure: it can identify the circumstances by which resources and time are utilized ineffectively. This is because a properly conducted management audit challenges decisions and the original basis for them, thus ensuring that the *status quo* is constantly challenged in the light of changing business and technological circumstances. The professional auditor challenges decisions and the factors on which they are based but never challenges the person who made them because that is counterproductive to the performance of the audit. It is a Golden Rule to never challenge the person being audited. (See Appendix 1. *"12 Golden Rules"*).

No organization can expect to have an effective continuous improvement programme without implementing a comprehensive management audit programme. (See Part 2, Chapter 1. *"Continuous improvement programmes"*; Part 2, Chapter 2. *"Value-added auditing"*.)

5. To improve communications and motivation.

Since the audit report reaches the senior management directly, it promotes communications between the lowest and the highest levels within the company. It enables employees at all levels to suggest improved methods of operation. The lowest echelons are those most closely involved with the actual product and service supplied and are normally in the best position to see the truth about the practical implementation of the official management systems. All such systems inevitably become outdated and it is often difficult to find the time to update and upgrade them. This tends to result in the systems losing credibility with the lower echelons, who often see them as something imposed from above, without consultation. By consulting people at all levels, an audit can make them feel that they are genuinely involved in managerial decisions, that management is interested in their suggestions and that their opinion is going to reach senior management unexpurgated. This improvement in communication can raise morale and motivation at all levels. If the people's ideas are acted upon as a result of the audit, they may feel more committed to making their suggestions work.

6. To assess individuals' performance based on facts.

An audit produces an unbiased assessment of each individual's training needs and of each individual's effectiveness at his or her job. Many managers do not enjoy the routine of the annual appraisal. They dislike the feeling that they are sitting in judgement on their subordinates, some of whom may perhaps be closer to friends than mere business colleagues. Moreover, where some are concerned, personal feelings may cloud the issue and render the appraisal less than accurate. The audit not only helps to take any personal colouring out the annual appraisal but also helps to safeguard the subordinate's position, in that any personal dislikes between subordinate and manager will not be taken into account.

7. To assess the status and capability of fixed assets.

An audit assists in obtaining an unbiased assessment of the status and capability of equipment and other fixed assets throughout the enterprise: their physical condition, their maintenance requirements, their repair and fault history as well as the need for new or modified equipment and facilities to perform new processes. It can also help to show how effective the preventive maintenance or condition monitoring systems are and assess whether or not, in the light of technological advances and competitors' activities, the equipment wastes time and resources (such as manpower, floor space, or energy) in use. This may be the case for, even though the equipment is still serviceable, it may now represent a liability to the company's competitive position. (See also Part 2 Chapter 2 *"Value-added auditing".*)

8. To assist with training of company staff.

An audit can provide useful training for the personnel who participate as observers. The observers see the various departments' interaction as well as the function and location of each individual department. They quickly gain knowledge of who does what, how they do it, what they need and the operational interfaces with other functions which demonstrate the reality of the organization's management systems in action. This familiarization afforded to the observers makes them more productive in a shorter space of time than would otherwise be the case if they are merely given a copy of the firm's manuals and procedures and expected to learn by osmosis!

9. To prevent management and business problems

All businesses have problems, indeed, within any given organization, all departments continually have problems. The tasks of management at whatever level in the organization are to identify possible sources of problems, to plan preventive action in order to forestall the problems and to solve them, should they arise. If this were not the case, managers would not be needed. When reduced to fundamentals the vast majority of the problems are, in essence, quality problems. They are problems concerning the quality of work being performed, the quality of work that has been performed, the quality of items being received, the quality of information being communicated, the quality of available equipment, the quality of decisions made.

All problems have a cost associated with them. It, therefore, follows that the avoidance, prevention and resolution of these problems equates to the prevention and reduction of unnecessary costs. The costs are avoidable if appropriate preventive measures are taken. The old adage of *"an ounce of prevention being worth a pound of cure"* can be rewritten as *"a few cents worth of prevention will save many dollars worth of avoidable costs".* Clearly, the prevention of business problems and their avoidable costs must be considered the prime task of management.

The following example amply illustrates the cost benefit of performing audits.

> A large utility decided to build a new complex which would cost $350 million. The design work for this installation was subcontracted, a very small management team being set up within that utility to provide overall control of the design contractor. Several months into the design work, the project manager felt unhappy with the performance of the design contractor and

considered having an audit performed. The audit was costed out at approximately $35,000. The project manager decided that this was too expensive and refrained from proceeding further. As the project progressed, avoidable rework and delays amounted to a $15 million loss for the utility. This loss would have been totally avoided, had a systems audit had been conducted on the contracting organization at the outset.

The whole philosophy and purpose of effective management is to prevent problems before they occur, to identify and correct them swiftly if they should occur, and to uncover the root cause. The accent is on prevention first rather than on actions designed merely to find problems that have occurred. Management audits are central to effective management because they are tools that provide forewarning of situations that will lead to problems: they identify the real root causes and the risks associated with leaving them uncorrected.

Over the years, I have found that there are only six real causes of business problems. These are discussed in Chapter 18 and consist of-

♦ Lack of organization.
♦ Lack of training.
♦ Lack of discipline.
♦ Lack of resources
♦ Lack of time.
♦ Lack of top management support.

The management auditor is looking for any of the many symptoms of these real causes of problems as well as for avoidable costs. The latter is discussed in greater depth in Part 2, Chapter 2 *"Value-added audits"*.

Analogies

The word *"audit"* was in use two thousand years ago to refer to a hearing of oral evidence. Its more modern usage is found in the Oxford English Dictionary, which defines an audit as *"an official examination of accounts with verification by references to witnesses and vouchers"* and states that to audit is *"to make an official systematic examination of* [accounts]". Management audits contain several of the characteristics here ascribed to financial audits. To be specific:

♦ Management audits are official in that they are authorized by top management as part of policy.

◆ They are carried out systematically.
◆ They verify by referring to objective evidence (such as items made, equipment used, documents and data created).

Management auditors must be independent of the activity being audited. A financial auditor has to **ascertain** that the accounts present *"a true and fair view"* of the financial state of an auditee company. The management auditor has to **present** a true and fair view of the efficacy, status, and implementation of the management systems as well as the capabilities of the auditee. (See Appendix 1. *"12 Golden Rules"*.) The value of a properly performed management audit is precisely that it presents a true and fair view, not one that subscribes to palatable fictions. The similarity of the management audit to the financial audit is so great that in some company departments, such as receiving, purchasing and stores, the financial auditor and the management auditor may be asking identical questions. This explains the efforts being made towards *"Converged Audits"* or *"Operational Audits"* which combine management and financial auditors into a single team. However, in one important aspect the management auditor is very different. The financial audit by its nature looks at past events and results: it is a form of inspection. That one cannot inspect quality into a product is now widely recognized as much as a financial auditor cannot honestly inspect profit into past loss. The management auditor can advise the auditees at all levels of the following:

◆ The risk of continuing present practices in tomorrow's world.
◆ The probable efficacy of planned strategies, practices, systems in preventing avoidable loss.

It is my firm view that management audits differentiate themselves from inspections in being future focussed. Management auditors look to the future, not the past as do traditional inspections and other forms of verification activities.

What is a *"management audit"*?

It was no accident that caused the first edition of this book, written in 1978, to be given the title *"Management Audits"* for experience had convinced me of its appropriateness. In that edition I wrote that when reduced to fundamentals quality assurance equates to good management. With that in mind it seemed logical that one needed to perform management audits.

A management audit is an independent examination of objective evidence, performed by competent personnel, to determine:

a)   Whether or not the auditee:

♦   Is assisting or is capable of assisting the company to achieve its policies and objectives.
♦   Is capable of or is assisting the company to fulfil its contractual and legal obligations.
♦   Has integrated management systems to do so.
♦   Is effectively implementing those systems.
♦   Could eliminate avoidable costs and continuously improve.

and, b)

♦   The risk of continuing present practices in tomorrow's world.
♦   The probable efficacy of planned strategies, practices, systems in preventing avoidable loss.

It is also:

♦   The true and fair presentation of the results of such examination.

One cannot present a true and fair set of results unless they are based on verified and verifiable facts. The audit is a fact gathering exercise and, when conducting an audit, it is vital constantly to remember that one's aim is:

FACT FINDING NOT FAULT FINDING.

Obviously, there will be occasions when faults will be found - but that is a fact! (See Appendix 1. *"12 Golden Rules"*). Fact finding denotes the correct attitude, fault finding does not.

Everybody in the organization has a product. Everybody is responsible for the quality of his or her product, as well as the costs they incur, and must, therefore, manage both their own work and themselves properly. Effectively this means that everyone is a manager, regardless of whether staff control comes under their delegated responsibilities. This is a basic principle of *"Total Quality Management"* (TQM) programmes, which used to be referred to as *"Company Wide Quality"* (CWQ) programmes, in years gone by. The independent audit, therefore, serves the needs of people at all levels since it provides them with information concerning *their* management of *their* work.

11

But the organization cannot survive or flourish if at each and every level of internal activity people effectively control their work tasks (processes). This cannot be achieved unless the individual, too, regularly audits the efficay of his/her own management systems and management practices. Self management audits, or more simply, *"self audits"*, are essential. The individual should not await the arrival of the independent person to audit their activities to determine if the practices are satisfactory or not. Ascertaining the effectiveness of one's own systems and practices, determining root causes of problems and deciding upon desirable corrective action is the essence of self control and personal continuous improvement. (Self audits are described in Chapter 2.)

In sum, regardless of who is performing it:

> A management audit is a fact finding exercise which provides management information.

What type of organization should perform management audits?

All companies and enterprises, regardless of size, can benefit by examining their activities and management systems. This applies no less to local government, civil service, commerce and the service industries than it does to manufacturing industry.

Managers often say"*I can't afford the time to perform audits because I have too many problems*". Performing an audit can lead most speedily to solutions and relief. When one has problems and time appears to be pressing, it is exactly the right occasion to perform an audit which will identify the real cause(s) of those problems, presenting solutions that will prevent the future recurrence of them. The manager, will thereby be presented with real opportunities for improved performance, opportunities which he or she would be foolish to ignore. Audits are one of the finest, yet under-appreciated, problem solving techniques available to business today. Fact finding, identifying root cause and offering solutions.

Management audits should be tiered. At the highest level is the *"President's Audit"*, which is further discussed in Part 2, Chapter 7. From the senior levels downwards, audits are directed at ascertaining that the subordinate levels are setting and working towards objectives that are consistent with those that have been delegated to them (as well as the matters described above under *'What is a "management audit"?'*). Such appraisals also ascertain that the lower echelons are performing their own similar audits properly, an activity which helps to give reassurance that any problems can be identified and corrected promptly before they occur. The basic audit is a self audit, described in Chapter 2.

In-house or hired auditors?

A company will inevitably have to consider the value, or otherwise, of employing a permanent staff whose duties will consist solely of auditing. The decision depends upon a number of factors including the size of the company, the product or service supplied and the type and number of contracts with which it is involved. Large companies can generally justify and sustain the cost of in-house auditors. Small companies, however, may find it cheaper and more beneficial to hire a management auditor from an external source (a consultant or someone employed by a consortium or joint venture partners). The major benefit of outside auditors is their independence. Other benefits include the experience of other types of systems, the absence of in-bred company habits and the freedom from preconceived ideas. Professional auditors from outside sources will be less likely to be biased and political manoeuvering, unafraid to present an honest picture.

It is also beneficial and cost effective to train people from various parts of the organization to perform audits, thereby gradually obtaining a pool of auditors that the managers can use to audit different departments. In this way a measure of independence is assured. When asked *"How large should be the pool of auditors?"* my experience is that approximately 8% of the full time permanent payroll staff drawn from all levels and functions has given optimal results. Problems of staff turnover, sickness, absence, vacation are minimized by developing such a size of pool. Building up such a pool also enables the company to audit more effectively at all levels of auditee activity whether at the executive suite or the "shop floor".

Costs of audits.

The benefits of management audits discussed here must be weighed against the costs of performing them. The cost consists of:

♦ The audit team's time spent preparing, performing, reporting, following-up and completing the audit.
♦ The auditee's time spent participating in and following-up the results arising from the audit.
♦ Overhead costs of materials, travel, accommodation, support staff and logistics.

13

The greatest costs arise when the audit is performed by untrained or unsuitable auditors, as anyone who has been subject to this experience can testify. Such auditors are unlikely to produce constructive analyses; often they leave a trail of destructive criticism and mayhem in their wake. Hence good training of management auditors is an important factor in determining the cost of the audit. Sadly, good training has been a rarity in the past. In some cases, people have suddenly been told that they have to perform an audit, without having any system, methods or much idea of what to do let alone what to look for. An auditor can hardly be expected to produce meaningful results if he or she is not given the tools needed to achieve them. Good auditors do not just "appear" - they evolve as their training and experience hones their skills. But, training and performance of audits alone does not create a good auditor. More is required, as discussed in Chapters 14 and 22. It is the auditor's knowledge that is central to obtaining a cost-beneficial audit, a value-added audit. For this, continuous development of the auditor is essential.

The auditee's investment

During the on-site portion of the audit, the auditee normally invests at least twice as much as the auditor. This can be simply explained as follows: at any workplace time is consumed as an auditee employee answers questions and produces objective evidence for the auditor; the escort's time is also taken up just by being present. (It is normal practice to have a knowledgeable escort present at all times, as further discussed in Chapter 10.) Given that a minimum of two of the auditee's people are thus present throughout the audit proceedings, the man-hours involved are twice as much, assuming that only one auditor is present. Even when more than one auditor is present, the investment made by the auditee must be respected. Additional auditee costs are incurred when supervisors are present, on a purely observational basis, to see how things are going and when the auditee gathers its people together after the audit to review the audit results and act on corrective action requests. In general, the auditee incurs a far higher cost for the audit than does the auditor. It represents an investment that must be respected by the audit team delivering a value-added service. This is at the core of value-added auditing, discussed in Part 2 Chapter 2.

Accordingly, the audit needs to be conducted professionally. For his investment, the auditee is entitled to a good return, some constructive criticism and valuable conclusions from the audit. Failure to achieve this is costly for both the auditor and the auditee organizations. In the case of external audits, the cost is eventually borne by the auditor's organization. The auditee's costs inevitably become incorporated in the unit price of the product and are passed on to the auditor's organization. Ultimately the latter passes, or attempts to pass, the costs to its customer and society. There is no guarantee they will be accepted, when they are not, business is lost, not safeguarded.

When one considers the investment in the audit made by the auditee, one must regard the auditee as a major customer of the auditor, deserving a value-added service performed by competent people in a constructive way. If one does not regard the auditee as a principal beneficiary of the audit effort, there is little point in conducting management audits at all.

The cost of incompetent auditors

Incompetent and ill-trained practitioners cause auditing and quality management to fall into disrepute. The attitude of many auditors also leads to inadequate results. Some of them revel in their apparent power and abuse the authority vested in them: they are irresponsible. They believe that their job is to search for auditee errors as opposed to evaluating the strengths. Moreover, upon discovering a problem, they tend automatically to think *"Let's put another piece of paper into this auditee's operation"*; or *"Shouldn't we have another procedure for this?"* That is wrong: many business and quality problems disappear when systems are simplified and paperwork is reduced. To suggest the introduction of extra "quality controls" and more paper is short-sighted and can have the opposite effect to the one desired.

> The North Sea oil industry instituted more formal auditing from the early 1980's onwards. The audits at first, and in most cases, performed by a mixture of former shop floor and construction yard inspectors. In reality, because of their backgrounds and inadequate investment in developing the auditors' abilities, many audits were what I call *"inspection nouveau"*. Although the North Sea industry and its suppliers spent a considerable amount of money in the performance of audits over the years, in general, they did not, I believe, obtain good value for money.

> At the time of writing this third edition, despite the good intentions of the "Big 3" members of the American automotive industry, that industry and its suppliers are mostly repeating the same error. They are not receiving the value for money they deserve from the "audits" being performed in the name of QS 9000.

The costs of audits mount up quickly and the benefit plummets when the auditors possess the wrong background. It is unreasonable to expect them to audit areas where they have no direct experience or competence in the techniques and products or services concerned.

In some audit environments, shop floor inspectors are inappropriate as auditors. This is not to denigrate them, they do have a very useful role to play. Some do fully comprehend contract processes, design processes, sales/ marketing, human resource and accounts functions, but many do not. Regrettably, the trend has been for managements to expect these people to audit such areas, often unassisted. It is an unreasonable demand.

It is always a question of horses for courses. Selection of the right auditor for the task, regardless of whether that person will come from internal or external sources, is a primary audit decision, as is discussed in Chapter 8.

Development of audits.

Audits, in the form adopted by a number of industries nowadays, were pioneered in the USA and began to develop after the Second World War in the military, nuclear and aerospace industries. These industries have two things in common: firstly that, they are capital intensive and secondly that in the event of a malfunction, there is a high safety-related risk. The audit developed as a result of the need to make certain that contracts were being properly performed. The earlier "audits", such as works surveys performed by various classification societies, concentrated on hardware and physical and manufacturing capabilities of a company: they were not audits as we understand the term nowadays.

At present, more and more industries are recognizing the benefit of audits as part of a quality management programme and it is reasonable to suppose that in the future the techniques will spread even further, especially as the fashion for complying with such standards as ISO 9000, ISO 14000 and QS 9000 continues. Some industries have reeled as a result of the frequency and number of audits to which they have been subjected by outside organizations. This has led to the emergence of so-called *"Third Party Assessments"* (TPA's), described in Chapter 2 and a supporting service industry in the hope that multiple assessment will disappear. It won't. It is conceivable that in the future, a more extensive interchange of audit reports between companies will develop in order to reduce the number of audits and the problems of multiple assessment. Eventually, organizations such as Dun & Bradstreet may include in their assessment of a company an analysis of the efficacy of the enterprise's business management systems and not rely solely on the results of traditional financial audits and posted reports of turnover and profitability. This might be based on information gathered by a management audit of the enterprise in question but, in my personal opinion, such audits are unlikely to be performed by all but a small few of the present day *"registrars"*, for the majority of them do not have the focus, methods or experience required.

The problem of multiple assessment.

The explosion in the number of audits being performed in many economic sectors of business activity has served to highlight even further the problems of multiple assessment, by which several companies operating in the same industry separately audit the same supplier with resultant excessive costs to them all and to their national economies. To reduce these costs, it would obviously be beneficial if schemes were introduced whereby an assessment of a company by a single organization would satisfy the needs of many. The ISO 9000, QS 9000 schemes *et al* have apeared but they still require various prerequisites in order to prove themselves acceptable.

A reputable assessment scheme must guarantee consistency in approach by all the organizations authorized to perform assessments; must have strict standards for the selection, vetting and continuous monitoring of those organizations; must have rigid standards for the performance of assessment and the competence of personnel (auditors). Even though this advice was written in earlier editions of this book one cannot but be dismayed with the general level of achievement by the ISO 9000 schemes in particular. The house magazines of recognized professional bodies, such as the British Institute of Quality Assurance, regularly and rightly record upsetting case stories of registration scheme failures, registrar inadequacy and incidents of incompetence. There remains much to do and one cannot but be disturbed when the emerging expression *"drive-by assessments"* is used not only by registered firms but also by some of the registrars themselves to describe the inadequate thoroughness with which many firms are *"assessed"* for registration purposes.

The reputation of individual assessment bodies is directly dependent on the quality of the auditors used and on the consistency of their approach. At the time of writing this edition problems in both areas plague them, though few would openly admit to it. Rigorous procedures for conducting the assessments, along with utmost integrity in the people involved, are crucial. In the final analysis, however, everything is dependent on the competence and attributes of the assessors, on the quality of training and on the methods of selection of the staff concerned.

Clearly, there is a need for professional training and qualification schemes. Training is only as good as the experience of those who perform it: auditing is a practical subject best taught by experienced practitioners, not by academics or recent recruits to the ranks of auditors. An auditor qualification scheme which is not dependent on verifying the competent performance of the auditor at work, in order to decide whether or not that auditor should be registered, must be regarded as unreliable and lacking.

The world has seen the emergence of various assessment schemes designed to reduce multiple assessment of companies in general. Their major plank is that applicant companies are assessed for compliance with a part of the ISO 9000 series of standards. Even though these schemes have now existed for nearly a decade, as at the time of writing this third edition of this book, the schemes credibility is not yet full established. As was noted in the second edition, however, it is doubtful that they will be of value if they remain based on the current version of the ISO 9000 series since that series leaves too much for interpretation, as described in Chapter 6 and elsewhere[4]. In short, different customers may have radically different contractual requirements, different firms may read the expressions differently for their circumstances and the problem of inconsistency in interpretation by the various registrars remains. Thus when an assessment body (registrar) investigates compliance with the standard, it will be considering *an* interpretation of the standard - and it will issue a certificate whose validity rests on that interpretation alone: assessment bodies do not, currently, have the authority to impose their interpretation of the chosen standard's words and expressions into the auditee's practices or management systems. Nor should they: it is for the industry involved to accurately specify its wants and needs. Accordingly, any company wishing to select a supplier solely on the basis of a registrar's certificate would be well advised to remain circumspect. This is further discussed in Chapter 2, in the comparison of supplier evaluations, external audits, pre-award surveys and "third party" assessments.

> The QS 9000 scheme, developed by the big three American automobile makers, Chrysler, Ford and General Motors and American truck producers, seems to have heeded the notes made in the second edition of this book. The scheme regularly releases sanctioned interpretations of its requirements defined by the industry itself, based on feedback of experiences, difficulties and circumstances.

2. Management audit categories, depth and scope

Like - but oh! how different!

Wordsworth.

There are three basic types of management audit and these vary in their depth and scope. It is important for an auditor to be clear about these points in advance because they affect the preparation and structure of the audit team required. The relationship between auditor and auditee will also vary according to the type of audit. It is often easier to have an open discussion when auditing within one's own company than it is when auditing or being audited by another organization.

Categories of management audit

Internal audit

This is a management audit performed by a company or a department upon its own systems, procedures and facilities. The auditors may be from the company's own ranks or hired from outside to act on its behalf. The internal audit is a technique whereby the management feels its own pulse and assesses the organization's performance, its needs, its strong points and its failings.

In the ISO 9000 industry, these audits are frequently dubbed *"First Party Audits"*, the expression deriving from terminology used in describing contractual matters whereby the customer is one party to a contract, the supplier is another. It was modified to suit the intention of the ISO 9000 series which defines what a firm must do. That firm is, therefore, regarded as the *"first party"* to the standard it selects; customers are then regarded as second parties to that choice. One of the stranger features of the ISO 9000 standards and its supporting industry is their inconsistency in using the expressions *"internal audits"* and *"first party audits"*. The body of requirements contained within ISO 9001/ 9002 etc. stipulate the performance of internal audits, making no menton of first party audits. The various registration schemes and its assessment community, though, refer to first party audits when setting and discussing auditor credentials. But, fear not,

19

gentle reader, if there is a difference (which there is not), just ignore it and regard the two as being the same thing!

Self audit

The self audit places mature responsibility onto one's employees. Since everyone is a manager, it is sensible for each individual periodically to determine the results of his or her efforts and associated needs for improvement. This is one area where the performance of a self audit is most useful. Although the ingredient of independence is lost, the extra values of self discipline and delegated trust fully compensate. Self audits are performed in addition to, not as a substitute for, independent management audits.

The techniques described in this book can be applied on a day-to-day basis by any person in order to determine the status of activities for which he or she is responsible. The question technique that is described in Chapter 13 can be used for obtaining information concerning such matters as peoples' needs, decisions, work, items and equipment. The task elements described in Chapter 4 can be used to guide the conduct of meetings and as an aid to communications in both written and verbal form. And so, the self audit is a particular type of internal audit performed by an individual upon his or her own systems, procedures and facilities in order to assess his or her performance, needs, strengths and failings.

External audit

External audits are performed by a company upon its own suppliers or sub-suppliers. The auditors may be either from the company's own ranks or hired from an outside source to act on behalf of the company. This type of management audit is performed in order to assess the status of contracts made with the company's suppliers and sub-suppliers, in order to determine whether the company will be receiving what it is paying for. In some cases, the line between the external audit and the internal audit may be rather blurred - as, for example, when the auditing company considers its suppliers as part of its own organization for the duration of the contract, providing technical guidance and support until the contract is fulfilled. This blurring of the boundary between the internal and external audit in no way undermines the basic distinction: where a contract exists, certain implications concerning rights of access and examination of goods necessarily follow.

The ISO 9000 industry dubs external audits *"second party audits"*, (for reasons explained in *"Internal audits", above*). But, at the time of writing this third edition, the ISO 9000 series does not require them to be performed.

20

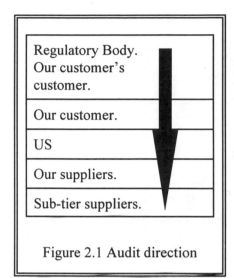

Regulatory Body. Our customer's customer.
Our customer.
US
Our suppliers.
Sub-tier suppliers.

Figure 2.1 Audit direction

Extrinsic audit

This type of management audit is performed either by a customer or by a regulatory body or an authorized independent inspection agency (or its representative). The title also covers such audits as those carried out by a customer on a company's suppliers or sub-suppliers.

Figure 2.1 shows the relationship between the various participants in audits. The arrow always points in one direction: it is not possible, as well as not done, to audit one's own customer, as much as frustrated suppliers would frequently yearn for the opportunity to do so! Anybody who is above *"US"* on the ladder is an extrinsic auditor: an audit from *"US"* to a lower rung is an external audit.

Figure 2.2. shows how the various management audits relate to one another. Notice the column marked *"Duration"*. The total duration of a full internal audit is measured in weeks rather than days because the internal auditor is able to go to a greater number of departments by performing a series of partial audits: he is able to examine a greater quantity of objective evidence over a longer period of time than an external or extrinsic auditor ever could. The latter are generally only allocated a number of mandays in which to perform the audit in question: this is why the duration of external or extrinsic audits is measured in days rather than weeks. (See also the discussion on time/benefit - Chapter 9, Figure 9.5.) Bearing this in mind, an external/extrinsic auditor will always regard the auditee's internal audits as activities that must be covered. Internal audits not only provide the auditee's management with the benefits described in Chapter 1, in the section *"Why audit?"*, they also create confidence in the customer that someone within the auditee's organization is continually appraising the efficacy of the operational systems. It follows, therefore, that if during an external audit the need for corrective action is identified, one must question why the auditee's own internal audits failed to discover this whilst investigating the effectiveness of and genuine authority vested in those internal activities.

Category	Auditor organization	Auditee organization	Scope	Depth	Duration
Internal	'Us' = own organization or hired auditor	'Us'	Full, partial (process, phase, department etc.), follow-up	Systems or compliance	Weeks
External	'Us' = own organization or hired auditor, consortium, joint venture partner	Our supplier, sub-suppliers, etc.	Ditto	Ditto	Days for each supplier
Extrinsic	Our customer, customer's customer etc., regulatory body	'Us', our supplier, sub-suppliers etc.	Ditto	Ditto	Days for each audit

Figure 2.2 Management audit category, depth and scope.

Management Audit applications

In addition to the types of audit just described, there are other audits often referred to in today's business life and publications. Even a quick analysis of them reveals they fall within one of the categories described above, internal, external or extrinsic. They tend to be labeled according to their application and examples are product audits, project audits, value-added audits, environment audits. Some particular applications are discussed in Part 2 of this book, *"Management Audit Applications"*. Most of these audit applications can be performed internally, externally or extrinsically as desired.

Audit depth

Systems audit

A systems audit probes whether or not there are organizational plans and management systems in existence and whether these were conceived to enable the various activities of interest to be accomplished as required. It assesses the adequacy of the management systems to meet the particular codes, standard and regulations invoked by a contract (for example an ISO standard, an ANSI standard or a national standard) or required by virtue of the legislation which applies to those activities and their products or services. The management systems must define the type of objective evidence to be produced as work proceeds, in order to provide information on the results obtained from their implementation. An auditor does not consider such a system to exist and operating unless there is objective evidence - i.e., proof - of its existence - which can only be obtained after the system is put into practice and assessed during a compliance audit, see below. Some standards, such as ISO 9001, require that the quality management systems are documented within a manual.

The systems audit does not ask whether the company complies with a system: it merely ascertains whether or not management has developed the systems needed to meet contractual and legal obligations. The mere provision of a tool is not guarantee that the tool will be used as it should be. The systems audit may be able to suggest improvements to the auditee's proposals but there is no guarantee that those improvements will prove to be effective in practice.

When to perform systems audits

It is advantageous to conduct a systems audit well in advance of the actual starting of an activity. The major purpose of that audit is to determine whether all the necessary organizational controls have been considered and whether the systems are in place, such that the decision to start the activity can be taken in the knowledge that the risk of loss has been minimized. The audit gives management the assurance that it is less likely to put good money after bad and that the methods which will be used to control expenditure of effort, time and resources have been carefully and thoroughly thought through. Such audits are timed so that in the event of inadequacies being identified, it is possible to implement corrective action. This philosophy renders systems audits akin to readiness reviews. Management is well advised only to release resources and expenditure upon the satisfactory outcome of such an audit. Although it makes little sense to commence work using methods which are likely to incur loss, the number of activities launched on such a basis is truly surprising. The timing of systems audits is shown in Figure 8.3.

Compliance audit

A compliance audit cannot be satisfactorily performed unless and until a systems audit has been done. This is because the auditor needs to understand the nature and requirements of the organization's and systems' composition if he is to assess whether or not the auditee is complying with them. Once it has been established that an organization and system has been provided, the compliance audit then investigates whether or not they are adhered to.

For the organizational arrangements, in order to answer that question, the auditor scrutinizes the objective evidence that should be generated by the implementation of the system, assessing whether or not they are effective. The auditor checks that the auditee works to the letter of the distributed information which describe them: they may or may not be in hard copy form - an increasing number of firms retain details of their organizational and systems arrangements within their computer files. Sometimes auditees do not work to the letter but still achieve the desired result. In this case, the auditor reports this fact as part of the audit report. Only the compliance audit can assess the real efficacy of the organizational arrangements and management systems in practice. The auditor can determine where improvement is possible or corrective action is needed based on tracking down the root cause of problems unearthed by the audit. The audit may reveal that the auditee's personnel are deviating from the authorized procedure or system. This is not necessarily a bad thing and is further discussed in Chapter 17.

When to perform compliance audits

The compliance audit is done to best effect shortly after actual work has begun using the system intended for it. At this time a small, yet highly significant, sample of the results produced will be available. If the compliance audit then reveals the desired results are not being obtained, there is time to take corrective action without having wasted too much in manpower, time and other resources. Losses are thereby minimized. The timing for compliance audits is shown in Figure 8.3. When a compliance audit is performed at the end of a work phase or upon completion of activities for which the system was intended, it amounts to nothing more than an inspection, dealing with past events and unable to influence their outcome. Losses are maximized in such situations for, if corrective action is revealed as being necessary, the auditee is faced with having to redo work and expend additional resources that could be as great or even greater than those originally allocated and used.

Whereas the compliance audit is performed to verify that activities are being accomplished in accordance with the systems authorized by the auditee's management, it must not be confused with an *"inspection"*. The latter is concerned with product acceptance and release for further processing. The former concerns itself with verifying that management systems are being implemented satisfactorily.

Audit scope

An audit's scope refers to the number of the auditee's activities the auditor wishes to see in order to meet the objectives of his audit. It will vary from audit to audit according to the information required.

Full audit

A full audit (sometimes called a *"cradle-to-grave"* audit) covers all the activities and departments involved:

1. in the execution of a particular contract or project; or,
2. in the development and supply of a particular product line/ range including after sales service throughout the lifetime of the product concerned; or,
3. company wide, including all line and staff activities.

In the case of 1, compliance audits with a full scope are very difficult to carry out on a single contract unless the contract has already been completed. If problems are discovered, it is costly and difficult to resolve them but the lessons to be learned will be of value for the future handling of similar contracts/ projects. (This is, of course, true only in the case of a compliance audit. It is entirely possible to perform a full audit to a systems depth.)

Similar remarks can be made in the case of 2. Where the particular product line or range is to be made on an on-going basis, areas of opportunity might be identified, after completion of the audit, which will be of benefit for its future supply and customer service.

Partial, mini, or phased audit, (process audits)

This is performed only on certain tasks (processes) or departments which are of particular interest. It may cover only those activities up to and including completion of design or it may cover only a particular process capability of the auditee, such as product encapsulation or financial lending, other activities (such as buying, design, sales, or planning) being excluded from the audit because they are not of equal interest at that time. This is not to say that these other activities will not be audited later nor that they have not been audited on previous occasions.

Follow-up audit

A follow-up audit is performed to verify and assess the efficacy of corrective action taken as a result of a previous audit. These audits are almost always partial audits (see above). However, a follow-up audit is not the only means of verifying the efficacy of corrective action. There are many other perfectly good and, perhaps, more cost effective means of performing follow-up action. This is further discussed in Chapter 21.

Informal audit

Sometimes people want to call an audit "informal". Any auditee, who is told that *"This will only be an informal audit"*, should demand that the audit be formal and on the record. If it is not, he should refuse to participate. By implication, if the audit is "informal", its results are not binding and have no weight. In view of the costs of audits, it is unreasonable to expect an auditee to allocate time and money to participating in such an audit unless assured of some benefit. In any case, the "informal" audit generally ends up by becoming formal if the auditor sees some deficiencies that require corrective action.

Bearing in mind the magnitude of investment in the audit made by the auditee, described in Chapter 1 (see *"Costs of audits"*), informal audits offer an unsustainable loss and should not be countenanced.

> One quality manager who enjoyed calling certain audits *"mini-informal audits"*. The individual concerned had no real authority and respect within his own company and was afraid to tell an auditee the truth. Many of his suppliers were in very poor shape but because the purchasing department in his company was extremely powerful, and concerned solely with matters of price, he was afraid of *"rocking the boat"*. The audits were called *"informal"* to make them appear more acceptable but they ended up simply causing a lot of annoyance. Having had shortcomings indicated to them, the suppliers' departments could not go to their own managements demanding corrective action because the audits were "informal". In some cases, there was not even a written audit report and the whole time-consuming process produced absolutely no benefit either to the suppliers or to the auditing company itself.

Unannounced Audit

Recent years witnessed an increase in the number of unannounced audits being performed, especially by registrars responsible for issuing applicant clients with ISO 9000 and QS 9000 certificates. The practice is to be disdained and discouraged. It shows, in my opinion, a distinct lack of professionalism on the part of the auditor(s) concerned. If the auditor does not feel confident in the reliability of the systems in practice, one must question the audit method, its efficacy and the competence of the auditor. The attitude of *"dropping-in to see if they can be caught out"*, of just arriving unannounced is, in my view, unacceptable. In any event, the auditor ought be aware that he probably does not have right of access for the purposes of auditing on an unannounced basis. Most contracts between customer and supplier include terms that specify access at *"reasonable times"* and, even then, with prior notification and arrangement. Arriving unannounced is not *"reasonable"*. It is certainly unmannerly. Registrars should reflect, if they believe the auditee cannot be trusted by them, readers of their certificates cannot rely on the worth of the registrars' certificates either. Their certificates are rendered worthless. (See also Chapter 12 in the discussion concerning *"clean-ups"*).

> I was contacted by a company requesting help with one of its customers who had gained access to the premises on the pretext of a visit and a brief meeting. During that visit, the company concerned had brought along an auditor who, whilst *"looking around"*, had spotted a few deficiencies which were not to his liking. Thereupon he had issued a couple of corrective action request forms. Since there

was no contractual requirement for the implementation of a particular quality management programme, the company that had been "audited", naturally, had felt rather perplexed. The issue was resolved by agreeing to institute the actions required providing that formal corrective action requests were rescinded. That auditor's attitude had caused resentment, upset and embarrassment for each organization.

Supplier evaluations, third party assessments and pre-award surveys

Pre-award surveys

Although the terms *"audit"*, *"survey"* and *"assessment"* are sometimes used interchangeably, I prefer to reserve the latter two to refer solely to a quasi-external audit performed *before* awarding a contract to a supplier. Hence I regard a pre-award survey as:

A visit to a potential supplier's premises for the purpose of assessing both his ability to supply items or services in accordance with the purchaser's anticipated requirements as well as to evaluate the amount of assistance that may be required from the purchaser in order to help that potential supplier comply with the purchaser's economic requirements.

There are two parts to that definition:

♦   The assessment of the supplier's ability.
♦   The amount of assistance.

This separation of issues is deliberate: all potential suppliers can be considered acceptable for the execution of a contract but some will require more support to enable them to comply with the contract requirements than others. A particular potential supplier may be able to deliver product which meets the fitness for purpose requirements, but, in so doing, may incur excessive avoidable costs, for which the purchaser will ultimately pay. There may well, therefore, be an opportunity for the purchaser to obtain an even better price by providing assistance to that potential supplier in order to reduce those avoidable costs. (Avoidable and unavoidable costs are discussed in Part 2, Chapter 2.) In short, the surveyor is asking the vital question: *"How well would this potential supplier spend my company's money?"*

One must always remember that a supplier does not have any money of his own - he only has his customer's with which, in the event of a contract, he is being entrusted.

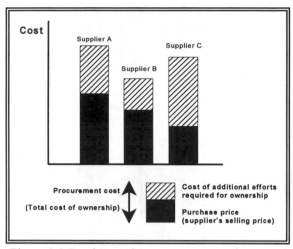

Figure 2.3 Purchase price versus procurement costs

In order to evaluate a tender properly and to determine the most economic source, one must consider the amount of effort (i.e. cost) should the contract be awarded. Suppliers have varying capabilities and these will have a cost impact on one's own company through the execution of the contract. As part of the pre-award survey, the surveyor must give an estimate of the assistance needed. The estimate may be in monetary terms, such as dollars, or in an equivalent, such as mandays of effort required, according to the company's standard practice. The above describes the difference between purchase price and procurement cost, depicted graphically in Figure 2.3.

The type of additional assistance could be categorized and estimated using a worksheet, such as the simple, and rather basic example, shown in Figure 2.4 to illustrate the points just made. The variance between budgeted and actual costs would be applied to the bidders' prices to compare them and to determine the most economic source. The activities listed in that type of worksheet would reflect those creating the total cost of ownership and procurement of the supplies concerned.

Supplier evaluation

A pre-award survey is not what is sometimes called a *"supplier evaluation"*. A supplier evaluation is an appraisal that also takes into account commercial, quality management and technical factors but it does not necessarily involve a visit to the supplier's premises. A supplier evaluation is :

an appraisal to determine the ability of a potential supplier to supply items or services in accordance with the purchaser's anticipated requirements as well as of the amount of effort that may be required by the purchaser to administrate the contract concerned.

Supplier Support Activities Estimate Sheet

Supplier:	Survey Date:	Product I/D:	Sheet......of......
Contract:	Surveyor:		

Activity	Budgeted	Estimated actual	Variance
Product design support			
Product design reviews			
Prototype testing/ validation			
1st piece verification			
Incoming inspection			
External auditing			
Regulatory support			
Supplier training			
Total			

Sophia Boot Street Cleaning Inc.

Distribution: Project Mgt./ Purchasing./ Quality Dept./ Design/ Production/ Finance.

Figure 2.4 Abbreviated worksheet for estimating potential supplier support required.

The quality management aspect of that appraisal may be carried out in a number of different methods, as shown in Figure 2.5. It should be clear from Figure 2.5, which shows the various components of supplier evaluation, that the process is not akin to an audit: whilst a pre-award survey may be performed as part of a supplier evaluation, the two procedures are not equivalent.

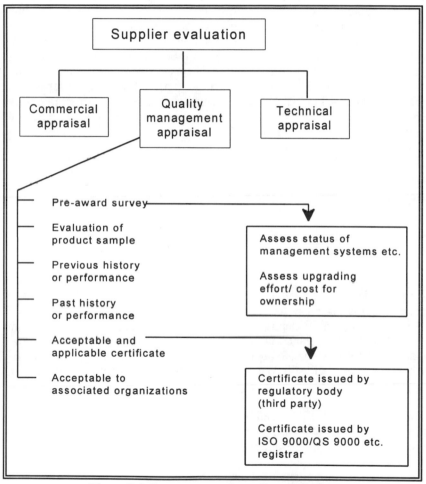

Figure 2.5 Components of supplier evaluation

Third party assessments

Present day conventional wisdom, extant in the quality industry, regards third party assessments as being performed by organizations accredited by a nationally authorized body, such as the American RAB or the British UKAS, that considers them both as competent to do so and as knowledgeable in the auditee's field of activity. The purpose is to perform an audit on behalf of the auditee's potential customers, who do not wish or cannot afford the expenditure of surveying or auditing external organizations themselves. The normal outcome of a successful assessment is the issuing of a certificate which states the auditee's compliance with the requirements of a pertinent standard such as ISO 9000 or QS 9000. The assessment body is engaged by the auditee as an allegedly impartial external body to perform this compliance audit. I stress the term *"compliance audit"*, for one can hardly consider these particular assessments to have any validity if they are performed before any product has been made. In my view, they are a form of internal audit (see above) because the auditee chooses:

♦ Whether or not to request the assessment.
♦ The actual assessment organization (and, frequently, the assessors too).
♦ The terms of reference for the assessors.
♦ The selection of standard to be assessed against.
♦ The scope of the assessment, the timing of the assessment.
♦ The budget available to the assessors.

Any certificate issued by an assessment body is worthless if the audit has gone no further than a systems depth. To make an assessment on the basis of a review of the quality manual, its referenced procedures and little more than a quick walk around the auditee's premises is obviously unwise, but too many do precisely that. Nobody would feel comfortable, given that the various systems might still be in a state of gestation or might never have been implemented.

The essential service provided by an assessment body should be to inform those *"whom it may concern"* that they can have full confidence that the products furnished by the auditee:

♦ Are economic and reduce the risk of loss to all concerned.
♦ Are fit for purpose.
♦ Are made strictly in accordance with *reliable* systems.

Back in the 1960's, the American Society of Mechanical Engineers (ASME) recognized the truth of this argument. It insisted that, in order to obtain recognition by the ASME, the applicant auditee must produce a qualification piece of work produced by means of the management systems that have been implemented in accordance with a quality manual submitted to and approved by the ASME. ASME have the backing of statutory regulation in the United States which requires all pressure vessels installed and used in the USA to be designed and constructed in accordance with ASME requirements including a quality assurance programme meeting prescriptions laid down by ASME. Thus, in the modern context of assessments, ASME authorized auditors are not like the so-called "third party" assessment body (registrar) of the ISO 9000/ QS 9000 type of scheme - they are more akin to a regulatory body and, accordingly, within this book an audit by ASME authorized auditors is considered to be an extrinsic audit and a genuine third party assessment. (As this third edition is written, to the best of my knowledge, I do not believe the ASME's position has fundamentally changed with regard to approving suppliers of pressure retaining equipment.)

A *real* third party assessment is one whose performance, timing and conduct is decided by a regulatory body possessing the authority to interpret the applicable regulations/ codes/ standards as required without intervention by the auditee. The body is backed by statutory powers of enforcement.

In the ISO 9000 industry, it is increasingly the case that many "third party" assessments take the form of:

a brief visit to a company to assess its ability to supply items or services in accordance with requirements that the company has selected, the assessment being performed by an organization that has been engaged by the company appraised but which is not owned by it.

A major problem is that the assessment body might not have the authority to interpret the meaning of a particular standard's words and must assess strictly against the letter of the standard selected by the company being assessed. There is thus the real risk that the unwary customer could believe the supplier to possess capabilities that the latter does not. For an example of this, turn to the discussion in Chapter 6, *"Pitfalls in practice"*. The wisest advice for any company to adopt when reviewing a certificate issued by a "third party" assessment body (a registrar) is that of *caveat emptor*.

Differences and comparisons

The differences between a pre-award survey (PAS), an assessment, performed by an ISO 9000/ QS 9000 type of registrar (RA) and an external audit are summarized in Fig. 2.6. and are discussed as follows:

ITEM 1. A PAS is performed at the discretion of the customer: the internationally recognized quality systems standards, such as ISO 9000, do not require one to be performed. In some industries, however, an external audit is mandatory because the standards require that audits be performed to assess all parts of a quality programme. RAs are performed at the discretion of the vendor.

ITEM 2. PAS is performed prior to contract placement whereas external audits are performed post contract. This seemingly trite point has implications for the teams involved, (see ITEM 4). RA can be performed at any time but, to have relevance, it does need to be performed once saleable product has been completely produced. The customer might have no knowledge of when and under what circumstances a RA has been performed.

ITEM 3. A PAS helps a customer to generate his own list of suppliers together with the goods or services for which they are considered acceptable sources. Such a list is generated on the basis of supplier evaluations, a method of which is the PAS. The external audit, on the other hand, may help to remove a supplier from the qualified supplier's list if it reveals that the supplier's performance has been unsatisfactory, that corrective actions have not been taken or that goods and services do not meet the customer's requirements. In the light of such removal, the company's buyers would no longer be authorized to procure goods or services from that supplier.

RA is a device which the vendor hopes will assist the potential customers to place that vendor on their own lists of acceptable bidders. It does not necessarily mean the vendor will be placed on a list of qualified suppliers, which is a different entity. (In its documentation concerning its QS 9000 initiative, the American automotive industry makes clear that compliance with or RA registration to the QS 9000 requirements does not guarantee the supplier concerned will be considered acceptable for procurement contract purposes.)

Pre-award survey	External audit	Assessment by registrar
1. Customer discretionary.	Mandatory in some industries; Not required by ISO 9000.	Supplier discretionary.
2. Prior to placement of contract/ purchase order.	After contract/ purchase order placement.	Timed to suit supplier, not related to any specific contract.
3. Helps to generate customer's qualified bidders list.	Might help to 'de-generate' the customer's qualified bidders list.	Might help customer to generate his qualified bidders list. Might help an industry to do the same.
4. Survey team is broader based.	Audit team generally restricted to quality department staff supported by process/ product specialists.	Team depends on registrar's professionalism, available resources and costs agreed with supplier.
5. No contractual access right.	Contractual access right or right of 'examination' of product (depends on law of country).	Supplier has initiates access and decides the extent of access according to scope of assessment.
6. Objective evidence is not necessarily 'yours'. It may be considered as being another's proprietary information.	Own objective evidence available according to contract status.	Objective evidence available depends on state of work, type of product and restrictions imposed by current customers.

Figure 2.6 Comparison of pre-award surveys, external audits and registrar assessments (RAs)

35

Pre-award survey	External audit	Assessment by registrar
7. Systems orientated.	Systems and/ or compliance orientated.	Orientation depends upon practices of registrar.
8. Not too deep (generally time limited). Restricted time limit is false economy.	As deep as necessary - can be extended if time short; could be a series of partial audits.	Depth depends upon practices of registrar and costs agreed by supplier.
9. Preparation and planning are often not so extensive (depend on contract size, type and value, in-house information etc.).	Extensive preparation and planning - in-house information on progress and problems is available.	Preparation and planning depend on registrar's practices and costs agreed by supplier.
10. Checklist/ procedure not required by ISO 9000.	Checklist/ procedure mandatory in some industries.	Checklist/ procedure depends on registrar's practices, procedure and assessment standard used.
11. Competent/ trained surveyors generally not required if PAS is not part of the declared quality system. They are required if PAS is part of the quality system declared under ISO 9000.	Competent/ trained auditors mandatory in some industries. They are required if external audits are part of the declared system under ISO 9000.	Competent/ trained assessors depending on quality system standard selected and on registrar's practices.

Figure 2.6 (Continued).

Pre-award survey	External audit	Assessment by registrar
12. Method of reporting aimed at acceptability of the supplier, the content of report generally not so detailed. Surveyors have no right to require corrective action for inadequacies found.	Reports aimed at contract/ regulatory compliance; reports give details of deficiencies. Auditors have right to require corrective action for inadequacies with contract requirements (which are equivalent to breaches of contract).	Reports aimed at issuing of a certificate. Deficiencies *should* lead to non-issue of certificate. Report may be confidential to supplier alone.
13. Provides opportunity for additional contract clauses/ safeguards and milestone payment conditions.	Additional contract clauses/ safeguards are difficult and costly to back fit or impose.	No guarantee that additional safeguards/ clauses are not necessary - *CAVEAT EMPTOR.*
14. Report gives levelization estimate for bid adjudication (man hours, dollars etc.).	Future money value and regulatory/ requirements cannot be assessed reliably.	No guarantee that prudent levelization amounts are not required - *CAVEAT EMPTOR.*

Figure 2.6 (continued).

ITEM 4. Generally, a PAS team comprises representatives from various departments within the customer's company, those representatives being individuals directly involved on the contract concerned. As an example, in manufacturing sectors, the purchasing department's representative investigates the commercial acceptability of the potential supplier (items such as financial strength, current order book level etc.) and discusses the commercial terms of the proposed contract; the technical specialists (design engineers, scientists, computer programmers and the like) investigate the technical capability of the potential supplier in relation to the product technical requirements; the quality management representatives assesses the supplier's applicable management systems and the production engineer assesses the manufacturing facilities and capabilities. The outcome of the PAS is a consensus of opinion on the part of all members of the survey team which reflects the different standpoints that must be balanced in the supplier evaluation.

For an external audit, the team is primarily restricted to members of the firm's quality department (if any). This is for two reasons. The first of these is that the commercial and technical terms of the contract are of an on-going nature whereas the function of the external audit is to assess whether or not contract compliance is being maintained, and can be attained, by the management systems. The second factor - and this is what I refer to as *"the two-edged sword principle"* - is that the external auditors assess to what extent their own organization is performing in the manner required by the contract (that the correct information is passed on punctually to the supplier, for example, or that the communicating information has been generated in accordance with company policy, that the company has taken its own customers' requirements into account in the contract with which the supplier has to comply). Hence, if a design engineer were to audit the supplier's design department, the audit might reveal his own mistakes and so the basic principle of the independence of the auditor would be violated. In order to protect this principle of the two edged sword, where the lead auditor has decided that specialists are required as part of the audit team in order to conduct the audit properly, he will attempt to obtain that support from persons who are independent of the contract in hand.

RA teams depend on the assessment body's discretion and professional attitude. They also depend on the requirements of the standard against which the supplier is to be assessed and the terms of reference stipulated by the supplier, as mentioned previously in this chapter.

ITEM 5. There is a difference in contractual rights of access. Before a contract has been awarded, the supplier can refuse to have its premises and systems surveyed. The award of a contract changes their situation. Most contracts nowadays contain a contractual right of access to examine the goods being supplied. In some countries, such a clause may not even need to be written into the contract since the law of the land provides for it automatically taking the view that, since the customer is paying for goods or services, part of his property exists within the supplier's facilities and that legally a person has right of access to his own property. This right must not be construed as meaning that the audit team can wander at will over the supplier's facilities. It may, however, amount to the right to examine the goods being supplied and the associated equipment and services utilized in the supply of those goods, and to verify by examination of objective evidence that the goods are what they purport to be. It should be noted that "goods" refers not only to the hardware but also to the software and records that are part of the contract supply and for which the customer is paying.

RA access is not a problem because it is at the supplier's initiative.

ITEM 6. The PAS team must remember that the objective evidence they review (or would like to review) is not necessarily their own company's property. This is particularly the case when the supplier has no existing contract with the potential customer. Some objective evidence may relate to another customer's contract and that other customer may consider such objective evidence to be proprietary information. The potential supplier is, therefore, not in a position to divulge details of contracts upon which work is being done or to allow all items to be examined by the survey team. This is particularly true for a company working on defence contracts and governed by its national Official Secrets Act. However helpful the potential supplier wishes to be, it may simply not be within his power to disclose sufficient information for the surveyor to decide whether or not there is compliance with the management systems. It may only be possible to review the management systems that are allegedly in effect.

In the case of the external audit, the auditor is in a stronger position because, depending on the status of the contract, there will be objective evidence of contract compliance and of compliance with the supplier's own management systems. The amount of objective evidence may not be so great if the external audit is performed shortly after the awarding of the contract, but it will be significant (see *Compliance audits*, above). Nonetheless, the auditor will have contractual rights of access to that objective evidence. Furthermore, the external auditor will understand the nature of the objective evidence because he will be (or should be) intimately familiar with the details of his own company's contract. Thus, the pre-award survey tends, perforce, to be more systems oriented while the external audit is systems and compliance oriented (see ITEM 7).

RA objective evidence is basically whatever is available: this may well have no relevance to a particular customer's needs. There may be restrictions imposed because of Official Secrets Act or similar limitations.

ITEM 7. A PAS can do little more than assess the potential efficacy of the auditee's management systems so that the intended method of operating can be established. (Unless the procurement from the auditee of goods similar / identical to those already in production is being considered.)

The external audit is performed in accordance with the customer's interpretation, if any, of the standard as stated and agreed in the contract.

The terms of reference for a RA depend primarily on the supplier: the assessors can only assess compliance within the letter of the standard of interest and cannot consider all permutations of every customer's needs. The status of the management system depends on the vendor's interpretation of the standard's requirements as well as on the flexibility and limits of the standard's wording. That interpretation may be more consistent with the supplier's business needs and attitude rather than those of the customer.

ITEM 8. The previous point (ITEM 7.) contains implications for the time-scale necessary for the visit to the supplier's facilities. Since the PAS tends to be systems oriented, the examination of objective evidence often is not too deep, and a time limitation may have to be imposed by management in the interest of economy. If a company is considering bids from several companies, it can become very costly to spend a long time surveying each company on the basis of compliance. It is common to find that, at best, the PAS tends to be a "look see". (There are attendant risks in this, particularly when the company has embarked on a just-in-time policy, discussed later in this chapter). The spending of an inadequate amount of time during a PAS is foolish because it is generally difficult and expensive to change suppliers after contract signature when inadequate performance is discovered. PAS activities provide valuable information to management making the procurement decision and thoroughness of execution must be regarded as sensible preventive action. The external audit, by contrast, is often as deep as is necessary to get to the truth and, should the time limit run out, it might be extended. The external audit may consist of a series of partial (process or phase) audits and hence the time available for auditing each activity selected may be greater. Regrettably, though, it is frequently too late to discover a supplier's inadequacies for the contract during external audits. External audits have limited preventive value considering the costs associated with purchase order placement. (See also ITEM 12, below).

RA depth and time depend on the professionalism of the assessors and upon the supplier's willingness to pay.

ITEM 9. The preparation and planning given over to a PAS are often less extensive than for an external audit although this depends on the type and size of the contract in question and on the other information available in-house concerning the potential supplier. The amount of in-house information available will naturally be greater for an existing, rather than for an unknown, supplier. In the case of an external audit, a certain amount of in-house information concerning the contract progress and problems that have been encountered is available to the auditor for review prior to the audit. The in-house information may be in document form or expressed verbally by other departments who have experience of dealing with the supplier.

RA preparation and planning depend on the assessors' professionalism and the status of information available from the supplier prior to performance. The assessors' preparation and planning require an investment of time for which the supplier must be willing to pay. Many are not and, in the competitive business world of registrars, the expression *"drive-by assessments"* has appeared, reflecting the skimpy way in which some of them are done.

ITEM 10. The internationally recognized quality systems standards do not require a checklist or procedure to be used for a PAS. At the time of writing this third edition, ISO 9000 does not require external audits to be performed at all, so no checklist could be required. When an external audit is mandatory in some economic sectors, use of a checklist/ procedure is as well. The choice of a procedure or checklist for a RA depends on the professionalism of the assessors and upon whether they conduct their affairs in accordance with a particular standard.

ITEM 11. Some quality systems standards do not require that trained surveyors perform a PAS whereas only trained and qualified auditors should perform external audits. In the case of ISO 9000, since external auditors are performing a *"specific assigned task"* required of them by their management, they must be *"qualified"*. (The level of qualification is at the auditor's company's discretion, though.) This might limit the choice of personnel to make up the audit team. The RA assessors' training and competence level depend on their professionalism and on the standard to which they operate.

ITEM 12. The PAS report states whether or not the supplier is acceptable to the customer. The external audit report goes further, stating whether or not the contract and regulatory requirements have been complied with and whether or not the supplier's management systems are efficacious in this respect. Any deficiencies revealed by the external audit are included in the report. One major difference between the PAS and the external audit is that the former provides an opportunity for additional clauses and safeguards to be written into the contract. These additions may be of crucial importance and it is both extremely difficult and expensive to try to impose or back- fit such clauses and safeguards after two parties have signed a contract.

The RA report states whether or not the supplier complies with a standard that he has selected. The usefulness of the assessment report or certificate to any particular customer depends on that customer wanting an identical set of requirements and interpretation of the standard. The customer cannot possibly know such things simply from perusing the certificate.

ITEM 13. As seen in the definition of PAS, the report should give estimates of the amount of effort required to render assistance to the potential supplier, either in monetary units or in kind, to help bid adjudication. (A worksheet such as that shown in Figure 2.4 might assist the surveyor to determine the amounts involved). The external audit does not give such estimates: problems already encountered should be noted in other records which will be reviewed for the purpose of future bid adjudication and supplier evaluation. It would be pointless in any case for an external audit to give an estimate of future money costs in view of the unknown variable rates of inflation, federal reserve bank rates and international currency exchange rates that will affect them. Furthermore, it is impossible to predict the future requirements of unknown customers and of new or revised codes and standards. Future legislative requirements that have not reached the draft or discussion stage are similarly impossible to foresee.

In the case of external audits, though, there is one exception. If the auditor has found that corrective action is necessary, it may be prudent to include in the audit report a statement which quantifies the monetary equivalent of the risks of allowing the deficient situation to remain uncorrected. This is further discussed in Chapter 17 *"Corrective action decisions"*.

RA reports are not directed at costs.

Assessments performed by registrars and by real third party auditors

The differences between *real* third party assessments (TPAs), and those assessments performed by an ISO 9000/ QS 9000 type of registrar (RAs) are summarized in Fig. 2.7 which reproduces the RA column of Figure 2.6.

Just-in-time justifies time

The time allocated to the performance of pre-award surveys is normally substantially less than the time assigned to external audits. This can be considerably risky in the case of a company wishing to implement a just-in-time (JIT) type of programme, which increasing numbers of companies do. The financial benefits of JIT have been well documented. There are also, however, considerable attendant costs if the organizations that are supposed to supply a product *"just in time"* are unable to do so. This means that the management decision to authorize a particular supplier to supply products just in time has to be taken with some care. A cursory review of the potential supplier's activities is inadequate: management must be prepared to allocate the requisite time budget that will be required. Chapter 9, *"Audit Preparation"* discusses the importance of time budgeting and Figure 9.5 displays a benefit-time curve which illustrates this point. Most pre-award surveys (wrongly) operate at the low end of that curve. For JIT, the time budget in the pre-award situation must greatly exceed that which would be allocated for the normal external audit situation.

The size of team and the constituent members is also affected. Too often pre-award surveys and audits are entrusted to the people *"we can spare"*. In normal circumstances, this is unwise; for JIT decisions, it is foolhardy because they require the involvement of fully trained auditors/ surveyors of the highest calibre possible, sourced from the disciplines that are of interest.

Third party audit (assessment)	Assessment by registrar
Mandatory in some industries and for some products.	Supplier discretionary.
Can occur at any time during existence of business. Timing decided by TPA, not by auditee.	Timed to suit supplier, not related to any specific contract.
Non-approval by authorized TPA body might help to 'de-generate' the customer's qualified bidders list.	Might help customer to generate his qualified bidders list. Might help an industry to do the same.
Audit team generally restricted to process/ product specialists. Can also depend on professionalism of TPA and political factors governing its performance.	Team depends on registrar's professionalism, available resources and costs agreed with supplier.
Right of access to premises as well as right of 'examination' of product, company records and data probably enshrined in law of country, state or other jurisdiction.	Supplier has initiates access and decides the extent of access according to scope of assessment.
Objective evidence available according to trading status and longevity of business.	Objective evidence available depends on state of work, type of product and restrictions imposed by current customers.
Systems and/ or compliance orientated.	Orientation depends upon practices of registrar.
As deep as necessary, and as permitted by budget available - can be extended at auditor's/ assessors discretion, as applicable authority permits; could be a series of partial audits.	Depth depends upon practices of registrar and costs agreed by supplier.

Figure 2.7 Comparison of real third party assessments (TPAs) and registrar assessments (RAs)

Third party audit (assessment)	Assessment by registrar
Extensiveness of preparation and planning often depends on budget made available to the TPA concerned for the circumstances of the audit/ assessment. This might depend on jurisdictional political factors.	Preparation and planning depend on registrar's practices and costs agreed by supplier.
Checklist/ procedure mandatory in some industries, but may also depend on TPA's practices, procedure and governing policy/ regulation.	Checklist/ procedure depends on registrar's practices, procedure and assessment standard used.
Competent/ trained auditors mandatory in some industries. Also dependent on jurisdictional policy and practice.	Competent/ trained assessors depending on quality system standard selected and on registrar's practices.
Reports aimed at regulatory compliance; reports give details of deficiencies. Auditors have right to require corrective action for inadequacies with regulatory requirements (which might be equivalent to breaches of law).	Reports aimed at issuing of a certificate. Deficiencies should lead to non-issue of certificate. Report may be confidential to supplier alone.
Additional requirements/ safeguards can be imposed according to jurisdictional authority provided to TPA auditor/ assessor and associated laws/ regulations.	No guarantee that additional safeguards/ clauses are not necessary - CAVEAT EMPTOR.
Punitive action including prosecution, imprisonment and monetary fines might be initiated.	Punitive action is restricted to withdrawal of registration certificate.
Incipient/ future regulatory requirements can be assessed and auditee forewarned accordingly.	No guarantee that prudent levelization amounts are not required - CAVEAT EMPTOR

Figure 2.7 (Cont.)

3. Looking at the auditee's organization

Good order is the foundation of all good things.

Edmund Burke.

While visiting a service company in Norway, I came across the following story posted on a wall.

> *This is the story of four people :*
> *EVERYBODY, SOMEBODY, ANYBODY AND NOBODY.*
> *There was an important job to be done and EVERYBODY was asked to do it.*
> *EVERYBODY assumed that SOMEBODY would do it: ANYBODY could have done it but NOBODY did it.*
> *SOMEBODY got angry about that because it was EVERYBODY'S job.*
> *EVERYBODY thought ANYBODY ought to do it, but NOBODY realized EVERYBODY wouldn't do it.*
> *Finally, ANYBODY blamed EVERYBODY for failing to help NOBODY and SOMEBODY wisely concluded that NOBODY is the most helpful person in the company.*
> *If you want a job done make NOBODY responsible!*

This chapter aims to help auditors analyze the auditee's organizational plans, a task which can be a particularly difficult one for an inexperienced auditor. It helps to remember that all the problems, systems and machines that will be encountered can be divided, analyzed, solved and understood. Similarly, all that is necessary is to break down the organization into manageable units and apply simple logic in the analysis. Unless an auditor can accomplish this, there is very little chance that the audit will produce meaningful results.

What has to be done and who will do it?

Organizational arrangements can be determined by the sequence shown in Figure 3.1. All derive ultimately from the need to serve and satisfy the expectations and demands of the marketplace and the community. Product and strategic decisions, concerning the extent to which the product will be designed, created and distributed by the firm itself, dictate what has to be

Input data / information	Determine	Planned for by defining	Auditor looks for this data/ information
Customer and community expectations, needs and requirements.	Products and services to be sold; Products and services not to be sold. By-products (nuisances) to be avoided/ prevented.	Markets to be served; Markets not to be served; Product and service design features; By-product features.	Sales and marketing research data and plans; Product descriptions; Design specification. Environmental/ safety protection policy.
Sales and marketing research data and plans; Product descriptions; Design specification; Environmental/ safety protection policy.	Processes to be performed.	List of processes to be performed; Process requirements.	Process plan/ project plan. Process specifications.
Process plan/ project plan; Company strategy on vertical integration and outsourcing. Human resource policy	Grouping of processes. Teams	Organizational hierarchy. Reporting levels & responsibilities for each process and each group of processes/team.	Organization chart. Job descriptions (assignment briefs).
Process specifications. Job descriptions (assignment briefs).	Personnel abilities and attributes required for the process.	Job specification for each process.	Job specifications.

Figure 3.1 Factors determining organizational arrangements

done and who will do it. A company needs to allocate the responsibility for the performance of each work phase or group of processes to a person, who might in turn lead a team of people. Even if various phases and processes are to be performed by external organizations (suppliers), there must still be an assigned and defined responsibility somewhere in the company for ensuring that each and every one is properly executed by the suppliers concerned.

One job to one person does not necessarily mean that one person need only have one job. Far from it, the essence is simply that each job has been assigned to an individual. In some cases, such as in the auditing of accounts departments or software development projects, it may be necessary for the auditee to ensure that certain positions are kept truly independent i.e. performed by different individuals or departments. In these cases, the auditor will verify that the principle of independence has not been compromised (See also Part 2 Chapter 4). Independence of duties may have been stipulated in regulations and the auditor will need to ascertain what the particular requirements are as part of the audit preparation process.

Creating an organization chart, job descriptions and job specifications does not entail or incur excessive bureaucracy: they are the prime components of a corporate quality plan. In not applying careful consideration to each of these, a management is failing in its task to plan the running of the business correctly. Many companies 'organize in' their problems (and, hence, their avoidable costs) rather than organizing to prevent them. Good planning is an essential aspect of problem prevention and the avoidance of avoidable costs.

Figure 3.1 indicates an *"audit trail"* that extends from the basic data and information about the marketplace and community the company operates in through to the defining information about how the company is structured (or should be structured). The data and information the auditor should request is listed and this should have been used by the auditee plan his operation. The auditor must obtain it when preparing for an audit so that the extent of actual activities performed at the audit site can be ascertained. This permits better audit planning (see Chapter 9 "Audit preparation"). Accordingly, the auditor will:

- ♦ Verify that the various activities which must be accomplished, in order to properly serve the customer and the community and to ensure that the product and services will be fit for purpose, have been clearly reflected in the organization chart.
- ♦ Verify that there is a job description (assignment brief) for each position/ group of processes/ team.
- ♦ Verify that there is also a job specification for each position/ group

of processes/ team.
- Verify that they are all compatible with each other as further described within this chapter.

This analysis is repeated at each level in the organization, depending on the objective and scope of the audit.

Organization charts

The responsibilities and reporting lines within the auditee's company, division, department or project can be summarized on an organization chart. It must reflect all of the various work phases and key activities necessary to furnish satisfactory products to the customer and to the community.

Top management decides on the responsibilities and authority to be vested in each key position shown on the organization chart. Frequently these responsibilities and corresponding authority will be contained in job descriptions for the personnel. The auditor should review the organization chart and the associated job descriptions together to ensure that one job is assigned to one individual in such a way that there is no overlap or conflict of duties and to verify that there have been no omissions on the part of the management, which could result in nobody being responsible for a particular job.

The shape of the organization chart

For many years, companies tended to organize themselves on militaristic lines. This led to many hierarchical levels being created, often just to satisfy the egos of individuals rather than to correspond with real trading and operational needs. In large companies, these levels, known as the *"chain of command"*, (the very phrase sums up the attitude), inevitably led to :

- Top management gradually becoming out of touch with the real situation on the shop floor, actual product performance and quality, particularly as the company grew in size and range of products;
- Industrial dissatisfaction and lack of motivation in the staff.
- Internal politics.
- Inflexibility to the changing trading circumstances and market needs, brought about by excessive inertia which prevented quick response to those circumstances and needs.
- Loss of competitive position and markets.

Many people seemed to ponder over the mysterious successes of small to medium sized companies in comparison to those of large companies, when the reasons were very plain: they have shorter lines of communication which permit top managers and owners really to know both their staff and the day-to-day problems. The modern trend, even in large companies, is, therefore, to keep middle management levels to a minimum. This is often done by creating business centres within a company that are virtually autonomous. The auditor should examine the extent of hierarchical levels carefully to determine whether they are conducive or otherwise to achieving successful business results, market flexibility and quality.

Lack of autonomy can lead to conflicts of interest as the various departments compete for scarce resources or manpower. Where, for example, there are several sales departments, each dealing with individual products, they may all claim the services of a single manufacturing department. As conflicts of schedule develop, jobs get rushed and quality suffers. (Lack of time - one of the six real causes of quality problems.) The organization chart will reflect this possibility. The solutions can be either to provide separate manufacturing facilities / resources within the company or to outsource (i.e. subcontract). Other popular alternatives include setting up self-sufficient profit centres, product centres and teams each having the autonomous authority to operate as if a small company within the firm. The auditor should look for evidence of this type of arrangement and carefully check the small "inner" companies genuinely have the freedom of action they need and are not examples of old style organizations re-badged to appear as new.

Effects of "downsizing" and "re-engineering"

The attempts to reduce the number of layers in their corporate hierarchies, coupled with the desire to reconfigure their businesses, have caused some companies to over-zealously *"downsize"*. The remaining staff often have so many extra duties imposed upon them that they gradually become exhausted and the quality of their work suffers as less and less time is devoted to individual activities. Paradoxically, this is increasing avoidable costs for the very same firms who previously believed that downsizing and re-engineering would reduce their avoidable costs. All that they have succeeded in doing is to replace one type of avoidable cost with another. Whilst I do not dispute the need for downsizing and re-engineering, it is the foolish over application of them that is unwise. The auditor should weigh the evidence and be prepared to recommend some *"upsizing"* if it will prevent avoidable costs. A cost-benefit analysis may be required to make the final decision. (See also Part 2 Chapter 2 *"Value-added auditing"*.)

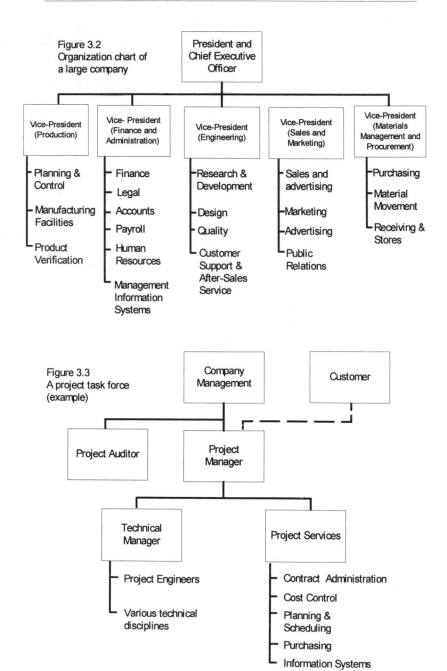

Figure 3.2
Organization chart of
a large company

President and
Chief Executive
Officer

Vice-President
(Production)

- Planning &
  Control

- Manufacturing
  Facilities

- Product
  Verification

Vice- President
(Finance and
Administration)

- Finance

- Legal

- Accounts

- Payroll

- Human
  Resources

- Management
  Information
  Systems

Vice-President
(Engineering)

- Research &
  Development

- Design

- Quality

- Customer
  Support &
  After-Sales
  Service

Vice-President
(Sales and
Marketing)

- Sales and
  advertising

- Marketing

- Advertising

- Public
  Relations

Vice-President
(Materials
Management and
Procurement)

- Purchasing

- Material
  Movement

- Receiving &
  Stores

Figure 3.3
A project task force
(example)

Company
Management

Customer

Project Auditor

Project
Manager

Technical
Manager

- Project Engineers

- Various technical
  disciplines

Project Services

- Contract Administration

- Cost Control

- Planning &
  Scheduling

- Purchasing

- Information Systems

The span of managerial control

There is a limit to the number of separate and distinct activities that anyone can manage effectively. For many years, it has been recognized that 7 or 8 is, in fact, the maximum. Beyond this, a manager begins to become remote as a result of the inevitable inability to devote adequate time to each one. Decisions can then be of precarious quality caused by this lack of time, combined perhaps with reduced effectiveness through exhaustion or overwork. Some individuals are capable of greater spans of control: most are not. The auditor should look at this matter.

Implications of the quality manager's reporting level

Figure 3.2 shows the organization of a large company that decided to design, manufacture and service its product but to buy in the various items needed for manufacture and to obtain data processing services from outside. The main functions have been shown on the chart. Within each of the divisions and departments, the auditor will verify the existence of similar charts plotting their own internal organization and reporting levels.

A point to note is that the company in question has decided that the quality manager will report to the Vice-President (Engineering). This might signify the following :

♦　　That the company does not recognize a quality programme is essential in every department, that it considers only the saleable product to need attention.

♦　　Accordingly, that there is no real company wide quality programme.

♦　　Quality matters are considered as being of subordinate importance and priority to financial assurance and technical matters. (This can have a negative effect on the controlling of avoidable costs.)

♦　　The likelihood of the staff believing in, or being committed to, an official quality programme is reduced.

In practice, the following often occurs, either of which lead to political squabbles, a difficult working atmosphere if not a state of non-cooperation to the detriment of continuous improvement:

♦　　The vice-presidents on the same senior level resent the subordinate of one of their peers having the authority to require corrective action and, perhaps, to stop work.

♦　　The same vice-presidents come to believe that the Vice-President

(Engineering) is considered to be superior to them by the President.

Figure 3.3 depicts a project task force. Note that there is no quality appointee reporting directly to the project manager. This does not violate the requirements of any internationally recognized quality systems standard. In fact this style of organization is to be preferred since there is genuine independence for the "quality" position which reflects the real function which is to provide management with the assurance that its company systems and policies are being properly accomplished on that project. It could indicate the existence of a management exercising the wisdom that the responsibility for quality rests with those who do the job although there is no guarantee of this. (This type of position is sometimes also dubbed "quality associate".) When auditing this type of company, the extrinsic auditor would need to investigate the company's circumstances and results to draw that conclusion.

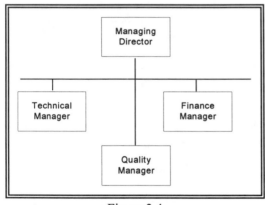

Figure 3.4

Figure 3.4 shows how a Scandinavian company depicted the organization at the top of the company. The quality manager was drawn at a slightly lower level than the other similar positions. When this was presented to me, I raised the question: *"Is this box drawn at a lower level because: a) the technical manager and the finance manager are unwilling to consider the quality position to be of equal importance or b) because the managing director does not consider it to be of such importance?"* The truth was that a) was the case. This led me to wonder who really runs the company: the managing director or his immediate subordinates?

The inference of titles

Titles can give an indication of the level of real interest and commitment by the top management towards quality. When the most senior person in the quality department is referred to as, say, quality controller, supervisor of quality or quality assurance coordinator, there is a clear indication that top management is not fully committed to the supremacy of quality as a priority in the company's business. The title should be consistent with the peer positions. When the finance or accounts functions are headed by the *"finance director"* or *"V.P. finance"* or sales is headed by the *"V.P. sales"* or *"sales manager"*, the quality position should be similarly headed by an equivalent title, such as *"quality director"* or *"V.P. quality"* or *"quality manager"*.

Quality managers and continuous improvement

Professional members of the quality profession have strived over the years to improve their companies' performance, by reducing defect levels and quality problems, attempting to prevent their causes before they could have their effects. They have tried to continuously improve business results. Their attention used to be restricted to conventional shop floor matters but, as top managements became increasingly aware of the full magnitude of potential savings and improvements, company wide attention to continuous improvement has increased. There is some evidence building up to suggest titles such as "quality assurance manager", "vice-president (quality)", "quality manager" and the like are being superseded by "vice-president - continuous improvement", "continuous improvement project manager", "business improvement manager" and similar. Such titles indicate to all employees and customers of the evolving nature of the corporate mission. They more accurately reflects the all embracing nature of the quality function when viewed on a corporate wide basis. Continuous improvement is the real goal of total quality management (TQM) programmes. The auditor should look for such position titles and review the depth and scope of their incumbents' responsibility and authority which should be directly linked to a corporate policy emanating from the most senior position in the firm. The continuous improvement coordinator should report to that most senior person. (See also Part 2, Chapter 1.)

However, regardless of the position levels and titles involved, it is the competence and abilities of the incumbent that really matter. When quality assurance became fashionable, many firms merely appointed their chief inspectors to the position of quality assurance manager. The individuals were *"rebadged"* but did not have the qualifications to really perform a quality assurance role. Accordingly, a majority dwelt on matters of conventional quality control and did not pursue quality management throughout the firm. Hence, the disappointing results experienced by their companies and the eventual discrediting of much "quality" activity. The same risks are now becoming apparent, as I write this third edition, in that quality managers are being retitled *"continuous improvement manager"*, yet possess not the range of skills and knowledge, especially business management tools, needed to really scrutinize the firm's operations and present cost-beneficial solutions for reducing avoidable costs. They are continuing to focus far too narrowly on quality systems, especially the mundane matter within ISO 9000 *et al*, believing it shows the way to some business Holy Grail. Their focus needs to be on projects that will deliver measurable business improvements and to quantify the results obtained as those projects progress.

Job descriptions

Associated with each position (group of processes), there should be a job description. (Job descriptions are sometimes also called *"assignments briefs"*.) These summarize, as a minimum, the duties, responsibilities and authority of each position also indicating the reporting level. In effect, they state the position's products.

Authority and responsibility need to be compatible. Although they should be inseparable, in practice responsibilities might grossly outweigh the delegated authority. In this situation, motivation is reduced because the discrepancy is a reliable indicator of management's distrust or undervaluing of its people. Furthermore, it does not assist the development of an individual, ultimately resulting in a political climate which is detrimental to product quality and avoidance of avoidable costs. Better qualified and able people, who want to move ahead with their careers, become frustrated and leave for better things where they feel appreciated and can grow.

When reviewing each job description, the auditor should verify that each subordinate's job description is consistent with that of his/her superior. This consistency ensures correct planning at each level commensurate with the company's strategic objectives.

Careful scrutiny of the job descriptions can reveal whether or not there is a genuinely company wide business improvement programme in place. Very often these programmes stop short at the so-called *"overhead"* departments within a company. These departments can contribute much towards overall efficiency and avoidable cost reduction through continuous improvement but few companies grasp the nettle and actually require them to do so.

Job specifications

Business achievements, product quality and the avoidance of avoidable costs ultimately depend on the person assigned to a particular task. Specifying and consequently selecting the correct personnel is the basis of any sound business. (See also Chapter 4, *"Person"*.)

Associated with each job description should be a specification of the level of competence and training necessary if the duties of that position are to be correctly accomplished. A job specification should contain the qualifications, experience, skills, training, special attributes which the ideal candidate should possess. If they have a direct bearing on the job, especially in terms of safety and customer sensitivities, age, sex and religious denomination might also need to be prescribed, but discrimination is unacceptable.

The auditor should look for the existence of job specifications and verify that the personnel assigned meet those requirements.

Work flow

The work flow will depend to some extent on the scope and nature of the contracts and whether the company is supplying goods or services. Nevertheless, all contracts, projects and products pass through discrete phases. These are not necessarily chronologically distinct: the purchasing department, for example may be booking long lead items and materials before detailed product design has been completed but at the same time as the production personnel are preparing their facilities for making the product.

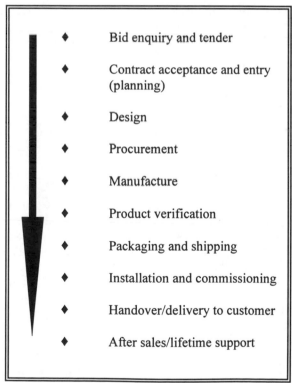

- Bid enquiry and tender

- Contract acceptance and entry (planning)

- Design

- Procurement

- Manufacture

- Product verification

- Packaging and shipping

- Installation and commissioning

- Handover/delivery to customer

- After sales/lifetime support

Figure 3.5 Typical contract phases

For a great number of contracts, the phases involved are as shown in Figure 3.5. In the case of a service contract, such as a design review service, the

57

handover phase will probably follow straight on from design. Some manufacturing service contracts involve only a manufacturing process (such as welding, heat treatment, coating, injection moulding, dynamic balancing, hermetic sealing) and, in this case, the design phase may not occur since the customer is procuring only those manufacturing processes. It is important for the auditor to understand the nature of the contract to gain a clear idea of the phases through which it is likely to pass. The list in Figure 3.5 by no means exhausts the possibilities so far as phase structure is concerned: the auditor must consider each individual contract afresh.

Once the auditor has determined the phases through which the contract will pass, (and are referred to as the *"primary system"* in Chapter 6), he can then decide which departments and tasks (processes) should be audited. There may be more than one department involved in supporting a particular phase, (these being referred to as the *"secondary system"* in Chapter 6): in the design phase, for instance, there may be a design office, a computer aided design (CAD) unit, a reliability analysis unit, a technical writing unit, a product planning unit, a customer support unit, a technical library, each of which has a distinct task or set of tasks to perform. Again, in the procurement phase, a purchasing department, a goods inwards area, a supplier monitoring function and material movement coordination may all be involved. The names of the phases do not reflect all the departments involved at each stage. An example of this in the procurement phase is that an item cannot be considered to have been procured until it has been received and found to be completely acceptable and in compliance with the purchase order requirements. This may or may not necessitate some degree of inspection and reporting, not just the issue of a purchasing order.

The unit concept

As stated above, before any phase can be considered complete there may be a number of different tasks that have to be performed. Each task can be considered as a unit performing a process (see Fig. 3.6). The unit requires an input and has an output. The output or product may be hardware or software or both: it may be a service. The output differs, however, from the input by virtue of the process performed. The input is either the output of the preceding unit or a feedback from a downstream unit's output. Together the units make a chain or a network of chains since there may also be units working in parallel with each other.

Whatever the arrangement of units, the work flows in one direction through the various phases, the whole chain being only as strong as the weakest link.

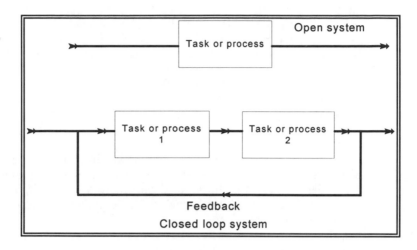

Figure 3.6 The unit concept (open and closed loop systems).

Problems of location and size

Geographic dispersion

Some companies, particularly large ones, have their facilities geographically dispersed, in that different task units are located in different towns, cities, or, in the case of multi- national companies, even in different countries. Sales, design, and procurement may be in the same central headquarters, for example; manufacturing, testing, and inspection may be carried out in a provincial factory; there may be distribution warehouses in other towns and after sales service units in others yet again.

From an auditing standpoint, geographic dispersion has the following implications:

♦   Careful decision making concerning the objectives and scope of the audit will be needed.
♦   Especially thorough planning of the audit programme and the composition of the team is required.
♦   Some companies have a policy of allocating only a fixed period of time (so many mandays, for example) for the performance of an audit. If this period does not include any allowance for the time spent in travel, a team of experienced auditors will be needed to

make the most of the time that will remain for the audit itself.

♦ Ideally, all the information required should be obtained on the first visit to each location, to avoid the expense and delay involved in having to return to gather more data later on. The auditor will need to be experienced enough to assess the type and volume of information required, not merely for the audit at that particular location but also for later auditing activities at other sites.

♦ Inter-team communication can become a problem. If the audit team is composed of two or three sub-teams, each responsible for auditing at a different location, it may not be possible for the audit team to exchange views by meeting every evening and telecommunications may prove inconvenient and expensive (particularly where a multi-national operation is involved). The outcome may be that the teams lack the information they need to co-ordinate their activities.

♦ The audit team must pay attention to the communication systems in operation between the various auditee facilities i.e. the methods by which information and data are passed. The risks are that business problems can arise through misunderstandings or vacuums. Geographically dispersed companies commonly rely heavily on electronic data transfer and the audit team will need to audit the management systems used for this. This will also include assessing whether or not adequate back-up has been considered and provided for the event of equipment malfunction, outage or power failure. Companies that operate with minimum or zero inventory and just-in-time policies are particularly vulnerable to communication disruptions.

The large industrial or office complex

Sometimes the auditor finds that the facilities he has to investigate are comprised of a vast and sprawling complex. There may be a large office block that contains the engineering department; a building for the sales department; another building housing the research and development group and so on.

This type of layout poses similar problems to those of geographic dispersion. It is wise to minimize the amount of walking about that the audit team has to do, not only to cut down on time wastage but also to avoid over fatigue and loss of efficiency. It may make sense to split the audit team into two or three sub- teams, so that each can concentrate on the activities being performed in one building alone, with a daily meeting being held to discuss progress. It is also useful to have a map of the of the organization's layout drawn up when the audit is being planned, so that the audit team can familiarize themselves with the terrain and avoid tiring and time wasting mistakes.

The small company

The small company poses its own unique problems. Within the small company, it is common to find "multi-functional" people - i.e. people responsible for performing more than one key function (an engineer who is also responsible for purchasing, for example). The idea of a unit may, at first sight, appear difficult to apply.

The efficiency of this type of company tends to depend particularly heavily on the capabilities the people involved since channels of information flow tend to be informal; their ability to keep themselves and others supplied with up-to-date information is also vital. Not everyone possesses the memory or organizational powers to achieve this and small firms often suffer from their lack of formal procedures. The attempt to do without the latter can prove a false economy and, as the boxed example shows, may put the small firm at a real disadvantage when competing for a large contract (especially in an economic sector such as aerospace or the nuclear industry where a lot of documents and records must be created and stored).

> One firm was virtually a one man company; the owner was the salesman, engineer, chief machinist, welder and draughtsman. The company had a good order book and produced a high quality product. However, it became obvious during a pre-award survey that the company would be unable to cope with the vast amount of paperwork necessary to handle a contract in accordance with the ASME Boiler and Pressure Vessel Code[1]. To make matters worse, the owner spoke very little English. The solution found was that the customer would prepare and institute all the procedures, instructions, and design calculations necessary for compliance with the ASME code. Fortunately, the associated quality assurance standard did not preclude the provision of such support.

One of the tasks of the pre-award surveyor should be to assess the work load and capacity of the company's personnel and to report on any support needed to handle the contract. In the foregoing example, it also became obvious that the owner was overworked and was omitting to keep himself fully informed of all the minute details of the potential contract.

Regardless of how small the company is, the precepts of organizational planning and of considering the task elements (See Chapter 4) for each activity still apply. This means that the auditor takes each task in turn, considering the inputs, outputs and the actual process itself within the limits of the responsibilities and authority which have or should have been assigned to that task. It is important to keep within the confines of one task (process) at a time and to ensure that the auditee does so as well: otherwise the audit becomes chaotic and unsystematic. Such lack of order eventually means that neither party can be sure of all aspects having been covered since the tendency will have been to "jump around".

The time required to audit to a systems depth is not too different in the case of a small company or of a large one: often the same number of activities are involved. Moreover, since small companies are frequently less formalized, there may be more sifting and analysis required of its management systems. Compliance audits can be a different matter, though, as there is more objective evidence to be studied in large companies than is the case in small ones, this because more people are using the same type of management system more times.

Virtual organizations, *"doughnuts"* and outsourcing

The last two decades have witnessed new shapes and style of organizations. Whereas the traditional structure may have been depicted as the pyramid, much has been written of alternative visual depictions of emerging and future companies. Charles Handy refers to one such shape as having the appearance of a doughnut. Others consider the trend towards outsourcing coupled with the increased availability of services obtainable from so-called teleworkers, who are linked by modern telecommunications' means to their clients and employers, will give rise to *"virtual corporations"*. Such firms would employ only a small central core of staff and would purchase the products and services needed to run the business from self employed workers and suppliers. A comparison of the traditional pyramidal company with these newer types is shown in Figure 3.7. Nonetheless, even at the core of the so-called virtual companies one finds a pyramid, albeit a very flat one having, perhaps, only two layers!

The auditor will audit these new structural forms in the same manner as the traditional ones for, regardless of the appearance of the structure, it still amounts to a coordinated set of tasks (processes) with a single person ultimately responsible for each group or set of them. It may be that the firm of the future will procure (outsource) more activities that it would traditionally have engaged its own permanent staff to undertake, even so, the precepts of purchase control systems will remain unchanged: someone has to do it and that someone is performing a task that can be audited. The phases shown in Figure 3.5 will remain the same, the only difference might be that some of them are wholly contracted out. But that is not new. Countless companies have sub-contracted chunks of work to external specialist businesses such as architects, project engineering contractors, licensed distributors and franchisees. For decades: automobile manufacturers have had vehicles designed and styled by external companies; the entire oil industry has relied on firms who design, construct and commission the oil platforms they own; every utility has acted in a similar way to obtain the fixed capital assets they use to earn their revenue; and national departments of defence have bought in (outsourced) what they need. Products and services have been supplied on countless occasions throughout the industrial revolution by joint ventures and consortia created for the specific purpose of the contract concerned, the joint venture or consortium being disbanded when the work is complete. Yet each of those types of business is auditable regardless of whether they possess characteristics ascribed to virtual companies or doughnuts!

Organizational feature	Conventional pyramid	New forms
Job task (process) assigned to	Individual	Team or set of individuals
Reporting levels	A single manager (except in matrix style of organization)	Team leader or *ad hoc* project manager
Job description	Applied to individual performing the task	Applies to a team or to a list of individuals
Job specification	Applies to the task. The individual must meet the requirements	Applies to the task; every individual must meet requirements
Communication	Via manager and to manager	Open, go find it/ get it from wherever you need
Longevity of skills	Possibly lifetime with some periodic updating	Short lived requiring constant updating
Predictability of daily tasks	High. Repetitious work affording full time employment as company specialist	Low. Individuals in full time employment need to be flexible and have many skills.
Promotion/ career path	Vertically through the hierarchy (perhaps on a "Buggins turn" basis)	Zig-zag. On demonstrated basis of willingness to continuously learn new skills
Security of tenure	Good if the individual performs satisfactorily and "keeps his nose clean"	Volatile and uncertain. Multi-career
Development of individual	By the employer firm	Some by firm but most by individual on own initiative

Figure 3.7 A comparison of traditional pyramidal organizations and newer styles of operation

4. The task elements

Each morning sees some task begin,
Each evening sees it close;
Something attempted, something done,
Has earned a night's repose.

Longfellow.

Introduction

Once the auditor has settled in his own mind the organization of work and the tasks (processes) involved in the auditee's enterprise, his next step is to analyze what each task involves so as to establish exactly what he should examine.

Many years ago, when I first became involved in management auditing, there were few standards or texts to assist an auditor in his work. The standards did not seem especially lucid and out of necessity I formulated the task elements and their sub-elements to guide me. Applying these

Task element	Is
Person	The individual who performs the task (process) or is responsible for its performance.
Item	A physical thing received for processing by the task or which has been processed by the task (process).
Equipment	Tools/ facilities needed to perform the task (process).
Information	Usable data and details needed to perform the task or which is created by the task (process).
Service	Outcome of a support activity needed when performing the task or which is supplied by the task to benefit others when they need it.

Figure 5.1 The task elements

65

elements and sub-elements has enabled me to analyze every work situation I have encountered in developing management systems and in auditing, from that of chief executive officers to workshop tasks, service functions and support staff roles, such as accounts receivable and R & D. They have never let me down and the many delegates from around the world and countlessly diverse industries who have attended my training seminars have subsequently had the same experience.

The task elements

With the exception of services every task unit comprises a set of up to five elements, which is necessary for proper performance of the task. The task elements are explained briefly in Figure 5.1.

Each task element has to be audited in order to audit the task unit fully. Figure 5.2 depicts the task elements with their sub-elements.
The chain of tasks that comprise a complete management system, whose function is to create a product or service, is only as strong as its weakest link. Each task element has to be performed correctly if the quality of products or services supplied is to meet the customer, user or community requirements.

The amount that one unit can accomplish also depends on the activities of the units upstream, which supply its input. Similarly, the given unit must satisfy the input demand of other units further downstream (its customers). One must remember that the computer maxim *"garbage in, garbage out"* (GIGO) is applicable to every task. One other important cause of *"garbage out"* is that the processing unit has processed correct input incorrectly.

The person

The most important of the task elements is the *"person"*. It does not matter how clever the quality management systems are, ultimately they all depend upon human intervention and effort for their success. People are the final determinants of how effective the business and its management systems will be in practice and therefore of how good the product itself will be. John Stuart Mill rightly observed:

"The worth of a state, in the long run, is the worth of the individuals composing it" [1].

Task (process)				
Person	Item	Equipment	Information	Service
Competence	Type	Type	Content	Type
Training	Condition	Condition	Condition	Characteristics
Identification	Capability	Capability	Edition	Presentation
Motivation	Identification	Identification	Identification	Identification
Attributes	Quantity	Location	Checked	Complete
		Environment	Distribution	

Figure 5.2 The task elements and sub-elements

Nonetheless, the auditee should have a system whereby the needs of those work activities being performed, the associated job descriptions and job specifications, are defined so as to assist with the correct selection of individuals for the particular tasks. Job descriptions and job specifications have been discussed in Chapter 3.

Person				
Competence	Training	Identification	Motivation	Attributes
Qualifications	Product	Unique	Internal factors	Physical
Demonstrated skills	Individual's contribution	Traceable	External factors	Personal values
Demonstrated ability	Skills, knowledge			
Applied knowledge	Department/ company capabilities			
	Management systems			
	Retraining			
	Future assignments			
	Career development			

Figure 5.3 "Person" task element, sub-elements and management topics

Audit procedure

When performing the audit, the auditor should leave the *"person"* task element until last. This enables him to ascertain the level of competence, attributes, motivation and training that the equipment, service, items and information require. It is then easier to conclude whether or not the auditee possesses them. For each person performing the task at the auditee's workplace, the auditor will then consider the sub-elements summarized in Figure 5.3 and described as below. (See also the discussion in Chapter 13 - *"Useful sequence for questioning".*)

Competence

The person who has to perform a task must be competent to do so. Every task requires a certain degree of experience: some may also call for formal qualifications. No person who falls below the level of competence required should be employed to perform the task in question. In some industries, there may be a need for the individual assigned to a particular task to have completed an examination specifically designed to evaluate the competence level achieved. Registered professional engineers, airline pilots, doctors, drivers of heavy goods vehicles and company accountants are all examples of this type of scheme.

Competence is the *demonstrated* ability of a person to perform a task correctly and completely, right first time. The type of competence that a person will require should be stated in the job specification, (see Chapter 3). Competence is established by means of evaluating the results obtained either by performing the task or by producing a prototype of the product. These are the only worthwhile means of qualifying a person to do any particular job.

The auditor should look for objective evidence that proves:

♦ The competence level required for each position is carefully determined.
♦ The competence level is consistent with the needs of that position (and the product that should result).
♦ The competence level is consistent with the codes, standards and regulations that apply to the task concerned.
♦ The person has demonstrated the ability to do that job properly.
♦ The auditee's management monitors the individual's achievements in order to verify that the requisite competence levels are maintained.

Training

No matter what their ability or experience, people should still receive proper training in performing the tasks assigned to them.

Training and competence are entirely different matters. Some people may undergo extensive training in the skills and knowledge required in a particular task but this does not guarantee that they have learned anything or that they can apply this knowledge such that the product will be made right first time.

The training requirements of an individual need to be defined in terms of:

♦ The function and requirements of the company's and the department's product.

At one supplier of servo-mechanisms, the assembly personnel were trained thoroughly in assembly of the servo-mechanisms. However, the inspectors, who were supposed to inspect the operators' work and to provide guidance on the assembly of products, had not been trained in assembling the servo-mechanisms. As it turned out, they were "trained" by the assembly personnel. Bad habits as well as good ones were learnt.

♦ The contribution of the individual to those products.

Training people to understand the contribution that they make to the final product is a good way of obtaining operator commitment, interest in the job and increased motivation.

A company was experiencing a general and widespread number of quality problems of varying magnitude. The workforce seemed to work reasonably well but did not appear enthusiastic about the work. With the agreement of the management, the entire staff was taken on a visit to see an example of the final product under construction at a customer's premises. Everyone was entertained to lunch, shown a film and models of the finished product and allowed to ask whatever questions they wished. After the return to work, it was remarkable the following week how people at all levels evinced a greater interest in the product by identifying their efforts with it. Quality problems rapidly disappeared.

♦ The skills and knowledge required for the actual task.

It is always dangerous to assume that somebody may have the level of basic knowledge that one possesses oneself.

Some years ago a friend of mine had been working on a large construction project in a third world country, nowadays referred to as an *"emerging nation"*. In order to create as much employment as possible, there was extensive use of local labour. Much of this labour had never seen such a construction site before and was unfamiliar with even the basic tools used. My friend recalled how one day he emerged from his hut to see two labourers with a wheelbarrow that contained concrete. Apparently there was one at the front of the wheelbarrow and one at the back. He gently persuaded them that it would be more convenient to make use of the wheel.

That is a somewhat dramatic example which has its modern equivalent.

I was once called to a manufacturer of microelectronic products that was unable to understand why the tiny components were experiencing extensive damage caused by static electricity. Earthing wrist bands for the operators, conducting work pads, tote pans and the like had been provided; everything was securely earthed to the bench. However, by standing back from the workplace one could see that the people had cut small rubber mats from some jointing material and placed them under the feet of each work bench. The reason was that they did not like the squeaky movement of the benches on the floor. They had effectively insulated the only electrical path to earth which would have prevented static damage. The rubber mats were left in place and the benches were correctly earthed directly through the floor. Investigation had revealed that the people had no knowledge of the problem of static damage and why maintaining the earth was so important. They each received subsequent training in such matters. The rubber mats were left in place and the benches were correctly earthed.

The nature of the task might be such that it is affected by statutory requirements for specific training, safety and emergency procedures, for example. The auditee must consider the circumstances and ensure knowledge of the regulations applying to the task is provided by means of proper training prior to the individual commencing the functions assigned to him / her.

♦   The capability of their department and the company.

One company became involved in a contract for the supply of pressure containing equipment to the United States. A condition of the contract was that the equipment must be certified according to ASME construction standards. The salesman who negotiated and signed the contract did not consult his quality assurance department

71

to ascertain whether or not the company had or could obtain an ASME certification. With only a few months to go before manufacturing was scheduled to begin, it was realized that obtaining such a certificate was going to pose major problems and create a major expense for the company. The pressure equipment was a standard product line made from a material not recognized by ASME. A complete switch in manufacturing and fabrication methods was required to accommodate such a major change. A complete reappraisal of the design was also necessary and much retraining of the employees involved in welding. The costs were horrendous. The salesman not known what signing such a contract would mean to the company or that a requirement contained in a clause two sentences long, occupying half an inch on one page, would be so significant. Had the salesman been trained in the company capabilities and product, the situation might never have arisen.

♦   The department and company management systems.

Many managements seem to suffer from the mistaken belief that this type of knowledge spreads through the company by some sort of osmosis, being absorbed automatically. The process of discovering how wrong this is can be very expensive. In spite of theories about telepathy, I have yet to encounter during an audit any person who possesses the attributes of a *"Midwich Cuckoo"*!

♦   Retraining.

Regular retraining of the person is also necessary whenever the competence level appears to diminish and whenever the job circumstances, such as the technology used, regulatory requirements or the product itself, alter: the auditor should verify the auditee's arrangements on this matter.

♦   Training for future assignments and career development.

Organizations must recognize adequately the need to train people not only for today's position but also for the position that management anticipates them holding in the future. Without proper training and preparation for the next position or promotion, there is the ever present likelihood that the *"Peter Principle"*, which avers people are promoted to their level of incompetence, will be demonstrated. Every function, from chairman of the board downwards, requires certain skills and knowledge for it to be performed properly and for its product to be right.

In sum, everybody in the company, regardless of their reporting level, needs continual training, retraining and training for tomorrow's circumstances. Training is an essential aspect of continuous professional development, or continuous personal development, (CPD).

Training often fails through the allocation of insufficient resources. Accordingly, the auditor should check that the requisite resources for proper training have been correctly defined and apportioned by top management. Benjamin Franklin shrewdly stated :

"investment in people pays the finest dividends".

Without proper allocation of the resources required for training, a company is failing to invest in its future. No matter how far or how fast technology moves and whatever new fangled pieces of equipment the company may buy, ultimately, people are always required: it is their skill level which will determine how well those technical resources are applied also fixing the return on investment. Sadly, though, training is one of the most neglected areas in most companies. It is one of the six real causes of operational and business problems, as listed in Chapters 1 and 18.

With these matters in mind, the auditor should look for objective evidence that proves:

♦ The skill and knowledge requirements for the successful accomplishment of the job are properly defined in its job specification.
♦ The training requirements of each individual are properly planned, budgeted and completed.
♦ The training is consistent with the requirements of the codes, standards and regulations that apply to the task and the product.
♦ The training is consistent with the needs of the product and is effective such that competence can be achieved.
♦ The auditee's management monitors the individual's development needs and achievements in order to verify that the requisite training programmes are effective.

Identification

Some system of identifying employees is needed because it is essential to be able to tell who has performed each task. There are various methods of identification: the person's name, employee number, initials, a special

73

number and stamp issued to each person, a user name for those using a computer terminal or an E-MAIL address.

Work must be traceable to the person who actually performed it. This is so that when the job is correctly accomplished and the product is fit for purpose, the person responsible may receive due praise and credit for his or her efforts. Likewise, so that when things go wrong, it is easier to determine who has been responsible and then to decide what further training is necessary in order for the person to achieve or regain the requisite competence. In Chapter 1, it was stated that one of the benefits of performing audits is the unbiased assessment of individuals by assessing peoples' performance regularly so as to provide appropriate reward and career development.

The auditor should look for objective evidence that :

♦ Means of uniquely identifying the individual assigned to a task are defined and communicated to those who need to know.
♦ Those means are solely used in practice.
♦ Those means are effective such that traceability of items processed, services supplied, equipment handled and information used or created by that individual is possible.

Motivation

Lack of motivation leads directly to poor quality output and tends to raise avoidable costs. Hence, it is something to which an auditor should be alert, (even though it is a matter to which quality systems standards seldom, if ever, refer).

Motivation can be affected by factors such as inadequate working conditions, obnoxious superiors, responsibility incompatible with authority, lack of career prospects, inadequate pay. People can become demotivated when they find comparable companies either locally or in the same industry, offer pay levels and conditions better does than their own employer. When staff find that they are required to use outdated equipment, that other organizations provide better training and staff development programmes or invest in new technology, they can become despondent and disinterested in their job.

An audit should ascertain how such factors are being assessed by the auditee. This could involve dealing with sensitive situations which are further discussed in Part 1 Chapter 13.

Motivation is not easy to assess but the "vibrations", reactions and body language of the individual being audited can be very telling. An indifferent attitude, avoidance of eye contact, body tension and hostility can all be signs that the motivation of the individual leaves something to be desired. (One must, however, be a little bit wary of over interpreting the meaning behind body language: *"He looked at me in a funny way"* is hardly the best kind of objective evidence on which to base conclusions and produce a sensible audit report.)   Individuals can be very hard to gauge during any audit and experience is the only valuable guide. There is much truth in Charles Dickens' words that people contain *"all those subtle essences of humanity which will elude the utmost cunning of algebra"*.[2]

With the above in mind, the auditor should look for objective evidence that :

♦   The auditee's management constantly monitors the employment conditions available in the same industry and in local industries.
♦   Work incentives which include career prospects and investment in individuals are not neglected.
♦   The auditee's management ensures that employees are treated with dignity and respect by their supervisors and others.

Correct attributes

The appropriate attributes will vary from task to task. Good eyesight is an example of an attribute commonly required in manufacturing industry and inspection, particularly nowadays, when microelectronic engineering may involve a product being assembled underneath a microscope. The requirement for good eyesight may entail not only acuity but also good colour vision - the ability to distinguish between different colours of electrical wiring or lamps on a control panel, for example, may be vital. Steady hands may be a necessary attribute for a different task: one would naturally be reluctant to employ a brain surgeon who suffered from *delirium tremens*. Hearing might be important - a tone deaf piano tuner would be unhelpful to a concert pianist. The needs of the product and the task performed might also require combinations of different attributes, such as eyesight and dexterity (a dentist filling a tooth) or eyesight and taste (a food grader).

Other attributes that may be important can include:

♦   Honesty, for those people who are handling money or other moveable assets (a matter of increasing concern, nowadays, with the advent of modern computerized accounts and stock control systems, which have led to the rise of computer fraud - See Part 2 Chapter 4). Honesty is an important attribute for anyone placed in a position of trust. This includes such people as police, lawyers, judges, bankers, government officials.

♦ Integrity, particularly in the case of those people who are performing audits. It is closely related to honesty and affects people placed in positions of trust.

♦ Health, where food or pharmaceuticals are being processed in any way or in the case of hospital staff, paramedics, doctors dealing with patients, for example.

An audit of a food factory revealed that its quality assurance manager found difficulty in understanding why there should be proper health checks and monitoring of staff coming into direct contact with the product to prevent any communicable disease or health hazard being passed on to customers. His argument *"It's never happened so far"* sounded hollow. He does not work there any more: management diagnosed that he carried a disease called stupidity, and decided that a "humanectomy" was the most appropriate corrective action!

Attribute levels, such as eyesight or hearing, might also be stipulated by the regulations that apply to the task. Insurance companies might have restrictions on inadequate attribute levels, such as health factors (heart disease, epilepsy, disabilities) that could affect the risks associated with the task: these need to be considered prior to assigning an individual to the job.

The system for control of most attributes can be adequately assessed by an auditor since so many of them can be tested. The auditor will investigate the stringency of acceptance criteria for those tests as well as the scheduled and actual frequency of those tests being performed. All must be consistent with the needs of the product, process and industry concerned. Assessing the systems which consider the honesty of employees is an extremely sensitive issue which requires careful handling through appropriate question technique. See Chapter 13.- *"Sensitive situations"*.

With these things in mind, the auditor should look for objective evidence that proves:

♦ The attributes required for successful accomplishment of the task are properly defined in a job specification.

♦ The attributes possessed by the person are consistent with the requirements of the codes, standards and regulations that apply to the task and to the product.

♦ Those attributes are consistent with the needs of the product and enable competence to be achieved.

♦ The auditee's management monitors the individual's attributes in order to verify that the requisite levels are maintained.

The item

The term *"Item"* is an all-embracing term that may refer to:

♦ A component, a part, a sub-assembly, raw material, an engineered system or a finished assembly.

♦ Ingredients such as foodstuffs being used to make saleable food products, chemical substances to be processed into raw materials according to a recipe or formula.

♦ Consumables such as the dye penetrant for dye penetrant testing; the filler material and flux used in welding; paint and coatings that are applied to finish or protect a deliverable product, such as a motor vehicle; the chemicals (ingredients, additives, starters) in process baths and chambers that, by virtue of the process, become part of the product delivered to the next work-station, user or customer.

♦ Fluids and liquids that are being processed into a saleable product (for example, milk being processed into cheese; gases being liquefied; blood being passed through a dialysis machine; wine being decanted; oil being centrifuged).

♦ By-products and industrial wastes whose "quality", or lack of it, could affect the company's costs and liability risks (for example, sludge; sewage; radioactive crud; heavy metals - of the non "musical" variety; smokestack discharges; toxic liquids, compounds and substances).

♦ Materials used for packaging and protecting the various types of items listed above.

Audit procedure

The auditor will first establish the items received at the auditee's workplace and the items to leave the auditee's workplace. For each one, he will consider the sub-elements shown in Figure 5.4 and described below. See also the discussion in Chapter 13 - *"Useful sequence for questioning"*.

Correct type

The correct type of items to be processed and any consumables required must be issued to the person who has to perform the task: clearly, they must be what the designer or specialist has specified. They must be selected in accordance with codes, standards or regulations that apply to the product, process or industry concerned. The type of item selected must also be compatible with the other items with which it will come into contact so that their mutual conditions are not impaired and so that there is no risk to safety.

Item				
Type	Condition	Capability	Identification	Quantity
Suitable	Safety	Chemical properties	Name	Process ready
Compliant	Process ready	Physical properties	Status	Reconciliation
Compatible		Biological properties		Compliant
		Compliant		

Figure 5.4 "Item" task element, sub-elements and management topics

The auditor will look for objective evidence which proves that:

♦ The correct type of item(s) is defined for the task to be performed and is communicated to the workplace.
♦ The type of item(s) is consistent with code, standards, regulations which apply to the task being performed.
♦ The type of item(s) is consistent with the needs of the task and ultimate product concerned.
♦ The correct type is issued to the workplace for processing.
♦ The correct type of item(s) is released from that workplace for subsequent processing or use.

Correct condition

An item must possess certain dimensional and similar physical characteristics, if it is to achieve the correct condition. Other features could include the item's chemical or biological properties such as inertness, acidity or asepticism, for example. Another important aspect of an item's condition is its readiness for the process and consequently matters such as the temperature, homogeneity, clarity, radioactivity etc. need to have been both considered and achieved. Naturally these considerations apply not only to the condition of the item on its arrival at the workplace but also on its departure.

Unless the items are in a condition suitable for processing or for use, money will be wasted. Examples of items in unsuitable condition might be those that are unclean or excessively eroded, corroded, bent, torn, scratched, damaged or otherwise unusable. To ensure that goods stay in a suitable condition, they need to be correctly handled and stored. Handling and storage are matters that are too often neglected in industry. It is not uncommon to find finished ferrous castings left to rust in the rain; expensively machined parts rusted up; chemicals or foodstuffs that have rotted or gone stale; rubber products, such as seals, that have been allowed to perish; clothing materials or garments that are dirty or stained being supplied to the fashion industry; food packaging that has become damaged or cosmetically impaired so that customer satisfaction and expectation is unfulfilled. The list is endless. The inadequate handling and storing of goods pours money down the drain. Thus one can see that the auditor is verifying that the auditee is protecting his company's (and hence the customer's) costs and assets. Auditors frequently identify inadequate handling and storing practices which provide an opportunity for the reduction of avoidable costs.

One crucial aspect is the safe condition of the item. This requirement applies to incoming items; items that are combined or come into contact with each other; items being sent out for delivery to the customer or user and by-products, such as effluents and discharges, that could affect the community or its environment.

The auditor will look for objective evidence that proves:

♦   The correct condition of the item(s) arriving at and leaving from the workplace is fully considered and communicated to the workplace.

♦ Only items that are in the correct condition are issued to the workplace.

♦ The correct condition of the items arriving at the workplace is protected at the workplace until the items are required.

♦ The correct condition of the items for delivery to the next process, customer or user, is achieved and protected by that workplace.

♦ Inherent environmental, health and safety hazards associated with the item(s) are known and controlled.

♦ Environmental, health and safety hazards that can arise through incorrect processing or by virtue of the process are both known and controlled at that workplace.

♦ Codes, standards and regulations concerning the condition of items are met at all times in that workplace.

Correct capability

There are three aspects of capability that are of importance, these being: the basic capability of the raw material used; the functional capability of the item achieved by virtue of its design; and, inherent safety capability.

Basic capabilities to be considered are those that arise out of the item's chemical, biological and physical attributes. Physical properties (such as melting point, boiling point, tensile strength, impact resistance, conductivity, resistivity, density, viscosity, elasticity, miscibility, coefficient of friction, atomic mass etc.) as well as chemical constituency and biological analysis are features that enable the functional requirements for the item to be achieved.

Form, dimensional size, finish and the like endow an item with load bearing, air or other fluid resistance, electrical resistance, capacitance, fatigue and creep resistance, along with other similar functional capabilities. Additional functional requirements such as reliability, maintainability, availability also need to be considered in the case of those items that will become the equipment at another workplace; these are discussed in the section *"Equipment - correct capability"* , below.

In order to achieve a safe condition, the basic materials used must possess capabilities which ensure their ability or inability to come safely into contact with, or be mixed with, other items. In the case of effluent, for example, the inherent capabilities such as radioactive half life, virulence or toxicity need to be considered by the auditee in order that the safe condition can be achieved, if necessary by encapsulating the item in specially designed equipment.

The auditor will look for objective evidence to prove that:

◆ The correct capability of the item(s) arriving at and leaving from the workplace is fully considered and communicated to the workplace.

◆ Only items that have the correct capability are issued to the workplace.

◆ The correct capability of the items arriving at the workplace is protected at the workplace until needed.

◆ The correct capability of the items to be delivered to the next process, customer or user, is achieved and protected by that workplace.

◆ Inherent capabilities that can cause environmental, health and safety hazards are known and controlled.

◆ Codes, standards and regulations concerning the capability of items are met.

Correct quantity

If 50 items are to be processed, the person performing the job must be issued with 50 items. All the items must be in the right place at the right time or - especially in the case of consumables - pressure of production deadlines may tempt people to substitute something that is not suitable. Giving way to this temptation can be a costly, even dangerous, mistake. (Whereas the auditee must receive all the items required, this does not mean they must all necessarily arrive at the same time. It is often more economic for the system to deliver sufficient items just in time for the process to proceed without being delayed. Hence the auditor must consider the appropriate size of batch arriving at the auditee's workplace but also verify that the sum total of all deliveries to the workplace is correct. See Part 2 Chapter 2, in the section *"Assessing the business performance of systems"*.

The auditor must be alert to the actual quantity of each item issued for it can be a good indication of quality process inadequacies and point to areas of opportunity for improvement. If, for example, when discussing the quantity issued to the operators, the auditor is told *"We always give them 3 extra because we know that on average 3 items in 50 won't turn out right. That means we will have the right quantity in the end"*, the question to be asked is *"Since that represents nearly 6% loss of yield what are you doing about trying to improve the process so that you can save this 6%?"*

A majority of auditees fail to understand that a few fractions of one per cent, lost at each work stage, accumulate into a substantial failure cost and loss of revenue by the time a satisfactory product has been delivered to the customer.

> Whilst performing a particular pre-award survey, I ascertained that the cumulative effect of all of such extras being absorbed by various processes amounted to some 8% loss. I promptly advised my client to press for an 8% reduction in the contract price since there is no justification in paying for scrap, the costs of which are undoubtedly incorporated in the unit costs. I also advised him to press for a quality improvement programme to ensure that defect free product would be supplied. The contract was worth in excess of $500,000 and my client obtained that 8% reduction. He also got his defect free supplies.

The quantity issued presents an immediate indication of the extent to which people get everything right first time and every time.

The correct volume of supplies is particularly important in some industries, such as the processing of nuclear fuels or the distillation of alcohol, since there are stringent requirements concerning the control and reconciliation of quantities. This is so that compliance with international laws, safety considerations or taxation requirements can be ascertained. Failure to comply with such matters can put a company at risk of loss. Another situation is one where the auditee has to pay a royalty or invoice to a commercial company on the basis of quantities actually used or consumed. The auditor needs to consider the systems and activities of the auditee in meeting his obligations accordingly in order to determine their efficacy.

The quantity of items at the workplace and in the system as a whole represents work in progress, balance sheet assets. The numbers present at or absent from the workplace can indicate major opportunities for the reduction of avoidable costs and improvement of the system's performance overall. (See Part 2 Chapter 2 *"Value-added auditing".*)

The auditor will look for objective evidence to prove that:

♦ The correct quantity of items is specified for the task concerned and communicated to the workplace.

♦ The correct quantity of items is issued to the workplace.

♦   The quantity of items used or consumed by the task is known.
♦   The correct quantity of items is delivered to the next process, user or customer.
♦   Code, standard or regulatory requirements concerning reconciliation of quantities are met.

Correct Identification

All items must be correctly identified either by means of a label on the item itself or its container or by a document accompanying it. A batch number, heat number, works number, contract number, or similar methods, including bar coding, may be used. In some cases, the identification may need to be unique to each individual item received by or released from the auditee's workplace. It is surprising how much material gets lost or is processed for the wrong contract or product line for want of proper identification.

A major purpose of identification is the need to trace the item to its information, the person who produced the item or the equipment used to produce it. The identification then permits any interested party to investigate further whether or not the item complies with its requirements in respect of type, condition, quantity and so on. In certain industries, such as food, pharmaceuticals or aircraft, where there is a risk to safety if an item does not meet requirements and is thereby unfit for purpose, the need for complete traceability of items is vital. Accordingly, the identification of the item may be constrained by industrial, market or statutory stipulations. Without a proper identification system, a product recall system will be difficult or impossible. It should, therefore, be readily apparent that identification of items is a matter which can affect the company's avoidable costs and liability position.

For some products, it is also useful for the auditee to develop a system of direct identification either on the item itself or by means of an accompanying document in order to indicate the individual who made it. This has the benefit of linking ownership to the person making the item, which can be a great motivator.

> A manufacturer of computers places a sticker inside the cabinet of completed machines. That sticker states the name of the person who assembled the machine and his home telephone number which the user is invited to call day or night if a problem occurs. Subtle!

Many hotels require their housekeepers to leave a small thank-you note in one's room, signed by whoever serviced the room.

Fender guitars released from the Brea factory bear a tag signed by the person who made the particular guitar purchased.

The auditor will look for objective evidence to prove that:

♦ A method for correct identification of items arriving at, used by and leaving from the workplace is defined and communicated to that workplace.

♦ The method is consistent with the requirements of the codes, standards and regulations that apply to the items used or produced by that workplace.

♦ Items are correctly identified in accordance with that method.

♦ The method used to identify the items does not impair the correct condition of the item concerned.

The equipment

"Equipment" is a term that embraces :

♦ Machines and process plant, such as lathes, presses, robotic welders, flexible manufacturing machines, vats and vessels, cracking columns, dialysis units, refineries, that are used directly to process items.

♦ Support facilities such as electrical generators, refrigeration or freezing plant, air conditioning and filtering plant, illumination devices and boiler plant.

♦ Buildings, including factories, warehouses and offices; structures, such as towers, chimneys and exhaust stacks; offices and access facilities, such as roadways, gangways, pathways, stairways, Jacob's ladders etc.

♦ Hand tools such as spanners, probes, brushes, scalpels; power driven hand tools such as solder irons, electric drills, saws, pneumatic grinders, paint spray guns.

♦ Process utensils such as pans, beakers, strainers, pots.

♦ Consumables and disposables including cleaning papers, swabs, tool bits; reusable fluids and liquids such as cutting oils, cooling water, recycled air or inert gas.

♦ Transportation machines including aircraft, ships, trains, conveyor belts; lifting devices including cranes, fork-lift trucks, elevators and hoists.

- Personnel clothing such as uniforms, space suits, diving suits, laboratory coats, surgical gowns, gloves, caps, helmets, visors and masks, boots and shoes.
- Administrative aids, such as desks, chairs, filing cabinets; data processing equipment including computers, visual display units, printers, disk drives, CAD facilities.
- Communications devices such as modems, telephones, telex and telefax machines, together with their optical and electrical cables.
- Instruments and devices used for the measuring and testing of items being processed and manufactured such as ammeters, voltmeters, micrometers, stop watches and clocks, analogue gauges, tensile test machines, Charpy test machines, Johanssen blocks, ph meters; intermediate devices such as templates and patterns; comparison standards such as colour and texture swatches, samples.

When a piece of equipment becomes an " item "

As the reader will no doubt appreciate, all of the above examples of equipment need to be produced before they can be used. When they are being produced by their suppliers or contractors they are *items*: only after they have been fully commissioned for their operational life at the customer or user workplace do they become *equipment* for it is then that they have become tools to help the customer or user *"person"* accomplish the task (process) assigned to him/her.

During its operational life, the equipment will need to be maintained. (For the purposes of the present discussion, maintenance includes such activities as repair, overhaul, refurbishment, calibration, restoration, capability assessment.) During maintenance, it is processed as part of a maintenance task. When the auditor analyses that maintenance task, the equipment being maintained is considered to be the *item* whilst the tools needed to perform that maintenance task are its equipment.

Simple examples of equipment

In the case of simple clerical activities, the equipment required may be nothing more than a pen, a desk and a chair upon which to sit. But a filing cabinet may also be required so that documents can be organized, retrieved readily and not mislaid. The auditor will not dwell on such equipment beyond noting that it has been provided, observing, perhaps the general capacity and condition, unless it is to be located in an environment

Equipment					
Type	Condition	Capability	Identification	Location	Environment
Suitable for process	Safety	Verified suitable for process	Name	Right place, right time	Absence of nuisances
Compliant	Process ready	Capacity	Status	Relative position	Maintained
	Maintenance	Known performance		Compliant	Monitored
	Cleanliness	Interface compatible		Ergonomics	Compliant
	Calibration	Reliability			
	Security	Maintainability			
	Handling	Up-to-date			
	Compliant	Compliant			

Figure 5.5 "Equipment" task element, sub-elements and management topics

which demands strict cleanliness or decontamination procedures in order to protect the condition of items being processed therein.

Audit procedure

The auditor will first establish what equipment needs to be supplied to the auditee's workplace and then what equipment will require maintenance (calibration). Even though the equipment may not physically leave the auditee's workplace for maintenance, the auditor will consider that it has been passed over to another task unit (process) for that purpose. The auditor will analyze that maintenance task separately if it is within the scope and objectives of the audit. For each piece of equipment the auditor will then consider the sub-elements shown in Figure 5.4 and described as follows. (See also the discussion in Chapter 13 - *"Useful sequence for questioning".*)

Correct type

It is essential that the equipment used to perform the process is of the correct type for the purpose concerned. The quality of the item being processed often suffers when substitute or "make do" types of equipment are used in an emergency or if the equipment is incompatible with the items with which it comes into contact. In certain industries, the type of equipment and materials used in the item's construction might be restricted by codes, standards and regulations. Even in the absence of such restrictions, the auditee's company or the customer might have its own standards that govern the choice available. Naturally, legal regulations will take precedence.

The auditor will look for objective evidence to prove that:

♦ The correct type of equipment for the task being performed is defined and is communicated to the workplace.
♦ The correct type of equipment is issued to the workplace.
♦ The type of equipment is consistent with code, standards, regulations that apply to the task being performed.
♦ The type of equipment is consistent with the needs of the task concerned.
♦ The correct type of equipment is handed over to those responsible for maintaining it or disposing of it.

Correct condition

Aspects of the equipment's *"condition"* which must be considered are: maintenance; calibration; cleanliness; handling; security and safety.

The equipment must be in the correct condition to perform the task, being handled in a manner that prevents degradation to itself and to the items and information being processed. The equipment must be marked to indicate its current condition, its maintenance or calibration status and its operability. For machine tools and other equipment, many companies operate either a planned maintenance system or a condition monitoring scheme. Maintenance and calibration of equipment are service functions. All equipment, especially sensitive instruments, gauges or machines, must be handled properly to avoid damage and inaccuracy.

> During one audit, it was noted that the master set of gauges were handled extremely roughly by the calibration department personnel. Upon close examination, the master gauges, a set of Johannsen blocks, were shown to be badly scratched and marked. (This type of equipment relies on the smoothness of its surface finish to be effective because the polished surfaces of the blocks are carefully brought together and, with a slight practiced twist, will unite as if one. Scratches cause air to leak between the surfaces preventing the blocks' assembly and causing inaccurate calibration. The blocks are held between gloved fingers or with a soft cloth or with specially provided tongs.)

Since equipment represents company assets, it is important to protect against pilferage or other forms of loss. One of the advantages of an audit is that the auditor can verify that the equipment which has been issued to a particular auditee is being properly protected and is still in existence.

In certain applications, the equipment may need to be clean in order that damage to or contamination of the item(s) being processed is prevented (in the food or pharmaceutical industries, for example). The auditor must ascertain what type of damage is unacceptable prior to investigating the effectiveness of the auditee's controls. Factors such as dirt, liquids, chemicals, microorganisms and detritus may all be unacceptable.

Equipment safety always needs to be considered. Some industries have regulations that relate to specific types of equipment such as aircraft, boiler plant, freezer rooms. These regulations generally cover inherent features that the designer and supplier must incorporate into the equipment as well as operational constraints. The person responsible for the task must be aware of, trained in and competent with regard to these. These operational factors might also include stipulations concerning permissible running hours between periodic maintenance and inspection tasks - the auditee will need some means of knowing when those permissible hours will be exceeded.

The auditor must determine what (if any) regulations, guides, codes and standards apply. In some cases, the auditor may discover that there are no specific regulations or such like for a particular piece of equipment. Nonetheless, in most countries it will be covered by a national regulation concerning general safety and associated practices such as the British *"Health and Safety at Work Act"*. Even if the scope and objectives of the audit do not specifically relate to safety, the auditor still has a civic responsibility to note any unsafe equipment or practice encountered during the audit and to bring this to the attention of the auditee's management.

The auditor will look for objective evidence to prove that:

♦ The correct condition of the equipment arriving at the workplace is fully considered and communicated to that workplace.

♦ The correct condition of the equipment arriving at the workplace is protected until the equipment is needed.

♦ The correct operational condition of the equipment is known at all times by its user and that the equipment is not used in any other state.

♦ Inherent hazards associated with the equipment are known and controlled.

♦ Hazards associated with use and incorrect use of the equipment are known and controlled at the workplace.

♦ Codes, standards and regulations concerning the condition of the equipment are met at all times in that workplace.

Correct capability

The equipment must have been tried out or established as suitable for the task required. New equipment must be shown to be capable of performing the task in hand, which might mean that it has been approved or licensed by a regulatory authority. Sometimes the qualification can be performed by processing the first piece. This is a commercial risk, a gamble that some contracts and some industries do not allow.

The capability of the equipment must be consistent with the task to be performed, with the items or the information to be processed. Thus size, capacity, payload, speed of response, flow rate of delivered fluid, height and reach, range, performance envelope, number of simultaneous users, are all types of capability that may be important. In the case of equipment used for preventing and coping with unsafe situations, its capability to do so, fire pump volume and delivery head, for instance, will be matters for regulatory compliance. In all cases concerning equipment capacity, the auditor needs to determine the appropriate units of performance measurement. In some cases, the auditor may discover that the capacity of the equipment is not being fully utilized. An example of this would be the excessive wastage of space in an office.

> The executives of an American company wished to hire new staff as part of the company expansion programme and thought it would be necessary to build a major extension to its offices. I accompanied one of the executive vice presidents around the offices and demonstrated that the staff were not using the space to best advantage. Result: approximately half million dollars' needless expenditure was avoided.

> A British company decided to introduce computer aided design equipment. The facility performed most impressively at first and the company quickly began to add more terminals for its engineers to use. As the response time started to deteriorate, they eventually came to appreciate that there is a limiting capacity to the machine and its software. An audit revealed that over a six month period the money wasted because high salaried design engineers had to sit idle, while the machine did its best to cope with the workload, exceeded the capital cost of buying an additional machine.

In the case of process equipment, its capacity to process the requisite quantity in a given period of time should be ascertained. For example, a conveyor belt which is required to transport 5,000 units per hour when, in fact, it can only deal with 4,650 units per hour will create a bottleneck. The capability of any production line is dictated by the slowest piece of equipment installed within that line. (This is discussed further in Part 2 Chapter 2 *"Value-added auditing"*.)

A variation of this occurs in the case of services relating to the capability to serve the anticipated number of customers at a counter or desk, at a supermarket, bank or fast food shop. The number of tellers, booking agents, sales assistants, clerks and associated equipment required will be dependent on the volume of customers arriving in any given period of time and on the length of time a customer accepts as reasonable to spend in a queue. In designing and specifying such equipment, queuing theory becomes important and the auditor may need to verify that it has been correctly applied and encompasses an assessment of peak load requirements. A feature that can be of particular importance is the capability of the equipment to deal with safety related situations. The width of access passages and escape routes in relation to the authorized number of customers that might be present in an emergency is a case in point. There could well be regulations affecting such matters: the auditor will need to investigate this.

The auditor will look for objective evidence to prove that:

♦ The capability of equipment is defined and verified prior to its commissioning and during its service.
♦ The capability is consistent with the needs of the task and with the capability of the equipment it interfaces with.
♦ The capability of the equipment has been communicated to the user and is known at all times.
♦ The capability of the equipment used by customers in a service situation is consistent with customer expectations and needs.
♦ The capability of equipment is consistent with regulations, codes and standards.

In the case of measuring equipment, the capability is determined by means of calibration, range, accuracy and precision being the principle matters of interest. Calibration of equipment must be compatible with the needs of the item being processed as well as the risks associated with the process involved e.g. accuracy and precision of the measuring devices needed to prevent damage to the item or hazards to the people using the equipment that it is helping to control. An additional matter to be considered is that of the regulations applying to the task and its equipment: regulations concerning weights and measures, for example, and quantities sold to the public. The checking of instruments used to control safety related activities, such as aircraft in-flight instruments or boiler pressure gauges is an instance of the same.

The auditor should look for objective evidence to prove that:

♦ The calibration of measuring and testing equipment is consistent with the needs of the task and the items or services affected.
♦ The calibration is performed in accordance with national codes, standards and regulations.

♦   The calibration is performed against known standards.
♦   The calibration status of the measuring and test equipment is
      communicated to the user so as to be known at all times.

Another and vital aspect of equipment capability which needs to be
established prior to commissioning and which requires to be continually
verified during routine maintenance is its reliability. This has particular
implications for equipment which can be safety related such as computers
required for air traffic control. The auditor must ascertain that the
supporting management systems for the maintenance of such equipment
are adequate to maintain the correct monitoring and reliability of the
equipment. This may also involve ascertaining that adequate back up has
been arranged in the event of equipment unavailability. Equipment
reliability and back up is a matter of considerable importance for those
companies which offer services as their products. Services are dealt with
more fully in Part 2 Chapter 5. Depending on the audit objectives, it may
be necessary to check the system used for equipment selection and the
methods used to specify its reliability.

The reliability of equipment directly affects its availability which, in turn,
affects profit. Unreliable equipment represents a cost to be avoided. The
inherent reliability of equipment may be satisfactory when it is new and
subsequently deteriorate during its life if the equipment is not properly
maintained. However, maintenance itself can take time and cause the
equipment to be unavailable in the interim. This represents a further cost,
part of which may be avoidable, depending on the maintainability of the
equipment. Maintainability of equipment is a particular capability which
must be correct and designed in. Equipment maintainability and back up is
another matter of considerable importance for those companies which
offer services as their products. Depending on the audit objectives, it may
be necessary to check both the system used for equipment selection and
the methods chosen to specify its maintainability.

Maintainability and reliability are features of equipment that are affected
by regulations in some industries. In the air passenger transport business,
for example, the reliability of aircraft and constituent parts such as engines
is a matter that needs to be demonstrated to the authorities prior to a
certificate of airworthiness being issued; in the nuclear power business,
the maintainability of equipment in a radioactively "hot" environment has
to be quantified and determined to the satisfaction of the regulatory
authorities involved.

Both maintainability and reliability are aspects of equipment capability that can render it obsolete as technology advances. Equipment that is still in perfectly good working condition can become a liability if competitors introduce more advanced types which reduce operational costs and thus improve their competitive price edge. In these circumstances, the equipment no longer possesses the correct capability even though its maintainability and reliability have not changed from what was previously acceptable. The auditor has a duty to advise the auditee management accordingly of the risks involved in not replacing the equipment. Those risks present a potential avoidable cost to the auditee. (See also Part 2 Chapter 2, *"Value-added auditing"*.)

The auditor will look for objective evidence to prove that:

♦ The correct reliability and maintainability of equipment is defined and verified prior to its commissioning and during its operational life.
♦ The reliability and maintainability are consistent with the needs of the task.
♦ The reliability and maintainability of the equipment is communicated to the user.
♦ The reliability and maintainability of the equipment used by customers in a service situation are consistent with customer expectations and needs.
♦ The reliability and maintainability of equipment comply at all times with regulations, codes and standards relevant to the tasks which the equipment is to perform.

Correct identification

Unless a piece of equipment is self-evidently exactly what it is, it should carry some form of exact identification - a works number, an inventory number or something similar. For example, in a ship's engine room, the machinery is often identified by its location so that when an engineer is told to start the "starboard for'ard generator", he knows exactly which generator is meant.

A major purpose of identification is the need to trace the equipment to its information, the products that it has helped to make, the service it has helped to supply and the people that have used it. The identification permits any interested party to investigate further whether or not the equipment complies with its requirements in respect of condition, type, capability, location etc. In certain industries such as food or pharmaceuticals, where there is a risk to health if the items produced or service supplied do not meet requirements and are therefore unfit for purpose, the need for complete traceability of equipment can be vital. Accordingly, the identification may be constrained by industrial, market, or statutory stipulations. Without a proper identification system, corrective action and further defect prevention would be difficult or impossible. It is therefore clear that identification can assist the company with its product liability prevention activities and, thus, help to avoid avoidable costs.

Correct identification assists in the management of the company assets and protection of the equipment from loss. It can also be important in the case of equipment that requires specific licensing such as aircraft call signs, motor vehicle registration numbers, pressure vessel tag numbers.

The auditor will look for objective evidence to prove that:

♦ A method for identifying equipment released for use is developed and communicated to the user.
♦ The method ensures compliance with the requirements of the codes, standards and regulations that apply to the equipment used and the tasks performed with it.
♦ Equipment is correctly identified in accordance with that method.
♦ Equipment released from the workplace to the next process, user or customer is identified in accordance with that method.
♦ The method used to identify the equipment does not impair the correct condition of the item concerned.

Correct location

It is part of the planning function to ensure that equipment is in the right place at the right time. There must be no temptation to substitute one piece of equipment for another.

The relative position of different pieces of equipment to each other can affect quality achievement. If, for example, a quenching tank is too far from a furnace, the items may lose too much heat during transfer to the pond and the correct condition after quenching will not be achieved. If an hotel kitchen is too far from the restaurant, the food may have become unacceptably cool by the time it is served to the customer. An illogical or inconvenient layout of equipment leads to excessive handling of items with all the attendant costs and risks of damage. Transportation of items is expensive given the equipment and energy, time, protective packaging, tote pans, pallets, labour and administration required to move the original articles. Major opportunities for cost reduction are often revealed during an audit by attention to such matters. Layout of equipment represents an important aspect of quality planning and when the decisions associated with it are of poor quality, the avoidable costs can be considerable.

The location of equipment is a matter of regulatory interest in some industries. For example, the authorized operation of a North Sea oil platform is contingent on the operator proving that the platform has been installed precisely where the authorities have approved it. In most countries, the construction of buildings on land is confined to precise coordinates that have been approved by local or national authorities prior to action commencing. In some cases, the location of equipment may be a safety matter governed by regulations such as avoiding the installation of a non-explosion proof electrical apparatus in an explosive environment; keeping cattle or pig pens at a certain distance from food processing areas; avoiding the placement of air intakes for air conditioning equipment near to fume sources.

Another feature is the ergonomic layout of the workplace itself. If the various types of equipment used are inconveniently located in relation to each other and to the person performing the task, the risks of operator fatigue (which can lead to quality problems) and the possibility of industrial injury can occur. Depending on the scope and objectives of the audit, the auditor may wish to pursue the auditee's controls on ergonomic design and layout.

The auditor will look for objective evidence to prove that:

♦ The correct equipment is issued to the correct location where the task is performed so as to be available when needed.
♦ The relative location of equipment used by consecutive tasks does not impair the correct final condition of the item concerned.
♦ The location of the equipment does not impair the service performed.
♦ The layout of equipment used at a workplace presents neither risk to anyone nor difficulty for use.
♦ Codes, standards and regulations that apply to the location of the equipment for the tasks performed with it are met at all times.

Correct environment

The environment in which the work or process is being carried out can affect the quality of the item involved. Environments include office space, chemical baths and tanks, protective and working atmospheres and they must neither contain nor present a *"nuisance"*. A nuisance may include, for example, noise, dust, vibration, static electricity, odours or contaminants. It may be necessary to take special measures to maintain the correct environment: a computer room will, for instance, generally require careful control of the temperature, dust count, pollen count and humidity, all within closely specified limits, records of the conditions achieved being kept for future reference.

The correct environment is, of course, most important in sensitive industries such as food and pharmaceuticals as well as in data processing or in the running of computerized equipment. As a case in point, a dairy factory may require close monitoring of the dirt, detritus and bacterial background levels in order to prevent contamination of the foodstuffs being processed.

Other features of the environment that may need to be controlled can include temperature, ph, pressure, draughts, electro-magnetic fields, static electricity, bacterial count or microorganism levels. Each of these might be too high or too low: some might be unacceptably uneven, stratified temperatures or concentrations of liquids in a processing tank, for example. Lighting levels can present a nuisance: inadequate lighting in a graphics design office or for the operator of a microscope can lead to eye strain, fatigue and mistakes; flickering fluorescent lights can lead to headaches and quality problems; neon lights can lead to changes in the appearance of colours used for coding of materials and thus to incorrect selection.

Regulations do govern the control of environments in certain industries where there can be a risk to health or safety. As part of the audit preparation, the auditor must ascertain which ones apply. The audit will then need to verify that the auditee has developed and implemented the systems and practices that will ensure compliance with those applicable regulations.

It is insufficient merely to check the condition of the environment for any nuisances. The audit must verify that the support systems necessary for creating and maintaining the correct environment have been thought through and are being properly implemented.

In a food factory's packing area, butter was fed through a chute onto the wrapping material and weighed. If overweight was measured, the operator removed some butter with his hands and replaced it in the chute ready for further feeding through. In the event that underweight had been registered, the operator scooped some butter from the chute with his hands and patted it down into the carton. The auditor noticed toilet facilities were available adjacent to the packing area. He visited these and emerged quite concerned because the hand washing facilities available were inadequate.

Inadequate environment can affect the quality of the product drastically. Quality problems are often designed in rather than designed out. As customer expectation and specifications become inexorably more stringent, the result partly of competition offering products of higher specification, environment and equipment that would have sufficed at one time become totally unsuitable for today's and tomorrow's business. Even though it may be in good working order, it is obsolete. This holds particularly true in service industries.

Deregulation of the UK bus industry allowed private companies to compete more with the nationalized bus companies. These private companies sought long distance routes and introduced state-of-the-art buses which featured video films, on-board steward services providing refreshments, air conditioning and so on. The nationalized company which had held a monopoly discovered that many customers preferred the equipment of its new found competitors and was thus forced to renew parts of its bus fleet which were probably still serviceable but effectively obsolete. Buses are not cheap acquisitions.

I have visited many food factories whose walls and floors are covered by shiny porcelain tiles. At the time those factories were built, it was genuinely believed that such materials were perfectly adequate to ensure an hygienic environment. However, as knowledge increased, it became recognized that porcelain tiles easily become cracked, that the joints between them are not impervious and that the risk exists of biological or other contaminants building up within cracks and joints. Environmental cleanliness is then difficult to maintain. (Some environmental cleanliness authorities now insist that all surfaces are lined with stainless steel.)

It is always a major decision to replace the materials and equipment totally with modern ones. For this reason, prudent management lays aside an amount of money from the profits and allows it to accumulate such that new facilities can be financed. Lack of resources is a real cause of operational and business problems. Whereas an auditor may feel some sympathy towards the auditee, it does not alter the fact that if the product is suffering, if legislation has changed or the market and external circumstances have evolved such that the environment and equipment is no longer suitable, he has a duty to bring this to the attention of the management and to require corrective action. The auditor is being paid to do just that.

The auditor will verify that:

♦ The correct environment for performing the task concerned is defined and communicated to the user.
♦ Environmental nuisances are defined and communicated to the user.
♦ The correct environment is maintained and nuisances are prevented and controlled.
♦ The environment defined and used does not impair the correct condition of the items contained within it or processed by it.
♦ The environment defined and used does not impair the service performed within it.
♦ The environment defined and used does not present a risk to those within it.
♦ Codes, standards and regulations that apply to the environment and to the tasks performed within it are met at all times.

The information

Information is of key importance to human workers, machines and robots. It communicates the results of decisions made by people and of activities performed by machines. There is a fundamental difference between data and information. These were most succinctly described in the British Standard 3527 :PART 1 :1976, in the context of data processing[3] as:

*DATA : "A representation of facts, concepts, or instructions in a formalized manner suitable for communication, interpretation, or processing by humans or by **automatic** means.*

*INFORMATION :"The meaning that a human assigns to **data** by means of conventions used in their presentation".*

Clearly from a quality point of view, fitness for purpose depends on ascertaining how a person will interpret and apply data i.e what does the user of data consider to be information. Within this book, however, the term *"information"* will be used to cover both information and data as well as documents. Information to be audited will be related to the task elements and their sub-elements information describing an item's condition, for example, information that records a person's training or competence; information describing the capability of equipment, information detailing the characteristics of a service and so on.

Documents are the most common means of transmitting information. A document is a written or pictorial means of conveying information. It describes, defines, specifies, reports or certifies activities, the requirements for performing activities or the activities' results. Sketches, specifications, procedures, instructions, records, CD-ROMs, radiographs, photographs, computer tapes and disks, computer print-outs, drawings, bar codes, invoices, labels, stickers, reports, purchase orders, process control charts and microfilm are all examples of documents.

Increasingly, however, information is also being communicated by means of visual displays, pulses of light and electronic signals. Whatever means is used, the sub-elements described later still apply.

Audit procedure

The auditor will first establish what information needs to be received at the auditee's workplace and then what information will leave the workplace for use by others. There will always be some information that a unit needs to keep for reference such as industrial standards, codes, agreed procedures, standard formulae: if statistical sampling is one of the unit's tasks, the sampling plans and associated instructions will remain within that unit. The resident documents may have been generated inside or outside the unit. The company expense procedure is frequently information that is resident in a great number of units throughout a company but which is generated by one unit, perhaps the accounts department. Instructions on the use of equipment, particularly concerning safety features and practices, is a further example of resident information. (I consider the test of residency is satisfied when it applies to information that is readily available to the workplace through databases, intranets and the Internet that the auditee can access immediately and directly from the workplace.) The auditor should ascertain what is resident and what is not; what is created by that work task and what is not as well as determining the origin of each piece of information that the unit does not itself create.

Information					
Checked	Content	Edition	Condition	Identification	Distribution
Self-checking	Based on user's wants and needs	Valid	Useable	Name	Economic
Based on classification	Compliant	Identified	Legible	Status	Based on user's wants and needs
User involvement		Stable	Protected		Archive/ records
					Compliant

Figure 5.6 "Information" task element, sub-elements and management topics

For each piece of information, the auditor will consider the sub-elements shown in Figure 5.6 and described below. (See also the discussion in Part 1 Chapter 13 - *"Useful sequence for questioning"*.)

Correctly checked

Checking is important and must not be abused. The auditor should be alert for *"you sign mine - I'll sign yours"* arrangements. Often auditees will fail to recognize that a major value of proper information reviews is that the preparer learns from any errors or omissions found. Reviews provide experience and assist in the raising of competence levels. This is an important part of training for the person charges with the responsibility of preparing the information. Failure to take checking seriously is often a cause of repeated mistakes which are costly. Frequently, supervisors are reluctant to verify firmly that their subordinates are capable of producing the right content of information first time around having assumed a level of competence and knowledge that does not actually exist. Such reluctance often stems from embarrassment about checking their subordinates' work or concern about appearing to be unreasonable or distrustful. That attitude does not help the staff to learn, develop and gain confidence: in the long term it is damaging both to the company, the subordinate and the supervisor.

Whereas independent review is valuable, essential in some industries, there should always be a *"self check"* performed by the preparer. The person performing a task is responsible for the quality of the work produced and should therefore not offer that work for acceptance without having first critically examined for completeness and correctness. It is wrong to waste one's colleagues' time by presenting unchecked work that contains avoidable mistakes. It is costly too.

A useful type of independent review is to ask the end user, wherever possible, to be involved. The end user determines whether or not the information really is fit for purpose. Accordingly, the auditor should consider whether the involvement of the user is feasible and ask the auditee whether or not it has been obtained. Some contracts or regulations might stipulate the involvement of the customer or a regulatory authority in the review process: the auditor must ascertain if such requirements apply. However, such involvements do not absolve the auditee of the responsibility for checking that the correct content of information has been achieved before its submission to them.

The extensiveness of the review and the degree of independence must be commensurate with the classification of the product and the task to which the information relates. (Classification is discussed in Chapter 8.) The auditor will look for evidence of planning the reviews and checks of information consistent with the classification required. Absence of such planning can prove both unwise and a false economy.

The auditor will look for objective evidence to prove that:

♦   The information checks are planned.
♦   The checks are commensurate with the importance and risk associated with the task and product to which the information relates.
♦   The planned checks include those required by the customer or regulatory body involved with the type of product or tasks to which the information relates.
♦   The methods of checking to be used are planned.
♦   The checking methods are commensurate with the importance and risk associated with the task and product to which the information relates.
♦   The checks are performed as planned.
♦   Those who will perform the checks are provided with all the background information prior to the checks being performed.

Correct content

Information must have the content required both for the unit to perform its task and to enable subsequent units to perform the tasks which they are assigned. Some information a unit receives may be for its own use and some may be for the use of a downstream unit (a workshop traveler, a quality plan, being examples which may contain instructions for an entire manufacturing or product creating sequence that comprises a large number of different units performing different processes): such information is passed through and is not necessarily generated by the particular unit. (The increasing use of company databases and intranets tends to reduce the distribution of information sequentially through successive departments, as hard copy disappears from use. Distribution to affected workplaces is often achieved simultaneously to all nowadays.)

The content of information must always be based on what the end user really needs as opposed to its creator's opinion of what those needs are. This is certainly true when the information is being created for the purpose of obtaining customer or regulatory approvals. Examples of this include

102

applications for licences; applications for design approvals for safety related equipment; extradition applications. Of course, the content may be prescribed in applicable regulations, codes or standards and the auditor will need to determine what does apply and to verify that the auditee complies with those requirements. The auditor should examine the system to verify that there is a direct feedback of information from user to creator in order that mistakes are avoided or promptly rectified.

Prior to the creation of the information, the task unit will need to be in possession of other information describing the background and what is required. This is further discussed under *"Correct distribution"*, below.

The content needs to be clear, complete and unambiguous. The essence of information is to communicate something to someone. Completeness can be defined and ascertained but clarity and ambiguity are aspects of style that the information's creator either does or does not possess. That style can be improved but only if the problems are pointed out in the first place. Hence, the need for good checking, discussed in the previous section.

The auditor will look for objective evidence to prove that:

♦ The correct content of information arriving at and leaving from the workplace is fully considered and communicated to that workplace.
♦ The content of information is based on the user's needs and is commensurate with the importance and risk associated with the task and product to which the information relates.
♦ The correct content of information is achieved.
♦ Codes, standards and regulations concerning the content of information are met at all times.

Correct edition

All information that is to be used to perform a task must be of the correct and valid revision. This is not so straight forward as it sounds. There may be a number of revisions that are valid throughout a company but only one of those may be relevant to a particular contract or project. This type of situation can arise with the ASME code which has addenda or revisions issued every six months. In this case, all the addenda can be valid since a contract is signed against a particular addendum and there may well be subsequent addenda in effect by the time the contract is completed: hence only one revision is correct for the particular contract, but a number of revisions are valid. It is the job of the unit responsible for generating particular information to distribute the correct and valid revisions to the units that require them and to stipulate which revision is correct for the task concerned.

The edition or revision of information must be clearly indicated by some means. An example would be drawings and specifications bearing a title block which contains the revision number or letter: approval certificates, licences and permits might bear start and expiry dates to indicate the period of validity. Computer files often show the last occasion on which the file was worked on and saved: the date and actual time of saving can be found using the computer systems' listings. For example, the File Manager in Windows software indicates such details.

Merely verifying that the correct edition is properly identified with that information is, however, insufficient. Upon discovering, for example, that a specification has reached, say, revision 9, pose the question *"Why does it take a minimum of 9 revisions to define the information that the user needs properly?"* Changing the information, checking it and distributing it is very expensive. Excessive revisions can be a good indication that the information has not been fit for purpose (although this is not always the case because sometimes the revisions show the continuing evolution of a product range throughout its saleable life). Often, though, constant revision highlights an area of considerable opportunity for cost reduction, improved efficiency and increased customer satisfaction. Constant revisions signal that the system is poor and there is a serious quality problem which deserves management's closest attention. The vast majority of effort in most companies nowadays relates to the creation, dissemination, absorption and use of information, activities which constitute probably the greatest part of the unavoidable costs and a most sizeable proportion of the avoidable costs. The auditor must always follow up to find out why such profligate waste has occurred. The reasons for so many changes must be unearthed by the auditor. (Computers and their software can sometimes prevent this useful information being obtained and the auditor might find nothing more than a *".bak"* copy in the system, assuming the auditee has not deleted the back-up or changed the identifier. Thus, there is no reliable indication of how many changes occurred before the current edition was released.)

The auditor will require proof that:

♦   A method for identifying the correct edition of information arriving at, used by and produced by the workplace is defined and communicated to that workplace.

♦ The information arriving at, used by or produced by that workplace is identified in accordance with that method.

♦ Only the correct edition of that information is used at or distributed by that workplace.

♦ Codes, standards and regulations concerning the edition of information to be used are met at all times.

Correct condition

Information can be transmitted by several types of medium nowadays and it is the medium that must be kept in good condition. The traditional medium has been documents comprising paper and ink which are susceptible to damage. Such documents need to be legible, clean and undamaged and stored and handled in such a way as to keep them in usable condition. One of the reasons why poor photocopies and indecipherable blue prints can occur is partly because in factories or on construction sites, they tend to be mistreated - left exposed to the elements, damaged by the rain, sun-faded, covered with dirty fingerprints or torn. Another cause of poor quality documents and one which applies to all sectors of activity, is inadequate clarity of reproduction achieved through using badly maintained photocopiers.

At one engineering company, the workshop papers were simply stapled together into a bundle. This was of such a size that a vast amount of thumbing through was needed to find any one document. Inevitably, the documents became grubby, torn, jumbled up, and unusable fairly rapidly, an inordinate amount of time having to be spent regularly checking the contents of the documents. The situation had carried on for so long and so many years that it had become accepted as the norm without question. By the simple expedient of changing the size and format of the workshop documents and putting them into a folder for issue to the shop floor, much time and effort were saved.

A similar situation existed at another company and was resolved by placing a computer terminal at each work station. Hard copy documents were eliminated, updates became immediately available on-line. Other benefits included elimination of paper shuffling, lost documentation, time spent tracking down originators' meanings within faded, indecipherable scrawl. The CEO estimated the cost of the terminals was paid for within six months due not only to the savings incurred from the foregoing points, but also from the increased efficiency shown by an almost immediate increase in factory throughput.

Where the information is distributed or stored in the form of magnetic media such as computer tapes and disks, this also means that proper protection must be provided to prevent degradation or damage which can be caused by physical abuse, stray electromagnetic radiations, heat, dirt, spilt fluids. Media such as floppy disks are easily damaged by careless handling, such as finger contact with the magnetic surfaces. Staff need to be informed that this type of contact must be avoided.

In some cases, the medium used is film, for example, radiographs, industrial or advertising photographs, microfilm records. Unless the films have been properly processed, there is a risk that the coating will be unstable and will degrade over time. It follows that for archive life applications, the auditee needs a condition monitoring system whereby the state of the files under storage is regularly assessed and compared to a control standard.

Damage and degradation can occur during use, storage or transportation: the above should have drawn the auditor's attention to the need to verify the methods and system used to protect information and to maintain it in a condition that is fit for purpose at all times. Information creation forms a major part of business expense and is an unavoidable cost nowadays: one can see that there are monetary benefits in protecting the condition of the media on which it is held so as to prevent the rise of avoidable costs.

The above describes various means by which information could be lost. Another possibility is loss by theft. Theft can occur when someone steals documents, films, tapes or disks. It can also occur when someone uses electronic transfer: this is discussed in Part 2, Chapter 4. Prevention of theft means that the auditee must design and implement a security system which covers physical and electronic removal of information. Loss can also occur when the information is destroyed before the statutory time for storage and retention has elapsed. The destruction may be either inadvertent or deliberate but it points to the need for security and a system whereby destruction must be authorized in writing only after a check has been made to ensure that legal or contractual requirements are not being violated.

The auditor will look for objective evidence that:

♦ The correct condition of information media arriving at and leaving from the workplace is fully considered and communicated to the workplace.

- The correct condition of the information media arriving at the workplace is protected by the workplace at all times.
- The correct condition of information media distributed to the other processes, customers or users is completed and protected by that workplace.
- Codes, standards and regulations that relate to the retention of information and the condition of its media are met at all times in that workplace.

Correct distribution

Distribution must be based on the finding out of who needs to know what, as opposed to the creator's opinion of who should receive the information. The auditor should ascertain that distributors advise potential users of the type of information that is available. With some products, it may be impossible to find out which users actually need information and some simulation may become necessary. The auditor should check how the distribution needs have been defined and how the organization then verifies that the distribution is in fact correct, such that all those who genuinely need to receive information have in fact been sent it.

Distribution can be excessive with people who do not really need the information being sent it anyway: distribution can be inadequate with people who need information being unaware that it exists and thus duplicating effort by creating their own version. Basing distribution on actual need is cost effective: it reduces the possibility for avoidable costs occurring. Audits can reveal unnecessary or inadequate distribution thereby contributing to savings, which can be considerable.

Information must have passed through the proper official channels before being released for use by any unit. No recipient should accept it without evidence that the correct approvals have been obtained if it does not appear to have been generated according to official practice. The unit responsible for issuing and distributing it should maintain a record or log of its distribution. Such a distribution list may be included with each copy of the information or it may be kept separately, depending on company practice and the appropriateness for the application concerned.

It is also important that the auditee distributes the requisite information to the store or archive in accordance with statutory or contractual requirements. In Britain, for example, a company's financial records must be stored for six years for tax purposes: in the nuclear industry, it is normal for various types of record to be stored over at least the operational lifetime of the nuclear installation to which they refer.

The auditor will require proof that:

♦ The correct distribution has been determined by ascertaining other processes, customers and user's needs.
♦ The correct distribution of the information coming to and going from the workplace is defined and communicated to that workplace.
♦ All information arriving at, used by or distributed by that workplace is correctly distributed.
♦ Codes, standards and regulations concerning the distribution of information are met at all times.

Correct identification

Information must clearly state exactly what it is and to what it relates. Common examples of unidentified documents include design calculations not linked to any particular contract, product range or batch and that are therefore just an impressive looking collection of figures and equations; drawings that do not relate to a product line or a particular contract for which the items have been purchased. Similar problems are found with spreadsheets created on desktop computers; floppy disks that are left unidentified or with indecipherable file names that have not been indexed or created under a formally established identification coding system.

In some circumstances, the identification might be constrained by statutory requirements such as tax codes, social security numbers or other numbers allocated by the local or national government. In such cases, the identification system and practices must incorporate those requirements.

The identification that must be available concerns:

♦ What the information is (its name).
♦ When it was created and which edition it is (see *"Correct edition"*).
♦ Who created it and who authorized its release (see *"Correctly checked"*).
♦ Where it belongs (in order to ensure its traceability to the person, services, item, equipment or other information to which or whom it relates).

The auditor will look for proof that:

♦ A method for correctly identifying the information arriving at, used by and produced by the workplace is defined and communicated to that workplace;.

♦ All information arriving at, used by or produced by that workplace is correctly identified in accordance with that method.

♦ Only correctly identified information is used at or distributed by that workplace.

♦ Codes, standards and regulations concerning the identification of information to be used are met at all times.

The service

The Oxford English Dictionary contains the useful explanation that *"service"* is *"conduct tending to the welfare or advantage of another"*, which presents obvious overtones of quality including safety, price and timeliness. *"Service"* has also been proclaimed as being *"work done for someone else [1]"*. Bearing in mind that both a company and an individual are each considered in law to be a legal *"person"* and putting together the above, I consider a service to be :

"Work performed for someone else in a manner that tends to the welfare or advantage of that person".

This definition provides some useful guidance for both auditor and auditee alike, containing a prescription that can be applied to everybody's work in all companies by denoting a desirable attitude to adopt. The definition does not restrict its application to contractual instances and is, thus, also consistent with my long standing view that customers are those who receive the result of one's efforts and suppliers are those whose efforts are directed at satisfying one's needs. (Every task unit must define its suppliers and its customers: see Chapter 5.)

Audit procedure

The auditor will establish what services need to be received at the auditee's workplace and what services the auditee is expected to provide to others. For each service, the auditor will consider the sub-elements shown in Figure 5.7 and described below. (See also the discussion in Part 1 Chapter 13 - *"Useful sequence for questioning".*) The services may well be coupled with another of the task elements. For example, incoming information needs to be supplied to the auditee with a certain degree of

		Service			
Type	Characteristics	Presentation	Identification	Complete
General	Price	Image and style	Name	Quantified
Specific	Safety	Speed and timeliness	Availability	Measured (accurate and honest)
	Legal	Staff conduct	Status	Verified
	Reliable	Treatment of customers		Compliant
	Consistent	Safety		
	Customization	Legal		
	After-care and customer support			
	Tangible/ intangible			

Figure 5.7 "Service" task element, sub-elements and management topics

timeliness, at an acceptable price and completely. Similarly, the auditee will be expected to serve his internal and external customers in a like manner.

Correct type

The auditee must be providing the correct type of service for the customer. The type of service may be expressed in general or specific terms. As examples, general types of service may be the provision of insurance or provision of a civilian police force. Both will have their own specific types of service such as, respectively, providing private motor vehicle insurance or performing a police street patrol. Figure 5.8 presents a hypothetical example of an insurance service and has been expressed in fairly broad terms. The auditor will:

♦   Ascertain the specific type of service the auditee is performing.
♦   Verify that the person responsible is informed of the correct type of service required.
♦   Verify that the correct type of service is being carried out.

Correct characteristics

a)   Price

The quantity of service that a customer receives in relation to the price affects the value for money perception of the customer. Price is in itself a characteristic that requires consideration by the auditee. The overall price charged to a customer incorporates the unavoidable costs of the auditee's task, the avoidable costs incurred through waste and a charge levied to provide for profit. Profit level is discretionary, though, in that the management decides upon its amount. Clearly, this decision is of importance for charging too much cannot be considered as tending to the customer's welfare or to his advantage since it reduces value for money which is a matter of concern for business customers and general public customers alike. Getting the price wrong affects goodwill which is of vital concern for any company, particularly when the customer is captive, as in the case of compulsory state education, a national health service or other nationalized industry: loss of the public's goodwill can affect the particular concern's ability to survive the vicissitudes of political fashion. Investigating matters of pricing policy may be a topic that can only be covered during a president's audit (see Part 2 Chapter 7.): it is a matter unlikely to be explored by the external auditor but could well be a topic of interest to an extrinsic auditor, such as a regulatory body.

111

b)   Safety and legality

In tending to the customer's welfare and advantage, the auditee must recognize that, when the service is performed, the customer will also be influenced by the way in which it is performed. Of concern to a customer will be such characteristics as safety, legality of method, the reliability with which the auditee performs the task and the consistency of its outcome in satisfying the customer's needs. Cases in point include a customer using an airline's services naturally wanting personal safety to be secured at all times during his trip; a customer seeking a home insulation service wanting to know that the materials provided comply with legal regulations dealing with fire retardant capability and absence of carcinogens such as asbestos; a company using the services of a chartered accountant wanting the financial audit and account preparation to comply with statutory requirements; a person buying a house wanting his attorney to ensure that all legal necessities governing the acquisition and registration of the property and the transaction are met.

c)   Reliability and consistency

Reliability and consistency are two further key characteristics. Travelers, for instance, always desire a service that can be relied on to depart from and arrive at the places advertised and at the times stated on all occasions. Similarly, customers always want to be able to trust the consistency of the task results: the processing of holiday photographs, for example, will not be entrusted to a someone who is known to produce variable results.

d)   Customization and its bandwidth

The service may need to cater for the individual requirements and circumstances of the customer. This may not always be possible and it is vital that the foreground task is informed of the extent to which the service can be customized. This is rather similar to placing tolerances onto a manufacturing drawing and is a matter to which the designers of service should have paid special attention as the management should have done in formulating the job descriptions and procedures. The limits beyond which the individual customer's requirements cannot be satisfied must be known to the auditee. These limits establish what I refer to as the *"bandwidth"*, an important service characteristic.

e)   After-care and customer support

Customer satisfaction can be influenced by the after-care characteristics which occur when the central part of the task is completed. Illustrations of this include a chimney sweep, a house builder or a plumber who does not remove his debris and mess: a surgeon who omits to remove all the surgical instruments used in an operation will be unpopular with the patient or residual relatives - according to the results. After-care and control of by-products are characteristics that require planning, training of the staff, and provision of the equipment to facilitate the process of cleaning up.

Customer support including help lines are important features for the auditee to offer its customers, both internal and external to the company.

f)   Outcome - tangible and intangible

The outcome of the service is another key characteristic. In many cases, the outcome is a tangible entity. The entity may be a document containing information (an insurance policy, for example, a bill of lading, a will, mortgage deeds) or an item supplied (a cooked meal, for example, a cleaned garment of clothing, transfused blood or a transplanted kidney). Equipment may have been subjected to the service and, so, for example, a repaired refrigerator, an office that has been painted or a car that has been cleaned could each constitute the entity; equally a person who has undergone an examination might be that entity. Each of these are, of course, instances of the other four task elements: their own sub-elements must be in accordance with a specification laid down by the customer or by the auditee as well as by regulatory bodies. To do so is in itself an important characteristic of the service

The outcome of the task can in some cases be intangible: the excitement a customer feels after a roller coaster ride, for example, or after watching a football match, a ballet, a rock concert or other spectacle. Another intangible is the knowledge obtained by the customer when a task has been completed. This knowledge can take several forms: in the case of an airline trip, the customer knows fairly quickly whether or not he has arrived at the right destination; in the case of training services, the customer will sense the extent to which a foreign language has been learned from a language teacher or the degree to which the rigging on a boat is understood after attending a training course on sailing. A customer will also know if any part of the service caused personal annoyance.

The major difference between the tangible and intangible outcomes of a service is that the tangible ones can be subject to process quality control actions by the auditee either before or during delivery of the service to the customer. Intangible aspects can only be judged by the customer and the auditee must devise mechanisms whereby feedback from the customer is obtained. Quality controls and customer feedback are discussed later in this chapter.

The auditor will look for objective evidence to verify that :

♦ The characteristics of the service have been defined and communicated to the workplace.
♦ Those characteristics are consistent with the needs of the customer and market location concerned.
♦ Those characteristics are achieved correctly by that workplace prior to completion of the task.

When there is a tangible outcome, the matters to be investigated by the auditor have already been described in the other task elements. When there is an intangible outcome, the auditor will investigate the quality controls and customer feedback mechanisms.

Correct presentation

a)   Image and style

A crucial feature of service presentation is the image which is projected. Colours, logos, design and layout of facilities as well as packaging all help to satisfy the customer's expectations. They affect the appearance of equipment such as delivery trucks, aircraft and premises; uniforms; information and documents; Internet web sites, as well as items delivered to the customer. All must be kept in smart order so that a desirable image is maintained. The auditee should be wary when designing logos that another company's trade marks or copyright have not been infringed.

The style of presentation also affects the perceived image and it must reflect the social issues, values and tastes of the target audience. Advertisements involving say, the human female form clothed solely in a bikini may be unacceptable in one country but acceptable in another; consideration for the environment by avoiding the use of packaging materials that are thought to pollute or otherwise damage it may be highly desirable; apparent failure to care for the environment when the target audience perceives a greater degree of care for others' environments could provoke a negative response. Of course, society is constantly changing and circumstances can impose a need for swift action to protect image.

A few months after the *"Herald of Free Enterprise"* passenger ferry disaster in 1987 in which nearly two hundred people were killed, that same vessel was still featuring in an advertisement for Townsend Thoresen, the vessel's operator. The advertisement was carried in one of the UK's Automobile Association's brochures which advertised the latter's *"5 Star Service"*, claiming that they were the *"No.1 CAR FERRY COMPANY"*.

The spectacular rise of activity on the Internet stimulated thousands of new customers to subscribe to the America Online company's services. At the beginning of 1997, the demand outstripped the company's ability to serve satisfactorily all of its customers at peak periods. The firm was criticized for continuing to advertise its wares when the problems were being widely reported in the media. It quickly offered compensation for customers who were disputing that they actually received the level of service portrayed by the advertisements. Twenty or so American State Attorney Generals concurred with that argument; some threatened legal action.

b)   Speed and timeliness of delivery

The speed with which the actual service is offered or accomplished characterizes the attitude of the company towards customer satisfaction. The speed of response to the customer's requests and the promptness of delivery of the service could involve, in the case of a telephone company, for example, matters of queue time, time to answer the telephone or the time required for the customer to have the number connected. In certain activities, however, over-promptness can be a bad thing: restaurant diners do not wish to be rushed through their meals, for example; people attending a doctor's surgery might not appreciate hasty diagnoses of their ailments; trainees attending a course may wish to have time spent on difficult matters.

c)   Conduct of staff, treatment of customers

Key features of the presentation involve the conduct of staff and the way in which the customer is treated. Helpfulness, pleasant and polite manners, personal hygiene and habits, body language, improper language, eye-to-eye contact, patience, tenderness, sympathy and understanding could all warrant consideration as would the sincerity with which the auditee expresses those factors - is the smile genuine or contrived, the sympathy patently false, the delivered speech reminiscent of that obtainable from a trained parrot? Achievement of such expressions is largely dependent on the auditee's competence and basic attributes which would be enhanced by training.

d)   Safety and legal issues

The service must not only possess the characteristics of safety and legality but also must be presented in a way that appears safe and legal. This consideration affects the visual condition of equipment and the methods used by the auditee in performing the duties.

The auditor will look for objective evidence that :

♦   The features for correct presentation have been defined and communicated to the workplace.
♦   Those features are consistent with the needs of the customer and market location concerned.
♦   Those features are accomplished properly prior to completion of the task.

Complete performance

a)   Quantifying deliverables

A vital characteristic in the case of services such as electricity supply authorities or telephone/ telex companies which do not have a physical item, is the quantity of service supplied. Telephone companies sell time and distance; electricity supply companies provide, of course, electric power. The meters placed to record the power units or period of time over which the customer has used the service, require proper calibration performed by instruments whose accuracy and precision is known and is traceable to national measuring standards. Most countries have enacted legislation concerning weights and measures which will probably govern this matter. Alternatively, where a public service has been created by the government, its charter or Act of Parliament might place restrictions on fair trading and accuracy of measurements. In some cases, full traceability of meters to national standards may not be necessary provided reasonable accuracy can be established. This will vary according to the nature of the measurements to be taken, a computer bureau that charges its customer on the basis of computer connect time and processing power used, for example may only have to demonstrate accurate logging and reliability of the machine. The particular circumstances must be ascertained by the auditor who will investigate further and as necessary in the manner contained in the discussion about *"Equipment"*.

When the service involves human effort, the auditee will need to devise a system for the accurate and honest recording of manpower used. The units might be logged to the nearest man-day, man-hour or quarter-man-hour but whatever they are, the personal attribute of honesty is central to customer satisfaction. The auditor will investigate the system accordingly.

Certain of the service's aspects cannot be measured to determine if they have been performed completely in relation to what the customer will pay. Quality controls can, however, help the task, verifying that everything has been done. Visual inspection of information for completeness, using a checklist as an aid to ensure that all pertinent details have been covered might help. Quality controls are discussed further later in this chapter.

The auditor will look for proof that :

♦ The service's aspects that would constitute its complete performance have been communicated to the workplace.
♦ The service is performed completely for the customer.

Correct identification

a) Availability and status

Some aspects of a service cannot be identified by a label or sign but their availability can be denoted by logos, labels, shop signs, advertisements or by the self evident appearance of what is being done (a cleaner polishing a table, a refuse collector handling garbage). The existence of the service and whether or not it is the right one can be gleaned from verbal announcements (air crew announcing the correct flight number and aircraft's destination, for example). All of these constitute information, which is one of the other task elements, and the auditor will investigate the matters relating to it as described earlier in this chapter.

An alternative way of identifying the service is by virtue of the equipment used or worn by the auditee, uniform and badges, for example. These can be investigated as described under *"Equipment"*.

The auditor will look for proof that :

♦ The methods to be used for identifying the availability and status of the service have been communicated to the workplace.

♦ The service is identified according to those methods.

Task - Provide Insurance cover

Service: Insurance sale

Type: Motor vehicle insurance

Characteristics:
Nationwide availability.
Office sale (face-to-face with customer).
Accurate premiums as per insurer's tables.
A selection of insurers for customer to choose from, but also catering for customer's other personal preference.
Credit card or cheque payment
All company outlets to operate in consistent manner.

Presentation:
Max. Waiting time 5 mins. Customer care during wait.
Individual attention without interruptions.
Private consulting room if requested.
Immediate written quotes.
Immediate coverage.
Pleasant, friendly atmosphere. Smiles, eye contact, calm, confident manner and absence of raised voice.
Do not rush the customer. Helpful - nothing is too much trouble.
Comfortable clean rooms at stable 70 deg. temperature
No form of discrimination whatsoever.
Standard local office hours. After hours telephone and Internet assistance messages.

Perform completely:
Customer welcome procedure.
Privacy procedure if needed.
Refreshment and courtesy procedure
Provide all information requested by customer.
Transaction forms fully completed. Customer receipts provided immediately.
Mailing list update, if required.
Customer farewell procedure.

Identification:
Company colour and logo to identify offices, staff uniforms, documents and computer displays.
Labeled sign placed on motor insurance officer's desk.
Motor insurance documents and computer screen displays to be titled as such.

Figure 5.8 Example of Service task element applied to an insurance organization

5. Looking at departments

Their appearance and their works were as it were
A wheel within a wheel
Ezekiel, I, 16.

A essential part of the preparation for the audit (see Chapter 9) is to draw up a list of all the departments affected by the objectives of the audit and to select those to be audited. If time is at a premium, a judicious selection of appropriate departments may allow the audit team to form an overall opinion of the state of management systems' implementation throughout an entire organization. If the audit objective is to determine the auditee's ability to comply with a particular quality systems standard, the auditor must recognize that not all of its clauses will apply to every department and so he must decide which clauses affect which departments. Figure 5.1 shows a sample analysis of the type that can be performed.

In analyzing the management systems that apply to the work of any department, the auditor has to structure his questions. The following is a suggested way for doing this:

♦   Determine the department's function (products and services).
♦   Determine its customers.
♦   Determine its suppliers.

A simple example is shown diagrammatically in Figure 5.2.

1. What is the function of the department?

In other words what is the department's product? The product might be any combination of the following, as described in Chapter 4 : items; services; information (contained in records, specifications, sales orders, drawings); equipment (for example, after performing planned maintenance or calibration services for others) or people (after completion of training

ISO 9001, Section 4, Clause	Contracts Department	Design Department	Purchasing Department
4.1.1			
4.1.2.1	x	x	x
4.1.2.2	x	x	x
4.1.2.3			
4.1.3	x	x	x
4.2.1			
4.2.2	x	x	x
4.2.3	x	x	
4.3.1	x		
4.3.2	x	x	
4.3.3	x	x	
4.3.4	x	x	
4.4.1		x	
4.4.2		x	
4.4.3	x	x	x
4.4.4	x	x	x
4.4.5		x	x
4.4.6	x	x	x
4.4.7		x	
4.4.8		x	
4.4.9	x	x	x
4.5.1	x	x	x
4.5.2	x	x	x
4.5.3	x	x	x
4.6.1			x
4.6.2			x
4.6.3		x	x
4.6.4.1			x
4.6.4.2			x
4.7	x	x	
4.8	x	x	x
4.9		x	x

Figure 5.1 Applicability of ISO 9001 clauses to auditee departments

ISO 9001, Section 4, Clause	Contracts Department	Design Department	Purchasing Department
4.10.1		x	
4.10.2.1			
4.10.2.2		x	x
4.10.2.3			
4.10.3			
4.10.4	x	x	
4.10.5		x	
4.11.1			
4.11.2		x	
4.12	x	x	
4.13.1	x	x	x
4.13.2	x	x	x
4.14.1	x	x	x
4.14.2	x	x	x
4.14.3	x	x	x
4.15.1		x	
4.15.2			
4.15.3			
4.15.4			
4.15.5			
4.15.6	x		x
4.16	x	x	x
4.17			
4.18	x	x	x
4.19	x	x	
4.20.1		x	
4.20.2			

Figure 5.1 (Continued)

123

services or as a result of providing interview and selection services to a company department).

The function might be established in job descriptions, manuals, procedures or work instructions: it might not, however, have been formalized by such devices, merely being understood by mutual agreement with other parts of the organization. See also Chapter 3 *"Looking at the auditee's organization"*.

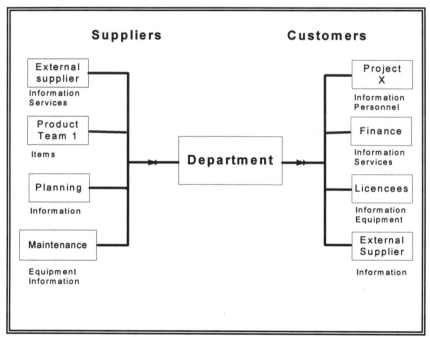

Figure 5.2 Simple analysis for imaginary company department

2. Who are the department's *"customers"*?

Here it is necessary to define the recipient(s) of each of those products. In the case of information, a copy may be distributed to a number of recipients both inside and external to the company. Similarly, an item may be routed to a downstream production unit within the company, to a vendor for further processing or to the final customer. As before, the *"customers"* might be described in job descriptions, manuals, procedures or work instructions, if these exist.

3. Who are the department's *"suppliers"*?

This question really has three component answers:

♦ The department may act as its own supplier in some respects.
♦ It probably requires input of personnel, items, services, equipment and information originating either from other departments within the company.
♦ It might require personnel, items, services, equipment and information originating from sources outside the company.

In determining the answers to these questions, once again the auditor will be guided by those job descriptions, procedures *et al* if they exist. If not, the actual on-site portion of the overall audit will need to allow time to establish the answers.

In defining the department's *"suppliers"*, the following questions are relevant.

a) In respect of the department acting as its own supplier:

♦ What must the department generate itself in order to accomplish its duties?
♦ What type of person should perform each task (thinking in terms of competence, training and personal attributes required)?
♦ What equipment needs to be used and what environment is necessary?
♦ What information must the department prepare for its own use before the task is performed?

(b) In respect of the department's needs that are served from within the company:

♦ What information, equipment, personnel, services and items does the department need from within the company to perform its function?
♦ Which other departments are or should be responsible for supplying each of them? (Within a machine shop, for example, the information may include a workshop document package compiled and then issued by the production planning department whilst the items needed may be raw materials received from the store; within an accounts payable department, there will probably be no items but there will be information such as

purchase orders, delivery notes, invoices received from other parts of the company, perhaps *via* a mail room.)

c)   In respect of the department's needs that are served from sources outside of the company:

♦   What information, equipment, personnel, services and items does the department need, that are not available from sources within the company, to perform its function?

♦   What sources outside the company are responsible for providing them to the department prior to its performance of the tasks? (These sources may include the supplier, the customer, a regulatory body, an inspection agency and such like. Suppliers are often responsible for supplying items such as those listed in Chapter 4; a customer may have to supply free issue materials, assemblies, or parts. The customer or a regulatory body may require a witness to be present during execution of the task and hence become responsible for supplying that person. The customer may insist on his own equipment being used to accomplish a task and may therefore have to supply measuring gauges or transport.)

It is always beneficial - particularly for an inexperienced auditor - to draw up a written analysis of the department's input, output and process in order to understand the activities the department has to perform. Two simpleexamples of this type of analysis are now described.

Example 1: A receiving bay

Figure 5.3 summarizes how one company's receiving bay operates. On the input side are items of material received from suppliers and various types of information generated both inside and outside the company.

On the output side are items and documents sent to the receiving inspection area and documents for the supplier's driver.

The employees within the receiving bay itself need to have different attributes and experience. The clerk must be numerate and literate; the crane driver and the fork-lift truck driver have to be trained by the work's transportation department so that they know how to lift and sling items as well as how to drive their equipment. The equipment required is regularly maintained, not only to prevent damage to items in case of a drop but also for safety reasons.

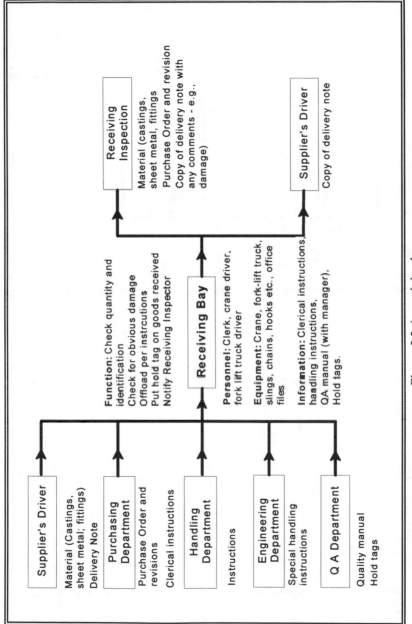

Figure 5.3 A receiving bay

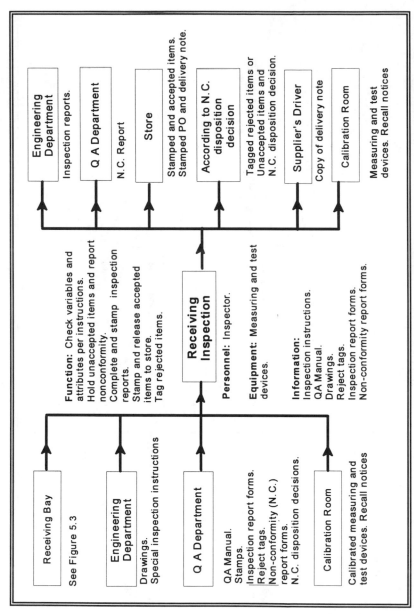

Figure 5.4 A receiving inspection area, downstream of the Fig. 5.3 receiving bay.

128

From the analysis in Fig.5.3, it is possible to determine which clauses of the applicable quality systems standard relate to the receiving bay. Figure 5.5 shows which clauses of ISO 9001 should apply.

Example 2: A receiving inspection area

This is the unit immediately downstream from the receiving bay analyzed in Fig. 5.3. Its operations are shown in Fig. 5.4.

All the items on the input side are the output of the receiving bay. Information in the form of documentary input comes from various other departments within the company. On the output side are accepted items (sent to the store) and unaccepted ones (which wait in a holding bay until their fate is decided). Information in the form of documentary output goes to other departments such as quality assurance and engineering. The receiving inspector within the unit has to have special training in the use of equipment and inspecting techniques. He also needs good eyesight. The inspection area itself needs special equipment, good lighting and an inspection bench.

After completing the analysis shown in Fig. 5.4, the applicable quality systems or management criteria can be determined by analyzing the quality systems standard invoked for the contract, as shown in Figure 5.5.

It can be seen from Fig. 5.5 that within the receiving bay and receiving inspection area, many of the quality systems standards' criteria are applicable. Hence, during ISO 9001 compliance audits, when time is at a premium, it often pays an auditor to concentrate on these areas in order to obtain an indication of the state of management systems' implementation throughout the company. It is strange how many companies underrate the importance of these areas, failing to appreciate the value of employing high-calibre staff within them. From an auditing standpoint, both the receiving bay and the receiving inspection area can be good barometers to indicate the quality programme of the company. (The auditor must remain aware, though, that this type of sampling naturally imposes limitations on the reliability of any conclusions concerning the overall status of the firm's compliance with the standard.)

ISO 9001, Section 4, Clause	Receiving Bay	Receiving Inspection
4.1.1		
4.1.2.1		x
4.1.2.2		x
4.1.2.3		
4.1.3		
4.2.1		
4.2.2	x	x
4.2.3		x
4.3.1		
4.3.2		
4.3.3		
4.3.4		
4.4.1		
4.4.2		
4.4.3		x
4.4.4		x
4.4.5		
4.4.6		
4.4.7		
4.4.8		
4.4.9		
4.5.1	x	x
4.5.2	x	x
4.5.3	x	x
4.6.1	x	x
4.6.2	x	x
4.6.3		
4.6.4.1		x
4.6.4.2	x	
4.7		
4.8	x	x
4.9		

Figure 5.5 ISO 9001 (Section 4) clauses applicable to the Receiving Bay and Receiving Inspection area shown in Figs. 5.3, 5.4, respectively

ISO 9001, Section 4, Clause	Receiving Bay	Receiving Inspection
4.10.1	x	x
4.10.2.1	x	x
4.10.2.2		x
4.10.2.3	x	x
4.10.3		
4.10.4		
4.10.5	x	x
4.11.1		x
4.11.2		x
4.12	x	x
4.13.1	x	x
4.13.2	x	x
4.14.1	x	x
4.14.2	x	x
4.14.3	x	x
4.15.1	x	x
4.15.2	x	
4.15.3	x	x
4.15.4	x	
4.15.5	x	x
4.15.6		
4.16	x	x
4.17		
4.18	x	x
4.19		
4.20.1		x
4.20.2		x

Figure 5.5 (Continued)

The kind of analysis set out in Figs. 5.3, 5.4 and 5.5 can be performed for each task unit within a company and the results combined into an overall matrix. Such a matrix can be very useful too in helping a company plan its own internal audits and quality programme. Companies that perform such analyses tend to have better management systems which show a better degree of control and provide better assurance that contractual conditions are implemented.

Analyzing each department's functions, determining the management systems that it serves and by which it needs to be served is an essential part of the preparation for and conducting of an audit: it is pointless auditing a department unless the auditor knows what he ought to be looking for and hence how much time can be devoted to auditing each task (process). Finally, without such an analysis, there can be no guarantee that a thorough audit of any department has been performed.

Resource management

Other department functions include the proper and efficient use of resources which will be comprised of manpower (persons), equipment needed within that department, as described in Chapter 4 and items that are being processed, since they represent work in progress and cash flow. The sum total of the resources equates to money and the budget for the department concerned. The auditor will:

♦ Investigate the basis on which the department determines its real budget needs.
♦ Verify that the basis is consistent with the company objectives.
♦ Assess the management systems employed by the department to monitor its use of resources.
♦ Assess the system used by the department to analyze the areas of opportunity for resource savings which are not to the detriment of quality achievement.

Over the years, the quality assurance auditors have ignored this aspect of auditing but it is of real importance and is discussed in Part 2 of this book. The allocation, use and monitoring of resources represent management decisions which can be of quality or can be inadequate. As stated elsewhere in this book, the fundamental product is the *"decision"* and when decisions are of inherently poor quality, avoidable costs result, as they do when defective items are produced.

Lack of resources is one of the six real causes of quality problems. (See Chapter 18.) It behooves the auditor to investigate how resources are managed. (See also Part 2, Chapter 2.)

Time management

Lack of time is another one of the six real causes of quality problems. It also behooves the auditor to investigate how time is managed. (See also Part 2, Chapter 2).

The proper allocation, use and monitoring of time are also functions of each department. Time is required to perform the various activities such as processing items, creating or reviewing information, providing a service, training people, cleaning or maintaining equipment. It needs to be quantified for each task that is to be performed within the department then allocated and monitored in order that management is continuously aware of progress and problems that may affect it. Since lack of time is a real cause of business problems (see Chapter 18), time management is essential, but it is all too frequently ignored by the management systems: it is certainly not given the prominence it deserves by the existing quality systems standards. Accordingly, the auditor will scrutinize the management systems to :

♦ Investigate the basis on which the time budget really required by each task is determined by the department;.
♦ Verify that each such basis is consistent with the organization's objectives (whether that organization is the company or a particular project).
♦ Verify that the department monitors its use of time.
♦ Check the department analyses the areas of opportunity for time savings which are not to the detriment of quality achievement.

Non-conformities and corrective action systems

An essential feature in any department is the ability to cope when things go wrong. This means having a non-conformity systems ready for immediate use. The auditor must verify that the auditee has prepared for possible contingencies. However, failures and problems can also provide an area of opportunity if the auditee takes the trouble to analyze the non-conforming situations and determine the real root cause. The cause may lie within the auditee's own department or somewhere else. In the former case, the auditee should have its own corrective action system and, in the latter case, the auditee must become an integral part of the firm's overall corrective action system. All quality systems standards stipulate requirements for non-conformity and corrective action systems.

Preventive action systems

Another essential feature in any department is its resolve to prevent problems from occurring at all. There are two aspects to "preventive action".

♦   Action taken to prevent recurrence of a problem that has occurred.
♦   Action taken to prevent a problem occurring at all.

Only the latter can really be regarded as preventive action since, in the case of the former, avoidable costs have occurred and lost for ever. Preventive action is designed to avoid avoidable costs.

A host of analytical tools are available for the auditee to employ as part of his preventive action effort. They include, *inter alia*, failure modes and effects analyses (FMEAs), fault tree analyses (FTAs), simulation, modeling, queuing theory, linear programming and other operational research techniques.

But effective preventive action is not limited to the application of mathematical techniques. It requires planning the process, the task elements and their sub-elements that will apply during the process and ensuring the six real causes of business problems are considered and avoided. All of these have to be considered in relation to the product. Never lose sight of the product.

The auditor needs to verify:

♦   The process is planned before it is started.
♦   The task elements and their sub-elements are included in the plan.
♦   Avoiding the six real causes of business problems (see Chapter 18) is a goal incorporated in the plan.
♦   Operational research and similar mathematical techniques are considered and, if beneficial, are applied during the planning process.

Continuous improvement programmes

Nothing remains perfect. If perfection is obtained, it tends to be a fleeting accomplishment in a world of change. New knowledge emerges at an ever increasing rate and is disseminated ever more swiftly around the globe.

Modern communications make and guarantee this as a fact of life. Competition guarantees that new knowledge will be applied, that present and past perfections become regarded as inadequacies, as showing opportunities exist for further improvement. Opportunities? Not really, more like necessities, if the firm wishes to survive the long haul.

The firm is, of course, a composite of departments within it. Each department must play its part in the overall continuous improvement effort. But to improve requires knowledge of the existing status of the department's activities as well as knowledge of new ideas, equipment, techniques, materials etc. discovered in the outside world. In order to ascertain whether improvement has been obtained, after efforts have been made towards it, the auditee must have some means of comparing results with previous levels of performance. The auditee needs some type of measurement.

The continuous improvement effort cannot, therefore, be a haphazard affair. It requires a planned programme that defines:

- Current levels of achievement.
- Goals for achievement and how they will be measured for success.
- Disciplined analysis of options that can be taken in order to realize improvement.
- The option selected for pursuing the goals.
- The resources required to pursue the goals.
- The time required to pursue the goals.
- Who is responsible for pursuing the goals.

The auditor will investigate those matters. (Continuous improvement is discussed further in Part 2 Chapter 1 *"Continuous improvement".*)

Performance monitoring methods

A department that does not monitor its performance is a department out of control. It jeopardizes the business. Not only does such a department not know what it is achieving, it cannot know how to plan or budget for the future, nor can it set in motion any meaningful continuous improvement programme (although the best one in this situation would be to introduce a performance monitoring system!) Performance monitoring is assessed by the auditor during step 6, of my seven step method described in Chapter 11.

How stringent should be the controls?

Every department needs to determine its own controls so as to ensure it does not incur avoidable costs. The stringency of the controls, including checks, reviews, verifications etc. will depend on the department's product. It will depend on the value of its work.

As an example, a design department has a highly valuable product for every department, following along after it has completed its work, will be striving to make what has been designed. Purchasing will commit contractually to buying items and equipment selected by the designers; production areas will commit their own resources and time to make what has been designed; customer support personnel will provide advice based on the designers' decisions and output, and so on. Design departments are generally at the front end of the primary system (primary systems are described in Chapter 6).

Whereas departments downstream might have problems, their cost and effect can be less than those of the upstream ones. If a production department creates a batch of scrap product, the batch could be remade, there is a good chance it might be found before release to the marketplace, but if the underlying design or its concept are faulty, countless batches could be made, sold and used by society. The costs of meeting defective product claims (product liability claims) might be unthinkable. It pays to be thorough up front. (As is being increasingly appreciated, working to the letter of ISO 9001 will not guarantee faulty products are not released into the marketplace. Relying on that standard to safeguard the company's product liability position is a highly risky practice, one that cannot be recommended.)

My general rule is:

♦ The nearer the front end of the primary system the auditee department is, the more critical its product, so, the more stringent must be its preventive action and its controls.

The auditor should consider the relative position of the department in the primary system when assessing the stringency of the auditee's controls.

136

6. Looking at management systems

A fail safe system fails by failing to fail safe.

John Gall

Codes, standards and regulations always state requirements that an auditee must meet but it is rare for them to stipulate specific methods. ISO 9000 series of standards, for example, repeatedly uses the phrase *"establish and maintain documented procedures"*.

The responsibility for compliance with a standard clearly rests with the auditee, as does the freedom of choice in the methods to be adopted, unless an authority or the customer has intervened and imposed its own interpretation on an auditee, either by contract or by code/regulation. Assuming that no such intervention has occurred that freedom of choice does not rest with the auditor: he retains only the freedom of choice as to the audit method to be used and has the right neither to impose any particular system on the auditee nor require changes to a system that meets the standard, simply because he does not like it. In all cases, however, compliance with a standard has to be demonstrated, which means that objective evidence must be created by the auditee and presented to the auditor for consideration.

It is one thing to establish a system, quite another to maintain it. Maintaining a system entails knowing how well it is performing and obtaining feedback on its results. Feedback involves the provision of information, perhaps in the form of documents, perhaps within a computer system. Information is objective evidence and it is objective evidence that the auditor is looking for. Objective evidence is required to prove both that some activity has been *"established and maintained"*and that management has *"ensured"*. Feedback systems and their associated documents have gained, and will continue to gain, increased prominence and attention in dealing with product liability issues (particularly with the concept of *"strict liability"*). As Greville Janner states[1]: *"Every court knows that memory is an unreliable guide to the truth. Documents - notes, memoranda, diary entries, letters, contracts and the like - made at the time are far more likely to reveal the truth."* This has been extended recently by some courts admitting the content of E-mail as evidence in various actions concerning race relations, fraud, product design.

Types of system

There are two types of system that can be implemented as part of a quality programme: an open system or a closed-loop one. Only the closed-loop type of system provides feedback of the results obtained when an activity has been performed. If there is a closed loop model then the system is capable of being maintained and the system will *"ensure that"* an activity will yield the desired results (eventually, but perhaps not on a first time basis).

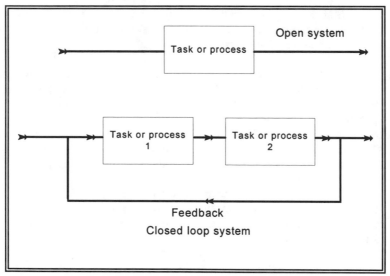

Figure 6.1 The unit concept (open and closed loop systems).

Open system (Fig.6.1)

Here, there exists an input, a task being performed and an output from that task. Assuming that the task is correctly performed, the input controls the output. If both input and process are correct, the output will be correct. If the input is incorrect and the processing correct, then the output will be incorrect. Correct input and incorrect process will also yield an incorrect output. And, of course, incorrect input and process will also produce incorrect output. Unless, however, the task process receives information that states *"Your output is wrong"*, it will carry on wasting time and money in yielding an incorrect output: avoidable costs will be increased. Regardless of how well the system is set up initially, there is no guarantee

138

that it will maintain itself and consistently yield the right results without intervention. This is the risk all open systems run. They are unreliable.

Closed loop system (Fig. 6.1)

This is an open system that has been closed by providing it with a feedback loop (engineering examples include overspeed governors on engines). Once feedback has been provided to a unit to the effect that its output is incorrect, it is then possible to analyze the root cause of the problem, apply corrective action and maintain the desired results. The root cause must necessarily be either that the input is incorrect or that the task process itself is being performed incorrectly, or a combination of both, just as for the open loop system.

The input and the task process can themselves be analyzed into the task elements (see Chapter 4) in order to determine which individual elements or combination of elements are resulting in the unit's output being incorrect. This is the principle of trouble shooting. Once the problem elements have been determined one can then begin asking *"why"* they are incorrect, move towards uncovering the root cause of the problem and finding a solution to prevent its repetition: this is the principle of determining efficacious corrective action. Effective corrective action would prevent repetition of the problem but it is not truly prevention because the process first incurred an avoidable cost in having produced unacceptable products/ services.

The needs for the input and the process must be determined first on the basis of ascertaining what the recipients of the output (i.e. the *"customers"*) want and expect from the task. This allows the task process to be properly planned and the constituent parts of the systems feeding the process with its input supplies also to plan how they will serve those needs. This is the principle of prevention.

Tools for analyzing systems

Information is easier to assimilate if it is presented in a visual form such as a   diagram   or   flow   chart.   These   illustrations   can   make

---

Indication of Inspection Status

Applicability and objectives

This procedure applies to the requirements for indication of inspection status on items in the various stages of production. Its main objective are to ensure that production stages are applied in a logical and systematic manner and that progress beyond one inspection stage does not occur until satisfactory.

Inspection marking system

A colour band code shall be applied at each inspection stage.

A "Yellow" band shall be marked on each item that is to be prepared for processing. The colour band shall be approximately 10mm wide. The inspector shall place his initials and the date inspected next to the yellow band.

A "Blue" band, of similar dimensions to above and adjacent to the yellow one shall indicate acceptance of the preparation and that the process may proceed. The inspector shall place his initials and the date inspected next to the blue band.

A "White" band, of similar dimensions to above and adjacent to the blue and yellow bands, shall indicate that the process has been performed correctly, is visually acceptable and has passed the necessary quality tests. The inspector shall place his initials and the date inspected next to the white band.

A "Red" band, of similar dimensions to above and adjacent to the yellow and blue bands, shall indicate that either, the process has not been performed correctly, is not visually acceptable or has not passed the necessary quality tests. The inspector shall place his initials and the date inspected next to the red band.

No further work shall be conducted on the affected item(s) until all unsatisfactory areas have been determined and the correct repair procedures determined.

The colour band status code shall be commenced from the "yellow" step and followed until a satisfactory process has been performed. All repairs shall be recorded on a "non-conformity" report and processed as required by Chapter 17 of the Quality Procedures Manual.

Figure 6.2 Example of a procedure for analysis during an audit

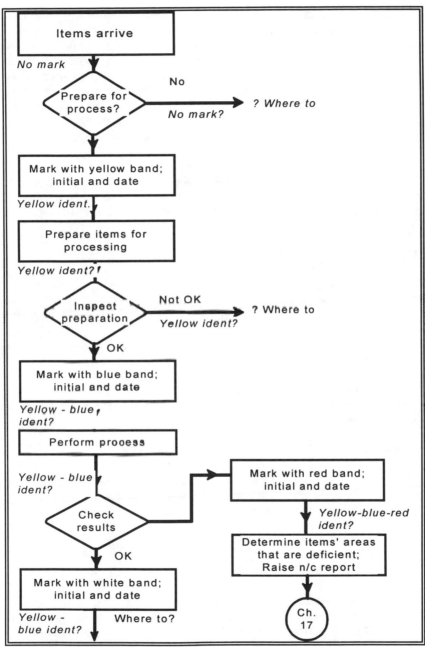

Figure 6.3 Flow chart for procedure described in Fig. 6.2

explicit the logical connections between different parts of the system and, by presenting the auditor's line of thought graphically, they can save a lot of unnecessary misunderstandings. It may be particularly useful to present the frequency of occurrence of trouble spots in a system or their magnitude by means of a diagram such as a pie chart or histogram, while flow charts and family trees can express in different ways a system's internal logic and can help to pinpoint possible origins of problems. Figure 6.3 is an example of a flow chart analysis of a system, that at a first quick reading of its procedure, as reproduced in Figure 6.2, appeared to be reasonable: the flow chart reveals a different picture.

If the auditor finds it necessary to draw a picture in order to analyze the auditee's system, he should reatin it as part of his working papers for future reference because it will help to refresh his mind at a later date (see Chapter 12).

What requires a system?

Each of the task elements - the person, the items produced, the service supplied, the information and the equipment - requires its own feedback system. The flow chart in Figure 7.11, relating to control over the selection of an operator performing a task, was matched by other charts relating to the items being processed, the information and the equipment. In the case of a service a similar chart would have been produced.

The management system must be designed to serve the needs of the task being investigated: that task may in turn serve another or the same management system.

Systemantics

John Gall's witty book [2] observes the refractory nature of systems and dubs them *"systemantics"*. It contains a number of valuable precepts for the auditor to bear in mind, including the following:

♦ Always be wary of systems that are allegedly *"fail safe"*. The example shown in Fig 6.2 was presented to me on such a basis. As John Gall states, *"a fail safe system fails by failing to fail safe"*.

♦ When considering corrective action, the auditor should always recommend simple systems, preferably by building on the strengths already available in the auditee's existing systems. (An example is described in Chapter 17, whereby existing systems were enhanced to control CAD tapes, disks and changes made to them). If one finds that a simple system has been implemented and works, that system must be respected and not tampered with. As John Gall says, *"The systems that work best are the simple ones. Simple systems cost least in time, money and grief"*.

Analyzing systems

Systems audit depth

If the auditor is using my *"Seven Step"* method, described in Chapter 10, he will have first analyzed the organizational arrangements to gain an understanding of who does what, what their responsibilities are and so on. To do so is to perform Step 1. Much of this information may have been displayed in organization charts and job descriptions. Proceeding to Step 2, the auditor will then analyze the systems and to do this the auditor should :

♦ Determine the objectives of the system (i.e. the product and its associated requirements).
♦ Determine where those objectives originate.
♦ Look at the final task involved at the end point of the management system where it delivers its intended product/ service and determine which of the task elements apply there.
♦ Review the organization plans and procedures to determine where each of those elements originates (who is responsible for them).
♦ Repeat those steps progressively back to the origin for each of those task elements. (Note that there will be supporting elements identified at each task and that the auditor should keep to the main track of the principle task element being traced before going on to look at others).

If the auditor is trying to ascertain whether the system would meet the requirements of a standard, such as ISO 9001, he would use the following tools:

♦ A flowchart, to ascertain the logic (or lack of it) in the way the system has been designed.
♦ A criteria checklist (to keep focussed on the precise words and expressions within the standard, (see Chapter 7, *"Criteria checklists"*).

At this point the auditor would know what the system is capable of achieving (or what it is not capable of achieving) if implemented as planned. The systems *capability* is not equivalent to its *reliability*. A capable supplier is not necessarily a reliable one.

Compliance audit depth

When performing a compliance audit, the auditor first analyzes the system as just described (i.e. performs Steps 1 and 2 of the seven step method), then moves to Step 3. The auditor should:

♦   Repeat the actions detailed above for the systems audit.
♦   Check at the final task involved that those requirements are being achieved. (This is similar to an inspection but it merely ascertains that the system can work and that the auditee has the capability to supply product to certain requirements. Note that ISO 9001, 9002, 9003 are concerned with a supplier's *"capability"* which is of limited value in the modern business world.)
♦   Then trace through to determine if each task involved in the system operates as the system requires.

At each task (process) the auditor will examine a sample of objective evidence sufficient to provide confidence that the achievements are consistently and constantly produced as expected and planned. (This provides objective evidence of the *reliability* of the system since the various weaknesses in application are identified together with facts concerning their frequency. Successful business results are concerned with the system's reliability as opposed to its *capability*.)

Primary, secondary and tertiary systems

In any project, company or organization there is a set of systems that become linked together often in a manner that makes them appear indistinct, perhaps messy. It is possible to *"rank"* the systems and this is something I do when looking at a whole organization. Once ranked, a clearer view of the sequence to analyze them each in and to trace them through during the audit is apparent. In most situations three distinct ranks can be defined and the systems labeled accordingly into: primary systems, secondary systems and tertiary systems. As an alternative, one could also regard the ranks as *"levels"*.

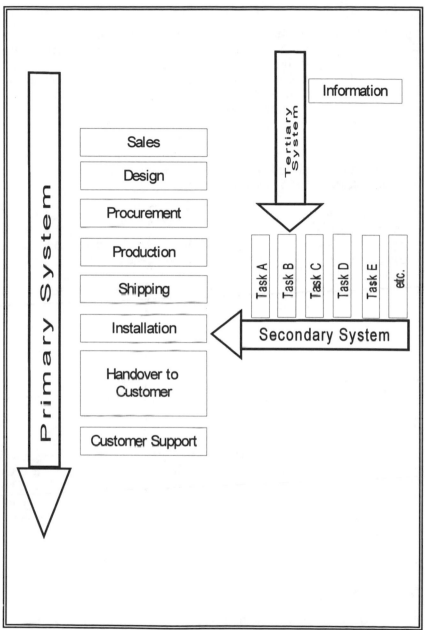

Figure 6.4 Relationship between primary, secondary and tertiary systems

The primary system:

There is always only one primary system in a company or business. It shows the way in which the customer's requirements are served by the firm by putting into order the main phases through which the work proceeds. The phases bear such labels as sales, product design, procurement, manufacture, delivery, post delivery service in the case of conventional manufacturing industries or, reservations, food and beverage supply, room services, check out in the case of a service such as hotel and inn keeping. Some people prefer to label these types of phases as *"processes"*, but it is preferable to regard them as *"macro processes"* to distinguish them from individual work processes (tasks) which could be then fairly described as *"micro processes"*.

The secondary systems:

These systems support the primary system by serving the needs of each work phase, or macro process. They are generally comprised of a sequence of tasks each designed to serve up a set of task elements (items, equipment, information, personnel etc., as described in Chapter 4) to a particular work phase within the primary system.

The tertiary systems:

These deliver an individual task element to a work process within a secondary system. The three ranks (or levels) of system can be envisioned as in Figure 6.4.

Audit procedure

I have defined a system as *"a set of interrelated tasks working towards a common end objective of customer satisfaction"*. It holds good at each level of primary, secondary and tertiary. Overall the full integration of all the levels of system creates a network. Proceeding in the manner described below enables the auditor to confirm the management systems (primary, secondary and tertiary) are truly integrated or are not.

The auditor would proceed as follows:

a)   Map out the primary system

♦   Obtain a clear definition of the end product and service to be supplied to the customer.

◆　　　　Find out how the customer's/ marketplace/ community's needs are to be satisfied or how the customer/ contract is to be *"processed"* mapping out the major work phases (macro processes) that will be required.

b)　　　Map out the secondary systems

◆　　　　Take in turn each of the macro processes and obtain a clear definition of what each will need and the sequence of processes (micro processes) embodied within them.　Map out that sequence.

c)　　　Map out the tertiary systems

◆　　　　Take in turn each micro process and break it into its constituent task elements needed for its successful accomplishment.
◆　　　　Find out how each individual task element is to be served to the micro process.

Using the trace back method (See Chapter 11):

If the auditor has decided to use a trace back method, for a full audit, the audit path will commence at the final work phase (end user/ customer enjoyment of the product/ service supplied) and, proceed in turn back through each of its secondary systems supporting that phase, back through each of the tertiary systems within the secondary system's micro process (task). The auditor will then go to the preceding work phase (macro process) and repeat this sequence. This will be repeated each time as the auditor moves back through each work phase in turn until he is at the origin of the prime system.

Using the trace forward method (see Chapter 11):

If using a trace forward method, the auditor would start at the first work phase in the primary system, say, sales, marketing or research and development, analyze its secondary systems, then their tertiary systems, move to the next work phase in the primary system and repeat that sequence and so on, ultimately ending at the last work phase dealing with end user/ customer enjoyment of the product/ service supplied.

Primary system activity	Secondary system activities
Reservations	Telecomms; personnel; training; accounts receivable; MIS
Customer arrives with own transport	Car parking; personnel; training; maintenance; security; accounts receivable; MIS.
Porterage assistance	Personnel; housekeeping; training
Customer check in	Reception; personnel; training; accounts receivable; MIS; telecomms; utilities; housekeeping; maintenance
Transport customer to room	Utilities; maintenance; safety; housekeeping; legal (licences)
Accomodation facilities	Utilities; maintenance; telecomms; housekeeping; personnel; training; purchasing (room supplies); accounts payable; MIS; security
External communications to and from office/ home	Telecomms; accounts receivable; MIS
Room service	Menu design; menu printing and distribution; food purchasing; food receiving; food storage; food preparation; telecomms; bell services; personnel; training; purchasing (cutlery, linens, china); housekeeping; accounts receivable; accounts payable; MIS; security
Entertainment in bar/ lounge	Utilities; housekeeping; food service (per Room Service) purchasing (food, beverages, glassware, bar supplies, furnishings); entertainment (programming, contracts, publicity and promotion); personnel; training; legal (licences); accounts receivable; accounts payable; MIS; telecomms; security
Recreation and sport facilities	Utilities; personnel; training; purchasing (equipment, furnishings); accounts receivable; accounts payable; MIS; telecomms; maintenance; security
Restaurant	Per Room Service; purchasing (furnishings); maintenance; personnel; training; accounts receivable; accounts payable; telecomms; MIS
Conference	Utilities; maintenance; personnel; training; purchasing (furnishings, visual aid equipment and materials); accounts receivable; accounts payable; MIS; housekeeping; telecomms
Light refreshments	Per Room service
Check out/ billing	As per check in

Figure 6.5 Primary and secondary system features for an hotel

148

Audit preparation

If the trace forward and trace back sequences just described seem lengthy possibly involving visiting and revisiting individual departments for different reasons, the auditor can look at the system network and list out all the macro processes and micro processes it serves in order to gain a view of its customers and their needs. Figure 6.5 shows a hypothetical set of systems and their constituent activities for an hotel. One can see that certain "departments" appear scattered throughout the network. By taking one of them, say, Management Information Systems (MIS), a table could be produced, such as shown in Figure 6.6, summarizing the service results expected of it by the hotel. An auditor assigned responsibility for auditing that MIS area would then have a clear idea of matters to be raised. The lead auditor would know whether or not the presence of a specialist is required on the audit team to deal with MIS and the matters that person must address during the audit.

If the lead auditor has a set of tables such as shown in Figure 6.6, and assigns the responsibility for auditing each one to an auditor, he can be assured:

♦   All contributory processes within the overall network of systems have been audited.
♦   The impact of problems, found in any of the processes on the primary, secondary and tertiary systems, can be determined.
♦   The importance/ magnitude of the problems found.

An alternative analysis can be performed by preparing a matrix which lists all of the primary system activities on one axis and all of the various departments and tasks on the other, with interfaces shown by a "tick" or an "x" in the applicable boxes created by the matrix.

Standards for management systems

Many contracts now involve one or other of the internationally recognized quality systems standards and the appearance of the ISO 9000 series will result in this particular standard gradually dominating the others. The involvement of quality systems standards can be either direct, through contract requirements, or by implication, when a company holds out that it complies with those standards and advertising that it has been successfully assessed against them. Quality systems standards specify criteria that are essentially no more than good management and present guidelines for formulating a company's management systems. They attempt to

MIS area	
Primary system interface	*Service required*
Reservations	Ability to create new customer account and database and enter data. Ability to retrieve existing customer details and account from database. Current and forward capacity and occupancy of hotel database.
Customer arrival	Data entry for customer account and database.
Customer check in	Ability to create new customer account and database. Ability to retrieve existing customer details and account from database. Data entry for customer account. Update current hotel capacity and occupancy database
Accomodation facilities	Data entry for customer account and database. Data entry for accounts payable database
External communications	Update telecomms database and service provider account. Data entry for customer account and database.
Room service	Update food and beverage database. Data entry for customer account and database.
Entertainment	Update food and beverage database. Data entry for customer account and database.
Recreation	Update guest services database. Data entry for customer account and database.
Restaurant	Update food and beverage database. Data entry for customer account and database.
Conference	Update guest services database. Data entry for customer account and database.
Light refreshments	Update food and beverage database. Data entry for customer account and database.
Check out/ billing	Data entry for customer account and database. Update current hotel capacity and occupancy database

Figure 6.6 Summarised contribution of MIS area (of hotel depicted in Fig 6.5)

150

communicate various features that the auditee's management systems must incorporate in order to provide an assurance that the contract requirements are being met and that the deliverable goods and services will be of acceptable quality. However, as with all forms of communication, they are open to misinterpretation. As a parody of the old wisdom about communication theory runs: *"I know you believe you understand what you think you read. But I am not sure you realize that what you read is not what could be meant."* The auditor must consider what the standards *really* say. If the purpose of the audit is to audit for compliance with the requirements of a particular standard, the auditor has no right to impose his own interpretation of that standard on the auditee.

Although the quality systems standards share a common aim, as described above, naturally they differ on numerous points of detail and in their phraseology. Some differences are trite: others can be significant. It is possible to get a grip on these differences by studying some of the comparison matrices available. Generating one's own matrix to compare two quality systems standards is a far more valuable exercise, however, and one that should help to highlight the full implications of the precise language each standard employs.

When studying the criteria contained in the quality systems standards, the auditor must free his mind of preconceptions and prejudices, particularly those based on practices in use within his own organization. In the ISO 9000 series, for example, one phrase that crops up time and again is *"establish and maintain"*.

The auditor must at all costs avoid reading his own experience into this phrase when interpreting the standard. A number of different systems might satisfy the standard's words. Some systems may be cheaper than others and some may appear better than others but seldom will a standard dictate the detail of any specific type of system. All they require is that some particular activity is performed. Two companies with very different systems may satisfy the standards equally well. This fact begins to indicate the risks of relying on assessments performed by registrars who cannot interpret a standard for a particular customer's needs. The more imprecise or weak the standard is, the lower the value of a registrar's assessment and its resultant certificate. (This is further discussed in Chapter 2.)

When reading the standards, it is also necessary to combine various criteria in order to see what is required for a particular task unit. In relation to training, for example, ISO 9001 does not say merely that training of personnel is to be *"established and maintained"* in one or two departments only: it requires training throughout the company. This is because it refers to personnel *"performing specific assigned tasks"*, an all encompassing phrase. Naturally, in every department of a company, everybody has been assigned certain tasks and therefore one sees that the requirement applies to everyone in the company. When discussing training, the standard also requires *"appropriate records"* to be maintained. The retention and control of *"quality records"*, as distinct from *"records of training"*, is treated in a separate clause. (Indeed the ISO 9001 is open to interpretation on this point and the definitions contained in ISO 8402 provide no adequate clarification of the differences between records and quality records, which in the contractual situation could pose difficulties. Frequently, though, training is considered to be a service and, therefore, the clause relating to *"quality records"* might apply but the auditor should approach this with some caution and feel sympathy for the auditee who cannot be blamed for the standard's vagueness.) If, however, the *"records of training"* are in document form then the ISO 9001 clause which concerns *"document control"* also applies to them.

An auditor must read the quality systems standards regularly. It is foolhardy to rely on memory or to assume that one knows them perfectly. It is a good practice to read the applicable standard before performing an audit, during the audit, and every now and then between audits. No auditor should be afraid of referring to the quality systems standards during an audit. Some auditors seem to think that they will lose face by doing so and appear to feel they ought to be able to quote the various paragraphs verbatim. In fact, the one sure way for an auditor to lose face is to assume that he knows the quality systems standard concerned and then to find that he has made a mistake.

Apart from the quality systems standards, the auditor must be aware of the other pertinent criteria that can apply by virtue of the industry in which the auditee is involved or as the result of a specific customer requirement. These might include :

♦   Statutes.
♦   Regulations.
♦   Codes of practice.
♦   Technical or professional standards.
♦   "Guidelines".

The auditor must know and understand what the applicable requirements are and carefully take the sum of them. The same illustrative comments described above in relation to ISO 9000 etc. also apply to the consideration of these specific requirements.

Pitfalls in practice

It is easy for an uninitiated auditor to misunderstand what a code, standard or statute says, attempting to impose his own interpretation onto auditees. The ISO 9000 series will suffice to illustrate some examples of potential pitfalls, (a complete analysis has been performed elsewhere [3]):

a).   Assumptions of consistency

♦   Whereas ISO 9001 requires documents and data to be controlled, data is subsequently excluded from its stipulations for review, approval and change control. Clearly, proper control of data in accordance with the precepts of document control would be a most sensible activity for any organization. Indeed, in an era being ever increasingly referred to as the *"information age"*, a company would be foolish to work strictly in accordance with the standard and ignore the need for full control of data. Failure to control changes in data fully, changes such as those pertaining to financial transactions and records or to safety related calculations could even render a company liable to prosecution. If an auditor is charged with auditing in accordance with that particular standard then this limitation of wording must be borne in mind such that an unfair corrective action request does not ensue.

b).   Assumptions of content

♦   ISO 9001 sets no time scale for implementing corrective action. Neither of the words *"immediate"* and *"prompt"* appear in that standard in connection with corrective action. Accordingly, unless otherwise specified by the prime customer, a supplier can take forever to implement corrective action yet still satisfy the standard. Commercial prudence, however, would dictate otherwise. Recognizing this problem, a satisfactory interpretation with the auditee has to be agreed.

♦   ISO 9001 does not require management reviews to include the assessment of the results of internal audits: it merely notes that it would be a normal practice thereby permitting the abnormal.

♦ It has long been recognized that quality management and quality improvement are primarily concerned with the prevention of quality problems through careful planning, the generally accepted outcome of such efforts being the quality plan: the benefits of such quality plans are well proven. No part of the series mandatorily requires the production of quality plans however. Whereas ISO 9001/9002 describe quality planning, they do not specifically require quality plans to be produced. They state that the company *"shall give consideration to ...the preparation of quality plans"* - but what does this mean? If the auditee states that he did consider the matter and decided against them, then that is the end of the matter for he has complied with the standard and nothing more can be said. (This has implications in terms of means to verify that quality is being achieved. In brief, both ISO 9001 and 9002 indicate that unless there is a quality plan there is no need to perform final inspection or testing: certainly the requirements about receiving inspection then become so open to abuse as to be positively dangerous in the case of certain products.)

c). Failure to cross reference.

♦ ISO 9001 requires internal quality audits to be performed. By cross linking with ISO 8402 (which is referenced, thus becoming an integral part of ISO 9001), these audits are to be performed by somebody who is independent of the activity which is being audited. However, there is no requirement whatsoever for them to be performed on a regular or a periodic basis. The ISO 9001 requirement is that they shall be scheduled but there is no indication as to the frequency of scheduling. An auditee needs only to perform such audits once every century to comply with the letter of the standard.

Sensible compromise not senseless confrontation.

The above illustrates the need for an auditor to prepare properly and to take great care when applying the precepts of any code, standard or regulation. Over the years, there have been fruitless arguments, pointless squabbles and enmities caused by ignorant auditors attempting to interpret the meaning of such documents unilaterally and to dictate the actions which an auditee ought to take. Whenever there is any doubt, the sensible course is for auditor and auditee to agree upon a compromise understanding. This should also be the case for statutory auditors who might have the right to invoke a particular interpretation but do not have the right to abuse their authority and should always recognize that an honest mistake can be made by an auditee. To engage in a battle over an ambiguous, inadequate or imprecise standard is pointless. If the article of contention is a statute or regulation, legal interpretation or case example might be needed. Such potential points of misunderstanding should, however, have been identified and resolved prior to a contract.

> The ASME code [4] has been in existence for many years. ASME wisely recognized that it is impossible to write a standard that will fit all circumstances on all occasions. It therefore developed the *"Code Case"* system. Whenever two parties disagree on the interpretation of any part of the ASME code, they have the right to appeal directly to the ASME to obtain a ruling on the interpretation of its code. This ruling is decided by a panel of experienced and learned practitioners, their decision then being officially published as a Code Case which becomes the interpretation of the ASME Code for future purposes.

In light of the level of interest shown in the ISO 9000 series, perhaps similar *"code case panels"* should be appointed for specific industries. (As was mntioned in Chapter 1, the QS 9000 scheme has elected to issue at regular intervals authorized interpretations of its requirements.) This development might serve to enhance the series' reputation but a better course of action would, however, be to rewrite it and reissue it.[5]

7. Audit guidance tools

A great artist can paint a great picture on a small canvas.

Charles Dudley Warner.

Introduction

No auditor should want to perform an audit without taking along a guidance tool that indicates the matters to be investigated. Without such a tool, there is a real risk that essential issues will be forgotten, that objective evidence will not be recorded in any systematic way and that future reference to the actual proceedings will be impossible.

There is a host of different tools available for the auditor to choose from. Each has its own advantages and disadvantages, as this chapter will show.

The usefulness of audit tools

Benefits for the auditor

1. They act as a guide to the person performing the audit.

The word *"guide"* is important. The audit tool must not rigidly dictate exactly what is to be audited. It often happens that, while carrying out an audit, the auditor is put on the scent of a problem and needs to deviate from the content of the audit tool in order to assess the depth and significance of that problem with a view to considering what corrective action may be required. So their usefulness does not lie in providing an exhaustive list of questions and matters for the auditor to ask during the audit. (In fact, a criteria checklist, described below, on its own provides no useful questions at all: each question it poses will need to be broken down into each of the task elements that may be applicable to the unit responsible for implementing the criterion concerned.)

2. They provide objective evidence that the management audit was performed, that it was performed in accordance with an audit guidance tool (i.e. the matters to be raised were planned) and that all applicable aspects of the business programme were verified.

Inevitably the auditor is himself audited sooner or later (i.e an extrinsic audit is performed). To retain the audit tool used on file is important since an audit report alone does not answer all the questions that the extrinsic auditor might need to ask.

3. The checklist is very useful as an *aide memoire*.

An auditor engaged full time on auditing activities will find it very difficult, if not impossible, to retain in his mind the details of every audit. When a question is raised some time after the audit has ended, the audit tool will serve as a useful reminder of what happened, what objective evidence was examined, the results and so on.

4. The checklist provides information to the auditor's successors, facilitating continuity of the audit work.

When subsequent audits have to be planned, the new auditor will find it useful to refer back to the audit tool to get an idea of what was done before, what problems were encountered, what objective evidence was examined and so on. Incomplete records may be a serious embarrassment.

5. They provide very useful places to collect and collate notes during the audit (see Chapter 12).

6. The information the audit tool contains helps the auditor to prepare for the exit interview and the audit report (see Chapters 19 and 20).

Benefits for the auditee

1. They reveal the auditor's guidelines and help the auditee to prepare for the audit.

The audit tool must always be forwarded to the auditee before the audit to help him make the proper preparations (see Chapter 8).

2. It helps the auditee train his own staff.

It is quite common for an organization to copy or amend another company's audit tools. This interchange of experience and information can be very beneficial. No auditor should take exception to it if the auditee copies them with a view to performing his own audits: this is one level of guarantee that the auditee will try to audit all relevant aspects of management applicable to the product, project or work being undertaken.

In the case of an external audit, the supplier might be considered part of the auditor's own firm and one might argue that the auditee is entitled to use the company's information. By studying the audit tools, the auditee's staff can familiarize themselves with what is required by their customer's contract, learning exactly what applies to the various departments. Eventually this could improve the auditee's processes and products and, perhaps, lower the price: both developments should benefit the external auditor's company.

3. They provide a useful *aide memoire.*

The auditee may find it helpful to refer to the audit tool later, during the exit interview, when reviewing the audit report or when implementing corrective action, since the checklist contains the information upon which the auditor's conclusions and corrective action requests have been based. With the audit guidance tool to assist him, the auditee can explain to the affected departments within his own organization exactly what the audit procedure and conclusions were: he is in a strong position to address the auditor's requirements.

4. Objective evidence is provided to show that the system has been independently audited.

A word of warning is called for here. Some organizations claim credit for extrinsic audits *in lieu* of their own internal ones. Until there is an internationally credible and recognized auditor qualification scheme that an guarantee consistency of approach and repeatabillty of audits (and at the time of writing this third edition none of the existing schemes can do that), this is dubious practice unless the members of the audit team and the circumstances in which the audit was conducted are both known to be acceptable. (Quality systems standards have disallowed this use of extrinsic audits either by implication or by edict - ISO 9001, for example, requires that the *"supplier shall carry out....internal audits".*) Potential customers, too, should be wary about accepting the findings of an unknown audit team as constituting an assurance that the management systems in use are of an adequate standard unless it is the customer's policy to accept certain certifications - such as an applicable ASME certification, or an ISO 9000 registration performed by a known and trusted registrar - as evidence of the state of management systems *in lieu* of a pre-award survey. (See also Chapter 2.)

Hard copy or electronic medium?

The advent of powerful portable computers, laptops, notebooks and the like, has made possible the elimination of audit tools presented in hard copy form. While layout, style, identification remain important, the portable computer removes limitations on size of paper that once prevailed. The audit tool can be prepared using standard applications software readily available by mail order or from store.

When this type of equipment is used, the audit tool can be sent by E.Mail to the auditee, always assuming the auditee possesses the requisite equipment to receive it.

As the audit progresses, the auditor enters data just as would be the case when using hard copy. However, scanning for details already entered can sometimes be more difficult than quickly thumbing through hard copy sheets. There is also the ever present risk of losing of data due to damage to the computer (dropping and similar accidents), and power loss. Waiting for the computer to boot up at each workplace can add to the time required for the audit. Battery life can provide problems, too, and the auditor will be well advised to have spare packs at the ready - fully charged!

While this type of equipment has its benefits, entering data while the auditee is actually talking might be considered impolite unless the auditor is an accomplished typist and can maintain eye contact, which I like to do, for one gets subtle clues as to the auditee's integrity from this practice. On balance, while I enjoy having my laptop computer available for the audit, I use it off-site during the evening, and prefer to carry hard copy with me for taking quick hand-written notes.

Types of audit tool

While other types do exist, the following types of audit tool are frequently used:

♦   Checklists
♦   Flow charts
♦   Matrices
♦   Tables

Each is now discussed in turn.

Checklists

The key tool for most audits is the checklist. It is mandatory to use a checklist (or a "procedure") when performing an audit in accordance with the requirements of some industries or regulations. In the case of ISO 9001, ISO 9002 although there is no requirement for a checklist, internal quality audits must be *"planned and implemented"* in accordance with *"documented procedures"*, a statement which is open to interpretation. Even in cases where a checklist is not specifically required, it is none the less sensible to generate one in view of the benefits they produce, as described later in this chapter.

The criteria checklist

This type of checklist is structured in accordance with the management criteria of the regulation, code or standard applicable for the contract concerned. As Figure 7.1 shows, the questions are generally a transposition of the content of the standard's various criteria. In Figure 7.2, an extract from a checklist of this type is shown.

ISO 9001: 1994 (Clause 4.4.9)	Checklist question
All design changes and modifications shall be identified, documented, reviewed and approved by authorized personnel before their implementation.	Are all design changes and modifications identified, documented, reviewed and approved by authorized personnel before their implementation?

Figure 7.1 Example of criteria checklist question

A criteria checklist can be used for any type of audit (internal or external) for any depth of audit (systems or compliance) and for any scope of audit (full, partial or follow-up). In each case, the auditor must indicate clearly which departments were audited to which criteria so that someone later reviewing the checklist can draw legitimate conclusions about the extent to which the criteria are being implemented throughout the auditee's organization.

Checklist question	Yes	No	Comments/ notes
Has the supplier established and maintained documented procedures for the control of verification, storage, and maintenance of customer-supplied product provided for incorporation into the supplies or for related activities? Is any such product that is lost, damaged or is otherwise unsuitable for use recorded and reported to the customer? (See 4.16)			

Figure 7.2 Part of criteria checklist based on requirements of ISO 9001: 1994 (Clause 4.7)

A criteria type checklist is preferable when auditing against a specific standard, code or regulation. In these circumstances the basic question and the objective of the audit is to determine *"Do they or do they not comply with such and such?"* The end result must be an unequivocal yes or no statement made by the auditor. Regulations, codes and standards generally comprise various sub-set requirements. Thus compliance with a complete standard entails compliance with all of its constituent parts. It is, therefore, advisable for the checklist to separate out the individual topics to be addressed.

When compiling a criteria type of checklist, it is important to recognize that any particular sentence of a standard can contain a variety of questions. Answering yes or no to one particular feature in the sentence does not guarantee that the entire matter has been covered. Accordingly, an alternative way of producing a criteria checklist from that shown in Figure 7.2 is to break the requirements into greater detail as shown in Figure 7.3. The structure shown in Figure 7.2 is only recommended for the well experienced auditor.

Checklist question	Yes	No	Comments/ notes
For product provided by the customer, for incorporation into the supplies or for related activities, has the supplier established documented procedures: a) For control of verification of that product? Are those procedures maintained? b) For the storage of that product? Are those procedures maintained? c) For the maintenance of that product? Is any such product that is lost, damaged or is otherwise unsuitable for use recorded? Is any such product that is lost, damaged or is otherwise unsuitable for use reported to the customer?			

Figure 7.3 Part of criteria checklist based on requirements of ISO 9001: 1994 (Clause 4.7)

When preparing the overall checklist, the auditor must remember that the various criteria can apply to various departments. (See Chapter 6.) It is for this reason that a table of the types shown in Figures 5.1 and 5.5 should be prepared in order that the auditor does not fail to apply any of the relevant criteria to any relevant part of the auditee's organization.

Tiering the questions

Using the criteria type of checklist requires a tiering of questions. A regulation may, for example, contain many different criteria. One of these might be that the organization shall document and implement a programme that meets the requirements of the regulation. The checklist question concerning implementation can only be answered after all of the others contained within the regulation have been addressed: violation of any one of the criteria clearly means that the answer to whether the auditee has implemented the regulation must be *"no"*.

Advantages	Disadvantages
A1. Provides ready assessment of compliance with relevant code, standard or regulation of interest. A2. Focuses auditor's mind on the words of the code/standard etc., and not the auditor's opinion of their meaning. A3. Saves argument with extrinsic auditors about inadequate questions.	D1. Inconvenient when auditing on departmental or individual task basis. D2. Requires experienced, trained auditor to relate requirements to an individual department or work task. D3. Does not tell inexperienced auditee what the auditor wants.

Figure 7.4 Advantages and disadvantages of criteria checklists

Figure 7.4 summarizes the advantages and disadvantages of the criteria checklist. It is worth explaining a few of these in more detail here. The notes D1, A1 and so on) refer back to the figure.

D1. Audits are always performed on a departmental basis. When more than one department has to satisfy the criteria invoked by a code or standard, it can be very difficult to reflect the true state of affairs on one checklist. The more departments to which the criteria should be applied, the harder the task becomes. It may be necessary to attach explanatory notes to the checklist, and if these should subsequently be detached or mislaid errors of interpretation may be made.

D2. Before using this type of checklist, the auditor has to be able to analyze the quality programme needs of each department (see Chapter 5). An inexperienced auditor may be able to do this perfectly adequately but someone with experience should review the analysis to check that nothing has been overlooked. The alternative is to run the risk that some aspect of the code, standard or statute will go unaudited.

A2. Anything that helps the auditor to keep an open mind is of major benefit to any audit.

A3. Some extrinsic auditors are prone to argue about the adequacy of the company's audits unless the checklist produced is responsive to the standards, codes and regulations that apply to the business. Some management systems standards, for example, require that audits be performed *"to determine whether or not the management system conforms to planned arrangements...including the requirements of this International Standard.."* If that quality programme is dictated by the management systems standard and the checklist reflects the standard (as criteria checklists do), then arguments with the extrinsic auditors should be kept to a minimum. (Similar remarks can be made concerning assessments performed by registrars.) Hence, even though the codes, standards or regulations do not specify any particular type, format or content so far as checklists are concerned, it may foster good relationships with customers, regulatory bodies or other external agencies if one adopts the criteria checklist format.

The departmental checklist

Departmental checklists are structured according to discrete departments and reflect the managerial or operational matters of interest in those departments. This type of checklist an be used for every type, depth and scope of audit. Figure 7.5 lists the advantages and disadvantages of this type of checklist. An extract from a departmental checklist, based on the *"Item"* task element, described in Chapter 4, is shown in Figure 7.6.

D2. The compiler must not write in questions which reflect his previous experience or preconceived ideas on that type of department's organization.

A3. The auditor retains a full set of departmental checklists. When the need arises to carry out a new audit, he can select the checklists which apply to the departments that are to be audited and combine them into an overall checklist for the audit. Each departmental checklist sheet may thus be considered as a building brick and a number of such building bricks can be combined to form the desired new audit checklist.

Advantages	Disadvantages
A1. Convenient when auditing on an individual task or departmental basis. A2. Flexible, can be tailored fro the company/department being audited by using 'building-brick' sheets. A3. Good for training inexperienced auditors. A4. Tells the auditee what the auditor wants in a particular area. A5. Useful for partial audits; aids in phased audits and timing in a contract/project.	D1. Does not provide ready assessment of compliance with the code/standard/regulation of interest. D2. Can reflect preconceived ideas of the auditor who compiled it. D3. Content may be debatable with extrinsic auditors.

Figure 7.5 Advantages and disadvantages of departmental checklists

A3. An experienced auditor often feels uncertain about what to investigate in a particular department. Studying departmental checklists provides useful training and indicates the type of question that could be asked within the department.

A4. This is important when dealing with an auditee who has not previously encountered audits or studied the code or standard in force. The auditee is told exactly which departments are of interest to the auditor as well as those aspects of the departments' work that are of concern to him. This helps the auditee both to inform the appropriate personnel of an impending audit and to prepare for it.

A5. By its very nature, the departmental checklist reflects the scope of the management audit performed. This makes it particularly valuable aid in assessing the overall implementation of required practices and policies throughout the auditee organization. At the end of a series of phased audits, for example, it will be readily apparent that all departments have been covered and that the state of affairs throughout the company or a project is known. Furthermore, all interested parties can easily verify that all aspects of good management practice have been verified by the audits.

Companies that do not work to a particular quality systems standard or that have special criteria or activities to verify generally find the departmental checklist more suited to their needs than the criteria checklist described earlier.

Question	Result
Items: a) What items must this department/task receive to perform its work? Are all those items received? Are they all of the correct type? Are they all correctly identified? Are they all in the correct condition when received? Do they all have the correct capability? Are the correct quantities received?	
Comments/Notes:	

Figure 7.6 Extract from a departmental checklist used for general purposes

The company standard checklist

Some companies maintain sets of ready-made checklists (either criteria or departmental or both) for use during audits. The advantages and disadvantages of these are shown in Figure 7.7.

A4. This has become a rather trivial advantage in an era of desktop publishing.

Advantages	Disadvantages
A1. Uniform questions for company audit teams. A2. Train auditors in company requirements. A3. Evidence of consistency for extrinsic auditors. A4. Economy of printing in bulk. A5. Quick review by company personnel.	D1. May not be suitable for all audits. D2. Stereotyped auditors; inflexibility; problems in dealing with different audit objectives.

Figure 7.7 Advantages and disadvantages of company standard checklists

D1 and D2. The recent years' explosive growth in ISO 9000 registrations and associated quality progammes' audits has caused most companies to focus their audits on compliance to the standard selected for registration purposes. This has led them to concentrate solely on the criteria checklists, an understandable response. An emerging problem for them, however, is their difficulty in addressing matters such as continuous improvement, an essential aspect of business management, (and which is a mandatory requirement in QS 9000 situations). The existing standard types of criteria checklists have stereotyped all involved. Progress will only be made when the audit programmes are adjusted to include not only compliance audits for assessing the status of implementation of the chosen standard, but also genuine departmental audits guided by departmental checklists, which might be company standard checklists or of special/ custom format created for each audit.

The special or custom-built checklist

If the standard company checklists do not fit the circumstances of a particular audit, it may be necessary to generate one specially. The advantages and disadvantages of special checklists are shown in Figure 7.8.

D2. Familiarity with the layout and content of a checklist encourages fairly rapid review and standard company checklists will be prepared with this in mind. A special checklist may be slower to assimilate because its content and format are unfamiliar to the reviewer.

Advantages	Disadvantages
A1. Shows the auditee exactly what the auditor wants. A2. Prepares the auditor well. A3.Good for training inexperienced auditors.	D1. Some extra work involved. D2. Review of checklist is not so convenient.

Figure 7.8 Advantages and disadvantages of special or custom built checklists

Layout and format of checklists

Question and response

Some checklists are laid out in question-and-answer style, the answer being either *"yes"* or *"no"*. The criteria checklists shown in Figures 7.2, 7.3 adopt this style. Checklists like this are quick to review since the eye can scan the page and will only stop to consider the significance of *"no"* answers. This is an example of the application of the *"management by exception"* principle: if everything has a *"yes"* answer, all is well and no further investigation is needed. For a large company with numerous audits to perform, such a format has obvious advantages. However, the *"yes/no"* answer does not allow for the shades of grey that inevitably colour most audits. An untrained auditor, looking for a yes or a no answer can get confused. If, for example, a criterion is applicable to eleven departments and the auditor finds that five of them are a definite *"yes"*, five a definite *"no"* with one wavering in the balance, it becomes difficult to answer *"yes"* or *"no"* without some qualifications.

Another style of checklist is the question-and-results type, an example of which is given in Figure 7.6, the departmental checklist. With this format, against each question the auditor has to write in his assessment of the situation and any additional remarks. Alternatively, the results can be broken down into *"satisfactory"*, *"unsatisfactory"* and *"not applicable"* with space being provided for the reviewer's comments alongside. In the case cited in the preceding paragraph, the auditor would state that five departments were satisfactory, five unsatisfactory and one borderline. It may be hard to review this type of checklist quickly, which can be a disadvantage if a lot of audit reports and checklists have to be handled.

169

Space for note-taking

Regardless of its layout and format, the checklist must always provide room for writing notes and for collecting and collating the information upon which the auditor's conclusions have been based. All the examples of checklists in Figures 7.2, 7.3 and 7.6 allow room for this purpose.

Identification

Like any other document, the audit checklist should carry some identification. The front cover, and possibly every page of checklist, should indicate the date of the audit, the auditor and the auditee, so as to avoid the possibility of mistake or misinterpretation later on.

> An auditor employed by a large corporation was carrying a box of audit reports and associated audit checklists to a new office to which he had been moved. This entailed using a large open staircase to get from one floor to another. The stone floors had just been washed and were rather slippery: the enactment of Murphy's Law caused the auditor to slip and discharge the loose-filed contents of the box over the banister. Hundreds of sheets of paper showered down as if confetti. Few were identified and it was impossible to reconstitute accurately the audit files. (Murphy is still at large and his law remains unrepealed.

Size

Most checklists being used, nowadays, are written in portrait style and on A4 size paper (or 8.5 inches by 11 inches, in the USA). This need not be considered a rigid convention. I have found landscape style and A3 size to be most useful on occasions. The essential point is that the auditor should be allowed to lay out the checklist in whatever manner he or she feels most comfortable with for achieving the audit objectives assigned. The checklist is a tool: it is the auditor's tool for the auditor to hone.

Other checklists and their uses

Checklists provide a very useful tool for a variety of activities other than audits. They constitute evidence that an activity has been accomplished and indicate what was performed as part of that activity. Checklists present an orderly view to any extrinsic auditor and provide useful guidelines to the personnel responsible for performing the activity concerned.

It can be extremely helpful to draw up a checklist for each of the presentations that occur during an audit, entry and exit interviews, for example, and to refer to these lists to make sure that all relevant points have been covered. Where the exit interview is concerned, a checklist has the additional advantage of making it easier to ensure that the presentation is true and fair. Examples of checklists for the entry interview and the exit interview are shown in Figures 10.2 and 19.3 respectively.

Flow charts

Standards, such as ISO 9001, generally require their audits to be performed in accordance with a documented *"procedure"*, the content of which is seldom defined in anything other than vague expressions. (The ISO 9000 series of standards relies on definitions contained in ISO 8402, which considers a procedure as being: *"specified way to perform an activity"*. Since an audit is an activity, it must be conducted in a *"specified way"* which might or might not require the use of a checklist or any other guidance tool, as the auditor's organization chooses to prescribe.) If we consider an audit tool as being a document that describes the matters to be examined then its content and layout can be whatever the auditor desires. In my experience, a most useful layout is the flow chart.

The advantages and disadvantages of flow charts are listed in Figure 7.9, which shows their advantages outweigh any disadvantages.

The flow chart is drawn up as part of the audit preparation while reviewing the auditee's description of the management system. It is very useful in analyzing the systems that the auditee has allegedly implemented and in determining the various decision points that may have been (or should have been) incorporated. Thus, for example, when an item has been inspected, there is a decision to be taken: is the item acceptable or not? Two routes are open, one of which, in the case of an unacceptable item, leads the auditor to analyze the auditee's non-conformity and corrective action system. Absence of such a decision point immediately shows that either there has been an oversight or that the auditee has decided to make this decision at a later stage and take the risk of processing possibly unacceptable items. (Such a decision is not precluded by ISO 9001, 9002, even though it is a wasteful practice.)

Once the system has been mapped out as a flow chart, this may be used for a compliance audit at a later date.

171

Advantages	Disadvantages
A1. Convenient when auditing integration of activities comprising a management system. A2. Graphically reveals the logic/lack of logic of the system's design. A3. Reveals opportunities to avoid/reduce avoidable costs. A4. Provides ready assessment of compliance with the management system requirements of the code/standard/regulation of interest. A5. Deters preconceived ideas of the auditor who compiled it. A6. Good for training inexperienced systems auditors. A7. Tells the auditee what the auditor wants in a particular system. A8. Useful for partial audits; aids in phased audits and timing in a contract/project.	D1. Might take greater time to prepare than is the case for a checklist.

Figure 7.9 Advantages and disadvantages of flow charts

D1. It can be rather time consuming to draw up a flow chart, such as the one shown in Figure 7.10, but the exercise can prove highly worthwhile, especially when performing an audit for continuous improvement purposes or when performing a value-added Audit. (See Part 2, Chapters 1 and 2 respectively.)

The flow chart can be marked up as the audit progresses to show those areas which are completely satisfactory and those areas which are not at all. An example of a marked-up flow chart is shown in Figure 7.11. The benefit of marking-up is that one then has a graphical illustration which depicts at a glance the strengths and weaknesses within the auditee's systems and which can be presented to auditor and auditee management. It will immediately highlight those matters which require corrective action. This is particularly useful at the exit interview. It is not uncommon to find that managers do not fully understand some of the parlance and terms which auditors may use: the marked-up flow charts can be printed onto foils which facilitate display and discussion. To assist in the promotion of better communication with the auditee, such graphical presentations are without equal.

A2. Flow charts have the considerable advantage over checklists in that they immediately show the logic or lack of it in the system. An example is provided in Figures 6.2 and 6.3 and shows how a procedure that, at first sight, may have appeared satisfactory would cause problems in execution.

A3. Flow charting a system enables one to see those areas which present an opportunity for the reduction of resources and time spent and, hence, to spot the opportunities for potential reduction in avoidable costs. A flow chart reveals areas which are superfluous to the real need and which could, in fact, be modified. Figure 7.12 depicts in simplified form a "before and after" situation in a company and illustrates how resources were saved, throughput time reduced and costs improved as a result.

Recent years have witnessed a burgeoning and improved amount of easy to use software dedicated to producing comprehensive flow charts by means of a personal computer or a laptop computer. These software application programs should be considered an indispensable aid for the auditor. (See also Chapter 11, *"The well equipped modern auditor"*.)

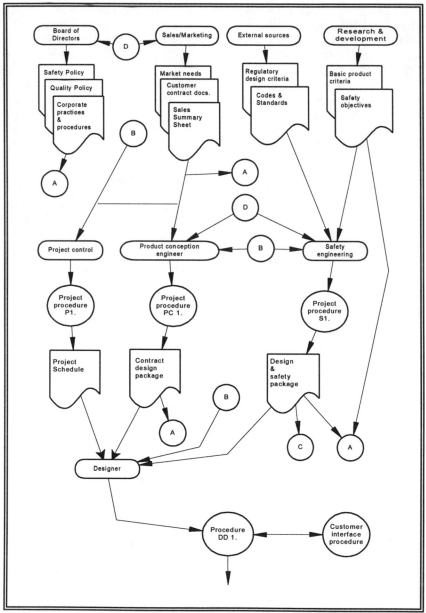

Figure 7.10 Wizz-Kids Design Services Inc. Flow of design information

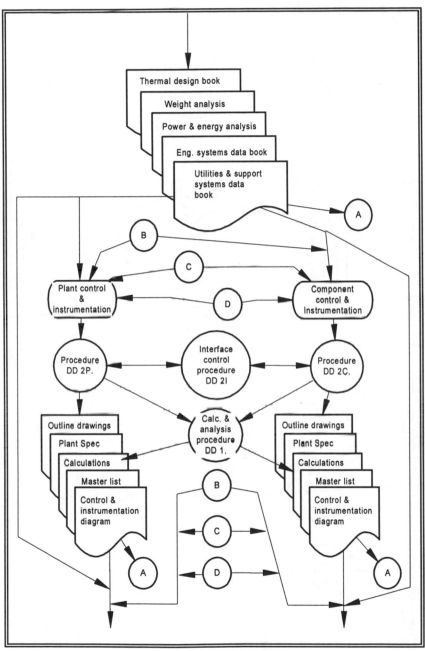

Figure 7.10 (cont.)

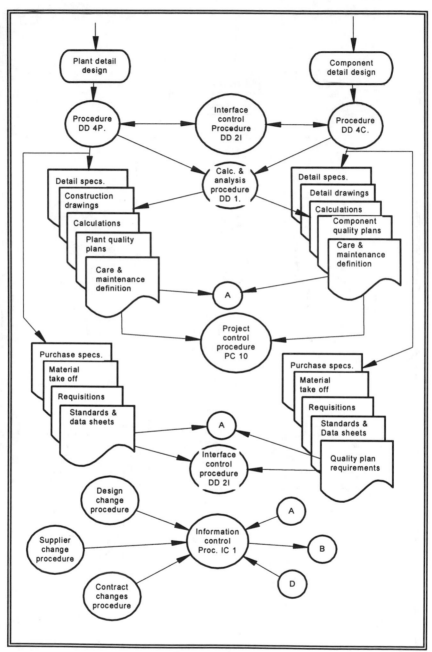

Figure 7.10 (cont.)

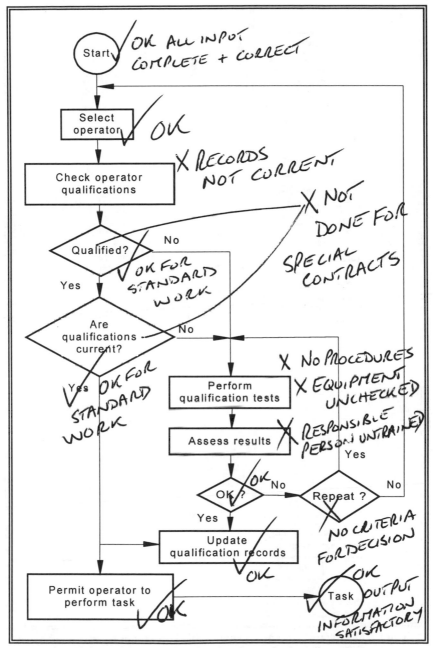

Figure 7.11 Example of a simple marked up flow chart

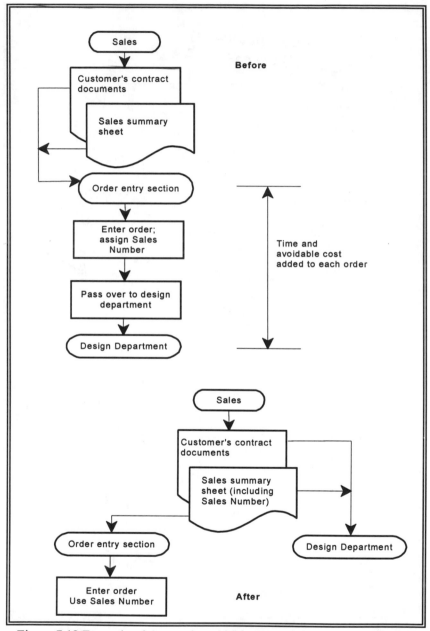

Figure 7.12 Example of time and avoidable cost reduction identified by an audit

Task element matrices

An alternative tool is the matrix laid out on task element basis. Figure 7.13 lists the advantages and disadvantages of task element matrices. One major advantage in the modern era of data processing and of good database management system software is they lend themselves to easy creation of a database and use within it. The task elements and their sub-elements are each readily form fields and records. A reduced sized example is shown in Figure 7.14. These can be produced in blank format, as depicted in Figure 7.14 on an international A4 or A3 size sheet (minimum size 8 ½ " x 11" in the USA) and completed specifically for a particular department on the basis of reviewing the documented systems description as shown in Figures 7.15 and 7.16. These have advantages similar to the flow charts in that they can provide a picture of strengths and weaknesses of audited areas.

Advantages	Disadvantages
A1. Convenient when auditing integration of activities comprising a management system. A2. Graphically reveals the logic/lack of logic of the system's design. A3. Reveals opportunities to avoid/reduce avoidable costs. A4. Provides ready assessment of compliance with the management system requirements of the code/standard/regulation of interest. A5. Deters preconceived ideas of the auditor who compiled it. A6. Good for training inexperienced systems auditors. A7. Tells the auditee what the auditor wants in a particular system. A8. Useful for partial audits; aids in phased audits and timing in a contract/project.	D1. Might take greater time to prepare than is the case for a checklist.

Figure 7.13 Advantages and disadvantages of task element matrices

Task audited	Inputs	Outputs	Audited by: / Audit date: / Sheet.......of......
Person			**Task function:**
From/to:			Reports to:
Competence			Description:
Training			
Identification			
Motivation			
Attributes			
Items *(Description)*			**Resources:**
From/to:			Defined:
Type			Allocated:
Condition			
Capability			Monitored:
Identification			
Quantity			
Equipment *(Description.)*			**Time:**
From/to:			Defined:
Type			Allocated:
Condition			
Capability			Monitored:
Identification			
Quantity			**Non-conformities:**
Information *(Description)*			System:
Checked			Understood:
Content			Implemented:
Edition			
Condition			
Identification			
Distribution			
Notes/comments:			

Figure 7.14 Example of a task element matrix

1.0 Operator qualifications and receipt of items

1.1 All operators shall be pre-approved using Company Procedure 23 for qualifying and training paint operators.

1.2 Prior to issuing for painting all manufactured items should have been inspected for cleanliness and surface preparation. This inspection should have been recorded on the Quality Plan that accompanies the items. The inspector's signature should have been recorded on the Quality Plan.

2.0 Painting

2.1 The paint shall be thinned for application using a standard lacquer reducer. Proportions to be 1 part paint to 1 part reducer. The paint shall be issued to the paint operator by the Stores but the operator shall check the paint's shelf life date and ensure that it has not been exceeded, prior to use.

2.2 Exterior finish paint coat shall be applied to a thickness between 0.75 and 1mm using Company colour grey enamel paint. Interior finish paint coat to be applied to a thickness between 0.75 and 1mm, using white enamel paint no. En-30. All paint shall be applied using the spray guns and the operator shall ensure that the equipment is kept clean at all times. Thickness templates shall be used by the operator to check the wet thickness as painting proceeds.

2.3 The finish paint coat shall be air dried for a minimum of 24 hours prior to releasing the items to the production assembly area. The items shall be left to dry in the drying racks. All thicknesses shall be checked by the operator, by means of Elcometer, who shall record and initial the readings on the Quality Plan.

2.4 The Quality Plan shall be kept with the items at all times to maintain their identity. Excess paint shall be returned to the Stores.

Doc. No. : 86	Description: Painting Procedure
Revision No: 2	
Prepared by: P. Brown	Sheet: 1 of 1.
Issued by: Design Engineering	Approved by: J. Black
THE PEELIN PAINT COMPANY INC.	Issue Date: 14 October 1996

Figure 7.15 Simple procedure for a painting task (process)

Task element matrix

Task audited: PAINTING	Audited by: JOE SMITH	Audit date: 1 MARCH 1997	Sheet 1 of 1
	Inputs	Outputs	Task function:
Person			Reports to:
From/to:	OPERATOR – JOHN DOE		Description:
Competence	PROCEDURE 2.3 ?		MIX PAINT, APPLY
Training	PROCEDURE 2.3 ?		INTERNAL/EXTERNAL
Identification			COATINGS, CHECK
Motivation			THICKNESS, RECORD
Attributes			READINGS
Items (Description)	ALL ITEMS PAINT PAINT REDUCER	PAINTED ITEMS PAINT	Resources:
From/to:	INSPEC STORES STORES	PROD. ASSEMBLY	Defined:
Type	GREY C. WHITE EN-20		Allocated:
Condition	CLEAN SHELF SHELF	DRY 3/4–1mm coat	
	PREP LIFE LIFE		Monitored:
Capability			
Identification			
Quantity		EXCESS TO NEEDS	Time:
Equipment (Description.)	PETE TRAVELLER TEMPLATE ELCO RACKS		Defined:
From/to:	SPRAY		Allocated: 24 HOURS
Type			FOR DRYING
Condition	CLEAN		Monitored:
Capability			
Identification			
Quantity			Non-conformities:
Information (Description)	WKS. TRAV. PROC. PROC.	WORKS TRAVELLER	System:
Checked	OPERATOR ✓		Understood:
Content	2		Implemented:
Edition	legible		
Condition	86		
Identification	FROM INSPEC FROM DESIGN 2.3	INPUT PLUS THICKNESS READINGS	
Distribution	PAINT PROPORTION – REDUCER = ONE TO ONE	TO PROD. ASSEMBLY	
Notes/comments:			

Figure 7.16 Task element matrix, shown in Fig. 7.14, completed from information available in procedure of Fig. 7.15

Tables

These can be usefully employed during audits to assess the auditee's extent of compliance with a standard, code or regulation. They compare the applicable criteria against the auditee's departments/processes/projects and are used to summarize the overall picture obtained from the audit.

An example is shown in Figure 7.16, which the reader will recognise is identical in its basic concept to Figure 5.1. The content is built up from a set of criteria checklists, as depicted in Figure 7.17. The columns can be "ticked" against each applicable criteria being assessed, yes/ no entries might be used, or OK/NOK is another alternative.

ISO 9001	Department				
Clause No.	A	B	C	D	E
4.1.1 4.1.2.1 4.1.2.2 4.1.2.3 4.1.3 4.2.1 4.2.2 4.2.3 4.3.1 4.3.2 Etc					

Figure 7.16 Extract example of table used to summarize findings across departments

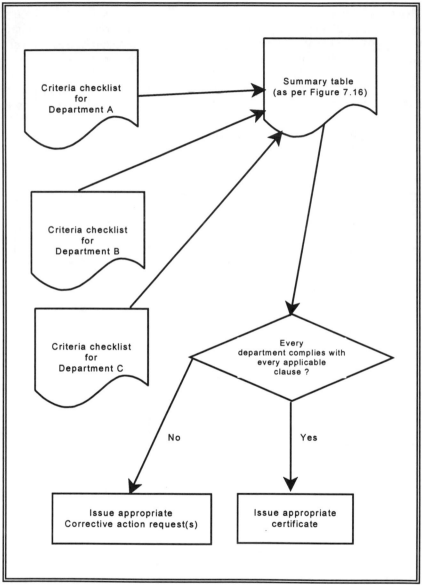

Figure 7.17 Summarizing compliance audit findings from criteria checklists.

8. The audit decision process

Before you begin, get good counsel;
then, having decided, act promptly

Sallust.

Information affecting audit decisions

Important decisions that have to be made before preparing and performing a management audit. In order to make the correct decisions, one needs accurate information about the issues listed in Figure 8.1 and discussed below.

1. The scope of the contracts involved (those between the customer and the company as well as those between the company and its suppliers).

In simple terms this reduces to asking the question *"What is the product?"* Auditors must remember:

NEVER LOSE SIGHT OF THE PRODUCT.

Each contract may invoke a particular quality system standard (such as ISO 9001, QS 9000, ISO 14000 or any other of the quality system standards cited throughout this book) or certain regulations to be met. The standard will describe the management systems that have to be developed, documented and implemented as a minimum by the company and its suppliers and thus it tells the auditor some of the things for which he must look. Regulations may be applicable by virtue of the product and the industry to which the organization belongs.

Every contract contains specifications for the product, defining what will make it fit for purpose, the delivery timing and performance expected of the supplier. The specifications denote what the auditee, its organization and management systems must achieve in order to satisfy the customer and be paid.

185

---

1. Details of contracts.
        Customer contracts/ supplier contracts.
        Standards involved.
        Product specifications and requirements details.

2. Product classification.

3. Current work status and delivery dates.
        Product/ project plans and schedules.
        Progress reports.

4. Auditee's previous performance.
        Customer complaints.
        Warranty costs analyses.
        Non-conformity reports.
        Previous audit reports.
        Pre-award survey reports.
        Supplier evaluation reports.
        Management review meetings' minutes.

5. Audit schedule.
        (See Chapter 9, Audit preparation).

6. Pending decisions.
        Contract award/ contract acceptance
        New and changed products/ projects.
        Process upgrades.
        Mergers/ acquisitions.
        Plant/ facility expansion/ contraction.
        Capital investment, asset enhancement.
        Staff development.
        Strategic plans, long range goals.
        Corporate reengineering/ reorganization.
        Continuous improvement programmes.

Figure 8.1 Information affecting audit decisions.

2. The classification of the product that is involved.

The product's level of importance can and should be classified. The classification can range from essential, safety related (or dangerous in the case of by-products) to non-essential or non-hazardous. Some products' management systems may not need to be audited at all unless work is over-running the budget allocated to it, in which case, the decision to audit may be taken on economic grounds. The matter is different with products that carry a safety risk unless they are up to standard. Here the company may have no sensible choice but to carry out regular audits to make sure that the terms of the contract are being fulfilled and that the company will not be liable to litigation as a result of defective products, inadequate practices or poor contract performance.

(The ISO 9000 series alludes to the need for classification of products, and its daughter standard ISO 9000-1 offers some basic ideas which would need substantial refinement to become practical definitions within the firm: it provides little to help the reader. The weight placed on each of the key criteria that it suggests will be a matter of decision for each company concerned. This raises the prospect of auditors and auditees arguing interminably over what is, essentially, subjective opinion. It is inadvisable for any auditor to get enmeshed in subjective opinion: always work on the basis of objective evidence.)

3. The current work status of the product relative to the contract progress and delivery date.

The amount of objective evidence available increases as work and contracts progress. It is unwise to audit only when the delivery or completion date is imminent: if problems call for corrective action at this stage, delivery dates may suffer and the company may run into penalties for late delivery, loss of customer good-will, warranty problems and so on. It is equally unwise to embark on a major new phase of the work unless one is sure that the release of resources entailed is a wise decision.

4. The content of files detailing previous auditee performance.

These files will contain results of customer complaints, warranty costs, non-conformity reports, quality costs, previous audits and pre-award surveys and hence may indicate likely problem areas or specific corrective action required in the past. In the case of a supplier, the files may also contain that supplier's rating (although not all firms make use of this type of scheme).

5. The audit schedule.

If one has been prepared, it should not only indicate the dates possible for the audit to take place but may also give a clue about the priority assigned to other auditing commitments which may affect the preferred dates.

Internal factors	External factors

*Staff capabilities
*Equipment capabilities
*Technological:
    Company state-of-art
    Company R & D.
*Product(s) developments
*Product(s) capabilities
*Product(s) quality track record
*Customer bid enquiries
*Existing order status/ Order book status
*Incipient contract/ order
*Resource availability:
    Manpower
    Equipment
    Financial
*Corporate relationships:
    Subsidiaries
    Licensees
    Joint ventures
    Agents
*Continuous improvement programmes
    Status and efficacy
    Goals and time frames for
      achievement
	#Legislation:
	    Fiscal
	    Safety
	    Environmental
	    Other product liability related
	#Market place:
	    National and global trading
	    patterns
	    Competitor activities
	    Customer expectations
	    Economic strength
	#Technological:
	    General state-of-art
	    Competitors' developments
	#Economic:
	    Policies of available sources of
	    finance, in general and towards
	    the company
	*Suppliers
	    Availability
	    Capability and reliability
	    Existing and planned products
	    Prices and cost to the company
	#Political
	    National
	    International

* Factor that is auditable	# Internal practices used to determine these factors, are auditable

Figure 8.2 Major factors in strategic decision making.

6. Pending decisions.

Both the internal and external auditor need this knowledge in order to single out particular activities, management systems or other operational features that will need to be fully effective in the future and which therefore merit special consideration.

Since audits provide input for management decisions, it makes sense for management to inform the auditor of those decisions which it eitherwishes or is forced to make as a result of changing circumstances in the business environment. Some decisions are made in response to internal factors. Others are dictated by external circumstances and events in the world outside. These factors can have a significant effect on the company's business strategy for survival and are summarized in the Figure 8.2. Auditors must always strive to keep ahead of the business circumstances rather than merely providing a history lesson.

Audit decisions that must be taken

1. Do we need an audit?

It is not always necessary to perform an audit for every contract or for every item or service involved in it. At the beginning of a major contract with a customer, it is wise to classify the items and services involved according to the necessity or desirability of auditing them and thus to generate an audit schedule for the whole contract. This type of schedule is particularly important for a complex project.

2. What must be the objective of the management audit?

Since the prime purpose of a management audit is to obtain information, it is important to establish clearly exactly what sort of information management expects the audit team to obtain. This knowledge is essential for performing audit preparation activities described later in this chapter. Embarking on an audit without knowing the objective is pointless. Managements which sanction the performance of an audit must define both the terms of reference and the objectives. It is poor management which authorizes the expenditure of resources for unknown and undefined benefits thereby giving the auditor a blank cheque. To do so can also cause annoyance for the auditee who has a right to know exactly why the audit has been commissioned and what he is expected to allocate resources to in order to facilitate its performance, in the hope of getting some return. Where there is no clearly defined objective, there can be no purposeful preparation and no meaningful results.

The objective of an audit can be stated in simple terms. There can be several objectives, in which case, each of these needs to be carefully and unambiguously defined. Examples of this could be:

♦ *"To determine whether the auditee has documented and implemented management systems that meet the requirements of......", or,*

♦ *"To determine whether the systems used to allocate and monitor resource usage ensure the product development plan will meet prescribed targets", or,*

♦ *"To determine whether the practices and procedures used by the auditee comply with the requirements of the latest edition of the Environmental Protection Act and Codes of Conduct", or,*

♦ *"To determine whether the practices and resources used within the company will prevent hackers and viruses from entering corporate data processing and computer facilities."*

One particular audit that I was engaged to perform had the following objectives defined by the management: *"To assess the status and effectiveness of the design department's management systems in serving the company's needs and to make recommendations for the improvement or simplification of the same".*

There is a wide variety of audit objectives dealing with matters such as: resource management; energy usage; time management; safety practice; environmental controls; by-product management; forward planning and strategic decisions; system improvement; continuous improvement; cost improvement opportunities; project planning and performance, and so on. In short, if there is a business matter the management wishes to address and about which its wishes to have information, there is, potentially, an audit objective. This is not to suggest an audit would be performed instantly a question arises, rather to point out the wide variety of applications possible for the management audit tool. (Part 2 of this book discusses particular audit applications.)

3. What must be the type, depth and scope of the management audit?

The classification of the goods and services involved may dictate answers to these questions, but it is always worth considering whether or not a series of partial audits might be more beneficial than a full audit. In some cases, either the industry's requirements or the prime contract with the customer will specify that internal, external or extrinsic audits are all to take place. Although extrinsic audits are the customer's or a regulatory body's responsibility, the company must still be aware of them in case it needs to integrate these with other audits.

The type of management audit (internal or external) will be fixed but the actual depth and scope may vary according to the audit objectives and management information to be sought. So far as scope is concerned, perhaps a partial audit on a particular phase of the contract, such as design or product validation, may be the best arrangement. The depth may depend partly on the capabilities of the auditee. For example, if the latter has not yet implemented the management systems required, the likely depth would be a systems audit. Later on, when the system should be working effectively, a compliance audit would be performed. (See also *Systems audits* and *Compliance audits*, Chapter 2.)

The depth of the audit is directly affected by the risks involved in not having reliable information available for the management to use as the basis for its decisions. If, for example, the company wishes to introduce a just-in-time (JIT) system with respect to a particular supplier, then the risk of authorizing a go-ahead entails accepting that a complete production line may come to a halt if the supplier is not capable of reliably delivering fault free product whenever required. To obtain confidence that this risk is minimized, the audit will need to take greater samples of the auditee's work than would otherwise be necessary.

(A common misconception about the value of ISO 9000 registration is that, if a supplier has been awarded a certificate associated with the schemes available, it means or implies the registered firm has reliable management systems. It does not. ISO 9000 requires the applicant firm to have the *capability* of meeting its requirements, not *reliability* in so doing. The firm's systems are, therefore, assessed for capability, not reliability and the sample size selected and the assessment time spent by the registrar reflects this difference. One would be ill-advised to place a supplier onto a JIT programme solely on the basis of an ISO 9000 certificate. (Similar remarks apply to the QS 9000 scheme of the automotive industry.))

4. When is the management audit needed?

To obtain management information in advance of key decision points dictates the need for proper timing so that the full cost benefit potential of an audit may be realized. Figure 8.3 depicts a simple project that passes through distinct phases. The starting of each phase entails a decision to release resources in the hope that they will not be squandered and that the requisite quality of product or service will result. The prudent manager would want to be confident that the risks involved in taking such a decision, particularly the risk of loss, have been minimized. Only the

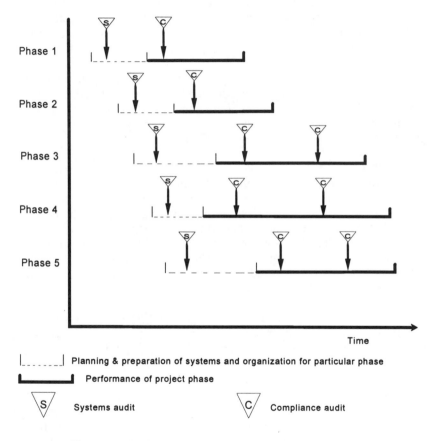

Figure 8.3 Basic internal audit plan for a simple project

performance of a thorough management audit can give that confidence. Sensible advance timing should enable any corrective action that the audit reveals as being required to be properly implemented. Avoidable costs are thus minimized from the outset. Forewarned is forearmed and appropriate timing of an audit forewarns the manager.

It is essential to plan the audit for the proper work phase. It is useless to perform audits solely when the item is about to be handed over to the customer, or the service is about to be delivered. As indicated earlier, errors detected at such a late stage are extremely expensive and embarrassing to put right.

Limiting factors such as holiday arrangements or previous auditing commitments may make it impossible to carry out the audit during the period preferred. A request by a customer for an extrinsic audit may also disrupt the planned schedule.

5. What are the risks involved if the audit is postponed and major problems then found during its course?

These are questions that too few managers ask. It is unwise to postpone an audit continually until there is no time left in which to perform it or to correct major problems without incurring considerable expense: to do so is also bad management. Of course, one must ask whether or not it is likely that major problems will come to light during the audit. The answer depends on the previous performance of the auditee. An auditee who has either a poor record or little experience of the product or contract requirements is more likely to suffer from a number of deficiencies, some of which may be more major problems. This point must be considered when the audit is scheduled and planned.

6. Who must perform the audit?

The personal and professional commitments of the auditors are important here. X may be the ideal person to perform the audit but circumstances may none the less dictate that Y is the only person available. The best rule, however, has to be the question *"Who MUST go?"* as distinct from *"Who can we spare?"*, which is a far too common management policy. The right expertise is essential for the successful conducting of the audit and to obtain the cost benefit required from its accomplishment. That expertise must be provided regardless of the level at which it might be found in the company. If the management is unwilling to make it available from within its own ranks, the alternative is to hire it in from outside. The cost benefit of the audit will dictate that this is advisable.

It also worth remembering the auditee wants, and is entitled to, a good return on his investment being made in the audit. Nobody enjoys being audited by an inappropriate auditor possessing insufficient ability, knowledge and experience in the processes concerned. Everyone likes to feel they are assessed by people they can respect: assigning the best calibre of auditor is a mark of respect towards the auditee that is appreciated in the end.

7. Can the audit be combined with a hold point or some other type of quality control activity to avoid duplication of effort?

In order to ensure that particular expertise is available during the audit, it is worthwhile determining whether or not the audit can be timed to coincide with another activity at which specialist personnel from the auditor's organization will be present. If, for example, a design review is scheduled then the particular engineers will be present: they will be able to examine objective evidence produced by the auditee to determine whether or not it shows the adequacy of the design output and the efficacy of the design control systems implemented by the auditee. In these circumstances, the audit is likely to be a compliance audit, but, it could also include a systems audit of the management systems to be used for the next stage of the work to be performed by the auditee.

I am certainly not proposing that hold points or verifications should replace audits - far from it. One problem associated with such a move is that the quality control activities tend to occur when a task has been completed, which does mean there is a risk that the whole affair will merely serve to confirm that the product has suffered as a result of one or more of the six real causes of business problems (see Chapter 18). A major purpose of auditing is to forewarn management that such causes do exist and require corrective action *before* the product suffers, for this is the best way of ensuring that avoidable costs are indeed prevented. Furthermore, whereas an inspection or other quality control activity can reveal that the product meets requirements, it does not necessarily determine whether the systems can be simplified or whether time and resources are being used inefficiently. This is hardly conducive towards achieving useful continuous improvement.

If, however, the specialist personnel are to be present for a quality control activity that is unrelated to the objective of the audit in hand, having the best of both worlds is then possible.

Who makes the decisions?

This depends upon the individual company's policies and organizational structure. A small company, for instance, may not have a quality department and, in the absence of a quality manager, the company owner may make the decisions. Some companies adopt a policy of actively involving top management in making the audit decisions as a part of the company's annual plan while other companies delegate the decisions to the quality department or to a quality committee made up of representatives from various departments within the company. Some companies do not make any such decisions at all because they have no auditing system. (This does not necessarily mean that the management is in default for it may well have been decided that a system of audits is not required. Although that decision can be considered to be unwise, for the reasons stated throughout this book, the situation is much more dangerous if management has simply failed to face up to whether or not it would benefit the company for audits to be introduced.)

It is essential that management is directly involved in making the audit decisions. The level of management will depend upon the use to which the information obtained from the audit will be put. If, for example, the objective of the audit is to determine whether the company has the capabilities to satisfy the requirements of a new market sector that the company wishes to enter, then the audit report would assist a strategic decision which is, in most companies, the duty of senior executive management, perhaps even the board of directors. That level of management or the board of directors would, therefore, make the audit decisions. Figure 8.2 summarizes the external and internal factors affecting strategic decisions and indicates those that are auditable. It can be seen from that figure that audits can provide significantly influential input of great value.

According to the objectives of the audit, some decisions concerning timing, scope etc. can be delegated. For example, if the company has appointed a safety officer, that person can and should be authorized to make the decisions about safety audits. But this does not invalidate the argument that top management or the Board should have been the ones to decide in the first place both that such audits will be carried out and that they wish to receive the audit reports. Managerial *"cop out"*, its being uninvolved in the making of the decisions described in this chapter, is unacceptable and an abrogation of responsibility. See Part 2, Chapter 7.

In the case of external audits, assuming that a quality department exists, its manager together with the quality management coordinator or lead auditor for the product line/ project/ contract concerned are generally charged with the decision making, possibly first consulting the purchasing department, line department personnel and others directly involved in the product/ service of interest. The responsibility for the decisions rests with the quality department's manager (or project quality manager, in the case of project procurement situations), however, and he is also responsible for approving the audit schedule and the manpower allocated to all audits.

In the case of internal audits, top management from the line and staff departments should make the decisions themselves, being advised and guided by the corporate quality manager or a quality committee. This can be best achieved as a fixed agenda topic for the Management Review meetings, thereby guaranteeing the continuous relevance for the firm's needs of the audit programme.

When are the decisions taken?

External audits

It is advisable to compile an audit schedule that will list those suppliers to be audited, or made subject to a pre-award survey. The suppliers will be those that are regularly used and those that the purchasing department knows will be used in the near future. Such a schedule should be compiled as a minimum on an annual basis and then kept regularly updated. In the case of a particular contract or project, the schedule needs to be formulated at the beginning or, at least, well in advance of procurement activities required to make the product or furnish the service involved. Audits should integrate with the sub-contract activities as undisruptively as possible, in such a way as to provide the most useful information obtainable. Special care must be taken if the suppliers concerned are to be required to operate under a just-in-time policy given the slim margins for error. The results of pre-award surveys are especially important in helping to determine the frequency, timing and objectives of such audits. Obviously, the decisions can and should be reviewed at a later stage, if fresh developments and problems occur, as is all too likely to in the context of a rapidly changing environment. It should be routine to review audit decisions along with those in other areas when any new situation arises.

Internal audits

The value of drawing up annually an internal management audit plan as part of the corporate annual plan is already recognized in many companies and increasing numbers of organizations are formalizing their internal audit planning in this way. Project management should also define its own audit schedule at the outset of a project. The audit can provide valuable guidance to the project manager with regard particularly to the question of whether the resources and time budgeted to each activity will be wisely spent/have been wisely spent/have not been wisely spent. Strangely, many project managers take great care in defining the cost and schedule reports that they want in order to *"control"* their projects but never ask for a report which will inform them of what they got in return or what they will get in return: that is precisely the information that an audit can provide. Such project audit schedules must be drawn up immediately the project is started, that is to say at the same time as the project is being organized and planned. In some cases, this might even occur when the company is bidding for a contract.

The same remarks and arguments apply in the case of a product development project stretching from basic research and development through to product introduction.

Ad hoc audits

Ad hoc decisions to perform audits may still have to be taken occasionally if an unexpected situation develops but this sort of fire-fighting exercise should be the exception, not the rule. There is a severe risk that auditors who possess a trouble making attitude will use ad-hoc audits as a *"catch them out"* exercise. (See Chapter 12 and its discussion of clean-ups.)

The role of the board of directors :

Every company's board of directors should require an audit to be performed annually on its behalf. Such a requirement is fully consistent with the duties and responsibilities vested in it and failure to do so would be most peculiar. Financial figures are totally historic in nature. When the financial accounts reveal that things have gone wrong, the underlying problems may be irreversible unless dramatic surgery, which can substantially affect the shareholders' interests (which the board of directors has a duty to protect), is taken. If a board wishes to protect the future interests of the shareholders properly, it is vital that, in authorizing certain strategic decisions within the company, the board itself is fully informed as to the company's capabilities. The management audit can give that information.   In discussing the fact that he specified the performance of audits, A.P. Sloan wrote [1]:

"...and I do not mean audits in the usual financial sense but one that contemplates a continuous review and appraisal of what is going on throughout the enterprise...This audit function...is of the highest value to the enterprise and its shareholders. I cannot conceive of any board of directors being better informed and thus able to act intelligently on all the changing facts and circumstances than is the board of General Motors".

(Part 2, Chapter 7 discusses *"President's Audits".*)

Involvement of the quality department

In a company that has set up a quality department, a management audit system and an audit schedule, the information described earlier in this chapter should automatically be circulated to the quality department. In practice, it is surprising how few quality departments actually receive the data they need as a matter of course: it is not uncommon for them to have to ferret out the facts for themselves even after notifying other departments of the information they require. Companies setting up their audit system must arrange for information to be sent directly to the quality department. The major sources of information will be either the sales or the purchasing departments (depending on whether the audit is internal, external or extrinsic) and the company management.

The alert extrinsic auditor will note the extent to which the quality department receives this information as a matter of course. Failure to keep that department fully involved and informed about the company's business is an indicator, (and a quite reliable one, too), of lack of commitment by the top management to quality. It can signal the existence of a cosmetic quality department - which is all too often the case.

9. Audit preparation

As the proverb says "a good beginning is half the business,"
and "to have begun well" is praised by all.

Plato.

Preparation is essential to satisfactory audit performance. Unless it is done thoroughly, all the time, effort, and expense of carrying out the audit may be wasted - a situation that is unforgivable should it be allowed to arise. Some organizations, unlucky enough to have experienced only ill-prepared audits, understandably become sceptical about the value of auditing at all. This frustrating and disillusioning experience need not and should not arise if the proper steps are taken before the audit begins. The aim of this chapter is to spell out exactly what these proper steps involve. First of all, however, it is worth saying a little more about the value of good preparation to all parties concerned in the audit.

The benefits of proper preparation

When the auditor is actually at the auditee's workplace or site, time is the great enemy, especially if insufficient time allowance has been made. Time usage must be maximized by avoiding any unnecessary activity that could have been accomplished prior to the auditor's arrival at the auditee's premises. The benefits of preparation are severely curtailed when insufficient time is devoted to or allowed for preparation. Management must be made aware of this for it is false economy to deny adequate preparation time.

The over-riding purpose of preparing the ground thoroughly before the audit's fact gathering phase is to permit the auditor to use the time available to the best possible advantage. Failure in this respect will slow down the proceedings or render the results less valuable. This is obviously undesirable from the auditor's point of view but the auditee will suffer too: the longer the audit drags on, the greater the disruption to ordinary work and the worse the nuisance. As far as the auditee is concerned, any auditor who arrives to carry out an audit without the background information needed, (contract terms, delivery dates, standards and so on), can be regarded as unprofessional and a nuisance.

> On one occasion, I and another representative of my company were scheduled to be observers while a supplier audited a sub-supplier. It became apparent within a quarter of an hour of starting the audit that the supplier was completely unprepared. There was no checklist, plan or programme, the contract had not been reviewed, the status of the contract was unknown, as were the delivery dates. My colleague and I, although scheduled as observers, quickly decided to take over the audit. We had already made the necessary preparations (in the course of preparing to act as observers), so we knew the scope of the contract, the delivery dates and the various parameters involved for a deliverable product. It was only because we possessed this background information that we were able to take over and perform a meaningful audit.

> The whole experience was illuminating - rather than a two-edged sword, a three-edged sword principle applied. We were able to see that our own company's departments had performed their functions properly; that the sub-supplier had developed and implemented satisfactory management systems and that our supplier had a very weak auditing ability. This last piece of information was passed on to the next of our audit teams to visit the supplier; they made a thorough review of the supplier's audit system, with the expected results. The major part of the problem was simply that the supplier's auditor had performed very few audits, had never been trained and did not realize the importance of proper preparation.

Tactically speaking too, it makes sense to be prepared for an audit. On the auditor's side, it shows that he has done his homework and means business. Members of the auditee's organization are less likely to try and bluff the well prepared auditor who seems to have all the facts and figures at his fingertips. On the auditee's side, good preparation (particularly for an extrinsic audit) can pay off by showing the auditor that the auditee knows what is required of him and takes his obligations seriously.

Audit preparation saves everybody time, money and grief. In some fields, companies are subject to so many audits by customers, regulatory bodies, inspection agencies and consultants that they employ full-time escorts whose sole responsibility is to accompany the various extrinsic audit teams. (The problem of multiple assessment are discussed in Chapter 1.) Ordinary work still has to be done sometime. No auditee is likely to have so much time at his disposal that he feels magnanimous about having it wasted by an inefficient auditor - particularly if the auditee then has to catch up on his work by doing unpaid overtime. When one considers the auditee incurs greater costs than does the auditor organization during the typical audit, poor preparation will cause less return on the auditee's investment than might otherwise be the case.

Perhaps, and worst of all, one cannot expect an ill-prepared auditor to draw any meaningful conclusions concerning the auditee's performance if such basic matters as determining the audit objective, the areas to be visited, the processes to be assessed, the questions to be asked and such like have not been decided upon.

A golden rule for auditors is: always be properly prepared, (see Appendix 1, 12 Golden Rules).

Audit schedules

Some companies draw up audit schedules on an annual basis, others on a quarterly one, others constantly update theirs on a day-to-day basis. (Audit scheduling is a mandatory requirement of ISO 9001 clause 4.17, which states scheduling is to be done *"...on the basis of the status and importance of the activity to be audited...".* It is an implied requirement of ISO 14001, which requires an *"...audit programme, including any schedule...",* for the semantic differences between a schedule and a programme are not worth bothering about.) An audit schedule has two significant benefits:

♦   It forewarns people throughout the organization of the audits to be done, of the time allocated for their performance as well as of the personnel, products, projects, products and contracts involved. This helps people to plan their work schedules, also helping departments to determine their manpower loading.

♦   It can be produced in extrinsic audits as objective evidence that audits are planned and a standard, such as QS 9000, is complied with.

In the example shown in Figure 9.1, we can see the top sheet of a simple management audit schedule appearing in tabular form. Week numbers are shown on the left hand side (it is this fictitious company's practice to use week numbers rather than calendar dates). The issue date on the top right-hand side tells recipients which revision they hold and whether it is the latest one (it is the company's practice to update the audit schedule every month). The updating period should be whatever best suits the

Hyper-Quality Company Inc.
1997 Audit Schedule

Issued Nov. 1996

Week No.	Auditee	Contract No.	Description	Product class	Audit scope or type	Duration (days)/ team size	Lead auditor	Buyer/ Engineer
1								
2	S.C. Rap Metal Products Inc.	1234	Gizmos	1	Full	4/4	OF	A. Connor/ P.I. Stone
3	CAD	1432 1433	Wotnot Mini- wotnot	1 2	Internal	1/1	BA BA	
4	Taquee Services Inc.	4321	Software Engineering	1	Partial	2/2	BR	C.P. Yu/ Buz Barr
5								
6	Sonia Boot Inc	3456	Cleaning Services	2	Full	3/3	OF	D.C. Flow/ B. Rush

Figure 9.1 An audit schedule

company's purposes and all recipients must be informed of the time scale of this updating period so that they can be assured of having the latest revision.

The audit schedule should indicate all internal and external audits being performed by the company. The column marked *"Contract number"* identifies the contracts that will be audited. The *"Description"* column will help those within the company who are not familiar with the contract number system (perhaps shop-floor staff only know about the Gizmos from S.C. Rap and not about contract 1234, for example).

The company operates a product classification system that reflects the importance of different products and services. The audit schedule shows the product classification so that people are aware of the product's importance.

The schedule should indicate the scope of each audit, its duration and team size. In Figure 9.1, three days for four people (twelve man days in total) have been allocated to perform the S.C. Rap audit. The initials of the lead auditor are shown together with those of the buyer and product designer to notify these people of their involvement in the particular audit.

Notice that in Figure 9.1 the external audits are to be performed two weeks apart. This really is the minimum time that should be allowed between external audits, in view of the need for the lead auditor to be able to report on one audit and prepare for a future one. Auditing is not the sort of activity one can perform week in, week out. Quite apart from the importance of allowing time for preparation, an overworked employee whose desk is always piled high with a backlog of paper work is not able to work effectively for very long. As a rough guide, the time needed to prepare and to follow-up an audit is generally about the same as the time actually taken to gather the facts at the auditee's workplace.

Audits may be scheduled on a basis of costs, of customer complaints or of customer requirements, according to the company's circumstances, as described earlier in Chapter 8, *"Audit decisions"*. The audit schedule may be compiled by the quality department manager, by the managing director/president of the company or by a management committee (such as a material review board or similar), depending on company policies and practice.

The audit schedule is distributed to each department concerned. The department manager is the usual recipient and it is then his responsibility to notify his staff accordingly. The audit schedule must be kept up-to-date and revised in the light of new developments. Provided that revisions are issued regularly - once a month, for instance - the audit schedule will be an authoritative document upon which departments throughout the company know they can rely. Thus, if a particular manager encounters quality problems with the product being supplied to his department, he can advise the lead auditor that the matter needs to be investigated further if an upcoming audit of the area responsible is shown on the schedule.

If any person does approach a lead auditor, claiming the prospective auditee is responsible for business problems, defective products or services needed by the person's department, the lead auditor must always request examples and proof of the allegations made. It is pure folly to accuse an auditee of errors without being able to cite verifiable proof. It is not uncommon for people to make insupportable allegations about others for mischievous purposes; the lead auditor must not become enmeshed in others' feuds, squabbles and political battles, to do so quickly destroys the lead auditor's credibility and professional standing.

Steps in preparing the audit

The sequence of steps required when preparing for an audit is shown in Figure 9.2. Some of the steps explained below may seem obvious but it is amazing how often some are left out of the audit preparation, with unfortunate results. All are necessary for a thorough preparation.

Step 1. Obtain details of the audit decisions

Chapter 8 contains details of the principle audit decisions that need to be taken before embarking upon the preparation of an audit. The outcome of these decisions must be in their entirety passed over to the lead auditor. The relevant information concerns:

♦ The objectives of the management audit.
♦ The type, depth and scope of the management audit.
♦ When the management audit is needed.
♦ The likely impact if the audit is postponed or major problems are uncovered during its course.
♦ Whether or not the management has decided on particular personnel who must perform the audit.
♦ Whether or not the audit is to be combined with a hold point or other quality control activity.

Step	Action	Input needed	Output produced
1	Obtain details of the audit decisions	Objective; type; depth; scope; timing; assigned personnel	
2	Notify the auditee		Audit notification
3	Gather preliminary information from the auditee	Questionnaire; Manuals; Procedures; Layout; Annual reports	Audit guidance tool(s) in "skeleton" form
4	Obtain and review all available information	Contract; Product details; Auditee file; Reports; Product performance records.	Outline of the audit programme
5	Decide audit team size and members		
6	Develop the audit guidance tools (checklist/ flowchart etc.)		Completed audit guidance tools
7	Develop the audit programme		Completed audit programme
8	Distribute the programme and guidance tool to auditee and to audit team		Audit programme; Audit guidance tools
9	Hold briefing session		
10	Make any last minute changes necessary		

Figure 9.2 Sequence of audit preparation steps

It could be that some of this information will be decided by management as a result of the audit preparations described below. Accordingly, some re-iteration is possible.

No audit can be adequately prepared or performed unless the management authorizing the audit clearly states the objectives, as described earlier in Chapter 8, *"Audit decisions"*. Knowledge of the objective is vital because the latter affects the information to be reviewed, the selection of the audit team, the content of the checklist, the amount of time required and the scheduling of the performance of the audit.

A golden rule is: always know the audit objectives. (See Appendix 1, *"12 Golden Rules".*)

The prime purpose of an audit is to obtain information to assist people to succeed better in their work and to make proper management decisions. It makes little sense to obtain vital information if the decision that it would affect has already been taken. The timing of the audit must depend on the classification of the auditee's product and upon the importance of the decisions to be taken as a result of the information obtained from the audit. Figure 8.3 depicts a simple project whose systems audits have been timed so as to be well in advance of new work phases being started. This is so that if the audit discovers any problems with the systems planned for use during the particular work phase concerned, management has adequate time to implement corrective action. Trying to backfit essential controls on the job loses time and money: it is often a futile exercise. Similarly, the compliance audits are planned to be in advance of completion of those phases so that management will know whether or not the system is being properly implemented and is creating the right results and product. As stated earlier in this chapter, it is best to perform a compliance audit for a work phase shortly after it has begun. At that time there will be a small but highly significant sample of the results being obtained from the auditee's practices and, if corrective action is necessary, not too much of the auditee's time, manpower and budget will have been wasted on the unsatisfactory procedures used. This minimizes the build up of avoidable costs.

Step 2. Notify the auditee

It is the responsibility of the lead auditor to see that the auditee is notified that an audit is being planned and prepared. The key considerations to bear in mind are listed below.

Timing :

The lead auditor must decide how much advance warning the auditee will need and make sure he gets it. The more warning one can give, the better - the minimum advance notification should be measured in months, not weeks or days. By providing the auditee with several months advance warning of the audit, the lead auditor will attain two benefits:

♦ The auditee is less likely to have alternative commitments that might cause a postponement and impact other audits within the auditor's organization's audit schedule.

♦ If the audit reveals problems, the auditee cannot claim to be in the process of resolving them and, complain if the audit had been performed just a few weeks later, these problems would have been eradicated. The auditee is well aware for quite some time that its organization is to be assessed against a defined requirement (the audit objective) and when problems are then seen during the audit, the lead auditor can legitimately question the real commitment of management to avoiding avoidable costs, to its quality programme and its responsibilities.

Figure 9.3 shows a typical audit notification letter for the lead auditor to complete and forward to the auditee through the appropriate channels. Using a standard form offers the advantage of saving time for the lead auditor and enabling a rapid review on the part of the recipient (purchasing agent, departmental manager and so on). It is not necessary for the notification to be sent in hard copy form, Fax, E-Mail, memorandum are all acceptable means of notifying the auditee. It is the content that is essential.

Information to be supplied :

The auditee should be given as much of the following material as is available, including:

♦ The dates proposed for the audit, which will also indicate the time that the lead auditor anticipates as being required. (This will be further confirmed when the lead auditor has determined the amount of work involved, as discussed below).

♦ The basis for the audit, that is to say, on what grounds access to perform the audit is being requested. Such grounds may include a contract requirement (in the case of an external audit) or a

Hyper-Quality Company Inc.

Audit Notification

To:
Date:
From:
Auditee involved:
Product(s) involved:
Please be advised we wish to perform an audit:

The audit objective is as follows:

The basis for this request is: (Delete as necessary).

      Company policy
      Customer order requirement
      Regulatory requirement
      ISO 9001   QS 9000   ISO 14001
      Other (specify)

The auditee is requested to supply the following information to help the audit preparation process: (Delete as necessary)

      Quality/ operations manual.   Organization chart(s).
      Management procedures/ instructions.   Annual Report.
      Response to attached questionnaire.   Plant layout.
      Copies of applicable certifications/ licenses/ approvals.
      Other (specify)

Our audit team will comprise the following persons:

The auditee is requested to confirm the acceptability of the proposed dates on or before:

                                      Lead Auditor

Figure 9.3 Audit notification

requirement of the company's quality programme (in the case of an internal audit).

♦ The audit objectives and the documents/information of prime interest in the audit such as the operations manual, code or standard invoked by contract, the procedures and instructions that describe the management systems and practices required of the auditee.

♦ The names of the audit team members if this has been decided. The auditee has to know who to expect and may indeed be acquainted with some of the proposed audit team.

♦ A blank questionnaire for providing advance details of the auditee's operation, if it is a company practice to issue one. The questionnaire might cover points such as the range of products or markets; industrial approvals held; turnover; quality systems standards, codes and regulations in force; plant layout; plant size; number of employees; name of the management's representative on quality matters; process capacities and types, and so on. This information can be useful if the auditing company has no prior knowledge of the auditee's operation. (Such questionnaires apply more in the case of external audits. As a preference and superior practice, they should have been sent to the supplier concerned before any pre-award survey was performed because they request information frequently essential for making sound purchase order placement decisions).

Channel of notification:

The notification must always be sent through the official, formal channels used for the product, service or project concerned. What these are will vary from company to company. In some cases, the lead auditor may be allowed to pass the notification directly to the supplier (in the case of an external audit); in other circumstances, he/she may have to pass through the purchasing department, contract manager or project manager, as applicable, depending on company policy. In the case of an internal audit, the notification should be sent by one departmental manager to the other concerned.

One reason for using the official channels is to set an example to other persons and organizations in this respect. Furthermore, new information may have been received by some person in more recent communications with the auditee. It may transpire that the proposed date of the audit would be inappropriate because, according to the latest information, the contract/project/work will have been completed earlier. In this case, the lead auditor will have to put forward an alternative date.

Confirmation:

The auditee must be asked either to confirm in writing that the proposed audit dates are suitable or to propose appropriate alternative dates, together with the reasons why the original ones were not feasible (one such explanation being, for example, that the auditee would not be able to make persons available during the audit because of holidays or other prior commitments).

Notification and confirmation of the audit dates should take place before the audit schedule is finalized. Changes may have to be made to the schedule in the light of the auditee's response to the notification.

Many companies are putting their audit schedules onto a central database accessible to all. Some show proposed audit dates in one colour, confirmed dates in another (red for proposed, green for confirmed and agreed seems to be a popular choice presumably because red typically alerts us to something risky, while green means proceed). Some differentiate by arranging for proposed dates to be shown as flashing data on the computer screens. Whatever suits one' purpose is fine.

It is just as annoying to arrive at a supplier's premises to perform an audit only to find that his sales department has not informed the other departments that an audit is to take place, as it is not to be informed by one's own sales department that a customer is arriving to perform an extrinsic audit. The lack of information may not be too serious if all the people concerned are available, but it is common sense and plain good management to keep people informed. The old maxim *"Do as you would be done by"* is a useful one to apply here. Thus, whoever is responsible for organizing the audit arrangements should also be responsible for keeping other departments and individuals informed of the decisions that have to be taken.

> I myself had the experience of not being told until the morning it was due that an audit had to be performed. My manager had made all the other arrangements for the audit, omitting to tell me that an audit was required and that I was to be the lead auditor. It is a practice I cannot recommend for the results obtained in these situations are always less than totally satisfactory regardless of the best efforts made by the hapless auditor.

Step 3. Gather preliminary information from the auditee

Although this section applies mainly to external and extrinsic audits, sometimes the auditee also has to send preliminary information to the lead auditor and audit team before an internal audit too. This is likely to be necessary if the company's departments are geographically dispersed so that information about outlying operations is not readily available at the auditors' offices. Alternatively, if the company has hired auditors from a consultancy or from an outside agency to perform the audit (as is the case with hiring registrars), they, too, may require information about the auditee's facilities in order to plan the proceedings satisfactorily.

The preliminary information the auditor may need includes the following:

1. A completed standard questionnaire, if any was forwarded with the notification (see above).

2. All the material - such as a copy of the operations manual, quality manual, job descriptions, organization charts, quality plans, procedures and work instructions - required for adequate preparation to a systems depth, if this is not already available at the lead auditor's desk.

The copies should preferably be controlled versions, that is, versions which are automatically updated when amended. This is more likely to be the case when the auditee retains all such information in electronic form and sends it to the Lead Auditor by E. mail or makes read only access to the lead auditor for the purposes of preparation. Using this technology enables the auditee to continually maintain up-to-date all the management systems descriptions without burdening recipients with mountains of hard copy. It is a preferable practice.

When preparing for an external audit the lead auditor should check whether or not the contract requires a controlled copies to be submitted. If the contract does not contain such a requirement, the auditee is perfectly entitled to issue uncontrolled copies.

The American automotive giants, Chrysler, Ford and General Motors and truck manufacturers who are party to the QS 9000 initiative require their QS 9000 suppliers to go electronically on-line so as to facilitate information/ data transfer during contractual activities. It seems reasonable to surmise that the preliminary information required for audit preparation, cited above, should be available to the customers' auditors on-line eventually

211

and for it to be maintained as *"live"*, especially considering the growing application of flexible organizations and systems responsive to customer needs and urgent changes.

3. Layout of the facilities

This helps the lead auditor to assess the physical size and spread of the departments/ processes that are to be audited. (For the auditing problems that physical size can cause, see Chapter 3, *"Problems of location and size"*.) Sometimes a layout of the facilities used to be provided by the auditee's company as an appendix to the quality manual, but this practice has, largely, died out in recent years. In the case of a resource audit, a value-added audit or an audit for continuous improvement purposes, such information should be requested, provided and reviewed.

4. A copy of the company's annual report or other profile material.

Although this information is more frequently of use in the preparation of external audits, it may also be used in the case of internal audits of company business centres or divisions that the lead auditor has not encountered before. Such material often contains photographs of the facilities and the equipment in use. This can give the audit team valuable clues as to the auditee's policy regarding replacement and maintenance of equipment, house keeping and other facilities but they should take these pictures with a small pinch of salt. The photos might also depict new equipment which the lead auditor can see will require the presence of a specialist as part of the audit team.

> One company had a most impressive profile book containing glossy pictures of a very orderly looking department. When the audit team later walked through that same department, they could hardly recognize it: the housekeeping was atrocious. When the audit discussed the housekeeping with the particular department manager, the latter effused at length about the impracticality and impossibility of having everything shipshape and shining. One member of the audit team quietly said to that manager *"We know you can do it. Here's your photograph of it."* When the picture was placed before him the manager went rather red and then claimed that the photograph was taken before his time. Patently true but his statement did tend to compound his sins!

5. The names of the official contacts who will be available during the audit such as the department/ divisional manager, quality manager, contracts administrator, project manager or salesman concerned.

6. The normal working hours of the various departments to be audited. This is important information since it can affect plans for travel and for the carrying out of the audit, particularly when the working hours in different parts of the organization are not the same. In an hotel, for example, the banqueting/ conference department might work different hours from the catering department or the housekeeping department; similarly, the reservations department of an airline might work different hours to the maintenance crews; in the case of a manufacturing facility there may be various shifts covering most or all of the twenty four hour day.

> Too few audits are performed to assess the systems and practices of night shifts. This possibly reflects a common unwillingness on the part of auditors to work what they consider as being unsocial hours. None the less, if an auditee is to be fairly and fully assessed all working hours and shifts must be audited sooner or later. It is my experience that these shifts are often used to complete urgent or late work, that management systems are frequently ignored on them because of the reduced presence of the firm's quality departments, its auditors and its top management. To discover less assiduous application of the quality programme and its systems on night shifts etc. is to find a less than thorough commitment to quality by the auditee's top management. (To the best of my knowledge, at the time of writing this third edition, virtually no registrars take the trouble to assess ISO 9000/ QS 9000 applicants' night shifts.)

In the case of a foreign auditee, it may also be prudent to enquire about possible clashes with the anticipated dates for the audit caused by national holidays or events.

> When I lived in Britain, I was once asked to audit an American company in Los Angeles and discovered that the start date proposed would be impossible because it coincided with the anniversary of George Washington's birthday, which is an American national holiday.

> On another occasion I was asked to audit a firm in Ireland but discovered the proposed dates would clash with the debut match of the Irish soccer team playing in the World Cup tournament. I was advised that on such an occasion Ireland always experiences a leap in the number of alleged funerals of grandparents that, naturally, have to be attended, as would the wakes which fortuitously would take place in a location that happened to have a copious supply of

213

Guinness and a television that might, by pure coincidence, happen to be tuned into the game.

Step 4. Obtain and review all available information

The lead auditor must review all the information listed below when preparing for the audit. After the team has been selected and mobilized (see step 5 below), the individual auditors may not each need to review all the details but the more each one can review, the better. The lead auditor should decide exactly what information each individual is to review as part of the audit preparation. The list below applies to both internal and external audits. (In the case of an extrinsic audit, when a company's lead auditor may be assigned to act as escort for the extrinsic audit team, the same information should be reviewed. Since it will be relevant to the extrinsic audit team's terms of reference.)

Information to be reviewed:

The information to be reviewed is as follows:

1. Contract and specifications, standards and codes invoked therein, details of the contract performance schedule and any milestone payments.

The milestone payments may be conditional upon satisfactory audit findings. This could well be the case where a pre-award survey team has required that special contract clauses and safeguards be included, coupled to a milestone payment. In these circumstances, the audit team must be aware that, upon completion of the audit, the chief buyer (in the case of an external audit) or perhaps the sales manager (in the case of an extrinsic or an internal audit) will ask the team whether the milestone payment can be either claimed or made.

2. If available, the manuals, procedures and work instructions describing both the management systems and methods of implementation.

In some cases, this information may not be available. Some external auditee insist that copies of the documents will be made available only at their own premises, on the grounds that they contain proprietary information which is not for release to external organizations. This possibility should have been clarified before contract signature and the auditor's organization should be aware of when and how access to such information for review purposes will be provided. It is extremely difficult to prepare for an audit without reviewing this information and, should it be unavailable, the time allocated to carrying out the audit may need to be extended to allow for the team's reviewing of it at the auditee's premises. If information is forwarded to the auditor before the audit, it must be reviewed and any apparent or potential deficiencies noted.

As auditees become more familiar with the idea of management audits, it is not so often, nowadays, that auditees prefer to not provide this information claiming its proprietary nature. This is mainly because the types of management systems being required by such standards as ISO 9000 have led to fairly common practices which can hardly be considered as being proprietary considering hundreds of others operate virtually identical methods for such matters as information control, corrective action systems, management reviews and the like. None the less, legitimate areas, where proprietary restrictions could be claimed, relate to process instructions that might be of a patented and protected nature or to the innovative use of technology or to applications of the auditee's own research, development and investment to product and service supply. Auditees also recognize the extra costs incurred hosting an audit team at its premises to do audit related preparation it could have performed at its own place of work.

The foregoing remarks apply more to external audits for it is rarely the case an internal audit would be refused access to auditee information in order to make its preparations.

When reviewing manuals and similar documents, one should make allowances for any possible language barrier, given that the auditee's mother tongue might not be the same as the auditor's. It would be unfair and unreasonable to assume that simply because the wording of grammar is poor, the management systems are automatically deficient. They may indeed be deficient but it is the task of the auditor to verify that fact during the audit and not to prejudge the issue. Furthermore, it is good practice to advise the auditee of the correct phrasing if any accuracies or obscurities have been noted. (If language problems are apparent from this information, it could herald the need to allow for language barrier difficulties during the audit: possible courses of action are described later in this chapter.) The other side of the coin is that it is not safe to assume that because documents/ information appear to be satisfactory in every respect, the systems are implemented and efficacious.

During a trip to Stavanger, I received a telephone call shortly after at my hotel from an individual whose acquaintance I had never made before. The caller asked if he and a colleague could visit me to discuss aspects of their management systems. They brought with them a copy of their company's *"quality manual"* and presented it to me requesting my comments. The company, too, was unknown to me. After I had scanned through the document I asked how long the systems had been in operation and was informed implementation had been satisfactorily underway for some months. I also asked how they had produced such a piece of work and was told proudly, it was all their own work. My visitors were considerably embarrassed when told I could recognize my own work and writings especially since a substantial proportion of the content had not long been in existence and my company's name was still included in the text. An unsuccessful attempt at plagiarism, or is it theft?

During an audit in New Zealand, a line department manager working for a major international oil corporation, and who I had never met before, presented to me the company's *"Internal Audit Training Manual"*, claiming it as being all its own work. It was most certainly not for much of it had been extracted, without permission, directly from the second edition of this book and from copyright material presented by me in Wellington during a seminar attended by some members of that company's staff. The actual audit being performed soon revealed the company's internal audit programme as a non-existent fiction.

The lead auditor should check whether the documents/ information have been reviewed previously within his department or company, determining what deficiencies, if any, were noted by the reviewer. This does not mean that a previous review by another person(s) excuses the lead auditor and audit team from carrying out their own review. This is not only because the earlier review may have been incorrect but because the omission of such a review would be an abrogation of the duty of the whole audit team to perform the audit properly, and to present a true and fair view of the auditee's systems and their implementation.

3. The auditee file.

This will contain information about the auditee, copies of previous audit reports, survey reports, reports of non-conformities and problem histories, maybe even an auditee rating. It may be especially useful to know about areas previously found to be deficient and about recommendations previously made. In the case of an external audit, it is important to know of special safeguards required by a pre-award survey for inclusion in contracts with the supplier as well as to know the names of personnel who have been associated with (who should, therefore, be familiar with) the supplier.

4. The information sent by the auditee.

This will enable the audit team to plan how to overcome problems created by geographic dispersion or by a large complex, also permitting them to work out the sequence in which the various departments/ activities. Processes in the scope of the audit should be visited. Other profile material can yield useful information, raise questions that need to be resolved during the audit or indicate the need for particular expertise within the audit team. (Geographic dispersion is discussed further in Chapter 3.)

5. Product service and field reports.

It is a grave and all too common error to neglect these reports, which should be on file somewhere. The product service and field personnel are in a unique position to assess the true quality and fitness for purpose of the product and services being supplied. These files may contain plaintive reports about recurring deficiencies, reports that have not been acted upon or that have required previous action. In any case, the files will indicate to the audit team areas that should be examined, with a view to preventing repetition of the deficiencies.

6. The corrective action request file (if one is kept).

It is advisable to maintain such a file and it should be kept in the quality department, for periodic review to determine if any issues are still open and require action to be taken accordingly. This procedure gives a bite to the corrective action system both for suppliers and for internal departments. The file may reveal some trends in deficiencies. The audit team should select some closed-out corrective action requests in order to verify that the auditee is taking continued corrective action. It is not necessary to devote a great deal of time to this side of the audit but it is good practice to show the auditee that corrective action should not be considered a one-time action or expedient. A common problem of corrective action systems is failure to get to the real root cause of the problems unearthed and to extirpate it. Many auditees experience a recurrence of problems they believed were resolved on a once-for-all basis. The audit team must test the real efficacy of the corrective action system by selecting a few, allegedly, "closed-out" issues.

The corrective action file should be information reviewed regularly by management as a fixed agenda topic for its management review meetings. It is not the sole preserve of the quality department to be regularly reviewing the contents of that file.

7. Product performance records, warranty claims.

These can provide useful guidance on the actual performance of the auditee's product when in service, namely, whether or not it really is fit for purpose, also detailing manifestations of problems that the auditee should have addressed or should be addressing.

All the information listed in 1-7 above should be available within the quality department since it is essential for the satisfactory execution of its quality support duties.

8. Other useful sources of information to be tapped.

There are many other sources outside the quality department which can provide useful information for the preparation of an audit.

a) In-house sources

Various departments within the auditor's own organization can provide useful background about the auditee, the work or contract's/project's status and any problems to be anticipated. Various departments, for example, may have difficulty in obtaining from the auditee the information required for review purposes or have experienced problems with its content.

> During the preparation of one particular external audit, a design engineer complained that an inordinate amount of time was being spent correcting the design calculations submitted by a particular supplier. These contained not only misinterpretations of the industrial standards applicable for the contract but also mathematical errors. The engineer furnished quite a few examples to substantiate his claim. The audit team suspected that, although the calculations submitted carried a signature alleging that they had been reviewed , they had in reality been signed without having been reviewed at all. This was verified during the audit and brought to the supplier's attention.

Other personnel may have various concerns regarding the quality of work being supplied by the auditee to them.

The purchase department (in the case of external audits) should always be consulted and asked about their experience of the auditee's past performance, about the buyer's understanding of the present status of the contract (which may not agree with the actual status encountered during the audit) and about any contracts that are being considered for award to the supplier concerned. If future contracts are under consideration, which may have different requirements from those at present, the audit team could state that any incapabilities exposed by the audit will not be acceptable during any subsequent contracts, this statement forming a necessary part of the audit report. The buyer should be asked about any imminent milestone payments or any other points of concern. It is important, for example, to know if the buyer is having problems obtaining the information, that the supplier is required to submit for the approval either of the auditor's organization or of the auditor's customer.

The customer service and product support staff (Particularly those out *"in the field"*) should be consulted if the audit affects items or services with which they have been or are involved. These are the people who see the true picture of the quality of the product supplied to the customer and the efficacy of the management systems used in the execution of the business. They stand first in the firing line when irate customers complain of deficiencies: it can be a chilling and unpleasant experience. They may know of problems with products or services being obtained from a supplier or from the auditor's own organization; there may be deficiencies or inadequacies in the information to be used; equipment might not have the requisite capability of providing customer satisfaction; the supplier's personnel in the field may be inadequately trained and perform badly. Whatever the case, these customer service and product support people are quick to appreciate any help from an audit if it will make their lives easier, as it frequently can.

> Prior to the performance of some major work at a customer's premises, a partial audit was planned and executed. The audit was performed at a time that permitted adequate opportunity to correct any deficiencies found. Some quite serious inadequacies were discovered and put right before the work commenced. When the actual work did begin, it was behind schedule by several weeks. However, as a result of the audit a number of improvements were made that affected management systems, equipment and information used: eventually everything was completed several weeks ahead of schedule.

The document control area (if one exists, and they are a rapidly disappearing feature of business organizations) can provide document numbers, information identities and revisions received. A selection of identities must be taken on the audit in order to verify that the correct versions are being used in the execution of the auditee's work and, if the auditee is responsible for submitting documents/ information for approval, that the latest editions have indeed been submitted for review.

b) External sources

In the case of an external audit, the company may have some consortium or joint venture partners who have agree to exchange audit reports. Recent reports may provide useful information or alert the audit team to a potential problem. The auditor's company may be a contributor to a scheme in operation within its own industry which pools external audit reports: perhaps, information is available from that source. Even so, the company may still perform additional research of its own on the supplier of interest.

c) Reconnaissance visits.

Occasionally, it may be decided that the lead auditor should visit the auditee before the actual audit. Such a decision would depend upon the company's policy, the location of the auditee, the costs involved (related to the nature of the contract and the classification of the product or service involved) and the status of the work. The purpose of this type of visit would be to obtain information to assist in planning the audit, an assessment, perhaps of the size of the auditee's facilities and the sequence in which the various departments and task units should be tackled. Discussion of previous visits to the supplier's facilities by other persons within the auditor's company may also produce useful information: the lead auditor should not neglect this possibility.

d) Telecommunication

A telephone call, telefax or E. Mail communication with the auditee can sometimes provide the extra information that the audit team requires to prepare for the audit.

It should by now be apparent that there is no shortage of information available if the audit team and the lead auditor care to look. The only excuse for failure to collect it is in the understandable situation whereby management requires the audit to be performed at such short notice that preparation is absolutely impossible.

e) The Internet

The Internet has given customers the opportunity to air any grievances they might have, concerning the auditee's products and services, to a global audience for little more than the cost of their time spent creating a web site, posting notes on electronic bulletin boards and setting up news group on the 'Net.

> Two owners of Ford automobiles were unhappy when their vehicles burst into flames. Others were too and an *"Association of Flaming Ford Owners"* eventually set up a web page of information airing their views. Ford became involved in the largest ever recall of vehicles experienced in the automotive industry (estimated at some 8.7 million units and costing $300 million, apparently.) [1]

> McDonald's, the fast food company, became plaintiff in a civil action brought against two unemployed people over the defendant's allegations about them. It appears that some 1800 secret McDonald's files eventually became available on the Internet at some point during the trial, files that McDonald's apparently did not want revealed. The trial has become (at the time this third edition is being finished) the longest ever in the history of UK civil disputes.[2]

> EPS Technology experienced three Internet sites complaining about them. That company wanted to act properly and acknowledged the complaints raised, which included late deliveries, incorrect deliveries and poor customer service.[3]

Step 5. Decide the audit team size and the team members

Although this decision should be the responsibility of the lead auditor, it is often dictated by others. It is my contention both that the lead auditor, who will, after all, be held responsible for the satisfactory execution of the audit, should have the authority to require the participation of such personnel as he considers necessary and that it is the duty of the auditor's management to do everything possible to make those persons available. The lead auditor's decision on team size and membership can be broken down into five stages.

1. Decide how much work is involved.

This depends upon the audit objectives; information received and reviewed; the type, depth and scope of the audit; the experience of the auditor(s); the number of contracts/ projects involved; geographic dispersion and plant layout; as well as the departments and processes to be audited.

2. Decide who is needed.

As stated above, the management must do its best to make available the people required by the lead auditor. It is a false economy to take so few people that the audit cannot be satisfactorily completed. The team may consist of a permanent full-time auditor plus a quality controller for the contract/project concerned. It makes sense to include the last person because if problems arise, he/she will be held responsible for verifying that corrective action has been satisfactorily accomplished. Thorough familiarity with the auditee's systems and any problems that require resolution can do a great deal to help quality controllers to carry out their duties. This holds true for internal audits as well as for external ones.

Many companies are adopting the policy of requiring the individual performing the work to be audited to be responsible for his or her own process quality management. If this type of policy is the case for the auditee concerned, the quality controller would not be part of the audit team, auditing his/her own process, since the aspect of independence would be lost.

In deciding who should make up the audit team, the lead auditor will naturally be constrained by company policy and the costs involved.

Use of specialists:

There is a mistaken belief that if somebody understands the principles and techniques of auditing, he or she could audit any type of operation. An auditor must never lose sight of the product: it is the very thing for which the management systems are created. In order to assess whether or not these systems are suitably stringent, it is essential that the auditor completely understands the product, the industry and their needs. Nobody can be an expert in everything. Different activities have different products. Few people are fully experienced in the product of every department in a commercial organization. To ensure that the audit is properly conducted, in preparing for the audit, the lead auditor will decide which areas will require particular expertise and will structure the audit team so as to contain the necessary specialists. It might not be essential for an individual specialist to be present throughout the entire audit: a specialist need only attend for that period of time in which his or her particular knowledge will be brought to bear.

Interpreters:

One type of specialist that might be necessary is the interpreter. Knowing that the auditee's mother tongue is a foreign language, the lead auditor must choose from the following options:

♦ To include in the audit team one or more auditors who are proficient in the auditee's mother tongue.
♦ To obtain a member of the auditor's organization's personnel who is proficient in that language to act as an interpreter.
♦ To hire in an interpreter for the duration of the audit.

If none of the above is possible or if management will not permit the hiring of a translator, there exists one final option:

♦ To rely on the integrity of the auditee organization to provide *bona fide* translations for the audit team.

In the event of the last option being necessary, the lead auditor should impress on his management the potential limitations both on the audit and on the veracity of the results. Working in a foreign language may also dictate the need for extra auditing time to secure the requisite amount of objective evidence and coverage. If the audit team has to rely on that option, the lead auditor must qualify the audit report with a statement such as *"The results are contingent upon the audit team's need to rely on the auditee to provide* bona fide *translations of the objective evidence presented to the team."* (Such a statement suggests to me the audit results could be worthless, and the audit team was witness to a theatrical event.)

Audits are not cheap exercises. Considering the benefits that can accrue from them, it is foolhardy for any management not to support the lead auditor's request for experts. The apposite question must always be *"who must go?"* not *"who can we spare?"*

Whereas it is generally impossible for an individual to audit everything effectively without expert assistance, it is possible for a competent lead auditor to lead (or manage) the auditing of any type of organization. Such

---

Hyper-Quality Company Inc.

Audit Programme

Auditee: S.C. Rap Metal Products Inc.
Audit dates: 8-13 January 1997   Auditee location:
Big Bone Lick, KY, USA
Purchase Order No.:   1234   Product(s)
involved: Gizmos
Audit team:
        Sub-team A: Ozzy Fry   Lead auditor
H-QCI.

        F. Flintstone   Specialist Auditor
H-QCI.

        D. Bailey   Customer's Observer
Candle Power Corp.

        Sub-team B: Ms. Dinah Shaw Sub-team leader
H-QCI.

        B. Rubble   Specialist Auditor
H-QCI.

        R. Robertson   Customer's Observer
Candle Power Corp.

Audit objective: To determine the extent of compliance with the requirements of Hyper-Quality Inc. purchase order of the S.C. Rap Metal Products Inc. management systems, to assess the extensiveness of the auditee's business improvement programme and verify the results of the same.

The basis for this audit is: H-QCI company policy and contract requirements of our customer, Candle Power Corporation.

Figure 9.4 An audit programme

```
                          Programme

              Sub-team A                    Sub-team B

Wed 8 January
09.00    Arrive at S.C. Rap Metal Products Inc.
09.15    Entry Interview. Brief description of organization, contract
         Status by S.C. Rap personnel.
09.45            Contracts                  Receiving Bay
                 Conceptual Design          Supplied product
                                                verification
                 CAD                        Stores
16.00            Completion of first day's activities
                 Evening team conference


Thursday 9 January
09.00    Reconvene at S.C. Rap facilities to continue audit.
         Short briefing session for S.C. Rap management representative.
09.15            Purchasing                 Heat treatment
                 Warranty & Customer Support   Special coatings
                 Business Improvement        Final Verification
16.00            Completion of second day's activities
                 Evening team conference


Friday 10 January
09.00    Reconvene at S.C. Rap facilities to continue audit
         Short briefing session for S.C. Rap management representative
09.15            Information control         Machine Bay No. 1.
                 Archive & Records          Packaging &
                                                despatch
                 Calibration Laboratory     Production
                                                planning & control
16.00    Completion of third day's activities
         Evening team conference (preparation for Exit Interview)


Monday 13 January
09.00    Exit Interview, presentation of audit findings to
         S.C. Rap management
10.30    Departure of audit team
```

Figure 9.4 An audit programme

225

a person understands the principle audit matters that need to be covered: they include the task elements described in Chapter 4. To give an example: in any department a lead auditor will know that the content of information must be correct but he may not be able to judge the correctness of the information's content when it is presented to him. Similarly, the lead auditor may be unable to decide whether or not equipment has the right capability for a particular process - again, a specialist can be asked to advise the lead auditor at the time he is confronted by such circumstances.

3. Check on the availability of the potential team members.

The ideal team from the lead auditor's point of view may be unavailable because of vacations, sickness or prior commitments (such as other audits, business trips or meetings).

4. If sub-teams are to be used, the lead auditor must decide on the team leaders.

In making this decision, he will take into account the experience of the individuals involved because each sub-team leader must have the experience and training to be able to lead those in his sub-team satisfactorily.

5. Notify the actual team members accordingly.

Step 6. Develop the checklist/ audit guidance tool

It is the responsibility of the lead auditor to decide upon the format and content of the tool that will be used to guide the audit (whether checklist, flow chart or matrix) checklist and to generate it accordingly (see Chapter 7).

When the lead auditor has decided on the type of specialists that may be required to help perform the audit and once management has agreed to make them available, they should be required to assist the lead auditor in ensuring that important matters have been covered in the guidance tool to be used.

Step 7. Develop the audit programme

An example of a programme is shown (without checklist) in Figure 9.4. While developing the programme, the lead auditor should:

1. Decide the amount of time required for the audit.

Audits fail to deliver their full potential results when inadequate time budget is allocated for their performance. (Lack of time is as much a cause of quality problems in auditing as it is in any other activity.) Time shortage is a false economy.

Figure 9.5 depicts the results benefit obtained during an audit. There is an initial period during which the benefit being obtained is low. As audit time increases, so does the quantity of objective evidence seen by the audit team. The more objective evidence obtained, the greater one's knowledge of the reliability of the auditee's management systems, and the auditee's capabilities. This affords greater benefit arising from the audit. Eventually, a point of diminishing returns is reached beyond which the expenditure of extra time merely reveals more of the same type of objective evidence.

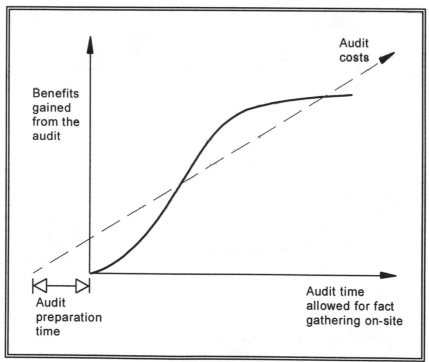

Figure 9.5 Audit cost-benefit vs. time

If one considers the costs associated with the audit, one obtains a pictorial representation of cost-benefit similar to that shown in Figure 9.5. For simplicity the costs associated with audit preparation are assumed linear representing only the costs of the lead auditor's time, although in practice they tend to be more saw-toothed as the various members of the audit team are mobilized, travel costs are incurred and so on.

Since the early 1980's, the North Sea oil industry took quality management more seriously than ever. As a result, large numbers of audits were performed. However many of these audits were allocated a totally inadequate time budget, the vast majority being allowed little more than a couple of days in which to audit an entire company fully. The North Sea industry did not receive benefits commensurate with the vast amount of money and manpower expended, principally because a prime objective of these audits seems to have been to accumulate evidence that *"somebody went there"*, as opposed to examining the auditee's management systems critically and determining which could be simplified as well as how to save on resources, time and cost. If more time had been devoted to the audits, the benefits would have been considerably greater.

Frequently the above has reached absurd proportions. I recall an encounter with an acquaintance one day and, from a brief conversation, one ascertained that he was assigned to audit a complete company in the morning, have lunch, drive to a second company, thirty miles away and audit it during the afternoon.
My observations of the American automotive industry grappling to comply with QS 9000 in the second half of the 1990's leads me to draw identical conclusion to those just expressed in relation to the North Sea oil industry. In this case the objective seems to be to *"get something on file for the registrar to see we do audits so we can get the QS 9000 certificate"*. Many firms pursuing ISO 9000 certificates have done and, at the time of writing the third edition of this book, continue to enact the same false economy folly. *Plus ca change*!

It is especially distasteful to discover registrars being parties to the same foolishness by agreeing to an inadequate period of on-site time to perform their assessments. The value of their certificates is substantially reduced by spending inadequate time gathering facts. Their customers, the auditees, should not pressurize registrars to reduce their prices citing competitor registrars as offering a cheaper deal.

The auditor must plan the audit time so as to be able to work within the positive cost-benefit area of the graph. Once meaningful conclusions can be drawn, based on a fair sample of the work being done by the auditee, it will be time to move on to the next matter on the audit programme: dwelling further merely reveals more of the same and moves the auditor into the negative cost-benefit area once again.

The time needed for audit performance depends mainly on the following factors, which the lead auditor should determine when formulating his audit schedule.

♦ The depth of the audit (system, compliance).

♦ The objectives (such as the follow-up of corrective action requests or the introduction of a just-in-time (JIT) philosophy. The importance of the decisions taken by management as a result of the audit must also be considered).

♦ The number of different work activities/ tasks/ processes and departments to be audited.

♦ The typical amount (sample size) of objective evidence that the auditor might wish to see in order to obtain a certain level of confidence that a true and fair view has been obtained.

♦ The availability of specialists and whether or not sub-teams will be used.

♦ The speed or experience of individual auditors. Every auditor develops his or her own methods and question technique. This has considerable effect on the speed with which the auditor can cover any particular area.

♦ The size of the auditee's facilities and whether there is any geographic dispersion between principal activities to be audited. If the latter is the case, then the lead auditor needs to allow time for traveling between them. (See Chapter 3 under the discussion *"geographic dispersion"*.)

A formula for calculating the time required:

I calculate the time required for performing the audit by means of the following formula:

$$T = \frac{t \times N \times F}{H \times S}$$

Where,

> T = Total number of days for the audit
> t = Average time per process/department/function audited
> N = Number of processes/departments/functions to be audited
> H = Hours per audit day
> S = Number of sub-teams used
> F = Factor, which depends on the audit objectives.
>> (The factor is never less than "1".)

Example:

A supplier has to be audited. The number of processes to be audited is 18. The lead auditor estimates the, on average, each process will require approximately 2.5 hours to audit. Knowing that the auditee works a 7.5 hour day, the lead auditor wants the audit team to work a 7 hour day in the auditee's premises. Thus, the total time required for the audit is:

$$\frac{2.5 \times 18 \times 1}{7} = 6 \text{ man days (approx).}$$

However, the lead auditor's management says that fact gathering part of the audit must be completed within 3 days. Therefore, the total number of sub-teams must be 2. The end result can be seen in the programme shown in Figure 9.4.

If the audit objective was to assess the suitability of the auditee to be placed on a just-in-time programme, the formula would become as follows, since I use a factor of "2" for such objectives.

$$\frac{2.5 \times 18 \times 2}{7} = 12 \text{ man days (approx).}$$

In this circumstance, to complete the work in 3 days, as the management requested, the total number of sub-teams would be 4.

230

Fit in with the normal working hours and allow at least half an hour in the morning for the auditee's people to open mail, allocate work to their departments, start up machines, sign letters and so on.

This half hour's grace makes it less likely that proceedings will be interrupted by the auditee's staff requesting decisions on routine or urgent problems. It also permits the auditee to make it known that he does not wish to be disturbed during the course of the audit unless absolutely necessary.

3. Never plan a late afternoon finish if there is a major local event occurring.

It is sometimes unavoidable that in order to complete auditing in a particular are, the audit team's work extends slightly beyond the auditee's normal working hours and, hence, the auditee's personnel go home later than usual. If some special event like an important sports event, a parent/ teacher meeting, a carnival or a parade, makes it particularly likely that staff will want to get away from work on time, it is only reasonable and human to try to avoid a late finish that would cause inconvenience and possible undue annoyance to the auditee's personnel.

4. Allocate the work.

The lead auditor will have decided what can be done, given the actual manpower and time available, and will have listed the departments that are to be audited accordingly. It may be necessary to select departments and processes so as to get the best "feel" in the time available for the auditee's management systems and their efficacy. (See Chapter 5). If auditing a manufacturer the lead auditor may decide to have one team audit all the activities in the works while another team audits the offices (the software, namely). This sort of hardware/software split is shown in the example of an audit programme given in Figure 9.4. If auditing a service organization, the lead auditor may decide on a foreground/ background split - see Part 2 Chapter 2.

Step 8. Distribute the programme to the auditee and to the audit team

1. Prepare at least two copies of the checklist (audit guidance tool) and programme for the auditee, in the case of an external audit. For an internal audit, a single copy should suffice.

2. Attach a copy of the checklist (audit guidance tool) to each copy of the programme.

3. Prepare one copy of the programme and checklist (audit guidance tool) for each member of the audit team, that is, one copy for each of the auditors and one for each of the observers who may be participating.

When forwarding the programme to the auditee, the lead auditor should adhere to the following:

♦ Always use the official, formal channels (see earlier section on notifying the auditee).
♦ Try to ensure that the programme will arrive at the auditee's facilities at least two weeks in advance of the audit.

This gives the auditee's people a chance to assimilate the programme to contact the auditor if they foresee difficulties. Make some allowance for postal delays where the auditee is located overseas. (This is not such a problem if fax communication is possible, as is likely to be the case nowadays, or if E. mail contact is possible). While compiling the programme, the lead auditor should have in mind a target deadline for forwarding the programme to the auditee.

3. Never forward untidy or illegible documents.

Scruffy documents create a bad impression and can make it difficult for the auditee to understand fully what the audit team wants. The results may be delays or difficulties during the audit. (See also Chapter 7 " *Hard copy or electronic medium?*")

4. State which of the auditee's key personnel should attend the exit interview.

It is desirable that the auditee's senior managers should be forewarned that their attendance at the exit interview would be appreciated. The more senior a person is in a company, the more valuable his or her time may be and the more important it is to forewarn that person.

In the case of an external audit, the auditee's senior management is generally interested in learning of any problems that the customer has encountered and, therefore, makes every effort to attend the exit interview. There is something seriously wrong with a company if its senior management is not interested in its customer's impressions of its management systems, facilities and products or in his assessment of whether the contract conditions are being met or not.

At the beginning of one audit, the auditee's quality department manager informed the audit team that the company's vice-president would not be available to attend the exit interview because he was away attending a meeting in another city for the entire week. Later that morning, while the team were busy auditing in a department, a secretary came to the department's manager to give him a message that the vice-president wanted to see him immediately in his office. The lead auditor turned to the department manager and said *"While you're with him, would you please remind him that the exit interview is on Friday and that we will be pleased to see him there?"* The escort's face wore an expression of acute embarrassment. The moral of the story is that if you are going out of town, make sure everybody knows that you are out of town, and then remember to be out of town!

Step 9. Hold briefing sessions

The importance of holding a briefing session depends upon many factors, among them company policy, the audit team member's experience and abilities , the scope of the contract/project/work being done by the auditee, auditee history, the extent and complexity of the audit, personal relations with the auditee, participation of third parties (consortium partners performing joint audits, inspection agencies, customers, other observers) and the geographic dispersion of the audit team members. Sometimes the relationships between customer and supplier or - in the case of an internal audit - between the auditor's department and the auditee's department are such that it is simple common sense to forewarn the members of the audit team of potential friction. This must not be taken to mean that they should turn a blind eye to any deficiencies, merely that they should be alert to possibly sensitive areas and adjust their conduct accordingly.

Prior to one particular audit, it was necessary to inform the audit team that another contract with the supplier concerned had reached the stage at which the companies' attorneys were exchanging letters. Although the dispute had not spread to the contract with which the audit was concerned, the team was advised that any discussion of the contentious contract might be prejudicial both to audit execution and to the company and should therefore be avoided.

233

Sometimes, when a customer, a regulatory body or an inspection agency is participating as an observer, its is advisable to hold a briefing session so that everybody understands exactly what their duties are in the execution of the audit. This will show the observers that the auditor's company takes its audits seriously.

When using specialists, one must make sure that they are aware of the need to keep their feet on the ground. They must not let matters of idle curiosity allow them to lose touch with the real needs of the audit and its objectives.

If not all the team are able to attend the briefing (perhaps because of geographic dispersion), those unable to attend should be informed of what happened during the session. (Sometimes the briefing session can be performed with a conference telephone and speaker 'phone enabling those located elsewhere to listen in and to ask their questions. Another alternative is to make use of video conferencing, if such facilities are available.) It may be possible for the audit team to meet for a briefing session during the evening before the audit, once they have all arrived.

Special attention has to be paid to the "new auditor", as described later in this chapter.

Step 10. Make any last minute changes necessary

Occasionally the audit programme may need to be altered in the light of input received from the auditee, from the customer, from work/contract/project progress or from the briefing session. Any substantial changes must, of course, be communicated to all concerned, namely, the auditee, the audit team and the departments/processes affected within the auditor's company. It may be necessary to indicate the changes at the entry meeting (see Chapter 10). In more serious cases, the audit may have to be postponed but this course should only be adopted if no other alternative presents itself.

Work out what to take

No job can be performed properly without the right tools: an audit is no exception. The following items are typical of the things that it is useful to have on hand for the performance of the audit.

1. Contract(s), specifications and standards. If the contract is very bulky, a photocopy of the relevant pages will suffice. The specifications or

standards should always be of a convenient size to tuck into a briefcase. An increasing number of these types of information are retained in electronic form and can be copied onto floppy disks for downloading into a computer during the audit if reference to them is needed.

2. The audit programme and checklist (guidance tool): it is surprising how many auditors forget these things. These may already contain certain mark-ups, such as quality manual references and other memoranda, that the auditor will want during the audit.

3. A selection of information identities that are applicable for the product, service and processes concerned as well as a note of their edition status.

4. The copy of the manuals, procedures and work instructions etc. that were reviewed as part of the audit preparation. It cannot be assumed that the revisions reviewed are in fact those that are being implemented.

5. Personal checklists and *vade mecum*. Many auditors find it useful to take along a notebook in which to jot down abbreviated details of findings and experiences during an audit.

6. Entry interview and exit interview attendance forms. This is rather gilding the lily but I make a point of taking a blank form for each meeting to serve as a reminder that an attendance list should be generated.

7. Corrective action request blank forms. If corrective actions should be required as a result of the audit findings, they will have to be written up and presented at the exit interview. A supply of blank forms is therefore necessary.

8. A tape recorder and blank tapes. A tape recording of the exit interview is a useful way of informing those who could not attend of what was said. It also helps the auditor to check the actual phrases used at the exit interview which can save time when compiling the audit report and prevent arguments about who said what in sensitive situations. A small pocket recorder is the easiest machine to use for this purpose.

9. A notebook computer. This type of machine is especially valuable nowadays for storing volumes of information that would in days gone by be carried in hard copy form. It can be used to quickly compile the checklists (during the audit preparation phase), the audit report, to transmit the results to one's home office by means of a modem, to flow chart the auditee's management systems during the audit, perform statistical

analysis of data obtained and for a host of other purposes. They are, in my opinion, indispensable devices which I only wish had been available in years gone by to assist audit performance and communications.

10. Several spare floppy disks. These are useful for storing any of the auditee's data/information needed for future reference and obtained from the auditee's computer systems. They are also useful for providing the auditee with copies of the audit report, flow charts, audit tools etc. created during the audit.

See also Chapter 11, *"The well equipped modern auditor"*.

Preparing a new auditor

There is always a first audit for every auditor. It can be a nerve-wracking affair because the auditor is not certain of his duties or what to look for. The lead auditor can prepare his new colleague in the following ways.

♦ Give the auditor a departmental checklist (see Chapter 7) and ask him to mark in the clause numbers of the codes, standards or regulations concerned against each question. Alternatively, give him a criteria checklist and ask him to mark in the departments involved.

♦ Ask him to review the auditee's operations manual(s) and other information describing the management systems against the checklist to suggest areas requiring particular attention.

♦ Ask him to mark up his checklist against those manuals and other information describing the management systems, showing their identities and paragraph numbers, exhibit numbers and other references to them.

♦ Review his marked-up checklist and explain any errors before getting to the auditee's premises.

The fourth point tells the lead auditor whether the new recruit understands the audit's aims, is aware of the contract/project/process requirements and can interpret whatever standards, codes and regulations apply to the auditee's work. Thus, the lead auditor can decide whether or not the new auditor will need special guidance during the audit. The review must be done before reaching the auditee's premises so as to spare the auditor the embarrassment of exposing any misconceptions publicly. This precaution will also protect the entire audit team from losing face with the auditee, as they may if the auditee feels that the team is composed of people who do not know what they are doing.

10. Entry interview

Speak thy purpose out;
I love not mystery or doubt.

Scott.

Upon arrival at the auditee's premises, a meeting between the auditee and the audit team takes place. This meeting is sometimes called the entry interview

	Auditor Organization	Auditee Organization	
		Internal audit	*Extrinsic audit (performed by customer)*
Must	All auditors who will audit that location, Lead auditor/ team leader, Observers for that location	Manager of area to be audited and/ or area supervisor	Quality manager, Customer account manager Contract specialist, Contract administrator/ sales person/ customer interface representative
Optional	Specialist(s)		Managing director/ CEO/ Product V.P., Technical manager, Production manager, Sales manager

Figure 10.1 Entry interview attendees

237

Lead auditor/ team leader	Auditee
	1. Welcome audit team and introduce personnel (more applicable for an external audit).
2. Distribute attendance list. Introduce audit team. Explain each individual's function in the audit and contract/ project/ process activities of interest for the audit concerned.	
3. State the audit objective, the basis for requiring the audit and confirm the intended audit programme. Request auditee confirms current actual status of the contract/ project/ process work activities.	
	4. Explain current actual status of contract/ project/ process work activities.
5. Request auditee confirms the current actual status (i.e. edition level) of information submitted to audit team for preparation purposes (see Chapter 9).	State/ confirm current actual status of that information.
If current edition levels differ from those used during preparation, ascertain reasons for and nature of changes.	Briefly explain reasons for and nature of changes (if requested).
Decide impact on audit matters planned to be raised. (Consult the checklist or audit guidance tool for this purpose.)	

Figure 10.2 Proceedings for entry interview

Lead auditor/ team leader	Auditee
6. Ask for a knowledgeable escort for each team (more applicable for external audits).	
7. Ask for a meeting room to be reserved for the team's use, if necessary (more applicable for external audits).	
8. Confirm working hours, shift changeover times, staff refreshment times. Request a quick lunch, please, (more applicable for external audits).	
9. Fix a time for each day's summary meeting with the auditee.	
10. State the tentative time for the exit interview and which members of the auditee's management should attend, if possible (see Figure 19.2).	
Invite auditee's questions (and answer all that arise).	
	11. Question time
12. Ensure all present have signed attendance list.	

Figure 10.2 (Cont.)

Attendees

Figure 10.1 shows the levels and types of personnel who, ideally speaking, should attend the entry interview. In the case of an audit that is proceeding simultaneously at two locations, the lead auditor can only be available at one of them so the sub-team leader conducts the entry interview at the other. Similarly, the auditee will be unable to have certain of the personnel indicated on the table present at both locations. In this situation, the auditee usually makes arrangements for appropriate personnel to be present at each location. In the case of an external audit, for example, the quality manager (or *"management representative"*, as is sometimes referred to in ISO 9000 and other similar programmes) may be present at the location where the lead auditor is conducting an entry interview whilst his senior management systems representative is in attendance at the second location. Some suppliers require that the senior management be present at the entry interview to meet an extrinsic audit team, to give it a warm welcome and assimilate what will be happening during the audit. It should also be noted that certain attendees in my chart are purely optional. Their attendance will depend on the needs of the audit, company policy or perhaps simply on them happening (or not happening) to be at the auditee's premises at the time of the entry interview.

Proceedings for entry interview

Figure 10.2 shows the typical sequence of proceedings for an entry interview.

Explaining the role of observers

During the proceedings, the lead auditor or team leader must make clear to the auditee that an observer is an observer, a guest rather than a participant as of right (unless the contract or regulations specifically states otherwise). This is particularly important when the auditor's customer is attending as observer. The auditee then knows that all comments and questions coming from the observers will be directed to him through the audit team. Observers should act in the manner expected of guests and the audit team should not be afraid to remind an observer of his role. However, if the customer is performing an extrinsic audit as of right, then the customer is running the audit and is responsible for taking such actions as are necessary to obtain the information required (provided that those actions are within the contractual limits).

> At one external audit, the audit team's customer was to be represented by an inspector who, it had been agreed, would act as an observer. That inspector's superior (the quality assurance manager) arrived and stated that he would also be an observer during the audit. Relationships between the audit team's customer and the supplier being audited were extremely strained because of that quality assurance manager, who had previously caused many unnecessary problems for both the audit team's company and for the supplier by acting beyond the limits of the contract. Knowing that the individual's intent was to cause trouble, the lead auditor immediately refused to have him as a participant during the audit. When the quality assurance manager refused to leave, the lead auditor stated that unless he did so, the audit would be postponed and no observers from the customer's organization would be allowed. The gentleman concerned was finally removed from the premises. The audit then proceeded smoothly and satisfactorily. The lead auditor knew the prime contract conditions, was acting within his company's rights and received the full support of the supplier and his own management.

Allaying fears

If this is the first time a company has audited a particular auditee, the latter possibly being unfamiliar with the mode of procedure, it is wise to explain the methods and the purpose of the audit exactly in order to put people's minds at ease. It may be that the only meaning of the word *"audit"* previously encountered by the auditee is in the context of the financial auditing of books.

> One company had been extremely unenthusiastic about providing access for audits to be performed by their customer and had put forward reasons for postponing the audit several times. An ultimatum was finally issued to the effect that the audit must take place by a certain date and, reluctantly, the company was forced to agree. When they arrived at the auditee's premises, the audit team were told that the managing director would be completely

241

unavailable for the week because he had suddenly been taken ill: arrayed in front of the audit team were nearly thirty individuals from varying levels of management of the company. Also present was the financial director. It very quickly became apparent that the auditee believed the audit to be some kind of meeting leading up to an apocalypse for the company's management. When the lead auditor explained the purpose of the audit, the expressions of relief visible on everybody's faces were most memorable. The next day, the managing director appeared to have made a miraculous recovery from his illness and was back at work.

It must be remembered that an audit can make some people so nervous that they go sick rather than face it. This not necessarily indicates that they have something to hide - they may simply be so concerned about getting things right that they "worry themselves to death" in case the audit should reveal some minor deficiencies which would reflect adversely upon themselves. The entry interview can do much to assuage these feelings and fears.

Meeting rooms

Item 7 of Figure 10.2 advises the audit team to request a meeting room, if necessary, for its use during the audit. Although some teams enjoy having such facilities at their disposal, it is not my practice to require a meeting room. Team meetings are best held during the evenings, off-site: holding team meetings during the day cuts into the time budget, which is always of a tight nature. While the audit team is at the auditee's premises it is essential to spend as much time as possible with the auditee's staff, gathering objective evidence by attending at the actual work processes as they are performed. Audit team meetings during the day do not assist this form of fact gathering.

Attendance list

At the entry interview, especially one held before an external audit, the audit team must always initiate an attendance list, which all present should be requested to sign. If, during an extrinsic audit, the audit team does not initiate an attendance list, the auditee should do so. The entry interview is an official, formal meeting that could have contractual implications should points of contention later arise as a result of the audit. It is therefore

242

advisable to record exactly who was present to represent the various parties involved.

Auditee speakers

The entry interview is the first occasion for the audit team to encounter the auditee: much useful information can be gleaned from it. Note should be taken of who speaks on behalf of the auditee since this may well reflect the real power structure within the auditee's company or department. This informal organization (which may be miles away from the formal structure laid down in the organization chart) may be of crucial importance in determining what actually gets done within the company: anything that helps to indicate that company mode of operation will be very valuable to the audit team. The informal methods of working may or may not be efficacious for the contract/ project/ work being undertaken. The audit team will have to try to determine exactly what really happens and decide whether or not this is satisfactory. Quite frequently, it is at this stage that the first indications emerge of lack of top management commitment to quality. Seemingly innocent remarks, of the type listed in Chapter 12 *"Indicators of lack of top support"*, can provide the clues.

The entry interview may also produce other valuable impressions - who seems to know what, how the various departments interact and so on. The conduct of the auditee's representatives can provide hints as to what tactics the audit team should adopt when dealing with particular individuals or departments. It is not uncommon for the entry interview to be a platform at which some people want to *"make it clear from the start that this audit team will see what I say they'll see"*.

The audit team (and especially the lead auditor) must make it clear from the outset that they have a job to do. This can be achieved quite politely although the team must be prepared to be firm if necessary. Provided they act within the limitations of the contract, the audit team should have no problems in the case of an external audit. For internal audits, the firm's auditing policy and the audit objectives state the limitations of the audit team's authority.

Escorts

The lead auditor must tell the auditee who, ideally, should act as
an escort (see Figure 10.2 item 6). It is unwise to become
overloaded with too many escorts (one really is enough for each
sub-team). The escort should be knowledgeable about the
management systems operating within the various areas to be
audited. He should also have sufficient status to ensure that the
auditee's personnel give the maximum co-operation while the
audit is going on.

> During one audit, it was decided that the quality assurance
> manager and quality assurance engineer would
> accompany the audit team. At some point, it was noted
> that the audit ensemble had swelled to 12 people: the
> team leader, an auditor and an observer, two escorts, the
> contract manager (who had caught up with the audit *"to
> see how things were going"*), the supervisor of the
> particular department being audited, one operator who
> was actually being audited, the patrol inspector at that
> particular location, the shop labourer (who had stopped
> sweeping to listen and try to help with what was going
> on), and two other bodies who had simply appeared from
> somewhere. The audit had reached a contentious point,
> with everybody trying to help by explaining to everybody
> else what should and should not happen as well as what
> had probably occurred. Absolute pandemonium ensued.
> Order was restored when the lead auditor asked the escorts
> to request that everybody not directly concerned leave.

The escort does not answer the auditors' questions, that is for the
auditee's staff member responsible for the function actually being
audited. The escort will:

1. Ensure the audit team get to the processes they want to
    see, when they want them.
2. Ensure the audit team receives full cooperation from the
    auditee's staff.
3. Assist with arranging changes to the audit programme as
    and when they occur.
4. Use the copy of the auditor's checklist (or other
    guidance tool), sent prior to the audit by the auditors
    (see Chapter 9), to record details of the objective
    evidence seen by the auditors.

5.   Act as host for the audit team to ensure the smooth running of the audit.
6.   Not answer any of the questions posed by the auditor to auditee staff members.
7.   Be able to explain to auditee staff and management, after the audit has been completed, why the audit results took the nature they did, the basis for any corrective action requests received, and potential improvements to systems and practices discovered during the audit.

Duration

Unless there are some particularly contentious points that must be clarified during the entry interview, half an hour or thereabouts should be quite adequate to cover the proceedings described in Fig. 10.2.

11. Audit methods

Knowledge advances by steps, and not by leaps.

Macaulay

With increasing experience, each auditor will develop his or her own method of performing an audit. A common trait in inexperienced auditors is the absence of a structured approach to auditing individual tasks and hence the entire auditee activities: they appear to believe that if they keep asking questions as inspiration occurs, then, when they cannot think up any more, everything must have been covered.

STEP 1	Analyze auditee's organization
STEP 2	Analyze auditee's management systems
STEP 3	Assess auditee's compliance with organization and management systems
STEP 4	Decide efficacy of management systems and organization
STEP 5	Decide if management systems/ organization could be improved or simplified
STEP 6	Assess auditee's performance monitoring methods
STEP 7	Decide if there are improvement opportunities

Figure 11.1 Seven step audit method

The vain hope that, by their running around at random, the job will get done, is busy-ness as opposed to business and does not provide any degree of assurance that all necessary matters have been treated.

THE AUDITOR MUST DEVELOP A SYSTEMATIC WAY OF WORKING.

The following method is suggested since it has provided me with pleasing results over the years. Figure 11.1 lists seven distinct and sequential steps which constitute a gradually increasing depth of investigation. These seven steps are applied at each level in the auditee's operation, that is, across the entire company, across complete divisions and departments as well as in individual task units. Objective evidence to be collected is discussed in Chapter 12 *"Information Collection"*.

STEP 1: Analyze the auditee's organization.

The starting point must always be to investigate the auditee's organization plans. Organization planning is the first stepping stone on the path which leads to a successful enterprise: without this foundation, business problems and chaos will result. The auditor has to assess whether or not the organization has been properly conceived in relation to the basic needs of the product and the business. Figure 11.2 shows those matters which the auditor must bear in mind. The very first is the vital question *"What is the product?"* The auditor must

NEVER LOSE SIGHT OF THE PRODUCT.

It is the needs of the product, the importance of the product (classification) and strategic decisions that will prescribe the organizational needs of the auditee. The type of objective evidence to be sought is listed. In assessing the auditee's organizational proposals, the auditor will review the information indicated in Fig. 11.2, keeping in mind the principle concerns shown. The good auditor will never read his own opinion into what a statute, regulation or standard says. Thus, when considering the auditee's organizational plans for compliance with such documents, one must always work to the letter and retain an open mind. See Chapter 3. for a discussion of organizational matters.

STEP 2: Analyze the auditee's management systems.

Once the status of the auditee's organizational plans has been established, the auditor then examines the auditee's management systems. Figure 11.2 lists the objective evidence that the auditor will peruse to determine whether or not the auditee's proposals for those systems are satisfactory. The auditor will continue to be aware of the matters raised in Step 1 as well as of the precise words of the statutes/regulations/codes or standards which apply. The existence of a reliable planned audit trail, between the various task elements and interfacing work activities, traceable back to the

	Major questions to keep in mind	Typical objective evidence to assess
STEP 1	What is the product/ service? What is its importance/ classification and it quality requirements? What do the applicable codes/ standards and regulations SAY?	Organization charts. Job descriptions. Job specifications. (See Chapter 3.)
STEP 2	As per Step 1, plus the need for an audit trail back to basic product/service requirements.. Is the system designed to ensure processes can be completed completely, correctly, economically and on time?	Operational manuals. Flow charts. Procedures and work instructions. Proforma used. Computerized "help" facilities. (See Chapter 6.)
STEP 3	Is the alleged audit trail followed?	State of the task elements at each process. (See Chapter 4.)
STEP 4	As for Step 3. Are there any problems present or incipient problems? Can processes be (are they being) completed completely, correctly, economically and on time?	As for Step 3. Results noted in the checklist (or other audit guidance tool - see Chapter 8).
STEP 5	Do the systems, organizational arrangements waste time or resources? What is the product's importance/ classification?	As for Step 4. Auditor's experience.
STEP 6	What are the avoidable costs that would be incurred by delivering deficient products/ services?	Customer requirements analysis/ market research/ customer feedback and product expectations. Benchmark analyses. Tally charts; process control charts; measles charts; non-conformity reports; corrective action requests; quality control reports; minutes; energy consumption reports; schedules; Pareto charts and histograms etc.
STEP 7	As for Step 6.	As for Step 6. Auditor's experience

Figure 11.2 The seven step method showing matters of concern and typical objective evidence to be sought

customer, regulatory body or other pertinent requirements must be verified. (See also Chapter 6.)

The examination of the auditee's organization and system proposals should have been completed as part of the preparation of the audit particularly as those proposals are generally contained in documentation. Upon arrival at site, to maximize time usage, the auditor will merely investigate those matters revealed by the preparation to require clarification.

Depending on the audit's objective, the auditor may also wish to investigate the systems for estimating, allocating and monitoring resources and time to each task (process). As has been stated in Chapter 1, lack of time and lack of resources are real causes of business problem. Time and resource management are inseparable and essential components of quality management: see also Chapters 7 and 18.

The auditor also need to determine the business performance of the management systems. This is an important aspect of value-added auditing and is discussed more fully in Part 2 Chapter 2 in the section *"Auditing the business performance of systems"*.

STEP 3: Assess auditee's compliance with organization and management systems.

Having assessed the organization and system, the next step is to investigate the extent of compliance with them. Compliance audits are only possible once work has actually started except when the auditee, either because of the sensitivity of the product or for staff training purposes, decides to have a dummy run or to produce a trial version of the final intended product or service. In some industries and for some products, this may be neither possible nor practical. By going through the task elements at each particular workplace systematically, the auditor will examine objective evidence furnished as a result of the various tasks being performed. While checking compliance, the auditor must follow the audit trail already assessed in STEP 2, above.

STEP 4: Decide efficacy of management systems and organization.

The objective evidence obtained in step 3 enables the auditor to decide whether or not the organizational arrangements, system and practices are effective. Figure 11.2 shows the principle matters to be kept in mind: these remain directly related to the product. The product requirements and the audit trail should not have been violated. Job responsibilities should be acted upon, not avoided or abrogated; authorities should be commensurate with assigned responsibilities. Evidence of either present or incipient problems must be noted.

Organizational plans and management systems can appear to be impressive on paper but the litmus test of their effectiveness is the product to emanate from their application and the extent of avoidable costs incurred.

STEP 5: Decide if management systems/ organization could be improved or simplified.

The possibility for improving or simplifying systems or processes must now be considered. Audits must be of a constructive nature and the auditor has a duty to be helpful at all times. It is all too easy to tear systems apart but offering constructive criticism for improvement requires true professional competence. The proficient auditor has a duty to help the auditee and to provide advice. Improvements or simplification[s] which would be unwise given the classification of the product must not be proposed. (It is worth repeating that the product comes first: never lose sight of the product.) The essential question is:

♦ On the basis of the objective evidence studied, do the implemented systems and organizational plans appear to waste time or resources?

Flow charts are of great assistance in answering that question. Specialists may be able to offer some advice concerning new techniques or equipment that are available to help reduce costs, save time and resources whilst maintaining or improving product quality.

It is very important to try to help the auditee at every opportunity. As stated in Chapter 1, the auditee is investing in the audit. Resentment and hostility towards management audits develop when auditees do not perceive much real benefit from their investment. Incompetent auditors tend to be nitpickers, destructive critics who thrive on confrontation. By offering advice and constructive help to the auditee, the auditor will help to reduce barriers of resistance substantially, creating a spirit of co-operation which is of benefit to both auditee and auditor alike. See also Chapter 14.

STEP 6: Assess auditee's performance monitoring methods and continuous improvement efforts.

The next step is to investigate the auditee's methods of monitoring his performance. The auditor will examine the data capture methods, the non-conformity and corrective action systems and an example of the information created by them. There are three key questions:

1. *What aspects of performance are being monitored by the auditee?*

Performance data do not need to be quantified in monetary terms: monetary equivalents, such as percentage yields, errors per document processed, tally counts, rework hours, downtime figures, grade to rework ratios, utility consumption data, quantities consumed, revisions per finalized document and the like will suffice. The essence is to ascertain whether or not the auditee and its management really are aware of the costs of each process they are responsible for. The absence of a performance monitoring system means those people are not managing the process effectively: the area is out of control. The performance data captured assists with identifying opportunities for improving efficiency, outgoing quality levels and reduction of avoidable costs. Without this data, opportunity is lost and ultimately the business is at risk or, in the case of the civil service, taxpayer's money is at risk. As Harold Geneen rightly states:

"the drudgery of the numbers will make you free....The numbers are there to reflect how well or how poorly your business is doing".[1]

Naturally, the quality cost systems should not cost more to operate than the potential benefits which can accrue. The auditor should not look for unreasonably complex and costly methods of capturing such data. The data might exist in tally charts, process control sheets, non-conformity report forms, corrective action requests, quality circle reports or minutes of meetings - whatever. Each of these provides feedback which identifies opportunity.

2. *What was the basis for selecting the performance aspects being monitored?*

Although it is important to capture data in order to ascertain the opportunities for improvement, it is even more essential to ensure the right data is captured in the first place. The data of prime concern must be that relating to the customers' needs and product/ service acceptance. The auditor must, therefore, verify what communication the auditee has had (and continues to have) with the customer[s] to find out what aspects and features of the product/ service the customer regards as important. These affect the manner in which the process should have been defined and designed so as to be responsive to customer needs, requirements and expectations. The performance monitoring methods and data must be consistent with these concerns. There may be other matters that deserve attention and performance monitoring, but, if one were to grade the data to be captured and process controls to be instigated, all else would be rated as secondary to that deriving from prime customer concerns. Failure to design the process, its quality controls and performance monitoring methods to serve those prime concerns renders the process out of control. It is a cardinal deficiency. It puts the business at risk.

3.   *What does the auditee do with the data?*

It makes little sense for the auditee to be accumulating data for the sake of it. The data must be put to productive use - it must become information. Information is the prerequisite for improvement. The auditor must ascertain:

♦   Is the data analyzed?
♦   How often is the data analyzed?
♦   What methods of analysis are used to improve the process and to improve the product?
♦   Do those methods get to the root cause(s) of the problem?
♦   What levels of improvement in product and in process is the auditee achieving?
♦   Over what period of time have these improvements been obtained?
♦   Are those levels validated?

The sum of those questions enables the auditor to conclude the existence or otherwise of a continuous improvement programme and its efficacy at the auditee's workplace. But the data might also enable the auditee to conclude the existence of a problem elsewhere in the system. The key matter, then, is what is done to improve the system's upstream processes (i.e. those processes within the system that are suppliers to the auditee). The auditor must determine:

♦   Is the data provided to the auditee's suppliers?
♦   How often is the data provided to them?

♦ Is the auditee actively involved in analyzing the data together with the auditee? (i.e. is there a team effort).

♦ What methods of analysis are used to improve the suppliers' processes and to improve their products?

♦ Do those methods get to the root cause(s) of the problems?

♦ What levels of improvement in product and in process is the supplier achieving?

♦ Over what period of time have these improvements been obtained?

♦ Are those levels validated by the auditee?

The sum of those questions enables the auditor to conclude the existence or otherwise of a continuous improvement programme and its efficacy at the auditee's suppliers' workplaces. Obviously, when these questions are addressed at each workplace (process/task) continuously throughout the audit, the auditor will see the depth, breadth and effectiveness of the company's/project's continuous improvement programme and policy. (Continuous improvement is also discussed in Part 2 Chapter 1.) Absence of a continuous improvement programme means the auditee is not effectively trying to reduce avoidable costs and improve the quality of product and service delivered to the customer. This, too, puts the business at risk in the end. (Avoidable costs and unavoidable costs are described and discussed in Part 2 Chapter 2 *"Value-added auditing".)

There is a multitude of problem solving techniques available for the auditee's consideration and use. They include, *inter alia*,: failure modes and effects analyses; fishbone diagrams and fault tree analyses; flowcharting; histograms; scatter diagrams; design of experiments; Weibull analyses; scatter plots; Pareto diagrams; process capability studies, for determining Cp and Cpk. Whereas many of these techniques used to involve repetitious, tedious to perform calculations and graphing, modern software application tools and low cost personal computers have removed much of the drudgery in using them. Nowadays, the auditee is able to obtain almost real time data analysis and information using some of the techniques just listed.

STEP 7: Decide if there are improvement opportunities.

Provided that there is a system for performance monitoring, the results of its operation should be reviewed to identify trends or potential opportunities for improvement. The competent auditor might be able to bring extra experience to bear, interpreting the auditee's data in a different way from that of the auditee, potentially giving rise to opportunity. Even if a formal system does not exist, the auditor should consider carefully the objective evidence of the auditee's management systems and level of accomplishments to try to identify areas that could constitute an opportunity for the saving of resources and time. Clearly, such improvement would need to improve quality or, at least, not compromise it. (See also Part 2 Chapter 2 *"Value-added auditing"*.)

Following the system

There are various paths that the auditor may take through the departments/processes involved in the management system, as the work passes through the various contract, project or product phases (see Figure 11.3). They relate to those activities within the auditee's primary system, as described in Chapter 6. Each of the following three methods has its advantages and disadvantages (see Figure 11.4).

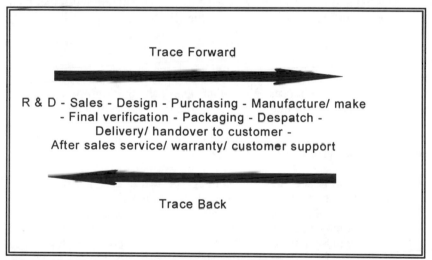

Trace Forward

R & D - Sales - Design - Purchasing - Manufacture/ make - Final verification - Packaging - Despatch - Delivery/ handover to customer - After sales service/ warranty/ customer support

Trace Back

Figure 11.3 Trace forward and trace back methods of auditing for following the management systems

Trace forward

In the trace forward method, for a full audit, the auditor starts auditing within research and development, sales or product concept creation area, selects the product or order(s) of interest and follows it (or them) through the various departments and work areas associated with the phases of the product/ project/ contract through top the despatch/ shipping department or other point at which the product or service is handed over to the customer. In the service industry, an example might be in auditing an hotel's management systems by following the path encountered by a guest from reservations, porterage and reception through to check-out and departure. (See Chapter 6, *"Looking at management systems"*.)

Trace back

This method works in the opposite direction to the trace forward method. For a full audit, the auditor retraces the steps involved in completing the chosen contract right back to the sales department. Trace back is particularly useful when auditing services: in the case of a fast food store, for example, the auditor might start at the point of consumption, work back through point of sale, food preparation and back towards, say, receipt of foodstuffs in the store. Thus the delivered product and service results are seen first and their "genealogy" established: any illegitimates can then be readily identified and banished from the family!

Random department

Here, the auditor visits all the departments or units that are of interest in whatever order he chooses. With this approach, the auditor has to be especially careful not to miss a unit or department that is of interest.

It is important to remember two points when a particular contract is selected for the performance of a *full* audit.

♦   In order to see the whole contract, project or product life cycle, it is necessary to select one that is *completed*. In the case of an external audit, this is probably *not* the auditor's contract and the audit may run into proprietary information problems or national Official Secrets Act limitations which are imposed on the auditee and hence on the auditor. In the case of an internal audit, the selection of a completed contract, due for hand-over to the customer, may also present difficulties: it may be difficult, because of financial considerations or internal politics, to persuade management to institute corrective action at such a late stage, even if deficiencies have been discovered which affect the quality of the product. This is a matter of top management support and attitude which the auditor may be unable to alter.

	Advantages	*Disadvantages*
Trace forward	Shows logical system through the company/ project/ process activities.	Logical flow broken if people unavailable for short period.
	Easy for training.	Not so flexible
	Aids pre-planning of arrival times at particular processes/ departments.	Not practical for partial audits, since trace back is also required.
	Deficiencies at front end found more quickly (these can have greater cost impact).	Effects of system problems not so apparent during compliance audits, since effects .on customers not immediately seen.
		Root cause discovery not so easy.
Trace back	Can start in any department and hence is suitable for partial audits.	Logical flow broken if people unavailable for short period.
	Easy for training.	Not so flexible.
	Aids pre-planning of arrival times at particular processes/ departments.	Sometimes difficult to use for systems audits depth prior to work commencing.
	Results (objective evidence) of department's/ processes work seen prior to arrival. (Provides knowledge of customer's actual experience of department's/ processes quality achievements). Thus,	Front-end software/customer requirements/ product or project definition not seen until the end of the audit; time shortage for auditing front-end processes needs to be avoided.
	Makes discovery of root cause easier because it is generally located in direction the auditor is heading.	Front-end might not be seen at all during partial audits.
Random sequence	Very flexible; minimizes disruption.	Requires experienced auditor.
	Audit programme not upset if people are unavailable.	Can mean avid note taking.
	Gives broad picture fairly quickly.	System breakdowns/ organizational problems can be missed/ not be readily apparent.
	Good for pre-award surveys.	
	Good for partial audits.	Root cause discovery is difficult.

Figure 11.4 Audit methods: Advantages and disadvantages

♦ When carrying out a full audit, the auditor tends to get to know the particular product/project/ contract intimately and the explanations given by the auditee acquire unique nuances for him. This "feel" for the auditee's work can speed up the proceedings and reduce the amount of note taking required.

In light of the foregoing, it is, therefore, quite common for a phased audit to be planned in order to monitor the progress of a particular contract/ project/ product life cycle.

Obtaining objective evidence

There are three principle methods of obtaining objective evidence. They are:

♦ Examination of documents, data, reports, computer print-outs and screen displays, items and their details, equipment and their details as described in Chapter 12 *"Information collection"*.

♦ Observation of performance. The auditor requests the auditee to demonstrate how the work is performed by processing an actual example at his workplace.

♦ Re-performance of the task. This can be useful in the case of, say, design calculations. A specialist member of the audit team can quickly re-check calculations to see if the same or similar results are obtained.

While auditing a mechanical equipment design, I decided to re-check certain stress analyses quickly since my original specialism is mechanical engineering design. A number of errors which could have affected safety of the components concerned were found. These were corrected. However, the real problem was that since the calculations bore evidence of review and approval, I could not have much confidence in the efficacy of the review and approval work. This led to a whole series of different questions being raised, but with the auditee's manager, not with the auditee who had performed the original calculations.

Similarly, while auditing a hygiene laboratory at a food factory, I asked a food technologist on my audit team to re-check some culture plates, to compare his results with the laboratory's. That person possessed that area of expertise : I did not.

An approval signature on a document provides no guarantee that the work was properly checked. In order to gain confidence that the signatory's work has value, a spot check is necessary.

Spot checks

The auditor must have spot checks carried out on items that have allegedly been inspected, tested, reviewed, checked or otherwise verified. It is essential that he should select the sample of objective evidence to be spot checked - this makes it impossible for the auditee to "fix" the spot checks in advance by choosing specially prepared examples. (See *"The fixed ballot"*, Chapter 15.)

Information must be spot checked for availability and compliance with requirements of the management systems, particularly when a pre-award survey is being performed (subject to the limitations discussed in Chapter 2.).

Sample sizes and sampling plans

The auditor must remember that for compliance audits, whatever is selected is probably only a sample of all the items/information/equipment etc. that are available. Hence, even at the best of times, the auditor is only spot checking. The auditor may wish to have some level of confidence of unearthing any significant business problem by following a statistical sampling plan (such as Mil-Std-105E [2]), when choosing which examples to check. To follow such a plan may involve checking a large number of items or documents and, in my experience, a relatively small number of spot checks is sufficient to reveal a major problem, such as a management system deficiency.

The auditor must try to assess the true magnitude of any problem he encounters and avoid making an issue out of trivial deficiencies, isolated mistakes and human errors. Depending on the audit objectives and the criticality of the decisions that will be taken as a result of its completion, it may be reasonable to select, say, six or ten of as a particular type of objective evidence and to leave the checking there, provided that absolutely no defects are found within the sample. If, however, the sample shows up one or more deficiencies, then the auditor must either spot check further examples or ask the auditee to purge the items/documents/equipment types to discover the true extent of the problem. The justification for this practice is as follows:

◆ If out of the sample, no deficiencies are found, then there is as a system present, working, and known to the personal concerned.

◆ If one deficiency is found, then the system, rather than simply not being implemented, may be in as a period of gestation (having been just introduced) or may need to be further instilled into the personnel affected.

◆ If further spot checking reveals that the deficient information/ item/ equipment from the first sample is the only one, then the problem is more likely to be human error (that is an isolated occurrence). (See Chapter 17 for further discussion.)

The need for re-inspection or re-testing depends on the product, project or contract status and on whether a hold point has been integrated with the audit. Combining the audit with as a hold point can have tremendous value (as discussed in Chapter 8). The acid test of the management systems is that the product or service is fit for purpose and complies with the contractual and legal requirements involved as well as customer expectations. This means that the product is both what the customer wants and what society, through legislation, requires it to be. The hold point results in a decision that the product is acceptable or unacceptable in its present from. The decision of unacceptability in the product's present form does not necessarily mean it is scrap - it may be possible to render it acceptable by further investigation, suitable efficacious reworking or repairing. Whatever happens to the product, though, the auditor will be concerned with ascertaining why unacceptable results were obtained by the auditee. This will lead to an investigation of root cause, discussed in Chapter 17.

Look and see

Upon entering an office, warehouse, factory, construction site or other auditee place of work it is my practice to stop and:

◆ Look up.
◆ Look down.
◆ Look around.

This enables me to assess the following: the size and dimensions of the work place; materials of construction; layout of work operations and processes as well as their proximity to each other; lighting levels; noise levels; vibrations; the temperature levels; the humidity levels; odours, smells and airborne matter; whether people seem happy, communicative with each other or uneasy; general housekeeping disciplines; style of furnishings, their condition and state of property maintenance; safety hazards.

These types of details offer an indication of pride in the workplace (and hence in the work being done), general treatment of staff, the working "atmosphere", environmental nuisances and controls, overhead and underfoot and environmental health or safety risks, the possibility of a shortage of funds to invest in the workplace, materials handling and process paths. They relate to the task elements (see Chapter 4) and to the six real causes of business problems (see Chapter 18).

Many auditees "engineer in" their business problems by virtue of the way they build their facilities, lay out the processes within them. See also Part 2 Chapter 2.

Two-level auditing and pattern recognition

It is easy to become so engrossed with as a particular auditee's processes that one fails to see the overall implications of what is being seen. The auditor must work simultaneously on two levels:

♦ At the level of the particular process being investigated/ assessed.
♦ Looking down at the audit process to see the implications of what is being found, said and the reason for asking the questions put to the auditee.

The second level, of looking down as if an observer of the audit process itself, helps the auditor to form an overall picture of the auditee's complete operation and its management. One looks for patterns in the findings being discovered. One also considers the impact of one process on the others within the system and on the system's efficacy as a whole. It is better to categorize findings according to common types rather than viewing each as a separate entity. This helps to see isolated errors and trivial issues for what they are as distinct from regarding them as definitive of the entire auditee situation. See also Chapter 17.

Cyber auditing

See Chapter 16

The well equipped modern auditor

As mentioned previously, recent years have witnessed a growing and improved amount of easy to use applications software. These software application programs should be considered as increasingly indispensable:

◆ Word processing and/ or desk top publishing.
◆ E. Mail.
◆ Spreadsheet.
◆ Database management.
◆ Flow chart.
◆ Virus protection.

The cyber auditor would also need the following software:

◆ Video conferencing.
◆ Data encryption.
◆ Computer linkage.
◆ Internet and web browser (maybe).

I consider a powerful laptop computer as essential nowadays as a portable tape recorder has been for years. Equipped with fast modem, CD Rom drive, capacious hard drive, floppy drive, colour screen, universal voltage power supply, spare battery and interface cables. Multimedia capability may be desirable according to the nature of auditing being undertaken and the auditee's business methods. A portable ink jet printer is useful too for printing a hard copy audit report, corrective action requests (if any are to be issued), and overhead view foils, if these will assist communication during the exit interviews for face-to-face audits. In some cases the printer is not needed as auditees have printing facilities the auditor can use.

If the foregoing might seem to be a formidable, bulky and weighty lot of hardware, the inconvenience of carrying it around is offset in many cases by the reduction of hard copy paper since a growing number of auditees are able to send the information requested during the audit preparation phase (see Chapter 9) on disk, CD Rom, via E. Mail, over the Internet etc.

> I recall the amount of paper I sometimes had to carry to audits. One audit in New Jersey entailed the review of some 150 kilograms of documents of which about 40% had to be taken to the auditee's site from my (then) office in Hampshire, England. The airline's excess baggage fees were considerable, and fortunately not to my account! Modern portable computers *et al* are most welcome.

12. Information collection

Now what I want is, Facts. Facts alone are wanted in life

Dickens.

Many auditors are unsure about what information to gather and how to collect and collate it. The two precepts below are guiding principles.

♦ Never trust your own memory: so much information has to be collected during an audit that it is doubtful whether even a chess grand master could carry it all in his head. Write down the information as the audit progresses.

♦ Do not clutter up your mind with trivia. Keep only the essential information in your head: store the detail in written form.

Use of the audit guidance tools

Whichever of these aids is used, be it checklist, flowchart or task element matrix, it should contain plenty of space for the auditor to note down the various types of objective evidence seen. Facts gathered during a management audit must be noted down. This has the following advantages:

♦ It keeps the notes and doodles together.
♦ It reduces the risk of losing the notes (jottings on the back of cigarette packets, bus tickets and odd scraps of paper do rather tend to get lost and are difficult to file at a later date).
♦ If the information is written in against the appropriate checklist question, it is there to refresh the mind later on.

The quantity of objective evidence to collect

Some auditors agonize over the quantity of objective evidence to be obtained i.e. the sample size. A statistical sampling plan is helpful when selecting, say, examples of documents for scrutiny (Mil-Std-105E [1] is often suitable): large samples needed to create the desired confidence level in the system, however, will incur considerable time expenditure which may not have allocated in the audit preparation. Sampling tables are only of real value during compliance audits. For systems audits, used to decide whether to commence an activity or not, there may not actually be any objective evidence of compliance available

What to record

If a matrix of the type shown in Figure 7.14 is used, then the type of information to be recorded becomes self evident for it relates to the task elements and their sub-elements (see Chapter 4), as indicated below.

1. The key person(s) interviewed.

The auditor will probably meet quite a number of auditee personnel and it may be hard to remember every name. Should corrective action be required in a particular area, it is a sensible move to record which representative of that area was present when particular problems were discussed and corrective action, perhaps, agreed. It is not necessary to take the name of absolutely everybody interviewed. Generally, that of the area supervisor, or perhaps just the escort, should suffice.

2. Information details.

This will include identities and editions, the place where that information was found along with a description of the information type (process specification, training records, purchase order, drawing, quality control report, process control chart etc.); similarly for computer program or data listings, details of disks, tapes, file, application program version, change date/ time and the like should be recorded as well as information concerning access to them at the workplace being audited.

The purpose of recording these details is to enable the auditor to verify at another location that the issuer and the recipient are using the same information.

3. Equipment details

This will include identification details taken so that the auditor can check on the performance of those areas responsible for serving the process currently being audited. The services can be such as calibration, preventive maintenance, cleaning, routine replacement/ change-out, process analysis. The quality of those services has to be directed at the needs of the process currently being audited. The auditor will check that the equipment is serviced, its condition is in accordance with process requirements. If the service records for calibration, preventive maintenance, cleaning etc. are retained within the auditee's process area where the affected equipment is used, the auditor need only make a special note of the equipment identity details if discrepancies arise (in which case the severity of the discrepancies should be recorded).

4. Item details.

Items might be identified by part number, heat number, batch number, contract number/name or such like. The identification may be on the item, on a document (possibly a bar code) accompanying the item, on the container that contains the item or on the shelf upon which the item is resting. Item condition (damage/ deterioration/ degradation) will be noted together with quantities of good and bad seen. This will help the auditor check that items received and specified are the same or otherwise. The efficacy of packing item protection will be seen and noted. The auditor will be able to check the known physical, chemical and biological characteristics of the items to determine their compatibility with the processes they will experience and the service requirements of the final product.

5. A selection of the information/equipment recipients as specified on the distribution lists.

It is not usually necessary to check all recipients, particularly in the case of a lengthy distribution list. If, for example, there is a total of five recipients, it may be sufficient to verify that, say, three of those five have received the correct edition of the information, or the equipment concerned.

6. Identification of personnel.

The identification may be the person's name, works/employee number, initials or a unique stamp issued to the that person. The auditor will verify that the stamps in the person's possession are the ones issued to him and that their condition is not such as will damage the items which are stamped (some metal stamps, for example, have sharp edges or are damaged in such a way as to create stress raising notches or electrolytic cells on the item).

The auditor must verify that the training and qualification records are traceable to the person concerned and, in the case of stamps, that the person has his own stamp, no-one else's.

At one manufacturer's premises one person had a stamp with the number 6 on it. When turned upside-down, the stamp could be mistaken for a 9. With a mischievous twinkle in his eye, the person whispered in the auditor's ear: *"If the job is good, it's a 6"*. The possibility of mistaken identity was quietly eliminated by withdrawing the 9 stamp.

In the case of people using computers, check that passwords are unique and maintained securely. Some programs automatically maintain a log of those people who have gained access to the program, also recording the time of access and whether any updates were changed, detailing the nature of the change if any has occurred. This permits ready traceability of work to an individual. Similar remarks apply to the use of magnetic pass cards for gaining access to secure areas or offices.

The auditor should verify the efficacy of security systems when people are required to sign for items/information/products/service etc. using a digitizing tablet. These tablets cause the signature to be captured in digital form and stored in electronic/ magnetic media. The signatures must not be used for anything other than the original purpose known to its owner. Using even the simplest of computer programs makes easy the unauthorized transfer of a signature to documents and records unbeknown to the signature's owner: to do so would be a dishonest and criminal practice the auditor must not tolerate.

7. The appropriate revision and paragraph number of references in the operations manual/procedure/instructions etc.

These details should in any case have been marked into the checklist as part of the off-site preparations for the audit. Differences between that which was available for audit preparation and that which is actually being implemented, are to be noted. If some aspect of an activity is found to be in a state of non-compliance with documented requirements, it is essential to accompany any request for corrective action on the auditee's part with a reference to the paragraph(s) concerned.

8. The condition of the environment.

The auditor should make a special note of any poor conditions, bad housekeeping and nuisance levels. These may not only cause damage or impair the quality of the product: they may also result in personnel fatigue, which leads to lack of concentration or poor performance, thus, affecting the job adversely. This is especially true in the case of people using word processors and computer terminals which require lengthy periods spent gazing at a visual display unit.

In recent years, the phenomenon known as the "sick building" has been recognized to cause poor quality work and excessive staff fatigue. The sick building phenomenon is common in modern open plan offices which rely upon air conditioning systems of doubtful effectiveness. Outbreaks of so-called Legionnaires disease have been found to originate from infected air conditioning systems.

9. Flow charts, system doodles and scribbles.

Often, during the course of the audit, in order to understand or explain the management system, the auditor or auditee may make a sketch or doodle to indicate how the system works, how information is routed, how particular problems are solved. These should not be thrown away: they are often very useful for reference at a later stage.

Mental notes

Information about many points not apparently directly related to management systems can prove relevant because of their effect on the work produced. All the points below may fall into this category.

1. The employee's workload.

When people have too much to do, they may become physically and mentally fatigued and there is a consequent risk that they will try to cut corners and fail to implement the system correctly. The result is poor output.

In some cases, overwork can lead to eyestrain - an obvious cause of substandard output. Most people need good vision to do their jobs.

> At one company, an inspector had the task of examining mass-produced printed circuit boards for visual defects. In the middle of the afternoon, the auditor noticed that after looking briefly at each circuit board, the inspector tended to rub his eyes for a moment. This prompted the auditor to question the true quality of the inspected work and to enquire whether the auditee regularly checked the eyesight of the inspectors. A re-examination of that day's boards revealed that inspection errors had increased throughout the day.

The employee's workload may also be such that there is the risk of folk rushing the job *"to get it out of the door"* or *"to keep up with schedule"*. This inevitably leads to quality problems and avoidable costs one day. An equally serious possibility is that an unsafe product is made or that unsafe practices emerge. (In the air transport industry, this problem is well recognized, a fact which explains the limitations on the number of hours that airline pilots can legally be allowed to work before relief. The trucking industry in some countries restricts the number of hours a driver can run the vehicle: installation of a tachograph sometimes being required, tampering with which is a criminal offence.) See Chapter 18 under *"Lack of time"*.

2. People's reactions, attitudes and the working atmosphere.

Do the work force seem involved in their work, keen to produce high quality products? Some individuals may feel little interest in their job, the management systems and quality matters in general. The cause may be lack of motivation, lack of discipline or lack of respect for quality itself.

Some people take the view that *"near enough will do"*. These people tend to make decisions that are beyond their competence, without resorting to the proper authority. This may result either in a product which becomes unsuitable for use at a later stage or in delays, caused by the need to rework. See Chapter 18, under the discussion *"Lack of discipline"*.

3. Do the employees seem to know their jobs and are they organized?

4. Does the place look orderly and is the housekeeping satisfactory?

Once on the spot, the auditor can often from a rapid judgement as to whether or not it would be desirable to take a thorough look at the housekeeping systems in operation at a particular location. There is an old Clydeside saying that one can *"judge a man by the way he wears his overalls"*. It frequently happens that if a place looks orderly, few deficiencies, if any, are found to be there. A disorderly work place where desks are piled high with dusty documents and littered with unwashed coffee mugs, where filing cabinets support kettles and teapots, where product samples lie around gathering dust and rust, where the cracked window pane is patched up with peeling drafting tape, heralds the sort of chaos that is, in my experience, often a sign that the people are not over-proud or over-conscientious about the quality of the work they produce or the performance of the business they are involved in.

The personal filing system, which only one person can understand, may well be found in this setting, with the inevitable result that information is frequently mislaid.

> This is becoming a particular problem accompanying the spread of desktop personal computers at the workplace. Floppy disks are unlabeled, scattered around and tossed about almost with abandon. The files stored on them often have no comprehensible structure, even for their owners and creators. Data gets lost and might have to be reproduced thereby incurring avoidable costs.

Disorder indicates a lack of organization and a lack of discipline, both of which are discussed further in Chapter 18.

5. Does the superior/ manager want to answer all the audit team's questions.

The auditor wants to interview the person who actually does the work: the person who *"owns the process"*. However, some supervisors and managers want to answer all the questions, either in the fear that their subordinates will commit an error which will reflect adversely on themselves or because they feel it is their right and responsibility to speak up since they know what is going on, (their belief that they know what is going on can often be an act of self-delusion). In this situation, the auditor must make it clear to the supervisor or manager that the "worker" should be the one to answer the questions, explaining that this is because the purpose of the audit is to see what is actually being done and to verify that the management systems and organizational plans are being implemented. He must make it clear that it is of benefit both to the auditor and to the auditee's management to allow the "worker" to give the answers.

> On one audit, a manager was insistent on providing answers to the audit team and persisted with interruptions despite being requested to allow his staff to speak. When the lead auditor asked the "worker" to operate the equipment involved in the process and demonstrate the way things were done, the manager stepped in to perform the demonstration. Within a matter of seconds it became apparent to all concerned he did not know how to do the job and, feeling self-humiliated and embarrassed, he slunk away to his office. The audit then proceeded as desired as the "worker", with an enigmatic smile on her face, performed the process to perfection.

6. Do the people interviewed really not speak English?

Some auditees try to play the language game (see Chapter 15). This type of attitude reflects a lack of concern for the organization and may indicate a fundamental attitude problem or dislike of quality programmes in general.

7. Does the auditee try to bluff his way out of a tight corner?

The auditor must make it clear that he is not fooled by bluff, indeed, that bluffing is likely to have an adverse effect on the audit report. An auditee who is honest enough to admit to uncertainty on some points, promising to find answers later, deserves full marks for co-operation and concern for the management systems and product involved. An honest attitude is likely to evince itself on the job: a major problem is the person who cannot own up to not knowing and being unwilling to find the information he or she needs. However, the auditor must bear the auditee's promise in mind and ask for the answer at a later stage of the audit. See also Chapter 15, *"Amnesia"*.

8. Do the people know the operations manual or associated procedure? Do they know where to find this type of information? Do the people know what is in the contract/ specifications/ codes/ other product requirements?

If employees have trouble locating relevant passages when they need to refer to the manual or other information, this may well be a sign that they look at it rarely, if ever. Where this happens, it is not uncommon to find that the person believes the information to contain and what it actually contains are totally different.

9. Do the employees act promptly when some deficiency or other problem comes to light?

Prompt attention is generally a sign of a genuine desire to please the customer and/or to mitigate the potential reaction of their own management. It can also herald a genuine pride in work. Failure to act promptly can indicate problems with motivation or with top management support for quality (or lack of it) being reflected in the work force attitudes. An old saying is *"the fish rots from the head"*: attitudes do precisely that.

10. The general condition of the equipment (lifting slings, machine tools, buildings, broken palates, stockyard, facilities and the like).

This is very similar to *4.* above. An auditor may, for example, find that a couple of items of equipment are in poor condition while similar equipment elsewhere is generally satisfactory. In these circumstances, an isolated rather than a general problem exists. The general state of the equipment can provide an impression of the management's equipment replacement and investment policy. Failure to update, upgrade and maintain equipment is indicative not only of an attitude problem on the part of top management but also an inadequate concern for safeguarding the business' future. It can mean too much of the profit has been milked from the firm over the years, causing a lack of resources and terminal decline. Equipment condition affects directly process capability and, hence, avoidable costs.

11. Access space.

> A manufacturer of air conditioning equipment won an order to supply a complete module that would be used to control the accommodation environment on an oil platform to be installed in the North Sea. The module was duly erected in the company's workshops. However, on completion, it was found that nobody had considered the need to get it out of the workshop for shipment. Two stark choices presented themselves: either to demolish the whole of one side of the workshop building or to dismantle the module totally, ship the parts to site, re-erect it, replacing all the cabling that would have to be scrapped as a result and incurring a penalty charge for the late installation of the re-built module. The latter was chosen. The supplier incurred a heavy (avoidable) loss on the contract.
>
> A company won a similar order to the one described above. Recognizing that there was insufficient floor area within its buildings, it considered that the product could be successfully erected immediately outside its workshop, in the open. To *"protect it from the weather"* a scaffold covered with tarpaulins was erected over the work area. A seasonal storm ripped the tarpaulins off and a deluge of rain ruined a substantial amount of electronic equipment. The company accepted that it had been unwise and replaced the damaged parts. However, when the product was ready for shipment it was discovered that it was wider than the company's access road. Enquiries established that there was no crane capable of lifting the whole thing over the top of the

company's buildings. It was dismantled and re-built. These potential problems had been brought to the a management's attention in an audit report. The company's owner had, however, chosen to ignore the warnings, dismissing them with the statement *"We know what we are doing."* Perhaps he knows a little more now.

Poor layout and inadequate access are common causes of business problems which generally have their roots in a lack of resources required to do the job properly. In service industries, for example, it is common to find pure clutter in the behind-the-scenes activities that the paying customer should never see.

12. Are all the requisite stickers on the parts? Are the job cards with the parts? Are the drawings and other information formats covered with "red ink"?

By comparing the picture the company presents of the external auditor's contract with what seems to be the general state of affairs in other areas, the auditor can sometimes arrive at a conclusion as to whether or not the auditee has "cleaned up" (see Chapter 14) before the audit. There is nothing wrong with cleaning up in this way but after the audit, problems can arise when the situation reverts to a more normal state. It makes sense, therefore, to note how well things are being done in areas unrelated to the particular contract, project or product of interest.

> This type of problem is frequently visible in companies having an ISO 9000 or QS 9000 registration certificate *"on-the-wall"*. Many tend to specify to their registrars particular projects or product lines for the assessment: others remain untouched by the disciplines of the quality systems standards. Few assessors take into account the balance of workplace realities.

Extensive use of red ink mark-ups is often a good pointer to management systems that are inadequate and partially replaced by fire-fighting expedients.

13. The informal organization.

Companies that embark on a quality campaign generally appoint a quality manager (vice-president, director or some equivalent title) and allege in their quality manuals that all kinds of vital authorities are vested in the position which is nominated as *"management's representative"*. In reality, this is no guarantee that the person is considered to be of the same importance in the company as, say, the finance director, marketing manager or other such appointments. Carefully noting the location of offices, style of furniture, company cars and other facilities made available to the quality manager can be quite revealing.

During an audit of a company based in the north of England, I had occasion to visit their quality manager's office. It was located at the farthest corner of the works: the office furniture was literally falling to pieces and the only chair available for his visitors had no back, this having broken away some years previously. The place was grimly decorated and situated immediately outside was the company's garbage tip on which the kitchen waste from the work's canteen was deposited. My visit occurred during the height of summer, the refuse tip stank and was infested with flies and vermin. The place was most unpleasant. The main office block, however, was comprised of an attractive modern building which housed not only senior management but most of the middle management as well. Having established that the quality manager was the only one not to be given a decent office, I asked the managing director why and received the reply that *"Because he has to deal with the product, it is the most appropriate location for him to be convenient for the works."* To this, I immediately replied why, if this was the case, the production manager and works managers' offices were not similarly located since there was adequate space for them. I received no reply.

If the company believes that financial management and financial assurance is important for company survival, then why does it not show similar belief in quality management and quality assurance? The latter two are the *sine qua non* for the former. Whereas the quality department is powerful in theory, it is often other departments who really rule the roost paying indifferent attention to quality matters.

At one company, an audit team found that the receiving inspectors were releasing critical material to production despite the fact that the quality manual forbade this. When questioned, the inspector replied *"It's more than my life is worth - if production tell us to release, then that's the end of it."*

In one large company, an audit team found that the purchasing department controlled the operation to such an extent that the quality manager had to give up his office to a buyer (the latter supposedly having to carry out such complex and confidential monetary negotiations that a closed door office was necessary).

The quality department received very little support from the members of the purchasing department and this state of affairs was, unfortunately, endorsed by the senior management. It was not unknown for a buyer to waive the quality programme requirements for a contract: in some cases, where essential safety-related equipment was being purchased, the buyer had even waived the requirement for submission of a quality manual for assessment.

14. The REAL practice.

While visiting a major computer manufacturer, I was invited to go into the *"clean room"*. Cap, gown, boots and mask were provided, to be put on prior to entering. Upon entering, a relatively low air pressure was noticeable as a gentle draft gently blew through the entry door - the wrong way. Once inside the room, an unofficial entry door to the area was discovered. It was open virtually all the time and provided the real main point of entry and exit for people wandering in and out, not always correctly dressed with their caps, gowns, boots and masks.

During a visit to a food processing plant, the works manager offered to take me into the processing areas and escort me around them. As he arose from his desk, he automatically picked up his cigarettes and lighter and put them in his pocket. Smoking is not allowed within the food processing areas. He paid no heed to the policy.

A friend of mine was auditing a supplier of steel stock. While in the records department, he noted a clerk was faking a certificate by altering the material properties stated on it. The clerk smiled and quickly tried to ease my friend's concern by saying *"Don't worry Jimmy, it's not for your job!"*

During an audit of a German company, I was checking a file of performance reports and various certificates for my client's contract. Whenever I discovered some documentation missing, the production manager informed me it was in his office awaiting his check and he would fetch it immediately. He would leave the records office and I would carry on with my sample selections, After a few minutes I would hear a photocopying machine busy at work, it would stop and the manager would reenter the room. At one juncture I decided to slip out and follow him. Busy in his office was a typist and a clerk making up the *"missing certificates"*. I asked if they were any good at faking bank notes!

The contract was removed from them on the basis of malpractice discovered during the audit.

15. Clean-ups.

Keep an eye open for obvious *"clean ups"*. One reason for forewarning the auditee of an audit is to give him a chance to put his house in order to some extent. It is perfectly natural that he should do this and it should give the auditor more cause for concern if the auditor makes no effort to clear up a messy operation before the audit begins.

The school of though that advocates an unannounced audit as a means of catching out the auditee will, I hope, soon fall into disrepute since it is based on a totally misconceived notion of the purpose of auditing. It signifies an unhelpful and negative approach on the part of auditors which I regard as disgraceful and amateurish for it denotes the actions of a troublemaker, not a professional person.

There is normally no need to worry about the clean-ups that the auditee carries out before the audit team arrive. Clean-ups rarely solve major problems. A major problem is generally of a magnitude that is equivalent to implementing a new management system, which is always a lengthy process, and it is doubtful whether any auditee would be able to solve major problem between the time of notification of an audit and the arrival of the audit team. A false clean-up is a good thing to spot, however, because it indicates the probable normal state of affairs. If the latter looks unsatisfactory, a pertinent remark would be quite in order.

> The receiving and storage area of a company was of corrugated steel construction and in a poor state of repair. The lower parts of the steel sheets had corroded to such an extent that draughts and moisture were entering whilst the wall were damp with condensation. During the audit, however, it was noticed that the metal storage racks had neatly typed labels taped onto them describing the contents of the shelf. The adhesive properties of that type of tape quickly deteriorate in a moist, damp environment and so the auditor knew that these labels were, at the most, two or three days old. In parts of the stores, a number of the labels had fallen off. Although areas of the shelves had been dusted, the items themselves had not. It was apparent that a false clean-up had been attempted. The auditee's quality manager shook his head and said *"Well, it was worth a try"*.

A clean-up shows the auditee is concerned about the outcome of the audit. The audit team is not on a fault finding exercise, and if a clean-up achieves the right result, why worry? The auditee has performed his own internal corrective action. Obviously, if the clean-up has not achieved the right result - a permanent change to the way things are done - then the auditor will, in any event note the deficiencies.

> Every firm embarking on an ISO 9000, a QS 9000 or a continuous improvement quality program has resolved to engage upon a clean-up, albeit with official management initiation and as a matter of public declaration to all inside and outside the company. The idea is (or is alleged) as being a permanent new way of working.

Clean-ups are easy to spot - you can *"see the join"*! It is impossible to backfit new or revised systems and practices to everything done in the past. When the auditor takes a meaningful sample of objective evidence the join makes its presence evidence. The auditor might see examples which lead him to remark *"I note that you have started using a different data entry method in the last few weeks: the old ones are different to the new. Why did you decide to make the change?"*

16. Indicators of lack of top support.

The auditor should be alert to the words and phrases employed by the managers and supervisors at all levels in the company. They can indicate the real feeling towards a quality programme and the true degree of understanding of the importance of quality. To cite a few examples:

♦   *"Of course quality is important but it does cost a lot of money"*.
♦   *"It causes a paper monster"*.
♦   *"Naturally we have a quality programme, we've done inspection for years"*.
♦   *"We work to quality systems standards whenever the customer specifies it"*.
♦   *"A quality programme? OK, if you are prepared to pay for it"*.
♦   *"We were forced into it by our customers"*.
♦   *"Of course we believe in quality, we've bought a quality manual because we're going for ISO 9000"*.
♦   *"Our quality programme must be effective, we've passed ISO 9000"*.
♦   *"If it were our choice, we would use our commercial systems"*;
♦   *"Can you tell us where we could buy a quality manual?"*;

♦ *"Yes, we do have a quality programme - we appointed a quality manager".*

♦ *"That's the responsibility of inspection".*

Collect the information as you go

Throughout the audit, the auditor should watch, look and listen. It is especially important to listen to explanations of how the system works because these may vary from department to department. The auditor can often obtain answers to some of the checklist questions without even having to ask, purely by paying attention to what goes on around him throughout the audit. The simple act of walking through the premises, for example, can give the auditor a picture of the equipment, the conditions, the housekeeping and overall orderliness of the work place as well as of the general atmosphere.

> One auditor noted that when he entered each of the workshops or stores, a fork-lift truck horn would sound twice and when he left it would sound once. It soon became quite apparent to the auditor that the fork-lift truck drivers were warning everybody within the workshop that management representatives were about. The industrial relations within that particular company were very poor.

13. Question technique

Questions are never indiscreet. Answers sometimes are.

Oscar Wilde

Naturally, every auditor develops his own style and technique of questioning which evolve with experience and are worked out on the basis of past successes and failures. The latter are bound to occur at some point, particularly when the auditor is relatively new to his task and liable to errors of both commission and omission. Past experiences like this can be turned to advantage if only the auditor is willing to learn from them. For this reason, the auditor should always try to devote a few minutes to a *post mortem* shortly after the audit is over. As the old saying goes: *it is a bad man who never made a mistake and a worse man who never profited from one.*

Inexperienced auditors naturally tend to rely heavily on the checklist (or other audit guidance tool), unaware, perhaps, that none of those tools asks all the questions which are necessary to arrive at the truth and draw a balance set of conclusions from the audit activities. They may also feel unsure about how to pose questions correctly. I hope this chapter will be particularly useful in suggesting ways in which they can overcome their initial difficulties.

Six friends

The beginning of Rudyard Kipling's poem *"The Elephant Child"* goes as follows:

> *"I keep six honest serving men*
> *(they taught me all I knew).*
> *Their names are What and Why and When*
> *and How and Where and Who".*

These six words - how, what, why, when, where and who - are six friends for the auditor and must figure in all the auditor's questions. When used properly, the six friends force a response. Asking *"Do you have a copy of your company price list?"*, for instance, may elicit the answer *"yes"* but

279

this is to ask only half a question since the auditor has still to verify the existence of the price list by a further enquiry. A more detailed question (*"Where do you keep your copy of the company price list"*) forces a more specific answer, such as, (*"in the filing cabinet"*).

This answer tells the auditor three things:

♦   The auditee *knows* that he should have the price list.
♦   The auditee *alleges* that he has received the price list.
♦   The price list is *allegedly* protected (in the filing cabinet).

An even more valuable question for the auditor to ask might be *"Who provides you with your copy of the price list?"* An answer such as *"I receive my copy direct from the sales manager"* tells the auditor the following:

♦   The auditee *knows* that he should have the price list.
♦   The auditee, *if the answer is correct*, knows where the price list actually comes from (this may be at variance with the operations manual, management system, procedure or whatever).

If the auditee's answer is at variance with the system/manual/procedure, the auditor knows that one or both of the following is true, either :

♦   The auditee does not know the system. Or,
♦   The system, as implemented, does not tally with the system as documented.

Questions framed in a judicious manner (encompassing the six friends) can yield much verifiable information within a short space of time. Remembering that time is the enemy of the auditor, one must never ask two questions when one good one is enough.

The seventh friend (the crunch question)

This is the simple request, *"show me"*. Properly used, it will enable the auditor to verify the auditee's response to the kind of question described above. The auditor in the example above might ask *"May I see the price list?"* or *"Could you please show me the price list?"* The answer has to be *"yes"* or *"no"*, either the auditee has the price list or he does not, either it is either in the filing cabinet or it is not.

The prime purpose of an audit is to verify that a system has or has not been developed, documented and implemented: verification cannot be achieved unless at some point the auditor poses a *"Show me"* question. An audit is conducted by examination of objective evidence: if objective evidence has not been requested, it cannot be examined and therefore an audit is not being performed.

The unit concept (analyzing the process)

The auditor must relate the six friends to the unit concept relevant to the task (process) being audited. He needs to ask *how/ what/ when/ where/ why/ who* in relation to the input, the output, and the task or process being performed, finally verifying with the crunch question *"Show me"*. For example:

"From where do you receive information?" is related to the input side of the unit (process).
"Where do you keep information you require?" is related to the information residing at the workplace.
"To where do you forward the information? " is related to the output of the unit.

The answers to all these questions are important in helping the auditor determine how well the unit understands its role as part of the chain of units involved in the product, project or contract being audited. In the case of a trace-back method of auditing, the auditor may want to ask where the work output goes and then work back to ascertain the source of the input.

It is always vital to request *"Show me what you do/where you put that/how you do that, please"* when checking at the compliance level. (See Chapter 11, *"Audit methods"*). The auditor then watches, quietly noting whether or not the methods are at variance with the system description and/or contract requirements. If the auditor notes some variation between procedure and practice, he must then ask *"Why do you do it that way?"*

It is of great value in auditing to keep the unit concept clear in one's mind, to split the work into input, process and output and to ask questions on each of these individually and in turn.

The hypothetical question

In some cases - particularly during a pre-award survey, where there may be little objective evidence available - it can be useful to ask questions of the *"What if..."* or *"Let us suppose..."* variety. The answers often expose the depth of understanding of the systems in operation as well as the amount of thought invested in creating them.

> I once had to perform a pre-award survey on a company about which I was told *"they are a very new company and have brand new premises."* Upon arrival at the supplier's location, I discovered that this advice was an understatement. The facilities consisted of a huge workshop which contained nothing but an overhead gantry crane, a few offices, a telephone line, a typewriter and a desktop copier. Even though the company had written its quality manual, there had to be quite a bit of *"What if-ing"* and *"Let us suppose-ing"* during the pre-award survey. In this case the "What ifs" were designed to elicit whether the parent company's practices (which were known to my company) were known to this subsidiary and were likely to be implemented.

The best way to use the hypothetical question is in conjunction with one of the six friends. An example might be *"Let us suppose that the information you receive does not contain the correct content you need for your job, what would you do (or who would you notify)?"* After the auditee has made some reply to the first question, the auditor might then ask *"Can you please show me the instruction to that effect?"*

An example is often a useful means to help the auditee understand the auditor's line of thought. Without one, the line of questioning may seem obscure or far-fetched. Sometimes an example suggests itself naturally, if for instance, the auditor has encountered a problem at another location that he would not wish to see repeated in the unit being audited. Using this type of example may at least alert the auditee to the possibility of some problem arising and may spur him on to take preventive action.

It is unwise to lose sight of reality by overdoing the "what if": it can make the auditor appear rather foolish.

"I don't understand..."

If the auditee's explanation or response is either unclear or unsatisfactory, the auditor should not be afraid to say: *"I'm sorry but I don't quite understand. Could you explain that again please?"* Some people are reluctant to ask for an explanation or an answer to be repeated for fear of appearing dimwitted. The auditor must put aside this fear. He must always continue questioning until he understands the answer and is satisfied that the truth has been obtained. He should, for example, always ask *"Can you show me another example please, I think I'm beginning to understand but I want to be sure"*. An auditee is very seldom unwilling to repeat or to rephrase an explanation or answer for the auditor.

Systematic questioning

The auditor must develop his questions in a logical sequence, not jump about between disconnected topics. As a rule, the questions should follow the sequence of work in the unit being audited. *("OK, you've done this, this, this then how/where/when/why/who.....")*.

It is good practice for the auditor to voice his understanding of how the system works, so that the auditee can correct any misconceptions. For instance, the auditor may say *"OK, so you do this, then this, and then..."*, and the auditee may interrupt with *"No. We actually do this, this, this, then that, and then...."*. Acting in this manner helps the auditor to keep an open mind about the situation and places him in a stronger position later on to say *"But when I told you of my understanding of the way that unit works, you did not correct me at that time. Why not?"*

The silent question

Silence can be extremely powerful because some people find it uncomfortable and to break it they volunteer something they should not. When the auditor looks at the auditee, saying nothing, the latter may feel that a response is expected of him, and because he is not sure quite what the response should be, he may say more than he otherwise would. This type of question often produces information of use to the auditor.

Non-questions

The auditor must avoid falling into the habit of asking the auditee a question and then answering it himself. He might just as well not ask a question at all as do this. Furthermore, he may well supply an incorrect answer, which the auditee may be reluctant to put right. The erroneous assumption may not be exposed until much later on (when the auditee will say, at last, *"We never told you that"*, or, *"You said that, we didn't"*), whilst the auditor's misconception may have put his investigation off course in the meantime. This is simply not conducting the audit properly.

The obvious or "dumb" question

The auditor should never be afraid to ask a question, even if the answer seems so obvious that it is scarcely worth asking. The obvious question may turn out to be the very one that the auditee is dreading because some glaring deficiency is about to be revealed. The obvious question may seem very similar to the non-question. Do not think to yourself, *"It's ridiculous to ask that, even a fool would....."*, and feel embarrassed to ask. Ask the "dumb" question and then hear a pin drop!

The unasked question

In the course of examining the objective evidence, the auditor will find that some questions are answered before they have been asked. In such cases, he should answer the unasked questions out loud (*"OK, I see on this purchase order, the prices, delivery dates, specifications, the acceptance criteria and the references to the company standards"*). The auditor is not asking the auditee to point out what is under his very nose: he is informing the auditee that he is noting the content of the objective evidence. Analyzing the evidence aloud like this helps the auditor to follow the system and the auditee to follow the auditor's line of thought. It also informs all concerned that the auditor knows what he is looking for, that he is not missing anything and that he is thorough. It may be that the auditee has included various details in one set of documents purely by accident, and that they will not be found in another set of documents in another area: from the auditor's words, the auditee now knows that deficiencies will be found in the other area. This often happens when the auditee is in the process of developing and implementing the management systems i.e. during the period of gestation.

Inverse questions

One often encounters auditees who are resentful of being either audited or subject to the strictures of a management system. In order to deflect attention from their desire to work their own way regardless of others, they may claim that the systems restrict their creativeness (a common plea of designers, software engineers, computer programmers) or could reduce their operational scope to the detriment of the company (salesmen often claim, for example, that the paperwork and formality of involving line staff could prevent a sales order being obtained). When auditing such people, I have found it useful to pander to their ego initially by starting my questions as follows:

"Can you please tell me if you are getting all the co-operation that you feel you need to do your job?" This is not what the auditee expects and the response might be:

"I'm not sure what you mean."

The auditor continues, *"Well, are you receiving all of the latest information that you need?"*

Auditee: *"I think so."*

Auditor: *"You don't sound too sure. What exactly would you like to have?"*

The auditee now perceives that someone has finally realized his position at the centre of the universe, relaxes and starts to specify his utopian requirements.

The auditor will then ask who might be able to provide that information: the auditee will express his state of knowledge about the organizational interfaces and how the system works. The auditor will then ask for examples of exactly what *"they"* are currently providing for the illustrious auditee. There is often a shortfall, so the auditor asks:

"How have you told them of what you need?"

The auditee is forced to present objective evidence of his requests or to admit that there has been no communication. In the latter case, the auditor will suggest that direct contact is made by the auditee with those interfaces in order to get the information:

"They clearly do not understand the vital nature of your position, perhaps you should go and see them yourself to explain precisely what you need."

That inverse questioning of asking a peacock if he/she is getting all the co-operation it needs, rather than asking for elaboration on how they are a slave to the system, breaks the barriers down.

The auditor will use similar questions to ascertain the items, equipment, training and so on that the auditee feels he requires, and then uses similar questions to determine whether other people have informed the auditee of their needs of him. If not, one will then suggest that he makes direct contact with the downstream interfaces. In the event that the auditee feels resentment about helping others to do their jobs, by going to them to ascertain their needs, a picture of an unfair attitude can be presented. Generally, however, the auditee is intelligent enough to realize what has happened and will become more co-operative.

Comparison questions

This type of question, much used in compliance audits, compares the content of the information, such as the work instructions, with actual practice. It is posed *after* the other questions have been asked and actual practice established. Apart from establishing how well the people know the contents of the information, the use of the comparison question is to determine the desirability of an amendment to that information in cases where the words do not reflect actual practice, provided that the actual practice is in accordance with customer, product and legal requirements. *("I see that you operate in such a such manner but the work instruction/ procedure says this, this, this. Since your method of operation is in compliance with the contract, I suggest that you amend the instruction/ procedure to reflect actual practice")*. Obviously, if the practice is at variance with the instruction/ procedure and any of those requirements, then this may warrant a formal request for corrective action. (The acid test has to be the state of the product. If the product is not at risk, if it meets the requirements of customer, project/ contract and the community (i.e. society's legal requirements), I would not issue a formal request for corrective action preferring instead to ask the auditee to update the procedures/instructions to reflect actual practice.)

It is a serious error for the auditor to attack the auditee with a question such as *"Why aren't you following the procedure?"* I prefer, instead, to "attack" the procedure with a question such as *"Why is the procedure at variance with practice?"* since this is the correct priority. Procedures are supposed to show practice (quality systems standards such as ISO 9001 show this to be the case) and the crucial issue is for management systems to be responsive to the needs of the product *et al.* When the auditee's product is as intended and as desired by the marketplace, the management system as implemented has served its needs: that is what matters, first and foremost. I take the view that the auditee has exercised necessary corrective action, as part of process control to ensure product quality is achieved: the procedure/ instruction should now be updated to state actual practice. Never lose sight of the product. (This is discussed more fully in Chapter 17.)

The comparison question is of particular use when auditing foreign companies that do not speak the auditor's mother tongue and have difficulty finding the right wording to use in their documents. Here, the auditor should explain why the word or phrase is wrong and suggest a suitable alternative that would describe actual practice more accurately. In some cases, it may transpire that the auditee has misunderstood the particular requirements because of imperfect understanding of the language used. It is the auditor's duty to correct such misunderstandings without making a big issue out of them.

A useful sequence for questioning

Questions should be related to the actual work flow. When auditing the compliance aspects of any particular task (process), a useful sequence is:

1.   Ask organizational questions concerning the function of the task and responsibilities of the person. (That is Step 1 of the seven step method - Chapter 11.)

2.   Ask questions concerning each of the task elements (see Chapter 4) taken in turn but relating to the system's flow. (That is Step 2, then Step 3 of the seven step method - Chapter 11.)

♦   The order in which the task elements are taken is irrelevant although questions concerning the *"Person"* sub-elements should be left until last because at that point the auditor will have a better understanding of the demands the task (process) place on the person responsible for it. The demands affect the auditor's understanding of the competence, training and attribute requirements of the auditee.

♦   In the case of a trace forward method, the questions concerning inputs are posed first, followed by questions concerning the outputs. The auditor will use the "six friends" followed by the seventh *"Show me"* once the process details have been drawn from the auditor's statements. (This relates to Step 3 of the *"seven step"* method - Chapter 11).

3.   Ask comparison questions. (These relate to Step 4 of the seven step method - Chapter 11. They also relate to Step 5 in that the auditor can also use them to compare the auditee's management systems, methods and controls with the auditor's own experience and knowledge to draw the auditee's attention potential improvements he should consider.)

4.   Ask hypothetical questions. These are used as described above to determine the existence and efficacy of:

♦   The process controls intended for dealing with possible out-of-control situations before they can have their effect. (This helps the auditee ascertain the extent to which preventive action has been considered and is taken).

♦   Non-conformity systems.

♦   Corrective action systems.

5.   Use the six friends and "show me" to asses the effectiveness of the auditee's performance monitoring controls. (This relates to Step 6 of the seven step method).

6.   Ask comparison questions. (These relate to Step 7 of the seven step method - Chapter 11 - in that the auditor can also use them to comment upon the auditee's monitoring data and its capture systems and methods with the auditor's own experience and knowledge to draw the auditee's attention potential improvements he should consider.)

An example of question technique

Auditor: *"What is your function and how do you know what your duties are?"*

The auditee will describe the product(s) of his efforts and the associated responsibilities. The auditor will take appropriate notes.

Auditor: *"In order to be able to do your job, what items and materials do you need?"*

The auditee will describe the various items (viz. Materials, ingredients, assemblies, components, sub-assemblies, consumables etc.) that he believes he needs. The auditor will record these on his checklist.

Auditor: *"Let's take each of those items in turn. Please tell me where does item A come from/ who supplies you with it?"*

The auditee states the upstream interfacing department/ process: this discovers the auditee's understanding of his internal/ external suppliers. The auditor notes this detail to help build a picture of the system, (possibly by starting to sketch a flow chart relating to the item supply side system).

Auditor: *"In doing your work what would make that item A unacceptable to you?"* .

This is a key question because if the auditee does not know what is or is not acceptable for the process and his workplace there is the considerable risk that defective items will be worked on, thereby wasting money, time and resources and creating avoidable costs. Riskier still, the auditee might not realize the existence of a danger to the environment, health or safety. By asking the question suggested, the auditor is proceeding in the manner described in Chapter 5 to ascertain the extent of the auditee's knowledge. Lack of knowledge would show the auditee is incapable of really controlling his process.

Having obtained the auditee's response, the auditor then investigates the sub-elements applicable to item A, and then would proceed with:

Auditor: *"Thank you for that information. Please show me some examples of item A"*. The auditor will make his own selection from the examples at the workplace and note the quantity and identity of the samples taken together with the results obtained, including discrepancies, as the audit proceeds.

Auditor: *"Now let us consider item B. Please tell me where it (they) come from/ who supplies you with it/ them?"* The auditor repeats the question format just pursued for item A, once again taking notes of the results obtained.

This format of questioning and verification is repeated for each and every one of the items listed by the auditee. Having then finished dealing with incoming items, the auditor now turns his attention to another of the task elements (but not the *"person"*, for reasons described in the preceding section), say, equipment.

Auditor: *"Would you please tell me what equipment do you need and use to do your job?"*

The auditee will describe the various pieces of equipment that he believes he needs. The auditor will record these on his checklist.

Auditor: *"Let's take each of those in turn"*.

Auditor: *"Please tell me where equipment A comes from/ who supplies you with it/ them?"*

The auditee states the upstream interfacing department/ process: This discovers the auditee's understanding of his internal/ external suppliers.

The auditor notes this detail to help build a picture of the system, (possibly by starting to sketch a flow chart relating to the equipment provision/ maintenance/ calibration systems, according to the nature of the equipment being dealt with).

Auditor: *"In doing your work what would make that equipment A unacceptable to you?"*

This is another key question again because if the auditee does not know what is or is not acceptable for the process and his workplace there is the considerable risk that defective or unsuitable equipment will be used, thereby wasting money, time and resources and creating avoidable costs. Riskier still, the auditee might not realize the existence of a danger to the environment, health or safety. By asking the question suggested, the auditor is proceeding in the manner described in Chapter 5 to ascertain the extent of the auditee's knowledge. Lack of knowledge about the equipment to be used for the job would show the auditee is incapable of really controlling his process.

Having obtained the auditee's response, the auditor investigates the sub-elements applicable to equipment A, and then proceeds:

Auditor: *"Thank you for that information. Please show me equipment A".* If there are several examples of equipment A, the auditor will make his own selection at the workplace and note the identity of the samples taken and the results obtained, including discrepancies, as the audit proceeds.

Auditor: *"Now let us consider equipment B. Please tell me where it (they) come from/ who supplies you with it/ them?"* The auditor repeats the question format just pursued for equipment A, once again taking notes of the results obtained.

This format of questioning and verification is repeated for each and every one of the pieces of equipment listed by the auditee. The auditor then continues by ascertaining what environmental nuisances must be avoided: he details them and records the fact of their existence or otherwise.

Having then finished dealing with equipment needed to perform the task/ control the process, the auditor now turns his attention to another of the task elements, say, information (but not the *"person"*, for reasons described in the preceding section).

Auditor: *"In order to do this work, what information do you require?"*

The auditee will describe, in the manner of a list, the information (including documents and data) he believes is necessary. Once again, the auditor will:

◆ Note the answers in his checklist.
◆ Take each one in turn and ascertain where it comes from/ who issues it: This discovers the auditee's understanding of his internal/ external suppliers.
◆ Find out what the auditee's acceptance criteria are for each one.
◆ Ask questions addressing each of the applicable sub-elements for each one.
◆ Ask the auditee to show examples of each one and make his own selection from the examples present at the workplace.
◆ Verify the actual status of the selected samples is consistent with the auditee's description.
◆ Note the identities of each sample and the findings, both good and bad.
◆ Repeat this question and verification sequence until all the types of information listed by the auditee have been analyzed.
◆ Move to the next task element ("services", according to the example being described) and repeat the entire sequence again.

Having now ascertained the status of all incoming task element matters (items, equipment, information, services supplied to the workplace, but still holding back questions concerning the "person"), the auditor will now investigate the actual work process.

Auditor: *"Would you please show me how you actually perform your task/ process"*.

The auditor will then proceed to perform his or her job. The auditor will note the methods that are used, any deviations from the intended management system and:

◆ The attributes of the person (dexterity, eyesight, strength, carefulness etc.).
◆ The competence of the person in doing the job.
◆ Process controls exercised during execution of the task.
◆ Reports/ records produced during execution of the task.

The auditor will not interrupt the auditee until the particular task is finished.

291

Auditor: *"How do you identify that the product and information were produced by you?"*

The auditee will state the method used and the auditor will verify the efficacy of this, making appropriate note on the checklist.

At this point the auditor will raise any questions that may have arisen from the methods actually used on the job and check that the activity actually matches with the job descriptions/procedures/instructions the auditor reviewed as part of the audit preparation (see Chapter 9). It is important not to attack the auditee (as described in the preceding section *"Comparison questions"*). The auditor will satisfy himself with the answers and then proceed to ask questions concerning the task elements, related this time to the output side of the auditee's process. A similar structure to that used for assessing the input side will be used. For example:

Auditor: *"What items do you release from your workplace"*

The auditee will list them. The auditor will take each in turn asking:

♦ *"Where do you send it/ them to?"* (This discovers the auditee's understanding of his internal/ external customers.)
♦ *"What would make that item unacceptable to that/ those customer(s)?"* (This discovers the auditee's understanding of customer requirements and, hence, the needs of the product and process he is responsible for.)

The auditor will ask the auditee to show examples of each one and:

♦ Will make his own selection from the examples present at the workplace.
♦ Verify the actual status of the selected samples is consistent with the auditee's description.
♦ Note the quantity and identity of each sample and the findings, both good and bad.
♦ Repeat this question and verification sequence until all the items listed by the auditee have been analyzed.
♦ Move to the next task element and repeat the entire sequence again and again until all the task elements have been dealt with, except *"person"*.

He will then proceed with *"what-if"* questions such as .

Auditor: *"What if any of the items/equipment/information you receive are incorrect, what do you do/ who do you notify/ how do you do it?"*

The consistency of such actions will be checked against the responsibilities and authorities in the job description.

According to the level of person being audited and the audit objectives, the auditor might now proceed along similar lines with questions concerning the estimation, allocation and management of time and resources.

Having seen the actual practice and the needs of the task (process), at this point, the auditor now knows:

♦   The auditee's understanding of the inputs needed for the job.
♦   The actual state of inputs received at the auditee's workplace.
♦   The auditee's way of doing the job.
♦   The auditee's understanding of the outputs expected from the job.
♦   The actual state of outputs ready to be sent from the auditee's workplace.
♦   The auditee's understanding of what to do if things go wrong.
♦   The extent of the non-conformity/corrective action systems' implementation at the auditee's workplace.
♦   The demands the task places on the person doing it and, hence, the type of competence, training, attributes, motivation etc. required for its successful accomplishment.

The auditor can now proceed with such questions as: *"With what training have you been provided?"*

The auditee will describe the training (if any) that has been received. The auditor will note this information, obtain objective evidence and do likewise for attributes such as eyesight checks by asking a question such as:

"How often does the company ask for your vision to be tested?"

For competence assessment the auditor could ask *"What tests, qualifications, skills, experience did the company expect of you to be able to do this job?"* The auditee will describe the company's demands (if any)

293

and the auditor will note this information, verifying the statements by obtaining objective evidence from the person's records, wherever they are kept.

When finished at the workplace the auditor will thank the person for his or her co-operation.

Presentation of questions

Always direct the questions to the person who *performs* the task being audited, *not* to that person's superior. If the latter tries to answer all questions personally, the auditor must politely put a stop to the interventions.

The auditor must never talk down to anyone. Any auditor who acts as if he knows it all and is superior to the auditee is unlikely to get the auditee's full co-operation. Such a state of affairs makes it much harder to obtain valuable information and results. Without the auditee's help, a cost-beneficial audit cannot be done. It is a worthwhile exercise to *"talk the person's language"* (but not bad language). An operative may not understand much about the finer points of management system theory and its *lingua franca* or about the statutory requirements, but he will know about the things with which he has to deal every day. The auditor should try to phrase his questions with this in mind, incorporating, for instance, some concrete examples relating to matters with which the operative will be thoroughly familiar.

Always speak clearly and carefully - this is a basic principle of effective communication. If the auditee cannot hear what the auditor is saying, he will find it very difficult to produce a useful answer. He may well end up answering a different question altogether. If the auditee seems not to have heard or understood the question, repeat it, rephrasing it if possible. As a corollary to this, the auditor should look at the auditee, not to the side or at his own feet when talking. In a busy, noisy environment, failure to look at the person to whom you are talking can render you inaudible. Apart from that, the auditee's facial reactions and body language can be valuable guides to the veracity or otherwise of the responses made.

Active listening

It is equally as important for the auditor to listen carefully to the auditee's responses and statements as it is for the auditor to carefully phrase his questions and to speak clearly. The essence is to communicate effectively and this is another golden rule. (See Appendix 1, *"12 Golden rules"*.). Active listening requires concentration and its is advisable to look directly at the auditee and not to be distracted by reading the next question from the checklist or some other extraneous matter. The old story of two people is that the first was speaking while the other merely waited to speak: this type of interaction is unproductive. The auditor must weigh carefully the auditee's remarks and decide the next question on the basis of what has been said: is clarification need or not, should the matter be investigated more deeply, is the auditee's response coherent to the point that the next topic/ task element/ aspect of the system can be addressed?

One useful method of ensuring you have heard and understood what the auditee has said in response to your questions is to repeat back to the auditee your understanding of what was said. *"OK, if I understand you correctly, you do this, this and this by means of...Is that correct?"* This advice is particularly important when dealing with an auditee who does not speak your mother tongue and language difficulties might occur.

It is also frequently the case that auditees express themselves poorly, are not too articulate, yet produce fine products and services controlling well their process.

Sensitive situations

Certain matters of a sensitive nature might need to be raised during an audit. An example of this would be auditee's checks on the honesty of personnel who are assigned to tasks where such an attribute is vital.

For internal audits such situations are best handled by, say, the quality manager auditing the human resources manager on a one-to-one basis. This would mean that other internal auditors need not concern themselves about such a sensitive matter. Obviously, in these circumstances, confidentiality is especially vital and thus dictates the need for the audit to be performed by senior management, such as the quality manager himself/herself.

On external audits, the matter is even more delicate because the auditee may consider the auditor to be prying into matters which should not be any of his concern. The external auditor has to act diplomatically to avoid raising hostility. A useful ploy is to present a realistic scenario to the auditee. The auditor might, for example, postulate that his own organization, in providing free issue material, is naturally concerned about security and might then gently ask how pilferage or unauthorized dissemination would be prevented. Alternatively, the auditor may stress that certain data which will be provided to the auditee is of a highly confidential nature and must only be brought to the attention of selected trusted employees on a *"need to know"* basis. From this position, the auditor can raise the matter of the security screening of those people who may be involved. Naturally the scenario that the auditor describes has to be realistic and based on actual need. The auditor must avoid areas which will not be directly related to his legitimate prime concerns.

Personnel security checks are becoming increasingly common as the number of businesses providing services to customers, such as banks, insurance companies, computer aided design, payroll processing, product launch, graphic design and marketing has grown. Where companies are offering design services to customers that issue them with confidential data, security is naturally important. Companies offering data processing services where monetary transactions are being handled also necessitate the investigation of such sensitive matters. Another field in which security is of concern is national defence.

Always give praise where it is due

Always give credit where credit is due. A compliment (*"nice job"*, *"orderly office"*, *efficient operation"*), sincerely given, goes a long way towards eliciting auditee's co-operation. Naturally, this should not be overdone to the point where the auditee sounds sycophantic. An essence of good management is to ensure that work is done correctly. When evidence proves that this is so, the auditee deserves some expression of appreciation. After all, when things are not so good, that type of news is quickly relayed back but the opposite is not always the case in life.

Personal demeanour

The auditor should not only look interested in the auditee's work and responses - he must *be* interested as well. Genuine interest is more likely to enlist the auditee's full co-operation, particularly in the case of people engaged in mundane tasks. On an internal audit, the auditor is more likely to elicit constructive suggestions for improvements from the people if they know that he is interested enough to follow their suggestions through: this is good for motivation.

At all times, the auditor must be courteous and helpful. When asking to see objective evidence, he must say *"please"* (*"Could you show me the records, please?"*). Another point of good manners is not to look

296

distrustful of people or to regard their responses with suspicion. The auditor should not adopt an air appropriate to dealing with a back street garage.

Always apologize for unduly interrupting people (*"I just want to ask a few quick questions, please"*). If the auditor has to return to an area to obtain more or fresh information and finds the auditee engaged in other activities, such as a meeting, he should not assume he is entitled to break in without some justification or apology. It is unreasonable to interrupt peoples' refreshment breaks. It is good practice to note the time of such breaks and to suggest the audit team removes itself from the workplace then for a cup of tea or coffee. If it proves impossible to avoid interrupting the break, always apologize (*"I'm sorry to interrupt you, but please show me...?"*). If the auditor is known to be reasonable and courteous, people are more likely to co-operate and say *"No trouble at all"*.

It should virtually go without saying that the auditor should both be and appear to be impartial and unemotional in his dealings with the auditee (an audit is supposed to deal with verifiable facts, not emotions, after all). Having said that, no auditor should be afraid to relax and appear human. Many auditees are nervous of audits, especially if previous audits have turned out to be quasi-witch hunts and finger-pointing exercises. Try to put the auditee at ease by taking a seat or suggesting a cup of coffee, perhaps. Break the ice by mentioning the weather, some sports results, the football team, a picture on the wall or such like. An occasional quip can help.

Unavailable information

Sometimes the information that an auditor wants is not available when he requests it. This does not necessarily mean that something is wrong either with the system or with its implementation. The audit is being conducted in a live working environment (even when the service being audited is that of the local embalmer!): others may be using the information requested. The auditor should not waste time, he should simply say *"OK, could you find out for me, please, and let ne know the answer/ bring it to me when it comes back to you?"* This gives the auditee an opportunity to look for the answer/ objective evidence or to search the area concerned in order to get to the true facts of the situation.

Gathering opinions at grass roots level

It is most enlightening to ask people for their blunt opinion about the practices and the management systems, their uses, their benefits and impact on day-to-day tasks, their shortcomings, as well as for any changes that they may care to suggest. Most folk are delighted to get the opportunity to speak out and what they say may be illuminating not just for the auditor but for the auditee's management a well. It is not uncommon for constructive and cost-effective criticism concerning the implementation of the management systems within the company to be produced. These suggestions should be given serious consideration. In the case of an internal audit, it is a good practice for the audit team to inform people of the outcome of their suggestions and to give the reasons why any were discarded. It encourages employees at all levels to feel involved in the business if they are given proof that their opinions are considered important. This is good for motivation, for morale and for industrial relations. Furthermore, if suggestions made at grass roots level are implemented, the people will have a vested interest in making them work: they will feel ownership for the ideas and responsibility for their successful accomplishment.

No continuous improvement programme can flourish without this action being taken during audits.

The constructive approach

It is a cardinal sin for an auditor to produce destructive criticism of an auditee's system. The auditor who justifies his existence by fault finding and the number of corrective action requests he issues is never welcome - from an audit of any kind, the auditee gains nothing. Constructive criticism, by contrast, can benefit everyone and an auditor who is known to produce useful suggestions will enlist the co-operation of management easily. He will find the auditing work goes more smoothly too: people will be more willing to talk frankly to him and will waste less time covering up, if they know the auditor is not simply interested in finding fault. Always remember that the auditor is meant to be

FACT FINDING NOT FAULT FINDING.

So, the golden rule for the auditor is to *always help the auditee*. (See also Appendix 1, *"12 Golden Rules"*.) When a deficiency has been found, the auditor must always suggest examples of corrective action that would satisfy his organization (*"As corrective action you could consider these alternatives...* "). This gives the auditee a choice between a number of courses, any of which would satisfy the auditor and quality requirements. This is obviously a much more sensible approach for the auditor to take than to require corrective action without suggesting what form it should take, then rejecting the auditee's proposals at a later date. The last method wastes time, is annoying to everyone and is also indicative of crass bad manners.

If the auditor can perceive a way of improving the auditee's system, he should tell the auditee about it, tactfully. He might say:

♦　　　*"Have you ever tried or considered....?"*
♦　　　*"Would it be better to....?"*
♦　　　*"Although you meet the requirements of the product/ code/ standard etc., how about...?"*

Constructive suggestions may help the auditee to improve efficiency, to reduce avoidable costs that have hitherto not been recognized as such. This could lead to lower prices or to greater competitiveness, regardless of whether an internal or an external audit is being performed.

So, the auditor's organization has much to gain as the auditee by approaching the audit in a constructive fashion. Such an approach is central to the success of value-added audits, described in Part 2, Chapter 2. It occurs when the auditor executes Steps 5 and 7 of the seven step method contained in Chapter 11.

Two-edged swords

It is not uncommon for the auditor to find that his own organization has been the root cause of a problem discovered during an external or internal audit. If the responsible person from the auditor's organization is present during the audit, then the auditor must question him right there and then.

Audits are two-edged swords. The auditor sees not only what the auditee is doing but also the results of work performed in his own organization. Answers to all of the following questions and more may come to light:

♦　　　Has the auditee been provided with the correct information?
♦　　　Does the information show evidence of the correct reviews and approvals?
♦　　　Has the auditor's organization's management system been bypassed?

♦ Have the auditor's customer's requirements been properly incorporated into the information provided to the auditee?

The auditor must never assume that his own organization is perfect. He must demonstrate to the auditee that he is open-minded and determined to get to the truth, whatever this may be, and that he is prepared to question members of his own organization. People are more responsive to individuals who are known to be unbiased and fair in their dealings with all.

The auditor's stature

If the auditor discovers that he has been wrong in his assumptions or conclusions, it is best to admit it to the auditee and to apologize. This may happen, for example, if fresh evidence throws a new light on earlier findings. In these circumstances, the auditor must say something like, *"Well, in the light of this evidence, it appears that my earlier conclusions were wrong. I'm sorry for that misunderstanding and pleased that you showed me this new information"*. Someone who is big enough to admit to being wrong, and apologize for his mistakes shows his fair-mindedness and maturity. Such an attitude elicits co- operation and respect from the auditee. Moreover, it is far better to be corrected for any misunderstanding and misinterpretations of the objective evidence found before the exit interview is performed and before the audit report is written and distributed for all to see.

14. Auditor conduct

"And how did little Time behave?" asked Mrs. Cratchit.
...."As good as gold," said Bob.

Charles Dickens.

Auditing conduct and question technique frequently overlap. Indeed, it may be difficult to make a clear distinction between question technique, auditing methods, information collection and question technique. I shall include under the heading *"conduct"* means that the auditor may choose to adopt in order to achieve the audit's objective. Hence conduct includes many more forms of behaviour than simply question technique.

Projecting the right image

One of the most valuable things for the auditor to do is to try to project an appropriate image of himself and his organization to the auditee. The first five precepts listed below are all important in this respect.

1.   Look the part.

As a representative of his company (and his department), the auditor should dress so as to reflect credit on his organization. A smart, tidy appearance creates a favourable impression on the auditee and also boosts the auditor's confidence in himself.

2.   Remain calm and courteous.

The auditor sets an example to others by his own conduct during the audit. If he allows himself to become flustered and emotional or to engage in heated arguments, the proceedings are likely to go downhill fast. By remaining calm and polite in all circumstances, he gives himself the best chance of obtaining useful results from the management audit.

3.   Be punctual.

A punctual auditor gives the impression that he means business. A chronic late arriver irritates everyone and also wastes valuable time. Time is always at a premium during an audit and the auditee incurs a greater cost than does the auditor during the fact gathering phase, as described in Chapter 1: it is wrong to waste the auditee's time and money by arriving late and it is discourteous.

4.   Be precise.

Loosely phrased questions or requests can cause a lot of confusion. The auditor should consciously strive to convey exactly what he intends in all communications with the auditee. Failure to do so wastes time and can lead to misunderstandings that can directly affect the end objective of presenting a true and fair view of the auditee's activities and achievements.

5.   Be prepared.

An auditor who has made proper preparations in advance (Chapter 9) gets off to a flying start. He has no need to waste people's time ascertaining details he should have checked in advance and he earns the auditee's respect by knowing what he is doing. An ill-prepared auditor will find it much harder to enlist the full co-operation of the auditee.

An example of ill-preparation is readily seen when the auditor arrives, asks to see the auditee's procedures and then proceeds to review them: the review should have been done as part of the preparation phase and the edition reviewed confirmed at the entry interview (Chapter 10).

Conducting the proceedings properly

Many of the items under this heading read rather like moral prescriptions. However, tactically as well as ethically, it is always good to adhere to them. By adopting the right approach, the auditor will avoid making mountains out of molehills and in doing so will smooth his own path.

6.   Keep a sense of proportion.

The auditor should not make it his business to ferret out examples of human error. These will inevitably turn up if you dig deep enough in any organization since everyone (even an auditor) makes an occasional mistake. This evidence of human fallibility should be of far less interest and concern to the auditor than evidence of a real deficiency in the management systems. If the evidence suggests that general control in an area is satisfactory, the auditor should accept this and move on to a new area, not linger in the hope of digging up a few faults. The magnitude and significance of a deficiency is the vital issue: to pursue unimportant errors indefatigably is to waste time and effort and to risk alienating the auditee as well. Remember the prime objective is to obtain a true and fair view. Isolated incidents of error do not necessarily reflect fairly on the overall situation. (See also Chapter 17.)

7.   *Make allowances.*

If some deficiency is detected and human error is the cause, the auditor should always try to put the error in perspective. He should, for example, consider what pressures the auditee was under at the time the mistake happened - poor working conditions, fatigue, domestic difficulties, personal troubles, fear of losing the job during a threatened downsizing exercise and so on. Even the most diligent folk can make mistakes when the pressure on them grows to become too great: their minds become distracted away from the job at hand and their concentration is impaired. It may be that the auditor can do something to improve the situation discretely without having to issue a formal request for corrective action. By so doing, he may be able to foster a good working relationship with the auditee's staff and enable the rest of the audit to run smoothly.

8.   *Be honest.*

An auditor should never try to cover up for his own organization. If the latter is to blame for a deficiency, he should admit this. Similarly, he should not try to conceal his own ignorance or uncertainty on any points raised by the auditee nor should he try to gloss over his past mistakes. If he ignores this advice and subterfuge subsequently comes to light, it can have a very detrimental effect on the course of the audit. The auditor's credibility is damaged and his integrity becomes questionable.

9.   *Be human.*

Some auditees still view the auditor as something of a bogeyman. If the auditor can manage to break the ice somehow - with a joke, possibly - he may make the auditee to relax and get things moving. If a difficult situation arises - one involving a deficiency on the auditee's part, for example - the auditor must try to defuse it. He might truthfully say, for instance, that he has come across the same mistake made by other organizations in the past. Proceedings can be held up if the atmosphere becomes tense, emotions get too high or personnel become over-anxious. The auditor must get everyone to focus on finding an efficacious solution and to regard the fact the problem as being unearthed as good thing, as an opportunity to improve and to reduce avoidable costs. This approach is of the essence in value-added auditing and continuous improvement programmes. Finding a root cause does not mean finding someone to blame.

10.   *Be determined, decisive and direct.*

It is always a good idea for the auditor to display his determination to get the business of the audit conducted efficiently and promptly. The auditee must not be allowed to think he can get away with presenting incomplete information or delaying the proceedings unnecessarily (see Chapter 15). When sufficient evidence has been collected and sifted, the auditor should not hesitate to come to a conclusion on the basis of it and he should then convey his decision directly to the auditee. Once there is enough evidence to form the basis of a sound judgement, there is no point in going over and over the same ground or in watering down conclusions. Bear in mind the cost-benefit graph displayed in Chapter 9, Figure 9.5, for the auditor should feel comfortable that he is in the positive cost-benefit area: wasting further time, wastes money and moves the auditor into the negative cost-benefit area again.

11.   *Get on with the job.*

The auditor should avoid spending a lot of time in unnecessary or irrelevant conversations. Here, again, he can set an example to the auditee and demonstrate his resolve to get the business of the audit conducted as efficiently as possible. One of the reasons I do not favour having a meeting room put at the disposal of the audit team is that the discussions that take place within them are best held during the evening, after the day's fact gathering activities. (See Chapter 10.) If a meeting room is to be used, use it during the audit evening, not during the audit day.

12.   *Be fair.*

The auditor should always be fair in the way he approaches the different departments he audits, not go to one specifically to find fault. Personal dislikes or prejudices must not be allowed to influence his investigations If he shows a bias, the auditor will lose the auditee's confidence and future his audits could be tainted with the suspicion of reflecting personal prejudice, bias and political maneuvering. You might not like the auditee you are dealing with, but you must respect him if you are to respect yourself.

13.   Be independent.

The auditor, not the auditee, should be the one to make the decisions as to what will be examined (bearing in mind the constraints mentioned in Chapter 11 namely, whatever is seen is only ever a sample. If the auditor allows the auditee to choose what is to be seen, he may well end up being led by the nose. (See also Chapter 15, *"The fixed ballot".*)

14.   Use your powers of deduction.

Sometimes the auditor will run up against a brick wall in his pursuit of information - this is often the case, for example, if the person he needs to see is temporarily unavailable. In this situation, it is worth trying to deduce the missing information by examining the evidence in units (processes) upstream and downstream of the unit concerned. An auditor may be able to reach some conclusions as to the unit's performance by examining units downstream of it or units it supplies with feedback. By auditing upstream, he may be able to deduce with what information the unit is supplied. The interaction between the units means that an auditor may have a fairly good idea that a deficiency exists long before he actually arrives to audit the unit in question. If, for example, goods of the wrong quality are being received , the auditor may suspect that the purchase orders are incorrect because the purchasing department is omitting certain key quality requirements. By auditing units upstream of purchasing, the auditor can determine whether the information purchasing receives is reflected in the purchase orders (if the auditor will have examined copies of purchase orders in the auditee's incoming goods receiving area). If there are any variances between the quality requirements conveyed to the purchasing department and those involved in the actual purchase placed, the auditor can conclude there is a problem within the purchasing department without even visiting it. However, this would still need to be verified in order to be certain, and, if a problem does exist in that purchasing department, the root cause would still need to be found.

15.   Know who's who.

An auditor should master not merely the names but the positions and interrelationships of the auditee's personnel. If he does not do this, embarrassing mistakes can occur.

> One external auditor was discussing a number of deficiencies with Mr. A. A further meeting had to be arranged the following morning

in order to continue the discussions. At the next day's meeting a Mr. B entered the discussions. His knowledge was not as extensive as Mr. A's, a point which the auditor commented on to Mr. A. Unfortunately, B was, instead of A's subordinate, his superior.

16.   *One swallow does not make a summer.*

If the auditor finds a couple of deficiencies in the area being audited, he has two alternatives. One is to recommend a purge of the area in order to get to the truth, assess the magnitude of the problem and put the deficiencies into correct perspective. The second alternative is to perform the purge himself, if time permits and if he doubts the auditee's good intentions.

It makes sense to give the auditee an opportunity to perform the purge himself unless the auditor feels he cannot be relied upon to do so properly.

> During an external audit of a supplier's design department, a few incorrect design calculations were found. A purge of the contract calculations was recommended and was performed by the auditee. The latter requested that all work be stopped in order to give the design department an opportunity to correct the deficiencies that had turned up in other calculations and to assess the impact on the contract itself. In this case the auditee took the initiative, acted responsibly and demonstrated his desire to get things right to the satisfaction of his own company and of the customer auditing him. Investigation showed an inadequate review being performed by a senior engineer assigned to that review task: the calculations were being "signed off", not properly checked. The root cause of the problem was found to be an excessive workload placed onto the senior engineer because of under staffing in the design department. (Two of the six real causes were acting in tandem: lack of resources and lack of time, see Chapter 18.)

The point to remember is that it is in the auditee's own best interests to ascertain the extent of any problem which arises and to instigate prompt and effective corrective action. Failure to do so may lead to more serious problems at a later stage, as the avoidable costs inevitably increase, and to incurring the displeasure of senior management in the auditee's organization. The basic instinct of self-preservation can often be relied upon to make the auditee take the purge seriously. In the few cases where the auditee does play down the problem in public, knowing very well that it is more extensive than he says, he will generally go away quietly to rectify the situation at the earliest opportunity. In any case, the auditor will probably be issuing a formal request for corrective action which will, in due course, be followed-up on. The auditee will be in an indefensible position if the follow-up reveals the auditee did not act responsibly and in good faith. The result is usually the same in the end and it is the result which counts.

> During one internal audit, three out of a sample of ten non-conformity reports were found to have a common deficiency. A purge of a further 100 documents revealed one further case of the deficiency and nothing more. The nature of the deficiency was found to be inconsequential - the non-conformity reports were used for statistical purposes and as a record - so a formal request for corrective action was not issued.

17.   *Discuss any problem immediately, on the spot.*

Doing this saves the auditor any arguments later on, when people's memories have grown hazy, and allows him to clarify the problem and to collect fresh evidence relating to it. If the discussion reaches an impasse, the auditor should not get involved in an argument. He should agree to differ from the auditee and refer the problem to a higher echelon of the auditee's management. Another advantage of discussing a problem on the spot is that it helps the auditee understand the nature of the auditor's doubts and may suggest a solution. Even if this cannot be determined, it is of great help for all concerned to have the problem, clear in their minds before the exit interview (see Chapter 19). Moreover, the operative concerned may be able to suggest effective corrective measures and, since he might not be present later at the exit interview, this on-the-spot discussion may give him his only chance to make his voice heard. Whether the suggestion is the one finally implemented or not is less important than showing that his ideas are considered of value. (If the suggestion is not adopted, the operative must be told the reasons and thanked for his efforts by the auditee's management and, if possible, by the auditor.)

18.   *Investigate fresh evidence supplied by the auditee.*

Be prepared to return to an area, if necessary, to obtain fresh evidence or to reassess the activity in the light of fresh evidence or to reassess the activity in the light of fresh evidence supplied by the auditee. Willingness to go back and re-audit an area shows that the auditor has an open mind and helps enlist the co-operation of the auditee's staff.

During one audit, it was found that certain documents were not being processed as the available procedure described. It was not possible to determine the reason for the variance between procedure and practice because the man responsible was temporarily inaccessible. It transpired during a discussion with the quality manager that the procedure had been changed without the person concerned being given a copy of the new version. In order to determine whether there had been compliance with the correct effectivity point, the audit team returned to the area concerned, looked at the evidence again and found that the person responsible had, in fact, complied with the old version. The problem was not caused by a failure to comply with procedure but rather by failure to issue the correct version to the person who needed to use it.

19.   Beware union relationships.

The auditor should be aware of whether or not the area being audited comes under the *"jurisdiction"* of a trade union. If so, he should ask for a shop steward to accompany the audit team around the area concerned. This prevents operatives complaining to their trade union and, possibly, exacerbating a delicate situation, if one already exists. It is particularly important to have a union representative present if there is to be a locker purge (i.e. the operatives' lockers are to be opened and examined for uncontrolled items, equipment and information). As audits have now become more commonplace, those representatives and the employees tend to understand the reasons for such activities and are generally unconcerned. It is always preferable to have present the locker's actual user.

My experience has convinced me that disharmonious union relationships herald business problems and excessive avoidable costs: there are numerous examples available that amply demonstrate disharmony is avoidable with effective management and internal communications.

20.   Hold audit team conferences each day.

It is vital for the audit team members to conduct a private conference amongst themselves. In the case of an external audit, the meeting generally takes place in the evening, perhaps in the motel or hotel at which the audit team is staying. Each auditor must remember that his colleagues do not communicate by telepathy. The information that has been obtained during the day's proceedings must be exchanged and analyzed.

One audit team thought it could usefully employ cellular phones to communicate with each other during the day at the auditee's premises. The practice was soon stopped when each began complaining to the others of interruptions to answer their telephone calls.

The meeting is so important because it enables the team to review progress and, if necessary, reassign tasks. Some members may be ahead of schedule, other may have encountered problems and had to spend more time in a particular area than was originally anticipated. In this case, those who are ahead of schedule might be able to take on auditing some of the departments previously assigned to other team members, provided, of course, they have the expertise and experience of the auditee processes involved.

It often works well to hold the progress meeting after the team has had an opportunity to take a shower or a bath to refresh themselves and to read through any documents provided by the auditee during the day (such as procedures relevant to the areas to be audited next day or something similar).

The audit team members must be sure to exchange the information that they each require for the following day (information, equipment, item and service identities and details, people's names/ Identification mechanisms and other data relating to the task elements seen - see Chapter 13 "An example of question technique" and Chapter 12). They should also discuss the occurrence of general problems which are found to be cropping up across a number of the auditee's departments/process areas. The problems will be in groups, each coming under the heading of one of the task elements' sub-elements, and then further assigned to one or more of the six real cause of problems. (See also Chapter 17, "Frequent errors".) Deficiencies discovered in a number of areas, for example, might be traced back to lack of training in the various management systems or to poor methods of handling products due to a lack of resources. It is important to categorize the defects in preparation for presentation at the exit interview. In categorizing the errors, the audit team is beginning to operate on the two levels described in Chapter 11, "Two-level auditing and pattern recognition". To coin an expression, the audit team is seeing the forest *and* the trees.

21.   Know thy time.

Time is the enemy of the auditor. It is also one of the greatest assets available to gather the facts. The auditor must be aware of the overall progress of the audit so as to avoid wasting precious minutes and hours on trivia. It is better to spend time auditing the more crucial areas, investigating those few vital problems than the trivial many. The audit team must, however, not allow the schedule to dictate to them if they feel that the problems encountered warrant deeper investigation. A word of warning, though: in certain countries (such as Switzerland) people will expect the audit team to make an appointment for meetings and to arrive strictly on time. If the decision is made to depart from the original schedule, the audit team must inform the auditee and request that information be passed on to the departments which may be affected by a late or early arrival. The audit team's escort should be asked to ensure this is done. In any case, this practice is simply a matter of courtesy in any country. If the lead auditor feels it is necessary (in the light of discoveries already made) to spend more time than is planned on the audit, then he should notify their own organization of the situation, explaining why he believes more time will be needed.

22.   Dispense with unnecessary escorts and hangers-on.

The auditor must only have the escorts and attendance he wants and needs in the area being audited (see Chapter 10 "Escorts"). If he finds he is collecting too many followers, he should ask them to disperse: the actual assigned escort's assistance may be needed to achieve this. They will simply obstruct and slow down the proceedings while their presence raises the costs of the audit quite unnecessarily, reducing its cost-benefit.

23.   Brief the auditee's management each day.

Once a day, let the auditee's representatives have a brief summary of what has been happening (without commitment to the final conclusions that might be drawn from the audit gathering further information from the areas remaining to be audited).

This summary is a courtesy measure that is always appreciated by the auditee's management. It also rules out the need to make embarrassing revelations at the exit interview and in the audit report by forewarning those involved of the nature of any deficiencies encountered. There is nothing creditable in saving the deficiencies for the exit interview with a view to gloating over people's surprise and embarrassment.

It may turn out that the auditee is already aware of the problem and has already instituted corrective action. In this case, the auditor must verify that corrective action is under way, that it addresses the root cause of the problem, that it has been recorded and approved by an appropriate authority level in the auditee's organization. (See Chapter 17.) If the auditor determines that the corrective action proposals would not be efficacious, the auditor will report the deficiency as a formal corrective action request issued by his own organization.

If the auditee is unaware of the problem, the forewarning provided by the briefing meeting permits the auditee to communicate to the appropriate level of management that certain findings have been made and to consider what corrective action could be proposed at the exit interview. The senior management, who will be present at the exit interview, will appreciate the forewarning and the chance to formulate their own proposals after performing their own investigation of root cause. If the auditor has a good idea of the sort of corrective action which would be effective, thereby satisfying his own organization's expectations, it is constructive for him to pass the information on to the auditee at this point.

Sometimes the senior management present at a brief summary meeting will appreciate a private discussion with the auditors or lead auditor - an example of this would be if they may have sensitive information which they feel the audit team should be aware but which is not for general dissemination. If this is the case, the audit team must indicate that this confidential information will not alter the audit's outcome since it will have to be regarded as hearsay, albeit much appreciated hearsay.

> During one audit I was called to the auditee's managing director's office for a private discussion. He asked me bluntly whether or not I thought the company's quality manager was suitable for the position he held. I answered honestly that I felt the individual was unsuitable since he lacked the requisite knowledge and personality to provide the essential support for implementing the firm's quality programme. The managing director stated that this accorded with his own opinion and that the quality manager was to be replaced soon, his replacement having been selected, but the news had yet to be broken to the quality manager himself.

Confidence of this kind must not be betrayed: the details must not be included in the audit report which will be disseminated throughout both the auditee's and the auditor's organizations. One must bear in mind that they are hearsay as opposed to factual evidence. Nonetheless, they are confidence and must remain so, which means they must not be loosely disseminated anywhere.

An important benefit of the daily briefing is that it can destroy rumour and gossip. Many organizations contain individuals who enjoy exaggerating events to cause alarm or dismay to others. The exaggeration might be malicious, it might be playful teasing, but it can be harmful and introduce an unhelpful atmosphere into the audit. Some managers might become aggressive, waiting for imagined battles and ready to engage immediately in an argument with the auditors. The briefing presents a factual account of what really has been occurring and an uncommitted view as to the direction in which events are going, conclusions might be drawn.

24.   Remember Murphy's Law.

Murphy is sometimes regarded as the patron saint of auditors! It is uncanny how an auditor finds the one superseded document still in use when all others have been withdrawn, the one and only batch of items outside of shelf-life in a store containing thousands, the single occurrence of un-maintained equipment in a preventive maintenance system that has correctly dealt with all other similar pieces in the auditee's operation, the isolated human error in many situations. Since the auditor is generally sampling he cannot hope to see every item, piece of information and person involved in the totality of the auditee's activities.

> During one audit, it was found that all the work areas were clear of uncontrolled materials. The auditee had, immediately prior to the audit, been around the various areas and attempted a purge of all uncontrolled material. This was a daily occurrence in the shop concerned. In spite of this, when the audit team arrived in the area where its contract work was about to start, a pile of uncontrolled material was found in a cupboard.

The auditor could be guided by Murphy and, upon finding a deficiency that may indicate a possible problem, require a purge. However, if on the basis of a limited sample the auditor finds all to be satisfactory, he could leave it at that. The reader can decide for himself, on the basis of past experience, how wise this last course would be.

> I was attending a courtesy visit at a book printer's premises in Michigan and was invited to examine a large collection of books printed at that plant, as examples of the firm's quality. The very first selected from the shelving was found to have been bound upside down, to the amusement of all! Murphy was present.

But Murphy also knows where to be for maximum impact, and does have a sense of humour. I supplied a number of books to the British Institute of Quality Assurance some years ago. The delivery was taken from a recently completed very large print run and still wrapped in packages of 12. When Penny Crick, of the IQA, opened the packages delivered to her, she found a few books bound upside down! My own checking of a number of packages had revealed no problems up until that time.

25.   *Good guy - bad guy approach.*

Some auditors believe a good method is to have two people on a team, one of whom adopts the *"tough guy"* approach while the other adopts a *"soft guy"* image. The idea is that the auditee's personnel will start to talk more of how things actually are. This method is unprofessional and betrays an attitude more befitting the thug than a professional auditor. It cannot be condoned and must be avoided. An audit is not to be regarded as an opportunity for confrontation. Such an approach benefits nobody. The good guy - bad guy approach does not alter the objective evidence available for perusal, a fundamental point to be made since audit results are not to be based on matters of opinion derived from fear - it is objective evidence that is needed.

26.   *The bribe*

Under no circumstances should the auditor offer to ignore certain problems, to omit them from the audit report or to refrain from issuing a corrective action request if the auditee will perform some favour.

A continental European auditor used to be quite direct in expressing his desires. Upon discovering a problem he would embark on a little routine as follows. Shaking his head in sadness he would say, *"This is bad. This is very, very bad. What should I do? I could report this and advise we will not accept your products and you would not be paid. Perhaps I should have you removed from our approved suppliers list."* (He had the authority to do this.) He would then express his wishes, on one occasion by saying, *"But you know, I need a new hunting rifle,"* and looking directly at the escort. He got his hunting rifle. On another occasion he finished his routine, presented to a different auditee's sales manager, *"But you know, my wife and I were thinking we would like to take a vacation in Bermuda this year."* The sales manager took his cue and said, *"I agree this is serious, but let us think overnight and perhaps we will find a solution by the morning."* The auditor agreed. Next morning, the auditor said, *"I was considering the problem in my hotel room last night. I do not think it is so serious as first appeared."* Later that year he and his wife enjoyed Bermuda. I also heard he had a profitable little side line selling copies of auditee's company quality manuals to firms desperate for such information.

The gentleman concerned was somewhat itinerant in Europe during the 1970's and back then I encountered many suppliers he had visited for his company. Several times I was asked by auditee's executives *"Do you know him?"* I would reply *"I know of him,"* and would be told, *"Yes he is very flexible."* It concerns me still whenever I hear an auditor dubbed as being *"flexible"*!

15. The auditee's conduct

Cunning is the dark sanctuary of incapacity.

Lord Chesterfield.

In the same way as there are right and wrong ways for an auditor to conduct the audit, an auditee can have a right and a wrong approach to the audit. Nefarious tactics are still occasionally used by some auditees or their personnel although this is growing rarer as audits become more commonplace. Some of the commonest tactics are listed below to help an inexperienced auditor recognize the symptoms. Of course, some auditees may display the relevant behaviour quite innocently, so the auditor should be discreet in concluding that the auditee is deliberately being obstructive.

There are 12 main tactics which obstructive auditees adopt. I call them the *"Dirty Dozen"*. They are listed in Fig. 15.1 together with a summarization of how to deal with each one. Various manifestations of each of these are now discussed.

Time wasters

1. The waffler.

This individual can speak at length, says nothing, and never answers a question concisely. Politicians indulge in such tactics. It wastes time and achieves nothing.

2. The "dog and pony" show.

This is a rather apt American expression for a lengthy presentation, generally during the entry interview, accompanied by impressive charts, slides, company film or video and exhibits. The content of the presentation may or may not be of use to the auditor. Even if it is, the auditor has to verify what has been said during the presentation, by the examination of objective evidence and thus, as the dog and pony show presentation is of no value to him, he should politely call a halt to the proceedings.

315

Tactic	How to handle
Time wasting	Tell the auditee you will extend the audit if progress is unsatisfactory.
The "Cook's tour"	If it has no value, stick to your audit programme.
Provocation	Remain calm and polite. Discuss the issues, not emotions.
Fixed ballot	Refuse and select your own sample of objective evidence.
Special case	Take extensive notes and wait till the auditee gets himself confused.
Trial of strength	Be prepared for the audit: know your facts; be firm; have the right specialists on the team.
Insincerity	Ignore it.
Pity	Show polite sympathy and then get on with the job.
Absentees	Call for the deputy, manager to explain the process. If no one is available, audit inputs and outputs to determine efficacy of the process concerned.
Amnesia	Go back and get it yourself.
Language barrier	Have a translator on team, or advise your management of the risks in advance. If you have to rely on the auditee's translations, qualify your report to reflect this fact.
Bribes	Refuse them, report it and stop dealing with that auditee.

Figure 15.1 The *"Dirty Dozen"* and how to deal with them.

3. The long lunch.

The external auditor is generally the recipient of this tactic, particularly in countries such as France or Italy where food is almost a religion. Instead of being allowed to take a quick lunch in the canteen, the auditor is faced with a four course meal, an aperitif, plenty of wine, and maybe a liqueur afterwards. This not only wastes time but also makes it difficult to concentrate during the afternoon.

There is a variation on this ploy, whereby the auditee tells the auditor: *"We know a delightful little restaurant just a short drive from here, where we would really like to take you because the food is excellent."* At lunchtime, there is a wait of five or ten minutes while the cars arrive, the short distance eventually turns out to be a thirty minute drive, the actual lunch takes two hours to consume, and a further thirty minutes is spent driving back to the auditee's location.

The auditor should obviously try to avoid offending the auditee when refusing the long lunch but he should none the less remain firm. It should also not be forgotten that in some companies the business lunch is regarded as a perk for the auditee's people, who seldom get the chance to dine out on the company and who look forward to it.

4. The late arrival.

The audit can be delayed if personnel arrive late for work or for their appointments.

> At on audit, the quality manager, who was the escort, arrived 45 minutes late each morning and delayed the audit team as a consequence. The lead auditor soon rectified matters by announcing on the third day that he was extending the audit to make up for lost time due to late starts and the like. The next day the quality manager was early.

5. The long way around.

Although it would be normal practice top use a short cut through a building to get from A to B, during the audit the escorts may use a circuitous route. This is a rather foolish tactic: the auditor will soon get his bearings and recognize when the long way is being taken. The auditor should suggest, for example *"Would it not be quicker if we cut through the stock yard?"*

6. The forgotten document.

One of the escorts "forgets" essential documents. Upon arriving at the area to be audited, he says: *"Oh, dear me! I have left the documents in my office. I will have to go back to fetch them".*

> A lead auditor noted that an escort did this twice. The company was of the large complex type and it was a full 15 minute walk from one end to the other. The third time that the audit team was starting out from the escort's office, the lead auditor noticed a particular document, which would be required later on, left lying on the escort's desk. He placed it in his bag. Sure enough, upon arriving at the destination, the escort smiled and apologized for having forgotten the document. The smile soon disappeared when the lead auditor produced it saying *"Don't worry, I picked it up for you".*

7. Interruptions.

It is the easiest thing in the world for an escort or manager to demand *"No interruptions until we're finished"*. An endless queue of visitors who drag the escort away for a few minutes at a time, phone calls demanding immediate attention and so on all waste time.

8. The "clean room".

With this tactic, everybody has to spend five or ten minutes putting on caps/gown/boots and signing the log sheet before entering the room because the escort says *"It's a strict rule, you know"*. However, upon entering, the auditor notes that one or two of the operatives are not acquainted with the *"strict"* rules, and that visitors who come in afterwards have not been obliged to follow the same *"strict"* procedures.

> On one occasion, an audit team had to get dressed in cap, gown and boots to examine the clean area. The quality assurance manager entered the area to see how the audit was progressing. He was wearing neither cap, nor gown, nor boots.

A variant of this is the trip to the medical department to collect safety spectacles, when it subsequently becomes plain that no one in the works wears safety spectacles and that no other visitor is obliged to wear them either. (I am not, however, suggesting that safety spectacles are unnecessary - rather that the auditee should have at the ready them and other things, such as head coverings, clean shoes, face masks, gloves etc.).

9. Lack of preparedness.

If the personnel are not forewarned by their management, the people whom the auditors need to see may be unavailable.

> A department manager complained bitterly to an audit team that nobody had informed him that an audit was to take place and that he was rather busy. To his credit, he quickly re-scheduled his work, made alternative arrangements and escorted the audit team while they audited his department. As it transpired, it was a most impressive area, under good control, and one where no deficiencies were found by the audit team. That company is in Switzerland, where people appreciate and expect an appointment to be made.

It is a good practice for the auditor to tell the escorts as the audit progresses roughly when he expects that they will arrive in the next areas and what will be done later that day. This helps preclude the possibility of people not being forewarned.

The "Cook's tour"

During the entry interview, the auditor may be presented with an audit programme constructed by the auditee. If the programme does not meet his own requirements, the auditor should politely convey to the auditee both the fact that it is not acceptable and the reason why. He should then state what he wants to audit, when he wants to go there, and who else should be present. The auditor should take care because in some companies and countries people expect adherence to a plan or procedure. This is why the auditor should supply an audit programme (see Chapter 9) prior to the audit so that the auditee can distribute it to departments concerned. Unless this is supplied, the auditee is bound to try to make his own arrangements or plans.

Provocation

According to this, happily rare, tactic, the auditee tries to make the auditor annoyed and argumentative so that the audit can be stopped.

> An auditor was becoming so angry and argumentative that the conversation was beginning to deteriorate to the level of personalities. The auditee knew that this particular auditor could be easily aroused. The lead auditor spotted the situation and quickly stepped in to prevent the auditee's quality manager from halting the audit by calming things down and asking the auditor to be quiet.

On another occasion, an auditor and auditee comprised an Israeli and an Arab. (I will not reveal which was which). As the lead auditor, I found that a considerable amount of diplomacy was needed to prevent a replay of the Six Day War.

The fixed ballot or loaded dice

The auditee may try to select the contract/item/operator/ document for the auditor to see. This can be similar to the *"Cook's tour"*, described above. As Chapter 14 points out, the auditor must always select the objective evidence that is to be audited.

The special case

When a problem arises, the auditee's response is always *"Ah yes, but this is a special case because...."* This may well be true if the auditor is auditing a contract that is not his own. However, unless the auditor is firm, every contract/document/ item becomes a special case. The auditor should politely ask the auditee exactly how many management systems and variations thereof are in effect and how the auditee manages to control the situation. In these circumstances, the auditee sometimes becomes so confused about the *"special cases"* that from department the explanations about each one start to conflict with one another. Once the auditee's confusion is highlighted, the auditor can suggest the auditee should implement a single, unified management system.

The trial of strength

The auditee, at some point and usually fairly early on in the audit proceedings, tries to test the auditor's resilience, knowledge or firmness. If the auditor fails this test, the auditee loses respect for him and the auditor may as well pack up and go home. Control of the whole audit is at stake.

If the auditor convinces the auditee of his ignorance about the process/project/contract/work/product in hand, the auditee might decide to have some fun playing *"apprentice jokes"* on the auditor. In any case the auditor is not in a position to surmise the effectiveness of the auditee's systems for he knows not how to judge them. In being prepared, knowing what applies to the auditee's processes and having the requisite specialists as members of the audit team will ensure a meaningful audit can be performed.

Insincerity

The auditee indulges in flattery, sycophancy and false admiration of the auditor which is designed firstly to make the auditor think more of himself and less of the audit and also to convince the auditor that the auditee's people are *"nice"* and very friendly, that they can be trusted without question. Variants of this are the unctuous look or the excessive hospitality attitudes that some auditees adopt to *"kill him with kindness"*.

> A senior manager in an auditee's company had been oozing humility, compliments and false admiration throughout an audit; they became increasingly obsequious as problems were revealed. At the exit interview, I confirmed that certain matters were deficient and that I intended to issue some corrective action requests. At this point, the tone changed and the manager concerned said unprintable words to the effect *"How can you be such a horrible person when I've been so nice to you?"!*

The auditor must not become affected by false admiration and must concentrate on the job in hand. The best way to handle insincerity is to be polite but ignore it.

Pleas for pity

Here, the auditee tries to make the auditor feel sorry for him so that the auditor will ease up or disregard his findings, either out of sympathy or the fear of having somebody commit suicide during the audit. The auditee may claim that he is unwell today, that he was sick last night, that the doctor said he really should not come into work at all (being a hero). Alternatively he may play the geriatric (*"When you get to my age...."*). The auditor should offer polite sympathy but refuse to be diverted from his investigation or discouraged from reporting his findings faithfully.

> A quality manager started to tell me a heart-rending story concerning the state of his health and how he had made a special effort to come into work that day. Strangely, at the outset of the audit, he had seemed perfectly cheerful and the tragic decline seemed to increase in direct proportion to revelations of deficient practices. I listened with sympathy and stated *"I really appreciate the special efforts that you have made in order to be here today. As a result, I would like to feel certain that I have done an especially thorough job so that you do not feel your sacrifice was wasted"*. By the time the audit was concluded and some suggestions for improvements had been made at the exit interview,

321

the quality manager was quite enthused and babbled on about his intention to do several things during the weekend and get matters advanced immediately. Whatever had been his malady, a miraculous cure had occurred once the quality manager had become more at ease with the audit.

The absentee or indispensable man

The auditee claims that the man who has the key/knowledge/book, whatever, is unavailable or away today. This may or may not be true. Of course, some people try to make themselves indispensable by refusing to pass on their knowledge to others.

At one South African manufacturing company, the production controller, who was really running the whole works, refused to write anything down and kept all his information in his head. His fear was that if he wrote the information down, he would become dispensable to the company and could find himself out of a job.

An audit revealed that an engineer had not adequately specified a product that was to be purchased. Although at the time the original purchase order was placed, an adequate specification appeared to be available, essential details to guide the vendor had neither been adequately included nor subsequently confirmed in writing. The investigations showed that the engineer in question lived in fear of losing his job because, in the straightened circumstances of his particular industry, redundancies, (in recent times euphemistically called *"downsizing"*), were common. He tried, therefore, to make himself indispensable.

These are human problems that can only be solved on a case-by- case basis. So far as the auditor is concerned, there is a job to be done. Except in a genuine emergency, the people needed should always be made available during the audit.

When the auditee claims that an absentee is indispensable, the auditor must ascertain who is the allegedly indispensable person's supervisor or manager. Then he must request that the latter comes to the workplace to explain how the area works and to show objective evidence of what is being done. Since any supervisor or manager is responsible for the processes and management systems in that area, that person must be familiar with them. But is he?

If this fails, the auditor must deduce the effectiveness of the absentee by assessing the evidence available from other areas (see Chapter 14, *"Use your powers of deduction"*). This latter course of action might not be perfect, and it has some shortcomings, but it is far better than walking away in the belief that no useful conclusions can be drawn about the effectiveness of the auditee's systems, practices and controls.

Amnesia

When this tactic is employed, the auditor has continually to chivy the auditee for the information that he has asked to be provided before the end of the audit. The auditee who acts in such a way may be hoping that the auditor will forget that the information was ever requested. The auditor must make it clear that he will continue the audit until the information is forthcoming.

If information is constantly not made available, the options are:

♦ To obtain the information immediately from wherever it has allegedly gone or whoever may be using it.

♦ To return to the area responsible for providing that information immediately on completion of the current aspects of the audit.

♦ To return to that same workplace upon completion of the entire audit, and prior to the exit interview, whilst making it clear that if this will entail an extension to the time required for the audit, so be it.

Language barrier

The options available for dealing with a genuine language barrier have been described in Chapter 9, under the heading *"Interpreters"*.

Some auditees exploit the language barrier by claiming not to speak the auditor's mother tongue. Unless the auditor speaks the auditee's language, this can create a problem and waste time. The auditee's aim may be to claim to misunderstand the explanation, questions and information discussed or examined during the audit. It is a quasi-political tactic.

> An auditor encountered an individual and asked if that person spoke English. The response was *"Nein"*. The audit proceeded in the auditee's language. However, at one point, the auditor noted that in the person's open valise was an English copy of *The Day of the Jackal* by Frederick Forsyth. At the end of the discussion, the

auditor remarked in English to the auditee that he hoped he would enjoy *The Day Of The Jackal*, since it was a good book that would help him to improve his English. The auditee looked surprised and embarrassed for a moment, then laughed. When the auditor next spoke to that particular individual, it was amazing how much English had been learnt.

An auditee had been conversing well with the auditor in the latter's mother tongue. All suddenly changed when some problems were discovered. At this juncture the auditee suddenly started to shake his head and lapsed into his own language claiming he did not understand what the auditor was saying. However, his international lingual ability soon returned when the auditor offered a simple solution to the problems!

Sometimes an auditor may find it useful to play the language game himself but for a different reason. The private chats and asides between auditee's personnel can be enlightening and help him to assess whether or not the auditee is acting in good faith.

A design engineer was being most unco-operative with an audit team. The quality manager, present as escort, spoke quietly to the design engineer and the auditor was able to mentally translate the words: *"Why do we have to drag every piece of information out of your nose?"* , which were accompanied by a plain language instruction to the engineer which one might loosely translate as *"Desist from playing games with us"*. The design engineer went fairly pale at being reproved by a senior manager. The auditor knew immediately that they were about to make better progress. They did.

The bribe

The auditor may encounter this distasteful practice when the contract is large or of critical value to the auditee. It may occur during the pre-award survey or during the external audit. Fortunately it is comparatively rare.

During a pre-award survey a potential supplier was so desperate to win the contract that a substantial bribe was offered in private to the lead assessor. The latter did not know how to manage this situation. After returning to his company, he consulted with a senior manager who promptly telexed the potential supplier stating *"We note your revised offer to be as per original less the discount offered to our lead assessor during the pre-award survey"*. The contract was, naturally, offered to an alternative source.

The bribe sometimes occurs during internal audits. It generally takes the form of promises (couched in terms that range from vague and implied to fairly direct) of promotion, raise, perks, favourable annual reviews. The reverse bribe takes the form of veiled or not so veiled warnings and threats affecting the auditor's prospects in the department or company.

Whatever from the bribe takes, it must be refused and reported to a senior level of management. In the case of an internal audit, the auditor should ask himself whether it is worth working for a company that would act in this manner, especially one that countenances threats when one is only trying to do an assigned job.

Registrars, especially, must not be swayed from doing their jobs by implied threats or inferences that they will lose the contract with the firm if, in the opinion of the assessed firm, their client, they are excessively rigorous and diligent.

The right tactics

Having looked at the tactics the auditee may adopt to hinder the auditor, it is necessary to mention those he should adopt to help him. These tactics will be the reverse of those just listed. Naturally, it is important to keep a sense of proportion here as elsewhere. I am not suggesting that the auditee should starve the audit team, deny them refreshments or give incomplete/terse answers to questions.

The auditee's escorts must be alert for the incipient use of the wrong tactics by the departments or units being audited. It should be remembered that an extrinsic audit provides, or should provide, an independent, unbiased appraisal of the auditee's practices, equipment, policies and so on. As such it is good *"free"* consultancy. An extrinsic auditor who is experienced, trained, constructive and helpful can be of great benefit to the auditee.

All too frequently, the extrinsic auditor is the only person who can elicit action and improvements in the practices and management systems from the auditee's management. This is because the extrinsic auditor has that all important lever: the customer's requirement/opinion or the regulatory body's endorsement/ approval of the auditee's practices or product This amounts to money and potential loss or gain of business for the auditee. It is commonly called *"customer pressure"* and, judiciously used, it can solve some apparently intractable problems.

> A quality department had struggled for a number of years with a workshop manager over the introduction of a material control system that would be up to modern standards. The spur for action came from my threat (as extrinsic auditor) to refuse to accept a complex safety-related product that had been fabricated for my company. My justification was that there was no evidence available to prove exactly what materials had been used in the welding process or to indicate the qualifications of the welders nor were there any test results to show whether or not the welds were satisfactory. To the workshop manager's credit, the situation was rectified in a very short space of time and a solution was found to analyze the materials that had been used in the fabrication of this complex structure.

Desperation

In difficult circumstances, the most punctilious of auditees can be driven to adopt desperate measures for dealing with an audit team.

> A Glaswegian friend of mine related an incident that occurred when his company was being audited. He had been the quality manager for over twenty years and ran a tight ship, so tight, in fact, that an extrinsic audit team were becoming increasingly frustrated, unpleasant and a general nuisance. Recognizing that they had to justify their existence, the quality manager waited till the team departed one evening and then went along to a department that was to be audited the following day. He instructed the foreman to remove a couple of calibration stickers on some measuring equipment and to scatter some spare material under the work benches. The audit team glowed with pure delight when they found this *"disgraceful set of affairs"*. Two corrective action requests were issued on the spot to my friend, who acted as if suitably chastened. The audit team then announced that the audit was complete. Immediately after the team left that *"filthy area"*, the foreman replaced the stickers and threw out the loose material.

I leave the reader to decide whether my friend's action was right or wrong.

16. Auditing and cyberspace

While from the bounded level of our mind,
Short views we take, nor see the lengths behind;
But more advanc'd, behold with strange surprise
New distant scenes of endless science rise!

Alexander Pope

The arrival of cyber audits

Outsourcing has increased the number of businesses in almost every country's economy. Small businesses are tending to use computers as an essential, if not central, part of their activities so as to be competitive. A growing number of supplier and customer firms are discarding hard copy in their quest to become paperless offices or, paperless partnerships. Many have succeeded, more will achieve that goal. Some large corporations are beginning to insist all communications between themselves and their suppliers are conducted electronically, that hard copy is eliminated.

National economies have grown as a result of the knowledge society; their firms selling only knowledge, not manufactured goods or services with tangible products. Inexpensive yet powerful desktop computers, laptop computers and modern telecommunications systems have enabled telecommuters to emerge and flourish. Some telecommunications firms, notably MCI of the USA, in their television advertisements, actively address this expanding business sector.

Telecommuters are process workers, just as much as the operative employed working on the shop floor of a conventional factory. They are subject to audit and assessment too. But, the audit might not need to be done on a face-to-face basis. The inter-connectivity afforded by modems and digital telephone systems means that the audit can be conducted regardless of how geographically remote the telecommuter (or auditee) happens to be. The magic of electronics puts the auditor alongside the auditee as if a face-to-face audit was in progress.

Cyber audits will increasingly replace the face-to-face audit, but will never totally eliminate them. They will be of particular benefit to firms globally

327

sourcing supplies, wishing to assess their suppliers' performance but not necessitating the costs of international travel incurred in face-to-face audits. At present day levels, one can obtain a considerable amount of international telecommunication time access to remote systems for the price of an air fare and hotel charges. For the company that uses the Internet, not even international telephone rates apply, merely the cost of a local call. In sum, one must expect an exponential rise in the use of cyber audits as the drive towards increased competitiveness and reduction of avoidable costs accelerates. One can present a powerful case that conventional face-to-face audits are entering ever deeper into the realm of avoidable costs in comparison to cyber audits using the Internet, video conferencing *et al.*

Most companies use computers to some extent. Many still maintain their desktop PC's isolated from each other, but the trend is towards internally linking all the company's machines to each other, to powerful servers and creating corporate Intranets. There is a burgeoning amount of useful and relatively economic software that enables these things to be done, to build a database the firm's working community can access and develop instead of passing around endless reams of hard copy paperwork. The paperless office is becoming a commonplace reality. Internal audits will need to become cyber based.

Although I never have found the tedium of examining paperwork to be a joyful experience and have strived to eliminate as much of the stuff as possible from the auditee's systems, in order to reduce avoidable costs, examining data displayed on visual display units offers no net relief.

The increasing use of computers as a central piece of process equipment simultaneously raises the following two issues, the answers to which are *"yes"* and *"no"* respectively:

♦ Are effective audits possible?
♦ Should the auditor proceed in any manner that is fundamentally different to that used when auditing traditional situations?

The following discussion relates to cyber audits performed *in lieu* of conventional face-to-face audits. It is not concerned with cyber audits performed to determine the efficacy of the auditee's computer and data security systems, policies and practices, although the auditor will gain an impression of this. (These are discussed in Part 2 Chapter 4.)

What is a cyber audit?

I regard a cyber audit as being:

a management audit of the auditee's work performed solely through the medium of computers and electronic communications.

What are the limitations of performing cyber audits?

Cyber audits are only of use when auditing processes whose product is the task element "information" combined with the other task element "service". Successful audits of auditees making manufactured goods require an element of physical examination during which the auditor's sentient skills are invaluable. Even though video conferencing is a useful facility, it is, at present, unsuitable for auditing factory floor processes. Thankfully, he Orwellian age of *"Big Brother"* is not entirely with us yet!

What kind of competence does the auditor need?

The auditor needs to be familiar with using computers, opening files, reading data much as many people do when using the Internet and *"surfing the world wide web"*. But, knowledge of the type of system architecture, the actual operating system and application programs used by the auditee is essential. It is unacceptable for the auditor to think an effective audit can be accomplished by learning the application on-the-job, constantly scrutinizing the available "help" facilities and user manuals. Although the auditee's tasks are not interrupted to the same extent as they would be during a face-to-face audit of the traditional type, when the auditor is doing this form of learning, the audit costs still become unacceptably high reducing the overall cost-benefit.

Where is the auditor?

It is not necessary for the auditor to be located at the same place as the auditee. The auditor can perform the fact gathering from any location in the world provided both auditor and auditee have the telecommunications equipment and facilities to link themselves. With this in mind, their is no reason why the cyber auditor cannot be a telecommuter or traveler performing the audit using a laptop computer while flying by aircraft to an overseas destination. The audit could be conducted through the Internet. By whatever method is used, the auditor will be on-line throughout the audit.

Audit preparation

The auditor will prepare just as Chapter 9 suggests. However, the information for review would be requested and received by means of E-MAIL, disks sent by the auditee using *"snail mail"* (conventional mail methods), or direct transfer made possible by linking together the auditor's and auditee's computers. If this latter method is to be used the auditor will need to establish the software, protocols etc. first, as described below.

By these means, the auditor not only can assess the information obtained from the auditee, but also can effectively perform a reconnaissance visit to the auditee's premises. Admittedly this would be a *"virtual reconnaissance visit"*, but the effect may well be the same as if an actual physical visit was undertaken.

The auditor's checklist (or other guidance tools) and the programme would be transmitted electronically to the auditee. The audit programme might include not only a list of the auditee's processes the auditor will want to examine, but also a list of computer systems, files and records that will be investigated. The auditee will need to know this so that appropriate access authority could be arranged.

What effect does the paperless office have on audit method?

Answer, none. The seven steps described in Chapter 11 can still be used as follows:

Step 1: Analyze the auditee's organization

The reader should note the remarks made in Chapter 3 in the section *"Virtual organizations,* "doughnuts" *and outsourcing"*. If the auditee is a telecommuter engaged by means of outsourcing either he/she is a member of a project team and reports within the project team structure or, the auditee is controlled by mans of a formal purchase order (contract) which will state the terms, conditions, performance requirements of the customer.

If the auditee is a member of one's own firm, the organization arrangements will be seen from the organization chart.

Step 2: Analyze the auditee's management systems

The auditor will investigate the management systems used by the auditee. Even though the auditee's product might be created electronically and all work and communications with upstream and down stream processes might be made by electronic means, in order to verify the effectiveness of the system to be used, the auditor can investigate the extent to which the necessary files are to be transferred between the processes, as well as the construction of databases and intranets set up for common use and development. The evidence might be available from systems flow charts, database design files.

Step 3: Assess the auditee's compliance with the organization and management systems

The auditor will verify the use of the system and its constituent files, databases and intranet by examining them on-line. The organizational authorities to release work will be seen from the various *"read" "write"*, *"execute" and "delete"* authorities given to the auditee's personnel.

Step 4: Decide the efficacy of the management systems and organization

This will, as usual, be evident from the objective evidence obtained from the previous step - compliance.

Step 5: Decide if the auditee's management systems/ organization could be improved or simplified.

The auditor's own experience will determine this. But, the precepts of *"Step 5"*, described in Chapter 11 nonetheless apply.

Step 6: Assess the auditee's performance monitoring methods

The cyber auditee needs to control his/her processes just as much as does anyone else. The controls must be based on what matters to the recipients of the cyber auditee's work.

Step 7: Decide if there are improvement opportunities

The advice of *"Step 7"*, described in Chapter 11, applies.

Interacting with the auditee

Face-to-face audits offer considerable benefits in that the effectiveness of communication between auditor and auditee is much higher. Regardless of whether one attributes this to mutual reading of body language, eye contact, "vibes" or whatever, it amounts to an inner sense developed over aeons of time during which evolution has had its effects on human nature. The cyber audit can be performed blind, just as is a telephone conversation. But the latter does at least provide listener and receiver with impressions gained from voice intonation, pauses, sentence construction, repetition and the like which, too, are processed according to the software of evolution.

On balance, the best way to perform the cyber audit is by means of video-conferencing which is increasingly affordable with the rise of the Internet, cheap yet powerful desktop and laptop computers, small video cameras, sound and video cards, low priced software to suit. Just because video conferencing is used during the audit, this does not mean the auditee has to stop work and observe the auditor in action. The great facility of current and emerging technology is that the auditor needs only to activate the link when a question arises for which a verbal response and personal interaction is necessary. In between times the auditor can examine the objective evidence available from the auditee's system and the auditee can go about normal revenue earning business but aware that the auditor is on-line.

Accessing the auditee's computer system

The auditor must be able to access electronically the auditee's files and data. This means it is essential to know the file structures, protocols, passwords and security arrangements necessary to gain access to the auditee's system etc. Obviously hackers might dispute that last statement, but one must distinguish between computer hacking, audits and covert examination of the auditee's files performed for security reasons without the auditee's knowledge. In that last comment lies a vital consideration: the management audit must always take place with the prior knowledge and agreement of the auditee. Auditee notification is essential, otherwise the essential element of trust is destroyed. The cyber audit must be prepared just as would be an audit in a non-cyber environment.

Security and auditor authority

One must always be concerned about security of data. Most firms are aware of the need to build fire walls to prevent hackers and viruses gaining access to its systems and data, and of the need to encrypt data being transmitted. These needs remain unaltered for the purposes of the cyber audit. The auditor has to address these issues during the audit preparation phase, as does the auditee. The auditor (or audit team, in the case that more than one auditor will be involved in the work) will need to be given the necessary authority to access the auditee's systems, files and data. If encryption software is to be used, its use must be mutually agreed together with the keys and method of using it.

There is nothing new in specifying the level of authority afforded to people using computer systems as being one or more of read, write, execute, delete. The auditor needs only the authority to *"read"*; it would be highly improper for the auditor to be able to add to or alter in any way anything within the auditee's system, files or data. But the auditor does not need the authority to read anything unconnected with the scope and objective of the audit and the auditee should not feel uncomfortable about restricting access to other material. If the information gathered during the audit reveals the need for the auditor to have access beyond what was originally envisaged as necessary for the audit, it becomes incumbent on the auditor to present the case for extension of the read authority. Should the circumstance arise that the auditee refuses to provide that extension, the auditor will qualify the audit report accordingly and express reservations concerning overall findings.

Hidden files

A delegate at one of my seminars questioned whether it is possible to know whether all the auditee's files are presented during the cyber audit because the auditee may have hidden files, barriers to entry or even files copied and removed from the system temporarily until the audit is complete. My response is that this has always been the case: auditees have always been able to remove hard copy files or to maintain two sets of data, the one "sanitized" for audit purposes, the other containing the real situation but withheld. The present discussion is not aimed at audits performed for the purposes of determining dishonest behaviour or criminality; it is to discuss audits for the purpose of business improvement.

The exit interview and the audit report

The exit interview can also be held by video conferencing, or by telephone (which is less than satisfactory, for reasons explained above). The format for the exit interview will remain as described in Chapter 19.

Audit reports and any corrective action requests (CARs) that need to be issued, can be transmitted by electronic means, just as has been the case for many years. There is no need for hard copy audit reports. Content not medium is what matters. See also Chapter 20 which describes the preparation, content and distribution of the audit report; Chapter 17 describes the issuing of CARs.

17. Corrective action decisions

And now remains
That we find the cause of this effect;
Or, rather say, the cause of this defect,
For this effect defective comes by cause.

Shakespeare (Hamlet)

After collecting all the evidence needed, the auditor's next move must be to analyze it, with a view to deciding:

♦   Whether or not corrective action should be taken.
♦   Whether or not a formal request for corrective action is warranted.
♦   What this corrective action might be.
♦   What the underlying root cause of the deficiency discovered really is.

The decision to require formal corrective action is not one the auditor should take lightly or without consideration of all the factors involved. This chapter outlines factors that he should have in mind when the moment comes to make such decisions.

Chapter 11 described an audit method and presented my *"Seven Step"* sequence that an auditor might use. Obviously there are occasions when any facts found during one of the seven steps shown in Figure 11.2 may be found to be deficient. The auditor then has to decide whether corrective action is necessary. Figure 17.1 enlarges on Figure 11.2 and each of the seven steps is now discussed.

STEP 1. The auditor should have ascertained the organization proposals within each department. Any problems encountered with the auditee's proposals for the structure and planning of his organization could be most serious. Where there is no organization, there can be either overlap or conflict of duties or unallocated responsibilities: everything is left vague. Upon encountering a potential problem, therefore, the auditor should follow the path described in Figure 17.2. Within that diagram, any aspect of organizational problems in any single department cannot be regarded as a trivial affair and should warrant the issuing of a corrective action request

(CAR) unless the auditee is aware of the problem and his proposed solutions are satisfactory to the auditor. Lack of organization reduces the reliability of the management systems because one cannot be sure people will know who is responsible for working within them and for the constituent work activities they embrace.

STEP 2. If the auditor finds problems with the management systems proposed by the auditee either for any department or in general, such problems usually constitute a situation which will warrant the issuing of a CAR. Provided, however, that the auditee can prove his awareness of the system problem and can satisfy the auditor by furnishing proof and efficacious proposals for redressing the situation, a CAR will not be issued, as shown in Figure 17.2. The potential reliability of the system depends on how well it has been conceived.

STEP 3. The auditor must not immediately rush ahead with the issuing of a CAR if non-compliance with the system or with the organization has been found. The auditee's personnel might have found the planned and documented *"system"* or *"organization"* to be inadequate when implemented. They might have found alternative and better ways of doing the job while still achieving the right results. This latter scenario is a common consequence of effective continuous improvement programmes which encourage everyone to constantly *"work smarter"* or *"to find a better way"* in doing things.

An overzealous auditor, keen to issue CAR's without due care and attention can do a lot of harm to such schemes. As mentioned in Chapter 13, the auditor will ask a question such as *"Why is the procedure at variance with practice?"* Recollect what the product's needs really are. Provided that the product as required is not suffering, the implemented system/organization is efficacious even though it may not be reflected correctly in the auditee's procedures/ organization plans. In such circumstances, the auditor should merely recommend that the auditee updates the organization and system descriptions to provide an accurate reflection of what is actually happening. At this juncture, inform the auditee that, in not having done so, he is *"selling himself short"*. (This is one particular area where some auditors would disagree with my advice but I take the view that it is the result that matters. Even though standards such as ISO 9001 require the quality system and organizational arrangements to be documented and implemented, my personal view is that the implementation is far more important than the documentation: ISO 9001 is supposed to be product focused and if the product is as required, then end goal of a sensible standard will have been attained.)

	Decision required	If yes	If no
STEP 1	Is auditee's organization OK?	Go to Step 2	Decide c/a
STEP 2	Is auditee's management system OK?	Go to Step 3	Decide c/a
STEP 3	Is auditee in compliance with organization and management systems?	Go to Step 4	Decide if the organization and/ or system are incorrect. If yes, make recommendation If no, decide c/a
STEP 4	Are management systems and organization arrangements efficacious?	Go to Step 5	Decide c/a
STEP 5	Could the management systems/ organization be improved or simplified	Make recommendation	Go to Step 6
STEP 6	Are auditee's performance monitoring methods OK?	If OK go to Step 7	Decide c/a
STEP 7	Do auditee's performance monitoring data indicate there are improvement opportunities?	Make recommendation	End

Figure 17.1 Seven step audit method and corrective action (c/a) decision

I consider it is wrong to issue a CAR to people who are merely doing what is required although they happen not to have recorded the exact details of how they do it. My experience is that when an auditee sees that he is receiving due credit for doing the right thing, for taking an initiative in the best interests of the product, in effecting continuous improvement, the recommendation is acted upon and the auditor is perceived as being fair-minded and maintaining the correct priorities. Receiving a CAR is a poor reward for diligent employees who, by their actions, have demonstrated their reliability for taking care of the product. No matter how well a system has been designed, or an organization has been conceived, its reliability is totally dependent on the reliability of the people entrusted with its adoption and use. Reliability to supply product that meets requirements is of greater importance than the capability to do so since it is reliability of practice which provides real quality assurance.

If, however, the objective evidence shows that the product is suffering and is not being furnished in accordance with requirements, then the auditor must go through the corrective action decision sequence as described in Figure 17.2.

STEP 4. A most critical decision is to determine whether or not each of the system and organization arrangements are effective. This is done on the basis of collecting and collating sufficient objective evidence: a sample whose size could be regarded as significant, indicative of the reality and a fair selection. If that evidence indicates that the system is not effective, the auditor should follow the sequence described in Figure 17.2.

STEP 5. As stated in Chapter 11, the auditor must be constructive and helpful at all times. Accordingly, the auditor has to consider whether the objective evidence and the analysis of the system and organizational arrangements show that there is room for improving or simplifying the latter two. The auditee may be achieving the right results i.e. a product that is fit for purpose and made right first time but the analysis of the system may nonetheless show that the methods used are inefficient in that they waste time or resources: they incur avoidable costs. The auditor's suggestions for improving or simplifying the system or the organization are not the subject of a CAR. The auditee is, after all, achieving the right result - so make a recommendation.

There may seem to be an exception to that last statement in the case of QS 9000 which requires the company adopting it to continuously improve: there is not. In the case of the QS 9000 audit, there are two considerations for the auditor to bear in mind.

Firstly, it is necessary to assess the auditee's system and organizational arrangements for pursuing continuous improvement. If this has been done using my Seven Step method, the decision to issue or not to issue a CAR will have been taken in the first four steps. Secondly, at Step 5, the auditee will be deciding whether or not even greater continuous improvements could be achieved by improving or simplifying the arrangements (system and organization) designed for them. One can reasonably assume that, at the next revision of the ISO 9000 standards, they too will, include the sensible requirement for achieving continuous improvement.

In the case of the current 1994 editions of ISO 9000, their body does not contain any mandatory requirement for continuous improvement in the way that QS 9000 does. The ISO 9000 auditor can rest content that, upon reaching Step 6 of my Seven Step method, he will see what kind of monitoring methods are used by the auditee. Since these should be based on feedback of what the customer wants and expects, the auditor will ne able to see to what extent the auditee uses the data obtained to improve performance.

Poor auditors do not take the trouble to perform this essential step (Step 5). They seem to regard audits as being witch-hunts or finger pointing exercises, which they are not. A pertinent recommendation provides the auditee with the stimulus to thought that so often leads to even better ideas for improvement. Many organizations tend to believe that the *status quo* cannot be improved but the mere challenge and demonstration that there could be room for improvement frequently makes folk think harder and arrive at even better suggestions. Obviously, every improvement benefits both auditor and auditee.

The best auditors all have one thing in common: they have personally defined, designed and commissioned management systems and organizations as opposed merely to being observers of other peoples' efforts. This enables them to understand fully the thought processes and difficulties encountered.

In selecting auditors it is useful to find out if they could take the proverbial blank piece of paper and design from scratch a management system and organizational plan that would govern the auditee's work and produce a product fit for purpose. If the auditor could not do that, he is not really suitable for the role. To be a management auditor, the person must think and act like a manager, understand the management process and have managerial experience. It is not enough to be able to repeat in a parrot like fashion the strictures of a standard such as ISO 9001.

STEP 6. As stated in Chapter 11, performance monitoring are an essential part of a corrective action system and of management (and process) control. They measure a system's reliability and highlight areas of opportunity. If data capture mechanisms do not exist, one can hardly believe that useful corrective action systems can be obtained. Under these circumstances, the auditor should follow the decision sequence shown in Figure 17.2.

STEP 7. Provided that the auditee has a system for capturing performance data, the auditor should peruse its results. It may be possible to interpret the data in an alternative way to the auditee. This may also stimulate the auditee's thoughts towards improvement and extra effort. Such circumstances justify a verbal recommendation as distinct from a CAR.

The corrective action decision

Figure 17.2 illustrates a sequence of decisions and actions to be taken.

Note 1:
Upon finding a deficiency, the auditor must either perform a purge of the area or, preferably, request the auditee to do this himself (as described in Chapter 14, in the section *"One swallow does not make a summer"*.). The object of the purge is to assess the frequency with which that particular type of deficiency occurs i.e. to assess the true scope and magnitude of the problem. The results of the purge will enable the auditor to decide whether the deficiency is an isolated or a frequent error, his decision needing to be based on a sample of sufficient size to permit confidence in his conclusions.

Isolated errors:

A common cause of isolated errors is found in simple human fallibility, due to somebody having an *"off-day"*. I do not believe in issuing a formal request for corrective action in such circumstance, provided that some means can be found to have the deficiency quickly and quietly corrected on the spot. If, for example, one or two items are found which carry no means of identifying their acceptance status but the auditor is aware that the normal methods are in use elsewhere, he should ask for the items to be rechecked and correctly identified there and then. If this sort of corrective

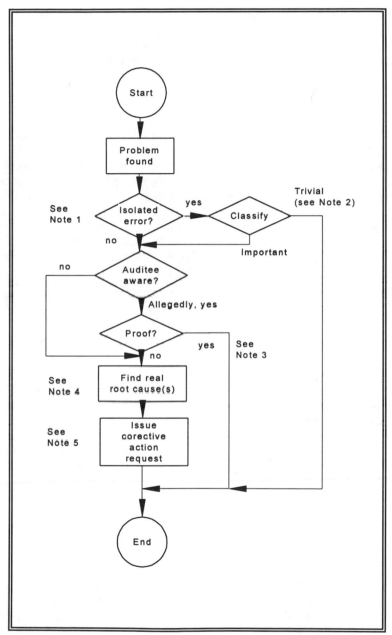

Figure 17.2 Corrective action decisions

action is taken, I act as if the auditee has just performed an internal audit and corrected the deficiency. In my view - and not all auditors would agree with me - it is the result that matters. My approach does have the advantage that when it is necessary to issue a CAR, the auditee will be aware that this is not done unfairly or without due deliberation as to the significance of the discovery.

Frequent errors:

Frequent errors occur as a result of one or more of the six real causes of business problems, mentioned later in this chapter and discussed further in Chapter 18. They also occur during the gestation period of introducing new organizational arrangements and management systems. (They can also occur when these are changed or upgraded.)

It is not my practice to issue a formal request for corrective action in the case of a gestation period problem or in the isolated instance of a new employee, who has not yet fully settled into the activity concerned, making a small error. Learning curve problems still occur when a system has been planned and documented, even, perhaps, partly implemented, if an individual concerned in the activity of interest requires further training in that activity. In these circumstances, it is only fair and reasonable to give the auditee a chance to put his own house in order.

Note 2:
Never lose sight of the product. Some problems may be found as a *"one off"*. The auditor must keep in mind the nature of the product and decide whether the particular problem can be considered either important or trivial. For example:

♦ An auditor selects and reviews 25 purchase orders and discovers one which does not show evidence of revision status. The objective evidence clearly indicates there is a system in practice, the system is effectively implemented but an isolated human error has occurred. At this point, the auditor will require that the purchase order is corrected on the spot and re-issued.

♦ An auditor reviews 25 purchase orders and finds that 3 are concerned with the procurement of safety related items. One of these three has not referenced the correct statute. Since safety is involved, the auditor should trace through the system and determine why such an omission was made, issuing a CAR to cure the real root cause of such a problem so as to prevent recurrence (that is unless the auditee is already aware of the problem etc., as shown in the remainder of Fig. 17.2).

♦ An auditor finds a new, inexperienced employee is maintaining an aircraft's navigation system. The employee is not fully trained, is still on the learning curve and is unsupervised. The auditor will investigate the organization and system used to select and assign personnel to their tasks and determine why the situation has occurred. A CAR would be issued to prevent persons whose competence has not been demonstrated being allowed to work unsupervised on such a critical task.

A crucial aspect of classifying deficiencies is not only the functional importance of the product but also the frequency with which that type of problem has been encountered throughout the entire auditee organization. For example:

♦ An auditor discovers that 2 invoice clerks out of 15 have not been properly trained in the detailed work methods required in their department; in the purchasing department the auditor finds that 1 buyer in 10 is not properly trained in the methods used in that department; in the field support department the auditor discovers that 2 new recruits out of a total staff of 20 have not been trained in the methods to be used within that department; in the sales department the auditor discovers that 1 salesman in 12 has not been trained in the methods to be used in that department. Further investigation reveals that all of those inadequately trained people have recently joined the company. Such circumstances will lead the auditor to diagnose an error that is widespread throughout the company (the correct training of new hire personnel) and to follow the remaining parts of the flow chart in Fig. 17.2.

To categorize the type of error and to determine whether a single incident constitutes a trivial or serious problem in terms of product fitness for purpose, the auditor will rely on the advice of specialists in the team. If such specialists are not present, the auditor should seek advice from his own organization as to the significance of his finding.

Note 3:
In determining whether or not the auditee already knows of the problem, the auditor should seek objective evidence demonstrating not only total awareness but also the action being taken. The latter must be directed at

343

curing the real root cause of the problem as distinct from the symptoms. Acceptable evidence includes corrective action requests, memoranda, minutes of meetings, internal audit reports, investigation reports.

If the action does not appear efficacious, it must be properly and fully discussed with the auditee. It may become necessary for the auditor to trace back through the system and determine the real root cause (or causes) so that a corrective action request can then be issued.

Note 4:
To discover the area from which real root cause of the problem originated, the auditor must trace through the system. There can be several contributory factors and circumstances (i.e. causes) that create an inadequate situation. When the real root cause has been unearthed, the true extent of the problem must be established. This will then enable the auditor to determine the necessity or otherwise of stopping the work. (Stopping the work in progress is further discussed later in this chapter, together with the factors involved in such a decision.)

Note 5:
CARs are only formally delivered during the exit interview after the auditee has been given every opportunity to correct the real root cause of the problem. The department/process or individual to whom the corrective action request will be addressed will be that responsible for the area(s) in which the root cause originated, not the area in which the root cause had its effect(s), unless the two are the same. This is discussed further below, see *"The appropriate recipient for a CAR".*

Corrective action prior to the exit interview

As pointed out in Chapter 14, the auditor should let the auditee know about his findings promptly to give him the chance to take efficacious corrective action before the exit interview (if possible). This course of action has many advantages, as detailed below.

♦ It saves the auditee's face. Since senior management is likely to be present at the exit interview, it may cause someone considerable embarrassment to have adverse findings disclosed there. Most people are extremely thankful to be given the chance to put their house in order discreetly even if they are initially hostile to the auditor's criticism.

♦ It gives the auditee the chance to display a genuine concern to improve matters. Underlying the concern may be either a genuine respect for quality or little more than the instinct of self-preservation. The people who are the real problem are those who evince no desire at all to put things right.

♦ It is good human relations. Giving the auditee the opportunity to correct the situation shows reasonableness, fair mindedness and humanity - the kind of qualities that will make it easier for the auditor to gain the confidence of those with whom he must deal.

♦ It saves a re-audit or follow-up, therefore saving time and money.

♦ IT IS THE RESULT THAT MATTERS.

Pre-empting a formal CAR should bring about the desired result more quickly than if the auditor insists rigidly on formality. If, for some reason, effective corrective action has not been carried out by the time of the exit interview, the deficiency will then be reported and figure in the audit report as a formal corrective action request.

Being constructive

After finding a deficiency, the auditor must always suggest corrective action that would satisfy his organization as being efficacious if implemented. The simpler the corrective action, the better, particularly if it builds on existing strengths. The following examples should illustrate this point.

An audit of a design department revealed that the engineers kept their own magnetic tapes and disks which contained the results of their computer aided design efforts. As they used each others' tapes and similar material at will, the procedure resulted in there being no record of the effective version of any particular design. The auditor suggested that the tapes and disks should be retained within the drawing store (suitably protected from damage) and that a log-out /log-in book be operated by the store. The design manager would separately authorize (in writing) the issuing of the software; he would also authorize all changes required, using the existing document change control system. The plotter was removed to the drawing store to be operated in there by the registry people so that proper numbering, recording and distribution of changes could be effected in accordance with existing practice. Thus maximum use was made of existing systems and virtually no cost was incurred.

A company was experiencing low yield with its products that were heat processed by passing them over a heated plate. The *status quo* had never been challenged since the company assumed that the low yield was a fact of life. An audit revealed that the heated plate gradually became covered with drips from the product until heat transfer to the product was impaired. Occasionally the product would knock off a lump of the burnt filth. The required process temperature was thus not being constantly achieved. Simply by issuing the operators with a scraper to clean the plate, the problem was overcome and yield was improved to over 98% from its previous best, which the supervisor estimated at around 60%. The underlying problem was found to be a lack of training of operators and supervisors in the process involved, the equipment used and the need for cleanliness. It took only a few minutes to inform them of this need and a simple sign sombrely stating: *"KEEP THE PLATE CLEAN AT ALL TIMES"* was mounted on the machine.

During one audit it was found that quite inadequate steps were taken to quarantine items whose status was either indeterminate or unaccepted. It was decided that a quarantine area should be built. The auditee was concerned about the cost of building a new room or structure and about the lack of space within the works and the manufacturing complex. The auditor explained that the quarantine area did not need to be elaborate. He proposed that the apprentices cut up and weld together some angle steel sections, cover the resulting structure with chicken wire or chain link fencing, make a simple door in the same manner and put a padlock on it: the padlock key should be held by a suitable member of the quality department. This structure was completed within a day and the apprentices had a lot of fun making it. It cost next to nothing but it achieved the desired effect.

In each of the three examples above, corrective action was taken prior to the exit interview and none of the deficiencies was reported formally in detail (either at the exit interview or in the audit report).

Drama is not necessary

While discussing the deficiencies with the auditee, the auditor should refrain from dramatizing or exaggerating the situation. A missing *"hold"* sticker very rarely portends an imminent apocalypse. It should, however, be made clear exactly why the deficiency is considered a deficiency. This is especially important with an auditee who is not used to audits, quality systems and programmes, or the particular product/product/contract requirements involved. It is the auditee who will have to implement corrective action and he can hardly be expected to do this efficiently and quickly unless he understands precisely why the situation demands it.

> Visiting the receiving inspection area of a medium sized company, an auditor asked *"What do you do with the goods until you receive all the certificates you have requested from the supplier?"* The supervisor immediately responded *"We know what you are leading up to - we don't have a quarantine store as yet but the management has authorized expenditure of £12,000 on the building of one"*. (That was £12000 in 1985 money.) The auditor asked *"Why are you building a quarantine store?"* The reply was that the company believed this was necessary in order to comply with its national quality systems standard. Knowing that standard well, the auditor stated *"That is not necessary, a simple hold tag systems and an area identified by painted lines marked on the floor, for example, would comply with that standard"*. A discussion followed for a few moments until the supervisor was convinced that the auditor was perfectly correct. The company wanted to do the right thing but had been advised by a "consultant" that only a structure resembling Fort Knox would suffice.

Always remember that cheap, simple, quick but efficacious corrective action is more likely to be acted upon promptly by the auditee, particularly if it sounds ridiculously easy to implement.

Is corrective action really required?

In some circumstances, the auditor may decide to dispense with corrective action entirely - if, for example:

♦ The area in which the deficiency turned up was one through which the contract/ product/ project of interest had already passed through, (provided evidence shows that the requisite system had been functioning properly at that time).

♦ The system will not be used in the future because the auditee has changed his operation effectively making redundant the system concerned.

In such circumstances the auditor may decide he can safely let the matter rest.

In performing a compliance audit of a supplier, an external auditor discovered that the date when calibration was due for a considerable number of gauges in an inspection area had expired. Examination of the works travelers proved that at the time the product had passed through the particular area, the expiry dates had not ben exceeded. The auditor decided not to issue a CAR since he was satisfied that the product could not have suffered and would not be affected because it would not pass through that particular area again. The auditee felt rather foolish at having allowed the calibration periods to overrun. A good calibration system was available, if only it had been implemented. Apparently, however, there had been a changeover in staff: the previous calibration room superintendent had retired and a much younger man had taken over and was still settling in. A recommendation was sufficient in this case as the product would not be affected.

The corrective action request form (CAR form)

A CAR form concisely presents the problem found, the justification or reason for recording it as well as the corrective action proposed, undertaken and verified to have been efficaciously implemented (see Figures 17.3 and 17.4). It provides objective evidence of follow-up and close-out of corrective actions and is standardized to permit swift review by the auditor's organization. When an organization is performing large numbers of audits, a standard form saves much time and money.

The lead auditor should write the CARs he intends to present to the auditee at the exit interview. They should be prepared on the eve of the exit interview to allow for any fresh evidence disclosed during the audit. This procedure avoids holding up the audit and minimizes distractions. Since CARs should be written to reflect common types of problems, writing the CARs at that time allows the audit team to categorize problems and effectively present common patterns of deficiencies. When deficiencies are grouped together by common type into individual CARs, they draw management's attention to the fundamental underlying issue, the magnitude of it and to the extensiveness of it throughout the organization. There are some points to note about Figure 17.3, detailed below.

Issued to: Within this box, the auditor identifies the person or organization responsible for the area/department/process from which the root cause of the problem originated. This will have been determined by the auditors tracing back through the system from the point at which the

Hyper-Quality Company Inc.	**Corrective Action Request**
Issued to: Issued by:	No: Date issued:
Non-conformity description:	
Auditee agrees with non-conformity description Signed: Date:	Non-conformity at variance with:
Recommendation(s) for corrective action:	
Corrective action commitment: Date for completion: Signed: Position Date:	
Follow-up and close-out action:	
The corrective action is verified as efficacious and this CAR is now closed.	Signed: Position: Date:

Figure 17.3 A corrective action request form (CAR)

problem's effects manifested themselves. (See also *"The appropriate recipient for a CAR"*; and *"Getting to the root cause"*, below.)

No: The CAR from is allocated a unique number (top right-hand corner), an identity, just as would be any other type of information requiring tracking and control.

Non-conformity at variance with: (The justification reference).
 This particular box on the form is extremely important. If one cannot clearly state what aspect of code, standard, regulation, instruction, procedure, company policy, contract or other requirement the auditee has violated, then the CAR is unjustified. This in turn indicates that the auditor acted improperly. The justification reference is also vital because the auditee will need to explain to his personnel, who must implement corrective action, exactly why and where they have deviated from requirements.

Auditee concurrence:
 This box is completed by the auditee to acknowledge that the CAR if fully justified. It is signed by the person to whom the CAR was issued, (identified in the *"Issued to"* box). A signature/ initials does not commit the auditee to a particular course of action, it merely signifies that the auditee agrees he must commit his organization to corrective action in the specified areas and matters raised by the CAR. Inclusion of such a box on a CAR helps to forestall misunderstandings concerning whether or not the CAR was accepted by the auditee. Providing the auditor has worked on the basis of facts, i.e objective evidence, it is unlikely that any auditee will refuse to acknowledge the truth of the situation.

In the case of an external audit, this concurrence is actually an acknowledgment the auditee is effectively in breach of contract, providing the auditor has been able to obtain facts that demonstrate the auditee's efforts are at variance with a contractual requirement, (see justification box, above). When issued to an external supplier, a CAR is a polite warning that effectively says *"You are in breach of contract, but we are willing to let you put matters right and, if you do, no further action will be taken"*.

Recommendation(s) for corrective action:
 As stated previously, the auditor must always make some recommendation concerning the type of corrective action that will

satisfy his organization. I hold the view that if an auditor cannot suggest how to solve a problem, he should not be auditing. It is easy to criticize others' efforts, to be destructive: being constructive is a different matter requiring judgement, intelligence and relevant experience. When audits are used as part of continuous improvement programmes, this advice has particular relevance, see Part 2, Chapter 1).

There are always two parts to a recommendation. They are:

♦ The action which the auditee could take in order to cure the root cause of the problem and prevent its recurrence.

♦ The action that the auditee could take in order to verify constantly that such action continues to be implemented.

Many auditees are unsure of the action to be taken so as to prevent business problems. This is particularly true in case of companies which are relatively new to the concepts of quality programmes and associated management systems. It is not very helpful to walk away from the situation by telling the auditee *"That's your problem. It's up to you to solve it and I'm not going to tell you how"*. Some external auditors hide behind directives, allegedly issued by their own legal departments, that they should offer no advice at all. A judicious disclaimer for such advice should be sufficient and would, generally, be understood by the auditee: but should that really be necessary?.

In an age when *"partnerships"* with external suppliers are becoming more commonplace, failure to offer advice is antithetical to the purpose of the partnership. If the customer really believes the supplier might take legal action over advice given, the relationship has problems that could not be resolved by any form of quality programme. There is the risk, moreover, that the supplier might decide to withhold advice concerning product design, manufacture or supply to the end marketplace on a similar basis of fear the customer might also take legal action for it. Effective partnerships require the building of trust, mutual respect and helpfulness - teamwork.

In the case of internal audits, however, any reasons why an auditor should not give advice to colleagues on how to cure root causes of problems, (and the problems themselves), remain a mystery. Even in the case of external audits, such behaviour is not conducive to the building of good teams. A customer needs its suppliers just as much as suppliers need their customers. A helpful relationship is far better than a destructive one.

351

I was engaged by a major international company to train members of its staff in auditing. I offered the advice just given: find and address the real root cause of the problems; always help the auditee, which are two of my twelve golden rules (see Appendix 1). After the first course was completed, the manager responsible for the firm's quality programme advised that such actions were contrary to that manager's policy and procedure, that I should present my course to reflect the firm's practice. It was a request (coupled with a pathetic threat to withhold more business from my organization if I would not accede to it), that I could not and did not countenance. The delegates unanimously agreed the helpful approach I advocate was what they wanted. It is all very well to serve the customer in the manner required but professional hypocrisy for the sake of money is neither ethical not acceptable practice. And the company? The manager stands Canute like as the auditors now act according to their unanimous resolve and their conscience.

I have seen some CAR forms that state *"corrective action required"*. They are not helpful. The benefit of making a recommendation is that the auditee can consider the auditor's suggestions and may be able to find something even better. *"Corrective action required"* can have a constricting effect on useful dialogue and it removes the onus of ownership away from the auditee.

Corrective action commitment: This space is reserved for the auditee to state precisely the corrective action to which he is prepared to commit himself. This commitment is designated and signed by the person who signed the *"Auditee concurrence"* box, described above. Note that the auditee has to commit himself to a date for completion of corrective action. The signer has accepted ownership and accountability for the corrective action and can be measured on the progress and the results.

Follow-up and close out action: This space will be completed by the auditor's organization to indicate the type of follow-up and close-out action that it will require in the light of the auditee's commitment. There is a space for the auditor to attest that the corrective action has been verified as efficacious and to cite the nature of the objective evidence on which this assertion is based. Until this attestation is made, the CAR is not

Hyper-Quality Company Inc.	Corrective Action Request
Issued to: *S.C. RAP METAL PRODUCTS INC.* Issued by: *H-QC INC.*	No: *SCR/97/1/01* Date issued: *13 JANUARY 1997*

Non-conformity description:
FAILURE TO PROVIDE AND IMPLEMENT MANAGEMENT SYSTEM FOR TRAINING OF PERSONAL HAS CAUSED INCORRECT TRANSFER OF DATA BETWEEN THE PRODUCT DESIGNERS IN THE COMPUTER AIDED DESIGN GROUP AND THE PACKAGING DESIGN SUPPLIER, "SUPERDOOPERPAKKER INC". THE END RESULT HAS BEEN DETERIORATION OF FINISHED PRODUCT (MODEL 62 GIZMOS) AWAITING DESPATCH AND IN THE DISTRIBUTION CHAIN. *Ozzy Fry, Lead Auditor*

Auditee agrees with non-conformity description Signed: Date:	Non-conformity at variance with: *H-QC INC PURCHASE ORDER 1234, SECTION 17, CLAUSE 3.2.1.* *S.C. RAP PROCEDURE 4.4.1; 4.18*

Recommendation(s) for corrective action:
DEVELOP AND IMPLEMENT A DOCUMENTED TRAINING PROGRAMME THAT WILL APPRAISE ALL CAD OPERATORS OF THE CORRECT OPERATION OF THE CAD EQUIPMENT, DATA AND FILE TRANSFER TO INTERFACING USERS, WHO USE SUCH EQUIPMENT. IMPLEMENT THAT TRAINING PROGRAMME AND REQUIRE EVERY PARTICIPANT TO DEMONSTRATE COMPETENCE IN APPLYING THE TECHNIQUES LEARNED BEFORE PERFORMING SUCH WORK IN FUTURE. RECORD EVIDENCE OF THE TRAINING AND RESULTS OF COMPETENCE DEMONSTRATION IN THE EMPLOYEE'S PERSONNEL FILE.

Corrective action commitment:
Date for completion: Signed: Position   Date:

Follow-up and close-out action:

The corrective action is verified as efficacious and this CAR is now closed.	Signed: Position: Date:

Figure 17.4 A corrective action request form (CAR) ready for issuing to the auditee

considered to be closed out and corrective action is not recorded as having been successfully implemented. (See also Chapter 21.)

Figure 17.4 shows how a form such as Figure 17.3 might be completed and issued to an auditee at the exit interview. A closed out CAR can bee seen in Figure 21.1.

The appropriate recipient for a CAR

Figure 17.5 describes the appropriate recipients for CARs issued during internal and external audits.

Internal audit	External audit
The manager responsible for the area/ department/ project/ division from which the root cause of the problem originated. If the organization is based on a "team structure", issue the CAR to the team (responsible for originating the root cause) as a whole. If the team has a designated leader, issue the CAR to the "team leader". If the problem is widespread or of a generic nature, the senior manager responsible for all the areas/ departments/ projects from which the problems are originating. This might be a vice-president, president, CEO or managing director.	Issue the CAR to whichever manager is considered responsible for the customer's contract (sales manager/ project manager/ vice-president/ president etc.) and who has the authority to commit the auditee's organization to corrective action. It is the responsibility of that person to obtain corrective action from whatever area within the supplier's company has created the root cause of the problem. (This will have been found by the audit team's trace back and analysis.)

Figure 17.5 Appropriate recipients for CAR's

Can we issue a CAR to the CEO?

I am often asked this question at seminars and conferences. The simple answer is *"yes"*; one might also respond *"why not"*. If a number of departments are affected by a common problem or policy look at where they all report to. If that person is the CEO, then issue the CAR to him/her for he or she is responsible for the performance of all those areas and the decisions guiding their activities. Professional audits are performed inside companies whose CEO supports them. CEOs in such places are seldom afraid to face facts and set an example through mature leadership. If the CEO does not willingly accept the CAR, take another hard look at the policy assertions boldly portrayed in the company credo, quality policy, manuals and the like.

Cure the deficiency or cure the cause?

The answer is simple: CURE BOTH

There is a significant difference between the Non-Conformity Report (NCR) and the Corrective Action Request (two documents commonly used in a quality programme). The former is directed at rectifying a situation and deciding what to do with a particular product that has been found to be defective. The decision may be: re-think the product; re-write; re-define; re-draw; re-compile; re-program; re-do; rework; repair; use-as-is; scrap; return to supplier. NCRs do not ask *"Why did this situation occur?"* The CAR, on the other hand directly addresses that question and proposes a solution to the underlying cause in order to prevent its repetition. When producing a CAR, the auditor's recommendations must be directed at curing the real root cause.

Curing the deficiency is a short-term solution. It is really a fire fighting exercise. The prime purpose of corrective action is to root out the cause of deficiencies. Such extirpation is the long term cure since it aims to prevent any recurrence of the deficiency.: it is fire prevention as opposed to fire fighting. Curing the real root cause of business problems increases the reliability of the management systems which in turn reduces the likelihood of avoidable costs occurring. Only by attacking the root cause of the problem will it be possible to achieve real reductions in avoidable costs that will benefit both auditor and auditee alike. It is a demonstrable example within a continuous improvement programme.

One question that must always occur to an auditor is *"How is it that I find these deficiencies and the auditee does not?"* In the case of an external audit, this should lead the auditor to examine the supplier's internal audit system and the training, ability and experience of the supplier's audit personnel. The auditee will have to continue to verify that corrective action is being implemented and for this he will have to rely on his own internal audit system. Similar remarks apply when an internal audit has been conducted: the department or unit should be performing its own audits and the auditor should question the effectiveness of these.

Getting to the root cause

The root cause of a problem always resides upstream or upstairs. Sometimes it reside in both. The auditor gets to the root cause as follows:

◆   Trace back through the system to the area in which the root cause originated. It might be found to have been born in a primary, secondary or tertiary system. A process that acted according to the requirements placed on it and achieved the output expected from it cannot be considered as creating the root cause.

◆   Use the six friends (see Chapter 13) and especially the question *"why"* until all of the contributory problems have been brought out into the open and one or more of the six real causes, discussed below, have been arrived at. The auditor asks, *"Why did A happen?"* The auditee responds, *"Because of B."* The auditor asks, *"Why did B happen?"* The auditee responds *"Because of C"*. This is repeated on and on, the auditor verifying in turn each of the reasons given.

I am indebted to Joe Molozzi of the Digital Equipment Corporation's Colorado Springs plant, who attended one of many seminars performed for that fine company, and likened the continuous asking of *"why"* as being akin to peeling the layers of an onion. The auditor eventually gets to the core of the problem. Those who know how to peel an onion correctly will also prevent the likelihood of tears! (Keep it cool!)

Who should find the root cause?

The auditor, not the auditee. The reasons for this position of mine are manifold.

356

♦ The auditor cannot assume the auditee has the capability of unearthing a root cause because he has failed to do so up until now. The audit decision sequence (see Figure 17.2) shows the auditor will have ascertained the auditee either is unaware of the problem or has not determined root cause and commenced any corrective action effort.

♦ Even if the auditee were allowed to trace back to root cause, the auditor would not know where that cause originated and could not be sure the auditee has actually found it. Some companies operate in a manner requiring auditee's to submit their corrective action commitments/plans/proposals to the auditor's organization for review and approval. Whereas I do not believe the auditor should be asked to *"approve"* the auditee's plans, since this can and has been construed by some as effectively *"passing the buck"* to the auditor, the auditor is in no position to comment on the potential efficacy of an action addressing an alleged root cause he has not himself verified as being correct.

♦ Some auditees need the auditor's help to get to root cause because top management will either not permit the auditee's own people to find it or curtail the efforts if they seem to get *"too close to home"*.

♦ Some auditees become emotional or dispirited when a subsequent audit, a follow-up or operational events demonstrate the problem is being repeated, because their efforts addressed something other than root cause.

Far too many auditors are unwilling to accept the responsibility for hunting down the root cause of problems. Regrettably, this is frequently caused by their own inability to do so, personal inexperience of managing, laziness, wrong attitude to the job (in extreme cases smugness and a personal enjoyment in seeing others in difficulty). They comprise a cadre of inappropriate types of behaviour.

It is sometimes the case that the audit time budget seems to preclude the opportunity for investigating root cause. This need not be the case if the audit team is pursuing a trace back path or is comprised of two or more sub-teams (see Chapter 9). In the case of the former, the audit team will be heading towards the root cause area and has objective evidence it can present to let the auditees in that area appreciate the effects of their actions. In the case of the latter, a sub-team finding a problem can transfer

357

its details to whatever other sub-team is to deal with the area suspected of being at the root cause. If the matter really is so complex that time appears to be running out, the lead auditor can pursue the following options:

♦ Extend the audit and obtain the concurrence of both his organization and that of the auditee. This concurrence is frequently given since the cost-benefit of so doing is patent.

♦ Recommend an additional audit whose sole objective is the discovery of the root cause and formulation of solutions to effect a permanent cure. The recommendation will be made to the auditor's organization and the auditee. Again, the cost-benefit is patent.

As a result of performing numerous audits over the years, I have concluded far too many auditees and auditors do not realize just how close they often are to achieving a real breakthrough in identifying the underlying causes of their problems. Time and again one observes audit activities being curtailed just as they are on the brink of identifying major opportunities for slashing avoidable costs by following through on root cause analysis. An unsettling proportion of those organizations continue to give inadequate support to their audit programmes out of a belief they make marginal contributions to improvements, are *"something we have to do"* or are *"a necessary evil"*. Their views would be dramatically altered if only they allowed the audits to pursue root causes and avoidable costs. The purpose of performing audits should not be *"to have something on file so we can show auditors (registrars) we do audits"*.

The six real causes

The auditor must think each problem through, and analyze the system(s) as well as the checks and balances (control) involved. A deficiency may turn out to have multiple root causes and contributory problems, each having their own root cause. The root causes are as follows, and are further discussed in Chapter 18:

♦ Lack of organization: measures have not been taken top plan activities or to assign responsibilities, systems and methods for properly accomplishing them.

♦ Lack of training of the personnel: thorough training or retraining, as described in Chapter 4 has not been accomplished.

♦ Lack of discipline: individuals do not follow the systems, methods required to achieve quality or do not meet the responsibilities assigned to them.

♦ Lack of resources: *"spoiling the ship for a ha'porth of tar"* (or *"trying to make a silk purse from a sow's ear"*); inadequate or incorrect finance for the work to be done; insufficient manpower allocated to the work.

♦ Lack of time: rushing or being forced to rush the job, too much pressure of work, overwork or inadequate manpower. (Increasingly common as a result of radical downsizing efforts.)

♦ Lack of top management support: This is the most common cause for it evinces itself in the other five real causes.

Consider the side effects

Upon discovering the real root cause of the problem, the auditor should also find out what other areas have suffered, could suffer or are presently suffering. An example of this could be an auditor discovering a problem in the way that a particular customer's accounts have been processed. The root cause is found to be an inadequate system for reconciliation. Further investigation shows that several thousand customers' accounts have all been processed by the same inadequate system. Clearly this constitutes a serious situation which has enormous cost implications to the company.

The potential cost of failure to tackle a business problem has many aspects. The auditor's company, the auditee, the customer and the community may all suffer eventually.

In practice, very few companies accept contracts that contain clauses for consequential damages liability. The liability is usually limited to replacement of the item concerned. In an extreme case, it tends to be the insurance underwriter and hence the community, who bears the cost of defective products (although legislation on product liability is changing this situation). Whoever ends up picking up the bill for actual damage caused by deficient output, the deficiencies inevitably mean that time and money are wasted: avoidable costs are incurred.

Pre-award surveys and CARs.

As discussed in Chapter 2, because there is no contractual relationship between auditor and organizations, the former has no right to issue a CAR during a pre-award survey. However, the auditor can make a statement such as:

"In the event that my company decides to award this contract to you, we will require corrective action for the following." (The auditor will describe the corrective actions that require addressing.) *"Satisfactory completion of that corrective action will be made a condition of payment at the first contract milestone."*

The auditor's organization will then incorporate the requirements for corrective action into the contractual terms and conditions. Knowing the implications, the auditee then has the choice to accept or to decline the contract offered by his potential customer.

Registrars and CARs

The registrar's assessor has the duty to issue CARs to auditees who are seeking a certificate of qualification against a standard, code or regulation they have selected for their compliance, whenever the auditee does not meet *in full* the applicable requirements thereof. (See Figure 7.17.) It should be a part of a professional registrar's working procedure to ensure that this is done. It is not, however, necessary for a CAR form to be used although they are rather convenient vehicles of communication. The assessor could include the CAR details as shown in Figure 17.4 in the text of his report, but this practice has drawbacks and I do not recommend it.

Naturally, no certificate of qualification or compliance must be issued unless and until all CARs are verified as closed-out: in any case, only rogues and incompetent would do such a thing. Their certificate would be a falsehood that represents the assessed company's practices and pours discredit on professional assessment schemes.

Line Line Line
Read
Line Line Line

Limitations on the auditor's authority

A situation can be so serious that the auditor considers it necessary to stop work. Regrettably, the authority to do so may not have been vested in him. Similarly , there are occasions when an auditor is not allowed to issue a CAR. The auditor must be aware of the delegated limitations and act accordingly. This topic is discussed in Chapter 20, in the section *"Limitations on the auditor's authority"*.

Stop work decisions

The decision to stop work pending the implementation of corrective action is one no auditor should take lightly. He must be prepared to do so, however, if he judges that the situation demands this course of action. The key factors involved in a stop work decision include:

♦ Health, safety or legal implications. Whenever health, safety or legal requirements are being compromised, the auditor must promptly request stop work and seek the full support of his own management. In the event that management chooses not to support the stop work decision, it is vital that the auditor places his recommendations on the record in order to demonstrate that he acted in a responsible manner and discharged his duty of care.

♦ Financial considerations. Where substantial risk of loss, of avoidable costs, can be incurred by allowing the situation to continue unresolved, the auditor should advise his management and seek support for stop work. Whenever money is at risk, most managements are supportive of any saving action.

♦ Work status and delivery date. Where the auditor ascertains that a major milestone, such as delivery of product to the customer, is scheduled to occur before satisfactory corrective action could be taken, stop work must be required and management support obtained.

Consider the scope of the stop work

Before requiring stop work, the auditor should carefully assess the scope of the stop work necessary. Naturally as much useful work as possible should be allowed to continue and only those matters which are genuinely unacceptable and require stop work should be considered.

Information to provide to management

In deciding on stop work, determine the type of corrective action that should be taken in order that work could be restarted. When advising management of a stop work decision, give all the facts including:

♦ A full description of the problems found.
♦ The reasons behind and justification for stopping the work (safety or legal violations etc., as above).
♦ The scope of work affected by the stop work decision.
♦ The root cause(s) of the problems and their impact on the operation (avoidable costs).
♦ The recommended corrective action.
♦ The likely costs in terms of time and resources needed to effect the recommended corrective action.
♦ The circumstances under which work could be restarted.

I strongly recommend that an auditor informs his own organization of his intention to call for a halt in work, offering the information listed, above. This should be done before the exit interview so that he can ascertain to what extent his organization will support him. There is nothing worse for an auditor than to ask that work be stopped, pending implementation of suitable corrective action, only to find that senior management of the auditing organization have overruled the decision (perhaps for internal political reasons) and left him out on a limb. When this happens, it becomes all too obvious to the auditee that the auditor has, in reality, no backing from his organization at all. Sometimes the auditor's own customer/ inspection agency (real third party) may be able to exert pressure and support must be discreetly sought, if necessary. Regardless of whether the auditor's management declares its support for the auditor or not, if the latter feels that stop work is necessary, particularly in the circumstances involving safety, health and legal matters, he should put the affair in writing and his reasons on the record on his return to his office. The audit report is a correct and appropriate place for this information.

On several occasions, during my audit training seminars, some delegates have expressed concern that, in putting things on the record when management has refused to back them, they might be putting their jobs at risk. I always advise them of two important considerations. Firstly, in many countries a responsible person, such as an auditor, has a civic and legal responsibility to bring issues such as health, safety and legal risks to the attention of the responsible management, failure to do so could make liable to prosecution or damages the auditor. Putting such advice on the record helps safeguard their personal position. Secondly, if they cannot have the courage of their convictions, they should not be auditing. The decision on whether one wants to work for an organization whose management would adopt such an attitude is a matter for the individual.

Presenting a CAR to management

The auditee's management will need to have the following information before they take action.

♦ An evaluation of the significance of the problem and the need for its eradication. (See *"Consider the side effects"*, above.)

♦ The total cost saving from curing the cause and preventing a recurrence of the effects (this may or may not be in monetary terms - management is generally quite capable of working out the financial implications of a statement such as *"Twenty three percent of your deliveries are damaged or put at risk because of inadequate packaging"*; *"One sixth of your invoices do not get paid promptly because of inaccurate keying errors in customer discount calculations"*; *"One meal in eight is sent back from the restaurant because it has been improperly cooked or is not what the customer ordered"*; *"Inadequate equipment maintenance is reducing the yield by approximately 3 kilograms per batch processed"*).

♦ The reasons why a cosmetic or fire fighting exercise is of no use.

♦ How (and at what cost) the proposed cure will extirpate the problem.

Remember the following empirical relationship:

Saving - Expenditure = Corporate Action Speed and Help, (CASH)

In the final analysis, it all comes down to money; if there is no monetary incentive, very few managements are motivated to do anything. Altruism is not especially rife. The auditor should, therefore, not waste his time formally requiring corrective action for a trivial problem. The money involved in corrective action may be seen in terms of a current loss or a future potential loss. Either way, both constituent avoidable costs. In the case of an extrinsic audit, for example, the auditee's management may be aware that the customer's auditor may recommend, in extreme cases, that the auditee's company be removed from the qualified supplier's list, with consequential loss of business. Another potential monetary loss might be that caused by future action under product liability legislation - and this is an increasingly important factor as the awards in the courts rise in value.

America is an especially litigiously minded nation. A substantial proportion of most editions of the *"Yellow Pages"* telephone directories are devoted to attorneys and their services. Some of these people are proud to describe themselves as *"aggressive"* or *"no nonsense"*. They sit and wait the failures of the firm's organization, systems and practices as demonstrated through the products and services supplied and operational actions.

The corrective action request log and tracking files

The auditor's organization should always maintain a log (or tracking file) of the CARs that have been issued. The advantages of this are that the log provides a quick guide to the status of CARs, summarizes the auditee's performance and constitutes objective evidence as to the status of follow-up and close-out of corrective action: it can, therefore, be presented to any interested third party or registrar. The log should be maintained by the company's management representative dealing with its quality programme (usually the quality manager). It need not be in conventional hard copy form, a simple computerized record will suffice.

The details (fields) to include are:

♦ Identity of each CAR (a number or alphanumeric entity)
♦ Identity of the person/ organization to whom the CAR was issued.
♦ The date it was issued.
♦ The status of acceptance of the CAR by the person to whom it was issued (the auditee's concurrence).
♦ The status of whether the auditee has committed to corrective action or not and, if so, the date that action is scheduled to be complete.
♦ The timing and nature of the auditor's follow-up action.
♦ The date and nature of close-out of the CAR.

By employing the miracles of modern database management system software, some auditors also maintain details of each CAR issued (Problem description, recommended corrective action etc.) which can be linked to the CAR record. It is thus possible to obtain reports concerning auditees, common types of problems being found, closure dates and so on. This can be invaluable in effecting continuous improvements, training staff and auditors, and assessing auditees' performance.

The CAR log, or tracking file, should be reviewed by management as a regular fixed agenda topic of its *"management review meetings"*. The knowledge that this is done spurs everyone to take corrective action seriously. It gives a bite to the CAR system.

18. Typical problems and their causes

Sometimes we may learn more from a man's errors
than from his virtues.

Henry Wadsworth Longfellow

Throughout this book, many examples of business problems and actions taken to prevent or cure them have been given. Within the following pages, a further selection of typical problems that the auditor may encounter is presented. As should be apparent, not every problem constitutes a true deficiency. One of the recurring themes of this book is the need for the auditor to be aware of what the codes, standards, regulations etc. really require. Sometimes the wording of the relevant document is open to more than one interpretation - phrases like *"shall establish"*, *"ensure that"*, *"arrange for"* can each be satisfied by a number of very different systems and the auditor must never assume that only his preferred type of system is acceptable. An open mind is an essential asset when auditing.

The following examples are grouped under headings corresponding to the task elements discussed in Chapter 4. One extra category is included, namely, matters concerning the auditee's practices for dealing with corrective action and his non-conformity handling system. Unless otherwise indicated, the examples mentioned apply in internal as well as external audits.

Information

Problems, or apparent problems concerned with information and its control are various and are detailed below.

Correctly checked

1.   No objective evidence that the information has been reviewed is available on it.

This is a problem relating more to the use of hard copy (i.e. physical documents) than to information made available by electronic means. Objective evidence may be available in the form of a letter or a memorandum rather than as a signature on the document. This is quite satisfactory and should not count as a deficiency. Where information is contained on computer tapes and disks, an original signature on the software is, in any case, impossible. Alternative means such as memoranda or review reports are useful.

2.   A readiness review of an information package is not performed.

This requirement is not directly imposed by quality system standards. However, in the case of contracts that take several years to complete, it is advisable that the information packages collated during the execution of the contract be given a review prior to release. This is so because, in most organizations, the staff change continually and many fail to hand over a job properly to their successors. Hence there may be unresolved matters of which the successor is unaware.

> While performing an audit at a construction site, it was noted that the package of documents issued to the construction personnel contained a number of specifications that did not bear the requisite customer approvals; in some cases the documents had even been disapproved. Somehow, these documents had never been rewritten. Upon investigation, it was found that the personnel responsible for collecting the document package together had changed several times during the course of the contract concerned, which had been running for four or five years. The remedial action required fell into two parts: the correct and approved documents had to be obtained and issued to the site whilst an instruction had to be given that all packages of documents should be reviewed for completeness and readiness before being issued to the site.

This type of problem can be overcome by instituting a handover system and maintaining a record summarizing both the total contents required in a package and the status of review of each constituent part.

3.   There is no mechanism for obtaining the customer's review/approval of information/corrective action proposed by the supplier.

Before laying the blame at the auditee's door, the external auditor must make sure that the contract has asked for such a mechanism. If not, and should the auditor feel such a mechanism to be needed, corrective action may be required in the auditor's own organization after the audit is over.

4.   The quality department does not review information or changes to it.

Few, if any, quality standards impose this obligation on the quality function, and in my view, it should not be its role to carry out information reviews. (The practice of requiring the quality department to review information, was quite commonplace in the 1970's and early 1980's but, thankfully, it has gradually disappeared as the importance of process ownership and control has become appreciated. The practice derived mainly from the rebadging of inspectors as *"quality managers"* who, true to their roots, felt it incumbent on them to perform such reviews (i.e. inspections); from the expectations of early certifications, such as ASME 'N' and 'U' pressure vessel stamping schemes, contingent on satisfying the *"Authorized Inspector"*; and from primitive quality program expectations of various military departments of defence.)

5.   Information is reviewed after it has been released for use.

The auditor should make a note both of the date when information was prepared and of that when it was reviewed and approved: *"preliminary"* issues may sometimes prove still to be in use when the product is about to be delivered to the customer.

(Note that some quality systems standards only imply, rather than state explicitly, that a review is necessary prior to release. The auditor should check that the standard states a particular point at which information must be reviewed. A case in point is ISO 9001-1994 which requires design input requirements to be *"reviewed by the supplier for adequacy"* but does not specify that the supplier must perform such a review prior to the design activity being performed, even though one can readily appreciate the desirability of so doing. If the auditor discovers that the auditee only

369

checks information input for adequacy when checking the information awaiting release from a work activity (process), as many organizations do, he is in no position to issue a corrective action request, merely a recommendation.)

6.   Documents have been signed as reviewed without being reviewed properly.

If the code or standard concerned asks for a review of documents, it may only specify an independent review, which, provided that the reviewer is competent, does not necessarily rule out the *"Your sign mind, I'll sign yours"* agreement that flourishes in some places. Standards seldom state that the person who reviews the documents has to be the superior of the person who prepared it, as some auditors erroneously assume.

7.   *"Minor changes do not need to be authorized."*

The auditor should beware that this phrase---which some auditees write into their procedures---does not become stretched to the point of covering every eventuality. Most quality systems standards preclude it. (ISO 9001, for instance). Many auditees use mark-ups to indicate changes and quality systems standards recognize this to be the case: ISO 9001, for example, do not preclude the use of mark-up. It prescribes : *"Where practicable, the nature of the change shall be identified in the document..."*. A mark-up would clearly comply with that prescription.

8.   The final *"hold"* point does not require that the information, such as a record package, is checked for contract compliance before release.

The customer may well be purchasing not only physical items but also the information and records associated with them. In this case, one cannot be certain that the contract has been fulfilled unless that information is checked prior to release. This is simple common sense.

(In its clause 4.10.4, ISO 9001 only requires final inspection to be performed   *"In accordance with the quality plan and/or documented procedures..."*. Clearly, if neither the quality plan nor documented procedures specify such an inspection, it does not need to be done. Fortunately its clause 4.5.2 is a little more sensible in requiring documents and data to be *"reviewed and approved for adequacy prior to release"*. However, reading its clause 4.5.1 gives the impression that its clause 4.5.2

only applies to documents and data *"that relate to the requirements of [ISO 9001]...".*)

Regardless of the ambiguities contained in quality systems standards, every company should check deliverable documents/data/information irrespective of the form in which they are to be presented to the customer, particularly bearing the product liability point of view in mind.

Correct content

1.   The content of instructions is not appropriate to the circumstances.

The phrase *"appropriate to the circumstances"*, which figures in some specifications, codes and standards, is obviously open to interpretation and the auditor must take care to consider each case scrupulously on its own merits. The acid test is to discover what the user of the information considers as being *"appropriate"*. If the user feels extra information must be included, a CAR is warranted as the information cannot be regarded as fit for purpose; if the absence of details about the users' views, and the auditor believes additional or corrected content is required, a recommendation to this effect must be made. A formal corrective action request may be unwarranted in this latter circumstance.

2.   Rework and repair procedures do not explain the method of dismantling and re-assembly in order to prevent further damage to non-conforming assemblies being processed.

This is a particularly common complaint in the case of encapsulated or hermetically sealed components. Again, it must be remembered that instruction should be *"appropriate to the circumstances"*. If there is a requirement that procedures have to be *"acceptable to the customer's representative"*, this is a prescription that the auditor (who may be the customer's representative) should never abuse by adopting an unnecessarily rigid attitude.

3.   The qualified suppliers' list does not include suppliers of services.

While it is common practice for companies to keep a list of suppliers found to be acceptable for the supply of particular goods, the names of suppliers of services are often not included. The term *"services"* covers design, special processes, financial audit, training, transportation, catering,

371

cleaning, maintenance, calibration, waste disposal, vermin control, inspection, test, computing, installation-in fact, anything that affects the product and that the auditee subcontracts to an outside source: it also covers those services discussed in Part 2 Chapter 5.

4.   Forgeries.

The era of photocopiers and correction fluid has allowed the unscrupulous to fake certificates and records. The auditor must not hesitate to ask for originals or certified copies of originals.

5.   Digital forgery.

Photocopies and correction fluid are to scanners and pixel editing what bull carts are to the space shuttle. Technological developments have resulted in a host of readily available software and powerful PC's that can be used to produce forgeries whose authenticity is almost impossible to determine. The cinema and advertising media have used such tools, *"Computer Generated Imagery"* (CGI), to produce impressive movie films, such as Forrest Gump, use archive footage and animations and integrate them with newly shot scenes to produce an impression that the present day movie star is actually talking to deceased famous people. Advertizing bureaux have been quick to take advantage of the possibilities, producing amusing depictions of Fred Astaire dancing with a 1997 vacuum cleaner, Lucille Ball assessing modern day products in a department store or Jackie Gleason proudly demonstrating a new kitchen aid.

The auditor now has the difficult task in knowing what really is an original, what is a fake, a montage.
It is too easy for the forger to cover its trail. Whereas one could carefully examine all the auditee's files, as might be made available during the audit, there is no guarantee that the prime state of originals can be detected. I have no doubt that the technology will be used at some time for nefarious and criminal purposes, especially where an expensive product liability action is involved. The equipment and methods used to edit the Watergate tapes, that led to the downfall of Richard Nixon, were crude by today's standards, but it still required expert forensic analysis to detect the deception; the average auditor cannot aspire to competence in this field. In an age where music can be *"sampled"*, the text of recorded speeches can be rearranged to produce a completely different message the auditor is hopelessly compromised because even what has been seen during the

audit subsequently can be changed without leaving any easily discernible clues of the process used.

Should the auditor take copies of everything seen during the audit? In some sensitive situations this might be advisable. But, this is not really practical. The time and space required to gradually accumulate everything, the associated costs of doing so preclude it as a practical solution for the every day management audit. The auditor could look at the computer's system files, the auditee's back-up and archive system to see if they record the incidence of change (see also Part 2 Chapter 4). Sadly, though, there is no guarantee that this will be totally effective as system files can be altered, especially on personal computers operated by the actual forger.

I do not profess to have a ready answer to the problem for the busy and time pressed auditor and I will be pleased to receive readers' experiences, views and solutions.

Correct edition

1.   Effectivity dates/locations for changes are not stipulated.

Some standards (such as MIL-Q-9858A [1], AQAP-1 [2]) used to require such a stipulation: ISO 9001 does not. The auditor must check the applicable codes, standards, regulations for the wording involved. This is particularly important in the case of an internal audit because the company may be working to two or three different sets of requirements, each for a different customer. This can be confusing for the auditee's own staff, as well as for the auditor.

2.   Changes are made by means of "attachments",.

A lot of stapled or pinned attachments to the prime document is annoying and confusing for the user. The risk of some becoming detached and lost or of being disregarded also exists. The auditor should use his discretion: if the practice appears to be causing problems, he should recommend that attachments are not used.

3.   *"Superseded"* copies of documents found to be still in use.

Caution is needed here: the *"superseded"* copy may be perfectly acceptable for continued use. A standard product may, for example, still be being produced as a previous "model" that has been sold to a current customer. One classic example is the ASME Boiler and Pressure Vessel

Code [3] addenda, issued every six months. The auditor must check the particular requirements for the contract being audited.

Correct condition

1.   Information is illegible or damaged.

Some examples of these problems have been described in Chapter 4.

Correct distribution

1.   There is no acknowledging of receipt of changed information.

Some auditors ask the issuer of a document, *"How can you be sure that the documents have arrived there?"* The acknowledgment receipt method was developed by some auditees in response to this problem but there are other methods by which the auditee can make sure that the documents have arrived at their destination. (Quality systems standards tend not to require the recipient of information to provide a receipt to its issuer but they do require that documents are distributed and used at the location where the particular activity is to be performed.)

This is becoming less of a problem as companies move towards achieving a paperless office. Software can ensure a record of successful transmission of information to its recipients has been accomplished. Many E-MAIL programs feature an indicator against records of transmitted files denoting successful despatch and receipt; Fax machines log the complete arrival of transmitted documents together with the date and time of transmission. Auditors should recommend as much information as is possible is transmitted electronically to the intended recipients.

2.   The management system, as described in the firm's operations manual or procedures, has been bypassed.

The auditor should assess whether or not bypassing the system is significant before he issues a formal corrective action request. (See step 3 of the seven step audit method, described in Chapter 11.) If bypassing the system achieves the same result as required by the code, standard etc., then the auditor should simply recommend that the written procedure is changed. Never knock initiative: it is a precious commodity in short supply. If the auditee has found a quicker, better system to use then both his own organization and the auditor's may reap cost benefits. This has been further developed in Chapter 17.

An auditor discovered that a sales department issued contract documents directly to the line departments. The auditee's procedure required that, upon receipt of an order, all contract documents be routed through a small unit that would allocate a unique number to the contract. That unit had become progressively overloaded to the extent that a backlog of two months' work had accumulated, which obviously meant that time available for contract completion was being lost. In order to save time and get things going, salesmen had decided to phone the unit, have a number allocated, mark it onto the documents and then distribute those to the line departments themselves. Although the sales department was acting in a manner that conflicted with the official procedure, the end result was exactly the same as if they had not done so. The auditor recommended that the procedure be updated to reflect the actual practice.

3.   Updating of information is difficult or impossible because the current location of the original document, as issued, is not accurately known.

I once asked an auditee how he would find the documents issued on a particular job if, say, one of them had been revised. The company, which was geographically dispersed, had a computer that monitored the progress of every contract and all the information applicable in a number of locations. The auditee alleged that within two or three seconds he could locate any individual document in use and obtain a report of every location at which the document currently was to be found. He also offered to trace every contract and department that had been affected by any particular revision of that document as well as those *"superseded"* versions that could still be effective for past customers who were still using the products they had bought from the company. He proved his claims. (This incident occurred during 1977 in Switzerland when Steve Jobs and Steve Wozniak were still pottering about in their famous California garage. As I finish this third edition in 1997 it is sad to find relatively few companies are as well organized and punctilious, despite the ready availability of cheap PC's and databases that would achieve the same goals.)

At another company, a *"document control centre"* was asked a similar question to the above. The answer was *"We'll phone around to see if we can find it."* The next question posed was, *"What do you do if you don't find it?"* The response provided was *"Then it's lost, so why worry?"*

Tracing and retrieving information that is contained in computer files requires controls such as those described in Part 2 Chapter 4.

4.　　　　Information retrieval is not performed.

It may not be essential for superseded copies of documents to be returned to the issuing department for destruction-indeed, in certain cases this would be neither possible nor reasonable. Purchase orders, issued to a supplier, for instance, are irretrievable because they have certain legal implications concerning a contract as signed and agreed between supplier and customer: the supplier is unlikely to hand over such contractual documents. (Most quality systems standards do not require retrieval of information, their only stipulation being that the use of invalid/obsolete documents are not unintentionally used.)

> A company ran a number of tape controlled machines. Each particular process item had its own tape. When the item was changed a new tape was issued to the machine operators but an audit revealed that they did not destroy the old ones or return them to the design office, which produced and distributed the tapes. Investigation showed that superseded versions of the items were regularly being produced and then mixed with existing stock. There was no way of telling which tape was which or to which model an individual item in the store belonged.

5.　　　　Information exchange control is not centralized.

Some auditors assume that all document changing functions should be centrally controlled. There is no reason why this should be done. For software, a library can be essential (see Part 2 Chapter 4). (Quality systems standards generally do not specify centralization.)

6.　　　　The results of pre-award surveys or external audits are not fed back to line departments.

> During an audit of a geographically dispersed company, it was found that the works' quality assurance department was auditing and performing pre-award surveys of the suppliers of welding electrodes. At head office, it was found that the welding department engineers were specifying certain manufacturers' electrodes but had no knowledge of the pre-award surveys and audits being performed by the works QA department, let alone of the results. Some suppliers whom the works' QA department had

found to be unsatisfactory were still being called out in the specifications from head office.

Similar examples could be quoted for many other types of information that an individual department possesses but does not distribute, with the result that people make errors out of ignorance or *"re-invent the wheel"*. Knowledge of who-does-what, which is derived from good organization, can help to forestall these occurrences. PC and computer networks, such as company intranets, greatly facilitate the pooling of gained experience and knowledge such that avoidable costs of unnecessarily repeating work already performed is prevented. The auditor should suggest the installation of this type of equipment.

Correct identification

1.　　*"What is it?"*

Creating information is a costly process and it is surprising just how much is not fully identified in order that folk know to what it relates. Common examples include calculations that are merely a jumble of impressive looking figures; print outs of work, performed on desktop computers, that have not title or identification number; floppy disks that are unidentified; test records that do not specify a particular customer order.

The requirements (or lack of them) for specific identification of information in quality systems standards leave much to be desired and the auditor should tread warily here.

Equipment

Correct type

1.　　No objective evidence is available to show that the equipment has been qualified.

Remember that it may be practical to qualify the equipment on the job or by analyzing a first piece, made using the equipment, and which is for ultimate supply to the customer. Some codes and standards do not preclude this practice and the contract may well permit it.

Correct condition

1.   No planned maintenance records of plant and equipment are available.

The auditor should check to see that plant, such as cranes, is regularly maintained. Apart from such maintenance being, in most countries, a legal requirement to prevent accidents, most codes and standards generally imply that such control is necessary.

> An auditor was arguing at length with an auditee that the cranes, slings and handling equipment should be monitored, inspected and tested. The auditee disagreed and had no sooner finished making his point when the telephone rang to announce that a very expensive item had just been dropped and irreparably damaged. The auditee rapidly lost his *"it couldn't happen here"* attitude of a few seconds earlier.

> A supplier who was confronted by one of his customers with the need to check out lifting equipment, refused to admit the necessity for doing so. During a previous contract with the same customer, a safety related structure weighing about 100 tons had been dropped. Although the customer's representatives had witnessed the actual drop, the supplier's representatives were adamant that it had never happened and never could have.

2.   Items become damaged because of inadequate hand tools.

Hand tools should be maintained because they can directly affect the quality of the work. Examples of this fact include wire strippers and crimpers used for electrical assembly or installation work; surgical instruments; ladles, spatulas and the like used for preparing food. Many people pay quite close attention to capital plant and high value equipment but fail to consider the correct condition of such relatively small or low value articles: these are rather taken for granted and become abused, misused and damaged. In extreme cases, hand tools can deteriorate to the point that they become dangerous in themselves.

3.   The working condition of process equipment is inadequate.

The working condition of equipment is not only affected by its maintenance but also by the way in which it is controlled during operation. It is not uncommon to discover inadequate process controls on temperature, flow rates, feed rates, pressures, voltage, amperage, power levels, rotational speeds etc.; no reference standards for acceptable work; no guidance on the process conditions or no monitoring of the actual process conditions.

4.　　　The maintenance frequency is not based on the usage rate and the frequency is excessive.

In many companies, various pieces of equipment that are subject to calibration are only used infrequently. If possible, the auditee should consider calibrating his acceptance equipment on the basis of actual usage. This can be a real cost saver. The frequency of maintenance activities can be assisted by the use of process control charts containing the usual decision points based on known process capabilities. Quality systems standards cannot state what is a *"suitable"* frequency for maintenance activities, such as calibration. They do tend to use words such as *"periodic"* which are open to interpretation and abuse.

> At one company that considered its engineering products to be of high precision, it was found that the inspection and acceptance equipment was only infrequently calibrated. Some gauges had not been calibrated for as long as nine to twelve years. There was no means of positive recall and the internal audit system had never challenged the veracity of the inspection and acceptance equipment.

It is not uncommon to find that acceptance and inspection equipment is not traceable to a national standard despite the fact quality system standards ask for traceability to such standards. Occasionally, there may be some debate as to what constitutes a national standard.

> An auditee once informed me that his calibration equipment was traceable to a national standard. On looking at the documentary evidence brought forward to support this claim. I noted that the document was issued by a private company. After some considerable discussion, the man responsible for calibration had to admit that, although in his country this particular company was considered as a high authority on calibration, it was necessary that they be requested to attest that their own gauges were traceable to that country's national standard. Considerable difficulty was experienced in eliciting an attestation from that particular company, who were most upset by the request. No company should assume that its foreign customers are intimately acquainted with the company's supplier's national calibration system.

That incident was one of several identical ones I experienced whilst performing a series of audits during a visit to the UK some years ago. Subsequent visits revealed that the gauge suppliers had changed their certificate to include a statement to the effect that they also certified that the devices used to calibrate a customer's gauges were themselves of known accuracy, traceable to UK national standards. In spite of the fact that the auditees proudly displayed approval certificates from the British Ministry of Defense and others, apparently no one had ever queried the lack of audit trail to national standards before.

At another company, the veracity of its master gauges was questioned. The reply given was *"But they are XYZ company's gauges "*. I explained that this did not necessarily mean that the gauges were correct and, after some considerable discussion, it was agreed that XYZ company should provide an attestation that the master gauges supplied were traceable to a national standard also stating the accuracy and precision of the gauges supplied to their customer. The gauges in question had been purchased seven years previously and it transpired that no certificate of attestation was available. At my insistence, the gauges were sent away for calibration. The auditee was considerably embarrassed when the results came through.

A company had assumed for many years that its inspection equipment was accurate enough for its needs. Since there was neither a calibration system nor any master gauges, none of it was traceable to national standards. The company entered into a multi-million dollar contract which invoked AQAP-4 [4] and, contrary to my advice, took little action towards calibrating its equipment, building 26 high value items of machinery for its customer. Inevitably, the company was audited, with the predictable results, which led to the purchase of master gauges and to the introduction of a calibration system. To determine the correctness of the completed machines, every one had to be dismantled and, when the rechecking was performed, each was found to contain major components that were unacceptably outside the engineer's requirements. The affected components were replaced and the machines were re-assembled and re-tested for performance whilst the records reviewed and corrected to record the identities of the replaced parts. It cost a small fortune, many times the originally anticipated profit.

With all the attention that has been paid in recent years by the so-called quality profession to calibration systems and stickers on gauges one might

380

hope that the incidents of basic problems would be almost zero, especially for firms possessing ISO 9000 certificates. Sadly this is not the case.

> Shortly after my 1996 move to live in the USA, a major automotive parts supplier contacted me to enquire of the validity of a calibration certificate issued by a company based in Hampshire, England, and how the UK's national calibration systems works. The document in question, entitled *"Calibration Certificate"*, stamped by its quality control function, bore no evidence that the equipment it *"certified"* was traceable to the applicable British national standards or to an accredited laboratory. One must remain mystified how the firm achieved its ISO 9000 registration. *Caveat emptor.*

Audits regularly reveal that although the process equipment is maintained at prescribed intervals, the maintenance equipment used to check it is itself of unknown accuracy or precision. Another frequent occurrence is to find that, although an auditee has a calibration system for ensuring the accuracy, precision and so on of his inspection and test gauges, the actual tools used for production are not included in that system.

> A company introduced a well thought out calibration system for the inspection and test equipment. The management were genuinely puzzled when they found that this did not reduce the defect level of work coming from its production machinery.

> Another company purchased an expensive machine centre to improve production efficiency but decided to use it also to check out its inspection gauges. The managers were unable to understand why this was undesirable. Things finally came to a head when it was found that the gradual drift in accuracy of that machine centre was such that customers were complaining that the spares did not fit the products supplied some time before. The inspection records had naturally shown that the machine was maintaining its accuracy whilst the *"well known problem of inspection gauge drift"* in the company had been overcome by adjusting the gauges when they were checked against the machine centre!

Correct capability and identification.

Some examples of typical problems in these areas have been described in Chapter 4.

Correct location

1.   Substitute equipment is used.

Failure to provide the right equipment to the right location at the right time may tempt people to use alternative equipment more readily to hand. Substitute equipment may or may not be equivalent to that specified for the process. Under pressure to produce results or meet deadlines, people often gamble on substituting equipment which they think or claim to be equivalent to that required. Such equivalence must be verified prior to use.

> A sales force was sent to make a major presentation to a potentially large account. It had taken some years to win the confidence of the target client, to build up trust an convince its executive of its attention to detail. Much time, money and effort was spent preparing for this most important of presentations. An outside graphics designer was engaged to produce impressive visual aid material to be projected directly from a portable computer via a graphics tablet. Upon arrival, the team leader discovered the graphics disk would not work in the team's computer. It had been prepared using an Apple Macintosh system; the team had brought the wrong type of computer (an IBM compatible) without the correct applications software. The potential client was unimpressed and remains a potential client.

Correct environment

1.   Processes that involve chemical or biological baths have neither clean baths nor control of contaminants, stratification, sedimentation, solution strength, temperature, pH value and the like.

Examples of processes that can be affected by one or more of these problems are cleaning, pickling, etching, plating, developing of film, dip coating, sterilizing. These processes can be monitored easily by simple control charts but frequently are not.

I have always considered "environment" to include the biological, chemical or other fluids into which the items are completely immersed during processing. Shortcomings which crop up with persistent regularity include silt in the bottom of the baths; unmonitored solution strength; uncalibrated or unmaintained temperature control equipment; inadequately maintained pH monitoring equipment; no instructions provided to inform people how and when to add the solutions, how to mix solutions and how to test for the required strength, temperature etc. It is also common to find that, in certain continuous processing baths, make-up chemicals are introduced from only one side of the bath during processing and are inadequately mixed, with the result that part of the batch being processed is subject to excessive solution strengths.

Similarly, a vacuum is an environment in which a process is performed, and must be regarded as such by the auditor. One can encounter gauges that are out of calibration or are damaged; seals that are not maintained; the absence of any alarm to warn of high pressure.

2.   Cleanliness of work areas and storage is inadequate.

In the electronic industry, small circuits are very sensitive to dust and many other substances that can damage them.

> An auditor noted that one company kept a large number of ready made printed circuit boards within the stores. These boards were then assembled into modules for particular applications. The stores were unclean and the printed circuit boards were covered in dust. It not only took much time and money to try to clean these printed circuit boards but the success rate of cleaning was poor. In effect, money was being thrown down the drain. The auditor recommended that the stores be kept cleaner, with a suitable kind of atmosphere control, and that the printed circuit boards be protected in non-static bags or something suitable.

Vermin control is important in various industries such as food production, catering, pharmaceutical and health care.

> In checking the efficacy of vermin control in a food storage warehouse, I became well satisfied both that rat poison was used in the form of pellets being put out and that these were effective. The problem was that I found several decomposing rat cadavers in obvious places.

> At similar store, the frequency of checking the pellet trays was clearly inadequate: ancient cobwebs ere to be found woven across the empty trays. Strangely, though, the auditee's records showed a weekly check of the trays and constant replenishment of the pellets.

3.   The "clean" room is not clean.

The auditor should look for positive air pressure supply, a dust count, humidity control, handling access and nuisance control/prevention. The nuisances that occur in the clean room vary according to the product involved and might include static electricity, vibration, fumes, odours, drought, personal cosmetics or similar substances. In pharmaceutical and health industries, cleanliness also entails the provision of aseptic conditions. The auditor must determine what constitutes a nuisance for the particular contract concerned, see Chapter 4, *"Environment"*.

> Upon entering one *"clean"* room, the auditor noticed that one of its walls did not extend up to the building roof. The auditee explained that this was open to allow the overhead crane to enter and leave. Behind the wall in question was a workshop which was anything but clean: sparks and dust were being generated by grindings work and these were entering the clean room. A film of dust was everywhere.

> A company manufacturing visual display units was experiencing substantial defects with the external coating applied to the tubes. Although the tubes were carefully cleaned prior to the coating being applied in a clean room, dust and detritus still settled on the tubes and became encapsulated in the coating, with unacceptable results. The tube surface was prepared in an antechamber which was part of the clean room. An audit revealed that, after the cleaning operation, the tubes passed along a slow moving conveyor to the coating station above which was the air delivery tube. This air supply maintained positive air pressure to the clean room. Surrounding the air outlet were strakes of black filth which indicated that the air supply was unclean. The filters had not been changed for years. Examination of the ducting showed that, although changing the filters would be a relatively small task, the ducts downstream of the filters were thick with filth and cleaning them would be a major undertaking.

Audits are not exercises performed at a desk or by looking at pieces of paper the auditor has to be prepared to get his hands dirty, especially in "clean" rooms!

Items

Correct type

1.   Item design does not preclude incorrect assembly.

The auditor should look for one-way connectors, plugs, dowels and so on. This is particularly important for valve installation in pipework systems.

Again, it is not an explicit requirement of quality systems standards but it is a matter of common sense, especially to reduce product liability risks.

2.   Incorrect type of item issued.

The auditor should ascertain how the auditee ensures that only correct materials or versions of items are issued for processing. Issuing incorrect types of material is not only risky but also wasteful because the work may have to be redone. Waste is contrary to the objectives of a quality programme. Amazingly ISO 9001 permits this practice (as did the superseded BS 5750-1979 and the 1987 edition of ISO 9001) *"for urgent production purposes"* provided that the auditee can immediately recall and replace the items *"in the event of non-conformity to specified requirements"*. There are many situations when the pressure of work schedules could result in unsafe types of item being released innocently:

☐   *"Take heart, widow Smith, we replaced the items as soon as your husband's accident proved them to be the wrong type. Incidentally, we would appreciate a copy of the death certificate to support our corrective action files"*.

☐   *"Yes sir, Mr. ISO 9001 auditor, our system enables us to recall every patient who has been given a blood transfusion. So, if we do find the blood was contaminated with the HIV virus..."*

Correct condition

1.   Items are found to be in poor condition as a result of poor storage, handling or shipping.

Some companies perform inspections (often referred to as *"product audits"* - a misnomer) to assess the condition of their items after shipping and when they reach the ultimate customer. This is not a measure that will prevent avoidable costs, though it might prevent repetition.

2.   Handling and stacking arrangements for delicate items are inadequate.

An auditor found that completed items were simply thrown into a box and were handled roughly within the stores. They were being damaged as a result. It was decided to improve the stacking arrangements so that the individual items did not come into contact with each other after completion. This move saves a considerable amount of money.

When I moved my household items to the USA, in 1996, I engaged the services of Pickfords. Using their own special wrapping paper, the removal team carefully wrapped every individual piece of furniture and chattel and loaded my possessions into a standard shipping container which was sealed in my presence. Upon arrival, I attended the opening of the container at the warehouse of the American sub-contractor, selected by Pickfords. Its crew expressed amazement at the thoroughness of the wrapping and packing, innocently remarking it far exceeded the level of service their firm would provide. Nothing had moved during the road transportation from Hampshire to the UK seaport, the trans-Atlantic voyage, and the trucking trip from the American east coast to Michigan. Nothing was damaged in the slightest. (Based on the remarks of its own crew, I am not sure I would engage that sub-contractor to wrap, pack and ship my belongings if ever I was to move again.)

3.   Packing of the finished product which does not protect its condition.

During one audit of a truly clean room, it was noted that the pristine, clean assemblies, that were ready for dispatch, were packed into a wooden box full of straw. After such packing, it was found that the straw had covered the items in dust. They had to be re-cleaned.

4.   No provision is made for clean and protected storage after delivery.

At a construction site, it was noted that cleaned pipework was stored out in the open, with no protection whatsoever. Many items were covered in rust and filth.

5.   Inadequate control of shelf life of stored perishable items.

It is wise to have a first-in first-out (FIFO) rota in the stores and to maintain a list showing the date when items were received, the date of their manufacture and the extent of their useful life. Typical items that can deteriorate are rubber products, resins, insulations, foodstuffs, paints and coatings, photographic film and process chemicals. Most auditees quickly appreciate the fact that deteriorated stored items do not enhance product quality, readily accepting the need for a shelf life control system once this is suggested. Purchasing on a just-in-time basis can help to alleviate this problem but can prove uneconomic for small deliveries of consumables.

(The need to control shelf life is one of the implicit requirements of quality systems standards that may be open to debate. The auditor must ascertain the requirements of the particular standards and contract.)

6. Suppliers of particular categories of item are not audited.

Some auditees make the quite unjustified assumption that the items purchased from a big name company must be good and that the company need not be audited. In fact, even huge multinationals can periodically experience quality and safety problems with the items that they supply. (Not all quality systems standards, notably ISO 9001, require external audits to be performed and the auditor is advised to check this point.)

Correct capability and correct quantity

Some examples of typical problems have been discussed in Chapter 4.

Correct identification

1. Items bear no name or objective evidence of their identification to permit traceability.

Not all items need to be marked for traceability, so the auditor must ascertain this point before deciding whether or not the lack of identification is a true deficiency. The classification (or criticality) of the item should provide the key to determining whether or not complete traceability is required for every individual piece.

2. Items are marked incorrectly or inadequately to show their acceptance status.

Not being able to discern whether or not an item has been checked, is awaiting checking, is accepted or rejected, is safe, unsafe or of unknown safety can cause obvious costly problems. At best avoidable costs will be incurred processing something that is not right. At worst, an accident could occur. The auditor must check this point and advise of the auditee of the risks that can result from using items of questionable status. External auditors must, however, avoid assuming that their own company's systems are the only acceptable ones.

Uncontrolled items, information and equipment

When ascertaining the storage condition of items or when checking for uncontrolled items such as consumable materials and other essential material, the auditor must conduct a thorough search, looking behind and underneath things, boxes, tables, shelves and so on. He may find, in work areas, that material which should be of controlled issue is not recalled to the appropriate storage area after use, when an excess amount has been issued or when some remains after the work is completed.

> In one company, it was the rule that consumable materials were to be retained in the work areas. However, the auditor noticed, when standing back from the area, that some of these materials had been placed on the top of an air duct that ran horizontally above the work places.

The auditor should not be shy: he should feel free to ask the auditee to open a few cupboards to check for uncontrolled material, superseded documents or instruments not within the auditee's calibration system.

> A particular firm thought its work areas were completely clean and the audit party was about to leave when the lead auditor happened to open a cupboard within a restricted welding area. Inside, there were several different types of uncontrolled material. The company concerned had never thought to conduct a periodic examination of their personnel's lockers.

If it is decided that the lockers should be periodically examined for uncontrolled objects and superseded copies of information, it may be advisable to perform such an examination in the presence of union representatives, who do generally understand the need for a periodic examination and are most cooperative (in my experience). The examination must always occur with the presence of the locker's user. It is well known that some folk like to collect materials for performing home jobs (weld rods for making gates, repairing motor vehicles, for example). Knowing this, it is better to tell the work force that the company would prefer to let them take home a few electrodes (or other material they would use) for their hobbies rather than have them try to hide material in their lockers with the result that the company loses business or has unfavourable findings during extrinsic audits.

It is a mistake only to work in "two directions": all that is overhead might not be well either.

Following maintenance activities at a food factory, loose nuts, bolts and other miscellaneous detritus were left in precarious positions on the top of silos, pipework and ducts. That filth, which could easily drop into the prime product was only visible by climbing the access ladders provided in the factory.

The auditor must open up boxes: sometimes boxes or containers do not contain what the label claims they do.

An audit team leader discovered a large number of opened containers containing critical consumables. He explained to the auditee that these containers should be removed from the working area and destroyed after use in order to prevent the excess consumables getting into the wrong boxes. The auditee's department manager asserted vehemently that such a situation could not occur within his department. At that moment, the second member of the audit team produced several boxes, each of which contained the wrong material. The manager immediately ordered a purge of the area and all incorrect material and containers were removed and destroyed. The auditors later returned to the area and verified that the action had been completed. Trust and verify!

Persons

Correct competence

This has been explored on in Chapter 4.

Correct training

1.   The person is not suitably trained or prepared to perform his or her task.

The auditor must attend to the exact wording of the regulations, codes and standards concerned since this area can prove to be contentious. The words *"suitable"*, *"training"*, *"qualified"* and *"appropriate"* are all open to differing interpretations and do not necessarily call for formal classroom training or written tests. Often people invoke *"grandfather"* clauses, which are so flexible as to allow much abuse and licence.

It is essential that, apart from understanding the designated task for which he is responsible, the employee knows and understands the company's systems, capabilities and product, as these all affect his tasks.

A company found itself in almost insurmountable difficulties because a salesman signed a contract that invoked a particular type of industrial standard and quality system with which that company and its product were incapable of complying without major changes of administrative procedure as well as fundamental design and material changes.

Salesmen are particularly liable to this sort of error: their desire to clinch a particular sale or to meet their sales target can make them overlook some of the implications of the deal. It is essential for them to be fully aware of their company's true capabilities. In terms of product ans system, and to understand exactly ow the product has been designed and its manufactured.

An audit revealed that the auditee's inspection personnel, who were not taught how one particular product of the company was assembled, were the very people responsible for verifying that the assembly had been carried out correctly. In reality the operatives knew more about the product and assembly than the inspectors did. The inspectors relied on the operators to advise them of the correct manner of assembly!

Auditors (i.e. internal auditors) do not seem to find the deficiencies that the external auditor has.
It is a common fault among companies to tell a person *"Tomorrow you are an auditor, my son"*. Untrained auditors waste time and money both for their own organization and for the auditee (see Chapter 1). If the external auditor finds a number of deficiencies, the competence, training and experience of the internal auditors needs to be re-assessed.

2.   Objective evidence is not available to attest to training/certification/competence of the personnel.

This problem occurs regularly. The auditee should develop a system of employees' files, which should be kept from the moment of hiring and constantly updated to reflect new skills, training and the state of attributes such as eyesight. Whereas quality systems standards can be vague about the content of those records, certain industries' regulations are not. The auditor must ascertain the precise requirements.

3.   People believe possession of a *"certificate"* infers competence.

Nowhere can the folly of making such a silly assumption be so well demonstrated as in the so-called quality profession with its auditor qualification certificates and associated schemes. Competence and training are separate matters.

4.   People believe the absence of a *"certificate"* infers incompetence.

A lady had been the graphics illustrator and artist for a major Scottish university's medical faculty for a number of years. She lived overseas for a while and returned to Scotland. When reapplying for her old job she was told she was *"not qualified"* because she did not have a degree in art and graphics. The education authority had, apparently, changed its entry requirements, demanding possession of an arts degree as essential evidence of training for the particular position. Despite the intervention and energetic advocacy on her behalf by her eminent professor, who knew well her work, and wanted desperately to reengage the lady, and despite the fact that her previous work continued to be used in standard medical training texts, she was unsuccessful.

5.   People believe membership of committees infers knowledge of a subject and competence in its field.

A member of one of the working groups involved in preparing the *"Advanced Product Planning and Control Plan Reference Manual"*, for the American automotive industry's QS 9000 initiative, and named in the *"Acknowledgments"* part of those documents was incapable of explaining its requirements.

A member of one of the ISO TC 176 committees, responsible for preparing the 1987 edition of ISO 9004, could not produce a quality manual to comply with ISO 9000 for his employer, who had to hire in a consultant to do the work.

After claiming the credit for the firm's successful QS 9000 certificate and guidance of its audit programme, an American company's quality manager amazed and embarrassed an assembly by requesting an explanation of the difference between the expressions *"auditor"* and *"auditee"*.

Correct motivation

See Chapter 4.

Correct attributes

1.   Eyesight is not tested.

Some industries' regulations require this to be done. Even though quality systems standards do not state that eyesight (or other personal attributes required in executing a work task) must be checked, it is a matter of common sense that this should be so.

> It was found that a particular inspector's eyesight had deteriorated to such an extent that he was virtually blind: he certainly could not read the indications on the measuring equipment accurately. The inspector was an old man who was afraid of losing his job and becoming unemployed. Nobody had questioned him because he had been performing inspection for years but there had been a number of customer complaints about the quality of items being released.

> At the entry interview for one audit, I explained that a particular area of concern would be eyesight checks for both accuracy and colour. I mentioned the problem of the virtually blind inspector to which I referred above. The firm's quality manager found the story incredible: he could not believe that any company would fail to notice such a situation. The company was manufacturing an electrical product which contained a good deal of coloured wiring. In addition, the calibration system in use relied on colour coding of the instruments to indicate the calibration status. That evening, the quality manager was dining out on the story of a blind inspector. When he had finished, I asked: *"Do you know that one of your inspectors is colour blind?"* The quality manager was so surprised that he dropped his knife and fork onto his plate. It was, in fact, his chief inspector who was colour blind.

> A firm engaged a new inspector to examine pressure containing components by means of dye penetrant techniques. Almost immediately, the production department started to complain about the poor quality of items released after inspection (a rather curious complaint considering that it was the production department who had made them). It was found that the new inspector's acuity was so bad that he could not discern the small indications within the dye penetrant developer. When asked about his eyesight, the man grew very angry but he eventually agreed to go to the company's medical department for an eye check. He returned most apologetic and stated that he had not realized that his eyesight had deteriorated to such an extent.

A company engaged a manager reputed to possess special expertise which would help to revolutionize its methods. Since his work entailed careful deliberation about what to do, he was given his own office rather than a desk in an open plan area, so that he would not be disturbed. After lunch each day, he could be seen through the glass partition that separated him from the main office, reclining in his chair apparently deep in thought with an eye staring transfixed at the ceiling. Knowing the importance of his mission, nobody wished to disturb him. This state of affairs went on for some months until the company discovered the staring eye to be made of glass and the expert fast asleep. The quality manager wryly remarked that all experts should be included in the eyesight checks.

These examples show how common it is for eyesight to be neglected, both by operatives and by companies. Regular checks should be made for acuity and colour vision. In the case of products that are assembled underneath the microscope (as an increasing number are nowadays) or microsurgery it is particularly important to have regular checks on personal eyesight, which dictates the ultimate quality of the product.

Similar remarks can be made about other personal attributes (such as dexterity) that are necessary and which affect quality.

While attending at a large construction site, I witnessed a crisis. A bullying foreman had insisted a workman should climb up a tower crane with something or other for the driver. The person concerned was to be seen half way up in a frozen state clutching onto the ladder. The man suffered from vertigo.

One memorable night some years ago, I visited Buddy Guy's club, *"Legends"* to enjoy Buddy performing. A young (then, well known) rock band was visiting Chicago too. Its lead guitarist asked if he could jam along with Buddy Guy who, in his usual genial manner, cordially invited the young man to the stage for that purpose. Sadly, the visitor's guitar was out of tune. Despite Buddy Guy's halting of the number several times to afford him the opportunity to correctly tune the instrument, the young man could not do so: I believe the young guitarist was tone deaf! Buddy left the stage to revive himself with what looked like a glass of brandy. The rock band left the club.

2.   Personnel do not comply with a document's requirements.

This may be no bad thing, in which case the auditor should not stifle initiative. People who actually have to perform the job quite often proclaim the document/procedure/manual to be rubbish. If this turns out to be the case, the auditor must take a look at the feedback system, the internal audit system and people who generated the *"rubbish"*. Provided that the product results required by the contract or other requirements are being achieved, the best course is to change the document so that it reflects the actual practice and this is what the auditor should recommend. A recommendation is usually adequate because the people responsible generally recognize the need for their documents to reflect actual practice: few people like to admit to being out of touch with what actually happens within their own organization or to allow documentary evidence to that effect to exist after the situation has been drawn to their attention. A formal request for corrective action to change the document would be unfair. The real cause of the problem (in most cases, lack of a feedback system) is what could warrant a formal request for corrective action.

> A company was applying for its ISO 9001 registration. It had bought one of the numerous *"do-it-yourself"* sets of documents available on floppy disk, changed the file names, company names and so on. The quality manager was pleased with his efforts. The registrar's assessment team discovered the employees were not complying with the firm's quality manual and procedures. Apparently it was more important for the staff to comply with the documents than it was for the documents to reflect the actual processes and systems used!

Corrective action and non-conformities

1.   The conclusion *"use as is"* is excessively exercised.

Quality systems standards generally do not preclude excessive exercise of this conclusion. Even so, the auditor should look for the underlying reason why *"use as is"* figures so prominently behind the non-conformities discovered.

2.   Tolerances are widened.

Again, quality systems standards do not rule this out, but freedom must not turn into license. The auditor must investigate the matter further: there may be a perfectionist designer who has never learnt (or never been told) what the company's capabilities really are and who invokes excessively tight tolerances that are expensive to meet. However, should tolerances be widened, the effect on interfacing items, overall function and fitness for purpose must be assessed by the auditee. The auditor must verify that this is written into the design change control system, for it is often overlooked.

> During a seminar of mine in London, in the fall of 1989, I fell into a discussion with delegate, a production manager, who, having read of the Motorola initiative, expressed an interest in six sigma quality. After some thought about the matter, and with his deep knowledge of statistical process control, he said he could easily achieve it. All that would be necessary would be for the design department to widen the tolerances. (Six sigma is calculated by dividing a tolerance by the standard deviation of the process making it. If the process standard deviation is large one would need a correspondingly large tolerance.) I think he was serious.

3.   The corrective action file is not retained by management.

It is a very healthy sign when top management maintains such a file or gets involved with it, since this adds an edge to the corrective action system. Management's failure to do so can herald a lack of top management support for quality.

The auditor must remember that quality systems standards, such as ISO 9001, do not ask for such a file to be maintained (let alone say who should keep it). What they generally do require is that corrective action be reported to *"management"* for *"review"*. Just what level of *"management"* would be regarded as appropriate, is a debatable topic. The auditor must keep an open mind on the subject and reference to the organization chart and associated job descriptions may be of assistance.

4.   Either management does not ask for a breakdown of avoidable costs or there is no breakdown of such costs.

Any management that is unaware of its avoidable costs, their constituents and their origin is a management failing in its fiduciary duty. (ISO 9001 makes no mention of this matter even though it is the stuff of business and effective management systems.) See also Part 2 Chapter 2.

5.   Corrective action responses from sub-suppliers or internal departments are either not prompt or are not expedited.

Regardless of the prescriptions a quality systems standard may or may not have on this particular subject, taking prompt corrective action is essential if avoidable costs are to be reduced as quickly as possible. See also Chapter 17. For those firms indulging in a just-in-time procurement programme, tardiness in corrective action will wreck the benefits of the imitative and defeat its objectives.

Preventive management systems

1.   A corrective action system is regarded as equivalent to a preventive action system.

It is not. There is a significant difference between action designed to prevent a repetition of a problem and action designed to prevent a first occurrence of a problem. Only the latter can be regarded as truly directing itself at the prevention of avoidable costs.

(The wording of such standards as ISO 9001 is amazingly ambiguous on this matter. That standard requires *"The procedures for preventive action shall include...initiation of preventive action and application of controls to ensure it is effective"*. How lucid!)

Real causes of business problems

Many years ago, as a result of having performed a lot of audits, I detected a recurring pattern of six underlying causes of business problems that have constantly needed to be addresses through corrective action requests. They are:

- ♦   Lack of organization
- ♦   Lack of training
- ♦   Lack of discipline
- ♦   Lack of resources
- ♦   Lack of time
- ♦   Lack of top management support

Lack of organization

Lack of organization divided into three main components, namely:

- ♦   Undetermined responsibilities and authorities
- ♦   Undefined management systems
- ♦   Inadequate communications

Undetermined responsibilities and authorities

This has been discussed more fully in Chapter 3, *"Organization"*. The purpose of organization is to determine what jobs must be done in order to achieve customer satisfaction, by furnishing a product (or service) that is fit for purpose. The fundamental tasks of organizing are:

♦ To decide what has to be done.
♦ To decide who is going to do what.
♦ To decide what level of responsibility and authority will be required for each position.
♦ To select carefully the people with the requisite competence and abilities to discharge their assigned duties.

When auditing, one might find that the company structure has not been defined; that job descriptions have been inadequately conceived and lead to conflicting responsibilities and an overlap of duties; that delegated duties are inconsistent with the manager's assigned responsibilities.

> An engineering department manager responsible for over 100 highly qualified and well paid staff, amounting to a payroll of several million dollars, did not have the authority to purchase any item to an amount in excess of $500. It was during an audit that I encountered this particular gentleman in the early 1980's at a time when he had just struggled to get approval to buy the first desktop computer (an IBM PC) for the department. At that time, any computing service his department requested of the firms' mainframe, had to fit in with the demands of the company's finance and payroll department who had the authority to spend up to $20000 without reference to higher management. (Design computing was, therefore, performed during evenings and over weekends. For that purpose, the support staff had to be paid overtime rates!) The gentleman had finally got the PC, but had been instructed to put in a separate expenditure request for the applications' software, which was subject to the approval of the finance department. While the approval system performed its magic, the PC was lying idle (it had been that way for a couple of months) and the engineering manager was criticized for incurring an expenditure for an item that was not being used!

Undefined management systems

The management systems should prescribe the methods and means of communication so as to form a complete and continuous chain between the various departments, individuals and organizations, involved in or affected by the firms business. It is not uncommon to find in a company that the management systems have not been thoroughly thought through and are *ad hoc* in practice. Whilst it is increasingly important for companies to be agile and flexible, which entails delegation of considerable freedom in decision making and action to individuals, teams and departments, the core of the business still needs a basic framework of systems. Indeed, by setting up such a framework the firm will find itself able to respond quickly to market place needs. What it does not need is a tangled web of bureaucratic systems that offer no additional value to the bottom line or customer service. (The quality movement has much to answer for, in that the bulk of its citizens have promoted pointless bureaucracy for the last half century. Its standard response to business problems has been to suggest additional procedures, forms, verifications and records. It is only now as the millennium approaches that clear signs are developing that it is trying to concentrate more on effective business process control than pointless paperwork. Hurrah!)

Management systems are required regardless of the company's size. All managers are duty bound to decide how the work is to be executed and how the internal processes are to interface between themselves and with external organizations (and, especially, with the customer). The degree of formality must be consistent with prudent action. It is not always necessary for procedures to be written down. Their purpose is to help explain the methods used and to provide a training vehicle for staff. If alternative training methods can be used, they should be pursued provided that health, safety and product liability risks are not compromised.

Assessing the need for written procedures:

Far too many auditors, and registrars in particular, demand and expect procedures to be written down. They want documentation before determining if it is needed or not. For my part, what matters is the knowledge and ability to apply experience and expertise on the job. If an auditee can demonstrate to me that he or she can control the process under scrutiny, the absence of written procedures is unimportant. If having such procedures would offer some real benefit for the future, I will suggest they are formalized. If they would not, then there is little point in having them. Meaningful written procedures are a means of communicating knowledge, experience and expertise to those who do not have it. But there are other ways of ensuring effective communications. There is no point in asking a competent person to write down his or her procedures when no one else would be performing the process concerned. The same can be said for teams. If members of a team decide together how they will do their work, is it really essential to write things down that no one needs to read? No, it is not.

Blinkered ISO 9000 zealots, and registrars, should consider carefully the words the standard uses in relation to *"process control"*. Documented procedures are only required *"where the absence of such procedures could adversely affect quality"*. It is my view that the competent auditor will first ascertain the ability of those in charge of the process, and those performing it, to control the work. As the thousands of delegates to my seminars know, I advise a reliable sign of an incompetent auditor is he or she who, on arrival at an auditee's workplace, begins asking *"Can you show me your procedures/ have you got a procedure/ where are your procedures"* and such like. It is silly, it is rude.

It is silly because the need for a written procedure has yet to be determined. In any case, if the auditee lacks the knowledge and ability to effectively control the process, he or she cannot be expected to produce a meaningful, useful and reliable procedure. The person needs training. If the person does effectively control the process, the procedure would offer nothing new. The essence of auditing is to determine whether or not the auditee can control its processes to the benefit of the product and the business. Asking for a procedure at the outset is a mistake for these additional reasons.

♦ It signals to the auditee *"this is procedure day"*. The auditee may know well what is written in the procedure but would not normally work in that manner. Knowing the propensity the majority of auditors have towards issuing corrective action requests for those not complying with procedures, auditees *"do it by the book"* while the auditor is present. The auditor does not learn how things really are done - hardly a hallmark of effective auditing.

♦ If the auditee does produce a procedure, the auditor still would not know whether or not it is relevant, efficacious in practice. The auditor still has to verify what is actually being done on the job and determine the impact of practice on the product. It is the product that matters and, the auditor must never lose sight of it. One can never be absolutely sure a procedure will guarantee product quality.

Demanding at the outset a procedure is rude because the auditor is prejudging without any verification the auditee's competence and need for written instruction.

> February 1997, State of Georgia, USA: A QS 9000 registrar enters an auditee's work area and immediately demands a written procedure. The employee responds advising it is with his manager. The registrar comments that absence of the procedure at the workplace is a violation of the QS 9000 requirements, that a corrective action request will be issued and leaves the area. (Just another little story among the countless similar examples that are a plague on business. The registrar auditor is, of course, *"qualified"*, and probably has a certificate to prove it.)

In sum, absence of a written procedure does not mean absence of a management system.

The correct time to confirm the presence of a written procedure is when the auditor has finished examining how the process is performed. Then *and only then* can one sensibly decide:

◆   If a written procedure would be beneficial (i.e. whether its absence does or does not *"adversely affect quality"*).

◆   If a written procedure is furnished to the auditor at that point, they do or do not reflect the actual work practice, as distinct from imaginary methods cooked up elsewhere.

(One must also hope the written procedure is the same as that supplied to the auditor for the purpose of preparing for the audit. See Chapter 9. But, if it is not, this does not constitute the crisis some auditors would believe it to be - auditees have the right to alter their procedures at any time!)

Circular systems:

Sometimes an auditee genuinely believes that he has created a good management system. Careful analysis during an audit only reveals that it is circular in nature and is therefore useless. For example:

> During an audit of a chemical laboratory, I enquired of its manager, *"How do you calibrate your pH meter?"* The laboratory manager replied *"We check against buffer solutions."* I asked *"Where do you get these buffer solutions from?"* To this he replied *"We make them up ourselves."* I then enquired *"How do you make these solutions?"* The response was *"In accordance with government*

authority's approved procedures". These were checked out for correct content, revision, validity etc. The next question I posed was *"When you have made up these standard buffer solutions how do you check them?"* To this the laboratory manager replied *"Using the pH meter"*!

An analyst used a mathematical technique to perform his work. Verification was done by a department colleague using a spreadsheet program. The spreadsheet program had been prepared by the colleague who had passed it to the analyst for checking. The analyst had used his mathematical technique to check the spreadsheet program.

Inadequate communications

Methods of communication have to be thought through in terms of who needs the information that the company or any given department produces. Recipients of information may be either within the organization or outside of it: communication problems can arise from any of the following:

Language barriers:

Special care must be exercised when the information user's mother tongue is a foreign language.

Apparently, one of the contributing factors to the DC10 air crash outside of Paris, France, was that the instructions printed on the fuselage for closing the rear cargo door were in English on a Turkish airline's plane that was being serviced at Paris. It appears that the airport employee who attempted to shut the cargo door was unable to do so because he could not understand the instructions provided.

Certain communications must be in the language that will permit the recipient to understand, otherwise product liability risks can ensue.

Attitudes such as *"We won't talk to them"; "they never help us, they think they are so clever, let them find out for themselves"* confound good communications. No system will prevent this sort of behaviour for ever and the only remedy is to develop a responsible attitude as part of the corporate business culture. The example set by management is crucial for, when staff detect that their manager is feuding with another department, they naturally take sides and join in.

Attitudes such as *"We didn't know what they wanted"; "we didn't know they had it"* can each presage unhelpfulness, pure laziness or absence of team spirit, none of which builds up the right corporate culture. A must not only be encouraged to tell B of his requirements from B's particular work area: A must also be encouraged to inform B of services, knowledge and products which A could provide to help B.

Lack of training

This has been discussed more fully earlier in this chapter and in Chapter 4.

There is little point in carefully avoiding the problems described under *"Lack of organization"*, above, if the people in the company are not trained in the systems and methods that are to be used or if they are not told with whom they are to interface. Many companies spend a lot of money in produce business and operations manuals and distributing them. If, however the users have not been trained in its contents all that expenditure is pure waste. Arguing that the purpose of the manuals is to provide a training vehicle such that the people will know those matters is generally confounded by the reality of everyday life in the workplace: managers do not provide the time their staff need to read the manuals and digest the contents. Experience shows that people appreciate a briefing meeting at least to explain the contents, a forum in which they can raise on the spot difficulties and questions about implementation. Such training briefs tend to offer better training value than does issuing a manual expectantly hoping it will be read, understood, implemented and efficacious in practice.

Lack of discipline

Regardless of how carefully thought through the systems may be and how much training has been provided, people are the real determinants of how well things turn out. Self-discipline and adult attitude towards the job is of prime importance. The discipline can be affected, however, by a number of factors, principally:

♦ The example set by supervisors and managers.
♦ Company wide campaigns and culture.
♦ Personal attributes.
♦ Inflexible systems.
♦ De-motivating environments.

The example set by supervisors and managers

A major cause of staff not following the systems and methods as intended, arises from bad examples set by supervisors and managers. There is little point in spending much time, money and effort in carefully devising the systems and procedures that are to be followed if one knows that the manager will waive them in order to get a product out of the door in time to the customer. It is a constant temptation. Every organization knows that urgent circumstances inevitably arise at some time or other, so when the systems and methods are devised, they must also cater for those urgent situations. Failure to have considered that set of trading circumstances and operational conditions indicates either a lack of forethought or pure stupidity.

> Over the years and when advising my clients about the structure and parameters for their organization and systems, I have always said they should be set up on the basis that every order is urgent, so, cut out *"nice-to-do"* things that add no value to the product or service supplied. The reality facing modern business is that urgent situations not only inevitably arise, and must be catered for, but speed of service is an important feature: urgency has become the norm. A growing number of customers are practising or moving towards just-in-time programs: some even aspire to real time programs. They will set tough delivery deadlines expecting every order to be dealt with as expeditiously as possible. Firms are not being measured solely on the quality and price of their wares: timeliness of service is a key measurable that affect future buying decisions.

Waiving the systems sends a clear signal to the staff that compliance does not really matter, that systems are not sacrosanct. From that point on, the work descends into chaos and *ad hoc* practices. Nobody knows how their own and different departments will operate, what their needs are and what budgets are needed in order to execute the duties assigned to them. Moreover, staffing levels cannot be accurately defined, nor can people's performance be assessed since there is no yardstick for measurement. It is, therefore, vital that people in managerial and supervisory positions set an example by following the systems that have been designated for use within their areas, improving them whenever possible or necessary. But, if waiving the system is done genuinely in the interests of improving efficiency, the supervisor/manager must advise the staff accordingly that the new practice is now the norm.

Perhaps worst of all is the situation that arises when the supervisor/manager deviates from the systems that have been determined for the department and devised by the staff themselves. This is often taken as disregard for people's knowledge, initiative and efforts and as indicative of a by *fiat* style of management.

Company wide campaigns and culture

Unless a business improvement campaign extends company wide to include all staff and line activities, there is a considerable risk that the line departments will become disenchanted.

> I have met numerous people in line functions who no longer care about their company quality campaign, which they rightly perceive as unfair. Common criticisms take the form of *"They keep pressing us to take care of quality but our pay packets still contain errors/the sales force continue to send us incomplete information too late/those in the office still churn out the same rubbish to us and nobody tells them to do a better job"*.

> A company, concerned about drinking on the job, fired an hourly paid employee in whose desk was found a small bottle of whisky. The company CEO maintained a well stocked bar in his office.

Demotivators and frictions build up preventing effective team work and healthy attitudes.
The auditor should ascertain the true extent of the campaigns and culture, noting any simmering resentment such as that described above.

Personal attributes

Some people stubbornly refuse to follow the agreed methods or systems, insistent on working their own way. Such attitudes must not be encouraged. In the case of a company involved in the furnishing of safety related products, anybody who does not follow the necessary systems which are known to ensure a safe product must be stopped, unless their own methods do not jeopardize safety. Even in this case, they should be encouraged to consider further the impact of their methods on colleagues before continuing with them. In persistent cases, this could ultimately necessitate firing the miscreant from the company. For those people whose work is not safety related, its is incumbent on their peers and their supervisors to point out that, by not following those agreed methods, they might be causing difficulties and problems for their colleagues in other areas, a consequence which would both be unreasonable and unfair. It

404

cannot be tolerated for long because those diligent employees who are doing their best will view as unfair that somebody else is allowed *to "get away with it"*. Gradually, they start to say *"well, why should I bother?"* This ultimately leads to chaos and work being incorrect, incomplete or performed indifferently.

Inflexible systems

Management systems should not be designed so as to be inflexible. People are employed principally because they possess a brain and are able to think. They are employed for the experience and skill they can bring to the job and the day-to-day decision making capability they have. Regardless of their position in their organization, everyone makes decisions. When systems are too inflexible, they remove the great motivating freedoms to innovate and make decisions. People want to *"beat the system"* and find a way round it as a form of protest.

I contend that many within the so-called quality profession have much to answer for. By constantly seeking to make procedures ever more detailed and inflexible to cover all circumstances and contingencies that could possibly arise in the workplace, they have helped to demotivate staff. Why is it that managers have been justifiably critical of QA auditors over many years? Simply because whenever there has been a problem, instead of trying to uncover the root cause and curing the problem, the response has been to impose another piece of paper, adding further bureaucracy to the workplace. Not very helpful. Certain activities do need to be planned in fine detail, this being the case especially in high value, high risk and safety related situations, such as in the operating of a nuclear power station or in flying of a commercial passenger jet aircraft. Even in these situations, however, there comes a time when one needs to rely on people's ability to think quickly under difficult circumstances: there may be no time to read the procedure.

The probability that a procedure will be read is at best inversely proportional to the square of its thickness (Sayle's Law of Procedures!) The auditor must ensure by his approach and attitude that he does not become counter-productive by promoting inflexible systems, explained in tomes full of procedures.

Motivation

A central cause of lack of discipline is also a lack of motivation. It is important that any demotivator that can occur is prevented and extirpated. Motivation is discussed in Chapter 4.

> A well known company equipped its PC's with web browsers. Naturally the staff began to use this equipment. Sadly, however, it became known that the firm was monitoring what the employees were doing *"on the web"*. The staff felt this equated to a "spy system" displaying lack of trust. They subsequently used the facilities sparingly.

Lack of resources

Lack of resources can be caused either by pure wastage or by their inadequate estimation and allocation to areas where they are really needed. The allocation of resources needs to be properly planned and it is my contention that an essential part of the management audit is to investigate the basis on which resources are determined and allocated. (Use of resources is discussed in Part 2 Chapter 2.)

As stated previously, it is not possible to determine where the available resources really are required unless the company has first of all organized itself thoroughly and thereby defined the systems needed for the product that it intends to sell. Only by getting organized, can one define the resources required in each of the various departments. The enterprise as a whole requires a management system which ensures that resources are properly estimated, allocated and monitored in every department. The auditor must look for proof that:

- Such a system exists.
- That system has been communicated throughout the organization.
- That system is implemented.
- That system is effective.

Furthermore, every department, cost centre, division, process, project etc. must constantly look for ways by which resources can be saved although not to the detriment of quality since that would represent a false economy. Managers must also ensure that none of the following, which can starve individual areas of essential resources is allowed to occur:

- ◆ Over-complex management systems.
- ◆ Irresponsible attitudes.
- ◆ Unrealistic estimates.
- ◆ Uneven allocation.
- ◆ Inadequate re-investment.
- ◆ Failure to modernize.

Over-complex management systems

Problems can occur because an over-complex system devours valuable resources. The systems must be economic. Too few management auditors analyze the systems to see whether or not they use the resources properly. When a system is too complex, it wastes manpower and budget which could be put to effect in other areas. Auditors should be on their guard, watchful for any signs of this development. Many of the real breakthroughs and benefits that occur in business improvement programmes happen by identifying this form of waste. (See also Part 2 Chapter 2, *"Value-added auditing"*.)

Irresponsible attitudes

People can have a most peculiar attitude towards resources. No matter how much is allocated to them, they always want more. It is a kind of Parkinson's Law [5] in that individuals and departments concerned will always manage to devour completely whatever resources are allocated to them. It is well known, for example, that people in governmental organizations are loath to return unused resources for fear that their following year's budget will be cut accordingly. Hence, resources are always used up according to the allocation made. This is an unfortunate type of attitude and is one that is difficult to break down. Effective teamwork requires everybody to realize that excess resources should be returned for use in another area to greater effect. Everyone must appreciate that this will improve quality and results elsewhere in the organization and fund real solutions to problems, thus benefitting everyone eventually.

Unrealistic estimates

It is not uncommon to find that bids and tenders or product development plans are based on totally unrealistic figures. People can be over optimistic from the most well meaning point of view. (Over the years, I have found this to be particularly true of software supply projects - see also Part 2 Chapter 4.) This has the result that, eventually, in order to complete a job on time, something has to give and part of the job is rushed. It is a false economy and there are many examples that have been reported bearing testimony to this.

Uneven allocation

The actual allocation of resources can be most unfair. I have come across many instances of uneven allocation based on bad planning or pure favouritism. Often, one particular department or manager receives an over generous share of the resources either because his face fits, because he makes such a fuss that his management wants to keep him quiet or because the superior has a particular affection for the work being carried out there. Uneven allocation means that someone somewhere else is having to make do and is often cutting corners and encountering avoidable problems in his own department as a result. On several occasions, I have experienced favoured managers gloating over the difficulties of their fellow managerial colleagues. All of this leads to strains in the team and is a great demotivator. It sets up pointless rivalries in which people are pitched against each other at all levels, determined to be *"one-up"* on others, and being more concerned about politics than getting down to business, solving the company's problems and maturely working together as a team.

Inadequate investment

Business is generally cyclic and every company experiences good and bad profit years. Prudent management will use the years of strong profit and performance to reinvest in the company's future development. History can show many examples of industries that failed to do so wit the inevitable result that traumatic restructuring and rationalization becomes necessary in the lean years or as the product range becomes effete.

Today's business problems are the direct result of poor management decisions of the past. Securing future prospects means that the company must reinvest in new skills, new techniques, new equipment and new products. A total quality programme must extend into the strategic decisions made by the board of directors and the top management, encompassing reinvestment decisions. The average auditor will not have much opportunity to investigate this aspect of the business, but the President's audit can and must. (See Part 2 Chapter 7.)

It is unwise for one year's resource allocation to be based on the needs of the previous year(s) because product lines and trading factors change and continue on in a constant state of flux. To slash the following year's budget simply because the resources allocated for the previous year were not required in their entirety can be unrealistic for the same reasons. Remembering that business circumstances can alter, the successful manager who, without impairing quality and business effectiveness, has saved on resources allocated in the previous year should not be hamstrung for next year's needs which may be totally different. The performance of that department could deteriorate and problems the result of having to *"make-do"*.

Failure to modernize

There comes a point when equipment which may still be perfectly serviceable is a liability to the company because of new technology and developments. By not replacing the equipment, a company can find itself disadvantaged especially if one's competitors have already modernized. Failure to modernize means increased avoidable costs. It all ends up in the unit price or reduced profits. New equipment might not only incur reduced running costs by virtue of its greater efficiency but might also be able to work to higher specifications. This is also been discussed in Chapter 5 and Part 2 Chapter 2.

Continuous improvement requires a constant search for improved methods and potential applications for new technology throughout the organization. One finds many instances of people continuing to work in old fashioned ways when, for example, an inexpensive desktop computer or terminal could reduce their workload and allow then to work more accurately and productively.

A manufacturing company purchased a state-of-the-art machine for an essential process. The machine could work far faster than the one it replaced. Its operator was familiar with statistical process control techniques (SPC) but still used manual methods for recording and analyzing the process data as the machine operated. This was so slow that defective products were produced before the operator had a chance to effect minor adjustments to keep within the process acceptance criteria. To avoid the problem, the machine was run at slower speeds than its true capacity. An auditor suggested the operator should be supplied with a PC equipped with one of the many SPC software application programmes to speed up analysis. This was done and the increased productivity and lower level of defects made paid for the machine in less than two weeks. Better still, the operator was able to provide the engineering department with up-to-date information about the process performance, machine capabilities and tool life when the PC was linked to their own computers. This helped to improve product and tool design, resulting in further efficiencies.

Resources can be wasted not only because new equipment, techniques or new technology is not used but also because the investment is not understood. Frequently companies are found to have acquired new equipment which is lying idle or used ineffectively.

In one American company, a very sophisticated machine tool which cost approximately $1 million lay idle for nearly 18 months because people did not understand how to use it. Many excuses were proffered such as *"We did not have the right tooling"; "We are waiting for the machine to be finally installed and commissioned"*. An audit revealed the real reason was that the machinists were apprehensive about using new technology.

A service company spent $25000 on a desktop publishing system which lay virtually idle for nearly a year because the staff did not learn how to use it. They had pestered management for that equipment but when it arrived, they avoided proper training. It was used for minutes of meetings and simple one page lists that could easily have been produced on a typewriter. But the laser printer did at least make those lists and minutes look pretty and the management was thus fooled into thinking that the investment had been worthwhile.

Instances such as the above can occur when people either lack training in the type of technology that is available or when they also lack the time to learn how to use the technology properly.

A number of years ago, a company purchased a numerically controlled machine tool which worked from holorith cards. One day, whilst rushing to start the machine working, the operator accidentally dropped the box of cards. Quite innocently and quickly he gathered them up from the workshop floor and stuffed them all back into the box: he had no idea that the card sequence was critical. When the machine started it totally ruined a valuable piece of material. The holorith cards had been programmed to move the machine head to the next position on the basis of the previous position of the head as opposed to moving relative to a fixed datum. What had not been appreciated was that if the cards became mixed up the machine tool head would move to the wrong position. Investigation revealed that there had been insufficient investment in the training of people and inadequate time allocated for the people to learn grow to use and program that machine tool properly.

Resources need to be carefully planned on the basis of the company's trading strategy. As part of the plan, the acquisition of resources needs to be carefully thought through and proper capital appropriation needs to be plotted, not just in respect of purchasing new equipment or techniques but also in terms of training the people who will have to use it.

Lack of time

Time is a resource that I single out because of the prevalence of business problems deriving from inadequate control of it. Problems result when people are forced to rush their jobs. I regard time management as an essential part of quality management, indeed, a prerequisite for a successful quality programme, and, accordingly, over many years have directed auditors' attention to the necessity of asking questions as to how the auditee manages time. The answers generally reveal opportunities for improvement and cost reduction. Lack of time is the business management version of saying *"Marry in haste, repent at leisure!"* Despite its critical effect on quality and business performance, quality systems standards still fail to require systems for its effective management. The omission is all the more shameful and surprising considering customers increasingly demand it and use timeliness in delivery performance as a key measurement of their suppliers' performance, as mentioned earlier in this chapter.

> The fact that time management is not a criteria on its own within such standards as ISO 9001, reduces the usefulness of any certificate. Time is an important aspect of *"service"*, described in Chapter 4. It directly affects customer profitability just as much as does poor product quality. Timeliness of delivery can be regarded as a product and it deserves its own management systems.

Every enterprise requires a management system which ensures time is properly estimated, allocated and monitored in every department. The auditor must look for proof that:

♦　　Such a system exists.
♦　　The system has been communicated throughout the organization.
♦　　The system is implemented.
♦　　The system is effective.

411

Every department, division, process, project etc. must constantly search for ways in which time can be saved but not by sacrificing quality or business performance, for that also would be a false economy. Managers must also ensure that none of the following, which can deprive individual areas of essential time, occur:

- ♦ Over-complex systems.
- ♦ Irresponsible attitudes.
- ♦ Unrealistic commitments.
- ♦ Selfishness.
- ♦ Excessive workload.

Over-complex systems

Systems that are too complex can waste time, in that needless activities bureaucracy and checks eat into the time budget allowed for a job. Wherever possible, one must strive either to eliminate needless tasks or to design the system such that essential tasks are performed in parallel to the greatest extent possible. (That is, the systems should be two-dimensional, not one dimensional, whenever possible. See also Chapter 6.)

Irresponsible attitudes

Some people use as much time to do their job as is allocated to them. It is Parkinson's Law in that work will always expand to fill the time available for it. However, excessive time allocated to one person often means that somebody else has been denied the time he needs to do a good job.

Unrealistic commitments

Sales orders:

It is quite common to find bids and tenders that are totally unrealistic about the time required to effect proper delivery to the customer. Salespeople can be over zealous in the commitments they make on behalf of the company. Promising unrealistic delivery dates introduces the risks that corners are cut, incomplete or unsatisfactory products are delivered and that the customer becomes annoyed. It not only costs a lot of money to rectify the problem at the customer's premises but there is the real risk that further business will be lost and the company's reputation will be damaged. A salesperson might consider that he has done a good job in reaching or exceeding his sales targets but, if that achievement means he has committed the company to a trading loss, nobody benefits.

But sales staff also require help and its is equally vital that the company sets up its systems and organizes itself in such a way that it can provide its sales force with realistic and meaningful delivery times for presentation to the customer.

New products:

In a similar way, development plans for new products can be unrealistic or over optimistic. Sometimes design and development staff are coerced into making rash promises by the pressure exerted by top management.

Production deadlines:

Production people can also be unwise in predicting release dates for products, especially new lines. Unforeseen hitches can easily arise: they tend to do so more frequently when time pressure is exerted irresponsibly. Inadequate involvement of the production people in the design and development work will lead directly to that - such a phenomenon occurs with monotonous regularity.

A common problem encountered in the service sectors is that of support staff (who service or install new equipment required for supplying the service to the customer) underestimating the time required to get everything into proper working order. There is a particular tendency for this to happen when they are not involved in the design of the service itself. (See also Part 2 Chapter 5.)

Clearly, to ensure a responsible allocation, planning and commitment of time, people should work together as a team. The auditor can check how the various commitments are made. But sensible estimation can only be made if the core systems of the organization are carefully designed and adhered to. This being done, the estimators will know reliably the time the system takes to serve particular needs: it is a key capability.

Selfishness

Figure 8.3 depicts a typical bar chart representation for the various phases that work might go through in a company. They are examples of major constituents in a firm's primary system (see also Chapter 6). The people working at the front end of any set of activities, project or contract have a duty to ensure that they prevent any slippage of time as far as possible. What tends to happen is that the front end activities view the total time available for the complete project (or order) and say *"Well, if we lose a*

413

few days, the other departments will pick it up, so let's not worry. In any case they probably have more slack in their budget than us." A cancer develops as the subsequent phases reason, *"It was handed over to us late and we still want our rightful amount of time to do our job"* and then they, too, exceed their time budget a little, further reasoning if the previous department can do so, why can't they? Eventually, the poor souls at the end of the line are pressurized to meet the delivery dates and commitments that were originally made to the customer, having their time allocation slashed in the process. Although they do the best they can, they look for shortcuts, overlooking or waiving essential quality checks, for example. The product is shipped, the customer complains and more money is wasted. It is shortsighted and unfair to steal time allocated for a colleague's work.

"Fast track" projects gained some popularity in the 1980's. It was a catchy and seductive name that persuaded many managers into taking unwise shortcuts only to discover they incurred excessive long term costs. These can have great effect on the lifetime costing of the product (sometimes dubbed *"the cost of ownership"*) obtained from the *"fast track"* project. An alarming number of managers confided to me their regrets at not having tempered their fast track enthusiasm with wiser decisions. Trying to avoid important tasks can be a case of throwing the profit baby out with the bath water. Avoidable costs mount up.

Excessive workload

Another cause of lack of time is, of course, the excessive workload of certain individuals. Whenever the burden of work is too great, due care and attention to tasks in hand is reduced as people strive to get work finished. The familiar results, previously mentioned, then occur. The prime cause of excessive workload, however, is a lack of manpower resource which has already been discussed.

> The 1980's and 1990's witnessed countless examples of companies *"downsizing"*. This fashionable prescription for improving business results has been accompanied by increases in employee absenteesim and sickness brought about by overwork, overtime and inadequate time for a little rest and relaxation, domestic stress, and an inability to respond to market upswings. (See also Part 2 Chapter 2 *"Downsizing"*.)

414

Lack of top management support

The following can be underlying reasons for a lack of top management support:

♦ Poor attitudes/ motivation.
♦ Inadequate management education
♦ Inadequate time management.
♦ The cancer of complacency.

Poor attitudes/ motivation

A majority of managers regard *"quality"* as being a mundane topic not worthy of discussion at their exalted level: for them, it is not a *"sexy"* subject. It is treated in an assumptive manner, i.e. managers assume the quality of their work is good and that anybody who does not agree is automatically an uninformed critic and an adversary. If there are product quality problems, these are matters for the lower levels to resolve, for they have far more important matters demanding their attention. Moreover, quality is not regarded as a matter affecting their personal output.

Corporate attitudes emanate from the board of directors who show their priorities towards quality not only by the direct interest they take in it but also by the way in which they construct their board and select the senior executives, by the type of expertise they admit to their ranks. There is generally an imbalance at the top of companies: too many economists, accountants, legal advisors and the like, few of whom tend to know much about the product, what constitutes its quality and customer satisfying potential, how quality is achieved in any department and, thus, what the business needs really are. This is not to say they are inherently bad or irresponsible by nature - far from it. The problem is they lack the training and appreciation both of the nature of quality and that it is the essence of all management systems and of organizational and operational decisions. It seems paradoxical that many top managers have received financial training but do not fully understand the nature of avoidable costs, how they arise and how they are avoided.

The problem becomes particularly acute when the balance of the top management and board expertise is wrong. Overdoing the financial, economic and legal representation at either of those levels is unwise. After all, how many people does the business need to obtain financial advice? Surely no more than it needs the people who are there individually to provide the specific technical and product advice which is, in any case, the core of the company's business. A company earns nothing when its products cannot compete in quality terms. If a board of directors wants financial assurance, should it not also want quality assurance in its ranks?

The balance of expertise at the top of the company is not a subject in which the regular management auditor can easily involve himself: it is a topic for the President's audit to address. (See Part 2 Chapter 7.)

Top managements tend to look for the quick and easy fix. Some foolishly believe all of their problems will be solved if the company obtains some certificate or other from a registrar (an ISO 9001, 14001 or QS 9000 certificate). It won't and most have found this to be the case, although a surprising few will publicly admit the fact, whilst doing so in private.

> The quality profession's various house magazines have contained registrars' reports of their own customer satisfaction surveys claiming high levels of satisfaction with business benefits accruing from registration. My own sources tell me many respondents did not want to upset the registrars to the point they might jeopardize retention of the *"certificate on the wall"*. I find it hard to believe registrars would actually publicize any substantial dissatisfaction with their services! I approached certain registrars, who proudly proclaimed growing numbers of companies using their services, for the number of customers who decided not to renew their ISO 9000 contracts, who went elsewhere or abandoned the whole thing: each refused to supply that data since it was *"not available"*.

None of the so-called quality standards provide the answers that will be found through constant attention by top management to quality throughout the business at all times. Believing the only involvement necessary from top management is to sign policies, promote slogans and shake hands is wrong. They must become directly involved and remain so.

Management education

It is only relatively recently that business schools have begun to realize the necessity of teaching executives and managers both the importance of quality and means of achieving it. It is futile to learn sophisticated ways of calculating profit and budget if one does not know first of all how to earn revenue, how to create, satisfy and keep customers. It is easy to talk of the importance of market share, but more essential to know how it is achieved. Take care of the product and it will take care of the customers. Take care of the customers and they will take care of the shareholders, the employees, the suppliers and the community. Customers will not buy

416

rubbish. The prime task of the manager is to concentrate on achieving quality if the desired cash flow, market share, growth rate and so on are to be secured.

Business schools frequently taught how to manipulate numbers without teaching their significance, what lies behind them, what they indicate operationally. That is gradually being addressed. Good. Fancy ways of calculating cash flow and profit projections are useless if the product does not sell, if the avoidable costs are not prevented and eradicated if they do appear. A business plan that does not state how quality will be achieved is a worthless piece of paper and a pipe dream on which no responsible financier, banker, pension fund, investor or mutual fund should waste its time. Quality creates the cash flow that creates the return on investment. Nothing else does.

Time management

Many top managements would genuinely like to get more involved in the quality aspects of the business but find they do not have the time. This can occur through inefficient use of their time or as a result of staff cutbacks. Downsizing efforts have exacerbated the problem.

Frequently, however, the manager's lack of time arises from constant fire fighting in their attempts to mitigate the effects of business problems. It is a self-defeating circle.

> I advised the two owner-managers of a small company beset with problems to get directly involved in quality prevention. They replied they did not have the time because of all the quality problems they faced. The problems had been recurring for years. I suggested they set aside a two hour slot once a week for a meeting during which one quality problem would be resolved. The programme was referred to as *"One a week"*. I insisted they maintained focus on the one single problem for the week and that regardless of whatever other pressures that might beset them, they would not cancel the meeting and they would not drop the program for at least six months. With some reluctance and apprehension, they agreed and kept their promise. I visited them after three months to discuss progress. They were pleased and said the programme was successful to the point that fire fighting pressures were reduced enabling them to make available two such meetings a week. Staff motivation had soared, measurable avoidable cost were plummeting. They still hold their meetings.

The president of a large international company to whom I related that last case story, smiled ruefully when expressing his view that such a programme, whilst being suitable for a small company, would not work in his own. His view changed when I asked him to reflect on the fact that his own was organized as if a collection of small companies and that all departments were considered as profit centres. Each one could do the same. The programme was enacted with remarkable results.

Cancer of complacency

Too many managers use the argument *"We have been in business for the last three generations/50 years (or whatever) and the customers come back because we have a fine reputation for quality."* Their *"experience"* leads them to believe that customers will always return, they have a captive market and their reputation for quality will always support them regardless of future circumstances. History is filled with examples of firms who felt their previous successes were strong enough to withstand the future. In the UK, in particular, there used to be an almost unending trail of sick companies seeking government financial support when they found themselves unable to compete in world markets. The Margaret Thatcher administration put an end to that: it was painful for many, but economically worth while. In the USA countless businesses have been dumbfounded when losing market share to overseas competitors offering superior value for money.

So long as top management and owners believe their earlier reputation will carry them through, new competitors will smile inscrutably and ultimately put them out of business. The social costs and impact (plainly seen in such cities of Glasgow, Liverpool, Cleveland, Pittsburgh, Detroit) are ugly. The process is and will continue relentlessly. Even the mighty and much vaunted Japanese have found their arrogant assertions of quality can be undermined by emerging nations of the Pacific rim.

It is foolhardy to assume the customer will be prepared to fund inefficiency, outdated technology and waste. They won't.

When investors see a firm losing market share, its share price and value drops. When a nation's firms are collectively doing the same, its stock market will have major problems as foreign investors move their money elsewhere. The national currency drops in value and the attendant economic problems become enormous, not to mention the real risk of social unrest, disorder and increased crime.

418

19. The exit interview

"The time has come," the Walrus said,
"To talk of many things;"

Lewis Carroll

The findings and conclusion of the audit team are presented to the auditee in summary form at a meeting attended by both the entire audit team and the auditee's key representatives. This meeting is known by such names as exit meeting, exit critique, close-out meeting, wrap-up meeting, summary meeting and so on. In the case of an external or extrinsic audit, the exit interview must be regarded as a contractual or as a statutory meeting, according to the identity of the auditor's organization. Similarly, during a third party assessment, the exit interview can be regarded as a quasi-contractual meeting because the assessing body has been appointed by an existing or by a future potential customer. When the audit has been performed by a registrar, the meeting is not of a contractual nature because the audit is, effectively, an internal audit (first party audit), as explained in Chapter 2.

The meeting always takes place after all the fact gathering, investigative and analytical work of the audit has been completed. The exit interview is extremely important and the auditor must prepare for it thoroughly so that proceedings may be properly conducted. The purpose of this chapter is to suggest a framework and format to help the auditor with this task.

Attendees

Figure 19.1 shows the attendees for the exit interview. In one section are the people who must attend or those attendance may be desirable but not essential. The level of auditee management in attendance should be at least one level higher than the highest level of management to have been audited. Figure 19.2 depicts this. As was stated in Chapter 1, a prime objective of a management audit is to obtain information for use by management. It is clearly essential for the auditee's management to be present at the exit interview since at this meeting the audit team produces its conclusions as to the effectiveness of various departments audited in meeting the company's contractual and legal obligations or other matters that form the audit

	Auditor organization	Auditee organization	
		Internal audit (including assessments by registrars)	External audit
Must attend	All auditors (including specialists), team leaders and the lead auditor.	Managers/team leaders of areas audited, quality manager/ business improvement manager.	Escorts, contract administrator, management of areas audited and their immediate superior.
Optional attendance	Observers, auditor management representatives.	At auditee's discretion.	At auditee's discretion.

Figure 19.1 Exit interview attendees

objectives. The audit team will also disclose its assessment of the status of the management policies and procedures implemented in the area(s) audited, of the status of equipment, of the competence of personnel or of whatever related to the objectives of the audit. This information should be of prime concern to management and it would be foolish to dismiss the opportunity to be present when it is made public. This is particularly true in the case of external audits, it would be a strange company that was not interested in its customer's conclusions as to whether or not the firm was meeting its contractual obligations, even stranger if the audit was conducted by a regulatory body concerned with statutory compliance. As more and more organizations of every sort come to appreciate the value of professionally performed audits, the presence of senior management at the exit interview should become increasingly a matter of course.

The audit team may feel it necessary to have other personnel from their own organization present, either if specific problems have been encountered or if specific investigations have had to be performed. These colleagues feature among the optional attendees listed in Figure 19.1. Likewise, the auditee may wish to have certain individuals present at the exit interview for an external audit if their opinions are required or if topics particularly pertinent to their operations are to be discussed.

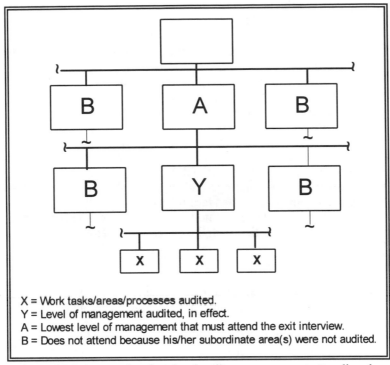

X = Work tasks/areas/processes audited.
Y = Level of management audited, in effect.
A = Lowest level of management that must attend the exit interview.
B = Does not attend because his/her subordinate area(s) were not audited.

Figure 19.2 Appropriate levels of auditee management attending the
exit interview

Preparation

Preparations for the exit interview are made continually throughout the audit.
The auditor may consider himself prepared after he has gone through the
following series of steps:

♦ Write down the details required in the original checklist (or audit
guidance tool), basing answers on objective evidence (verifiable
facts) that has been examined.
♦ Note who was present in each department audited and what
discussions concerning deficiencies were held at the time with the
escorts and auditees present.
♦ Analyze the business management systems, determining their
strengths and weaknesses.
♦ Discuss the findings (good and bad) with the audit team.

♦ Investigate the root cause of adverse findings/business problems revealed by the audit.

♦ Obtain and analyze fresh evidence if this is necessary to arrive at the truth and resolve disputes with the auditee concerning existing facts gathered.

♦ Hold a summary meeting between the audit team and the auditee each day in order to acquaint the latter with any problems, allowing him to institute his own investigation and corrective action, if possible.

♦ On the eve of the exit interview, discuss the position with the audit team and decide which findings, if any, must be presented as formal corrective action requests (CARs).

♦ Summarize these findings and write up the CARs on the audit team's organization's standard forms.

♦ On the eve of the exit interview, discuss and prepare the exit interview presentation with the entire audit team.

Some legal considerations

The audit team must take great care to choose its words wisely or misunderstandings - even litigation - may occur at a later date.

> One company reached the stage of its attorneys exchanging letters with its suppliers attorneys over a dispute concerning payment for their contract completion and contract compliance. As part of their claims and counter claims, each party submitted the audit reports to their respective attorneys.

When assigned to an external audit, the audit team, and particularly the lead auditor, must bear in mind that the audit reports may be used later on as a source of reference in order to resolve a dispute over whether or not the customer had been satisfied and, if not, whether it had discussed its dissatisfaction with its supplier. Since an external audit is normally concerned with the objective evidence to prove satisfactory contract compliance, it might be construed as an opportunity for *"examination"* of the goods and service involved in the scope of supply. Most purchase orders do contain a clause to the effect that any examination of goods and service will neither preclude subsequent rejection if they are found to be unsatisfactory nor relieve the supplier of its obligations under the contract but there may be cases where such wording will prove insufficient. In the case of extrinsic audits performed by statutory bodies, the possibility of legal defence by means of audit reports will depend on the regulations involved, on the associated power and duties of the auditors and on the legal precedents set in the country concerned. The liability of third party assessors, to the best of my knowledge, has yet to be established but, if history teaches us anything, it is that such liability will one day be clarified in a court of law. There abundant examples of financial auditors being sued and prosecuted and one can see no reason why third party assessors should, or will, remain immune from similar treatment. As for registrars, they are just as much a supplier to the applicant firm as is a company selling physical goods. However, the law of tort in many countries imposes on them a duty of care to those who may act on their advice and opinion. ISO 9001/QS 9000 certificates and the like are issued with the intention of being presented to *"whom it may concern"* that the registered company has been found to comply with the requirements of whatever standard against which it was assessed. The registrars have pursued their businesses by advertising the benefits of their certificates, *inter alia*, as being reducing the need for multiple assessment and their self-professed professionalism and competence. They have held themselves out as being competent to advise.

> While preparing for an exit interview, a principal engineer of an auditee's design department approached me in the desire to impart some *"vital"* information, claiming that it could substantially affect the results of an audit I had been engaged to perform. He alleged the company's chief engineer was overruling equipment selection and design decisions to such an extent that there was a resultant risk to safety at a particular petrochemical complex. To support these allegations, various documents were tabled before me. I decided that these allegations had to be investigated, that to do so was beyond the scope of my current activity (which had excluded that engineer's area) and that an independent investigation should be recommended. The statement made at the exit interview was carefully worded and considered beforehand. Furthermore, I resolved that the whole affair needed to be brought to the attention of the company's CEO.

To ignore that type of allegation would be to fail in one's legal duty of care. The statement made at the exit interview is described in Chapter 20.

If the audit has been properly performed, the exit interview becomes little more than a formality.

> In many governmental institutions, issues are discussed and resolved prior to meetings between the senior people. Everybody is informed of each other's stance and of the necessary compromises, resolutions and agreements expected to occur at the meeting. The meeting itself is little more than a rubber stamp session. This is a wise practice since top management time is always at a premium. No top manager wants

to be party to a brawl (and nor, indeed, should anybody else). What they want is an agreed summary of facts and concrete constructive proposals for action.

Duration

The duration of the exit interview varies according to the audit type, scope and objectives, as well as the extent and seriousness of any problems encountered. An hour should be sufficient in most cases. Occasionally the meeting may run to an hour and a half if there is a considerable list of problems to discuss. The only occasion I have ever been engaged in an exit interview that lasted for one and a half hours at a supplier was when there was a considerable language problem and, consequently, communication took time.

> The longest exit interview I experienced ever lasted nearly a day and a half. It was for a value-added audit to establish where the company was, what needed to be done and the opportunities for continuous improvement throughout the firm. All departments had been audited. The bulk of the time was spent in assisting the client formulate a detailed strategy to achieve the goals and to discuss options. The core of the exit interview, to present the actual findings, though, lasted only a couple of hours.

Attendance list

In the case of an external audit, the audit team should always initiate an attendance list and request everyone present to sign it. There should be a record of those who were present, just as there is at any normal meeting that is minuted. In the case of an extrinsic audit, if the audit team does not initiate an attendance list, the auditee should do so instead. Moreover, the audit team must then be requested to sign it.

The sequence of proceedings (agenda)

The suggested sequence for conducting the exit interview is set out in checklist from in Figure 19.3. The following points should help the audit team get through the business efficiently:

1.   When presenting the results, it is recommended that the strengths of the auditee's organization, systems and practices are mentioned first. This is good psychology. On hearing a barrage of criticism that seems endlessly to point out the problem areas, management tends to *"switch off"*. One can even read their thoughts, *"We know we have problems but surely not*

everything is bad?" As those thoughts develop, folk are not paying attention, resentment brews and communications barriers build up. However, if the strengths are tabled first, the auditee's personnel will be more receptive to hearing of any weaknesses that were uncovered. In these circumstances, people tend to think *"Fair enough, we have got problems but at least the auditor has recognized that we also have our strengths"*. The auditee will consequently be more willing to consider and hasten through the improvements required. Using this ploy, the auditor will present the good news first to ease the transition to the *"bad"* news, if any.

With the proviso that the auditor has held a daily meeting and kept the auditee constantly informed of his findings, good and bad, as the audit has progressed, people will be in the correct frame of mind to recognize that the *"bad"* news represents an opportunity for improvement and reduction of avoidable costs.

2.   Group similar deficiencies together (for example, under each of the task elements, or by department or by project). This helps the auditee to concentrate and to comprehend the extensiveness of the problems encountered and is a useful technique in getting corrective action undertaken.

3.   Report all deficiencies but ignore trivia. Instances of human error need only be mentioned in one umbrella statement such as *"A few cases of isolated human error were encountered but these are not considered significant and have been acted upon to the satisfaction of the audit team"* - provided, of course, that this is actually the case. Do not report isolated deficiencies: a purchase order, in a collection dozens, that did not bear a delivery date; a couple of gauges not labeled with a due date sticker; a couple of items outside their self life date in a warehouse containing thousands. See also Chapter 17.

> One reason why so few top managers attend exit interviews, these days, is that the performance of too many audit teams has led them to expect nothing more than nitpicks and trivia to be paraded at the meeting as if heralding an imminent apocalypse. Such matters could and should be dealt with at lower levels in the organization. ISO 9000/QS 9000 auditors have been especially prone to making such presentations.

4.   Report deficiencies that are being acted upon and about which the auditee knew before the audit team also discovered them. However, such matters must not be reported as formal CARs. It is enough to say that the audit team has considered the corrective action the auditee is attempting to

425

Lead auditor	Auditee
1. Initiate attendance list.	
2. State that the critique is based on objective evidence presented and does not mean that areas not within the scope of the audit, which were not seen or which are not mentioned are considered satisfactory.	
3. Request all questions be held until the presentation is completed.	
4. General impressions.	
5. Strengths of the auditee's activities noted by the audit team.	
6. Weaknesses and deficiencies. Presentation of CARs and recommended corrective actions. Stop work issues (if any).	
7. Invite questions from the auditee.	
	8. Ask questions and obtain clarifications on matters raised. Present fresh evidence if pertinent to the auditee's case.

Figure 19.3 Proceedings for an exit interview

implement and will verify its implementation and closure at a later date. Remember to compliment the auditee for having acted properly in that he discovered the problem(s) and initiated corrective action.

5.   If the auditee was able to resolve some deficiencies promptly before the exit interview, say so and praise the auditee's personnel for their efforts and action (see Chapter 17). An umbrella statement such as *"The audit team is pleased to report that some deficiencies noted during the audit were promptly resolved and need not be reported here. The prompt action of your*

Lead auditor	Auditee
9. Answer all of the auditee's questions. Consider fully any fresh evidence offered and determine its validity. Resolve points raised by auditee. 10. Present *"Position statement"*. 11. Explain CAR form layout and use (if any are being issued). Request auditee signs *"concurrence box"*.	
	12. Sign "concurrence box" of CARs to indicate agreement with the nonconformity/problem description.
13. Ensure everyone has signed attendance list. 14. Thank the auditee for hospitality, courtesy and assistance. 15. Depart.	

Figure 19.3 (Cont.)

staff in dealing with those matters is commended" consequently should do.

6.　　When presenting the CARs, describe, as a minimum: the problem found; the justification for issuing the CAR (i.e. the particular clause of the statute, code, standard, regulation, policy, procedure, manual or whatever that has been violated) and the audit teams recommendations for corrective action. The auditee is asked to sign the *"concurrence"* box on the CAR form immediately after the *"position statement"* has been made by the lead auditor (see below).

7.　　If necessary, report favourably or unfavourably on the attitudes of the auditee's personnel although it may be better to discuss sensitive issues privately with top management. If a private discussion seems desirable, the lead auditor should discreetly indicate this to the auditee's senior management. I have never known the latter to refuse.

8.   Remember that the prime responsibility is to present a true and fair view of the status of the management systems, procedures, equipment or whatever, in relation to the audit objectives. It follows, therefore, that the audit team *must* mention the good points, the operational strengths and impressive areas, as well as the bad, in order to present a balanced view. Too many auditors present only the gloomy side of the picture at the exit interview.

Method of approach

May exit interviews are ruined because of poor presentation by the audit team. Some key rules to follow are detailed below.

♦   Be prepared: the audit team must have its facts at its fingertips and its analysis of the situation complete and ready.

♦   Base the presentation only on objective evidence, not on subjective opinion. Most people are willing to bow to the force of facts. As Rensis Likert wrote:- *"People seem most willing and emotionally able to examine in a non-defensive way, information about themselves and their behaviour, including their inadequacies, when it is in the form of objective evidence."*[1]

♦   In making the presentation on behalf of the audit team, speak clearly, calmly and audibly. This is particularly important when the auditee's mother tongue is not that of the audit team. The auditee cannot be expected to implement efficacious corrective action if he cannot understand what is being said.

♦   Remain cool and unemotional. Do not get provoked into any heated arguments that would allow the auditee the chance to complain to the auditor's organization and declare the audit null and void (see Chapter 15).

♦   Be constructive and helpful if the auditee has questions or queries concerning the problems uncovered or if he wishes to propose certain actions.. When asked, the audit team must indicate clearly whether or not the auditee's proposals for corrective action would be acceptable to their organization.

♦   Be polite, firm, fair and reasonable.

Corrective action requests

The completed CAR forms are presented to the auditee at the exit interview - not before. The audit team must make quite clear that, whilst they will be pleased to receive one, they do not expect a commitment to any particular plan for corrective action at that time, only an acknowledgment that the description of the problem (non-conformity) is accurate and truthful in light of the objective evidence presented. (The CAR form should include space for a concurrence signature from the auditee's representatives - see Chapter 17.)

The auditee must be told how long he will be allowed to consider the commitment he is prepared to make to corrective action. A period of 30 days for consideration and commitment is generally satisfactory. However, urgent cases, such as stop work decisions, may call for speedier decisions. The audit team must consider each case on its merits.

If the auditee is unwilling to concur with the non-conformity description as presented on the CAR form, the basis for the refusal must be resolved there and then and, if necessary, fresh evidence sought. It is seldom that an impasse is reached.

Stop work decisions

Occasionally stop work may be considered necessary. When requesting that work be stopped, the audit team must explain the reasons that have led them to this decision. The issue can occasionally produce a fairly unpleasant situation, with much resistance from the auditee, which is why it is important for the auditors to have consulted with their own senior management beforehand (see Chapter 17). The limitations on the auditor's authority are described in Chapter 20. When requesting stop work the lead auditor must state:

♦ The reasons that led to the stop work decision.
♦ The extent of work that has to be stopped.
♦ The suggested corrective action to be taken (this will be described on the CAR form).
♦ The estimated costs of taking the corrective action suggested.
♦ The full extent of the problem, including the costs and risks of maintaining the *status quo*.
♦ The circumstances under which work could be restarted.
♦ The anticipated time required to accomplish the suggested corrective action.

Auditee questions

Auditors must answer or attempt to answer all the questions that the auditee may wish to pose. If they lack any of the information needed to produce an answer, they must promise to find out the facts for the auditee and must be as good as their word. This will often require the audit team to return to the auditee's process workplaces and seek out evidence to address the questions raised by the auditee. If the questions relate to policy or procedural matters within the audit team's own organization, it is always best to immediately contact one's office and determine the response.

Position statement

Whatever the type of audit, the audit team must always include a position statement in the exit interview. In the case of third party assessments, this is a formal necessity. It is a statement that summarizes the conclusions drawn from examining the auditee's objective evidence in relation to the audit objectives.

The position statement must be absolutely clear and unambiguous. A statement like *"The systems as documented and implemented fulfil/do not fulfil the requirements of such and such regulation"* will leave the auditee's management in no doubt about where they stand and whether or not their systems have achieved their objective or not. It is bad practice, extremely unprofessional and bad manners to leave the audite in the dark, especially when one considers the expenditure the auditee will have incurred hosting the audit.

An alternative and unequivocal statement would be:

"Based on the objective evidence that has been provided to the audit team and with the exception of those matters that are the subject of corrective action requests and excluding those areas that were not within the scope of this audit,
* *the company does meet the requirements of (the code/standard/regulation/policy etc.)*
* *the management systems do comply with the (XXX code/standard/regulations/policy)*
* *the operational manuals/procedures are complied with".*

The above can be modified by the audit team to reflect the objective of the audit.

If, during an extrinsic audit, the audit team does not offer a position statement, the auditee should first ask politely for one. If this is refused, the auditee should draw the audit team's attention to the fact that they have been provided with the necessary assistance on the basis of the audit team being charged with performing an audit for a particular objective. In the absence of any position statement, the auditee will indicate the view that the audit team has not succeeded in reaching the objective, the cooperation of the auditee is not in any dispute and, therefore, the audit is declared null and void as far as the auditee is concerned. The auditee should refuse to sign any formal CAR presented by the audit team until the position statement is forthcoming. The auditee is entitled to know where he stands.

Auditee speakers

The audit team should make a mental note of those who speaks and attends on behalf of the auditee. It is extremely valuable to note the atmosphere, response and reactions of the auditee's personnel since these may indicate stormy waters ahead. Neither an external audit nor an extrinsic audit is finished until the auditor's organization has verified that any corrective action requested has been implemented efficaciously. On occasions, this may give rise to a major battle. In the case of external audits, it is not unknown for an auditee to procrastinate about implementing corrective action in the hope that the auditor's organization will be forced to overlook problems if delivery of the product becomes critical. If the audit team picks up warning signs of such difficulties at a later stage, they must pass the information on to their own management.

(If the audit team is from a service company engaged by the auditee to perform the audit and advise of the need for corrective action, the audit is complete when the report has been submitted and payment has been received for services rendered. If the scope of the contract includes verification that efficacious corrective action has been taken, the audit will be complete at that point and when payment has been received for services rendered. Such an audit is an internal audit, i.e. a first party audit.)

Fresh evidence

If at any point during the exit interview, the auditee wishes to present fresh evidence, the audit team must go back and re-audit the contentious area and analyze it in light of the evidence presented.

In being allowed the opportunity to offer fresh evidence, the auditee is reassured that the auditor is genuinely concerned with obtaining a true and fair view. The auditee, therefore, has less justification to complain about the conduct of the audit and has been given a *"fair go"*, as Australians would say.

The auditor should remain firm, however, if the fresh evidence does not obviate the original findings. It is beneficial to explain why the fresh evidence is unsatisfactory, for altering the original conclusions the audit team had drawn from its investigations, because the situation could herald some confusion within the auditee as to what the deficiency actually is and what would remedy the situation.

If the evidence disproves the audit team's findings, they must:

♦   Apologize for the wrong conclusions that were drawn.
♦   Thank the auditee for presenting the fresh evidence so that the truth could be ascertained.
♦   Strike the original findings from their checklists and notes.

The third point is especially noteworthy. The reason why I generally complete my checklist in pencil is to make it easy to delete items if fresh evidence turns up to discredit the first findings. This is not done because I am in any way fearful that people might accuse me of inadequate auditing in the first place and want to *"cover my tracks"*! To let false findings stand in the checklist and notes is grossly unfair to the auditee: a third party, not actually involved in the audit, may subsequently review the checklist and notes and thereby gain a false impression of the auditee. In the case of over-zealous or officious extrinsic auditors, the discredited findings may provide grounds for lengthy arguments: deleting the relevant notes eliminates of all chances of this occurring and ensures the checklist contains only such data as portrays a true and fair view of the auditee for others to assimilate.

The hidden tape recorder

Auditors must not be afraid of allowing people to make a tape recording of the exit interview, whether this is done openly or surreptitiously. If they are not prepared to stand by their statement or if the statements are in any way incorrect, then the auditors are not prepared for the exit interview and ought to examine the efficacy of their audit method, for they have failed in their duties. If an audit team is confident that the audit has been performed in a professional, thorough and honest manner, then it is presenting a true and fair view and need not be concerned with such tape recordings. A similar attitude should be adopted towards video recordings of the proceedings.

> During one audit, I became aware that someone was secretly attempting to make a tape recording of the exit interview. In accordance with my normal procedure, I was quite openly recording the exit interview, only switching off the tape when certain remarks

were to be made off the record or in confidence by the auditee to which I was required to respond. Upon becoming aware of the activities of the person who was attempting to make a clandestine tape recording, I invited him to put his tape recorder on the top of the table beside mine and perhaps to sit nearer to me so that his recording would be of better quality. The person concerned went crimson with embarrassment and certain of the auditee' representatives went crimson with rage at his behaviour.

Before making a tape recording of the exit interview, I always inform the auditee personnel assembled for the meeting that the tape recording is only being made in order to help me when it comes to writing the audit report and that, should anyone wish to make any remarks off the record, the recording will be switched off at that point. In my experience, no one objects to tape recordings made upon these conditions. When I have finished with the tape, I use it for another audit; I do not keep them.

Interruptions

Before presenting the audit team's findings and conclusions, the lead auditor should request that any questions be reserved until the presentation has been completed, adding that the team will be delighted to answer them.

If the auditee interrupts the proceedings, ask whether or not the query can be saved until the end: if not, deal with it swiftly on the spot and carry on with the presentation. In my experience, it is rare for the presentation to be unduly or excessively interrupted. The most common cause of interruptions is difficulty in communicating when the auditee and audit team do not share the same mother tongue.

Copies of the auditor's audit guidance tools

Some auditees request that the auditors leave a copy of their marked up checklist, flowcharts, matrices and other working papers used during the audit. There need be no objection to this since the papers will only contain details of the auditee's own objective evidence accompanied by the auditors' own doodles, scribbles, shorthand notes, flowcharts, calculations etc. It is always disappointing to receive such a request because the auditee's escort should have been taking the same details as the auditors on his own checklist (or working papers). See also Chapter 23, *"Note taking"*.

Good manners

At the end of the exit interview, the audit team should thank the auditee for the assistance and hospitality they received throughout the audit, making it clear that achieving a meaningful and thorough assessment depends most crucially upon the response of the auditee's organization. Even if there were some contentious issues and the parties had to agree top differ and try to resolve their problems at a later date, the team should still indicate that it has appreciated the auditee's co-operation.

Private conference

If the CEO, managing director, president or other senior management cannot get to the exit interview (for an external audit), the lead auditor should try to arrange a short conference with them in private. Similar remarks apply in the case of internal audits if the requisite manager was unable to be present. This is particularly important if some points of contention have arisen or if obstructive behaviour has been encountered during the audit. A short talk with senior management gives the auditor the chance to put these points across discreetly.

> A few individuals had been adopting a belligerent attitude both towards the audit team and towards the audit being performed. The lead auditor decided to seek a meeting with the auditee's chief executive officer (CEO). This was arranged and the CEO's prompt response to the question was that he most certainly did not condone the attitude of those employees and that the auditor organization's contract requirements would willingly be honoured since they were perceived as most beneficial for the firm's future. He was as good as his word. It is worth recalling that an audit does remove the rose tinted spectacles! That CEO was not fully aware of the manner in which customers might be treated by isolated individuals.

Occasionally the top executive may wish to convey to the audit team information that is highly confidential and that cannot be aired in public at the exit interview (see the example in Chapter 14). At this sort of conference, only the lead auditor should attend on behalf of his organization. Any information transmitted in these circumstance:

♦ Must be treated as strictly confidential and not reported to anyone.
♦ Must not influence the lead auditor to alter in any way the findings and conclusions of the audit team, for whatever statements are made by that auditee, they should be regarded as hearsay and as unverified objective evidence.

The auditee

The auditee must be prepared to discuss the audit team's findings and, if necessary, refuse to sign or accept in any way a formal request for corrective action if he is unhappy about the construction the audit team has put upon the objective evidence. He must be prepared to offer fresh evidence and, if this fails to resolve the differences, pursue the matter with the audit team's senior management, particularly if he feels that the audit has been performed unfairly, incorrectly or by untrained or incompetent personnel. (This last advice is especially noteworthy when dealing with extrinsic auditors and registrars. If the registrar's management fails to act, the applicant might refuse to pay the invoice, take his business elsewhere, make a formal complaint to the body who accredited the registrar firm.)

Some auditors are guilty of exceeding their terms of reference, of going beyond the actual requirements of the codes, standards, regulations, policies etc. concerned in the audit objective, by trying to enforce their own subjective interpretation of the texts. In the long term, it is of benefit to the auditor himself to have these mistakes corrected. The situation can hardly improve unless the auditee is prepared to let the auditors' senior management know about their representatives' errors. A servile attitude towards the auditors is quite out of place, no matter what the organization to which the auditors belong or are employed by. The auditee is entitled to a true and fair view being placed on the record.

435

20. The audit report

Let us admit it fairly, as a business people should,
We have had no end of a lesson: it will do us no end of good.

Kipling.

The audit report is virtually a written transposition and summary of the exit interview. It summarizes the audit team's findings and conclusions as to the status and efficacy of the auditee's management policies, systems, procedures and instructions. If the exit interview has been properly conducted, there should be no problem with the audit report. This chapter covers the content of the audit report and suggests a format for it.

Responsibility for preparation and timing

The lead auditor, together with the individual team leaders (if there were any), prepares the report. Before it is released and distributed, the entire audit team should review it to check that the statements it makes are fair, complete and true. After this review, the lead auditor signs the audit report on behalf of the entire audit team since he is ultimately responsible for both the conduct of the audit and the veracity of the audit report. The report must always be written and distributed immediately upon the return to the auditor's premises.

Content and layout

These depend on company policy, the type of audit performed, and the lead auditor's practice. As the organization and the auditors themselves become more experienced in conducting internal and external audits, both content and layout tend to evolve. A typical audit report is shown in Fig. 20.1.

What to include

As a minimum, the report should state the following details.

♦ The auditee's name (internal department or external company name); the dates during which the audit was performed; the

437

location(s) at which the audit was performed (in the case of geographic dispersion, there may be a number of locations not involved in the audit) and the contract, project or product identification (number, name, or code).

♦ The objectives of the audit; the names of the particular departments that were audited and the basis or justification for performing an audit (e.g. standard, regulation/statute, code).

♦ The key personnel contacted during the audit.

♦ The names of the audit team members and their "rank" during the audit.

♦ The auditing qualifications of each auditor. (Some standards require that an auditor be qualified: ISO 9001, for example, requires this by virtue of the fact that auditors are performing *"a specifically assigned task"*).

♦ The identification of the checklist/procedure/flow chart that was used to guide performance of the audit.

♦ The results of the audit, including details of the CARs issued (these should, in any case, be attached to the report), the date of the exit interview and the attendees, any recommendations for improvements to the management policies, manual or systems, as well as any particular observations made at the exit interview.

♦ A true and fair position statement (see Chapter 19) that is consistent with the audit objectives.

♦ The audit team's appreciation for the hospitality and help received from the auditee during the audit.

♦ The distribution list for the audit report.

♦ A list of the attachments such as CARs, if any.

What not to include

There are a number of things that *must not* figure in the audit report. These include the details listed below.

♦ Deficiencies that were discovered, acted upon, and corrected by the auditee during the audit.

♦ Confidential information provided during a private conference.

♦ Anything that was neither discussed nor mentioned during the exit interview.

♦ Trivia.

♦ Subjective opinions: the report must deal only with verifiable facts.

♦ Information that is to be confidential to the auditor's company, in the case of external audits (on the basis of the two-edged sword principle, requirements for corrective action in house, for example; or remarks about the performance of individual auditors during the audit).

♦ Ambiguous statements.

♦ Antagonistic words or phrases (avoid pointless adverbs and adjectives).

♦ Abusive remarks; foul language.

Wording and style

The audit report needs to be written in clear, concise and unambiguous language. If the auditee's mother tongue is not the same as the auditor's, it is particularly important to keep the wording simple and to avoid using words that could be misinterpreted. The auditor's organization will not achieve the required actions if it fails to communicate these to the auditee. It is a very dubious practice deliberately to include - as some organizations do - loopholes that will enable the auditor to alter their position later on. If the auditor is not prepared to stand by the audit report, he has not carried out a proper management audit, and has not based his conclusions on objective evidence.

> One of the most ambiguous statements I ever saw was contained in the summary conclusions of a pre-award survey report. The assessor had advised *"Waste no time in placing an order with this supplier"*.

The audit report must not be a *"snow job"* that tries to cover up significant deficiencies still in existence when the audit team left the auditee's facilities. The snow job damages the auditor, the auditor's organization and the auditee.

Stop work

The audit report must state the reasons for requiring work to be stopped, the circumstances under which work can be restarted as well as the other matters listed in Chapter 19 on this matter. It is most unusual for an entire project or contract to be stopped as a result of deficiencies discovered during an audit. More often the deficiencies are confined to a particular area or set of activities. Hence, the audit report must state exactly what work must be stopped (e.g. machining operations, painting, house insurance policy issue, computer aided design, refueling operations).

Hyper-Quality Company Inc.

Audit Report

Auditee: Scrap Metal Products Inc.
Location: Big Bone Lick, KY, USA.
Dates: 8-13 January 1997
Purchase Order No.:   1234   Product: Gizmos
H-QCI customer: Candle Power Corporation.
Previous audit:
Audit basis: The basis for this audit is: H-QCI company policy and contract requirements of our customer, Candle Power Corporation.

Audit Scope: A full audit of all SC Rap departments and functions involved in execution of the purchase order.

Audit objective: To determine the extent of compliance with the requirements of Hyper-Quality Inc. purchase order of the S.C. Rap Metal Products Inc. management systems, to assess the extensiveness of the auditee's business improvement programme and verify the results of the same.

Audit tool used: H-QCI standard checklist #3 was used to facilitate auditing of discrete departments of SC Rap.

Key auditee persons contacted: The following SC Rap personnel were contacted and attended the exit interview which was held Monday 13 January 1997 at the auditee's premises.

S.C. Rap President and CEO
A. Brown   Quality Manager
C. Dawson   V.P. Engineering
E. Fowler   V.P.Contracts
G. Hawkins   V.P. Purchasing
I. Jones   V.P. Manufacturing

Audit team: Two sub-teams were formed as follows and included observers from H-QCI's customer, Candle Power Corporation.

Sub-team A: Ozzy Fry   Lead auditor   H-QCI.
                 F. Flintstone   Specialist Auditor H-QCI.
                 D. Bailey   ObserverCandle Power Corp.

Sub-team B: Ms. Dinah Shaw Sub-team leader   H-QCI.
                 B. Rubble   Specialist Auditor H-QCI.
                 R. Robertson   ObserverCandle Power Corp.

Auditor qualifications: Ozzy Fry and Ms. Dinah Shaw are qualified lead assessors as per the ASQC CQA scheme.   Page 1 of 2

Figure 20.1 Example of an audit report

Results: Performance of the audit resulted in the issuing of one (1) corrective action request to the auditee. This CAR is numbered SCR/97/01. The auditee did not make any specific commitment to a particular corrective action but has committed to respond with a proposal within thirty days of the exit interview. This is considered to be a reasonable period of time for the auditee to determine its course of action.

The following suggestion was made during the exit interview:

Increase the frequency of internal audits in all departments. Although present practice is in compliance with the purchase order requirement, it is considered that the present frequency of once per two years is inadequate.

H-QCI Position statement:

On the basis of the objective evidence presented by the auditee to the audit team, excluding the matter raised in the CAR and with the exception of those areas not within the scope of the audit programme, SC Rap Metal Products Inc is complying with the requirements of the H-QCI purchase order and its own business programme.

The design control and special coatings systems are particularly impressive, the latter being a six-sigma performer.

The cooperation and helpfulness of all SC Rap personnel was most appreciated throughout the audit.

Ozzy Fry,

Ozzy Fry
Lead Auditor, H-QCI

Date of Issue: 15 January 1997

Distribution:
(By E. Mail)
　　　　Purchasing department (3).
　　　　Quality Department (1)
　　　　H-QCI Field Representative.

(Hard copy)
　　　　Candle Power Corporation (1)

Attachment: CAR SCR/97/1/01

Page 2 of 2

Figure 20.1 Example of an audit report (continued)

Limitations on the auditor's authority

Stop work

When the auditor does not have the authority to stop work, when he has been engaged, for example, as a consultant to perform an internal audit, any situations that are serious enough to warrant further action by the auditee management must be drawn promptly to its attention.

In Chapter 19 mention was made of an audit during which an auditee's senior engineer made some serious allegations with severe legal implications. It was not the auditor's prerogative to make judgements. Accordingly, the matter was brought to the attention of the auditee's CEO and the audit report contained the following statement:

> *A senior engineer has made some serious allegations that essential designs have been altered without the knowledge or consent of the senior engineer responsible, such that installed equipment could present a hazard; design codes and material standards have been misapplied; recommendations made by an expert external to the company have been disregarded such that certain equipment may be unsafe.*

> *It is most strongly recommended that a full and totally independent investigation be undertaken immediately by a competent person or organization external to the company to determine the veracity or otherwise of these allegations and to identify any unsafe situations that might exist.*

If the auditor had not brought the situation to the attention of management he would have been failing in his legal duty of care. In this type of circumstance, it is essential that such matters be put in writing.

Corrective Action Requests

If the auditor does not have the authority to issue CARs, deficient situations must be stated in the audit report together with the auditee's recommendations for rectifying them and curing the root cause. In other words the auditor records the *"Non- conformity"*, justification reference and *"Recommendations for corrective action"* parts of the CAR form in the "Results" section of the audit report.

Naturally both of these situations will have been presented at the exit interview.

Supplier ratings

The audit report is generally not the place to state the supplier rating. This should be reserved for a separate communication, for the following reasons:

♦ In the case of some contracts, audit reports may be auditable by third parties. The supplier rating system is not generally the concern of such third parties: it is a matter between the auditor's company and the supplier.
♦ Most management systems standards (including ISO 9000 series) do not require the use of supplier rating schemes, so such schemes are not auditable.
♦ The omission helps to forestall pointless and time-consuming arguments with extrinsic auditors about the company's methods of supplier rating.

Distribution of the audit report

Timing

The advent of new technology and modern telecommunications systems and devices make entirely possible the production and distribution of most audit reports within 24 hours of completion of the exit interview. Auditors can use computer notebooks with audit report templates included within word processing software; modems permit fast transfer of the report to the auditor's organization by E. Mail; small portable ink jet printers enable the audit report to be printed out and most businesses, hotels and motels have fax facilities permitting rapid transmittal of the print-out if a modem and E. Mail solution is unavailable. Not many audits are performed high in the Himalayas, in the jungles of Borneo and the like. It is my contention every auditor organization should set its standard time frame for distributing its audit reports: I normally recommend 48 hours (or two working days) after completion of the exit interview as being entirely practical these days.

> Some years ago, I was engaged by an oil company having an operation in Aberdeen, Scotland, to audit a supplier in California, USA. The report was faxed to its quality manager within six hours of leaving the auditee's premises, having been written in my hotel room, dictated across the telephone to my (then) UK office which had typed it up and faxed it to my hotel for any final corrections. Corrections made, the fax was retransmitted to my UK office that made the adjustments I required and faxed the final copy to my client's quality manager in Aberdeen, copying it by fax to me in

443

my California hotel. Using my laptop computer and E. mail connection, the process today would be even easier. Hundreds of auditors now operate in similar fashion.

Distribution channels

The audit report, its attachments and copies thereof are forwarded via the correct formal channels (see Chapter 9) by the lead auditor, who may attach a covering memorandum or letter, according to company practice. The master copy of the audit report should be retained by the quality department: this enables further copies to be produced at a later date if they are needed.

The auditee's response

If the auditee does not agree with any part of the report, he must pursue the matter promptly with the auditor's organization. In the case of an external audit, there may be difficulties if the auditee delays his raising of objections beyond a reasonable time. It may be sufficient simply to notify the auditor that the auditee will disagree in due course and that he wishes to discuss the contentious issues in order to reach an amicable solution.

When the auditee disagrees with the audit report

This could be a most serious affair, depending on the nature of the disagreement. There is an entire spectrum of potential disagreements for an auditee to raise. It ranges from minor points of detail to outright refutation of the auditor's presentation.

If an auditee objects to the audit report the auditor's manager (or person in charge of the entire audit programme) should do the following:

♦ Ascertain from the auditee the nature of the complaint.
♦ Inform the lead auditor that the auditee does not accept all or part of the report.
♦ Ask the lead auditor to bring all the working papers pertinent to the audit (checklist, flow charts, information reviewed, notes, scribbles etc.) for review.
♦ Examine the information brought by the lead auditor.
♦ If, necessary obtain clarification from individual auditors and specialists responsible for auditing the areas which are the point of contention to the auditee.

♦ Go to the auditee's premises and meet with the auditee. Ask to see the areas and objective evidence offered by the auditee to support his complaint.
♦ If the evidence supports the auditee's complaint and disproves the audit report statement(s), apologize verbally and in writing to the auditee.
♦ Distribute that apology to all recipients of the offending audit report.
♦ Withdraw the offending audit report.
♦ Offer to conduct a new audit led by a different lead auditor (the manager or person dealing with the auditee's complaint).

An unjustified audit report is a most serious affair. Put bluntly, in extreme cases it could be considered a libel. In the case of external audits, pre-award surveys, it could damage the supplier's reputation resulting in lost business. In the case of internal audits it could affect the reputation and career prospects of individuals in the auditee's organization. If left un-retracted, it could mislead innocent parties not privy to the entire affair.

Failure to consider fairly and publicly an auditee's complaint sends an unfortunate message to all neutral observers about the professionalism and attitude of the auditor organization that is highly counter-productive in gaining future respect and co-operation. Its investigation is not a matter to be delegated to subordinates: it warrants the attention of the highest level of management because the auditors are acting (or should be acting) as the representatives of senior management with their implied authority.

When the auditor's organization is a registrar

One must hope a responsible registrar would act in accordance with the above advice. In any event, the company must draw their concerns to the registrar's management: it should also contact the registrar's accreditation body, such as the British UKAS or the American RAB, and describe the complaint raised. Unless this latter course of action is taken, it is impossible for accreditation bodies to weed out sub-standard registrars and raise the level of assessments done. The complainant should remember it may one day be at the receiving end of a certificate submitted by a potential supplier assessed by a registrar whose performance is unprofessional. The ramifications of this are fairly obvious, hence the various precepts concerning *"Third party assessments"* contained in Chapter 2.

21. Follow-up and close-out

It's a long road from the inception of a thing to its realization.

Molière.

There would be little point in performing audits, requiring corrective action or having an audit programme at all, if the auditee knew that the auditor would never verify that the corrective action has been efficaciously implemented.

Follow-up action

There is a commonly held and mistaken belief that the only acceptable method of performing follow-up action is by means of a re-audit of the areas found to be deficient and responsible for the root cause of problems. (This type of action is known, logically enough, as a follow-up audit.) This is not so and it is incumbent on the lead auditor to choose a cost effective method of verification based on the circumstances. Most management systems standards, including the ISO 9000 series, do not stipulate that a follow-up audit must be performed. (In fact the 1994 release of ISO 9001 only implies that follow-up action has to be taken but does not specifically require it [1].) Depending on the nature of the real root cause of the problems, the auditor's organization can check the implementation of corrective action in many ways including those listed below.

♦ A re-audit of the deficient area responsible for originating the real root cause of the problems found.
♦ Reviewing revised/ new documents (e.g. procedures, training records, manuals, policies, specifications and reports) submitted by the auditee, if such information was the cause of the problem.
♦ Verification performed at the next periodic management audit (if the original findings either do not demand urgent action or the problems are of such a magnitude it will take that amount of time between scheduled successive audits to eradicate the problems and introduce new systems and organizational arrangements).

♦ Verification performed on the next occasion at which a representative of the auditor's organization is present at the auditee's workplace or premises.

♦ Verification performed by a specialist from the auditor's organization (although depending on the nature of the corrective action required), during a routine meeting with the auditee.

♦ Verifying, on receipt of the next lot of products forwarded by the auditee to the auditor's organization, that the business problems have been eradicated (by, for example, performing a receiving inspection of items: or by checking the correctness and completeness of the work before further use). This method has the risk that the problem might have been dealt with by a non-conformity report (NCR) system and the incoming supplies might represent a temporary fix.

Close-out decisions

Who does this and on what basis?

This is the responsibility of the lead auditor. The CAR is closed out upon receipt of objective evidence that the corrective action has been verified as efficacious. The objective evidence may consist of an audit report, an inspection report, minutes of a meeting, a memorandum or letter from another department within the auditor's organization or anything similar. It should state what was done, what was seen, when the follow-up action was taken, observations made and who undertook this activity.

If evidence is acceptable

When this evidence has been received and found to be satisfactory, the lead auditor:

♦ Completes the *"closed out"* section of the CAR form, specifying the objective evidence received. (See Figure 21.1.)

♦ Sends a copy of the closed out CAR (or a letter, telefax, E-mail, memorandum stating that the corrective action is acceptable and closed out) to the auditee *via* the correct formal channels.

♦ Sends copies of the same to all other recipients of the audit report, so that they are properly appraised off the auditee's action and of the fact that the auditor's organization *does* take follow-up action. (This is especially vital if a regulatory body or customer was present as observers during the original audit.)

Hyper-Quality Company Inc.	**Corrective Action Request**
Issued to: *S.C. RAP METAL PRODUCTS INC.* Issued by: *H-QC INC.*	No: *SCR/97/1/01* Date issued: *13 JANUARY 1997*

Non-conformity description:

FAILURE TO PROVIDE AND IMPLEMENT MANAGEMENT SYSTEM FOR TRAINING OF PERSONAL HAS CAUSED INCORRECT TRANSFER OF DATA BETWEEN THE PRODUCT DESIGNERS IN THE COMPUTER AIDED DESIGN GROUP AND THE PACKAGING DESIGN SUPPLIER, "SUPERDOOPERPAKKER INC". THE END RESULT HAS BEEN DETERIORATION OF FINISHED PRODUCT (MODEL 62 GIZMOS) AWAITING DESPATCH AND IN THE DISTRIBUTION CHAIN.

Ozzy Fry, Lead Auditor

Auditee agrees with non-conformity description Signed: Chas, Dawson (V.P. Engineering) Date: 13 January 1997	Non-conformity at variance with: *H-QC INC PURCHASE ORDER 1234, SECTION 17, CLAUSE 3.2.1.* *S.C. RAP PROCEDURE 4.4.1; 4.18*

Recommendation(s) for corrective action:

DEVELOP AND IMPLEMENT A DOCUMENTED TRAINING PROGRAMME THAT WILL APPRAISE ALL CAD OPERATORS OF THE CORRECT OPERATION OF THE CAD EQUIPMENT, DATA AND FILE TRANSFER TO INTERFACING USERS, WHO USE SUCH EQUIPMENT. IMPLEMENT THAT TRAINING PROGRAMME AND REQUIRE EVERY PARTICIPANT TO DEMONSTRATE COMPETENCE IN APPLYING THE TECHNIQUES LEARNED BEFORE PERFORMING SUCH WORK IN FUTURE. RECORD EVIDENCE OF THE TRAINING AND RESULTS OF COMPETENCE DEMONSTRATION IN THE EMPLOYEE'S PERSONNEL FILE.

Corrective action commitment:
As per the 'Recommendation'; training programme will be developed and performed by CAD Group Leader and documented in the training database. CAD Group Leader will perform post-training assessment of individuals; results will be held in Human Resources database..

Date for completion: End February 1997	Signed: Chas, Dawson	Position V.P. Engineering Date: 20 January 1997

Follow-up and close-out action:

F. FLINTSTONE TO VERIFY AUDITEE HAS IMPLEMENTED CORRECTIVE ACTION AS PER COMMITMENT (ABOVE) DURING MARCH CONTRACT PROGRESS MEETING AT S.C. RAP PREMISES.

The corrective action is verified as efficacious and this CAR is now closed. *SEE MINUTES OF MARCH 1997 CONTRACT PROGRESS MEETING*	Signed: *Ozzy Fry,* Position: *Lead Auditor* Date: *March 10 1997*

Figure 21.1 A closed-out corrective action request form (CAR).

♦ If stop work had been ordered, the lead auditor states that work may now resume. (This has generally already been stated verbally, the lead auditor is now officially confirming that fact.)
♦ Updates the corrective action request log (or tracking file), see Chapter 17.
♦ Files the closed out CAR with the audit report.
♦ If the auditor's organization keeps a separate file dealing with the auditee's performance, also files a copy of the closed out CAR therein.

If evidence is unacceptable

When this evidence has been received and found to be unsatisfactory, the lead auditor:

♦ Leaves open the "closed out" section of the CAR form.
♦ Considers what the root cause of the auditee's failure to implement corrective is. This might necessitate a visit to the auditee's facilities. If the failure is caused by a lack of auditee management support for the original corrective action, the lead auditor should be prepared to make this the subject of an additional CAR issued to the senior person within that management structure. (This CAR would be processed as any other CAR and entered into the CAR log/ tracking file.)
♦ Considers the impact of the open corrective action and decides whether stop work is now required, if stop work had not been ordered before. (The basis for this decision is as described in Chapter 17 and the lead auditor should obtain the support of his management, providing it with the information described in that chapter.)
♦ Sends a letter, telefax, E-mail, memorandum stating that the corrective action is unacceptable and not closed out to the auditee *via* the correct formal channels. (If an additional CAR has been issued it will be attached to the communication.
♦ Sends copies of the same to all other recipients of the original audit report, so that they are properly appraised of the auditee's failure and of the fact that the auditor's organization *does* take seriously follow-up action. (This is especially vital if a regulatory body or customer was present as observers during the original audit.)
♦ Updates the corrective action request log (or tracking file), see Chapter 17.
♦ Files a copy of the additional communication with the audit report.

♦ If the auditor's organization keeps a separate file dealing with the auditee's performance, also files a copy of the additional communications therein.

The timing of follow-up action

The amount of time which the auditee should be allowed in order to propose, commit to and complete corrective action depends on many factors, among them the following, which all amount to the impact of the problem on the business and minimizing avoidable costs.

♦ The urgency of the situation. Stop work, for example is always an urgent situation.
♦ The severity of the findings that require corrective action and the avoidable costs associated with them.
♦ The work status. There may be, for instance, little time left before scheduled delivery date or a business opening date.
♦ Financial and legal considerations.

Some companies have a policy of allowing the auditee only 30 days to propose and commit himself to corrective action but generally this should be sufficient. This does *not* mean that the auditee has to *implement* corrective action within thirty days: he only has to state *when* corrective action can be completed and *what* corrective action is proposed.

If, after careful consideration, the audit team decide that the auditee's proposals for corrective action should prove efficacious if implemented, they must signify their agreement immediately. Any such agreement does not mean the auditor approves of the proposal or has taken any kind of ownership or responsibility for the outcome away from the auditee: the auditee remains fully responsible for achieving efficacious corrective action at all times. If the auditee's proposals do not work, no blame is to be attached to the auditors. The schedule for completion of corrective action is more likely to be a point of contention, depending on the situation at hand. If any aspect of the auditee's proposals is not satisfactory to the auditor's organization, the matter must be promptly discussed and resolved.

The schedule for verifying the implementation of corrective action will naturally follow from the agreement between both parties as to what corrective action appears suitable, and when it should have its effect.

Gestation problems

If a company implements a quality programme, the number of deficiencies existing at any one time in the auditee's area eventually reduces. During the gestation or development phase, however, it is quite common for the auditee to run into teething problems. The number of deficiencies that an audit would pick up during this phase may increase rather than fall in relation to the first audit. Personnel will still be learning how to work with the new systems and mistakes of the human error kind will probably heavily outnumber grave deficiencies. In the circumstances, it is asking for trouble to audit during this phase. Allow the auditee a reasonable time to get over the teething troubles without outside interference. It is good practice, however, to let the auditee know that the auditor's organization is happy to make help available if this is requested.

Figure 21.2 depicts the typical situation I have encountered over many years, that of a company which decides to embark on a quality programme that necessitates the introduction of revised management systems and organizational arrangements. This curve shows what inexperienced "consultants" often do not tell the auditee or do not know themselves!

As time elapses, the number of errors found initially increases as opposed to decreasing. It is crucial for the auditor and auditee to comprehend fully this phenomenon because managers tend to complain that they have more problems than they did before the campaign started: they prefer the *"old way"* and do not realize that the errors are being found because the system is doing its work. Many problems, that would previously have been accepted as *"the way things are in our business"*, become highlighted as business problems. They were always present but were not appreciated as being such. Operational changes are occurring in that the responsibility for reporting problems are now defined as is the responsibility for curing them; there is a standard for acceptability and rejection of a situation; there is a non-conformity and corrective action system specifically designed to bring such situations to the attention of management. Put together these changes are having their effect for previously hidden, unappreciated and ignored problems are being revealed and reported to management. Naturally the number of "problems" landing on the manager's desk is increasing. As noted above, the *"learning curve"* for the new practice makes its contribution to the number or errors found. These situations combine to produce the hump in the curve.

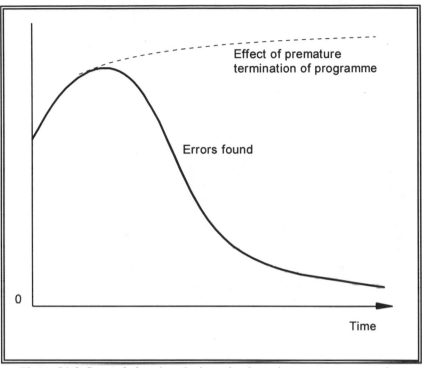

Figure 21.2 General situation during a business improvement campaign

As the problems are unearthed, management has the opportunity to eradicate them permanently. Eventually, the breakthrough point is reached and the number of errors found in any time period diminishes.

It is unwise and also unfair for a follow-up audit to take place during the gestation period since the auditee management is fully occupied in achieving improvements. Give the auditee the chance to get through this busy time.

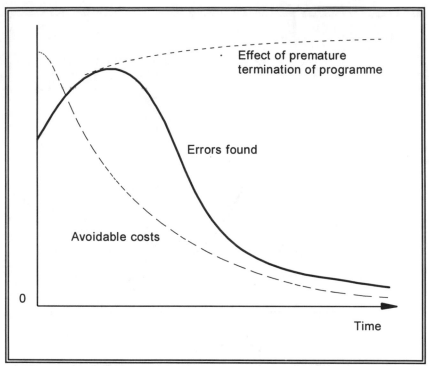

Figure 21.3 Typical avoidable cost trend during a business improvement
campaign

Figure 21.3 is Figure 21.2 superimposed on which is the typical effect of
the new systems and organizational arrangements on avoidable costs.
These show a virtually immediate drop as soon as the system starts to
operate and the auditee begins to get organized. This effect has to be
drawn to the attention of the auditee management (and also the auditor's
management, who may not be able to understand the benefits of the audit
and efficacious management systems either).

It is always advisable for the introduction of business improvement
campaigns to be coupled with the advent of a data capture system for
recording avoidable costs. This is achieved by implementing effective
performance monitoring measures at each and every process (macro
processes and micro processes) so that the auditee's personnel at all levels
can be reassured that real benefits are accruing from their efforts. The risk

that management may give up before the breakthrough point, a development which is unhelpful to all concerned, means that the auditor should recommend an appropriate system for obtaining the improvement performance data.

Subsequent audits

Unless there have been major changes, company re-organizations, take-overs or senior appointments, for example, subsequent audits seldom produce such dramatic results as first audits. The deficiencies they reveal tend not to be so major or so numerous. If the first audit was able to deal only with the auditee's systems (i.e. a systems audit), the next audit must deal with compliance with those systems.

When an audit team next visits an organization, it would be well advised to follow a different method of proceeding. It could, for instance, look at different areas or different sorts of objective evidence, consider different members of the same department or different product ranges or it could follow a trace-back rather than a trace-forward method. The audit team must check *quickly* that closed-out corrective action is still being implemented. The check should not take too long and the auditors should not dig around in any area with a view to finding trouble. The auditee's internal audit system should be particularly closely checked if the first audit revealed widespread problems. The internal audit system can investigate the auditee's business improvement programme far more thoroughly than an external audit team (see Chapter 2) and so it is extremely important to establish that it is working properly.

22. The Auditor

If you can fill the unforgiving minute
With sixty seconds run,
Yours is the Earth and everything that's in it,
And - which is more - you'll be an auditor, my son!

(With apologies to Rudyard Kipling!.

This chapter describes what makes a good auditor and points out some traits that do not. Figure 22.1 lists the desirable and undesirable attributes of an auditor and is in some respects quite daunting. Nobody is so perfect as to posses all of the desirable characteristics but the more the auditor has, the better.

Knowledge

The auditor must have the proper sorts of knowledge to be able to perform the audit concerned. The types of things he must know include:

1.   Business management practices for the auditee's industry or economic sector.

2.   Contractual and legislative requirements that apply to the auditee's product or service.

3.   The work processes that the auditee would use.

If the lead auditor does not possess this knowledge, then specialist help and guidance must be obtained for the audit.

There is a school of thought which says that if one is acquainted with the principles of auditing, one can audit any activity or department. According to this theory, a floor cleaner trained in the principles of auditing could audit, say, an accounts department or a factory making airplanes or pharmaceuticals. In fact, the unfortunate person would be almost certain to run into difficulties directly stemming from a lack of background experience in the area being audited. The "auditor" might not be able to interpret accounting systems or product specifications sufficiently well to

457

Characteristics and abilities	
Desirable	Undesirable
Good judgement	Injudicious
Open minded	Closed mind
Resilient	Gives in
Diplomatic	Argumentative
Self disciplined	Undisciplined
Honest	Dishonest
Unbiased	Opinionated
Listens	Won't listen
Patient	Impatient
Articulate	Inarticulate
Industrious	Lazy
Can communicate to all levels	Uncommunicative
Professional	Unprofessional
Interested	Apathetic
Inquiring mind	Gullible
Analytical	Accepts things at face value
Systematic, logical in approach	Chaotic
Unafraid of unpopularity	Wants to be liked by all
Human	Unreasonable
Sober	Drunkard/ drug addict

Figure 22.1 What to look for in an auditor

judge their adequacy. An unscrupulous auditee would then be able to capitalize on this situation. For this reason, the person chosen to carry out any audit should have a background of experience and expertise in the area concerned.

4.   How to organize and plan activities.

Unless the auditor works to a plan, the audit will be chaotic and haphazard.

5.   How to audit.

A person may understand all of the above points and still be unable to perform an audit because he knows nothing about the style of questioning, auditing methods, conduct and preparation required. No matter how knowledgeable the auditor may be in other respects, unless he has been properly trained in auditing, the money spent on the audit is wasted.

6.   New technology.

The expanded use of desktop computers, electronic communications has resulted in auditees moving towards employing paperless offices. Even when the auditee is not entirely paperless in his daily operations, much information will be kept in computer files. The auditor needs to understand the basis of the technology used, how to search the auditee's computer system and how to operate various applications programs commonly used (including spreadsheets, word processors, database management systems).

7.   The specific details relating to the contract/project/processes to be audited.

This information is obtained during the preparation phase of the audit, described in Chapter 9.

Training

Attendance at a formal course on auditing is one obvious method of training but this should always be supplemented in one way or another. However, there is a spectrum of audit training course available ranging from poor to value-added. Regrettably, in the so-called quality profession, too many rest at the low end of that spectrum and tend to pad out their time slavishly going through such standards as ISO 9001 or QS 9000, on a word-by-word, clause-by-clause basis. These are to be avoided and the mere fact they are "registered" courses is less than a guarantee of their worth: *caveat emptor*. It is advisable to select course run by practitioners having substantial experience (at least ten years) in management auditing. A practical subject, as is management auditing, is best taught by practitioners, not academics.

The value of on-the-job training depends upon the efficiency of the "experienced" auditor who is providing the training. Working with an experienced and competent auditor, either as an observer or as a member of an audit team, is extremely valuable although the trainees auditor will, in any case, probably pick up bad habits as well as good ones.

Before assigning someone to perform an external audit, it is sensible to have him participate in an internal one first, giving him a critique of his performance during that internal audit. This critique of performance should also be provided during the subsequent external audits to which the trainee is assigned. These reviews should always be given in private and not in front of the auditee. (See also Chapter 9 *"Preparing the new auditor"*.)

Much can be learned by observing poor and incompetent auditors. They handsomely show how not to do things. (A reliable sign of an incompetent auditor is the one who focuses on *"procedures"* first, as discussed in an earlier chapter.)

Independence

The auditor should be independent of the activity being audited, the only exception to this being the self audit which forms part of the tiering of audits, as mentioned in Part 1, Chapter 2. There is often some concern about the issue of an auditor being involved in the development of the auditee's management systems, the contentious point being that the auditor's independence might thereby become compromised. This debate has frequently descended into arguments about whether or not the auditor is, in reality, a policeman or a consultant. If the former is the case then the audits generally are perceived as being witch-hunts and confrontational positions rapidly develop which are not conducive to progress. Both the auditor and auditee erect their own Chinese walls and prepare to do battle while the product and all associated with it suffer the consequences. Constructive debate and continuous improvement benefits are unlikely in these circumstances.

From my own experience, the consultancy role has been proved time and again to be preferable. The auditor has certain concerns and knowledge that should rightly be brought to bear when the auditee is developing his management systems and organizational arrangements. These are at the core of effective prevention of problems. This has the considerable advantages of ensuring that the auditee's and auditor's legitimate interests are balanced at the outset, are appreciated by each whilst the systems and organization become fit for purpose earlier than would otherwise be possible. It is not acceptable for the auditor to actually draw up the organizational arrangements, to define and develop the auditee's systems and otherwise have ownership of such work done: to do so would be to allow the auditee to abrogate his responsibilities.

In giving advice and information, concerning types of system and organizational arrangements that would meet his business needs and an audit objective, the auditor has not relinquished any authority to require corrective action and the responsibility for achieving quality and implementing effective management systems still rests with the auditee. In fact, the auditor finds himself in an even stronger position if his audit reveals that the auditee has not heeded his advice and requirements with the effect that problems have emerged: the auditee was, after all, forewarned of the factors to be considered. It is the knowledge that the sanction to require corrective action exists that provides a deterrent. The mature auditor will not become compromised by giving assistance and advice.

Politics

An auditor must not allow himself to be "used" for the auditee's own political ends. His function is to assist in sorting out the auditee's systems, not to be enrolled in some covert power struggle.

Achievement

While it is not always possible to reward high achievement financially, a job well done should carry its own reward. The satisfaction of knowing that his work has been carried out professionally and thoroughly should be sufficient for any auditor.

Mistakes

Everyone makes them, auditors are no different. The essential thing is to learn from them. For this reason I always advise the auditor to perform a *post mortem* on the audit and assess what was done well, what did not go so well and how to improve. The only difference between newcomers to auditing and experienced professionals is their position on the learning curve. No one has reached the top for there is always something to be learned.

Continuous professional development (CPD)

Particular emphasis has been placed on CPD in recent years. It is nothing new. Neither the ascent of man nor scientific and technological progress would have occurred without it. The main difference, nowadays, is the accelerating rate of change in technology, working practices and markets which mean new knowledge is constantly arriving and arriving ever faster. Auditors must keep abreast of factors affecting business for they will affect the way auditee's perform their processes, the products themselves, legislation surrounding the work and management techniques, all of which are at the centre of auditing efforts.

Being challenged by the auditee

Whenever an auditee challenges the findings or conclusions of an auditor, believing them to be unfair or incorrect, it is not an occasion for heated disputes, resentment or sulkiness from wounded pride. As stated many times throughout this book, the auditee is entitled to a true and fair view on the file and it is the auditor's job to see that this is obtained.

An auditor should be at his most relaxed when challenged for he will then know the audit is going to be a success, for the following reasons:

♦ If the auditee can produce objective evidence to support his claims, the truth is known and a balanced assessment has been made.
♦ If the auditee cannot produce any objective evidence to support his claims, the auditor has an even larger sample on which to base the audit conclusions. Moreover, the auditee cannot complain at not being given the chance to present his case.
♦ There is less likelihood of being challenged once the audit report is on file. Such a challenge could have serious repercussions, as explained in Chapter 20. It is better to be corrected before going into print than afterwards.

Ethics and ethical standards

Few things can be as unpleasant as encountering an auditor lacking in ethical principles and conduct. A full discussion of ethical behaviour is more appropriate to a treatise on philosophy and out of place in a book such as this. Nonetheless, some precepts are worth listing. During my audit seminars I advise the following as having especial importance towards the ethical conduct of an audit:

♦ Know your subject.
♦ Tell the truth. Do not falsify the findings on the audit report.
♦ Use plain language. Do not use *"weasel"* words and expressions.
♦ Be fearless and do not get bullied or threatened by your management or the auditee.
♦ Do not abuse the auditee.
♦ Do not cover up dangerous, unsafe or illegal situations.

- Do not breach any confidential information, but ascertain what really is confidential and what is not.
- Do not steal.
- Do not steal or divulge to any third party any proprietary information or copyright material.
- Remember you are in a position of trust.
- Do not accept bribes.
- Avoid and do not accept assignments where there is a conflict of interest.
- Declare any actual or potential conflicting personal interests you might have affecting the auditee's activities.
- Serve your customer. Ask yourself *"who is my customer?"*

23. The Auditee

From the lowest place when virtuous things proceed,
The place is dignified by the doer's deed.

William Shakespeare (All's well that ends well).

It is just as appropriate for the auditee to adopt a set of guidelines to govern his conduct as it is for an auditor to do so. Where an extrinsic audit is concerned, the auditee should ideally display as many as possible of the characteristics listed as desirable in an auditor in Fig. 22.1.

Attitude towards the audit

While it is quite natural for an auditee to feel a degree of anxiety about being audited (particularly the first time), he should try not to become too tense and nervous. The higher levels of management can set an example to their staff by being as relaxed and calm as possible throughout the audit. This will help matters to proceed smoothly and efficiently.

Extrinsic audits can assist the auditee in several ways. The audit team not only provides fresh eyes which may see a new solution to familiar problems but can also help to convince the management that action is necessary. Extrinsic auditors can also provide very useful clarification of obscure requirements in the codes, standards or regulations affecting the auditee. The auditee should recognize the potential benefits of being audited and try to ensure by his conduct that these benefits are realized.

Such guidelines apply each and every time an organization is audited. Simply because no deficiencies were found at a previous audit, it does not follow that the management systems will be passed with a clean bill of health on a subsequent occasion. Practices, standards and legislation are all subject to change, and sooner or later the time will come when the systems operating within the organization will also need to change, as might its organizational arrangements. Hence an extrinsic auditor's findings should never be ignored, however many other auditors have found no deficiencies. No organization should consider itself above reproach: every adverse finding should be taken seriously and welcomed as providing an opportunity for improvement and for the reduction of avoidable costs.

Answering the questions

Do not volunteer any information that the auditor has not requested but do not be unco-operative. Only the question in hand should be answered and it should be answered in full. Be prepared for the auditor to use silence as an interrogative tactic (see Chapter 13), and don't talk yourself into unnecessary trouble.

Bluff

It is always risky to try to bluff your way our of a tight corner. It is far better to admit ignorance if you don't know the answer to a question. Bluff is very rarely convincing and it can cause a great deal more trouble than it cures. If an auditor realizes that he is being duped, his respect for the auditee will disappear; the auditor will no longer trust the auditee and will probably start to take larger samples of objective evidence, which is both time consuming and costly; his questions may also become more penetrating.

Taking action on the spot

If problems are discovered during the audit, the auditee should try to take corrective action immediately and show genuine concern about addressing the real root cause. By taking action on the spot, the auditee can save embarrassing revelations being made at an exit interview or in audit reports that will be submitted to the auditee's senior management. Of course, if the problem is such that only top management can resolve it, then the auditee should forewarn the appropriate level of management of the situation before the exit interview. The auditor's daily briefing might be used for this purpose (see Chapter 14). They may well appreciate some suggestions for corrective action.

> A peculiar and undesirable example of prompt action happened to me while auditing a manufacturer in a Mediterranean country. The checking of a material certificate revealed that the product's chemical composition was incorrect as per the specification. The auditee manager concerned looked aghast and put his hands to his face expressing shock. After a few moments, however, he regained his composure and, with a face of pure joy, proceeded to mark up the certificate with the specification's figures! His elation was short-lived as he was politely informed that life is not so simple.

466

Challenging the auditor

If it seems that the auditor has made a mistake, perhaps by scrutinizing an inadequate amount of objective evidence, the auditee should offer to present further objective evidence to correct the misinterpretation. If in doubt about the interpretation of requirements, the auditee should ask for the contract, regulation, standard, specification or code to be re-read, in order that he may establish exactly what they are. (This is a variant of the auditor's *"show me"* request.) Do not automatically assume mal-intent on the part of the auditor: auditors are only human and they *do* make the occasional mistake. As soon as it is apparent that the auditor is in this position, the auditee must draw the error to his attention. If the auditee does not do so, the auditor may be entitled to ask why the findings were not corrected at the first opportunity. It is in the interests of both the auditor and the auditee that a true and fair view is obtained.

Note taking

The auditee should make and retain his own notes, detailing the objective evidence seen by the auditor (e.g. information identity details, item identities, persons involved etc., as discussed in Chapter 11). These will be most important when the auditee has to follow up with corrective action, to answer the senior management's questions at the exit interview or to explain the nature of the deficiencies and why they *are* deficiencies to those individuals responsible both for the quality of their work and for taking corrective action to improve it. The notes will also serve to refresh his mind at a later date.

Preparation

It is important that the auditee is properly prepared for each day's auditing activities, a rule which applies especially to the escorts who will be on the spot during the audit.

Before the audit team arrives, the auditee and the escorts must be familiar with:

♦ The auditor's checklist and programme (so that the various activities are forewarned of the auditor's concerns and approximate time of arrival and so that they can prepare accordingly).

♦ The basic references that will be encountered e.g. regulations, contract/specification or their relevant parts.

467

- The relevant management systems and organizational arrangements, and where objective evidence of their implementation is to be found.
- The objective evidence available to demonstrate those organizational arrangements' and systems' results in each of the various projects, departments or processes (units) to be audited.

At a later stage, the auditee must prepare for the exit interview. This involves checking up on corrective action proposals and on the result of purges, so that these do not come as an unwelcome revelation to the senior management who will attend the exit interview or delay the proceedings.

Auditee's personnel

A responsible member of a department that is being audited should try to help the proceedings along. It is *not* helpful to intervene when the auditor is interviewing a member of staff (unless it is apparent that communications have broken down). The auditor needs to talk to the person on the job to find out how well he or she knows the job, what training has been provided and so on. The department head should stay in the background unless specifically asked for some information or help. Managers who are inexperienced in being audited commonly and mistakenly believe that in answering the auditor's questions, they are helping the situation. This is erroneous for not only might an untrue and unfair view of the actual state of things at the ordinary workplace be offered but also they can be deluding themselves about their departments' real effectiveness and needs.

If a deficiency is found, the audit should not be allowed to develop into a witch-hunt. The head of department should not try to allocate blame or ask for excuses there and then.

> An auditee's manager started describing his schedule for the internal audits for the coming year. He had only been talking for a minute or so when a subordinate challenged him. A heated argument flared up immediately. It was obvious that the two individuals disliked each other intensely and were continually feuding. I had to ask the "gentlemen" to quiet down: *"Please don't spill blood on the table, it will make a mess of my checklist and not look good in the file"*. This type of brawl is embarrassing for all concerned and must be prevented at all costs.

Obstructive tactics (see Chapter 15) should be stopped immediately, before they have time to sour the proceedings.

Corrective action requests (CARs)

When a justified CAR appears to be coming the auditee's way, it is a good idea for him to prepare some proposals for discussion with the auditor at the exit interview. If the nature of the findings makes this impossible, the auditee should try to elicit an opinion from the auditor as to what the options for corrective action might be. The auditee must not try to pass ownership of the solution to the auditor if the latter's suggestions are accepted and acted upon.

Marketing statements

The auditee must ensure that he can live up to the statements and commitments made by his salesmen. If salesmen are over-zealous and make rash representations and commitments, a company may find itself embarking on a contract which it lacks the resources to meet or which it can only fulfil by resigning itself to a loss (which may turn out to be worthwhile if it carries the promise of profitable business in the future). Whatever the company's motives, an extrinsic auditor will still expect the codes, standards and product requirements to be satisfied. It will be no defence to plead the high cost of doing what is required - if the cost of compliance is too high, the auditee should not have become contractually enmeshed in the first place.

Obvious deficiencies

Before the audit team arrives, the auditee would be well advised to carry out a purge of the areas concerned. There is nothing worse than to receive corrective action requests for obvious deficiencies such as superseded documents still in use, uncontrolled material and the like. The auditor will quite rightly assume that if the obvious is deficient, the not-so-obvious is also likely to be in a poor state. This can provide good grounds for suspecting that the auditee has a negligent attitude towards quality achievement and has a poor internal audit system.

Although the purge might be considered as a *"clean up"*, it is important for the auditee's management to make clear to staff that the *"cleaned up"* condition is to be considered the normal condition for the workplace and cleaning up should not be necessary. Staff can learn therefrom. (*"Clean ups"* are discussed further in Chapter 12.)

Escorts

If at all possible, the auditee should have a trained auditor available to escort the audit team. The benefits of making such a person available are that:

♦   Someone will be on hand who is able to talk the auditor's language.
♦   The escort will understand what is going on, what the auditor's method is, and what the auditor is looking for.
♦   The escort will be able to learn from watching another auditor in action.
♦   The escort will be able to see whether or not the internal audit system needs amendment and, if so, where.

A large company was being audited. The management decided that there would be no constant escort present at each location: each area audited would in turn accompany the audit team to the next area and leave it there to do its work. This rapidly proved to be unwise because when corrective action was required, the auditee's staff experienced difficulty in understanding the reasoning behind the auditor's request fully since the true extent of the objective evidence studied was not appreciated or recorded by them.

Regrettably, there is no guarantee that the auditor aspires to professional standards of auditing. This can obviously cause much upset to innocent staff and a knowledgeable escort can prevent this sort of occurrence. If, however, the audit team is known to be particularly proficient, an inexperienced person could also learn a lot by participating as an observing escort. The auditee should consider these points when selecting the escorts. (See also Chapter 10 *"Escorts"*.)

Appendix 1. 12 Golden Rules

Rules and precepts are of no value
without natural capacity

Quintillian

My twelve golden rules are offered now. There is no significance in the order they are presented here because each is as important as any other. The following *Golden Rules* must be adhered to by the auditor at all times if the auditee is to truly benefit form the audit and a value for money exercise is to be accomplished:

♦   1.   Never challenge a person.
♦   2.   Always present a true and fair view.
♦   3.   Go fact finding not fault finding.
♦   4.   Use systematic methods.
♦   5.   Never lose sight of the product.
♦   6.   Find out the auditee's interpretation not yours.
♦   7.   Always be properly prepared.
♦   8.   Always help the auditee.
♦   9.   Always define the audit objectives.
♦   10.   Communicate effectively with the auditee.
♦   11.   Find and address the real cause of problems found.
♦   12.   Always follow-up corrective action requests.

Never challenge the person.

The success of an audit depends on the auditee's willingness to co-operate and provide full and sensible answers to the auditor's questions. Verbally attacking the auditee, which is all too common, results only in the auditee taking a defensive posture which can range from economical presentation of the truth to outright hostility. When auditees feel challenged on a personal level barriers to effective communication are built, intransigent positions can develop and the audit is ruined as each side becomes loath to give way and admit defeat. The pride of the combatants borne from those formative years in the school play-yard take over. Auditing is not about confrontation: it is about co-operation and personal challenges yield little objective evidence of value. If there are business problems the auditor will never get to the underlying cause by challenging the auditee - the latter will close up like a clam, fear of punishment prevents openness. The auditor has to the underlying reasons for particular actions by understanding the auditee's circumstances, an objective that can only be achieved with a relaxed auditee.

Always present a true and fair view.

The expression *"true and fair view"* is unashamedly borrowed from the world of financial auditors who use it when describing their findings of a company's accounts. Auditors must not report lies or distortions, they must maintain a sense of balance. There are some auditors who want to *"get them on something"* in order to justify their existence, failing to examine a truly representative sample of objective evidence. It is wrong to present to management isolated errors as indicative of the norm, to generalise on the basis of minor incidents. The lasting impression left in the minds of management is that auditing is about fault finding and nit-picking.

Go fact finding not fault finding.

The purpose of an audit is not to *"get the auditee on something"*; the real purpose is to obtain a balanced picture of the auditee's operation. There are auditors who become discontent if they cannot issue a CAR at all and their total approach is towards finding fault with the auditee's practices and systems; they are wrong.

Weaknesses will never be eliminated unless the auditee's strengths have been found for it is only by building on those strengths that the weaknesses will be obviated. The auditor must approach the audit with an open mind and an absence of preconceived ideas. An auditor who says *"they've got nothing"* is an auditor who has not done his/her job properly for there are always some strengths. If the auditee really had "nothing" he could not have traded or survived as long as he has. Take stock of the auditee's capabilities and report them in a balanced way to management. That cannot be done by adopting a fault-finding approach.

Use systematic methods.

The auditor must know at all times, the precise status of the audit and just how far it has proceeded. This can only be done by adopting a systematic method of analysing the auditee's activities and systems and through a systematic questioning technique. Knowing the next question to ask the auditee is essential. Experienced, professional auditors have developed a proven system for conducting their audit. They do not walk away believing their job is done when standard matters such as checking revision numbers, calibration stickers, sign-off cross-dates, material batch numbers have been exhausted for they know the audit has hardly even begun. Inadequately trained auditors tend to "jump about" in their questioning, shifting from topic to topic and returning to matters already partly covered rather than dealing fully with one matter at a time. These people are unlikely to identify potential business problems and offer suggestions that will prevent the effects from becoming a reality.

Never lose sight of the product.

The whole reason for the auditee's activities is to furnish a product fit for purpose to a customer. Their management systems help them work towards the common goal, of customer satisfaction, achieved when a product fitness for purpose is delivered. The practices, or processes, that link together forming a chain or system unite towards that common goal. One can easily become bogged down by detail during an audit and struggle to decide whether some aspect of the auditee's operation is truly acceptable or requires corrective action. A moment's reflection along the lines *"What is the product here?"*, or *"What is the objective of this auditee's work?"*, or *"What should the auditee be achieving here?"* can help one to regain priorities.

Find out the auditee's interpretation not yours.

An auditor can be tempted to impose his/ her interpretation of a code, standard, regulation or statute onto the auditee. This pitfall traps the unwary. The main purpose of any audit is to find out what the auditee is doing and why he operates in the way he does. Obtaining an understanding of the decisions taken by the auditee therefore becomes vital. Quality assessments these days are increasingly directed at seeing if the auditee complies with some chosen standard from the ISO 9000 series or some other code/ regulation/specification, none of which is unambiguous.

The issue at hand during every audit is not how the auditor would choose to interpret and comply with the standard, rather it is to find out how the auditee has decided to implement the standard and why the decisions were taken as they were. By following this course of action the auditor will understand the auditee. Without this knowledge the auditor will be unable to really help the auditee by offering relevant suggestions for corrective action, if indeed corrective action is warranted and can be justified.

One often sees CAR's, alleging an auditee's violation of a code, standard or whatever, that actually amount to a violation of the auditor's ideas or shibboleths. Even though the auditee's practices are not to the auditor's liking, that is not the issue in the audit. The auditor must always work to the letter of the standard/code etc. It is most unreasonable to expect any auditee to comply with the concepts of a person who, until the time of the audit, he has probably never met and whose concepts have never been defined in writing beforehand. If the auditee is one's external supplier, he could legitimately claim the auditor's personal and hitherto unknown requirements constitute a contract variation. And the auditee would be correct for otherwise he is in an impossible situation.

A basis for sensible dialogue will be built up by finding out the auditee's interpretation and working to the letter of the standard. If the auditor does not like the manner by which the auditee is complying with the letter of the standard he/she must persuade the auditee of the benefits, if any, of adopting the auditor's ideas.

Always be properly prepared.

The entire success and value for money obtained from an audit hinges on the thoroughness of preparation. Without a sound knowledge of the objective, which areas have to be visited and why, what matters have to be investigated, what the auditee's procedures, manuals, policies, instructions say and what his organizational arrangements are alleged to be, the audit quickly becomes a visit, a walk around that benefits no one.

Proper preparation ensures that the right team is mobilised, the time budget is allocated and auditing efficiency is maximised. An incompetent and ill-prepared auditor is the fellow whose first question to the auditee, when on-site, is *"Have you got a procedure?"* This matter is investigated last of all; the auditor should already know whether such information is meant to be available. Immediate demands for the procedure are of little use for if he/she has not yet analysed the auditee's work process, the auditor cannot judge its content, relevance and efficacy. Spending time on-site by reviewing information that should have already been assimilated is unacceptable, it is wasteful for auditee and auditor organization alike.

Always define the audit objectives.

It is not possible to prepare properly, select the right team and ultimately provide management with the information it needs unless the auditor knows why the audit has been authorised and what the objectives are. No auditor can reach valid and valuable conclusions without this knowledge.

The auditor's management must define the audit objectives in unambiguous terms avoiding elastic terms such as *"suitably"* and *"where necessary"*: for it is unreasonable to expect the auditor to qualify these expressions and to make management's decisions for them.

Always help the auditee.

Audits are for the benefit of the auditee not for the benefit or aggrandizement of the auditor. In value-added auditing the auditee gains the most from the audit because the auditor adopts a helpful and constructive approach. An attitude of trying to *"get them on something"* is inconsistent with value-added auditing.

Unacceptable CAR's are ones that do not offer solutions to the problems found. Unprofessional audit training courses abound actually instructing trainee auditors never to offer solutions. A substantial proportion of auditees are not expert in business management matters and tend to look upon the auditor as the expert. Leaving the auditee in a quandary not knowing how to resolve an apparently unacceptable situation benefits neither the auditee nor the auditor's organization. Since the essence of the pursuit of progress is to constantly strive for continuous improvement, every auditor has a duty to contribute to that goal by offering helpful advice throughout the audit.

When positive suggestions arise, management values audits and pays greater attention to them. Being helpful also removes the incorrect and long standing image of the auditor being a policeman.

Communicate effectively with the auditee.

Central to the audit's objectives is the need to report on the auditee's actual status and capabilities. This cannot be accomplished unless the auditor and auditee understand each other. Effective communications are essential if relevant objective evidence is to be unearthed. Auditees who do not understand the auditor's questions cannot provide relevant answers. Auditees who cannot understand the content of a CAR and the solutions offered therein cannot quickly introduce efficacious preventive action.

Sound questioning technique and the ability to write clearly are vital attributes for every auditor and constitute skills that proper training can enhance. When an auditor has to constantly rephrase or repeat his/her questions the auditing efficiency is dramatically reduced, sometimes to well below 50% - and the value for money gained is far less than is otherwise possible.

Find and address the real cause of problems found.

Auditing is a preventive management tool aimed at reducing total costs. Opportunities cannot be realised unless solutions that extirpate real causes of problems are offered. Professionally trained auditors possess the skills for finding real causes and addressing them in CAR's. By practising Golden Rules 3 and 4 they reveal and suggest cures for root causes. See also Chapter 18 for a description of six real causes of business problems.

One often encounters auditors and auditees adopting quick fixes only to find that their managements become disillusioned with auditing when *"the same old problems keep occurring"*. For example, upon finding someone has the wrong edition of a document the preventive remedy is found by asking why the right one was not supplied in the first place: a quick fix would merely reissue the correct one and go no further. If Rule 9 is to be achieved this Golden Rule is a natural consequence.

Always follow-up corrective action requests.

Some auditees are less than willing to take corrective action if they believe the auditor will not verify that they have done so. In such situations the CAR's are irrelevant, the audit has no value. Sensible auditees are disappointed if follow-up action is not taken for they frequently want both confirmation that they have done the right thing and the kudos that attaches when an independent expert practitioner or a peer acknowledges their achievement. Thus an aspect of auditee motivation is obtained. If following-up is not to be the policy, one need not bother auditing and can abandon any ideas of business improvement.

Management Audits

Part 2

Management audit applications

1. Continuous improvement programmes.

Biased decisions are often so venerable, so reflexive,
so much a part of our second nature,
that we never stop to recognize their status as social decisions
with radical alternatives -
and we view them instead as given and obvious truths.

Stephen Jay Gould

Refocussing on the original mission

The drive for improvement in all facets of business and life is as ancient as mankind's existence. It has caused the so-called ascent of man, increased life expectancy, propelled us through the agricultural and industrial ages and into the information age. Mankind's working energies and intelligence have been directed at improving the individual's situation as well as those of the surrounding society. All goods and services that contribute towards satisfaction at each level in Abram Maslow's hierarchy of needs have been subject to the desire for improvement. Trying to get more out of less, trying to create larger profits from turnover and trying to reduce waste have been constant themes over the millennia. These efforts provide simple interrelated measurables for assessing their success: efficiency, profit ratio and avoidable costs.

The 1980's and 1990's may be recorded by some future business historian as being a time when much effort was diverted from those traditional efforts and expended on ISO 9000, QS 9000 and some other "thousand" registration scheme without producing measurable benefits of efficiency, profit increase and cost reduction that would compare favourably with those obtainable from alternative investments. Whatever arguments there might be, they become rather academic for competition will not disappear and the fight for business survival will intensify as the patterns of global trading change. The rise of the Asian economies and the spread of knowledge *via* modern means, such as the Internet, guarantee this fact. The net result is that business will be faced for ever with the need to continuously improve its product, processes, people and performance. But, even if they are all improved, there will be no guarantee that profits will increase because the seller is no longer able to set the price for its wares: that is being done by the buyer. (See Chapter 2.) The original mission will remain, though: continuously improve or wither away.

Quality standards, is registration necessary?

The short answer to this question is *"no"*. At the time of writing this third edition the ISO TC 176 committee is striving, through its turgid process, to revise the ISO 9000 series, the big three American automobile manufacturers (Chrysler, Ford and General Motors) are trying to press home a desire for their tier one supply base to be registered to QS 9000. Business leaders, when considering their essential purchases, still want the best value for the price paid - that is nothing new - and few really care how the supplier satisfies that requirement. If the supplier wants to formalize its management systems, "fine". If the supplier wants to pursue a paperless office, "fine". If the supplier wants to be vertically integrated, use outsourcing, use direct selling, use mail order, set up a state-of-the-art research and development facility or employ the man in the moon, "fine". All of these initiatives are "fine" with the customer/client/buyer or whatever as long as the price is right and the value for money is delivered.

It has become common for inter-company purchases to have contractual clauses requiring the seller to comply with or be registered to a quality systems standard, such as ISO 9000. Compliance with that standard might increasingly be the choice of the seller, not the buyer. In the case of the "big three", for example, since their central concern is for their suppliers to continuously improve products, processes and price so that their own costs are controlled, or even reduced, all that is really needed is a clause requiring a defined level of continuous improvement set at, say, 7% per annum. The target could be linked to an incentive clause, such as a withheld payment, activated once evidence of measured improvement has been validated by the buyer. The sum could be set aside in an escrow account or similar. The buyer would care less how the improvements are achieved. If the seller elects to comply with ISO 9000, to be registered to that standard, to outsource, to downsize, to become a virtual corporation, to pursue a six sigma programme, to implement "Japanese style" manufacturing techniques, that would be its own decision. If the seller felt such initiatives would assist towards achieving the continuous improvement target, it is its choice. The customer defines the targets required, the seller chooses how to meet them and retains the liability for the methods it selects. The simple instruction from buyer to seller would be *"The requirement is x% improvement this year."*

One thing is certain. Any firm believing in maintenance of the *status quo* will not maintain its customer base. In order to keep or expand the customer base, its management systems, processes, products, people and performance would need constant scrutiny for identifying improvement opportunities and constant change to realize them. Timidity in approach will cause the firm to be left behind. Aggressive continuous improvement is becoming the norm in international trade.

The role of the quality movement

Ever since it first appeared, the quality movement focussed its efforts on improvement of deliverable products, especially of physical products. This was achieved through independent inspection, end of line inspection, product testing and similar quality control techniques. The process only came under real scrutiny when the benefits of statistical tools were demonstrated. Through an evolutionary process the scope of business matters requiring attention, to really improve outgoing product quality, increased. The total quality management (TQM) concept was born. But the quality movement cannot truly claim any accolade for the broader view that TQM possesses. Others in the field of management science and business improvement deserve that recognition. As a result, the quality movement's knowledge is changing, albeit far too slowly. It is becoming better educated in a wider range of business management techniques. The knowledge required to be a competent quality professional extends far beyond gauging, limits and fits, SPC, non-destructive testing and ISO 9000's basic requirements. The traditional inspector with his traditional knowledge bank no longer makes for a quality "professional". He is becoming extinct. That type of verification effort is increasingly being assigned where it should always have been: to the person performing the process and creating a product.

The role of the quality movement is: to assist the company to continuously improve its products, processes, people and performance and achieve measurable gains in each.

The extreme majority within the quality movement have become seduced into believing the answers to that goal reside within ISO 9000 *et al*. They are wrong. The wording of the ISO 9000 series is so general that little of direct prescription is contained in it. It was intended to be that way. The quality movement and registration industry has adopted an approach of documenting company methods and chasing around after labels, stickers and revision numbers. This *"docs and stickers"* approach, as I dub it, is insufficient. Once the obvious benefits drawn from sensible practices of internal communications have been realized, for that is what much of that docs and stickers frenzy amounts to, what then? *"Bottom line"* measurable gains deriving from such concepts as just-in-time, real time supply, flexible organizations, Internet sales will be required to propel forward the company. These have produced measurable gains attracting the attention and commitment of top executives worldwide to a greater extent than have the ISO 9000 advocates' offerings with their seldom measured benefits and unfulfilled promissory notes.

As noted in Part 1 Chapter 3, titles such as "quality assurance manager", "vice-president (quality)", "quality manager" and the like are being superseded by "vice-president - continuous improvement", "continuous improvement project manager", "business improvement manager" and similar. They indicate to all employees and customers the corporate mission. The auditor should look for such position titles and review the depth and scope of their incumbents' responsibility and authority which should be directly linked to a corporate policy emanating from the most senior position in the firm. The continuous improvement coordinator should report to that most senior person. Particular attention must be paid to the background experience and qualifications of the person assigned to the role. He or she needs to possess at least the capacity to continuously develop professionally so as to learn and apply new business concepts and techniques as they emerge. A broad knowledge and experience of business operations is essential. Few in the so-called quality profession have that for their assigned tasks prevented it. Those who have not got it will need to get it. Especially management auditors.

The role of the management audit

Management audits are a tool whose benefits are recognized by a growing number of company executives. They distinguish themselves from the typical "audit" performed by much of the quality industry in being future focussed. (See also Chapter 2). Moreover, they search out opportunities for improvement, whether in process, system, product or task element. The best ones take nothing for granted, question the basis for decisions made and assess their ongoing relevance to current and future needs. In so doing, the management auditor makes a positive contribution to the firm's potential results, drawing to the attention of the auditee, the audit client and their associated management possible improvement projects with estimated benefits that might be accrued.

In that last statement lies an important point, the management auditor will report not only the nature of the opportunity identified, but also some estimate of the gain. The audit is an important first step in a proper cost-benefit appraisal of improvement projects and the auditor must be able to quantify his estimates: generalities and subjectivity are insufficient in the world of continuous improvement. No longer would such advice as *"Introduce improved material handling methods"* suffice. The auditor will need to advise in some detail:

♦   The existing situation.
♦   The recommended improvement.
♦   The reason for making the recommendation.
♦   Estimates of the costs and benefits of the recommendation, presented in quantified and measurable terms; i.e. the measurable gains believed as being achievable.

The line between consultancy and auditing will be blurred, perhaps non-existent at times.

Management auditors will be offering a greater value for money from audits designed to search out improvement opportunities than do the typical quality auditors (inspectors) so prevalent today in the quality industry. Business wants one thing only: value-added auditing. Survival necessitates it.

2. Value-added auditing

Opportunity has power everywhere;
always let your hook be hanging;
where you least expect it, there will swim a fish.

Ovid

There are few captive markets. Competition is ensuring the era of cozy clubs, cartels and cliques is passing. Any that still remain are living on borrowed time. Even in centrally controlled countries, protected monopolies cannot be relied on to last, international factors coupled with spreading democracy and human nature will conspire to change pragmatically their politicians' policies. (This can be detected in China too, as its "one country one system" gives way to "one country two systems" shown in the scheme for the 1997 take-over of Hong Kong and setting up of enterprise zones within the Chinese mainland. Eventually one of its two systems will wither. It will not be the free market and enterprise one! Events in Eastern Europe and totalitarian regimes have demonstrated this.) The free market is about free, not captive, customers. It gives the customer freedom but, paradoxically, reduces the supplier's freedom in some crucial aspects of business decision making. Notably in the determination of price.

Revisiting the elements of price

Delegates attending my management audit seminars of the last three decades are familiar with the discussions held in the very first session, concerning price and cost, during which this age old equation, is presented.

Profit = selling price - cost

The equation indicates the need to reduce costs as much as possible if profit is to be maintained or increased. However, the purpose of the firm is not only to deliver its wares, tangible and intangible, to the customer, but also to supply them at an acceptable price. Selling price is a characteristic about which the seller used to have greater control whilst requiring careful consideration. It could not be set too high but was put as high as possible until the customer squealed.

The overall price charged to a customer incorporates the unavoidable costs of the seller's tasks (processes), the avoidable costs incurred through waste and a charge levied to provide for profit. If profit level is discretionary, being fixed by the management, so too is the amount of avoidable cost, described below. If profit is set as a percentage of cost, the customer is hit twice: first for the avoidable costs and then again for a profit mark-up on those costs. Customers are aware of this as never before and are refusing to accept the situation. Being more savvy about the constituent elements of price they are stating what it will be. This is a fundamental and far reaching development. Old fashioned *"cost plus"* formulae whereby there was no incentive for the seller to reduce costs (both avoidable and unavoidable), because the buyer agreed to reimburse the seller on the basis of documented expenditure, are eschewed and increasingly rare: they seem to be destined for the academic museum.

The task element *"Service"*, described in Part 1 Chapter 4, describes *"price"* as a characteristic of the service supplied. Less and less often now is the price a matter for the seller's discretion; more and more often it is the buyer who dictates a target level. A growing number of customers are shopping globally, setting a budget for their purchases and rigidly adhere to it. An expanding free market allows them to do this. In sum, buyers now require sellers:

♦   To meet the target price the buyer has specified.
♦   To constantly reduce that selling price by sharing gains brought about by continuous improvement.

And so, the old business equation can now be rewritten as:

$$Price = cost + profit$$

One might say, *"So what is new about that?"*, to which one must fairly reply *"Nothing. But..."*. The "but" is the pressure for cost reduction which is higher than it has ever been. As the customer effectively says *"This is all you will get"*, it behooves the seller to spend wisely and avoid waste. But, when muscular industrial customers, such as major original equipment makers (OEMs) each say, *"This is all you will get. I will demand even better next time"*, and the stock market or owners simultaneously demand profit growth year on year, having compared the firm against a benchmark of others' performance, the pressure for continuous improvement is considerable. It is demanded, it is expected and the only place to find it is in the reduction of avoidable costs.

The nature of costs

Traditional costs categories, promoted and adhered to throughout the quality industry, are: failure, appraisal and prevention. Together with that industry's embracing concepts of the *"costs of quality"* they no longer suffice, if indeed they ever did, for they inadequately reflect business realities known through the ages. Trying to pursue cost of quality initiatives using those categories has caused too much debate, confusion and waste of available corporate effort. Ordinary employees have frequently found its concepts confusing and complex leading to arguments about what should be assigned to what category. Is a particular type of appraisal a sign of failure? Are certain types of appraisal actually a prevention cost? Is the fact that we need to take this action, to prevent defects being made, a sign that some process is inadequate and the action is actually a failure cost? Having witnessed countless dilemmas such as those in company after company, one cannot believe those categories facilitate ready comprehension or communication in the firm.

In my view, there are only two types of cost:

♦ The unavoidable.
♦ The avoidable.

Unavoidable costs are those that must be incurred if the business is to be successful and over which the firm has no real discretion. Avoidable costs are those which, by commission or omission, the firm has decided to incur and which are totally preventable. They drain the firm's resources and jeopardize its future. They reduce the shareholder's earnings, the employee's prospects and the customer's satisfaction. They are pure waste. They are targets for improvement projects.

Understanding the nature of those two types of cost directly affects one's way of thinking, managing and auditing.

What are examples of unavoidable costs?

One obvious example would be scrap or incorrect products. Another might be obtained by considering design and planning functions, which many in the quality industry tend to regard as residing within the category of *"preventive costs"*. Undoubtedly those activities are performed in the spirit and with the intention of preventing waste. But the healthy firm will want to review how much of those activities represent avoidable costs, how much of the processes used in the conduct of each is avoidable, how much is unavoidable. Such fundamental questions lie at the heart of successful value-added audits for they challenge the *status quo* and underlying decisions concerning the way things are structured and done, the way things are being structured and are intended to be done in the future.

The target

The target has to be zero avoidable costs. One cannot overstate how difficult is the challenge of achieving it: it is extremely difficult. Just as one thinks "zero" is within reach, an expenditure previously categorized as unavoidable can quickly become avoidable as technology changes, competitors change their methods and products, new forms of equipment appear in the marketplace, new and more efficient methods are devised elsewhere.

An essential culture

Regarding costs as avoidable or unavoidable has to become a way of thinking throughout the entire firm, at all levels and in all functions. The glaring past weakness of thousands of companies has been the belief that reducing waste, avoiding avoidable costs, is the preserve of management. It is not. Tapping the reservoir of knowledge and experience possessed by all employees is essential. In every company I have visited, a wealth of information and an unexploited gold mine of ideas and willingness to eliminate avoidable costs, which each employee can identify (if only asked), have made themselves apparent. This has been especially the case when one has taken a few moments to illustrate the difference between the avoidable and the unavoidable by citing some simple examples. (See also *"Gathering opinions at grass roots levels"*, Part 1 Chapter 12).

But the culture of avoiding avoidable costs cannot be built by conducting only an awareness programme of their nature, and it requires more than the "suggestion box", so beloved in past yars. It requires a double empowerment of the staff: empowerment to identify the avoidable; empowerment to eliminate it. Most suggestion schemes fizzle out and are discredited when management stifles ideas, fails to act on improvement suggestions (for whatever reason suits its whim) and fails to justify the decision with valid argument transcending the inappropriate edict of *"because I say so"*. If one wants staff to act in a business like way, one must offer business benefit explanations to them.

Continuous improvement and value-added auditing

Both continuous improvement programmes and value-added audits alike look for evidence of avoidable costs. Yesterday's unavoidable costs might be avoidable costs of today and tomorrow. Once identified they present an improvement project that can be planned and pursued.

The two ideas are inseparable. If the audit team does not offer suggestions for measurable improvement, no value has been added through its activities. The magnitude of suggestions determine the overall value received by the audit client and the auditee from the audit. They must exceed the audit costs. When one considers the investment in the audit made by the auditee, one must regard the auditee as a major customer of the auditor, deserving a value-added service performed by competent people in a constructive way. If one does not regard the auditee as a principal beneficiary of the audit effort, there is little point in conducting audits at all.

Future focus

As stated in Part 1, management audits differ from inspections in being future focussed. Management auditors look to the future, not the past, as do traditional inspections and other forms of verification activities. The only place where value can be increased is in the future. The only place where improvements can be realized is in the future.

Advertisements aimed at stock market investors always offer the prudent warning that past performance is no guarantee of future results. That advice reflects operational reality for every company since the stock market's potential is only as good as the prospects of the firms quoted within it. Sensible business owners, management and employees will eschew any advice that *"all is well"* or *"we comply with..."* when it is based on what has been done and achieved to date i.e. past results. Who can guarantee the situation will prevail in future?

As was noted in Part 1, Chapter 1, the management auditor can advise auditees, at all corporate levels, of:

♦ The risk of continuing as at present in tomorrow's world.
♦ The probable efficacy of planned strategies, practices, systems in causing or preventing avoidable loss.
♦ Opportunities for improvement.

Audit preparation

Value-added audits are prepared in the same general way as is described in Part 1 Chapter 9. One difference, though, concerns the background information required.

The value-added audit considers applications of new knowledge, techniques, alternative facilities and service available from outside sources, new materials in the marketplace and so on to determine improvement opportunities. The audit will use the information to identify emerging avoidable costs, costs that are currently regarded as being unavoidable but which will move into the realm of the avoidable.

Sources of information that can be tapped include the journals of professional associations, conference transactions and the Internet. In effect the audit will be assessing the auditee's past decisions against the benchmark of globally available knowledge to highlight opportunities.

The effect on the audit team.

The key to its selection and structure, as has always been the case, is the knowledge required to perform the audit. Process knowledge is in itself inadequate. Business management knowledge is also required as is the ability to apply the types of analytical tool mentioned below. Just as conventional auditors have on occasions found SPC, or flow charting to be useful tools, the management auditor will use those and other tools as and when required. An audit team's ability to understand the nature of extraneous factors and their effects on the auditee's processes, organization, systems, resources and management style is of especial importance. Knowing what is happening in the world outside of the company is vital, without that knowledge, it is unlikely that the audit team will be able to suggest new ideas possessing a value-adding quality.

The effect on the auditor

Knowledge that would once suffice is of little use, if any, for the future and performing value-added audits. Auditors not only need to know the range of tools described below but also need to be accomplished in cost management techniques, the use of spreadsheets and risk assessment. In addition to this, the auditor must be fully up-to-date with the latest business techniques, applications of technology and competitive trends.

When combined together, these knowledge and skills demands conspire to affect the overall basic training of the management auditor. The curricula and content of such existing schemes as the ASQC's Certified Quality Auditor (CQA) will be found lacking.

From where would such auditors be drawn?

The traditional sources of supply remain, these being: senior management, external consultants and the workforce itself.

The expression *"senior management"* may be inappropriate in the new millennium for new organizational forms. It may be more accurate to substitute the term *"central management"* or *"core business management"*. Employing consultants, nowadays referred to as *"intellectual outsourcing"*, will be particularly valuable for there will some who specialize in the auditee's sector and possess a broad base of knowledge of sector developments and trends. Savvy and well briefed consultants will be well worth their fees. But the type of consultant extant in today's quality industry will be unsuitable for undertaking value-added audits: most have already, and justifiably, been discredited.

The workforce will be a likely and preferred source. As the need for greater knowledge and business skills at "lower" levels increases and firms respond, these people will be able to offer greater value in the audits they are asked to do. Progressive firms have been pursuing this policy for more than a decade. (Digital Equipment Corporation, particularly its European arm, is one that immediately occurs to me).

Checklists and tools

Can we use standard checklists, must they always be customized?

The answer to these questions is yes and yes, respectively. The first *"yes"* to ensure ongoing application of value-added concepts by auditors: the second *"yes"* because of the risk of stereotyping auditors when the audit checklists are maintained the same regardless of the audit objective and the auditee's situation, (See Part 1 Chapter 7), and the need for the firm to be agile in a changing world. The custom built checklist can be built from the company standard one.

In practice the auditor :

1. Looks at the checklist question.
2. Obtains data relevant to it.
3. Applies appropriate analytical tools to the data in order to,
4. Answers the particular checklist question.

Analytical tools

Analytical tools that are sometimes useful include failure modes effects analyses (FMEA's), fault tree analyses (FTA's), flowcharts - if not already used, queuing theory, operational research techniques, design of experiments (DOE), evolutionary operations methods (EVOP's). Applying some of these might take some time.

The effect on audit time

Value-added audits take longer than those presently performed. This is because they cover more matters and in a deeper more fundamental way than most of the present day ones. The cost-benefit curve shown in Part 1 Figure 9.5 prevails. A considerable risk can occur when management fails to provide sufficient time for the audit team to thoroughly execute its duties: half answers and hasty cost-benefit analyses could prove dangerously misleading.

Some audits might proceed over a period of several months, stopping and starting as the audit team gradually builds up its view of things, waits for data to be gathered and provided by the auditee, goes away to analyze it, then returns to verify additional matters deriving from it.

Audit method

The seven step method can still used by the auditor, and is shown in Figure 2.1. Additional questions are posed, however.

Review past decisions.

A poster in my dentist's surgery portrays a number of beautiful yachts underway on blue water and proclaims: *"We cannot control the winds but we can adjust the sails."*. Good sailors carefully pay attention to weather forecasts in order to prepare for the conditions ahead. They read the sea and the sky, the conditions before them and they reevaluate past decisions, trimming sails, instructing their crews, preparing their vessels and setting course accordingly. The successful sailor acts proactively more often than he acts reactively after events have overtaken the vessel.

Successful businesses know they cannot control trading conditions, competitor's actions or the timing of others' innovative ideas. Ever changing circumstance is a fact of life and making adjustments so as to harness its force is essential. Systems, organization, methods, processes - and people -

	Audit activity	Value-added considerations
Step 1	Analyze organization.	Review historic basis for current organizational decisions. What changes could be made?
Step 2	Analyze management systems.	Review historic basis for current management systems' decisions. What changes could be made?
Step 3	Assess compliance with current organization and management systems.	Should any existing non-compliance be formalized because it improves upon existing organizational arrangements or management systems?
Step 4	Decide efficacy of current management systems and organization.	Will they be efficacious for the future? What changes are required for future needs?
Step 5	Decide if management systems/ organization could be improved or simplified.	What will be the costs of changes versus the benefits? In what time frame must the changes be made? What time frame will the changes require?
Step 6	Assess performance monitoring methods.	Review historic basis for current performance monitoring measurements and methods.
Step 7	Decide if there are improvement opportunities.	What will be the costs of changing the performance monitoring methods used and of obtaining the measurements versus the benefits of so doing? In what time frame must the changes be made? What time frame will the changes require?

Figure 2.1 The seven step method and value-added auditing

all must change. The value-added auditor constantly poses, to the auditee, the essential question : *"Would you do the same today as you did yesterday bearing in mind the circumstances and requirements of today and tomorrow's business as you now know them?"*. Once the underlying reasons for a past (and present) course of action have been unearthed, the auditor asks, *"Given the opportunity, would you make the same decision for present and future needs?"* The response is almost always, *"No, because...".* Clearly, it is time to change, and the auditee knows it. All too frequently, and because of the day-to-day pressures and apparent (or imagined) priorities, the auditee has little time to review its situation and decide the merits of revision. The auditor acts as a catalyst for change: the value-added audit provides a useful "time-out" to consider opportunities and develop action plans for realizing their benefits.

The roots of existing, historic decisions must be reviewed. The following types of question are helpful:

Step 1: Analyze the auditee's organization.

♦ What were the underlying reasons/data input for the setting up the organization the way it is?
♦ Are those reasons/data still valid, are they now superseded by events or developments?
      What aspects are extinct?
      What aspects are new?
      What are the emerging and upcoming aspects?
      What is the impact of those emerging, upcoming and new aspects?
♦ What effect will they have on the processes?
      Which processes will still be needed?
      Which processes will no longer be needed?
      Which processes require change?
      What is the nature of the changes required?

Step 2: Analyze the auditee's management systems.

♦ What were the underlying reasons/data input for setting up the management systems the way they are?
♦ Are those reasons/data still valid, are they now superseded by events or developments?
      What aspects are extinct?
      What aspects are new?
      What are the emerging and upcoming aspects?
      What is the impact of those emerging, upcoming and new aspects?

- What effect will they have on the systems?
  Which systems will still be needed?
  Which systems will no longer be needed?
  Which systems require change?
  What is the nature of the changes required?

Step 3: Assess the auditee's compliance with organizational arrangements and management systems.

- What were the underlying reasons for the past and existing instances of compliance and non-compliance (with the organizational arrangements and management systems)? (Why were/are things done as they were/are?)
- Are those reasons still valid, are they now superseded by events or developments?
  What aspects are extinct?
  What aspects are new?
  What are the emerging and upcoming aspects?
  What is the impact of those emerging, upcoming and new aspects?
- What effect will they have on the processes and systems?
  Which processes and systems will still be needed?
  Which processes and systems will no longer be needed?
  Which processes and systems require change?
  What is the nature of the changes required?

Step 4: Decide the efficacy of the organizational arrangements and management systems.

- Will the organization and systems be as effective as they need to be? If not, why not?

Step 6: Assess the auditee's performance monitoring methods?

- What were the underlying reasons/data input for selecting the past and existing measurements to be made and methods to be used?
- Are those reasons/data still valid, are they now superseded by events or developments?
  What aspects are extinct?
  What aspects are new?
  What are the emerging and upcoming aspects?
  What is the impact of those emerging, upcoming and new aspects?

495

♦ What effect will they have on the performance measurements and
methods of monitoring required?
Which of the existing measurements methods will still
be needed?
Which of the existing measurements and methods will no
longer be needed?
Which of the existing measurements and methods
will require change?
What is the nature of the changes that will be required?
What new measurements and methods will be required?

Can more be done with less?

This has been a theme of business improvement and increasing efficiency for
centuries. It has been the stuff of scientific management, operations research,
technological advances, innovations, inventions. It feeds the enormous
business consulting, education and conference industries. It will remain so.

"Less is more", runs an old saying. Less time needed to develop products,
bring them to market and serve customers; lower expenditure in executing
one's business; lower levels of manpower to perform needed tasks; lower
amounts of materials to make physical goods; lower amounts of energy to
perform particular processes and so on. All these reduce costs provided they
represent savings in avoidable costs, not a cut into unavoidable costs, into
corporate muscle.

The auditor will constantly examine whether all the auditee's resources and
assets can be used more effectively. Many candidates for examination have
been presented, throughout both parts of this book, particular examples
being:

♦ The auditee' organization, described in Part 1 Chapter 3.
♦ The task elements, described in Part 1 Chapter 4.
♦ Management systems, described in Part 1 Chapter 6.
♦ Operational problems and their real causes, described in Part 1
Chapter 18.

Other things to consider

In the light of the past decisions, their bases and present and future situations
facing the business, the auditor will consider the following during the seven
step method.

Step 1: Analyze the auditee's organization.

♦ Are all of the processes really needed? Which ones could be eliminated? Which ones add value to the business, which ones do not? Could other processes be amended so as to eliminate the need for a particular process?
♦ Can the organization be flattened and the hierarchic layers reduced?
♦ Do the existing levels of hierarchy cause delays in doing the work?
♦ Would empowerment help reduce or eliminate the delays?
♦ Would an alternative team structure be of benefit?
♦ Are the processes in each part of the hierarchy grouped together to the best advantage?
♦ What changes in responsibility, authority and reporting levels for the processes would reduce resources (time, budget and manpower) required.
♦ Which processes could be outsourced to improve results?
♦ Which processes should be relocated to other geographic locations?
♦ How could new technology improve the existing organizational arrangements?

Step 2: Analyze the auditee's management systems.

♦ Which of the management systems could be eliminated? Which management systems add value to the business, which ones do not? Could other management systems be amended so as to eliminate the need for a particular management system?
♦ Are the systems one-dimensional? Which systems could be redesigned to become two-dimensional?
♦ Where is the waiting time between consecutive processes? How can it be reduced or eliminated?
♦ What aspects of the system's design cause delays in processing the work?
♦ How could new technology be applied to the constituent processes so as to improve the performance of the management systems?
♦ What avoidable effort does the system impose onto the constituent processes?
♦ What extra and avoidable processes does the system itself create?

The auditor will also investigate the business performance of the systems, as described later in this chapter.

Appraising the nature of the costs

Value-added audits look for avoidable costs. They challenge what are regarded as unavoidable costs to determine whether they really are unavoidable, and can remain classified as such, or the proportion of them that should be reclassified as avoidable. Once identified, eliminating that proportion becomes a project with a measurable goal. When the goal has been achieved, the firm can legitimately claim to have realized a quantified improvement. The problem with many improvement claims is their unquantified and unmeasured basis - they tend to be of a subjective nature.

> A speaker at a 1997 ASQC section meeting stated that he considers an increasing or large number of non-conformities as a *"healthy"* thing and as evidence that his company is continuously improving. His statement represents bold assumptions that the non-conformities are not of a repetitive nature, that they contain prescriptions for curing their real root cause and the cost savings can be quantified. In response to questions from the attending audience the gentleman confirmed his company as being a tier one American automotive supplier registered as meeting QS 9000 requirements, but was unable to quantify the improvements obtained. He declined to name the company's registrar *"in public"*.

Yesterday's unavoidable costs become today's avoidable ones.

Examples of changes that have caused the old to give way to the new include the following, and the reader can probably add many more to the list:

♦ As service industries grow, traditional vertical integration gives way to horizontal integration, to outsourcing and partnerships in procurement. Failure to take advantage of the services available from outside the firm causes an avoidable cost.

♦ Just-in-time material management reduces inventory and associated costs of storage, insurance, handling, waste and damage. Failure to implement the concept creates an avoidable cost.

♦ Two dimensional systems reduce overall process time. Staying with one-dimensional systems creates avoidable costs.

♦ Employee empowerment and team building reduce managerial and supervision time, speed up decision making and help flatten the hierarchy by eliminating the number of superfluous intermediaries retained on staff.

♦ Ships are welded not riveted. Welding is cheaper, more flexible. The difference in cost between welding and riveting is avoidable for those who retained old methods: none have.

♦   Plastics replace metal fabricated components. Using traditional materials with their limitations can represent an avoidable cost.

♦   Large volume production of printed circuit boards is executed nowadays by surface mount technology not by hand soldering or flow soldering as was common in past years. It is a more flexible manner of production at lower overall cost. The cost difference between the old methods and the new is avoidable. The flexibility of set up increases the avoidable costs of not using this technology.

♦   The application of computer technology enables control of new types of equipment and production thereby making possible batches sizes of single units. The savings accrued through lower levels of material handling, storage, batch processing time *et al* are avoidable costs for those yet to implement the technology.

♦   Mundane activities can be performed by robots and automated equipment. The manpower cost savings possible are avoidable costs for those performing activities the old way.

♦   Desk top computers have greatly simplified records keeping and retrieval possibilities. Hard copy production and transmission costs are avoidable costs. The cost of their slow speed of distribution can be quantified; the benefits obtained form the speed difference between old and new is an avoidable cost for those sticking with the old ways.

♦   E-mail, intranets and the Internet make possible a reduction in the cost of hard copy document handling, distribution, delivery, filing and retrieval. They also reduce the possibility of people repeatedly creating information and data already available and they provide users with rapid access to useful banks of knowledge. There are now avoidable costs for firms failing to introduce these facilities.

♦   Modems, cellular telephones and laptop PC's enable faster serving of customer orders from remote locations. The lower efficiency experienced by not using these facilities represents an avoidable cost.

♦   Telex communications are replaced by telefax which is in turn replaced by E-mail and the Internet. (As examples: increasing numbers of stockbrokers advertise lower order handling fees for customers using electronic order placement systems such as E-mail or Internet; the number of teleworkers is increasing, reducing the cost of maintaining corporate office facilities.)

♦   Video conferences become cheaper and quicker than business air travel to fixed location meetings. Paging machines enable staff to be located and communicated with faster and more conveniently.

♦   ATM machines and on-line banking *via* the Internet reduce traditional bank telling costs and remove geographic barriers for customers wanting access to their own cash 168 hours per week.

♦ Incoming inspection is being eliminated as process quality controls become more reliable. Conventional inspection techniques present an avoidable cost to those retaining them.

♦ Three sigma SPC is giving way to six sigma. The savings realized by companies improving their process controls beyond traditional three sigma levels cause avoidable costs for those who do not.

♦ Emerging markets and developing countries (including designated enterprise zones, green field and brown field sites) can offer attractive cost advantages over existing locations used by the firm.

If many of the foregoing derive from applications of new technology, it was ever thus. Water power, the wheel and the cart, steam power, electric motors, telephones, materials technology and all forms of the application of science have been at the root of advance. Organizational structures and their constituent processes have always been devised to reap their benefits. When knowledge advances, processes must change or disappear to accommodate the new, old structures have to change, people within them have to change,. Human tragedy cannot be ruled out. Downsizing or redundancy may be required to pare off what has become excess corporate fat.

Cutting fat, not muscle

The effects of *"downsizing"* and *"re-engineering"* were described in Part 1, Chapter 3. While the auditor should, rightly, identify areas of opportunity for manpower savings, care must be taken to ensure cuts are made to fat, not to muscle. Healthy bodies do need a small amount of fat as an energy reserve.

Over zealous downsizing efforts of the 1980's and 1990's produced spectacular savings that became reflected in the stock price of many companies. Indeed the denizens of Wall Street seemed to approve of the methods which undoubtedly made their contribution to the extended bull run of the 1990's. But, as economic activity picked up some firms experienced difficulty in quickly responding to improving demand levels: they had insufficient reserves to take advantage of the opportunities offered by potential customers. Upsizing and rehiring began. Each company must make its own comparison of the costs incurred in first laying off staff, then rehiring and retraining, of lost trading opportunity as business activity accelerates again and of damage to morale and trust *versus* those incurred by the retention of some fat. It is a difficult calculation, but it is a necessary one.

Economizers and services

And yet, there are situations where some additional expenditure provides gains far in excess of its cost.

> Fossil fuel boiler plants create steam by burning combustible materials. The gases of combustion are lost after they are exhausted through a smoke stack, and they contain substantial amounts of heat energy. Some, but not all, of that waste heat can be recovered and put to good use by fitting a heat exchanger immediately before the smoke stack. As the combustion gases (smoke) pass through this heat exchanger they heat up cold water pumped through tubes fitted within it. This device is called an *"economizer"* for it improves the efficiency of the entire boiler plant making it more economic to run.

> The industrial revolution advanced greatly after James Watt (an alumni of the Royal College of Science and Technology in Glasgow, now known as the University of Strathclyde) realized that existing power plant (pumping engines being the largest application at the time) was inefficient and by adding a piece of equipment (the separate condenser) more useful work could be obtained from the overall plant. That discovery caused a great leap forward as steam engines fitted with the separate condensers made possible mass manufactured goods, locomotives, overseas travel unencumbered by the vagaries of the wind.

Embarking on "slash and burn" programmes is ill advised. One might believe savings can be made in equipment maintenance costs by removing the boiler's economizer or the separate condenser, but to do so would cause increased costs. Economizers and separate condensers should rightly be regarded as unavoidable, they provide a value-adding service. Organizations, too, need their forms of them. There are occasions when the auditor needs to recommend additional expenditure, personnel or equipment - investment - to reduce avoidable costs, to recover waste. The auditor has to fully appreciate the function and contribution of the process being audited. It is wrong to consider it as being an avoidable cost when it is demonstrably improving the business results. The key word, though, is *"demonstrably"*. It is only by examining objective evidence and performing a cost-benefit analysis that the auditor will be able to decide the worth of a process. There may, of course, be opportunities to avoid part of the costs within the process: part of the process may create avoidable costs.

Upsizing

The auditor should weigh the evidence and be prepared to recommend some *"upsizing"* if it will prevent avoidable costs. A cost-benefit analysis is required to make the final decision. Looking carefully at the objective evidence produced by the auditee's performance monitoring systems, as is done during step 6 of the seven step method, described in Part 1 Chapter 11, can provide useful guidance. If they portray a growth in problems and avoidable costs since the start of the downsizing process/re-engineering efforts, the magnitude of the increase needs to be drawn to the attention of the auditee's management. This advice, though, presumes the auditee has an effective performance monitoring system collecting the pertinent type of data listed below. If these are not available, the auditee has greater problems as it is operating as if blind. The full magnitude of the avoidable costs may not manifest itself until some time after the downsizing efforts were put into force. Indicators can include the following and are symptomatic of incorrect (or now invalid) past decisions:

♦   Increased defects and product failures.
♦   Increased warranty costs and customer complaints and returns.
♦   In a steady or growing market, a slow down in or cessation of the previous growth rate of :
        Sales enquiries;
        Customer orders.
♦   Gradually reducing numbers of sales enquiries received from a steady or growing market.
♦   Gradually increasing numbers of unsuccessful sales quotations in a steady or growing market.
♦   Gradual loss of market share.
♦   Loss of valuable employees; increases in rates of staff turnover.
♦   Increased rates of absenteeism due to sickness.
♦   Increased housekeeping problems.
♦   Increased equipment downtime and outages.
♦   Increased problems with suppliers and procured supplies.

Staff utilization and turnover

It has always seemed strange that companies who proclaim *"Our people are our finest assets"* so frequently under-utilize those assets. People need to be given every opportunity to fully display their talents. In order to grow they must given the authority to take decisions without constant recourse to so-called superiors. Like an unused or unmaintained machine, people can "rust". One cannot comprehend why hard-nosed business managers will demand the highest utilization of the company's fixed assets but not of their "finest assets". Just because people are kept busy, this does not mean their capabilities are being utilized to the full. Under-utilization of staff capabilities is one of the most serious avoidable costs a company can incur.

Part 1 Chapter 3 describes the importance of balancing responsibility and authority so that staff feel valued and trusted. Empowerment has become a popular theme of countless publications and conferences. It works. When it does not feature as a matter of corporate policy and culture, better qualified and able people, who want to move ahead with their careers, become frustrated and leave for pastures new where they feel appreciated and can grow.

This loss creates avoidable costs of the greatest magnitude. The costs of recruitment and hiring are sometimes estimated to be at least one half of the employee's annual salary. High staff turnover is not only an indicator of avoidable costs incurred, they point to avoidable costs of the future incurred by:

♦ The need to train replacement staff in the basics of the company's business and the job knowledge they need.
♦ The loss of knowledge investment possessed by former staff.
♦ The reputation earned by the company as a place to avoid if one wants to be respected professionally and advance one's career and earnings. (This might also lead to a requirement to offer more costly inducements to attract replacement staff.)
♦ The rate of progress in continuous improvement of products, processes and systems is reduced, stopped or, even, reversed.

Neither continuous improvement nor value-added auditing can reach their full potential benefits without motivated staff. Motivation can be improved by getting them involved in the efforts so as to increase their sense of achievement. This is only possible, however, when management acts on the opportunities presented to them by the staff. Auditors can help by involving the auditee in constructive dialogue and pursuing with management the agreements reached. By its attitude and leadership qualities, management, though, ultimately determines the fate of their efforts. It will get the both staff it deserves and the consequential results.

Auditing the business performance of systems.

Systems are not set up for the benefit of auditors. They are intended to benefit the business and must be assessed with this goal in mind. Part 1

Chapter 3 advised that the system will be of quality if it causes an end task (goal) to be performed completely, correctly, economically and on time. If a system has been poorly set up it matters not if the features so beloved by the quality profession are present - the system will not cause a smooth flow of work at a definable rate of execution at minimum avoidable cost. Whereas most auditors will look for waste reduction, scrap, prevention of defects and the like at individual workplaces (processes/ tasks) they seldom consider the avoidance of waste when viewing the overall system (indeed, if they view the overall system at all). This failure is one of the most glaring weaknesses in the "service" offered by financial auditors and quality systems auditors alike.

System efficacy is not limited to ensuring the quality of products made within it. The quantity of work that can be processed through a system and the operational cost of so doing are essential ingredients too. They are, of course, interrelated. The auditor must be concerned with reducing or eliminating avoidable costs regardless of their origin and many systems incur such costs without their owners realizing the fact.

The role of auditors

With few exceptions, the so-called quality systems auditors do not audit the performance of the system. They restrict their activities to verifying features within the system at individual processes, (calibrated gauges, editions of documents, personnel qualifications etc.), seldom, if ever, do they look at what the system actually achieves for business performance: profit or loss. Nor do they consider the avoidable costs engineered into the systems' arrangement. One cannot truthfully claim to have assessed the quality of a system unless its functional performance and business capability have been assessed.

Traditional financial auditors, too, concentrate more on verifying correctness of figures in terms of simple profit and loss, accountability for expenditures, audit trails between vouchers and matters of that ilk. They rarely question the way systems have been set up and are managed in terms of their performance results. Nor do they question whether the system serves its fundamental purpose so long as the numbers are right and there is no evidence leading them to suspect dishonesty.

The system is set up to serve the revenue needs of the business, just as is a product. In fact the system is itself a product, designed by the firm to serve its needs. The firm is the system's customer. Systems require the expenditure of money and other resources in order to operate. Whether or not that expenditure is optimized as well as possible is an essential question to be addressed by management and it is one for which the management auditor can provide valuable input, answers, improvement options and solutions.

Assessing the efficacy of the system is the role of the auditor, but so too is assessing the efficiency with which the system serves the business and the extent to which it incurs avoidable costs in the doing.

Interface systems capability

Business systems are concatenations of processes, chains which are only as strong as their weakest links (processes/tasks). Generally, the systems interlink, but the overall operating system will still only be as strong as the weakest process in it.

If a system can only perform as well as its weakest link, it follows that any link that is served by another system can only perform as well as the system it is served by. Thus, a primary system can only perform as well as the weakest secondary system serving it. A secondary system can only perform as well as the weakest tertiary system serving it. Put together, this means a primary system can only perform as well as the weakest tertiary system it is related to.

If a primary system has to meet a particular performance level, the secondary systems and tertiary systems must also be set up consistent with that performance level. (Primary, secondary and tertiary systems are described in Part 1 Chapter 6.)

The auditor must ascertain the end level of performance (output) required of the primary system in order to determine the demands that other interfacing systems must satisfy. This output dictates the performance of the various processes (outputs) within any of the systems. But, it is equally important to verify the demands made of the system. If they are greater than the least capable of the processes within the network of interfacing systems, problems will inevitably arise. As an example, accepting too many customer orders than the company's system can handle will cause the system to become overloaded. This common sense fact must be borne in mind.

What is the avoidable cost?

Traditional accounting methods consider in isolation the *costs* of a process, not the *value* of its work. The management auditor cannot afford to work as accountants do. If a process is halted for an hour, the loss incurred is not that of the process, it is that of lost production from the system the process serves.

Thus, although the process might cost, say, $100 per hour for the machine, operator, space, power, heating, maintenance etc., its value would be far higher. If the product sells for, say, $50.00 each and the process is supposed to make 500 per hour, the loss is $25000 per hour. Those in the oil industry know this well. They will willingly hire a helicopter costing several hundred dollars an hour to transport a spare part to an offshore production platform that needs it in order to return to operation. The value of the part greatly outweighs its intrinsic cost of purchase and delivery: its value is equal to the avoidable costs incurred in a complete shutdown.

The impact on audit time budgets

When discussing the audit time budget during my audit seminars, the delegates have always been made aware that the formula described in Part 1 Chapter 9 contains a "factor" which is determined by the objective of the audit. The factor is never less than "1". For an audit of a firm whose customer wishes to place it on a just-in-time (JIT) delivery basis, the factor is always "2" at least. The reason is that the supplier's systems must be fully assessed for their efficacy. Merely investigating such features as revision numbers on documents, the existence of written instructions or procedures, calibration tags and the like, so extant in the typical ISO 9000 audit, is most insufficient. If the information obtained by the audit is inadequate, there is the real risk the supplier may not be able to deliver JIT in practice with the consequence that the customer's entire production line will come to a halt. That is expensive, possibly disastrous for a customer operating on slim margins in a highly competitive field. For those organizations wanting to move to "real time" supply, the goal would be totally unachievable.

The auditor needs time to assess not only the features within a system and the control of the constituent processes themselves, but also the overall efficacy of the system. How well will the system achieve completeness, correctness, timeliness and economy of performance? What are the true capabilities of the system, not only in terms of product quality, but also business efficiency? A system that is highly productive yet managed in such a way as to produce volumes of unsold inventory cannot be described as helping the business to be efficient. Such a system increases avoidable costs inherent in the cost of inventory. Nor can one regard a system that operates in a stop-start fashion, pulsatingly producing variable quantities of product at spurious intervals, as being helpful. These tend to create unreliable delivery times, late deliveries and frustrated customers who eventually take their business elsewhere. Poorly conceived and executed systems detract from business results as much as (and often more than) the costs of defective products. Waste, deriving from whatever source, demonstrates a system is not of quality.

506

There are trade-offs between operating costs, inventory and the firm's investment in its assets. The assets include not only fixed assets, such as capital equipment, plant and facilities, but also its knowledge base and work in progress. The balance between these has to be optimized by the auditee. The auditor needs to investigate this.

The system's use of time

Time is money. So goes the well known saying. Considerable effort has been expended during the twentieth century to determine how time can be put to best use, how to detect and prevent the wastage of time, how to plan operations to be as time efficient as possible. The work of Frank and Lillian Gilbreth is well documented. The former spent his life devoted to eliminating needless work activities so that work could be performed more expeditiously. His fascination with work spilled over into his private life and the way his own household was organized, as portrayed in the film, *"Cheaper by the dozen"*, made some years ago. Time and motion study became a matter of concern for most managements, although the devious methods they used, so consistent with old-fashioned autocratic management styles, caused much industrial disharmony. One recalls the entertaining film *"I'm all right Jack"* in which the time and motion snoop is constantly confounded over productivity issues until a naive young Stanley Windrush, played by Ian Carmichael, enters the firm, causes chaos and a strike led by a pseudo-intellectual communist shop steward, played by the late and incomparable Peter Sellers.

For all their misapplication, some of the old time and motion precepts and tools can be of use, notably flow charting the sequence of activities and indicating all movements of materials, productive activities, idle times, operational set up times, handling activities and so on. It is not especially necessary to sit with a stop watch, as did the snoop in *I'm all right Jack*, there are other indicators of poor material flow, as discussed later.

Chapter 6 in Part 1 of this book mentioned some problems that can be found with the way systems have been constructed. One-dimensional systems take more time to complete than two-dimensional ones. Needless processes extend the overall performance time and deserve to be eliminated by some reorganization. The classic example of this in recent years, has been reducing the amount of receiving, in-line and end-of-line verification being performed, this being made possible through improved process control, amongst other things. Idle time, queuing time and the like all add needlessly to the overall system execution time - and avoidable cost. They tend to increase inventory - and its avoidable cost. They also make the product more susceptible to damage and deterioration - and, hence, that type of avoidable cost - unless extra protection is provided during those periods; that, too, adds to the avoidable costs. System time elements are discussed below.

Some indicators of system problems

Item - quantity :

The quantity of items present at a process workplace can indicate a problem somewhere in the system, upstream or downstream. When a process has a shortage of items for processing it can mean the upstream processes in the system are not issuing their products in the time frame required. When a process has an excess of items it might herald an inadequate processing capacity for them either at the immediate process or elsewhere further downstream in the system (the former is more likely) or that management has decided to produce an excess because of expected process waste so that the correct quantity will finally be achieved. This latter can be rather hit or miss and shows a need for improved process control.

The quantity of items also gives evidence of how well inventory is controlled. Excessive inventory is symptomatic of poor system control and management decision making.

Equipment - capability:

Interfacing equipment must operate at compatible speeds otherwise the recipient will have to speed up or slow down. If too much is being produced, a back-up of product can be seen. If too little is being produced, some spare capacity is apparent. This could indicate the equipment is operating at lower efficiency than otherwise possible, and hence at higher cost. But it might also be necessary in order to optimize the overall system in light of existing capacities. An imbalance in interfacing equipment capabilities can tend to cause stops and starts in production (i.e. the system's operation) and waves in the rate at which things are processed.

Waves:

Every road user has experienced waves in traffic flow as vehicles speed up, slow down, speed up, slow down with no apparent cause. On encountering these waves, one often expects an incident as being the cause of a slow down only to discover no visible reason, accident, road works, or slow moving vehicle when the traffic accelerates. Traffic waves can be seen from the sky, having been filmed from helicopters, and their phenomenon is being studied.

Some have said, rightly, that slowing down the traffic a little will enable more vehicles to use a given stretch of road. This can work to good effect in business systems too.

Road users are also familiar with badly designed road systems: the M25 motorway (freeway) encircling London became known as Europe's largest car parking lot because of its lengthy queues and hold ups; the autobahn system around Dusseldorf and Dortmund is notorious for hold-ups during rush hours; many American cities have helicopters as "eyes in the sky" at busy times. Poor road designs are brought about as a result of inadequate thinking and calculations. These systems need a larger processing capacity for the desired flow. (Since the first British motorway, the M1, was built in the late 1950's, the mantra seems to have been: *"three lanes maketh a motorway. If a road hath three lanes, a motorway it doth be"*. This foolishness prevailed for decades in spite of the exploding growth in registered road vehicles and the evidence of everyday experience showing that four or five lanes in each direction were necessary in certain stretches.)

Businesses, too, experience similar problems of capacity. Their management systems must be designed so as to prevent congestion and with a capacity for dealing with the throughput of work expected of them.

Sometimes, though, it is a slower moving vehicle holds up the traffic, a queue forming behind as each motorist waits in turn to overtake it. At other times there are too many roads feeding into a single one that cannot process all the vehicles arriving in a given period. An example of that can be seen in Surrey, England, where the A3 highway slims down from three lanes to two in the approach to Surbiton just as other roads join it. I have known the resultant queue to stretch back almost to the M25 some miles away in a southwards direction. Traffic feeding problems can be overcome by controlling the number of vehicles joining a road at a time. Many American freeways have traffic lights at their entrances to control the feed of incoming cars. The lights are operated by computers receiving data about the oncoming traffic stream and spaces between its vehicles on the freeway. When sufficient space becomes available between vehicles, the traffic lights are turned to green allowing for a computer calculated period of time so that a metered number of vehicles can join the freeway.

Similar mechanisms are available to the firm. Carefully controlling the rate at which new orders are accepted, material is released for processing, and information is distributed for use are similar methods can assist a system to process more orders overall, and with greater efficacy, and congestion can be avoided.

To return to the traffic analogy, newer traffic control innovations include the use of in-car equipment that advises the driver of congestion ahead and offers alternative routes. Information technology makes this available to the driver. Within the firm, too, information technology can distribute similar information to all the various processes within a system advising of incipient orders, active constraints on progress, alternative routes (such as outsourcing) to overcome temporary difficulties.

Within the firm, waves can be detected by looking at those figures that are concerned with the output of the various processes and the system overall. They should be coupled with details of working hours. Pulsations suggest (but do not prove) the existence of problems. The auditor must also look at the normal trading patterns the business experiences. Many businesses experience their seasonal surges and natural peak times: they might occur during lunch hours, at Christmas, at Thanksgiving, at Easter, approaching Valentines day, or during evenings and place increased demands on the system. Their associated demand levels should be extracted from the figures and considered as normal. As pointed out previously, the system should be set up to accommodate the actual trading pattern, and the auditor should verify this has been done. Accordingly, the auditor needs to ascertain:

♦ What is the normal trading pattern? When and where do the peaks and troughs occur?
♦ How valid is the pattern that is actually being used? When was the normal trading pattern last determined?
♦ Is the system designed on the basis of the normal trading pattern?

Whereas some processes operate at a fixed predetermined speed, others fluctuate causing ripples and waves in their output to the system. These waves are not ideal but almost inevitably occur. The auditee needs to plan its operation accordingly ensuring the capabilities of the affected processes can smooth out the waves so that as steady a stream as possible occurs. Stop-start histories indicate problems for the auditor to investigate. The auditor needs to identify the weak links and determine what can be done to improve the overall performance of the system. This begins by discovering:

♦ Whether or not the auditee knows the actual capabilities of each process within the system?
♦ If the system is planned according to the actual process capabilities?
♦ Which processes constrain (limit) the system capability?
♦ Whether or not the other processes' outputs are controlled according to the constraints?

The use of flags:

Systems that result in production waves are unreliable and cause customer dissatisfaction with delivery performance. Some firms try to remedy the situation by instituting "flag" indicators. These takes the form of stickers of various colours and shapes that are attached to work in progress. The colour or shape indicates the urgency of the work and is supposed to draw people's attention to priorities. (Some firms use information folders of different colours.) While being well intentioned they are often abused and also cause further problems.

> A medium size company introduced a priority indicator system. The staff were supposed to always give priority to matters bearing a red star. (The firm got the idea of using a red star from the express parcels service, formally owned by British Rail, bearing that name.) The staff did as they were told. Unfortunately other work tended to back-up as more and more work appeared bearing red stars. Eventually the backed-up "non-priority" work became so delayed, it too was given red stars. Few orders ended up without red stars. The firm failed to determine the root cause of the hold-ups and waves. Inventory piled high everywhere, nothing moved as organizational constipation developed. Orders and customers were lost, inventory costs grew, incoming revenue depleted. Work relations deteriorated as staff became frustrated by constantly changing priorities, endless panics, excessive overtime and weekend working, none of which seemed to produce discernible progress and a sense of achievement.

System time elements

To perform a process, two key elements of time expenditure are incurred:

♦ The time to prepare the process, to set up the equipment. (Set up time).
♦ The time to perform the process. (Process time).

But, other elements of time are also expended as a result of the process being an integral part of a system that provides it with inputs. These are:

♦ Time spent waiting for other inputs needed by the process. (Idle time).
♦ Time spent by the inputs awaiting their turn for processing. (Queuing time).

Expenditure of time represents expenditure of money. Needless expenditure of time is an avoidable cost and the auditee's systems cannot be viewed as being "of quality" if they incur such costs. The auditor should, therefore, carefully examine the underlying reasons for expenditure of time and determine opportunities for improvement. Each of the foregoing four time elements are candidates for investigation and possible improvement. They are constituent elements of the system's overall business performance. Put simply, each one affects the overall time to process a customer's order: the lower each one is, the faster an order can be handled thereby bringing greater cash flow and profit for the firm. By lowering overall time it becomes easier to meet target sales prices set by customers, or to reduce them and improve market share. Time management is a major battleground for business.

Lack of time is one of the six real causes of business problems, described in Part 1 Chapter 18. When these four time elements are not managed effectively the risk is twofold. Firstly, business cash flow is impaired, as described above. Secondly, work gets rushed in order to "make up for lost time" or to meet schedule deadlines and quality becomes impaired; this too increases avoidable costs and reduces business performance.

Set-up time

The importance and effect of set up time depends on the criticality of the process concerned. Those processes that determine the minimum completion time of an order are said to lie on the *"critical path"*. When a process is on the critical path for handling a customer's order, any increase in set up time will delay delivery, reduce the number of orders handled in a given period of time and, therefore, reduce cash flow too. When the process is not on the critical path, often referred to as being on a *"sub-critical path"*, set up time becomes crucial if it takes so long that it consumes the spare or *"float"* time available: in this unfortunate circumstance, the process can become "critical". Set up time can overlap with idle time, described below and not cause a problem if neither one of these time elements are part of the critical path.

The act of setting up is in itself a process which requires a combination of the task elements, described in Part 1 Chapter 4. In order to set up for the actual process the person responsible will need all those applicable task elements (equipment, information, services etc.), and sub-elements (competence, training, capable equipment, correct content of information etc.). Equipment design and personnel competence and training are especially important matters that can affect the setting up time.

The auditor should :

♦ Determine which processes lie on the critical path and which do not.
♦ Determine how the auditee decides and monitors the critical path processes within the system concerned.
♦ Determine how the auditee decides and monitors set up time for each process.
♦ Determine which of the task elements and sub-elements apply.
♦ Determine their effect on set up time.
♦ Determine how the auditee assesses their effect on set up time.
♦ Determine how the auditee assesses potential improvements and manages projects to secure them.

Idle time

The importance and effect of idle time also depends on the criticality of the process concerned. Just as is the case for set up time, above, if the process is on the critical path for handling a customer's order, any increase in length ultimately incurs avoidable costs and reduces the business performance. When the process is not on the sub-critical path, it only becomes crucial if it, too, consumes the float time available, thereby making the process critical. However, some idle time may be desirable in order to prevent the process from producing inventory that the remaining processes within the system cannot expeditiously deal with. In this latter case, the system's performance may have been optimized.

Idle time can be created by any of the task elements, being input to a process, not arriving when required. Accordingly, the root cause of idle time can vary. On one occasion it may be a lack of resources causing essential information to be delayed, on another it could be a lack of organization causing some incoming items to be delayed. The auditor should :

♦ Determine the inputs required for the process and ascertain the system responsible for supplying them to the process.
♦ Determine their effect on idle time.
♦ Determine how the auditee assesses their effect on idle time.
♦ Determine if the process lies on the critical path or not.
♦ Determine which of the inputs are also on the critical path and which are not.
♦ Determine how the auditee monitors the delivery of inputs for the process.
♦ Determine how the auditee decides and monitors idle time for the process and for optimizing the performance of the system within

which the process is a constituent.
♦   Determine how the auditee assesses potential improvements and manages projects to secure them.

Process time

The time taken to actually perform a process is, of course, dependent on the task elements and sub-elements that apply to it. Equipment capability, condition and reliability, personnel training, motivation, attributes and competence, and the quantity and capability of items to be processed in particular all affect it greatly. The auditor should :

♦   Determine if the process lies on the critical path or not.
♦   Determine how the auditee decides and monitors process time.
♦   Determine which of the task elements and sub-elements apply.
♦   Determine their effect on process time.
♦   Determine how the auditee assesses their effect on process time.
♦   Determine which of the outputs are on the critical path and which are not.
♦   Determine how the auditee monitors the delivery of outputs for the process.
♦   Determine how the auditee assesses potential improvements and manages projects to secure them.

Queue time

Queuing is accepted by many as an everyday fact of life. Queues become annoying when they seem excessively long and proceed slowly. They develop when:

♦   The customer demand for a service or product is greater than the system's ability to deliver.
♦   The number of items arriving for processing exceeds the capacity of the process concerned.
♦   The number of pieces of equipment awaiting maintenance or calibration exceeds the capabilities of those latter two functions.
♦   Information is awaiting review and action.

A queue is an "inventory" having economic consequences, namely:

♦   They cost money to maintain.
♦   Extra expenditure might be required in order to increase the capacity of a process (or system) in order to reduce or prevent the queue,

514

with the attendant risk that once it has been eliminated the system may lay idle for a while, thereby incurring additional expenditure.

Obviously the queue time and size are affected primarily by two key factors, although there are others which are beyond the scope of this text and are subject of specialists texts on the *"queuing theory"* which the reader may wish to consult:

♦   The quantity of input arriving in a given time to be processed.
♦   The capacity of the workplace to process that quantity of input at the rate of supply.

It makes no sense for upstream processes to deliver their supplies to the process at a rate greater than can be dealt as this only results in an increase in queue time, inventory and avoidable cost. What might be considered an "economic batch quantity" for an upstream process can be uneconomic for the system as a whole. In general, queue time must be eliminated to maximize the performance of the system and the business. (Many firms now realize this and are moving towards processing batch sizes/work volumes of one - single units.) Queuing problems reveal themselves by creating piles of inventory. The auditor should be alert to this and, upon discovering this situation, investigate the relative capacities (capabilities) of interfacing processes within the system that is creating the inventory that has been observed. The auditor should :

♦   Determine how the auditee monitors queue time and the capabilities of interfacing processes within the system concerned.
♦   Determine how the auditee decides on batch sizes/work volumes for each process.
♦   Determine which processes are involved in the system and create the inventory observed.
♦   Determine the effect of each on queue time.
♦   Determine the batch sizes/work volumes for each process that will prevent inventory build-up and queue time in the system. (This will ensure the processes within the system can be balanced with each other.)

Mathematical techniques

The theory of systems design is not new. Mathematical techniques for planning and ensuring optimum performance of systems have existed for decades and been included in the curricula of many university engineering degree courses. Within its School of Engineering, my own *alma mater*, the

University of Strathclyde, included them in its *"Operations Research"* classes more than thirty years ago. Linear programming, queuing theory, decision theory, critical path method, simulation and various other quantitative techniques featured in our studies. Over the years, I have found some of these useful when examining systems and commend them to those wanting to perform a business systems audit in a value-added way. A full discussion of the various techniques is neither possible, nor desirable, in this book and the reader is advised to obtain one of the many excellent texts available in public libraries and bookshops to gain a full appreciation of them. One must stress operations research techniques and concepts apply to all forms of system regardless of economic sector. They are concerned with business operations and few companies would not find them applicable.

Assessing resource utilization

Resources are required for providing the five task elements and their attendant sub-elements (described in Part 1 Chapter 4) as well as to support the management systems. The auditors are, in essence, looking at the waste prevention attitudes and associated management systems of the auditee. Waste can result from any of the following all of which have been discussed previously.

♦ Over complex management systems that waste time, manpower and finance.
♦ Non-conformities derived from any of the six real causes of business problems.
♦ Excessive handling of items
♦ Inadequate quantity control of items.
♦ Superfluous information content or distribution.
♦ Equipment of the wrong capability.
♦ Incorrect decisions.
♦ Obsolete decisions being maintained.
♦ Competence mismatch between personnel assigned to perform a task and the needs of the task itself.
♦ Poor utilization of space.
♦ Failure to modernize or reinvest in equipment of improved efficiency, capability or reliability.
♦ Failure to update attitudes or practices in line with developments.

Several of the foregoing derive from failure to change or from a resolute and irrational defence of the *status quo*.

The audit must check that the auditee has a policy and practice of self help which incorporates a system that defines, allocates and monitors resources and encourages the identification of opportunities for improvement. That system must ensure ongoing and continuous input of new ideas based on technological trends and developments. Of vital importance is the willing support of top management towards beneficial change.

Assessing energy management

Two separate issues must be considered by the auditor the first of these being the selection of the energy source, the second the actual usage of energy. Together they ensure that energy costs are optimized or are wasted.

Energy source selection

The key questions that the auditee must regularly address are as follows:

♦　　　Are we using the right type of energy?
♦　　　Would it be more economic to use a different source such as oil or gas (if, say, electricity is currently being used)?
♦　　　Would it be more economic to alter the work pattern to take advantage of off peak tariffs?
♦　　　If we were to change, what would be the pay back period?
♦　　　Are we too reliant on one type of energy source, a particular supplier, for example?
♦　　　Should we look for an alternative supplier source, perhaps an international one?
♦　　　If we are purchasing our energy from international sources, are we ensuring that our exposure to exchange rate fluctuations is minimized?
♦　　　Do we need an alternative type of energy source to minimize our exposure to risks of strikes, power cuts (which might affect manufacturing processes, computers or telecommunications links)? Should we install our own generators to reduce those risks?
♦　　　Is the energy source we use becoming an increasing liability in terms of its environmental impact and costs of reducing emissions, waste heat? Should we consider alternative sources such as windmills, solar panels?

As all engineers know, energy can be high grade or low grade: high grade energy sources can be completely transformed into other forms of energy, low grade sources cannot and result, therefore, in energy wastage. Electricity, for example, is a high grade source because it is completely converted into other forms of energy at a conversion rate that depends on the equipment efficiency; heat is a low grade source since a portion of it always remains unavailable, thereby constituting a loss. Such are the laws of thermodynamics.

Energy usage

Energy is required to operate equipment, maintain environmental conditions, perform processes, distribute items and information. The auditor will generally have an engineering background because energy balance and optimization form an important part of professional engineering training. Points for consideration are detailed as follows:

♦ The auditee needs to monitor energy usage at all points of his operations. It is also important that process capability together with equipment and workplace layout are carefully considered because they can affect energy consumption dramatically.

♦ The selection of particular equipment should always be based on the efficiency with which it converts energy to serve a useful purpose. Electric lamps, for example, can have greatly different light outputs for a certain energy consumption; electric motors can have different efficiencies over a given power range. The equipment will have been constructed from various materials whose inherent capability may or may not be conducive to energy efficiency. Cases in point might be the characteristics of insulating or conductive property or of reflective ability. When selecting equipment, the auditee should be considering such matters and obtaining suppliers' performance curves and other data.

♦ The process is affected directly by the capability of the items being used and their energy demands. Melting point, viscosity, specific heat, freezing point, hardness and other chemical and physical properties all have their effect on energy consumption. In designing the product, the energy conscious designer should have considered them all for they will constrain the processes required, the energy consumption levels and hence the unit costs, price and profitability. As part of the auditee's design control system, the features should have been analyzed.

♦ When the items or services have been designed, the processes which will be used to furnish them must be determined. The equipment that will be used and the interrelationship of the processes will affect the layout of premises in which particular environmental conditions will need to be maintained. Space and layout affect energy loads directly and the design must have considered this fact.

Thus the auditor will look for an audit trail between what exists and what was designed. Challenging the basic assumptions and the design decisions generally reveals the greatest opportunities for energy savings.

Designing is a decision making process whose product is controlled primarily by the *"person"* and *"information"* task elements. The auditor should verify that the auditee's design control system ensures that the design process is based on complete and correct input information and is executed by designers who are competent, trained etc.. If the design process uses equipment such as computers supported by software, the auditor should investigate computers by considering them to be *"equipment"*, as described in Part 1 Chapter 4 and should consider the software to be *"information"*. Where the software is used or has been developed in-house, the precepts of Chapter 4, in this Part 2, should be considered also.

The usage of energy can be measured and the auditee should be measuring consumption as well as input levels. The difference will represent a loss and reveal the inefficiency: it is thus a measure of the opportunities available. However, it must always be recognized that opportunity can only be realized by energy recovery and/or by initial savings born of improved equipment, processes or the demands made on them. Recovery is limited by the laws of thermodynamics and depends on whether the waste takes the form of high or low grade energy. The usage of energy can be reported in various forms, either descriptive or graphic. One graphic method that has been used for many years is the Sankey diagram (the origin of which has been attributed to Captain Riall Sankey [1]); another is the pie chart. The auditor will check that the auditee has a system for capturing and analyzing data on energy usage. Analysis and graphical presentation of the captured data is a simple matter for those having a personal computer installed with spreadsheet software having graphic display features.

Six real causes:

Wastage of energy is just another example of avoidable costs born of decisions of bad quality. Energy wastage is anathema to an efficient business just as much as scrap or reperformed work. Once again, the six real causes of business problems can have effects on energy efficiency.

♦ Top management needs to support energy conservation programmes both by expressions of encouragement and by direct action in the form of demanding regular energy usage reports and energy audits. It should appoint someone to be responsible for monitoring energy usage and sources who must report back on a regular basis.

♦ Lack of discipline over the use of energy leads to dissipation and waste.

♦ Lack of resources (budget) to obtain energy efficient equipment and practices will, ironically, lead to avoidable costs.

♦ Lack of training in energy conservation and awareness can lead to profligate attitudes caused by ignorance of the importance and cost of energy.

♦ Lack of time devoted to analyzing energy usage and sources means that valuable opportunities will remain hidden.

♦ Lack of organization in estimating, allocating, and monitoring energy leads to hidden costs derived from unknown waste.

Can a CAR be issued?

CARs can only be issued when the auditee has violated some formal requirement or other. As stated in Part 1 Chapter 17, the auditor must justify the issuing of the CAR by citing what aspect of the auditee's activities is at variance with a requirement such as a standard, company policy, customer contract, regulation etc..

Continuous improvement programmes

If continuous improvement is a mandatory requirement for the auditee to execute a CAR will be justified if the evidence shows any of the following:

♦ The auditee has absolutely no programme or policy for pursuing continuous improvement.

♦ The auditee has such a policy or programme but is not implementing it at all.

♦ The auditee is implementing such a policy or programme but has realized absolutely no improvement whatsoever.

Even the commonplace nonconformity procedure and its attendant forms show evidence of an attempt at continuous improvement, although the magnitude of accrued benefits is seldom apparent. So too do audit programmes, training programmes, introduction of statistical process control programmes, research and development, product upgrades and the like show attempts at the same.

It is unlikely that the auditor will ever encounter a company that has no continuous improvement efforts anywhere within it. Individual processes, though, might present a different situation. The auditor must proceed with caution before stating categorically the auditee is not pursuing continuing improvement.

Matters might seem to be clearer if a requirement for continuous improvement is coupled with a specified level of achievement, say to achieve six sigma quality within a defined period of time, or to reduce process time by 15% per annum in perpetuity. When this situation presents itself, the auditor must look for measurable efforts and quantified data as wells as examining the detail within the auditee's programme for reaching the specified goals. This takes time as the veracity of the objective evidence must be affirmed.

Value-added auditing

The auditor cannot and should not issue a CAR covering suggestions for improvement and opportunities for avoidable cost reduction. This is discussed further in Part 1 Chapter 17. The auditee has not violated anything, merely has not identified improvement opportunities.

If previously identified opportunities have been made the subject of a mandatory improvement project and the auditor is assessing its progress, a CAR might be justified. But, in this latter case, the auditor is undertaking a conventional compliance audit and is charged with identifying areas of non-compliance with established requirements, not with unearthing hitherto unknown possibilities. It is most unreasonable to expect an auditee to comply with the unknown!

Exit interviews

These can proceed as described in Part 1 Chapter 19. Attendance may need to be restricted depending on the level of confidentiality the audit client requires but ordinary level auditees must not be unduly prevented from attending if a failure to invite them would be counter-productive to morale.

The exit interview will be prepared in the usual way, but it generally takes more time to fully present the audit team's findings and recommendations than would be the case for an audit whose objective is to ascertain compliance with, say, ISO 9000. The audit team should expect and accommodate more questions from the auditee and the audit client.

Audit reports

The type of layout shown in Part 1 Chapter 20 can still be used as a template audit report. The general information sections, such as auditee location, audit dates, audit team members and so on are still required. The results section and position statement will be different, though.

The results should state the following:

♦ A comparison of the situation existing with the upcoming or the new.
♦ A summary of the risk analysis performed by the auditor, particularly:
the risks of continuing as at present,
the risks of the changes the auditor proposes.
♦ The nature of the opportunity identified by the auditor and
the impact of the new factors on policy, processes, organization, management systems, people and resources (both time and budget)
♦ Estimates of:
the avoidable costs to be incurred in continuing as at present,
the costs associated with implementing the auditor's proposals
(i.e. the investment required) and, hence,
the cost-benefit of those proposals.
♦ Estimates of:
the time frames involved for implementing the changes proposed,
the time frames involved for obtaining a payback on the investment required, and
the urgency of the situation.

A position statement is not really necessary, but a summary of the report along the lines of the following is generally appropriate:

Based on the objective evidence presented by the auditee to the audit team it is considered there are (or are not) opportunities for realizing quantifiable reductions in avoidable costs through changes in [the organization/ processes, management systems, plant or equipment, the introduction of new technology, using alternative materials, outsourcing....etc.]. The risk of not implementing change in the areas suggested is [.....]. The changes are required within a time frame of [....]. Detailed results and analyses are presented herein.

When audit time has been inadequate

Inadequate audit time could prevent the audit team from completing a thorough cost benefit analysis. In this situation it is necessary to indicate the opportunities that are available and recommend a thorough analysis of the potential benefits that a change might deliver. This must not be regarded by the audit team as a prescription for offering generalities, motherhood advice, as described below. A description of the past rationale for present courses of action and a comparison of it with the new or emerging situation together with the options to be considered when the full analysis is done, should be presented. Apparent risks and the urgency of need should also be indicated.

Distribution and confidentiality

These matters will depend, as ever was the case, on the instructions issued by the audit client to the lead auditor which the former must agree first of all with the auditee.

Follow-up action

The need for this depends on the audit client's policy. If continuous improvement is an explicit operational requirement, verification of improvement recommendations as agreed with the auditee may be necessary. Follow-up can be conducted as described in Part 1 Chapter 21.

Internal, external, extrinsic and self audits as part of the effort.

All types of audit have a contribution to make to the overall value-adding effort. The amount of each depends on the audit team's knowledge and experience as well as the scope of its work. Self audits performed by empowered staff imbued with the concepts of avoidable and unavoidable costs will be central to achieving continuous improvement.

From wherever the auditor comes, be it the workforce, process teams, customers or consultants all can contribute to some degree: some will be able to contribute more than others, but all offerings will add up. What is important, though, is for every one to act in a way that helps the auditee, this is one of my Golden Rules described in Part 1 Appendix 1.

Sharing the gains

Profits can only benefit when costs are reduced. So too should prices.

Chrysler, the American automobile maker, requires its suppliers to continuously improve and to share with them the benefits they accrue.

Passing along savings to one's customer has obvious competitive benefits. Such action shows the customer its supplier is demonstrably serving its customers' needs and acting in a way that tends to the welfare and advantage of the latter. This offers a real service to the customer, as measured against the definition of *"service"*, stated in Part 1 Chapter 4. It also serves well the shareholders and owners in defending market share and cash flow out of which earnings are derived. The savings must, of course, be greater than those offered by one's competitors!

Value-added audits and the registrars

It is likely that registration, to some quality standard or other, will lose its relevance. One can only speculate when that will finally be the case. Most registrations have been of a cosmetic nature designed to impress potential and existing customers and seduce them into believing the registrant's quality performance is better than others'. The basic idea of registration to the likes of ISO 9000 and QS 9000 is that it is supposed to provide a service to the customer and, *inter alia*, reduce the need for the customer to audit its suppliers thereby reducing the occurrence of multiple auditing.

It will be increasingly the case that the following two things matter to the customer and by which a seller's continuing suitability as a source of supply will be assessed:

♦ The quantified magnitude of continuous improvement achieved by its supplier.
♦ The velocity of improvement by the supplier relative to that of other potential sources of supply.

The question arises can registrars offer a useful service addressing these two concerns. It is unlikely for the following reasons:

♦ As markets become more volatile, technological change accelerates, customers need faster response to their orders coupled with constantly changing product and processes, the management systems, organizational arrangements will need to be more agile. The frequency between full assessments of the registrant will seem like an aeon: continuous improvement will have to be more rapid, assessment of it more frequent (and deeper) and value-added audits will be needed at short regular intervals. The information service the registrars offer will be too little too late.

♦ The "assessments" (audits) currently being performed by registrars (auditors) inadequately analyze the registrant's (auditee's) organization, systems, processes and operational management methods. As an example:

A QS 9000 registrar assessing a North American tier one automotive supplier in early 1997 asked an auditee's employee *"Do you have a job description?"* The employee promptly handed one over. (It had been typed up less than one hour before hand). The assessor noted its existence, did not read it or assess its content, did not validate its basis. The same assessor asked for evidence of continuous improvement, and was satisfied when shown allegedly closed-out CARs, but did not assess whether root cause had been addressed, did not visit the subject process to determine whether or not the close-out was justified. The firm retained its QS 9000 certificate.

(That example case is not atypical. My network of contacts has provided many more of the same in relation both to ISO 9000 and QS 9000 registrations.)

Registrars cannot perform the types of analyses continuous improvement programmes warrant because:

♦ They do not have the breadth of background needed. They are not specialists in the type of processes the registrants use and, even when they do possess some knowledge, it is of insufficient depth. Within the fees currently receivable, the registrar firms cannot afford to provide the knowledge their staff would need to perform effectively.

♦ Insufficient time is made available for the assessors to do little more than a quick tour of the auditee's premises. Competition from other registrars, trawling for business, forces them all to reduce price. When their price drops they face a stark choice, if they want to be profitable (or merely avoid a loss). They can either engage cheaper less proficient people or spend less time at the auditee's premises. Neither choice is conducive to offering a value-added audit.

To be fair to the registrars, performance of value-added audits is not within their current remit. And they can be placed in impossible positions. As an example, the QS 9000 initiative requires *"Third party auditors will identify opportunities for improvement (e.g. excessive scrap) as these become evident during the audit without recommending specific solutions."* (My italics.) An expression such as *"excessive"* is subjective when no defined targets, such as 25 parts per million, are available and one cannot be sure of possible cost-benefit (i.e. reduction in avoidable costs) unless and until a specific solution is decided upon. The timeless advice *"reduce scrap"* is of a motherhood and apple pie nature: such generalities are of little use (Americans refer to them as *"no-brainers"*). The value-added auditor distinguishes himself (or herself) from auditors who diagnose in generalities (no brainers) in being able to offer solutions and quantify the potential reduction in avoidable costs. Determining what is *"excessive"* requires the auditor to know what is possible from the type of process, alternatives, technology available, effects of interfacing processes and suppliers and so on. Few if any of the registrars' people can be expected to have the breadth of knowledge required to make a fair judgement. Moreover, they are allocated insufficient time to effect a thorough fact gathering exercise and analyze the information obtained therefrom. The demands of QS 9000, quoted above, are unreasonable.

3. Project audits

The greatest of faults,
I should say,
is to be conscious of none.

Thomas Carlyle

The nature of projects

Projects are becoming increasingly common and used for a variety of purposes such as:

♦ The development of new, changed or upgraded products.
♦ To provide a service to an external customer who either does not have the internal resources or expertise to produce the deliverables being purchased or does not wish to acquire them. (The supply of capital assets such as oil platforms, power stations are examples of such projects).
♦ Achieving specific business objectives. (A set of defined goals identified as an opportunity by a value-added audit would be an example; setting up a continuous improvement programmes to achieve a six sigma performance level would be another.)

Projects are undertaken by an assigned team, formed for the specific purpose of the project, which is disbanded when the end goals are achieved. They offer a service to others and the precepts described in Chapter 5 apply to them. They are of growing importance as companies increase the amount of outsourcing and, as the consequential rise of the service economy continues, there is a need to manage service contracts as a project. Characteristically it is essential for the service providers to plan, perform and execute their briefs within tight deadlines, especially when serving customers demanding delivery of the outsourced products and services on a just-in-time or real time basis.

The pressures for high levels of performance create a vital need for project audits since the management of all parties requires forewarning of incipient problems and a supply of information that enables proactive decision making. Accordingly, internal audits should be performed by the project team itself. Extrinsic audits, too, should be performed by the customer when the product or service involved is classified as sufficiently important. (See Part 1 Chapter 8 *"The classification of the product that is involved".*

The role of the auditor

Occasionally, there is some confusion between audits and reviews. A review is really an inspection of work performed, conducted for the purposes of acceptance or rejection, and is therefore a quality control. An audit, on the other hand, is aimed principally at ascertaining whether or not the management systems proposed for use on a project *will* prove effective in practice and/or the compliance with those systems and the determination of their efficacy. The audit is future focussed, as mentioned in the previous chapter. Auditing is a preventative action taken on behalf of management to determine that the release or use of resources is justified and the results desired from using those resources will be obtained.

During systems audits

If a systems audit is being performed prior to commencement of the entire project or of any phase therein, the auditor will be verifying that:

♦   The project is organized properly.
♦   The management systems have been properly considered.
♦   The necessary resources have been fully and properly budgeted.
♦   The time required has been carefully and properly estimated and allocated.

The information gleaned by the audit concerning all of those listed points will assist management in deciding whether or not to allocate the time and resources requested for the project, to commence the project or any particular phase and to know if the risk of loss or of avoidable costs has been minimized. The systems audit should be planned sufficiently ahead of the commencement of each phase to enable the project management to take any major corrective action revealed as being desirable or necessary before the initiation of the phase or project. (See also Part 1 Chapter 9, Figure 9.3.)

If the project is required to act in accordance with the supplier's standard project control procedures, the auditor will also:

- Verify the project has been organized, the systems have been developed, resources and time have been budgeted in accordance with those standard procedures;
- Obtain objective evidence from the project's performance in order to determine the efficacy of those standard procedures; and, of course,
- Require any corrective actions to those standard procedures that are considered necessary.

During compliance audits

Depending on the audit objectives, the auditor will, during a compliance audit, verify that the management systems are being carried out such that:

- The auditee is operating in accordance with the organizational arrangements and the management systems.
- Fitness for purpose is being achieved.
- Fitness for purpose will be achieved.
- The contractual and legal obligations are being met.
- Time and resources are being properly managed and justified.

The auditee's procedures may refer to various standards with which the personnel must comply. In this event, the auditor will also spot check to verify that the requirements of those standards are being met: this may entail obtaining and using the advice of a specialist on the audit team. One must stress again that such audits are not being performed as quasi-inspections. The main purpose of the compliance audit is to ensure that one can have sufficient confidence that the auditee is complying with basic project requirements, procedures and standards. The auditee should also be monitoring his own observance of those by means of process controls and verification activities and by implementing his own non-conformity and corrective action systems, if problems arise.

Conduct of the audit

Use specialists

Many people become very concerned and anxious when they are asked to lead an audit in a project environment. The essential point to remember is that the project can still be split into work phases and tasks from which the task elements and sub-elements can be extracted, described in Part 1 Chapter 1. Whereas the lead auditor may not have the competence or experience to determine whether, say, the content of a project design specification or of some calculations is adequate or not, he will recognize from the task elements that they are types of information whose content must be correct. This being a key matter that the audit must address, when preparing for the audit (see Part 1 Chapter 9) the lead auditor can arrange for a specialist to be a member of the audit team. That specialist can be asked, during the audit's fact gathering phase, to confirm whether or not the information content is correct and complete. The specialist will then use his or her skills and advise the lead auditor accordingly. There is no reason for an auditor who is inexperienced in the project's activities to feel any more anxious than an auditor who is inexperienced in, say, food manufacturing. All this means is that specialists must be co-opted onto the audit team and directed by the lead auditor.

General approach

Product and service development and the running of a project, regardless of its size, are activities that require proper management and, as stated in Part 1, need to be subject to a management audit. When conducting the audit, the auditor can be guided as per the various chapters in Part 1 of this book.

- ♦ The seven step audit method and question technique will both be as discussed in Chapters 11 and 13, respectively.
- ♦ Each department/ process involved in the project will be analyzed as per Chapter 5.
- ♦ Management systems will be treated as suggested in Chapter 6.
- ♦ Careful audit preparation as described in Chapter 9 is obviously beneficial as is the creation of a checklist, matrix or flowchart as discussed in Chapter 7.

So, for any particular task being performed in any phase of the project, the basic checklist, such as that described in Figure 7.6 or a matrix, of the type shown in Figure 7.14, (based on the task elements listed in Chapter 4, non conformity and so on), should be usable. If the auditee is supposed to comply with a standard, such as ISO 9001, the auditor needs to prepare a criteria type of checklist, as also described in Part 1 Chapter 7.

In performing the audit, the auditor will need to look for various controls that are peculiar to project management. The following sections attempt to give basic guidance on some particular features to be studied.

Project controls

Every project passes through various discrete phases. These can be depicted as shown in Figure 3.1, which can be seen to be very similar to the Figure 8.3, in Part 1. It is therefore clear that a project can be properly planned, indeed, if the quality of the deliverables is to be assured, it is vital that proper planning does take place. Each of the phases can be further divided into task units and hence into the various task elements and sub-elements.

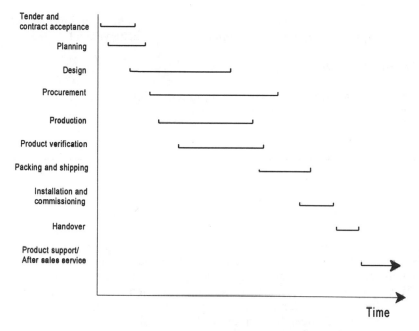

Figure 3.1 A simple project Gantt chart

Control of time

The auditor must verify that the project has been broken down into the various phases, such as those shown in Figure 3.1. (It matters not what method of planning has taken place whether it be by the use of a simple Gantt chart as shown in Figure 3.1, or by PERT or CPM means). Each of these phases will take a certain period of time for satisfactory completion. Remembering that lack of time is a real cause of business problems, the auditor will examine objective evidence to verify that :

531

◆ Management systems for the estimation of the time budget needed for each phase have been defined and communicated to the project management;

◆ The basis for planning and budgeting of time is consistent with the project objectives and customer requirements;

◆ The project has defined its systems for monitoring and recording its use of time and has communicated them throughout the project;

◆ All the foregoing management systems are implemented and are effective;

◆ The project analyses the areas of opportunity for time savings which are not to the detriment of quality achievement.

Control of resources

Resources that will be of particular importance throughout the project and which will require careful management are:

◆ Manpower resources
◆ Overall budget

Manpower resources:

A major reason for problems in the execution of projects is inadequate consideration of the manpower build-up that will be required as the project progresses. Professional and modern project management practice is to summarize graphically the planned and actual build-up of manpower. A number of tools including tables, histograms and charts are used. A plot of the cumulative total tends to form an elongated "S", and is frequently referred to as an *"S Curve"*: an example is shown in Figure 3.2 together with some hypothetical data for an imaginary project.

The auditor will examine objective evidence to verify that :

◆ Systems for the estimation of the manpower budget needed for each phase have been defined and communicated to the project management.

◆ The basis for manpower planning and budgeting is consistent with the project objectives and customer requirements.

◆ The project has defined its systems for monitoring and recording its use of manpower and has communicated them throughout the project.

♦ All the foregoing management systems are implemented and are effective.

♦ The project analyses the areas of opportunity for manpower savings which are not to the detriment of quality achievement.

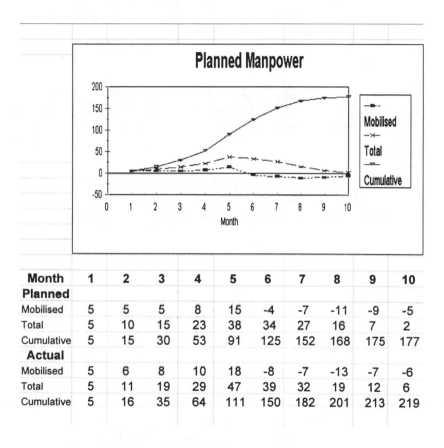

Month	1	2	3	4	5	6	7	8	9	10
Planned										
Mobilised	5	5	5	8	15	-4	-7	-11	-9	-5
Total	5	10	15	23	38	34	27	16	7	2
Cumulative	5	15	30	53	91	125	152	168	175	177
Actual										
Mobilised	5	6	8	10	18	-8	-7	-13	-7	-6
Total	5	11	19	29	47	39	32	19	12	6
Cumulative	5	16	35	64	111	150	182	201	213	219

Figure 3.2 Example of simple manpower resource report

The timing necessary to mobilize and demobilize project manpower, as and when required, must be carefully thought through by the auditee and based on solid estimates that are consistent with the tasks to be performed. As stated in Part 1 Chapter 18, lack of resources is a real cause of business problems and this is particularly true for projects, many of which have failed over the years because their managements did not adequately consider manpower build-up, with the result that cash flow requirements were seriously underestimated.

A person should have been assigned to each task and the *Person* sub-elements of Part 1 Chapter 4 can be applied. Prior to commencement of work, it is often advisable for the project team to be given training and familiarization not only with the project and contract requirements but also with the specific techniques, management systems and skills that will be used on the project.

Just as for any other audit, the auditor will examine objective evidence and confirm that those matters raised in Part 1 Chapter 4 have been planned and implemented.

Overall budget:

The sum total of all aspects of planning, namely, personnel build-up, purchases made, equipment utilization and acquisition costs will form a major part of the overall budget that the auditee will require in order to execute the project correctly for the customer. The auditor will examine objective evidence to verify that :

♦ Management systems for estimating the overall budget for all the resources needed for each phase have been defined and communicated to the project management.
♦ The basis for planning and estimating that overall budget is consistent with the project objectives and customer requirements.
♦ The project has defined its systems for overall monitoring and recording of its use of those resources and has communicated them throughout the project.
♦ All the foregoing management systems are implemented and are effective.
♦ Those resources and budget have been allocated by management that is authorized to do so (i.e. management that is acting within the constraints and authorities of its own job descriptions).
♦ The project analyses the areas of opportunity for overall resource savings which are not to the detriment of quality achievement.

Performance monitoring:

Vital aspects of planning concern the performance monitoring of the project as it progresses. (The reader will recall that assessing the performance monitoring method and measurements is one of the seven steps of the audit method described in Part 1 Chapter 11). It includes planning feedback reports not only on cost achievement, schedule achievement but also on quality, as listed in Figure 3.4. Many project managers avidly specify reports concerning the cost and time expended but rarely preplan feedback to tell them whether or not that expenditure is achieving the desired effect. It is futile to believe that one is within budget and time if the quality of the deliverables is wrong. To execute its duties properly, the project management must know whether fitness for purpose is constantly being achieved at each milestone, as the project progresses and whether it will be achieved when the project concludes. This fitness for purpose must be achieved as far as possible on a right first time basis. Naturally this means that management need to be forewarned of any problems that can result in wasted cost or wasted schedule. The type of feedback required, therefore, not only derives from inspection or test of completed work (which is after the fact and, as the saying goes, cannot put quality into a product) but also from management audits which will inform the project manager whether any problems either exist or are likely to develop by virtue of the manner in which the project team is working. The auditor will look for proof that :

♦ The project has defined its management systems for overall monitoring and reporting of its actual quality achievement and has communicated them throughout the project.
♦ The particular points at which quality achievement will be ascertained have been defined.
♦ The detailed methods to be used for each monitoring activity have been defined and that responsibilities for that monitoring have been assigned and communicated throughout the project.
♦ The foregoing management systems are implemented and are effective.

Project phases

Some matters that require attention are as described below. They relate to the typical project phases depicted in Figure 3.1.

Tender and contract acceptance

This will include the auditee's receipt of a specification from the potential customer, his decision to tender or not, his conduct of commercial negotiations and decision to accept or reject a contract offered. The product specification will fully describe what the customer is seeking in terms of performance and function of the deliverable goods and services. Contract information presented in Figure 3.3 forms the basic determinants of the matters listed in Figure 3.4.

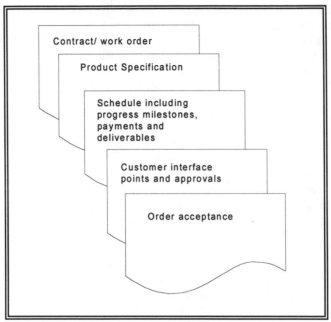

Figure 3.3 Contract information required

One must bear in mind that many customers do not have the technical knowledge to prepare an adequate product specification fully. In such circumstances, it is incumbent on the project team to institute a procedure whereby all of the key questions which need to be addressed (to obtain a complete and correct product specification) have been raised with the customer in an honest fashion: this should be done as a normal part of the tendering procedure. Regrettably, there has been a tendency over the years for rogue project organizations to regard an unsophisticated customer as an open cheque book. Responsible and reputable ones have a procedure whereby the customer's operational needs and circumstances are carefully analyzed. Such analysis is performed together with the customer and enables the supplier to prepare an adequate specification from which the cost and time impact for successful supply can then be accurately estimated and provided to the customer. It is of no help to either the supplier or the customer to find that the product specification had been

536

Principal matter	Detail to be planned
Project	Project schedule Project internal milestones and deliverables Tasks involved Manpower usage
Organization	Organization chart Responsibilities and authorities Project procedures
Equipment	Equipment selection Equipment acquisition
Staff	Staff selection Training and familiarization
Budget	Budget definition Budget allocation
Reports	Costs incurred for: Manpower, Purchases etc.
Reports	Time expended Milestones met Deliverables achieved Receivables in.
Reports	Quality achieved: Specifications met; Deliverables correct Receivables correct.

Figure 3.4 Principal matters to be planned

inadequately conceived such that extra costs are incurred to the detriment of all. The product specification also forms key information upon which the supplier will decide whether or not he has the capability of satisfying the customer's needs and whether or not to enter into a contract. The decision to enter into a contract must be based on the supplier being fully aware of his proven capabilities in relation to the customer's needs.

The auditor will look for objective evidence demonstrating that:

♦ A system, for ensuring that careful review of customer enquiries is performed, has been developed and communicated to the project;
♦ That system is followed and that commitments made to customers are consistent with the auditee's known capabilities;
♦ Only authorized competent persons are able to negotiate with the customer.

The various milestones for marking the progress of the project, the activity deliverables and payments associated with each one must be properly defined. This enables both customer and supplier to predict their respective cash flow requirements and for each to know the circumstances under which they will agree that fitness for purpose is being achieved. The customer may wish to become involved with the project team as the work proceeds. These interface arrangements, which may be for the purpose of reviewing design work or witnessing performance tests, must be adequately defined and will probably be linked to milestone payments.

The auditor will examine objective evidence to show that :

♦ Contractual milestones and interfaces have been properly considered, defined and agreed between the respective parties.
♦ The deliverable goods and services associated with each milestone have been fully defined together with the acceptance criteria for each.

For a contract to be legally binding, there must be both an order placed by the customer and the supplier's acceptance of that order returned to the customer. The terms and conditions of contract offer and acceptance should be consistent and agreed. In the event of any differences between either parties' terms and conditions, the courts of law will normally uphold those definitions furnished last, whether by customer or by the project organization, as being the ones to prevail in the event of a dispute arising. For this reason, the auditor will examine objective evidence to verify that :

♦ A system has been developed and communicated to the project, to ensure careful review of the contract prior to acceptance in order to verify that only the features tendered for and negotiated are included in that contract.
♦ That system is followed and contractual commitments made to customers are consistent with the auditee's proven capabilities.

538

♦ Only authorized, competent persons are able to make contractually binding commitments for the supplier to supply the software and other deliverables.

The auditor will use the unit concept and task element analysis when auditing each of the tasks involved in the tendering and contract acceptance phase.

Planning

Most of the planning should have occurred before the contract signature - after all, if the supplier has not planned how the project will be run, how could an honest tender be made? Figure 3.4 shows the principle matters that the auditee should have considered and planned if the project is to be properly executed. The overall schedule, discussed above, will indicate the major milestones that have been agreed between customer and auditee: from these milestones the particular internal ones, used by the project for monitoring its progress, should have been defined. The auditor must always be wary if the main schedule shows a lengthy *"maintenance"* phase since this is often a sign of an auditee who intends to finish developing and de-bugging his product while the customer's operational phase proceeds and consequently to charge the customer for the privilege of doing so. Frequently, this has the effect of the customer paying more than once for the same product and is a form of fraud. Legitimate product support and after sales service are entirely different matters since they help the customer to obtain better service from, and understanding of, a product which is fit for purpose and has complied with its contract requirements.

The various phases will contain specific tasks to be performed which should be properly defined. Associated with each one, the responsibilities and limits of authority should have been documented. The auditor will examine objective evidence and verify that the organizational matters raised in Part 1 Chapter 3 have been performed by the auditee. This includes verifying that :

♦ The auditee has planned his organization by defining all of the principle functions needed and their relationship to each other.
♦ Job descriptions and specifications for each of those key tasks and their deliverables have been produced and communicated to the persons assigned to them.

Detailed planning of each task should be by means of procedures describing the management systems which are to be used in accomplishing the tasks. The auditor will verify that these have been produced and that they appear effective. (The reader will remember that proof of efficacy can only be obtained by compliance auditing.)

Design

This might be the first major phase for which an audit team needs, within its midst, appropriate specialists who can provide advice on whether or not the content of information, for example, is correct. The auditor can consider design to be a process and then analyze its task elements (which will generally consist of person, equipment, service and information) and the sub-elements for each, as stated in Part 1 Chapter 4.

When proceeding with the audit, the auditor should bear in mind that the design input constrains the design output and there needs to be a direct trail from it to the contract information, shown in Figure 3.3.

Procurement

If the project team needs to procure any goods or services in order to perform its duties, or for onward supply to the customer, the normal types of control used in any commercial procurement situation should have been carried out. Once again the auditor is well advised to remember that procurement constitutes a set of tasks each of which can be broken into the applicable task elements, described in Part 1 Chapter 4. Whereas there may not be a physical item involved at the workplace of certain of those tasks, the remaining ones and their sub-elements will still apply. Figure 3.5 summarizes the principle information that is usually created. (See also *"Virtual organizations"*, at the end of this chapter.)

Production

The production phase principally involves the actual creation of the physical deliverables, required by the contract, in accordance with the design output. It consists of a set of tasks (processes) each of which can be broken into the applicable task elements etc. Assistance and support from a specialist, possessing knowledge of the particular processes being audited, on the audit team may be required to audit the sub-elements involved in them.

Information created by buyer	Information created by supplier
Material take-off/ list of services to be procured	Plans (project, quality etc.)
Long lead time list	Procedures
Purchase terms and conditions	Designs
Approved supplier list	Customer approvals
Bidder lists	Changes
Enquiries	Records
Analysis of bids/ tenders received	Manuals and technical information
Purchase orders and associated attachments	
Change orders	
Quality controls on suppliers' products	
Supplier surveillance programme	

Figure 3.5 Principal procurement information

Product verification

A verification plan is essential. It is extremely beneficial for the auditee to develop the plan in conjunction with the design so that as a particular feature of the product or service deliverables is designed, the designer is constrained to state how that design feature will be verified as being efficacious. It is important that the auditee plans before verifying. The plan should specify :

♦ Activities designed to verify that the deliverables do what they are meant to do.

541

♦　　　　Activities designed to verify that the deliverables do not do what they are not meant to do.

The latter is particularly important because unforeseen peculiarities could be most inconvenient or could, perhaps, result in an unsafe situation. As a minimum, the verification plan must state: who performs each activity; the methods to be used; equipment required for each activity; the acceptance criteria for the deliverables involved; and, the reports to be generated. It must contain or reference detailed procedures that describe each particular verification activity and the method for its performance. The content of reports required, authority for preparation and approval might be contained in auditees' procedures as a standard: the auditor should verify this point.

The auditor must examine objective evidence to ascertain that each verification activity is covered by a procedure. (This does not imply a need for separate procedures for each and every activity. A number of activities can often be adequately covered by a generic procedure relating to them all). If the auditor is performing a systems audit prior to any design or verification being performed, then the existence of a set of plans and procedures describing how these activities are to be controlled and accomplished, as described above, requires verification.

Packing and shipping

The auditor should verify that the arrangements for packing and protecting the product deliverables during shipping and delivery to the customer have been properly considered and planned. The auditor can use the task elements when analyzing the efficacy of the tasks (processes) and their associated management systems.

One thing that many auditors fail to consider is the linkage between the design function and the efficacy of packing and shipping activities. Products need to arrive in a known specified condition at the customer's premises and their protection necessitates careful selection of packing materials used and configuration of the surrounding packaging. This must not be an afterthought on the part of the project. Accordingly, there needs to be a direct audit trail between the design function and the packing and shipping activities. These latter will be constrained by the former. The auditor must verify the existence of that audit trail and its efficacy.

Installation and commissioning

As with the other project activities, installation and commissioning contain functions that can be broken down into the task elements and thereupon thoroughly planned, executed and audited. The auditor should look for plans describing how the deliverable is to be installed at the customer's or end user's work location and how it will be commissioned. This is particularly important if both customer and auditee are to be convinced that the product quality is delivered as required. As mentioned in the case of packing and shipping activities, installation and commissioning rely on the design activities: the auditor needs to verify the existence and efficacy of an audit trail between design and the installation and commissioning processes.

In some circumstances, the customer may have to install and commission the product without the presence of anyone from the project. If this is so, and it should have been made clear in the contract requirements, the project should have provided the necessary information (for example user manuals, instruction sheets, procedures, "help" facilities within software etc.) that will enable the customer or end user to do so successfully. That information should have been controlled as per its sub-elements, contained in Part 1 Chapter 4. The auditor will verify that the management systems required to furnish that information have correctly addressed those sub-elements.

Handover

The auditor should verify that handover activities have been carefully planned and agreed between the customer, user and supplier. This is because the results obtained from handover activities establish a baseline from which any warranty claims or deterioration of the product itself can be monitored and, as such, normally has a considerable influence on the final payments to be made by the customer to the project. A smooth handover which reveals the product's fitness for purpose and its compliance with the contract requirements is the acid test of the project's management systems and controls. Handover is the point at which each party will want to be convinced that everything is right. Its constituent activities also establish a datum that will be of great assistance to the user or customer in maintaining effective condition monitoring and maintenance systems.

Product support and after sales service

All five task elements are present during this phase. The auditor will ascertain that the after sales service has been designed and that the management systems that will be required to support the foreground activities are efficacious, as described in Chapter 5.

Virtual organizations

Although outsourcing is nothing new, for the procurement of goods and services is as old as trade itself, it has become a fashionable expression in the last two decades accompanying the rise of a service economy offering specialist support to firms. Vertical integration, so popular and common during the last one hundred and fifty years, is a less prevalent way of organizing companies. Highly educated entrepreneurs are driving forward the service sector by spotting and exploiting the potential of niche markets.

Modern communications technology now permits teleworkers to develop portfolios of clients and serve their needs from any point in the world they choose. Some contracts and projects can, accordingly, be completed by groups of small businesses and individuals banding together for that sole purpose. They can be geographically dispersed around the world. This is sometimes referred to as the *"virtual corporation"*. Pundits and academics continue to speculate on the shape of the virtual organization's chart and suggest a range of possibilities, one example being the ring doughnut. What the debate does not recognize is that these new forms serve only to illustrate the contractual relationships between the parties within them. They do not recognize the more important functional relationship that exists while the contractual work actually proceeds. In this latter case conventional pyramidal and matrix forms prevail. Pyramids, in particular, show who reports to who to get the work done, who is responsible for discrete chunks of the work and their deliverables. They also indicate to the client who has overall responsibility for managing and coordinating all the various parties involved.

The auditor can proceed as discussed elsewhere and throughout this book when considering the organizational arrangements. Outsourcing controls follow normal procurement controls with regard to source selection, qualification of the suppliers, contract placement, working interfaces, communications channels, records etc.

4. Auditing software and computer applications

for all our power and weight and size,
We are nothing more than children of your brain!

Kipling.

This is a subject becoming of increasing importance to management and to auditors. Given that in itself it is a very large subject, the following is only intended to provide some basic guidelines on how to approach an audit of a software supply project or an operating computer installation. The chapter must assume that the reader has basic knowledge of a typical computer configuration and the various pieces of equipment that it comprises such as the central processing unit, disk drives and terminals, the function of each one and how they link together.

The importance of software

Software is the life blood of a computer and if it is not fit for purpose, the computer's performance will be impaired. A computer is totally inoperative without software, which is the master for whatever work is done on it such as design or accounting calculations or the control of complex equipment. In the control of hazardous equipment, the quality of the software dictates safety, efficiency and operability. The potential size of avoidable costs incurred by failed software quality is considerable and if one considers the product liability costs that might arise in the event of an accident, one can speculate that inadequate control of a computer installation or its software could have disastrous results for a company and could financially jeopardize it.

Problems of procurement

Most organizations tend to purchase software from software houses which now proliferate in response to the enormous demand for their products. The software is supplied either on a bespoke basis or as a standard package, such as a PC operating system or an application package. In some cases, software might be "free" and downloaded from a the Internet

545

after being created by a software company who has no contractual relationship whatsoever with the users. As in every walk of life, some suppliers and creators are of doubtful integrity. They all allege that their product is of high quality but customers/ users often find that the software does not quite fulfil their needs and bugs are constantly being found. Quite commonly bugs are found by users after the software is installed and in end use. Some software suppliers encourage their customers to report problems and discuss how to use the product with one another and with them. People exchange information about the operational limitations discovered in the software and how their inconvenience was avoided or mitigated. Hopefully, the software house will often then release a new version of the software which addresses those problems that the original version was intended. What are often advertized as "upgrades" are little more than versions of software that have been corrected to do what the customer had originally paid for and expected from the purchase: the customer is expected to pay for that "new version". Good business for the software house but unethical nonetheless.

As in any type of purchase, the risk of using a disreputable source remains. What redress does a customer have if the software is unfit for purpose and there is a consequential loss? Most suppliers refuse to accept a consequential loss clause in their software contracts. Plainly, there is a need to control one's procurement activities carefully in respect of computer installations and quality. Pre-award surveys and audits will help but many customers may find they are in no position to perform these. This is certainly the case with the burgeoning industry that sells standard application software for desktop and portable computers.

Control of the quality of desktop/portable computers' application software must be left to the industry and the marketplace itself. The latter has, by and large, a good track record at weeding out the scallywags and advising the purchasing public of software packages that are of dubious quality. The abundance of media publications, analysts, beta testers, and Internet chat rooms, affording global dissemination of experience and views, is quite effective at rapidly informing actual and potential customers of the existence of problems and whether the product would or would not be a value-for-money buy.

This chapter will deal with bespoke software created for specific customer needs and intended to run on mainframes or corporate networks managed and controlled by a central management information systems department. It is addressed to those customers who are in a position to audit their software suppliers and, although it is written in the context of a contractual situation, the principles still apply to internal audits of software development and computer usage.

The role of the auditor

Occasionally, there is some confusion between audits and reviews. A review is really an inspection of work performed in the supply of software, conducted for the purposes of acceptance or rejection, and is therefore a quality control. An audit, on the other hand, is aimed principally at ascertaining whether or not the management systems proposed for use on a software supply project *will* prove effective in practice and/or the compliance with those systems and the determination of their efficacy. The role of the auditor will be as described in Chapter 3 *"Project audits"*.

Conduct of the audit

Many people become very concerned and anxious when they are asked to lead an audit in a computer environment. The essential point to remember is that computer assisted operations can still be split into work phases and tasks from which the task elements and sub-elements can be extracted. Whereas the lead auditor may not have the competence or experience to determine whether, say, the content of a software design specification or of some lines of code are adequate or not, he will recognize from the task elements that they are types of information whose content must be correct. This being a key matter that the audit must address, when preparing for the audit (see Part 1 Chapter 9) the lead auditor can arrange for a specialist to be a member on the audit team. That specialist can be asked, during the audit's fact gathering phase, to confirm whether or not the information content is correct and complete. The specialist will then use his or her skills and advise the lead auditor accordingly. There is no reason for an auditor who is inexperienced in computer applications or software developments to feel any more anxious than an auditor who is inexperienced in, say, the pharmaceutical industry. All this means is that specialists must be co-opted onto the audit team and directed by the lead auditor. Software development and the running of a computer installation, regardless of its size, are activities that require proper management and need to be subject to a management audit.

When conducting the audit, the auditor can be guided as per the various chapters in Part 1 of this book.

- The seven step audit method and question technique will both be as discussed in Chapters 11 and 13, respectively.
- Each department/process involved in the software supply project will be analyzed as per Chapter 5.
- Management systems will be treated as suggested in Chapter 6.
- Careful audit preparation as described in Chapter 9 is obviously beneficial as is the creation of a checklist, matrix or flowchart as discussed in Chapter 7.

So, for any particular task being performed in any phase of the software supply project, the basic checklist, such as that described in Figure 7.6, or a matrix, of the type shown in Figure 7.14, (based on the task elements listed in Chapter 4, non conformity and so on), should be usable. If the auditee is supposed to comply with a standard, such as ISO 9001 or the guidance standard, ISO 9000-3, the auditor needs to prepare a criteria type of checklist, as also described in Chapter 7.

In performing the audit, the auditor will need to look for various controls that are peculiar to projects and to computer installations. The following sections attempt to give basic guidance on particular features to be studied.

The need for controls

Software creation has been regarded as something of a black art for many years but nowadays software engineering techniques are extensively recognized and documented. Their associated basic procedures are well understood by the professional software engineers and there remains little excuse for producing poor quality software.

In order to ensure software quality and that the computer installation functions properly, it is essential that various management controls are put into place. These are :

1) Controls implemented during the supply of new or revised software.
2) Controls implemented during the operational life of the computer installation and the software.
3) Loss controls.

Loss controls (my own phrase) are an overriding discipline that are necessary during software development, supply and operations. It is essential that consideration of loss be taken into account from the

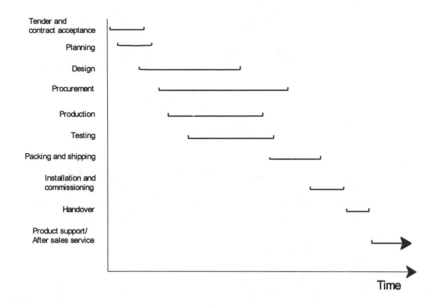

Figure 4.1 A software project Gantt chart

inception of a software development project so that the loss controls that will be required for the operational life will be effective.

1. Controls implemented during the supply of new or revised software.

The supply of new or revised software can be considered to be a project which passes through various discrete phases. These can be depicted as shown in Figure 4.1, which can be seen to be very similar to the Figure 3.1. It is therefore clear that a software supply project can be properly planned, indeed, if the quality of software is to be assured, it is vital that proper planning does take place. Each of the phases can be further divided into task units and hence into the various task elements and sub-elements of Part 1 Chapter 4.

The auditor must verify that the software project has been broken down into the various phases, such as those shown in Figure 4.1. (It matters not what method of planning has taken place whether it be by the use of a simple Gantt chart as shown in Figure 4.1, or by PERT or CPM means). Each of these phases will take a certain period of time for satisfactory completion. Remembering that lack of time is a real cause of business problems, the auditor will examine objective evidence to verify that :

♦   Management systems for the estimation of the time budget really needed for each phase have been defined and communicated to the project management;

♦   The basis for planning and budgeting of time is consistent with the project objectives and customer requirements;

♦   The project has defined its systems for monitoring and recording its use of time and has communicated them throughout the project;

♦   All the foregoing management systems are implemented and are effective;

♦   The project analyses the areas of opportunity for time savings which are not to the detriment of quality achievement.

Tender and contract acceptance

This will include the auditee's receipt of a specification from the potential customer, his decision to tender or not, his conduct of commercial negotiations and decision to accept or reject a contact offered. To check that this phase is properly managed, the auditor will look for the documents depicted in Figure 3.2. The most important documents affecting quality, are the Requirements Specification, which is the software equivalent of the product specification listed in Figure 3.2, and those defining the milestones and payments. The Requirements Specification will fully describe what the customer is seeking in terms of performance and function of the software or computer installation.

One can readily see that for software supply contracts, the management controls are no different from those in normal commercial contracts involving the supply of hardware or services. The auditor will use the unit concept and task element analysis when auditing each of the tasks involved in the tendering and contract acceptance phase.

The remaining comments, made in Chapter 3 *"Project audits"*, for tender and contract acceptance, apply also to the software situation. The auditor will verify the points made in that section.

Management	Independence
Determines policies and budgets	In review and approval of information/ documents
Reviews and approves plans and procedures	In testing and approval of new/ changed software
Selects and appoints staff	Of audits
Requires management audits	In following-up corrective actions identified
Authorizes corrective action	

Figure 4.2 Principal matters for the project's organization

Planning

Most of the planning should have occurred before the contract signature - after all, if the supplier has not planned how the project will be run, how could an honest tender be made? Figure 3.3 shows the principle matters that the auditee should have considered and planned if the software development project is to be properly executed.

The remaining comments, made in Chapter 3 *"Project audits"*, for planning, apply also to the software situation. The auditor will verify the points made in that section. Additional matters concerning organization are shown on Figure 4.2. When reviewing the organizational arrangements, the auditor should verify that those features have been incorporated into the project procedures and set up. An example of an organization chart is shown in Figure 4.7.

Performance monitoring

See Chapter 3 *"Project audits"*.

Design

This might be the first major phase for which an audit team needs, within its midst, appropriate specialists who can provide advice on whether or not the content of information, for example, is correct. Various features that

System architecture	At module level	General
Hierarchy of software modules	Screen layouts	Audit trail to Requirements Specification
	Keyboard commands	
Program/ data flow charts (if used)	Response times	Programming language used
Data dictionary	Reports, queries, print-outs needed	Standards and conventions
Definition of each module	Authorities/ security features	
Interfaces with other software systems	Priorities	Design quality controls (reviews, approvals, walkthroughs etc.)
Hardware configuration	Interfaces, data transfer protocols	Control of design changes
Central processing unit constraints	Data files involved	Corrective actions
Response and performance levels	Hardware requirements	Procedures and proforma
	Central processing unit constraints	Library controls

Figure 4.3 Various software design considerations

need to be considered in the design of software are listed in Figure 4.3. It is beyond the scope of this book to describe the content of each one and the reader should peruse any of the standard texts that are available. The auditor can consider design to be a process and then analyze its task elements (which will generally consist of person, equipment, service and information) and the sub-elements for each.

The auditor should also verify that the auditee's design management systems ensure that the loss and software controls outlined later in this chapter are fully considered and incorporated into the software design. Depending on the audit objectives, the auditor will verify then that those systems are both implemented and effective.

Procurement

If the software project team needs to procure any hardware or services in order to perform its duties, then the normal types of control used in any commercial procurement situation should have been carried out. Once again the auditor is well advised to remember that procurement constitutes a set of tasks each of which can be broken into the applicable task elements, described in Part 1 Chapter 4. Whereas there may not be a physical item involved at the workplace of certain of those tasks, the remaining ones and their sub-elements will still apply. Figure 3.5 summarizes the principle information that is usually created.

Production

The production phase principally involves the coding of the software in accordance with the design output. It consists of a set of tasks each of which can be broken into the applicable task elements etc. Assistance and support from a specialist on the audit team may be required to audit the sub-elements involved in this part of the software development project.

Testing

Since software cannot be seen, its testing is a vital check on quality achievement. The problem in relation to software testing was neatly encapsulated in the saying attributed to Edsger Dijkstra:

"Software testing reveals defects but not the absence of defects".

As for any other type of test, a test plan is essential. The software test plan should, however, specify :

♦   Tests designed to verify that the software does what it is meant to do.

♦   Tests designed to verify that the software does not do what it is not meant to do.

The latter is particularly important because unforeseen peculiarities could be most inconvenient or could, perhaps, result in an unsafe situation (in the case of control of hazardous plant, for instance.) As a minimum, the test plan must state who performs each test; the testing methods to be used; equipment required for each test (perhaps a simulator may be involved) and the reports to be generated. It must contain or reference detailed procedures that describe each particular test and the method of performance. The content of reports required, authority for preparation and approval might be contained in auditees' procedures as a standard: the auditor should verify this point.

It is extremely beneficial for the auditee to develop the test plan in conjunction with the design so that as a particular feature of the software is designed, the designer is constrained to state how that design feature will be verified as efficacious. It is important that the auditee plans before performing tests. If this is not done, there is a risk that the software testing will descend into a mish-mash of people playing at computer terminals. Test plans are required for each level of the software being developed or changed. Those levels are:

♦ Tests on individual software modules.
♦ Integration tests.
♦ Tests on the software system.
♦ Tests to verify compatibility and effectiveness of the software and hardware interfacing with each other.

The auditor must examine objective evidence to ascertain that each level of test and each test is covered by a procedure. If the auditor is performing a systems audit prior to any design or testing being performed, then it is important to verify the existence of a set of plans and procedures describing how these activities are to be controlled and accomplished, as described above.

Packing and shipping

The auditor should verify that the arrangements for packing and protecting the software during shipping and delivery to the customer have been properly considered and planned. The auditor can use the task elements when analyzing the efficacy of the tasks (processes) and their associated management systems.

Installation and commissioning

See Chapter 3 *"Project audits"*.

Handover

See Chapter 3 *"Project audits"*.

Product support and after sales service

See Chapter 3 *"Project audits"*.

2. Controls implemented during the operational life of the computer installation and the software.

During the operational life of software and the computer installation, controls are required for hardware, software, data and documents. The principle process controls for hardware amount to correct running and operation of the computer and its peripherals, together with the management systems required to support and maintain its correct condition. These include condition monitoring and planned maintenance.

Protection of magnetic media, back-up policy and practice

Since much operational software is retained on magnetic media, a principle feature to require attention relates to the care of master tapes and disks, as well as copies used for day-to-day operation. It is bad practice and extremely risky to use the master copies of software in a day-to-day environment although in certain circumstances, particularly in small applications, this is not an uncommon practice - however ill-advised. Where programs are of high value, the auditor should verify that there is proper protection of the masters. Then, in the event that the operating copy should become damaged in some way, a new working copy can be promptly made from the master. In the case of data, the auditor should verify, for batch processing in particular, that regular back-up copies are made so that if some transaction data has been lost, it will only be a loss restricted to the time period extending back to the previous back-up. As is touched upon later in this chapter, the auditor must ascertain that proper library controls are being implemented to prevent the risk of loss to software and data.

Correctness of input and output data

The major concern in the day-to-day running of the machine is that the correct and complete output is obtained. In a batch processing environment, this is totally dependent on the completeness and correctness of the input, once the fitness for purpose of the actual software and hardware has been proved. It is only in exceptional circumstances that incorrect output might be obtained even though correct input has been supplied. For present purposes of this discussion, it is assumed that the process hardware and software are completely reliable. The auditor will verify that the management systems for the maintenance of that reliability:

a) exist;
b) have been communicated to those that need them;
c) are implemented; and
d) are effective.

Method	Completeness		Correctness	
Batch totals	Input	Output	Input	Output
Checks of print-outs	Input	Output	Input	Output
Computer sequence checks	Input	Output		
Matching	Input	Output	Input	Output
Verify data preparation			Input	
Edit checks			Input	
Validity parameters			Input	
Control totals		Output		Output
Rejection control		Output		Output
Reconcile master and transaction files		Output		Output

Figure 4.4 Various methods for ensuring completeness and correctness of input and output during the operational phase

Figure 4.4 lists various methods that are used to ensure completeness and correctness of input and output. These types of controls are fully described in standard basic texts on data processing, which the reader who wishes to know more should consult and study. The principle matters that the reader should note are that:

♦ Various of these methods require human intervention (known as *"Manual controls"*) such as the checking of a printout to verify that the output is consistent with the input.

♦ Certain of these methods are performed by the software itself (known as *"Software controls"*). (An example of the latter might be in relation to validity parameters: if, for example, some technical software has been programmed to calculate the flow rate of a fluid through a pipeline, the software can be programmed to reject an input which claims the pipeline to be of negative diameter; in the case of a purchase transaction, the software can be programmed to reject a date such as 37th October.)

Audit method	Manual controls	Software controls
Visual examination of objective evidence	Yes	
Manual reperformance	Yes	
Observe reperformance	Yes	
Visual comparison with audit copy		Yes
Reperformance		Yes
Audit pack		Yes

Figure 4.5 Audit methods for manual and software controls

Audit methods that can be used in the case of manual controls and software controls are shown in Figure 4.5. When preparing for the audit, the lead auditor must determine the methods to be used. The first three, relating to manual controls, have been outlined in Part 1 Chapter 11 within the section *"Obtaining objective evidence"*. A brief description of the last three audit methods that relate to software controls is detailed below.

Visual comparison:

By this method, the auditor will compare a printout of the actual software used with the master copy of the correct software which is kept in a secure environment and used solely for the purpose of auditing. This rather lengthy process entails a risk of error by the auditor in missing differences between lines of codes of the two copies. If the program is comprised of several million lines of code, not only is the risk of error compounded, the time taken by this method and the associated costs are probably prohibitive and unacceptable. An alternative method is to load an audit copy of the software onto the computer with an instruction for the computer to highlight any differences between the audit copy and the one in use.

Re-performance:

By this method, the auditor asks the auditee to re-run the software in his presence. The correct data is loaded into the machine and the auditor then verifies that the same results are obtained. This can also be done by loading that data and comparing the results, obtained when it is processed using an audit copy of the software, with those obtained from the software edition used by the auditee. This method is not always suitable for auditing of computer operated/ controlled plant.

Audit pack:

By this method, the auditor uses special software which has been produced solely for the purpose of auditing. This software comprises a set of data or programs to be processed by the computer, the results of which are pre-known to the auditor. Alternatively, a simulation pack which creates known situations is used. If there are any irregularities in the results, the auditor will investigate the matter further. One particular problem with this method is that audit packs can cost a lot of money to develop and it is often only large companies or computer applications which can justify their creation. This particular method is much favoured by accountancy firms performing conventional financial audits.

3. Loss controls

Loss prevention is an overriding discipline that must be an integral part of both the software supply project and the operational life of the software and computer installation. I have found it convenient to categorize loss as being comprised of six principle types, each of which is further described below. They are:

♦ Damage.
♦ Deterioration.
♦ Sabotage.
♦ Theft.
♦ Fraud.
♦ Change.

Damage

One must not only consider damage that can be caused by fire, flood or tempest but also damage which can be caused by the working environment. This might include nuisances in the form of: high or low humidity; dust or airborne particulate matter; stray electro-magnetic fields that can damage magnetic media; high static electricity levels; high temperature or low temperature; vibration, which damages disk drives and other mechanical pieces of equipment. The reader will recall that *"environment"* is one of the sub-elements of *"equipment"*, see Chapters 4 and 18.

At various points of operation and development, the auditor will check the arrangements that are designed to prevent environmental nuisance from occurring. (The number of points at which the arrangements will be checked will depend on the audit objectives.) This activity will include:

♦ Checking the management systems that control the support utilities required to maintain correct environmental conditions.
♦ Checking the arrangements for fire protection and detection.

The latter will be required at each work station, in the computer room (in the case that the auditee is operating a mainframe or large mini-computer system) and also within the library itself (where magnetic tapes, disks, master listings, print-outs and log books are retained). Any damage in such areas can obviously lead to a high degree of financial loss both directly and indirectly as a consequence of the value of the software's, the information's and the data's content.

Deterioration

Things gradually wear out with use. This is particularly true of disk drives and magnetic tapes that may be continually loaded and unloaded from a computer. Disk drives and printed circuit boards have a finite life and they require constant maintenance. The auditor should verify that the auditee is operating a satisfactory, planned maintenance system, as well as a condition monitoring system, to cover all equipment used. (If this is an activity performed by a service supplier under contract to the auditee, the auditor should investigate the efficacy of the purchasing controls used to select the supplier, specify the service required, monitor the supplier's performance.)

A log book should be maintained by the auditee so that the number of times that a particular magnetic tape has been loaded on and off the computer is known. There should be arrangements to ensure that prior to the end of its predicted life, the tape's contents are copied onto a new tape to prevent the risk of loss. The content of the new tape should be validated before use and the old tape destroyed in order to ensure security of the data it contained.

Sabotage

One is not dealing here primarily with sabotage caused by explosive devices, although this must not be overlooked (particularly in the case of government, military or other types of secure installations that could be a prime target for terrorism). A more insidious type of sabotage occurs through the software "bomb" which takes the form of someone gaining access to a computer program or data, leaving some coded instructions designed to do damage to that software or its associated data at a future point in time: one is dealing here with the problems of malicious, mischievous (criminal) damage caused by hackers and viruses. Software bombs may be an action by a disgruntled employee. It is, therefore, generally desirable that any disaffected employee or any person who appears about to resign from a company, has his or her authorization to use the computer system or to access any part of the software, withdrawn immediately. If an employee decides to resign, the auditee may well be advised to ask the person to leave immediately and provide him/her with the appropriate remuneration due. These actions are as much to protect the innocent employee from the finger of suspicion as they are to protect the company from the risk of a software bomb. Accordingly, this will affect the auditee's human resources (personnel) policies.

The auditor will examine objective evidence that demonstrates that:

♦ An effective policy exists, concerning the authorization or removal of access to software in the case of new employees, resignations and transfers.

♦ An effective policy exists, concerning positive vetting of new staff prior to engagement and assignment to sensitive situations.

♦ An effective policy exists, concerning positive vetting of staff being transferred or promoted to positions requiring access to sensitive software and data.

♦ An effective policy exists, regarding constant monitoring of staff in sensitive situations.

♦ Management systems have been developed for implementing each of those policies and have been communicated to those charged with implementing them.

♦ Those policies and management systems are implemented and are effective.

Apart from careful monitoring and selection of staff, other essential controls include the maintenance of log books and signatures of personnel authorized for access to or use of specific tapes, disks, print outs, programs and so on. These should all be maintained in a secure environment within the library and there should be a regular check by the auditee to ensure that unauthorized alterations to the software have not taken place. In the event that access to the computer or its software can be obtained from an external site *via* a telecommunications link, there must be careful control over the issuing and security of passwords and over the authorization that each potential user might have to access any part of the system. The systems needs effective "fire walls". The points to verify have been outlined below under *"Theft"*.

Theft

Theft of hardware and hard copy can be prevented by normal security controls at a reception desk, for example. However, software or data theft can also occur by unauthorized transmission. Industrial espionage is a genuine problem and it is somewhat irritating to find that a new suite of software, a new design for a product or the company's accounts have been stolen by or on behalf of somebody outside one's own organization.

The auditor will verify that:

♦ Unauthorized print outs of programs and data are prevented.
♦ There are controls as to who can log into the computer, the company's network or its intranet, which include the use of

> security clearances, confidential passwords, encryption, user names and other firewall aids.

♦ Unauthorized transmission of data or software through telecommunication links is prevented.

♦ Alterations to programs, standing data or transaction data are only performed by authorized personnel on the basis of management approvals. This in turn means close monitoring of access to libraries to obtain master disks, tapes and other media that contain software and data.

♦ There is controlled access to every part of the computer installation and controlled use of the programs and data that the systems (the network or the intranet) may contain.

♦ Management systems to achieve the above have been defined, documented and communicated to those who need them.

♦ Those systems are implemented and are effective.

Theft can also occur by electronic eavesdropping on stray electro-magnetic radiations that are caused whenever a computer is operating or a data transmission line is working. This has particular significance for military and similar high security installations. With this in mind, the software development or computer operation might need to take place within a secure bunker, for example, that is completely electro-magnetically screened and secure; transmission may need to be scrambled or encoded. In these circumstances, the auditor may also wish to assess the protection systems that prevent stray radiations from being picked up by a foreign or potentially hostile power, or by an aggressive corporate competitor. Other matters that may require verification by the auditor have been listed in the section *"Sabotage"*, above.

Fraud

Fraud is recognized as a being a modern white-collar crime and is purportedly a "business" with a high growth rate. It can occur either by alteration of master tapes and programs or by alteration of standing data: it can also occur through improper use of, or access to, the computer or data. As the Internet grows apace and the boom in commercial shopping through its facility expands, the security of customer data, such as personal details, credit card numbers and identities, is taxing the inventiveness of software developers and Internet suppliers alike. The resourcefulness of thieves, hackers and mischief makers also seems without bounds.

Within the company, though, to deter fraudulent acts, the auditee should maintain log books recording who has had access to any part of the software or data as well as the formal authorizations for such access. Naturally, the auditee should also be regularly checking that programs and data have not been altered. The auditor must verify that such arrangements are being made and are properly maintained.

The other points which are listed under *"Theft"* and *"Sabotage"*, above, should also be checked by the auditor.

Where fraud could occur during actual use of a computer through batch processing, the operational controls, described earlier in this chapter, must be verified.

Change

Software and data can be changed either deliberately or inadvertently. Deliberate change is for the purpose of fraud, theft or sabotage which have already been mentioned. Inadvertent change often arises from good intentions: it is not uncommon, for example, to find that a programmer, trying to help the users, may alter a program, but in so doing has introduced other problems into the running of that software. Hence, there is a need to maintain a tight control on the configuration of the software. Inadvertent loss arising from change also requires:

- The implementation of rigid controls in the library.
- Planned authorizations regarding change to the software.
- The maintaining of log books.
- Strict control over personnel authorized to alter standing data that is maintained by the system.
- Independent auditing of all these controls.

Loss can also occur when parts of the hardware, such as printed circuit boards, are changed. Accordingly, when the computer system is being maintained, it is important that the auditee ensures that the same type of spare parts as in the original machine have been used. Without such control, there is the possibility that the software and hardware interface may become impaired.

Management	Authority	Independence
Determines policies and budgets	Operators not permitted: To write/ amend programs or system software; Access to program listings.	Library staff independent of operations/ development staff
Reviews and approves plans and procedures		Independent audit of library controls
Selects and appoints staff		Independent tests of new/ changed software
Reviews and approves controls' results	Development staff not allowed unauthorized use of computer	Independent audits
Requires management audits	Controlled access to: Library; Computer room; Terminals	Independent follow-up of corrective actions identified
Authorizes corrective action		
Authorizes development of new/ changed software and documents		

Figure 4.6 Principal organizational features for loss control

Organization requirements for loss control

Figure 4.6 lists various organizational requirements that should have been considered by the auditee in preventing loss. These features need be verified by the auditor when looking at organizations charts, job descriptions, job specifications and procedures. (This is when performing Steps 1 and 2 of the seven step method described in Part 1 Chapter 11.) The various loss controls, the task elements and the associated sub-elements are interrelated. Controls over the distribution of information, for example, are identical to analyzing the problem of controlling access to that information, which helps to prevent several of the categories of loss; control over the checking and the edition of information reduces the risk of loss caused by change; an important attribute of the people working on the systems, or developing the software, is honesty and integrity. The reader will by now appreciate that applying the task elements and considering the implications of the key sub-elements is essential if the risk of loss is to be minimized.

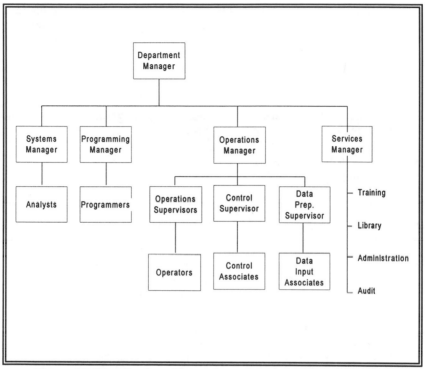

Figure 4.7 Organization chart - a large data processing department

Organization charts

Figure 4.7 depicts a rather large data processing department. Various of the organizational features described in this chapter can be seen in the diagram. An example of this would be to study the functional independence between the operations staff, the programming staff and analysis staff and to compare the independent positions of the audit and library from each other. Of course, it is not adequate to just look at such a chart, the auditor also needs to ascertain the names of the people charged with the responsibilities of each position in order to check that the same person has not been assigned tasks that could lead to a conflict of duties.

Virtual organizations

See Chapter 3 *"Project audits"*. When the software project is undertaken by this type of organization the auditor must pay attention to the manner in which the various project team members are managed to ensure the loss controls, mentioned above, are in place. The organization chart can be reviewed to ascertain the loss controls etc., described in this chapter are in place.

Control of resources

Resources that will be of particular importance throughout the project and which will require careful management are:

- Manpower resources
- Equipment
- Overall budget

Manpower resources and overall budget have been described in Chapter 3 *"Project audits"*.

It has been my experience that software development projects are particularly susceptible to overruns in their manpower budgets. The "S" curves, described previously, depicting planned and actual manpower usage appear as Figure 4.8. The auditor should examine carefully the divergence of actual manpower from planned manpower levels as this frequently indicates inadequate planning coupled with emerging quality problems. The cause and effects of those problems need thorough investigation so that management can be properly advised of remedial and preventive action for upcoming project activities. Examining such manpower reports and graphs, such as Figure 4.8, does not require any special knowledge of software technology and can point the audit team towards project activities that merit their special attention.

Equipment

In some cases, the customer or end user may want the software to run on equipment of a different type or make to that which the vendor has. It is important to verify that the auditee has correctly selected the computing equipment which will be used to assist with the software development. If the equipment does not have the same capability, condition, configuration etc. as the user's, the auditee will need to have made provision for the acquisition either by purchase, lease or rent of the right type of equipment.

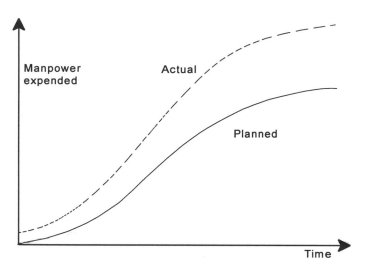

Figure 4.8 A typical software development project 'S' curve

This will incur expenditure of money which should have been properly estimated and allocated.

The auditor will examine objective evidence to verify that :

♦ Management systems for the estimation of the equipment budget really needed for each phase have been defined and communicated to the project management.

♦ The basis for equipment planning and budgeting is consistent with the project objectives and customer requirements.

♦ The project has defined its systems for monitoring and recording its use of equipment and has communicated them throughout the project.

♦ All the foregoing management systems are implemented and are effective.

♦ The project analyses the areas of opportunity for equipment savings which are not to the detriment of quality achievement.

5. Auditing service providers

Serve and thou shalt be served.
If you love and serve men, you cannot,
by any hiding or stratagem, escape the remuneration.

Emerson.

Introduction

Services are prevalent in all companies regardless of the industrial sector in which they operate. They permit specialization and are intended to reduce unit costs, thus increasing efficiency for the customer/user. To achieve this state of affairs, they must be efficient in themselves. They can only succeed by not incurring avoidable costs and are thus obliged to prevent problems associated with their own work, just as manufacturing functions are constantly required to.

Service companies are no different from any other. They have their problems, company-wide and in individual departments. Those problems also have their roots in the six real causes described in Chapter 18 and, just as for any other industry, services can benefit from management audits.

ISO 9004-2 is a standard that offers extensive advice. Released in 1991, its content reflects elements of the second edition of this book, written some years earlier. It outlines various basic controls and systems to consider and contains useful precepts for service organizations.

The importance of service quality

The service sector of all nations' economies forms an ever increasing percentage of most countries' gross national product and, since it is comprised of human beings possessing all the usual frailties, it creates an ever increasing percentage of each nation's avoidable costs. In the civil services, these costs are funded by the tax burden and one can only speculate how much one's own nation's tax burden could be reduced if those avoidable costs were reduced by 10%, 20%, 50% or whatever, if only as much attention were paid to quality improvement in these sectors as has been the case in many manufacturing industries. Alternatively, one might wonder how many more hospital beds and surgical operations would be possible if the money saved invested immediately in a nation's health service; or how far the incipient national pensions crisis could have been mitigated.

The quality of service received from departments within one's own company and from external companies is a major factor in deciding competitive advantage. A better service with minimized avoidable costs can mean an achievable lower target price; reduced marketing; repeat business; increased market share; increased profit and return on investment; increased share value. Concentrating on service is an area of opportunity for every company. Auditing can identify opportunities, as described in Chapter 2 *"Value-added audits"*.

What are the products of a "service"?

The traditional view of services is that they are comprised of activities such as banking, insurance, postal delivery, entertainment, tourism, transportation and the security sectors of the economy. Many other businesses also provide services including for example, design, storage, logistics management, specialized manufacturing, product repair, all of which would have been found at one time in-house at manufacturers' premises - indeed, many still are. Some activities are called services but comprise the delivery of a tangible product. Vending machines, for example, deliver a product and are more accurately described as process equipment in the way that power station boilers are. A vending machine is a robot that acts as a shop, delivery system and factory combined. It requires human tending and servicing just as a production line robot does. Plainly, services are *"work done for someone else"[1]*, regardless of any particular economic sector. One could view a motor manufacturer as a service company in that it does something for someone else. There is a tangible "item" involved.

Not all services result in a tangible product, however. Transportation of items or people does not cause them to exist, it merely removes them from one location to another; an insurance company does not cause its customers to exist, but, it does provide them with certain knowledge, information about which can be communicated in a document called a policy whilst contractual agreement about this information can be denoted by the issuing of a certificate.

What is a *"service"*?

See Part 1 Chapter 4 for my definition of *"service"* .

What is *"quality"* of a service?

As always, quality can be considered as comprising an amalgam of fitness for purpose, compliance with customer requirements and realization of customer expectations. Quality and price are not synonymous: they never are, even in the case of manufacturing. In all businesses, quality and price are inextricably entwined to form the concept of value for money which is a perception of the customer: so too with services, hence the importance of customer expectations. When considering value for money, the customer certainly expects the service to tend to his welfare and advantage for if it does not, the service will not be sought. Value for money and his own welfare and benefit are, therefore, important constituents of customer expectation. As in any business, the provision of services imposes contractual and legal obligations. In the final analysis, all of these considerations are, as ever, vital features of the service which must be defined.

The role of the auditor

An audit is aimed principally at ascertaining whether or not the management systems proposed for use in the development and supply of a service will prove effective in practice and at determining both the extent of the compliance with those systems and the systems' efficacy. As always, auditing of services is a preventative action taken on behalf of management to determine that the release or use of resources is justified. The audits assist management to make sound decisions by providing them with factual information.

Systems audits

If a systems audit is being performed prior to commencement of a service product's life cycle or before the start of any particular phase of that life cycle, the auditor will be verifying that :

♦ The service organization has been properly conceived;
♦ The management systems have been properly developed and communicated to those who will use them;
♦ The necessary resources have been fully and properly budgeted;

♦ The time required for the product to become fully operational has been properly budgeted.

Such knowledge helps management both when it is deciding whether or not to allocate further resources and to proceed with the subsequent activities as planned and when it is trying to judge if the risk of loss or of avoidable costs has been minimized. The systems audit will, as always, be planned sufficiently ahead of the scheduled start of each phase to permit any corrective action, revealed by the audit as being necessary, to be accomplished. The audit objectives will be determined as outlined in Part 1 Chapter 9.

Compliance audits

Depending on the audit objectives, the auditor will, during a compliance audit, verify that the management systems are being met fully, such that :

♦ Fitness for purpose is being achieved;
♦ Contractual and legal obligations are being met;
♦ Time and resources are being properly managed.

The auditee's procedures may refer to various codes and standards with which the personnel must comply. If so, the auditor will spot check the auditee's compliance with them. Should this necessitate the presence of a specialist on the audit team, then this must be arranged. The auditee should be monitoring his own adherence to those standards etc. by means of quality controls and audits and should also be pursuing his own non-conformity and corrective action systems when he discovers problems. The auditor's spot checks are primarily aimed at obtaining confidence in the auditee's diligence in such matters and are not in themselves intended as quality controls for the auditee's use. If those responsible for the service are required to implement any company standard procedure the auditor will also :

♦ Verify compliance with those procedures;
♦ Obtain objective evidence of performance in order that the efficacy of those procedures can be ascertained;
♦ Inform those responsible for authorizing those procedures of any corrective action to them that is considered necessary.

Conduct of the audit

If the audit's objectives include ascertaining the auditee's state of compliance with any particular codes, standards or regulations, then, as part of the audit preparations, the auditor must obtain the interpretation that has been imposed on or agreed by the auditee. The task elements described in Part 1 Chapter 4 will still apply to individual tasks in the service operation.

The auditor will split the auditee's work into phases and tasks in order to investigate the systems, as described earlier in this book.

♦   The audit method and question technique will be as per Part 1 Chapters 11 and 13 respectively.
♦   Each department can be analyzed as described in Part 1 Chapter 5.
♦   Management systems can be considered as per Part 1 Chapter 6.
♦   The vital importance of thorough preparation remains (see Part 1 Chapter 9) as does the advisability of using a checklist, matrix or flowchart etc., as per Part 1 Chapter 7.

Certain aspects peculiar to services are described in the following sections of this chapter. These aspects are concerned with :

1.   Organizational matters;
2.   Designing of services;
3.   Quality controls.

1.   Organizational matters

Key matters and decisions

In organizing his operation, the auditee should have analyzed his business and potential markets and then defined the following :

♦   Customers and their associated market locations.
♦   The services to be offered to each customer at each location.
♦   The market share, penetration and timing of that penetration at each selected market location.
♦   The target price for each location and associated cost maxima.

These are the key matters that should be decided within the framework of a management system which ensures :

- ◆ The basic information which has to be obtained to assist those decision makers is defined.
- ◆ The information on which those decisions are based is reliable, up-to-date and recorded.
- ◆ That information includes details of current finance, management, staff and technical capabilities available within the company.
- ◆ The information includes all relevant legislation and other restraints that would affect the company and its product at the individual market locations.
- ◆ The information is presented to those decision makers at the time required and in the manner specified.
- ◆ The absence of information required by those decision makers but not available is recorded.
- ◆ The constraints imposed on the decision making process are recorded.
- ◆ The people making the decisions are competent and trained in the skills and techniques required.
- ◆ Security of the information, its acquisition and the decision making process is maintained.

The auditor will look for objective evidence that such a management system exists, has been communicated to all concerned, is implemented and is effective. This may involve the consideration of matters which are best treated during a president's audit, see Chapter 7.

Once the decision has been taken to proceed with the supply of the service, it has to be designed and there will often be some iteration between the actual designing and the decision making process. The decisions mentioned above constitute key input to the design team and help to formulate its terms of reference. Accordingly, the auditor will check that this design input has been effectively communicated to that team and is consistent with the information provided to the decision makers, thereby verifying the existence of an audit trail.

Defining the organization

At this point or when the design has been approved, the auditee management should :

- ◆ Define the tasks involved in performing the service;
- ◆ Define the organizational structure including reporting levels, job descriptions, as mentioned in Part 1 Chapter 3. for

      a) the central corporate body, such as a business
           profit centre (if any),

      b) each service product,

      c) each market location to be served;

♦   Specify each task (as described below);

♦   Design the management systems and work sequence;

♦   Communicate these features to all concerned, perhaps by means of manuals or procedures. (It is not ncessary to use hard copy for this pupose - electronic means offers considerable advantages that should be reaped.

The auditor will look for proof that these things have been done and are consistent with the needs of the service as designed and approved.

Foreground and background activities

There are two distinct sets of activities involved in service companies and departments. I refer to those which come directly into contact with customers and end users as *"foreground"* activities and those which are behind the scene, supporting the foreground, as *"background"* activities. Both require organization and integrated management systems.

Examples of tasks that might be encountered in a company are listed in Figure 5.1. Every company will have its own individual differences, shades of gray and overlap between the foreground and background tasks listed above. Company image is especially sensitive to lapses in those who interface directly with the customer and personnel must be carefully selected, trained and assessed accordingly. The exposed nature of foreground tasks dictates the need for special care in their accomplishment which can only be achieved as a result of thorough designing and planning of the tasks before they are introduced. Company image can also be affected by the way in which individuals and departments interface and deal with other external bodies who are not customers. If, for example, purchasing officers are unpleasant with supplier staff, this can affect the company reputation. In this context, one can see that virtually everyone in a company has to be aware of the service aspects of his or her performance and that the precepts contained in the fifth task element *"service"* could, therefore, apply to all.

Resources and time

Remembering that lack of resources and lack of time are real causes of business problems, the auditor will also look for proof that the auditee :

Foreground tasks	Background tasks
Reception	Human resources
Marketing	Advertising
Sales	Storage/ warehousing
Telephone enquiries	Staff training
Customer support advice	Accounts payable
Customer equipment servicing	Technical library
New installations	Plant maintenance
Delivery to customers	Plant design
Customer training	Plant procuerment
Accounts receivable	Fleet maintenance
Contract/ project management	Legal
Technical information	Cleaning
Customer complaint	Finance
Customer equipment design	Records
	Research
	Product development
	Product design
	Materials managment
	Purchasing
	Distribution/ transport
	Packaging
	Item distribution
	Computing
	Management information systems
	Quality control
	Security

Figure 5.1 Examples of foreground and background tasks

♦ Has developed a management system for the estimation of time required for the development and introduction of the service.

♦ Has developed a management system for the estimation of resources needed for the development and introduction of the service.

♦ Has developed management systems for the monitoring of time and of resources.

♦ Has communicated those systems to the staff involved in the development and introduction of the service.

♦ Has implemented those systems.

♦ Can demonstrate that those systems are effective.

♦   Has allocated the resources necessary for the development and introduction of the service.

♦   Has allocated the time required to introduce the service at each location.

♦   Analyses areas of opportunity for saving time and resources which are not to the detriment of quality achievement.

The task elements and service providers.

When reading this section the reader is also referred to Part 1 Chapter 4 which contains some additional considerations.

Person: Competence

Formal educational qualifications can be irrelevant or of secondary importance to the person's achieved abilities and attributes. In services such as sports and entertainment, the competence of players and performers is of paramount importance since their abilities are a major attraction of the service, affecting customer satisfaction and business success: nobody pays to see a loser. In other services functions, such as serving in a hamburger store or selling insurance, the competence levels can be defined in terms of experience, formal educational qualifications, vocational certificates and the like, and can be prescribed in a job specification.

If the service involves the actual supply or hiring out of staff, the auditee must ensure that the candidates' competence and other personnel accomplishments are consistent with the customer's needs. This will necessitate a management system for the review of customer requirements, scrupulous attention to the selection of staff and a policy of ensuring that only those staff who meet the customer's needs are offered to that customer. Even though an employment agency or recruitment consultant may not actually employ the candidates, they are equivalent to foreground staff who reflect the quality of the service provided. Not only must the competence and other sub-elements relating to the persons responsible for selecting and interviewing the staff be controlled, so too must the procedures for selecting candidates offered to the customer. These considerations apply equally well to the work performed by human resource departments when screening job applicants. The auditor will pay attention to these points.

Person: Training

As ever, training is of vital importance. Special aspects of training that a person may require are mentioned throughout this chapter. The individual is responsible for the quality of his or her work and that of the staff for whom he or she is assigned responsibility. This is especially important in foreground activities and is a point that must be impressed upon the individual during training programmes. Considerable assistance can be given to foreground staff in the form of training programmes which present the expected standard of performance in matters such as courtesy, customer handling, personal appearance (grooming) and so on. Adequate performance in these matters should be a part of the assessment process to determine staff competence: regular re-assessment and training must also be considered and performed as necessary. The auditor can verify whether or not the auditee implements an effective system for the achievement of these aims.

Person: Attributes

The exposed position of foreground tasks means that special attention must be paid to defining attributes that the ideal person would possess. Amongst them might be behaviour; articulacy; the ability to work in a team; the ability to work under pressure; personal appearance and hygiene; self-discipline; self-confidence; ability to take criticism, both warranted and unwarranted; patience; flexibility/adaptability. Certain attributes such as behaviour, courtesy, presentation and attitude of staff can also be most important and can be improved by the process of training.

Items

Many services actually provide finished items for consumption or use by the customer. Fast food stores, restaurants, airlines, shops, supermarkets, photo studios, dry cleaners all do so, some of them actually making the item (e.g. snacks or meals), others using chemical or physical processes to provide the service (e.g. dry cleaners, photo studios). Attention to the quality of the item provided is, of course, a central part in achieving customer satisfaction. Obviously the sub-elements for *"Item"* require the auditee's careful consideration and control. A simple example of how item sub-elements might apply to a hamburger is shown in Figure 5.2.

Legislative constraints on the item must be obeyed and the management systems must ensure that their edicts are satisfied. Weights and measures regulations, for example, govern the quantity controls for the items provided to the customer. Compliance with them will depend on other sub-elements including personal honesty; equipment condition; correctness of information. The equipment, staff and information to which they relate might be either in the background or in foreground activities and the auditor must ascertain which.

Items: Correct condition

The condition of the item might have been specified by the customer (glossy finish to a photograph; ice cold beer; sharp creases in pressed trousers) or it might be specified by the service company and advertized as such (*"ice cold beer on tap"; "photographs ready mounted"; "cleaning includes pressing"*). For various services, the law may stipulate certain minimum conditions that the item must possess, most frequently in respect of health and safety (e.g. non-toxic food; insulation that contains no asbestos).

Care of customer property must be ensured at all times and, so that the company's liability position can be safeguarded, the condition of the items should be established on receipt. Any apparent damage should be pointed out and agreed with the customer, a note being made to that effect. (Furniture removal services note damage and broken items prior to their packing the same; prospective tenants will prudently note all damage and deterioration to fixtures, fittings and decorations in the accommodation they are considering renting.) If the condition is such that the service may cause damage or would not be effective, the auditee staff should make this known to the customer and if necessary decline to accept the work. Examples include badly packed parcels that the customer wishes to post; out-of-date film that the customer wishes to have processed; torn or stained garments sent to a dry cleaning agency. The auditor will check that the auditee has a management system to ensure these points receive attention and that the staff are trained accordingly.

Items: Correct quantity

Excess or short measure is always unacceptable. The meters, gauges, scales and other measuring devices used in background and foreground activities have to be true and accurate: in most countries, there is legislation affecting these matters. Hence, traceability to a recognized national (or international) standard is prudent and essential from the product liability and reputation standpoints. Certain quantities require equipment maintenance as opposed to conventional calibration of gauges:

Task - Serve hamburger	*Task - Provide Insurance cover*
Item: Hamburger	**Service:** Insurance sale
Type: 1/4 pound cheeseburger	**Type:** Motor vehicle insurance
Capability: To retain temperature of at least 110 deg. F. Up to 10 minu tes after cooking and packing	**Characteristics:** Nationwide availability Office sale (face-to-face with customer) Accurate premiums as per insurer's tables A selection of insurers for customer to choose from, but also catering for customer's other personal preference Credit card or cheque payment All company outlets to operate in consistent manner
Condition: As delivered to serving tray by kitchen Freshly cooked within last 10 minutes Meal hot Cheese melted Uncrushed Absence of oil or grease stains Ingredients stacked as per company standard Packaged in company standard carton	**Presentation:** Max. Waiting time 5 mins. Customer care during wait Individual attention without interuptions Private consulting room if requested Imediate written quotes Immediate coverage Pleasant, friendly atmosphere Smiles, eye contact, calm, confident mannr and absence of raised voice Do not rush the customer Helpful - nothing is too much trouble Comfortable clean rooms at stable 70 deg. Temperature No form of discrimination whatsoever Standard local office hours. After hours telephone and Internet assistance messages

Figure 5.2 Applying the task elements to different services

Task - Serve hamburger	Task - Provide Insurance cover
Quantity: Single unit comprising 1 hamburger slice of 1/4 pound uncooked weight Standard sesame seed bun 2 slices tomato 4 pieces pickle 2 slice lettuce 2 onion slices 1 slice chees **Identification:** Position in serving tray; visual appearance and pre-printed cheeseburger carton	**Perform completely:** Provide all information requested by custoer Transaction forms fully completed Customer receipts provided immediately Maling list update, if required Customer welcome procedure Privacy procedure if needed Refreshment and courtesy procedure Customer farewell procedure **Identification:** Company colour and logo to identify offices, staff uniforms, documents and computer displays Labelled sign placed on motor insurance officer's desk Motor insurance documents and computer screen displays to be titled as such

Figure 5.2 (Cont.)

in the case of a cash dispensing machine, for instance, there would be no thanks for short change. The auditor will ascertain the quantity control required and use this information when considering *"Equipment"*, discussed below.

Items: Correct identification

The customer wants to receive the items that he has selected. Identification might be by visual appearance which makes the identity of the item self-evident: it could equally well be on a package, as, for example, take-away food may be served in a preprinted package. Tags, ticket stubs, counterfoils, labels etc. could all be acceptable means of identification provided that they do not damage the item, reduce its quality in any way or present a risk to the customer.

Identification of status can also be important. The background and foreground staff must understand and use the same identification system. Embarrassment can be caused when the actual status of processing the item is not known by foreground staff and it is handed over to the customer incomplete, unready, unfinished or whatever. Where background and foreground staff work in close proximity to each other, these situations can develop when things get busy. The auditor should investigate how those embarrassments are prevented.

Equipment: Correct condition

The condition of the equipment used in foreground activities can affect the company image. It must be in a presentable condition that is properly maintained. Cleaning, painting, lubricating, overhauling may each be necessary to some extent and the frequency at which these actions are undertaken will depend on usage rate and service conditions. Passenger transport vehicles may require cleaning prior to each journey; sales offices may require cleaning, polishing and dusting every day and repainting every six months with carpets being replaced at least yearly; decorative plants may need weekly tending.

Similarly, background equipment will also require its own maintenance programme for daily, weekly, monthly actions or for routine maintenance every so many running hours. Hotel kitchens, for example, may require nightly cleaning whilst air conditioning equipment may require an overhaul, say, every 5,000 hours of operation.

In certain instances, the equipment condition might affect safety of customers and/or of staff. There will probably be various regulations and codes that the auditor must consider when covering this matter.

Equipment: Correct capability

The consistency of performance and reliability of the service are greatly dependent on the reliability of the equipment used by the customer or by the staff. The equipment must work correctly under all operating conditions and even under abnormal circumstances, such as when there is peak demand for the service. Such latter considerations must be taken into account when the service is being designed and equipment is being specified for procurement.

Higher levels of safety, faster transportation, better snow clearance in a municipality, entertainment machines capable of providing the customer with greater excitement or mental stimulation and similar demands for better services constantly necessitate higher specifications for the equipment. The auditee will render himself liable to needless avoidable costs if these matters are not considered.

Many service operations rely on computers. They are often a convenient scapegoat for staff who cannot admit their own fault or their own sloppy work. The computers must be capable of processing the volume of information required within a time frame that is acceptable to the customer.

In October 1986, the rules governing the buying and selling of stocks and shares in London were changed. The event was known as the *"Big Bang"*. As these rules were changed, so were the computer systems used to present information to the dealers. When trading began, the systems crashed because the demands on them exceeded expectations. Acute embarrassment and frustration was incurred by those responsible as well as by the users.

When programmed properly, computers can reduce the likelihood of error because of their ability to permit consistency of quality. Further discussion on controls on computer software and installations is contained in the previous chapter.

The explosive growth of the Internet has attracted ever increasing numbers of new customers to its possibilities. At peak times telephone companies are finding their local networks jammed by Internet users: the companies have begun to complain and even threaten to charge Internet users a premium for using local dialing facilities. The real problem is the failure of the telephone companies, many of whom are also enjoying the status of being an Internet service provider, to upgrade their systems to meet the demand they themselves have courted. Internet service providers, too, often are unable to serve all their customers at peak times: the response of some to user needs noticeably deteriorates on these occasions.

The situation became so bad at the beginning of 1997 that many customers of the company America On Line (AOL) began legal action because of alleged persistent inability to gain Internet access by that company, whose breathtaking growth had exceeded its equipment capabilities at that time. When trying to log on to AOL,

583

at peak periods, the customers would be advised to try the service later. The gridlock was so extensive various American State Attorney Generals considered filing legal suits against AOL.

Equipment: Location

Customers are seldom impressed when the necessary equipment for performing the service is not available at the right place at the right time. The auditee should consider the need for issuing complete sets of equipment to each of its foreground staff since sharing might cause inconvenience, delay and frustration.

Closely allied to this, is the consideration of the availability of equipment by virtue of its reliability, or lack thereof.

Equipment: Environment

The key principle is to ensure that nuisances do not arise: whereas in a manufacturing environment, a nuisance is one that affects the performance of staff, the condition of items or equipment, in foreground activities of the same sector, however, the "condition of the customer" also can be affected. Lighting levels, temperature and humidity controls, dust and dirt, noise levels, crowded conditions each play a part in customer satisfaction. Customer expectations for the environment must be considered since, if the environment does not meet the standards set by competitors or similar industries, business may be lost. It is wise to remember that the ready availability of international travel, news and communications afford opportunities for customers to compare standards with those elsewhere.

The auditee must take these factors into account when the environment is being designed and maintained. The auditor will investigate whether or not the auditee has done so.

Information: Content

All members of staff and all customers want correct information. Some information can be especially critical or sensitive, particularly when it relates to personal details. Customer records must be correct and complete and one can easily imagine the damage and upset caused if, for instance, a hospital's medical records are inaccurate (allergies are not listed; blood types are wrongly recorded; drugs prescribed to the patient are incorrectly stated; physical or mental ailments are listed incorrectly). Similarly, customers do not wish to receive someone else's account, to be billed for services which were not required or not received, to be billed without due discounts being applied or receive incorrect tickets or reservations.

The precepts concerning loss control described in the previous chapter are also important in service operations and the auditor should investigate such matters.

2.   The design of services

Designing anything is a task itself whose outcome depends on the quality of the input, the task elements involved and avoidance of the six real causes of problems. The latter two have been previously discussed in Part 1 Chapters 4 and 18 respectively.

Design input

Typical information that comprises design input is listed in Figure 5.3, much of which should have been the result of the business decisions described earlier in this chapter. Some matters obviously require particular attention. In considering *"who is our customer"*, for example, the auditee should bear in mind that customers may be manifold and that the term does not just include the person who pays for the service. "Customers" could be end-users; those who see the effects of the service and its results i.e. bystanders; regulatory bodies, banks, insurance companies, with which the company has to deal to secure loans or execute its business; colleagues in the chain of supply/consumption/system; even suppliers who receive the results of the service, as in the case of the company's own purchasing service. Any or all of these must receive due attention.

The fact that there can be many different customers involved can be illustrated by considering those telephone users who experience the service offered by a telephone company. They could include:

♦   Domestic subscribers; private and business.
♦   International visitors; private and business.
♦   Domestic call recipients; private and business.
♦   International call recipients; private and business.
♦   International interfacing organizations such as foreign telephone companies.
♦   International callers; private and business.

Design input from management	Factors for consideration	Principal design action
Who is our "customer"? What is our product? Where is the customer located? What would constitute fitness for purpose? Anticipated customer and market expectations Contractual obligations Legal obligations Target selling price, volume and market share Current company capabilities Available resources Time scale for introduction of the service Budget available	Assisting the customer in specifying requirements Customer behaviour Assumptions can be wrong Customized services Potential non-conformities Customer complaints Product liability	List the foreground tasks Define task elements and sub-elements for each List the background tasks, task elements and sub-elements for each Design the managment system that links the foreground and background tasks Define acceptance criteria for tasks Define quality controls for tasks (i.e. produce quality plan)

Figure 5.3 Service design factors for consideration and design action

Each customer has its own particular needs, some or all of which may be identical to others': these must be subject to careful analysis by the designers. The auditor will verify that the auditee has a system which :

♦ Provides the correct input information to the designer prior to commencement of the design.
♦ Ensures that the input is incorporated into the design.

586

Assisting the customer in specifying requirements

The foreground staff could be faced with a customer who is not completely sure about what he wants, cannot provide a detailed specification or merely wishes to explore the various options available. In these situations, the customer can be helped if presented with some choice or menu. A questionnaire form, checklist or set of prompts on a visual display unit which the foreground staff can discuss with the customer may aid the latter's decisions.

The auditor will look for proof that the auditee :

a) Has developed a design management system to ensure :

♦ Mechanisms for assisting the customer to select and specify his particular requirements are designed.
♦ Those mechanisms are properly checked prior to issue.
♦ Those mechanisms are communicated to the foreground staff.

b) Has communicated that design management system to those that will use it.

c) Has implemented that system and that the system is efficacious.

Customer behaviour

Customer behaviour can affect the employee response desired under normal circumstances. The customer's perception of that response and of the service might make his behaviour even more unpredictable. A vicious circle could develop leading to a breakdown in communication, antagonism and hostility, the effects of which might extend far beyond a lost customer. Customer actions and questions must be anticipated and planned. A dummy run with a member of staff assuming the role of a difficult customer can help the design process by highlighting unforeseen factors. This is similar to prototype testing which is often practised in manufacturing industry as part of design verification.

The design should, therefore, strive towards exploring and removing possible causes of unpredictability by ensuring that the customer will be managed from the time when initial contact is made. Layout of premises, of forms, provision of instructions and signs all help. A good example of managing the customer is to be found at Disneyland with its marvelous queuing and help systems: another excellent example is to be found at

Changi Airport, Singapore with its concept, layout, appearance and facilities. The environment in which the service is delivered also affects and conditions the customer to react in the desired way. Attention to nuisance avoidance is important. The way in which the customer is managed helps to prevent product liability claims.

The auditor will look for proof that the auditee:

a)   Has developed a design management system to ensure:

♦   The customer's possible questions and actions are carefully considered.
♦   Measures to deal with those questions and actions are developed such that customer dissatisfaction is prevented as far as could reasonably foreseen and anticipated.
♦   Those measures are checked properly prior to issue.
♦   They are communicated to the foreground staff.

b)   Has communicated that design management system to those that will use it.

c)   Has implemented that system and that the system is efficacious.

Assumptions can be wrong

Without a market survey or other feedback it is impossible to know completely what the customers' acceptance criteria are or will be. Even with this information, it is easy to misjudge the relative importance of individual features of the service to the customer. It is always possible that values within the auditee's company have influenced the market information obtained as the result of a failure to address certain matters which the customer considers important but which were neglected by the auditee or dismissed by him as being trivial.

The influence and effects of competitive sources

The company may also have misjudged how the customers regard the competitors' products, technological and other advances in the market or environment. A classic example of the impact of technological advances is the market change caused when television started to compete with cinema. Although film companies competed with each other, there came a time when they were also competing with technology - if convenience foods provided convenience eating, television provided convenience entertainment. Many failed to realize this. Amusement parks, that rose in popularity during the early 20th century, suffered a similar reverse in fortune as competition from motor cars and television increased. It took a new concept to revive such parks. This was due to Walt Disney's "theme parks" initiated in 1955 with the opening of Disneyland in California. The auditor will investigate whether or not the auditee's design management system ensures that the design considers and allows for erroneous assumptions.

Customized services

Customers always like to feel that they are receiving personal attention and are considered to be important. Foreground staff will want to be as accommodating as possible in satisfying the customer's particular needs or whims. It is obviously sensible that they do not commit others to a customized service which is beyond the company's resources or capabilities. Staff training and good communications are vital if the *"Yes, we can do that for you"* promise is to be honoured. The bandwidth will establish the limitations.

Bandwidth

In order to customize the service, it is essential that its "core" is defined at the outset. From this the bandwidth, or range of options possible, must also be defined. The bandwidth necessary can be based on the experience and feedback obtained during a rehearsal or from a market survey. The service designer must receive this information and study it. Similarly, the input information concerning the existing capabilities must be reviewed and the designers should consult with as many members of staff as possible to determine what really is possible as well as the particular requirements of each. (It is often useful for the designers to consult with the internal management auditors who can offer an unbiased view of the actual capabilities available within the firm - see also Part 1 Chapter 1.)

The auditor will look for proof that the auditee:

a)   Has developed a design management system to ensure:

♦   Detailed information of the core of the service is produced by the designers and is comprehensively checked prior to release.

♦   The service bandwidth is based on verified capabilities within or available to the firm.

♦ Detailed information of the service bandwidth is produced and comprehensively checked prior to release.

♦ All of such detailed information required by the foreground and background staff is communicated to them for their own further action.

b) Has communicated that design management system to those that will use it.

c) Has implemented that system and that the system is efficacious.

Non-conformity

An effective service must recognize that things can go wrong without warning and that *"Murphy's Law"* can strike, when, for example, equipment fails or, in the case of an airline, luggage is lost. Alternative causes of action must be available immediately for there will be no time to process a conventional non-conformity report form and no time to train the staff in how to handle the situation.

The auditee should have defined *"What-if"* situations and designed solutions for them into the service and into the management systems that will support the foreground staff in dealing with the difficulties. Flow charts, fault trees, Ishikawa charts, failure modes and effects analyses (FMEAs) are all useful tools that the auditee can employ when analyzing non-conformity scenarios and their associated risks. These tools help identify the need for alternative actions.

Contingency plans

Contingency plans, along with the arrangements and resources required for them are essential. Their associated details must be part of the training and competence level of staff. The auditee's design must specify what is entailed. When properly considered and prepared, contingency plans can head off loss of business or reputation as well as a product liability claim but, even with all this effort, the sad fact is that Murphy's Law can still prevail.

As an aside: students at the University of Newcastle, England, sought to verify one of the corollaries to Murphy's Law, that a slice of bread dropping to the floor will land jelly side down. After exhaustive testing of the proposition by means of dropping countless slices of bread coated with butter, the results were inconclusive: the slices landed on plain and coated sides with more or less equal frequency. The experiment was filmed for broadcast on British television and this led their eminent Professor to conclude that Murphy's Law was true in that when one wants it to happen it won't! Murphy is a difficult cuss!

The auditor will examine proof that the auditee :

a) Has developed a design management system to ensure:

◆   The design defines the operational situations that could lead to non-conformity.
◆   Each situation is analyzed to determine its likelihood and risk.
◆   Those that must be catered for have been specified.
◆   Alternative actions, contingency plans and arrangements, readiness requirements and the requirements for dealing with each of those specified situations and their non-conformities have been developed.
◆   Those contingency plans etc. are comprehensively checked prior to issue.
◆   They are communicated to the foreground and background staff with details of responsibilities for making them work successfully.

b) Has communicated that design management systems to those who will use it.

c) Has implemented that system and that system is efficacious.

Customer complaint

The design can help to reduce the likelihood of customer complaint but for those unforeseeable occasions when complaints do materialize, there should be a system for dealing with them courteously and promptly.

The auditor will examine proof that the auditee:

a) Has developed a design management system to ensure:

◆   The design defines the situations that could lead to customer complaint.
◆   Guidelines for dealing with each situation have been specified.
◆   Those guidelines are fully checked prior to issue.

591

◆　　They are communicated to the foreground and background staff, together with details of responsibilities for dealing with those complaints successfully.

b) Has communicated that system to those that will use it.

c) Has implemented that system and that the system is efficacious.

Product liability

The designer must consider breaches of contractual and legal obligations which could give rise to a product liability claim and then "design out" potential causes. Obviously it may not be possible to foresee everything that could happen but the risks can be minimized by performing the analyses previously outlined in the section *"Non-conformity"*, above. Contract notices, warning notices, descriptions, advertisements, security, equipment and information safety, tort, health, trespass, weights and measures are but a few of the matters to be considered. Legal experts must review the design and plans.

The auditor will examine proof that the auditee:

a)　Has developed a design management system to ensure that:

◆　　Legal requirements are defined.
◆　　Product liability risks are defined.
◆　　These are communicated to the designer prior to the design work being started.
◆　　The design defines the operational situations that could lead to infringement of legal requirements or incur a product liability risk.
◆　　The possible causes of those situations are analyzed.
◆　　The likelihood of those causes arising is prevented or minimized.
◆　　Arrangements for dealing with any such situation that might arise have been specified.
◆　　Those arrangements are fully checked prior to issue.
◆　　Those arrangements are communicated to all staff, together with details of responsibilities for preventing such situations and for dealing with them successfully.

b)　Has communicated that design management system to those that will use it;

c) Has implemented that system and the system is efficacious.

Service characteristics

The characteristics required to ensure the achievement of quality and customer satisfaction must be defined and it is essential that careful consideration is paid to defining them during the design process so as to develop a service specification. Service characteristics have already been outlined in this chapter.

The auditor will look for proof that the auditee's design management system ensures:

♦   The characteristics are defined and checked prior to issue.
♦   Acceptance criteria for each characteristic are defined and checked for adequacy prior to issue.
♦   Those characteristics and their acceptance criteria are communicated to those foreground and background areas affected by them.

The auditor will also look for objective evidence that the system is implemented and is efficacious.

Service presentation

A selection of features which constitute correct presentation have been mentioned earlier in this chapter. The design effort will involve specifying the presentation required and then defining how each feature will be achieved by foreground tasks and by the management systems that direct the efforts of background staff in support of their foreground colleagues.

The auditor will look for proof that the auditee's design management system ensures:

♦   The presentation features are defined and checked prior to issue.
♦   Acceptance criteria for each feature are defined and checked for adequacy prior to issue.
♦   Those features and their acceptance criteria are communicated to those foreground and background areas affected by them.

The auditor will also look for objective evidence that the design management system is implemented and is efficacious.

593

Service performance

In order for the service to be performed completely, the foreground task needs to know precisely what would constitute complete performance. The design must state those details and devise methods which can be used to assist all concerned in checking for complete performance. (This matter has been discussed earlier in this chapter.) A major problem is that when the service requires customization, the designers cannot readily allow for the completeness of performance although details pertaining to the core of the service will remain immutable and require their attention. The auditor will look for proof that the auditee's design management system ensures:

♦ The aspects constituting complete performance of the service are defined and checked prior to issue.
♦ Those aspects are communicated to those foreground and background staff affected by them.

The auditor will also look for objective evidence that the design management system is implemented and is efficacious with regard to these matters.

Service identification

Methods for identifying the service were described earlier in this chapter. They will be achieved by means of organizing the other task elements, *viz.* Item, equipment, information and person. The auditor will look for proof that the auditee's design management system ensures:

♦ The methods for identifying the service are defined and checked prior to release for use.
♦ Those methods are communicated to those foreground and background areas affected by them.

The auditor will also look for objective evidence that the design management system is implemented and is efficacious with regard to these matters.

Design output

The preceding paragraphs have outlined design output information, all of which has consequences upon both the time needed to introduce the service and the actual resources that will be needed to introduce it and to operate it successfully. When the design is complete, the foreground and background departments (processes) must organize themselves for their contribution to the overall service effort. They will be linked together by management systems that contribute to the common objective of assuring that the service will be of quality. The entire organization will be linked together by primary, secondary and tertiary systems, as discussed in Part 1 Chapter 6.

The auditee should have considered the design output and then planned the entire delivery cycle/process and those primary, secondary and tertiary systems interface requirements. Each of those systems within the entire delivery cycle should then have been broken down into the interlinking tasks and the task elements and sub-elements defined for each. These in turn can be used to determine:

♦ Efforts needed to introduce the service.
♦ Time required to develop and introduce the service.
♦ Resources needed to develop, introduce and provide the service.

These activities have been mentioned earlier in this chapter, in the section entitled *"Organizational matters"*.

3. Quality Controls

Quality control always provides useful management information in the form of feedback so that areas for improvement can be detected. However, control is similar to the examination of accounts: it deals in history. Items, equipment and information that are supplied as part of the service can all be assessed by means of conventional quality controls, such as inspection or statistical quality control. All quality control involves measuring, testing, inspecting, examining a product or otherwise performing some type of verification activity to decide whether or not the product complies with its acceptance criteria (which might be stated in a specification or a standard) and a decision either to release the product for further processing, for use, for repair/ rework and then further examination or to scrap the thing and make a new one.

Acceptance criteria

Performance standards are needed. Certain aspects of presentation and service characteristics can be measured, common examples of this being response time *versus* response rate; errors per transaction/ document. The acceptance criteria for both background and foreground activities must be specified since without this, management will never be in control of their departments.

Performance levels of background and foreground tasks mutually affect each other. The existence of an integrated management system linking them together at the primary, secondary of tertiary levels (see Part 1 Chapter 6) naturally has the effect that they reinforce each other's needs. Poor performance in a background task (i.e. a task within a secondary or tertiary system), however, will quickly result in poor performance in a foreground one (i.e. a task within a primary system) whereas the opposite is not automatically true.

> Like many other people, I have traveled extensively by means of air over the period of the last four decades. On numerous occasions the in-flight service received from well known airlines has been poor. The cause, with few exceptions, has always been a failure of the ground staff supporting the flight crew with the supply of meals, refreshments, baggage handling and routing. Flight crews generally do the best they can but cannot deliver what was never put on board the aircraft prior to departure. (The only airline with which I have never had any cause to complain about the service provided to me is Singapore Airlines.)

Some targets for performance can be specified and information may be readily available as a basis for setting improvement goals. Examples of data frequently available, if only the auditee were to take the trouble of analyzing them, are defective documents or data entries, customer complaints, records of average response time, equipment failure rates, maintenance costs, warranty claims and refunds, repeat business percentages, number of membership renewals declined versus number of new memberships obtained, volume available versus volume sold, occupancy percentages, services canceled per period, services delayed per period, staff turnover and attendance rates. All constitute simple measurements which can be used to establish acceptable levels of service performance for customers and between departments or to highlight problems whose root cause needs to be ascertained. Many of these can be further estimated during rehearsals. The target levels of performance and deviation limits permissible could well be 100% and 0% respectively, particularly where health and safety are concerned.

Although the intangibilities of service characteristics and presentation cannot be assigned units of measurement, the standard for acceptance can be indicated by means of audio cassettes, tapeslide programmes, photographs, training videos, visual demonstrations, interactive CD Rom training models and the like. Unacceptable standards can also be portrayed by similar means.

Auditee quality control techniques

A major problem with a service is that because certain of its characteristics and presentation are intangible, one cannot totally "inspect" them before delivery. For this reason, services also have to rely on prototype assessment, rehearsals, staff training and competence tests as well as feedback from customer surveys and opinion petitions. Staff knowledge and skills can be regularly tested and certificates of recognition can be awarded. Performance based incentive schemes or promotions are used by some firms to signify an acceptable level of achievement. Service activities can be observed whilst in progress but observation may affect performance. Some auditees may use anonymous assessors to act as customers in order to appraise the level of performance.

Foreground and background staff can check the state of readiness, of the equipment, of information and of items that they require both before and during the working day. Planned and periodic checks can also be performed by them. Records of complete activities and routine checks can be reviewed or audited.

Customers are the final arbiters on service quality and if their experience and views are obtained, a better guide becomes available. One must, however, appreciate that customer feedback often is only available after the event and does not present *real time* control on quality performance. (Stage entertainers performing to a live theatre or studio audience can get real time feedback, though. The consummate professionals know how to "read" their audience and make subtle adjustments to their performance as it progresses in order to get the reactions they want.) A wide variety of customer feedback mechanisms are used by auditees in service companies and operations, the most common include: questionnaires delivered by mailshot or with the "product"; telephonic, fax or E. Mail follow-up and personal interview; customer complaints obtained from regular contact with the clients and customers or from "hotline"/ emergency calls; repeat orders used to analyze each customer's buying trends, market share trends and media reports derived from product surveys, test reports, complaints, comparisons with competitor's products. The results of these techniques must be promptly fed back to the staff and can form a part of the personnel performance appraisal process.

Clearly, many quality control options are available to the auditee and, by examining the proof, the auditor should verify:

♦ The auditee has developed management systems which ensure that quality control activities are planned and used.

♦ Those systems ensure that acceptance criteria for the various tasks are defined and communicated to the workplace at which those tasks are performed.

♦ Those systems have been communicated to the areas responsible for performing those activities.

♦ Those management systems are implemented and are efficacious.

Self-control in foreground tasks

Service locations might be geographically dispersed to the point that the service is performed in the customer's home or office. Although the auditee could be tempted to produce voluminous procedure manuals, they are often of little help and are unlikely to be read by the foreground staff. A better approach is to give the foreground staff more discretion and freedom. This can lead to higher estimation in the eyes of the customer and is good for motivation, being a form of job enlargement. If the increased motivation also leads to lower staff turnover, this in itself is a saving of the avoidable costs to the company. On balance, it is preferable to pursue the concept of self help and self inspection/control, provided that safety and quality are not jeopardized.

Error analysis

Although it makes little sense to develop a quality control system to specify acceptance criteria and to capture information as a result, only to ignore the opportunities presented, a surprisingly large percentage of auditees do precisely that. Often the problem rests in failure to analyze the information and present it in a form that is easily assimilated. Pareto charts, graphs, pie charts, flow charts are all simple devices which can help. Modern software application packages for handling data and reports frequently have graphics tools and capabilities that remove the tedium of plotting data and drawing pictorial representations that was such a chore in past years.

With these points in mind, the auditor will check the improvement opportunity arrangements (mentioned as Steps 6 and 7 of the seven step method described in Part 1 Chapter 11).

6. Safety and environmental audits

*If you believe knowledge is expensive,
try ignorance.*

Anon

The importance of safety and environmental audits

Few people on this planet could be unaware of the growing prominence afforded to matters of safety and protection of the environment. Public awareness and education in these topics has raised their profile and made them a priority for business attention. Pressure for responsible attitudes come from all age groups, from politicians (ever aware of the vote impact of public concern), from ethical investors and from insurers trying to minimize their risk exposure. Court awards in some countries against miscreants are huge when punitive damages are included. The concerns about safety affect products, process performers, users and bystanders. Concerns for environmental protection go beyond saving rain forests and reducing gaseous emissions to influence, *inter alia*, the selection of materials used to make products and deliver services, so as to guarantee bio-compatibility, the recycling of wastes and by-products and the policies, structure and organization of the firm itself.

Adverse publicity about products, practices, pollutants, processes and policies can rapidly reduce sales, market share and prospects. No firm can afford to ignore the importance of safety and environmental protection. To do so entails the real risk that avoidable costs will be incurred, costs that could dwarf those related to conventional scrap and process waste, costs that could cripple the firm, costs that could bankrupt it.

Safety and environmental audits should not be regarded as optional *"nice-to-do"* activities. They are *"must-do's"*, offering

599

the real prospects of forewarning management of avoidable risks and costs, of enabling preventive action to be taken before disaster strikes. Their cost benefit is considerable. Prudent management derives substantial benefits from paying attention to them. By highlighting certain matters this chapter is intended merely to emphasize the auditing aspects that have been studied throughout both parts of this book.

Role of the auditor

The auditor's role will depend on the specific objectives of the audit. That role may be to determine the efficacy of the systems which affect the safety of products and services supplied into the community; it may be to determine the status of safety practices and procedures in the company; it may be as a consultant engaged specifically to recommend improvements in environmental policies and practices.

Whatever the objectives, the auditor is still representing management and must approach the audit with an absence of preconceived ideas.

During systems audits

If a systems audit is being performed prior to commencement of an environmental protection or safety programme, the auditor will be verifying that:

♦ The programme is organized properly.
♦ The management systems have been properly considered.
♦ The necessary resources have been fully and properly budgeted.
♦ The time required to introduce the programme has been carefully and properly estimated and allocated.

The information gleaned by the audit concerning all of those listed points will assist management in deciding whether or not to allocate the time and resources requested for the programme, to commence it and to know if the risk of loss or of avoidable costs that might be incurred if the programme is inadequate has been minimized. The systems audit should be planned sufficiently ahead of programme commencement so as to enable the project management to take any major corrective action revealed as being desirable or necessary before the initiation of the programme. (See also Part 1 Chapter 9, Figure 9.3.)

If the programme is required to utilize the company's standard procedures, the auditor will also:

- ◆ Verify the programme has been organized, the systems have been developed, resources and time have been budgeted in accordance with those standard procedures;
- ◆ Obtain objective evidence from the programme's performance in order to determine the efficacy of those standard procedures; and, of course,
- ◆ Require any corrective actions to those standard procedures that are considered necessary.

During compliance audits

Depending on the audit objectives, the auditor will, during a compliance audit, verify that the programme and its management systems are being carried out such that:

- ◆ The auditee is operating in accordance with the organizational arrangements and the management systems for the programme.
- ◆ Safety/environmental protection is being achieved.
- ◆ Safety/environmental will be continue to be achieved.
- ◆ The regulatory requirements and legal obligations are being met.
- ◆ Time and resources are being properly managed and justified.

The auditee's procedures may refer to various codes or standards with which the personnel must comply. In this event, the auditor will also spot check to verify that the requirements of their requirements are being met: this may entail obtaining and using the advice of a specialist on the audit team. One must stress again that such audits are not being performed as quasi-inspections. The main purpose of the compliance audit is to ensure that one can have sufficient confidence that the auditee is complying with the safety/environmental protection requirements, the programme, its procedures and related codes/standards. The auditee should also be monitoring his own observance of those by means of process controls and verification activities and by implementing his own non-conformity and corrective action systems, if problems arise.

Conduct of the audit

General approach

The preparation, performance and reporting of each of these types of audit remain as described throughout this book, especially in Part 1.

♦ Whichever type of audit is being performed, however, the auditor can use the task elements with their corresponding sub-elements, (see Part 1 Chapter 4), to considerable effect.

♦ The seven step audit method and question technique will both be as discussed in Chapters 11 and 13, respectively.

♦ Each department/ process involved in the project will be analyzed as per Chapter 5.

♦ Management systems will be treated as suggested in Chapter 6.

♦ Careful audit preparation as described in Chapter 9 is obviously beneficial as is the creation of a checklist, matrix or flowchart as discussed in Chapter 7.

So, for any particular task being performed in any phase, of the environmental protection or safety programme, the basic checklist, such as that described in Figure 7.6 or a matrix, of the type shown in Figure 7.14, (based on the task elements listed in Chapter 4, non conformity and so on), is usable. If the auditee is supposed to comply with a standard, such as ISO 9001, the auditor needs to prepare a criteria type of checklist, as also described in Part 1 Chapter 7.

602

The audit objectives, as ever, require most careful definition if the audit is to be successful. The audit can and must only be based on the examination of objective evidence. Facts are vital, hearsay inadmissible. This is a point of particular importance because each area of investigation, generally calls for specialist knowledge and expertise.

Effects on the audit team

Knowledge is the crucial issue. Safety and environmental audits are not for those unfamiliar with any of the following:

♦ The applicable Codes, regulations, standards, legislation and case law.
♦ Products, processes and services of the auditee.
♦ Analytical tools to perform risk analysis and probability assessments.

A strong familiarity is vital with legislation, and case law concerning its interpretation, as well as with acceptable preventative systems and measures. It may be prudent to engage the services of outside specialists, consultants. As always, careful selection and determination of experience, qualifications (i.e. the person sub-elements) is important. The saying *"you get what you pay for"* is especially apposite when hiring such people, but the associated costs do pale when measured against the cost of proceeding in ignorance of risk.

Safety and environmental protection programmes naturally involve the application of various sciences. Accordingly, the audit team will need members qualified in the relevant applied sciences which might include any of the following: engineering (all disciplines), geology, medicine, biology, botany, organic and inorganic chemistry, nuclear physics, meteorology.

Safety and environmental management are topics of such breadth that a full discussion of all aspects is not possible within the confines of a single book. The reader will be well advised to research other texts for specific matters related to those fields.

The following sections seek to provide some additional guidance to the points raised elsewhere in this book.

1.   Safety audits

Safety is a large subject, even more so if the additional context of health is introduced, but all in this realm can ultimately be reduced to the task elements etc. and the way in which they are or might be used, abused or misused. The reader will recall that fitness for purpose means careful consideration of the use, abuse and misuse to which a product may be subjected in service. Since fitness for purpose is a prime constituent of quality, it is clear that efficacious management systems will incorporate and address safety.

The systems must be based not only on the requirements of legislation but also on the hazards inherent in the work task, equipment, item etc. that is involved. Legislation is necessarily couched in the most general of terms and the auditee must have interpreted those terms accordingly.   The general legislative climate is also important.   Some countries operate more extensively on a strict liability basis than do others and this has a considerable effect on the depth of thought required in the designing or auditing of a management system. It is precisely for this reason that special expertise is required of the auditor: safety audits are not trivial matters in which amateurs may dabble.

The task elements and safety audits

The reader is also referred to Part 1 Chapter 4 when reading this section which contains some additional considerations.

Person

Safety is directly affected by the person performing a task. Lack of competence and training in the equipment used, items used or processed, the process itself or management systems can give rise to risks as can failure to inform others of what is required or of risks involved.

Items

The condition of the item(s) being processed or handled has to be considered. Items can be inherently dangerous (nuclear isotopes, acids, explosives etc.) or unsafe only when abused. Similarly, items can be inherently safe until they are mixed, combined or brought into contact with other items (such being the case in chemical reactions). The auditor needs to consider the operational circumstance and decide on the risks that could be involved: these factors set the objectives of the management system and of the corresponding audit. Naturally, the auditor will verify that the auditee has exercised the same thought process and acted responsibly on the results.

Item quantity can also give rise to risks. Excess quantities of items, for instance, can lead to unacceptable forces, weights, heat or other loads; in the case of certain nuclear substances, too much can lead to a critical mass; in chemical reactions, similar scenarios can develop. A variation on the problem of quantities is one of excess concentrations: the auditee should have considered these possibilities, designing and implementing his systems accordingly. The auditor will need to determine the correctness and completeness of the auditee's determination of acceptable quantities and then analyze the efficacy of the resultant systems and measures in use to control their potential effects.

Items need to be correctly identified in order to keep the user or bystander properly informed of their existence and status.

The correct type of item must be issued to the user and the auditee needs to develop systems to ensure that this is done. However, supplying the correct type also entails careful analysis of the circumstances in which the item will be used or placed. The auditee should have determined this as a prerequisite in developing management systems to ensure issue of the correct type of item.

Equipment

The reader will recall that, in Part 1 Chapter 4, I stated that the workplace's equipment was at one time someone else's item since it has first to be made or created before it can become usable equipment.

The selection of the correct type of equipment depends on the operational circumstances that it will encounter. It must be fit for purpose along the lines described earlier in this chapter.

Accordingly equipment must possess the correct capability for the task involved. It cannot be securely expected to operate beyond the limits of safety for which it was designed. Abnormal circumstance must have been considered in the selection process, together with transient conditions which can occur. The working loads, duties and stresses should each have been thoroughly scrutinized and their effects calculated prior to specification of the equipment itself. Failure modes assessed together with the reliability of equipment will affect such matters as the configuration of complete plant incorporating planned redundancy by the installation of stand-by equipment. The operational circumstances might include maintaining items or containing them so as to retain a particular condition (e.g. canisters, nuclear containment buildings, heat shields) or it may be to maintain a particular environment (e.g. fume extractors, heating and ventilating plant). The auditor needs to verify that these circumstances were properly considered, built into the equipment's capability and that the equipment is maintained so as to retain that capability. Naturally, the operating conditions must be such as to avoid exceeding those designed conditions. The auditor needs to verify this.

Equipment must be identified to inform the user and bystander of its existence and its condition status: "on" or "off"; "live" or "dead"; ready for use, awaiting maintenance, being maintained; safe, unsafe, under review. Hazards also need to be indicated: *"Danger - High Voltage"*; *"Do not place hands into machine"*, etc.

The auditee must have ensured that the right equipment reaches the right location at the right time, otherwise unsafe equipment might be substituted. Associated with this aspect is the requirement that safety and protection devices be available physically and operationally, not tampered with, overridden or immobilized. The auditor will pay attention to these points.

Environmental nuisances are to be controlled. Dangerous (slippery, explosive, badly lit etc.) or toxic atmospheres (fumes, leaked radiations, sour gas etc.) must be prevented. They can affect operator performance or the innocent bystander and might result from the condition of items or equipment in the area or perhaps from inadequate information or operator carelessness. The risks associated with undesirable atmospheres, as well as the potential sources, should have been analyzed by the auditee. The auditor will verify the completeness and correctness of the auditee's analyses and subsequent actions.

Information

When information is unchecked there is a risk that its content is unproven or unfit for purpose. Content could mislead, be ambiguous, dangerous or false. A user can also be misled and come into contact with unsafe conditions of equipment, items or practices if the incorrect edition of information is available. Likewise, when the valid period of personnel competence certificates or licences is exceeded without reaffirming ongoing competence, safety can become compromised.

Information must be presented in a usable condition which means that illegibility of documents due to damage, deterioration or small print sizes (in relation to the distance from which someone is expected to read the information) must be avoided by the auditee. A particular and unsafe condition of information is the instance where it is presented in the wrong language. The auditee should have based the information on the user's needs and circumstances but this can only be achieved if he has first ascertained what they are. The auditor will verify the validity of the premises on which the information has been created before going on to determine the efficacy of the auditee's resultant actions.

Closely associated with the last point is the necessity for proper distribution of the information. Improper or inadequate distribution that can cause people to be ill-informed or un-informed is unacceptable. The auditee must have analyzed exactly who needs to know the information, such analysis not being satisfied by his stating his opinion of who needs to know. The auditee should also have considered extraordinary circumstances and planned the distribution of information accordingly: product recall situations, for example, place particular demands on information distribution and the prudent auditee will have determined not only the distribution required but also the method of distribution in relation to the speed with which information needs to reach the target audience. The auditor will investigate the thoroughness and efficacy of the auditee's actions.

Services

The characteristics of the service place particular demands on the interfacing task elements. If, for instance, a certain level of safety risk is required, this will have a direct impact on the selection of the type of equipment and its capability. The auditee must have defined the safety characteristics and risk levels as a basis for determining the stringency of the supporting management systems. The auditor will investigate the decision making process surrounding this basis as well as the efficacy of those systems.

The method of presentation of the services can also give rise to or reduce the risks to safety. The presentation and potential safety risks affect the training of foreground personnel (see Part 2 Chapter 5), as discussed in Part 1 Chapter 4. The auditor will verify that the presentation and possible attendant risks have been analyzed, defined and effectively communicated to the personnel involved.

Failure to perform a complete service can also be unsafe. The auditee needs to ensure that his management systems prevent the attendant risks associated with incomplete performance. If, for example, a company is engaged to perform a cleaning or sterilization process, a risk to safety can arise if there is anything less than total thoroughness. Or, in the case of an airline, it really is rather inconvenient for the passengers to have the flight element of the service cut short in mid-air!

The six real causes

In addressing the need for corrective action, when it is found necessary, the auditor will trace through to the real root cause(s), a process which was described in Part 1 Chapter 17. Just as is the case for other business matters, safety problems have their root in the six real causes that were mentioned in Part 1 Chapter 18, some common examples of cause and effect being:

♦ Inadequate resources leading to inadequate training, staff levels, equipment and so on.
♦ Inadequate time leading to a lack of due care and attention to the work in hand.
♦ Lack of discipline in following procedures that affect health or safety having obvious results.
♦ Lack of organization leading to confusion and unsafe conditions or to difficulties in controlling them when they do arise.
♦ Lack of training in the safety aspects of a task and in the sub-elements causing accidents. Inadequate training in the handling of non-conformities can mean situations getting out of control.
♦ Lack of top management support for safety having potential repercussions that are unthinkable.

2. Environmental audits

Environmental protection is an enormous subject. It covers a host of topics including pollution prevention, waste creation and disposal, thermal and noise emissions, recycling, biodegradability of substances and many more. All in this realm can ultimately be reduced to the task elements *et al* and the way in which they are

609

organized, selected and managed, or might be used, abused or misused. The reader will recall that fitness for purpose means careful consideration of the use, abuse and misuse to which a product may be subjected in service. Since fitness for purpose is a prime constituent of quality, it is clear that efficacious management systems will incorporate and address environmental protection.

The systems must be based not only on the requirements of legislation but also on the hazards inherent in the work task, equipment, item etc. that is involved. Environmental protection legislation is necessarily couched in the most general of terms and the auditee must have interpreted those terms accordingly. The general legislative climate is also important. Some countries operate more extensively on a strict liability basis than do others and this has a considerable effect on the depth of thought required in the designing or auditing of an environmental management system. It is precisely for this reason that special expertise is required of the auditor, as noted previously.

Contracts and jurisdictions

Jurisdictional requirements vary globally, even though many nations were parties to the *"Rio Declaration"* (see below), they retain the right of self determination in environmental matters and laws. The jurisdictional requirements affect the product and process design, the selections made within the task elements. The requirements of the supplier's jurisdiction might be far removed from those of the user's. The firm should define all the market places it wishes to serve and which its own licensees or franchisees wish to serve. This forms an essential part of the design input for products and services. Also affected are the auditee's tendering procedures, contract acceptance reviews, records requirements and control systems, license application and maintenance programmes, and acquisition and maintenance of statutory approvals. The auditor must check these matters.

Organization

Organizational matters are described in Part 1 Chapter 3. Responsibility and authority must be established for:

♦ Normal working and business conditions
♦ Abnormal and unplanned incidents, including emergencies.

The speed with which decisions are made can affect normal operational situations and actually create an environmentally unsafe situation. And when an emergency occurs, timely decision making is also essential to prevent disaster or to regain control over a dangerous situation.

Emergencies

The constraints the management systems may place on the speed of decision making need to be ascertained. There is little point in having a comprehensive emergency handling system so tardy in application that effective action, supposed to mitigate environmental impact, is hindered. The auditee's system should be two-dimensional, not one-dimensional, and a just-in-time philosophy coupled with a value-added approach offers distinct benefits for the handling of emergencies in particular. The emergency system must be created in the framework of an organization that has considered how resources will be mobilized. Rapidity can reduce the cost of a clean-up, forestall customer and community complaints, adverse publicity and exposure to prosecution with its unique attendant risks of punitive fines. The auditor will investigate these matters.

Amongst the contingency arrangements the auditee should arrange, and which the auditor must verify, are:

♦ Enabling contracts. These are contracts agreed with suppliers who will be needed when emergencies occur. The terms and conditions are pre-determined as well as the performance criteria, such as speed of response, communications, management and logistic

611

arrangements, so that the work can be started without unnecessary delays. The auditee should have the usual procurement controls in place for selection, monitoring and regularly reviewing the readiness of the supplier.

◆ Procedures ready for use. The methods for dealing with an emergency situation should be planned in advance. The auditee's staff should be familiarized with the arrangements by means of training, practice runs, simulations. When trying out the procedures, the speed of application should have been carefully monitored and reviewed for adequacy, and improvements made if required: the procedures must have measurable targets for their performance.

◆ Records retrieval. Those charged with managing accidents and incidents require the prompt availability of records, containing details of the processes, items, equipment, premises and personnel involved. Speed of retrieval is often crucial in order to provide relevant information. The auditee should regularly verify the efficacy of his records retrieval systems in meeting pre-defined speeds of recovery.

◆ Language. Some auditees might operate in places whose mother tongue is not their own. Due consideration for the prevention of needless problems deriving from language barriers must be avoided. This can also affect the firm's domestic procedures when staff possess different language backgrounds.

◆ Emergency services. Arrangements for mobilizing local, national (and, maybe, international) fire, ambulance, coastguard and police services must be predetermined with responsibilities for their coordination defined.

◆ Media management. If the nature of an emergency could give rise to media attention, having a pre-assigned and trained spokesperson is a prudent action.

♦ Financial reserves. The auditee should have considered how financial resources can be appropriated, for time will be of the essence in obtaining the requisite resources (human, equipment, logistic and other support services, materials etc.) needed for effective prompt action.

♦ Readiness reviews. The auditee should regularly review the state of readiness of all the emergency arrangements, including those described heretofore.

♦ Risk assessments and incident probability analyses. By using such tools as FMEA's, FTA's etc., the auditee can determine the relative likelihoods and consequences of particular scenarios. These might include equipment failures, power outages, loss of essential utilities and supplies, transport vehicle accidents, communication breakdowns, supplier unavailability, excessive or abnormal demands on systems and resources, delays and so on. Risk assessments can help to determine the configuration of equipment and whether or not the installing of back-up systems would be a wise policy. (As an example, key pieces of equipment at nuclear facilities are sometimes triplicated in order to deal with incidents, the logic being one piece fails in operation, a stand-by piece happens to be under maintenance or repair at the time so a third piece will be required. In some cases a fourth piece is added just in case the third one fails to start when required by the incident, even though the probability of such a sequence of events is miniscule.)

♦ Criticality ratings which affect the environmental protection programme. The auditee should determine these from the environmental impact studies performed when the products, processes and services are being designed. They will help to decide the organizational responsibilities and authorities (and, hence, the tasks to be performed), the measurable performance criteria for the management systems as well as the design of those systems.

An excellent example of readiness management can be seen from the activities of Red Adair, the famous fighter of oil field fires and blow-outs. His company's success is based not only on accumulated knowledge and experience of its teams, but also on having tried and tested organization, management systems and task elements: people, items, equipment, information, services. This includes the preselection of known reliable sources of supplies for goods and services.

The task elements and environmental audits

The reader is also referred to Part 1 Chapter 4 when reading this section which contains some additional considerations.

Person

Environmental protection is directly affected by the person performing a task. Lack of competence and training in the equipment used, items used or processed, the process itself or management systems can give rise to risks as can failure to inform others of what is required or of risks involved. The motivation and attributes of individuals can vary and affect their attitudes towards environmental care.

Items

The reader will recall that the term *"items"* embraces not only materials and substances used to make saleable products but also by-products of the process activities. Many firms take considerable pains to develop and implement management systems to manage the creation of products, but regularly fail to have such systems for the management of by-products of their processes. They seem to forget they are as much responsible for making the by-products as they are for making the saleable products. Just because a by-product is something the firm does not want and cannot sell, it does not mean the company can abrogate its responsibility for "safe" disposal or storage of these things. The sub-elements apply as much to by-products as to other items.

The condition of the item(s) being processed or handled has to be considered. Items can be inherently deleterious (nuclear isotopes, acids, toxic chemicals, explosives etc.). Hazards can increase when they are mixed, combined or brought into contact with other items (such being the case in chemical reactions). The auditor needs to consider the operational circumstance and decide on the risks that could be involved: these factors set the objectives of the management system and of the corresponding audit. Naturally, the auditor will verify that the auditee has exercised the same thought process and acted responsibly on the results.

The following properties are all important and need to be established: chemical, physical, nuclear, thermal, biological, biodegradeability. These properties will have differing affects on flora and fauna, air, soil and water. A thorough analysis cannot be said to have been undertaken if one or more of those properties and effects on them are not known. Whereas it is now fashionable to refer to one's products as *"biodegradable"*, one of its crucial aspects is the rate at which the item degrades. Just as different nuclear isotopes possess different half-lives for decay, so too do other materials break down at different rates. This needs to be determined and the auditor should look for evidence that it is systematically done by the auditee.

Excess quantities of items can also give rise to risks. In the case of certain nuclear substances, too much can lead to a critical mass; in chemical reactions, similar scenarios can develop. The limited ability of the environment to cope with spillages and damaging releases can be exceeded; "safe" dispersion may become impossible. A variation on the problem of quantities is one of excess concentrations: the auditee should have considered these possibilities, designing and implementing his systems accordingly. The auditor will need to determine the correctness and completeness of the auditee's determination of acceptable quantities and then analyze the efficacy of the resultant systems and measures used to control their potential effects.

Items need to be correctly identified in order to keep the user or bystander properly informed of their existence and status. This is impossible in the case of gases and fluids after discharge from the auditee's premises or facilities, although audible alarms and media announcements might warn those communities local to the incident. It may be necessary to contain them or to implement a controlled release that does not cause safe levels to be exceeded. This affects the design and location of the auditee's equipment and plant, such as stacks, effluent pipework systems and burial sites.

The correct type of item must be issued to the user and the auditee needs to develop systems to ensure that this is done. However, supplying the correct type also entails careful analysis of the circumstances under which the item will be used. The auditee should have determined this as a prerequisite in developing management systems to ensure issue of the correct type of item. Substitution can create unknown or unascertained hazards.

Equipment

The selection of the correct type of equipment depends on the operational circumstances that it will encounter. It must be fit for purpose along the lines described earlier in this chapter.

Accordingly equipment must possess the correct capability for the task involved. It cannot be securely expected to operate beyond the limits of environmental protection for which it was designed. Abnormal circumstance must have been considered in the selection process, together with transient conditions which can occur. The working loads, duties and stresses should each have been thoroughly scrutinized and their effects calculated prior to specification of the equipment itself. The operational circumstances might include maintaining items or containing them so as to retain a particular condition (e.g. canisters, nuclear containment buildings, heat shields) or it may be to maintain a particular environment (e.g. fume extractors, heating and ventilating plant). The auditor needs to verify that these circumstances were properly considered, built into the equipment's capability and that the equipment is maintained so as to retain that capability. Naturally, the operating conditions must be such as to avoid exceeding those designed conditions. The auditor needs to verify this.

Noise control and abatement legislation is gaining in prominence. It affects all types of equipment, aircraft, power plant, musical concerts and public address systems being examples. The use of personal electronic pagers and mobile telephones in libraries and similar public places is often restricted.

> A seminar I was presenting in Singapore had to be halted because of constant interruptions caused when the pagers and mobile telephones, brought by several delegates into the assembly room, rang. Others applauded when I asked for the devices to be switched off or removed from the room. Bringing this type of equipment into restaurants and theatres is unnecessary posing and inconsiderate of others.

Thermal discharge of equipment is another matter attracting increasing attention. It can cool or heat the surroundings, according to its temperature. For several decades, savvy countries have required environmental impact studies to be undertaken when considering the siting of power stations because cooling water discharge into the neighbouring sea, lakes or rivers can dramatically alter their ecosystems, cooling towers, too, give rise to the familiar plumes of water vapour and smoke stack heights affect the dispersion of emissions. Office buildings, factories, plant and utilities will all have a thermal profile that could require careful assessment and affect their design and selection. Waste heat recovery systems can offer operational savings. Excessive discharges that cause a nuisance to neighbours could give rise to legal action for damages.

End of life disposal of the equipment may also be a matter requiring careful consideration as well as a programme to effect it. Contaminated equipment can require planned procedures and systems for its dismantling, decontamination, recycling or burial, as appropriate to its nature. The auditor must investigate these matters have been considered well in advance of their need. They should have been planned for when the equipment and its associated processes were first conceived and designed, but this is not always possible because unknown or unappreciated problems can surface with experience and use. Burial sites can be regarded as *"equipment"* and the sub-elements, described in Part 1 Chapter 4, can be applied when considering their selection, design and management.

The auditee must have ensured that the right equipment reaches the right location at the right time, otherwise inappropriate equipment might be substituted. Associated with this aspect is the requirement that environmental protection devices be available physically and operationally, not tampered with, overridden or immobilized. The auditor will pay attention to these points.

Information

When information is unchecked there is a risk that its content is unproven or unfit for purpose. Content could mislead, be ambiguous, dangerous or false. A user can be misled and inadvertently cause an incident if the incorrect edition of information is available. When the valid period of personnel competence certificates or licences is exceeded without reaffirming ongoing competence, environmental regulations can be infringed.

Information must be presented in a usable condition which means that illegibility of documents due to damage, deterioration or small print sizes (in relation to the distance from which someone is expected to read the information) must be avoided by the auditee. Environmentally unsafe conditions can occur where it is presented in the wrong language. The auditee should have based the information on the user's needs and circumstances but this can only be achieved if he has first ascertained what they are. The auditor will verify the validity of the premises on which the information has been created before going on to determine the efficacy of the auditee's resultant actions.

618

Closely associated with the last point is the necessity for proper distribution of the information. Improper or inadequate distribution that can cause people to be ill-informed or un-informed is unacceptable. The auditee must have analyzed exactly who needs to know the information, such analysis not being satisfied by his stating his opinion of who needs to know. The auditee should also have considered extraordinary circumstances and planned the distribution of information accordingly: emergencies, for example, place particular demands on information distribution and the prudent auditee will have determined not only the distribution required but also the method of distribution in relation to the speed with which information needs to reach the target audience. As was noted above, the speed with which records can be retrieved is of especial importance. The auditor will investigate the thoroughness and efficacy of the auditee's actions in these matters.

Warnings, labels, instructions, contact telephone numbers and help facilities can be important, especially for use by the emergency services fire, police, ambulance, lifeboat crews and coast guards.

Services

Failure to perform a complete service can be environmentally unsafe. The auditee needs to ensure that his management systems prevent the attendant risks associated with incomplete performance. If, for example, a company is engaged to perform a toxic waste process, a risk can arise if there is anything less than total thoroughness.

Acceptance criteria

One cannot determine the status of compliance of products, processes and services unless and until the acceptance criteria for their characteristics have been defined. This definition is also essential if the firm is to monitor the results of its continuous improvement efforts. To do this effectively requires a baseline or datum of performance to be established. This should be a part of the firm's policies and included in its management systems. The auditor will check for this.

The six real causes

In addressing the need for corrective action, when it is found necessary, the auditor will trace through to the real root cause(s), a process as described in Part 1 Chapter 17. Just as is the case for other business matters, environmental protection problems have their root in the six real causes that were mentioned in Part 1 Chapter 18, some common examples of cause and effect being:

♦ Inadequate financial resources leading to inadequate training, staff levels, equipment and so on.
♦ Inadequate time leading to a lack of due care and attention to the work in hand.
♦ Lack of discipline in following procedures that affect environmental protection having obvious results.
♦ Lack of organization leading to environmentally unsafe conditions and difficulties in controlling them when they do arise.
♦ Lack of training in the environmental protection aspects of a task, and in the sub-elements, causing accidents. Inadequate training in the handling of non-conformities can mean situations getting out of control.
♦ Lack of top management support for environmental protection having potential repercussions for the stakeholders that are unthinkable.

Exit interviews

These can proceed as described in Part 1 Chapter 19. Attendance may need to be restricted depending on the level of confidentiality the audit client requires but ordinary level auditees must not be unduly prevented from attending if a failure to invite them would be counter-productive to morale.

The exit interview will be prepared in the usual way, but it generally takes more time to fully present the audit team's findings and recommendations than would be the case for an audit whose objective is to ascertain compliance with, say, ISO 9000. The audit team should expect and accommodate more questions from the auditee and the audit client. Although there is the temptation for the audit team to plunge into technical terms, especially when dealing with the properties of items and equipment, this should be resisted if the auditee's management attending does not fully comprehend the minutiae of the detail. If technical reasoning is necessary, the specialists must present it in simple terms so as to communicate effectively.

When audit time has been inadequate

An inadequate amount of audit time could prevent the audit team from completing a thorough analysis. In this circumstance it can be necessary to indicate the risks of the gaps in knowledge obtained and to recommend a thorough on-going analysis. Apparent risks and the urgency of need should also be indicated.

Issuing corrective action requests

Whether or not corrective action requests should be issued is a matter of policy that must be determined at the outset of each audit and the position of the auditor will, clearly, have some effect on this. If, for example, an outside consultant or specialist is engaged, the management may require a report which only states areas for which corrective action is recommended. It will then be the decision of the company's management to issue corrective action requests or not. If the auditor is performing an extrinsic audit, as in the case of safety audits, it is probable that the statute which empowers the auditor to enter the auditee's premises for these purposes will also be translated into the authority to issue a formal corrective action request (or, more likely, a corrective action *requirement*).

Audit reports

The type of layout shown in Part 1 Chapter 20 can still be used as a template audit report. The general information sections, such as auditee location, audit dates, audit team members and so on are still required. The results section and position statement will be different, though.

The results should state the following:

- A comparison of the situation existing with the upcoming or the new.
- A summary of the risk analysis performed by the auditor, particularly:
    the risks of continuing as at present; and
    the risks of the changes the auditor proposes.
- The nature of the environmental concerns or safety concerns identified by the auditor and the impact of the new factors on policy, processes, organization, management systems, people and resources (both time and budget)
- Estimates of:
    the avoidable costs that might be incurred in continuing as at present; and
    the costs associated with implementing the auditor's proposals (i.e. the investment required); and, hence,
    the cost-benefit of those proposals.
- Estimates of:
    the time frames involved for implementing the changes proposed; and
    the time frames involved for obtaining a payback on the investment required; and
    the urgency of the situation.

A position statement is not really necessary, but a summary of the report along the lines of the following is generally appropriate:

Based on the objective evidence presented by the auditee to the audit team it is considered there are (or are not) violations (or risks of violations) of the following regulatory requirements/standards/codes/ contracts in respect of health/safety/environmental protection [.....]. These can be remedied through changes in [the organization/processes, management systems, plant or equipment, the introduction of new

622

technology, using alternative materials, outsourcing....etc.]. The risk of not implementing change in the areas suggested is [.....]. The changes are required within a time frame of [....]. Detailed results and analyses are presented herein.

Distribution and confidentiality

These matters will depend, as ever was the case, on the instructions issued by the audit client to the lead auditor which the former must agree first of all with the auditee. It is always advisable for the lead auditor to retain a copy of the report, the checklists (or other audit tools used) and other audit information, such as letters of engagement, on file. Matters of safety and environmental protection are of such sensitivity that one cannot rule out the possibility of the lead auditor and the audit team being called to give testimony in the event of an unfortunate incident. They might be called as expert witnesses and their own position must be safeguarded. Retaining copies or originals of the various documents used (but not necessarily of the auditee's documentation) is a wise policy for they can revive pertinent memories and improve testimony.

Video tapes

Modern video cameras are portable to the point they can be useful in recording the state of the auditee's processes and task elements. The tapes can be used to help secure effective communications during the exit interview and as important audit records. Bearing in mind the sensitive nature of some safety and environmental protection audits, the audit team might find it prudent to use these devices, naturally the auditee must be informed of this beforehand and a copy of the tape must be deposited with the auditee when the audit is finished. The tapes can have uses beyond the audit as aids to training the auditee's staff, but their use and display to third parties without the auditee's permission is highly improper, unless the third party happens to be a court of law and display is part of some legal proceedings.

Follow-up action

The need for this depends on the audit client's policy. Follow-up can be conducted as described in Part 1 Chapter 21.

Internal, external, extrinsic and self audits as part of the safety and environmental protection efforts.

All types of audit have a contribution to make to the overall effort. The amount of each depends on the audit team's knowledge and experience as well as the scope of its work. Self audits performed by empowered staff imbued with the concepts of safety and environmental protection, as relating to their particular assigned tasks, will be central to achieving set goals.

From wherever the auditor comes, be it the workforce, process teams, customers or consultants all can contribute to some degree: some will be able to contribute more than others, but all offerings will add up. What is important, though, is for every one to act in a way that helps the auditee, this is one of my Golden Rules described in Part 1 Appendix 1.

The Rio Declaration

This contains various points that the environmentally concerned firm, such as a transnational or multinational enterprise, should take cognizance of when defining its environmental protection systems. Its prescriptions can be found appended to the standard, ISO 14004: 1996.

Standards

The International Standards Organization (ISO) has issued a set of standards that attempt to deal with environmental systems management and the auditing thereof. These were released shortly before this edition of this book was completed.

624

7. President's Audit

Here is Edward Bear, coming downstairs now
bump, bump, bump, on the back of his head behind Christopher Robin.
It is, as far as he knows, the only way of coming downstairs,
but sometimes he feels that there really is another way,
if only he could STOP bumping for a moment and THINK of it.

A.A. Milne

Introduction

With the exception of matters of honesty, conventional financial audits, whilst checking for the existence of an audit trail between vouchers and the accuracy and verity of accounts, do not investigate and are not really designed to investigate, the performance realities that lie behind the figures. The president's audit is specifically intended to do so. They fill the void in most internal management audit programmes which only consider the efficacy of subordinates' actions whilst steering well clear of uncovering facts about the effectiveness of the work (i.e. decision making and forward planning) performed by the top management. A major benefit of these audits is their ability to increase staff motivation by demonstrating genuine leadership for the company's total quality management programme since they set an example for all to see.

Very few of the audits performed by registrars, to determine compliance with such standards as QS 9000 and ISO 9001, audit effectively the top management of applicant firms. At one prominent international automotive parts manufacturer, the QS 9000 coordinator tells the registrar's auditors what to ask the local president. The coordinator then advises the president what the registrar's auditor will ask for and doctors the necessary records ready for presentation during the audit. Knowing the QS 9000 registration industry as being extremely competitive and the kudos associated with the registrar being awarded the firm's account, the coordinator also advises the auditors how dissatisfied the firm will be with the registrar's services if any deficiencies are reported.

625

President's audits will gain in popularity. As the name suggests, they are authorized by the president or chief executive officer (CEO) of the company and in some cases are actually performed by that person. Generally, however, the audit team is hired from outside the company in order to ensure genuine independence as well as an absence of the inbred habits and beliefs which would inevitably occur if the team were to be derived from within the company's own ranks. These audits enable the CEO to determine that corporate policies and strategic decisions have been properly determined and delegated throughout the company and are being implemented. In addition, they obtain factual evidence concerning the current validity and correctness of earlier strategic decisions, also serving to determine the efficacy of those decisions. President's audits can reveal the true capabilities of the firm factually. Clearly, they provide a most valuable input for successful management at the top of the firm.

Auditees

The president's audit, by definition, is at the highest level within the hierarchy of the company's audits as described in Part 1 Chapter 1. The primary auditees are those managers who report directly to the president or CEO but, depending on the audit's scope and objectives, the auditees may be found at any level in the company whose participation is necessary to obtain the requisite facts.

Role of the auditor

The reader will recall that I regard the fundamental product in a company to be *"decisions"*. The most important decisions are the ones that are made at the top because everyone's actions stem from them. The president's auditor investigates the quality of the decision making process as well as the management actions that result from those decisions, verifying that an audit trail exists between the policies and strategic decisions made at the top and the actions taken at all levels. If no such trail exists, the possibilities of bad communications, incompetence, anarchy, but principally the suspicion that the management and workforce are out of touch with each other, are raised.

Certain matters cannot be effectively addressed by the regular auditor who is appointed from middle management or lower ranks of a company. Auditing the structure and membership of the top management, for example, is a job which must be left to the president or his directly appointed auditor. This is because some auditees would consider it to be either an impertinence or an embarrassment to be audited by someone from a lower level in the company. It is also unfair on the auditor himself since the sense of self preservation and embarrassment surrounding the questioning of those who hold superior positions in the company could render his performance less than adequate.

Conduct of the audit

General approach

The preparation, performance and reporting of each of these types of audit remain as described throughout this book, especially in Part 1.

♦ The auditor can use the task elements with their corresponding sub-elements, (see Part 1 Chapter 4), to considerable effect.
♦ The seven step audit method and question technique will both be as discussed in Chapters 11 and 13, respectively.
♦ Each department/process involved in the project will be analyzed as per Chapter 5.
♦ Management systems will be treated as suggested in Chapter 6.
♦ Careful audit preparation as described in Chapter 9 is obviously beneficial as is the creation of a checklist, matrix or flowchart as discussed in Chapter 7. The basic checklist, such as that described in Figure 7.6 or a matrix, of the type shown in Figure 7.14, (based on the task elements listed in Chapter 4, non conformity and so on), is usable. If the auditee is supposed to comply with a standard, such as ISO 9001, the auditor needs to prepare a criteria type of checklist, as also described in Part 1 Chapter 7.
♦ The precepts concerning value-added audits, described in this Part 2, Chapter 2 will be useful.

The audit objectives, as ever, require most careful definition if the audit is to be successful. The audit can and must only be based on the examination of objective evidence. Facts are vital, hearsay inadmissible.

In those cases where the president/CEO is to be a member of the audit team, it is important that he or she sets an example to all by being properly trained since, without this, a lack of discipline in the performance of regular management audits could easily ensue.

It is crucial that the right attitude be adopted during these audits. The president's audit must not only be a fact finding exercise that will present a true and fair view but it must be seen to be such otherwise much damage can be done. The audit has to be performed with a good degree of sensitivity as some auditee imagine hidden motives behind everything and their instincts of self preservation emerge at the slightest (imagined) provocation. Accordingly, the audit team must be especially careful to adopt the consultancy role advocated throughout this book. They must make suggestions and be helpful to the auditee at all times. Given that, the audit team is representing the president/CEO of the company, its actions and attitudes can easily be interpreted to be those of the president/CEO himself. Much damage to team spirit can result if an insensitive, incompetent and ill-trained audit team is let loose: such a disgrace can severely undermine a corporate team spirit that has been carefully nurtured over a number of years. For this reason, one cannot recommend that the audit team be comprised of anything other than auditors who have considerable experience of making such audits. The audit team must act responsibly, never adopting the attitude that it has a special position and extensive powers of censure, for it does not. It is merely a group of people authorized to go and gather facts, that is all.

The auditors must remember that they will obtain valuable results by challenging the framework within which those decisions are made. They must never challenge the person, (one of my golden rules), for to do so merely raises barriers. It is counterproductive and gives totally the wrong impression about the president's psyche. The president's audit is not an inquisition and it is vital that this is remembered because there will be natural apprehensions, fears and defensiveness to overcome in the auditees.

In most president's audits an element of auditee politics, personal motives and malicious attitudes surface occasionally. Phrases such as *"Well, of course, its not for me to say what his department is doing. I have no doubt you will see it for yourself"* which are accompanied by a "knowing smile" can easily inject subtle poisons into the mind of an inexperienced auditor but they are to be ignored. The audit team must be particularly scrupulous to ensure that it works only on rock solid objective evidence and that it does not report hearsay for some auditees try to seize on the president's audit as an opportunity to do harm to others and to benefit themselves. The *"dirty dozen"* tactics can occur (see Part 1 Chapter 15) and the auditor needs to deal with them effectively. When auditing senior managers, there can be a tendency for the trial of strength to take the form of a manager trying to browbeat the auditor by virtue of seniority of his position (although clearly this does not work when the auditors come from external sources). Implied bribes which stem from hints about using the auditor's company's skills for future contracts can occur - the auditor should simply ignore them and continue with the job in hand.

I was engaged to perform a particular president's audit and one of the auditee's top managers stated that he was a great believer in the value of such audits. He further ventured the opinion that I was just the kind of person that his company needed at the top and that he would express those sentiments to his CEO. However, once the exit interview was completed, he remarked that I was clearly not the type to work effectively in "his" team and that I was unsuited to be one of his managerial colleagues. The audit had revealed that his particular office was at the root cause of various business management problems involving non-implementation of corporate policies.

Typical objectives and topics raised

The following provides a selection of various objectives and matters which often arise in or from president's audits.

Long range plans

Vital to such audits is the fact that they verify the operational plans at all levels of the company are consistent with the corporate objectives set by the president. These objectives may have been defined in long range plans. The audits can ascertain the actual capabilities available in the company in order to assist the formulation of corporate strategy. To promote the determining of long range plans, the president's audit can also report:

♦ How quickly do the operational areas and departments respond in practice?
♦ How quickly could they respond to decisions made at the top of the company?
♦ What improvements are required to reach that level of response?

Audit trail between strategic decisions and actions

President's audits are fact finding exercises. They verify that the plans, policies and procedures set or authorized at the top of a company have been accurately translated throughout the various levels of the company and consequently implemented. They determine that there is consistency within the organization at the lower levels of the company. Like any other audit, they remove the rose-tinted spectacles to reveal the way things really are as opposed to the way that the president might believe them to be, a general impression based on information provided by his immediate subordinates.

Some of the matters raised during the president's audit will have been topics for discussion at top management in companies for many years. Those discussions can be of dubious value when they do not base themselves on reliable information obtained directly from the "coal face" where the work is actually being performed in the company. The president's audit fills the information gap that frequently exists between those discussions and the conventional management audit which often focuses on management issues but assumes the key decisions about the way the company is organized and operating to be correct and consistent with the corporate objectives.

To be genuinely integrated, the management systems must not only integrate with each other but also with those used to make strategic decisions. There must be an audit trail between those decisions and the operational management systems. The president's audit will, amongst other things, verify the existence of such an audit trail.

The main product of any level of management is, as remarked upon earlier, "decisions". Decision making is a task that principally involves the task elements *"person"* and *"information"*. In investigating the efficacy of the decision making system, the auditor will pay attention to those elements and their sub-elements. The basic premises under which decisions have been made need to be ascertained and evaluated in the light of changing circumstances. The issues are:

♦ Was the original decision right at the time it was made?
♦ Is that decision still correct?
♦ Have any of the basic premises, on which the decision was based, changed? If so, what is their impact?

(The section concerning *"Review past decisions"*, contained in Chapter 2 *"Value-added auditing"*, offers additional generic guidance for this activity.)

Management of resources and time

The audits are often aimed at ascertaining whether or not resources and time are allocated sensibly, used properly and are properly controlled. They can verify whether or not avoidable costs are constantly monitored at all levels in the company and whether or not efforts are made to reduce avoidable costs by the identification of opportunities. Closely aligned with this is the verification of continuous improvement efforts that do more than address trivial issues and make cosmetic changes. The value-added auditing approach described in the *"Value-added auditing"* chapter will be of use. Associated matters raised normally resemble the following:

♦ Do we know what our avoidable and unavoidable costs really are?
♦ Do we know how much time is really needed to satisfy the

- customers' needs?
♦ If not, what must we do?
♦ What improvements must be made?
♦ What does the improvement budget really need to be?
♦ If we took X% of the avoidable cost reduction opportunities identified during the audit, by what amount would this reduce the company's financing or borrowing needs?
♦ Alternatively, by taking those opportunities what target pricing levels could we meet, what would be the impact on market share, and on profit?

Legal obligations

The president's audit can question whether or not legal considerations are really respected at all levels, in areas concerning health and safety, trade descriptions, weights and measures, employee discrimination, environmental protection and the like.

Analyzing the organization

Henri Fayol spoke of the need to audit the organization of any enterprise regularly. The value of his shrewd advice remains undiminished over the years. He wrote [1]:

It would be most improvident not to make periodic inspections of all parts of a machine, especially a complex one. There would be a risk of poor output, accidents, even catastrophes. Daily (somewhat superficial) inspection is no guarantee. No less great is the need for periodic overhaul of administrative machinery....The following rule meets this need - 'Every year, in connection with the drawing up of the annual plan, a scrupulous study of the constitution of the organization is to be made with the assistance of summarized charts'.

The foundation for the company's effectiveness is laid by the organizational decisions taken by top management. The typical management auditor has little opportunity to investigate the rationale behind a particular organizational structure and conventional management auditing consequently tend to ignore this vital aspect which determines the business performance of the company. Naturally this must be addressed during the president's audit. The decisions behind a particular organization must be questioned in terms of the basic information upon which they were originally made. Trading circumstances and product needs are constantly changing and no company can assume that particular organizational structure will adequately serve its purposes for ever without any change. Organizational features

631

which can be investigated have been described in Part 1 Chapters 3 and 18. The information obtained from the president's audit creates such reflections as:

♦ If we still had only the facts on which the original organization was based, would we still structure it the same way?
♦ In light of the facts now available concerning our product range, market places, business objectives, legislation and so on, would we structure the organization in the same way?
♦ If not, how would our decisions be affected and what changes need to be made?
♦ Are our direct sell or licensing policies still valid?
♦ Considering the current status and capability of our equipment, our financial strengths and people resources, not neglecting commercial and technical trends, should we re-invest or buy in the goods and services we currently create ourselves? Should we revise our levels of outsourcing and change our vertical or horizontal integration status?
♦ Is the way in which we are organized consistent with the needs of the marketplace and the customer? How well does the existing organizational structure respond (in terms of speed and cost performance) to their needs?

Management systems, effectiveness and information

The audit will examine the company management systems to determine if:

♦ Cross-company management systems are compatible.
♦ They are implemented in a consistent way across the company.
♦ They are effective in securing the company's objectives.

Management effectiveness issues often raised consist of questions such as:

♦ Are individual managers effective?
♦ If not, what training or other actions should we take to improve their performance?
♦ Do those managers avoid decisions? If so, why?

At the executive management levels the following questions are exceedingly valuable in helping the president/CEO and top management put their own actions and achievements into perspective:

♦ Is the company executive/am I responsive to department needs or

are we/am I out of touch?
- Do I/we really know what they need?
- Do I/we serve them properly and on time?
- Do I/we engender fear or defensiveness?
- Do I/we communicate with them effectively? Or, do I/we communicate *at* them?
- What must I/we do to improve my/our performance?

These audits frequently uncover motivation and team attitudes by addressing such matters as:

- What is the real state of motivation throughout the company?
- What is the real state of motivation in a particular department/project/group?
- Do we really work as a team?
- Is information communicated effectively?
- Is integration of interfacing systems really achieved?
- What is the timeliness of inter-department (inter-process) supply?
- Is there joint effort on problem solving?
- Do we work by personal contact or through petty minded memoranda and E-mail?
- Do we have too many meetings and, if so, why?
- How well do we conduct our meetings?
- Are assigned actions really taken and followed-up?

Every executive likes to believe that he or she is in touch with what is really happening and that his or her information systems achieve those laudable aims, but the president's audit can look at the truth of the situation by addressing such matters as:

- How effective or accurate is the normal reporting system?
- Do we and our managers really know what the shop floor problems are?
- Are their management reports accurate, reliable and timely?
- How quickly do we and our managers respond to problems?
- Can that response be improved?
- Are we preventive minded or are we fire-fighters? In other words, are we managers or are we fixers?

Exit interviews

These can proceed as described in Part 1 Chapter 19. Attendance may need to be restricted depending on the level of confidentiality the audit client requires. Ordinarily, the president/CEO and his immediate reports, involved within the scope and objectives of the audit, would attend.

The exit interview will be prepared in the usual way, but it tends to take longer than would be so for conventional management audits. And it generally takes more time to fully present the audit team's findings and recommendations than would be the case for an audit whose objective is to ascertain compliance with, say, ISO 9000. The audit team should expect and accommodate more questions from the auditee and the audit client. President's audits address major business, strategic and operational matters and they can, occasionally, be quite complex, which is why the preparation for and delivery of the exit interview takes longer. They are not dealing with simple matters of compliance which essentially conclude *"the auditee does or does not...."*, which is a *"yes/no"* result. Since the outcome of the President's audit can influence the business direction and prospects and create substantial avoidable costs if poorly conducted, careful analysis of facts gathered and presentation of results is vital.

Corrective action requests

Whether or not formal CARs should be issued to cure problems identified during an audit is a policy matter which tends to vary between companies. Some enlightened CEOs willingly receive CARs placed on themselves if the root cause of problems is identified as resting with them. In authorizing the performance of such audits, the president/CEO must realize that there is always a possibility that particular inadequacies in the company may be directly traceable to his own efforts or lack of them. Honestly and openly admitting to any personal shortcomings or inactions that the audit may identify, as opposed to counter-productively *"shooting the messenger"*, is an act that requires personal stature and integrity. It does, however, set a model that is of enormous benefit to the company's operational and business objectives. Not everyone possesses such worthy attributes.

> A president's audit in a consumer products supplier resulted in a number of problems directly attributable to the CEO's efforts. The CEO accepted the conclusions and recommendations and decided on a plan of action to remedy the deficiencies. The firm's staff were skeptical of the CEO's ability to receive well any seemingly adverse findings since the general morale was low, relationships with top management strained and a generally negative culture extant. The CEO let the findings be known, accepted responsibility and actively pursued change. It was a turning point in relationships. The internal culture became positive and caused a leap forward in overall performance.

CARs cannot be issued unless the audit uncovers evidence that some established requirement, a policy regulation or standard, has been violated. Many of the matters addressed by the president's audit do not necessarily involve assessing compliance with that sort of thing. In such circumstances, a CAR could not be justified. Frequently the audit team will describe shortcomings and the recommended solutions in the audit report, not in CARs.

Audit reports

The reports must be concise and to the point. The audit team must not be afraid to state facts plainly because that is precisely what they have been engaged to do (or should have been engaged to do). The Aldous Huxley quote in Part 1 Chapter 1 should be borne in mind by auditor and auditee alike.

The type of layout shown in Part 1 Chapter 20 can still be used as a template audit report. The general information sections, such as auditee location, audit dates, audit team members and so on are still required. A position statement is not really necessary, but a summary of the report addressing the audit objectives is always appropriate.

Distribution and confidentiality

These matters will depend, as ever was the case, on the instructions issued by the president/CEO to the lead auditor. Often the president's audit report will have a restricted circulation although it may be sent to the senior management and to the board. This will depend on the policy for such audits and also on the audit's objectives. If, for example, one of the objectives has been to examine the performance of a particular senior manager, it would be singularly inappropriate for his colleagues to receive a copy of the report. If, however, the objectives are not of a particularly sensitive nature then restricting the distribution could in itself be a demotivator.

Follow-up actions

Should the audit identify various corrective actions as being required, it is essential that follow-up action be taken to determine the effectiveness and completion of those actions. When the audit has identified the need for corrective action on the part of the president/CEO, the latter should ensure that follow-up action is seen to be taken to verify the efficacy of the results. Being prepared to act in this way sets a shining example to the company.

References

*It is not wide reading but useful reading
that tends to excellence.*

Aristippus

Chapter 1.

1. Sloan, Alfred P., *"My years with General Motors"*, Doubleday & Co. Inc.
2. Fayol, Henri *"General and industrial management"*, Pitman.
3. Geneen, Harold (with Alvin Moscow), *Managing*, Avon Books, 1984, New York.
4. Sayle, Allan J., *"Meeting ISO 9000 in a TQM world"*, Second edition, AJSL, 1994, ISBN 0-9511739-3-6.

Chapter 4

1. John Stuart Mill, *"On liberty"*.
2. Charles Dickens, *"Hard times"*.
3. British Standard 3527 :PART 1 :1976. *"Glossary of terms used in Data processing: Part 1. Fundamental terms"* British Standards Institution, Park Street London W1A 2BS. (Note that standard is the British edition of the ISO standard ISO 2382, Section 01 - 1974 "Data processing vocabulary: Fundamental terms").
4. Juran, J.M., *"Quality Control Handbook"*, Third edition, 1974, published by the McGraw-Hill Co., New York, USA.

Chapter 6

1. Janner, Greville, *"Product Liability"*, 1979 Business Books Ltd.
2. Gall, John, *"Malice in Blunderland"*, 1973, McGraw-Hill, New York
3. Sayle, Allan J., *Meeting ISO 9000 in a TQM world,* Second edition, AJSL, 1994, ISBN 0-9511739-3-6.

4. American Society of Mechanical Engineers Boiler and Pressure Vessel Code is published by the American Society of Mechanical Engineers, 345 East 47th Street, New York, NY 10017, USA.
5. Sayle A.J. *"ISO 9000 - progression or regression?"* QA News, Volume 14 No.2 February 1988. Published by the Institute of Quality Assurance, 10 Grosvenor Gardens, London SW1W 0DQ

Chapter 8

1. Sloan, Alfred P., *"My years with General Motors"*, Doubleday & Co. Inc.

Chapter 9

1,2,3. These reports and claims were made during CNBC's *"Power Lunch"* programme 25 February 1997, interviewer - Bill Griffeth. At that time, the *"Association of flaming Fords"* web site was found at www.flamingfords.com and the site dealing with McDonald's was at: www.envirolink.org/mcspotlight/home.html

Chapter 11:

1. Geneen, Harold (with Alvin Moscow), *"Managing"*, Avon Books, 1984, New York.
2. Military Standard Mil-Std-105E, *"Sampling Procedures and Tables for Inspection by Attributes,"* 1963. Government Printing Office, Washington, D.C., USA.

Chapter 12

1. Military Standard Mil-Std-105E, *"Sampling Procedures and Tables for Inspection by Attributes,"* 1963. Government Printing Office, Washington, D.C., USA.

Chapter 18

1. Military Specification Mil-Q-9858A *"Quality Program Requirements"* 1963. Government Prnting Office, Washington, D.C., USA
2. AQAP-1 *"NATO requirements for an industrial quality control*

system". Edition No 3 May 1984 issued by the NATO International Staff - Defence Support Division.

3. American Society of Mechanical Engineers Boiler and Pressure Vessel Code is published by the American Society of Mechanical Engineers, 345 East 47th Street, New York, NY 10017, USA.

4. AQAP-4 *"NATO Inspection System Requirements for Industry"*, edition No. 2 June 1976 issued by the NATO International Staff - Defence Support Division.

5. Parkinson, C. Northcote, *"Parkinson's Law"*, Penguin, Harmondsworth, 1965

Chapter 19

1. Likert, Rensis, Harvard Business Review July/August 1959 pp 75-82.

Chapter 21

1. Sayle, Allan J., *"Meeting ISO 9000 in a TQM world"*, Second edition, AJSL, 1994, ISBN 0-9511739-3-6.

Chapter 2 - Value-added auditing

1. Lyle O. *"The efficient use of fuel"*, H.M.S.O. Third impression.

Author's note: Whereas technological advances have rendered obsolete some of its content Oliver Lyle's book was a veritable tome of timeless wisdom about the economic use of energy. Its companion *"The efficient use of steam"* (an H.M.S.O. publication also written by Oliver Lyle) similarly contained precepts of value.

Chapter 5 Auditing service providers

1. Juran, J.M., *Quality Control Handbook*, Third edition, 1974, published by the McGraw-Hill Book Co., New York, USA.

Chapter 7 President's audit

1. Fayol H. *"General and Industrial Management"*, Pitman.

Standards.

Throughout the book, the text refers on a number of occasions, to several standards including the ISO 9000 series and QS 9000.

The ISO 9000 series is published by the International Organization for Standardization, (ISO), Case Postale 56, CH-1211 Geneva, Switzerland, and includes, amongst others:

ISO 9001: 1994 *"Quality systems - Model for quality assurance in design/development, production, installation and servicing"*.

ISO 9002: 1994 *"Quality systems - Model for quality assurance in production, installation and servicing"*.

ISO 9003: 1994 *"Quality systems - Model for quality assurance in final inspection and test"*.

ISO 8402: 1994 *"Quality management and quality assurance - Vocabulary"*.

The ISO 14000 series, also published by ISO, above, includes:

ISO 14001: 1996, *Environmental managment systems - Specification with guidance for use.*

ISO 14004: 1996, *Environmenal management systems - General guidelines on principles, systems and supporting techniques.*

ISO 14010: 1996, *Guidelines for environmental auditing - General principles.*

ISO 14011: 1996, *Guidelines for environmental auditing - Audit procedures - Auditing of environmental management systems.*

Quality system requirements QS-9000 is available from AIAG at (810) 358 3003; in Europe available from Carwin Continuous Improvement at 1708-861333.

Index

If that thou wilt not read,
let it alone;
Some love the meat,
Some love to pick the bone.

John Bunyan